KAHLIL GIBRAN

SELECTED WRITTEN WORKS BY KAHLIL GIBRAN

Nubthah fi Fan Al-Musiqa (*Music*), 1905
Ara'is al-Muruj (*Nymphs of the Valley*, also translated as *Spirit Brides* and
Brides of the Prairie), 1906
Al-Arwah al-Mutamarrida (*Spirits Rebellious*), 1908
Al-Ajniha al-Mutakassira (*Broken Wings*), 1912
Dam'a wa Ibtisama (*A Tear and a Smile*), 1914
The Madman, 1918
Al-Mawakib (*The Processions*), 1919
Twenty Drawings, 1919
Al-'Awasif (*The Tempests*), 1920
The Forerunner, 1920
Al-Bada'i' waal-Tara'if (*The New and the Marvelous*), 1923
The Prophet, 1923
Sand and Foam, 1926
Jesus the Son of Man, 1928
Al-Saniibil (*The Spikes of Grain*), 1929
The Earth Gods, 1931

POSTHUMOUS, IN ENGLISH
The Wanderer, 1932
The Garden of the Prophet, 1933
Lazarus and his Beloved (play), 1933
Tears and Laughter, 1947 trans. A. R. Ferris
Nymphs of the Valley, 1948 trans. H. M. Nahmad
Spirits Rebellious, 1948 trans. H. M. Nahmad
A Tear and a Smile, 1950 trans. H. M. Nahmad
The Processions, 1958 trans. George Khairallah
The Broken Wings, 1959 trans. A. R. Ferris
Lazarus and his Beloved (play), 1973
Dramas of Life: Lazarus and His Beloved and The Blind, 1981

KAHLIL GIBRAN

BEYOND BORDERS

by Jean Gibran and Kahlil G. Gibran
in collaboration with the Interlink Gibran Project

foreword by Salma Hayek-Pinault

Interlink Books

An imprint of Interlink Publishing Group, Inc.
Northampton, Massachusetts

First published in 2017 by

INTERLINK BOOKS
An imprint of Interlink Publishing Group, Inc.
46 Crosby Street, Northampton, Massachusetts 01060
www.interlinkbooks.com

Library of Congress Cataloging-in-Publication Data
Names: Gibran, Jean, author. | Gibran, Kahlil, 1922-2008, author. | Hayek,
    Salma, 1966- writer of foreword. | Interlink Gibran Project.
Title: Kahlil Gibran : beyond borders / by Jean Gibran and Kahlil George
    Gibran in collaboration with the Interlink Gibran Project ; with a
    foreword by Salma Hayek-Pinault.
Description: Northampton, Massachusetts: Interlink Books, 2016. | Includes
    bibliographical references and index.
Identifiers: LCCN 2016022408| ISBN 9781566560856 | ISBN 9781566560931
Subjects: LCSH: Gibran, Kahlil, 1883-1931. | Authors,
    Arab--Lebanon--Biography. | Authors, Arab--United States--Biography.
Classification: LCC PJ7826.I2 Z664 2016 | DDC 811/.54 [B] --dc23
LC record available at https://lccn.loc.gov/2016022408

About this book: Building on the foundations of the 1974 work, *Kahlil Gibran: His Life and World*, this
volume has been developed and produced as a collaboration between Jean Gibran and the Interlink
Gibran Project: Michel Moushabeck, publisher; John Sobhiea Fiscella, editor and project coordinator;
Dr. Hani Bawardi, research advisor; Ann Childs, assistant editor; Pam Fontes-May, designer; Jennifer
Staltare, document manager and proofreader; Judith Charvat Watkins, bibliographer and researcher;
Abdul Mohsen Al-Husseini, translator and researcher; Joelle Solé Maguire and Raghad Qattan, assistant
translators; Karen Gracie Kowles, indexer; George Lynde/Art Imaging, photographer and proofreader;
Whitney Sanderson and Meredith Madyda, proofreaders.

Printed and bound in the United States of America

10 9 8 7 6 5 4 3 2 1

Toward homecomings beyond borders

CONTENTS

Foreword by Salma Hayek-Pinault   ix

Preface by Kahlil George Gibran   xi

Introduction by Jean Gibran and the Interlink Gibran Project   xvii

I

1   Born in Bsharri   3

2   A City Wilderness   21

3   Bookmaking and Bohemia   37

4   Beirut   59

5   "Pegasus Harnessed to an Ash-Wagon"   79

II

6   "A Gallery of Gracious and Novel Heads"   99

7   *Al-Musiqa*   111

8   "The Presence of a She-Angel"   125

9   Rebellious Spirits in Paris   145

10   Frontiers of Friendship   169

11   From Boston to New York   187

12   Growing Partnerships   207

13   Work Made Visible   227

III

14   War and Famine   255

15   A People's Poet   285

16   Awakenings in the Immigrant Press   303

17   No Longer Apart   329

CONTENTS

18 "O Mist, My Sister" 353
19 "After All the Debts Are Paid" 369
20 The Final Years 383
21 Homecoming 411
Legacies 433

Notes 437
Bibliography 477
Acknowledgments 509
Index 514

Foreword

A LOVE AFFAIR WITH LIFE

When I was small, I was very close to my Lebanese grandfather. One of the things that I remember about him is that on his bedside table there was always a little book with the image of an enigmatic man on its cover. And I knew that that book was very important to my grandfather. Unfortunately, he died when I was only six, and it wasn't until I was in my teens that I saw that book cover again. I realized that the book I had seen was *The Prophet*, by Kahlil Gibran, and I read it for the first time. I was immediately captivated by its beauty and power, but I also felt personally connected to it. In reading *The Prophet*, I felt like I was learning more about who my grandfather was. I felt he was talking to me through this book and that through the book he was teaching me about life.

Throughout my life, I have returned to the book many times, and its words have always nourished my heart and my soul, while also helping me stay connected to my memories of my grandfather. While I have a personal relationship with the book, I know that in this I am not alone. Since its initial publication in 1923, readers of all ages have turned to *The Prophet* in times of celebration and of sorrow. The book has sold millions of copies around the world, in dozens of languages, and is one of the most beloved books of all time. To each of us who have experienced this book, Gibran has given us an enduring and priceless gift.

And beyond *The Prophet* and Gibran's other works, Gibran's life itself is an inspirational story, mainly because Kahlil Gibran loved life. What he evokes and describes in his poetry and prose is a love affair with life—in both life's joy and its challenges. And sharing and spreading this kind of love for life may be a key to ultimately helping save the world from its problems. I believe that there is goodness inside of every single one of us, and artists like Kahlil Gibran help us to discover and nurture that goodness in ourselves and in others.

As a kind of "love letter" to Gibran and to my Lebanese heritage, I collaborated on an animated film called *Kahlil Gibran's The Prophet.* The film was always intended to be a celebration of Gibran's poetry by a group of artists—including directors, animators, musicians, and actors—from around the world. During production of the film, I learned much about Gibran, not only through his works, but also through this thoroughly researched, beautifully illustrated biography.

It is my great pleasure to invite you to discover, or rediscover, Gibran's life and work.

—Salma Hayek-Pinault

Preface

BETWEEN WORLDS

The need to explore the world of Kahlil Gibran began for me in 1932 when I was ten years old. His death the year before had profoundly affected my family. N'oula Gibran, my father and the poet's cousin, felt most bereft. They had grown up together in Lebanon, and when my father finally made the long voyage to America ten years after Kahlil and his sister Marianna, he also gravitated to Boston. There he met and married my mother Rose Gibran, another cousin. Not only was he their best man, but "Uncle" Kahlil also named my brothers and sisters: Horace, Susan, Hafiz, and Selma, and me, Kahlil.

We grew up huddled in the Syrian-Lebanese enclave of Boston's South End. Poor during the twenties, we hardly noticed the difference when the Depression became official. The only event that relieved the dreariness of those tenement days was a visit from Gibran, who was then living in New York. We would all descend upon "Aunt" Marianna's Tyler Street apartment, and for days there would be feasting, laughter, and talk.

I remember his room late at night, dense with smoke, redolent with the licorice smell of the *arak* liquor. I can hear the melodies of the *oud* (lute) and *nay* (flute) played by neighbors in homage to the man who was celebrated as a writer and artist. Many mornings I would deliver bread to the Tyler Street studio, when it was deserted except for Kahlil and his sister. He talked with me and encouraged me. Once he gave me parts of a broken clock to reassemble. I can visualize the paint box in which he taught me to mix colors, and even the slippers he wore as I sat and watched him at his easel or writing table. One especially vivid picture remains. We all attended the Quincy School, as he had. It had just let out, and as I was rushing away I spotted him. He was standing across the street, in front of the Denison House, our local settlement center, dressed in a white suit and holding a cane. He looked far removed from my dingy world—but he saw me and shouted to me in Arabic, and I knew somehow that he was not apart.

When he died, we lost someone who had brought a certain flair and style to our lives. I treasured the little trinkets he had given me, but it was not the material gifts I really missed. After his death Marianna left for Lebanon. When she returned, the liveliness that I had known in her house was replaced by her memories and her tears. She was close to us and good to us; and in return we treated her, the closest one of all to the poet, like a matriarch.

She had moved out of the South End, and we made trolley-car pilgrimages to her house in Jamaica Plain. There, one weekend, I became an unwitting conspirator in the destruction of evidence about the man we had all revered. While Marianna was abroad we saved her mail, some of which was addressed to Gibran. Enough accumulated to fill a shopping bag. When she returned, she at first ignored the letters. But one drowsy afternoon, she asked me to go through them with her. She could not read, and I was her eyes. I would dip into the cavernous bag, retrieve an envelope, and read aloud the name of the sender and return address. If she did not recognize the source, she laid aside the envelope, unopened. That night we burned the voluminous unread correspondence—probably two hundred unexplored letters, decorated with stamps from all over the world. All of these deliciously perfumed, sealed, and embossed covers encased documents that attested to Gibran's life beyond us. They were destroyed, and I stood and wondered what I had done.

~

Years passed. My childhood adulation of an exciting relative was superseded by my own concerns as an art student and then in my own work as an artist. Yet an urge to understand the man I had known, whose name I bore, was always present. Oddly, the growing body of publications about him made it harder for me to reach this understanding. The books and articles were either embarrassingly reverential or offensively lurid. My curiosity had to be content temporarily with the material remnants of his life given to me gradually by Marianna: his clothes, his watch and cigarette lighter, the pigment chest, the paintings stored in Boston, letters and manuscripts, even his death mask, all became mine. Neither owning these things nor listening to the endless reminiscences of my family was an answer to my questions. How did a penniless immigrant not only adapt to the Boston slum, but within a few years have enough of a following to bridge the social chasm between the South End and the Back Bay? I knew that his literacy was no magical happening, as one biographer stated, nor was it due to an enlightened family environment.

As my personal career developed, my quest for Gibran's identity became more imperative. As his namesake and a creative artist in an allied field, I was constantly besieged by inquiries about the man. Inevitably confusion arose. I even considered changing my name. Somehow pride prevented me.

By 1966 the complexities of my own life had been resolved. I was recognized professionally, and independently of my relative. Entrusting me with articles, books, and letters, my father had added to Marianna's gifts. I had my own family, and the time to stop and assess what to do with the mass of Gibran material that had arrived.

I turned to an outside depository. Years before, Marianna had showed me letters from Gibran's friend and mentor, Mary Haskell Minis, in which she stated her decision to give all her Gibran correspondence, as well as her journal, to the University of North Carolina. At last I could begin to put together the pieces. At this stage, my wife Jean joined forces with me, and we began to explore the 615 letters and 47 diaries that spanned the years from 1904 to 1931. Reading the material through twice, we learned about Gibran's beginnings in Boston and achievements in New York from a fresh perspective. Although the long passages of the Haskell journal abounded in leads, the basic puzzle of Gibran's earliest introduction into the world of arts and letters remained unsolved.

Finally, in the early seventies, my wife and I decided to stop midcareer and devote ourselves full time to research, however long it might take. We were in possession of two primary clues—an extraordinary photograph and a packet of letters. The stunning large print of a young Kahlil dressed as a Bedouin had hung over Marianna's sofa for as long as I could remember. When I asked her about the photographer, she responded with vague stories of an impressively elegant Mr. Day. Fred Holland Day's significance in the poet's life had always been limited by biographers to his role as the owner of a studio in which Gibran's drawings were shown in 1904. However, Gibran's youthful appearance in this portrait convinced us that Day was an important force at a much earlier period. The letters were mostly written during the most obscure time in Gibran's life—when his mother, his sister Sultana, and his half-brother had died—and were addressed to an unidentified "Brother." How Marianna had received them or why she had so carefully saved them had never been clear.

We made inquiries about Day, and Peter Bunnell, then working in the Alfred Stieglitz Archive at Yale University, suggested that we visit the Norwood Historical Society, formerly Day's home. In 1972, at the Day House, our serious research began. On our second trip there, we verified that the packet of letters, written in stilted English, were unquestionably addressed to Day. Moreover, although we could locate no further correspondence from Gibran (leading us to suspect that Day had returned such notes either to the poet himself or to Marianna after Gibran's death), other letters to Day demonstrated his early sponsorship of the precocious adolescent. One note linked the entire chain of people who contributed to Gibran's success. In 1896, a sympathetic social worker had requested Day's collaboration in helping "a little Assyrian boy Kahlil G." No discovery in all our research moved us as much as this early letter.

Also at the Day House was correspondence from Josephine Preston Peabody to her publisher. As early as 1898, it began to mention Gibran's name. We then realized that at the turn of the century, Day, photographer, publisher, and avid collector, did not deserve characterization as an "opaque" figure. On the contrary, when Gibran met him, he was a colorful tastemaker and entrepreneur whose function and significance had disappeared as the twentieth century became louder and bigger.

With the engaging personality of Josephine Peabody added to our list, we began to look for material relating this talented poet to Gibran. We were led eventually to Harvard University's Houghton Library, where her beautifully executed diaries revealed a completely new dimension of his experience. Through her sympathetic eyes were recorded his most tragic years. The myth was becoming reality. The story of Gibran would necessarily be the story of Gibran and his contemporaries. To reflect accurately the period and set his life firmly in a meaningful world, we would have to describe and recreate the vivid characters of Day, Josephine Peabody, Mary Haskell, Charlotte Teller, Emilie Michel, Ameen Rihani, Rose O'Neill, and others, by then nearly all forgotten.

Some of his biographers had resorted to imagined conversations about the major events of his life. With the discovery of the Peabody diaries and the wealth of material in the Haskell journal, fiction became unnecessary—all conversations and descriptions appearing in our text originate from either eyewitness accounts or letters. Previous allusions to relationships and incidents that have not been corroborated by primary source material have remained unmentioned. For the most part, we have footnoted only direct quotations. Gibran's English letters abounded in grammatical errors and misspellings. We have not noted his obvious mistakes unless they interfere with textual meaning.

Both Josephine Peabody and Mary Haskell kept two sets of diaries, the second set being more private "page-a-day" or "line-a-day" books. We have depended heavily on these intimate accounts. In them, unlike the more self-consciously literary journals, one may trace visits, mail, and the pertinent details of daily life. When Mary relied upon the phonetic spelling of names, we have supplied the correct version.

Probably the greatest problem in dealing with Gibran's life was his duality. Constantly, the theme of divided loyalties to two languages, two careers, two often conflicting sets of associates, dominated his development, with the result that biographers and historians have been biased, aware of one perspective and neglectful of the other. The hundreds of articles appearing posthumously in Middle-Eastern publications have analyzed his contribution to modern Arabic literature, while American accounts, flawed with careless scholarship and little documentation, have concentrated on the implications of his popularity. We have attempted in our work to show Gibran's several worlds, and the way he lived in them all.

—Kahlil George Gibran (1922–2008)
with additional comments by Jean Gibran, Spring 2016

Photo of young Kahlil Gibran by Fred Holland Day. (Courtesy private collection)

Introduction
A BORDERLESS CITIZENSHIP

Exiled between the cultures and conflicts of the Middle East and the West, Kahlil Gibran's life and art crossed divisive boundaries to embrace a borderless citizenship. This biography, *Kahlil Gibran: Beyond Borders*, honors Gibran's spirit and legacy. Building on the foundations of the 1974 work, *Kahlil Gibran: His Life and World*, which introduced people and events that formed his worlds, this volume portrays how those people and events inspired his body of work. Retelling the story of his creative life and art, it testifies to Gibran's remarkable capacity to embrace and reconcile dissonant and opposing worlds, turning loss into promise.

From the rich spiritual inheritance and material poverty of his childhood in Mount Lebanon to the urban wilderness of Boston's South End tenements in the 1890s; from the recognition of his talent by settlement house social workers to the loss of his family to illnesses afflicting immigrants to America's cities; from his apprenticeships in the creative circles of Boston, Beirut, Paris, and New York to his art and activism for "Greater Syria" and Syrian-Lebanese immigrants; and from his friendships, loves, and partnerships to his emergence as a people's poet—both in Arabic and English—Kahlil Gibran crafted an expansive vision of shared humanity treasured in many languages.

~

In the fall of 1916 at the age of just thirty-three, Gibran suffered a physical and emotional collapse. Exhausted from overwork and from tensions among his Syrian-Lebanese colleagues, he grieved for Mount Lebanon and Syria, as famine wore down his homelands. Anti-immigrant sentiment was in full swing and within a decade would lead to the 1924 Origins Act, cutting off entry to the U.S. of people from the Middle East and rupturing ties and communication among generations of loved ones. Viewing World War I as a way to liberate his homelands from Ottoman

Turkish rule, Gibran was torn between supporting that devastating conflict, along with his fellow Syrian nationalists, or maintaining his ties to his American pacifist friends associated with *The Seven Arts* magazine in New York. To rest and recover, he returned to a house on Jerusalem Road in Cohasset, Massachusetts, near the sea and where his few close family relations would spend time together. Confiding to a friend about his health, he wrote:

> I am ill in bed…Overwork and the tragedy of my country have brought a cold, dull, pain to my left side, face, arm and leg…Here I sit in the sun all day turning the left side of my body to its warm, healing rays. And the left side of my face is darker, much darker than the [right] side. The effect is strangely queer—not unlike the jesters of the xvth Century![1]

While convalescing, in the afternoons after resting he drew sketches, without any idea of what they would be and hardly knowing what he was doing. Freer in form than his past work, many of them vibrant in color, a series of images coalesced around three motifs: centaurs, mothers and children, and dancers, "just the human form in relation to other forms—trees, rocks—other forms of life."[2] This expression of an elemental unity between human beings and our natural environment became for him a turning point. Gibran sought creatively to transform displacement and exile into art and a borderless sense of belonging. How this search led to the universality of his art is at the heart of this story.

~

After his death fifteen years later in 1931, myths surrounding Gibran's life and art would proliferate with his rising popularity. The passage of time and dynamics of culture and the marketplace in the West would often strip Gibran of aspects of his identity. This volume is an attempt to renew our views of Gibran in the context of his culture and times, while reconsidering the people, relationships, and events of his life and art from the vantage point of our own, seeing how his story always was—and continues to be—enmeshed in larger ones.

This expanded edition has been developed and produced in collaboration between Jean Gibran and Interlink Publishing, as part of its commitment to global voices in art and literature, and to Gibran's story, in particular. In this effort, the contributions of scholars and local historians, devoted to recovering the untold histories of immigrants to the U.S. from the Middle East at the turn of the twentieth century, have been invaluable. Their work shows his story to be an earlier chapter in the continuing American and global saga of migration and exile. It again demonstrates how those of Gibran's generation from "Greater Syria" more than a century ago struggled to find work, care for family and loved ones, establish networks of faith and support, and send remittances back to their towns and villages. But it also reveals that, even in the face of immediate survival challenges, they sought to contribute to their adoptive country, find ways to hold onto and renew their own culture, and support the aspirations of people in their conflict-ridden homelands.[3]

Also, key to our search for historical perspective are this edition's photos and artwork, gathered thanks to the assistance of numerous archives and collections. Including over two hundred black-and-white and color images, these designs, illustrations, paintings, and drawings span Gibran's entire life and artistic contribution, forming a miniature gallery of his legacy. Our desire was to accompany Gibran home; to help return his life story and art to the histories and cultures from which they grew, to better appreciate the timeliness of his legacy.

~

Gibran recognized the necessity of boundaries and nations, yet he strove toward a borderless citizenship that transcended geography. One of his favorite expressions of encouragement to his friends was that we are "far greater than we know" and that "all is well." That we are greater than we know, we are often reminded by the resilience, sacrifices, and creative labors of humanity in exile, far from—or within—their homelands. Although his expression's corollary, that "all is well," may seem inconceivable, the passionate story of Gibran's life and art encourages us to imagine—and attempt to create—ways that it might be so.

—Jean Gibran and the Interlink Gibran Project

I

View of Bsharri and Mount Lebanon. (Courtesy *Aramco World Magazine*, July–August, 1940.)

1

BORN IN BSHARRI

"Of time you would make a stream
upon whose bank you would sit and watch its flowing."[1]

Bsharri in the late 1800s was very much like it always had been: a fortress-like village, secure by itself in high, lonely, limestone hills at the edge of the Qadisha Valley of Mount Lebanon. Five thousand feet above the Mediterranean, tucked in the northern corner of the 120-mile strip that is now the Republic of Lebanon, Bsharri's origins lie far back in prehistory, when early inhabitants first settled there in caves that still beckon today.

Mount Lebanon—literally "the white," from the Semitic word *lubnan*, which evokes the whiteness of milk—describes the mountain range that rises abruptly from the sea along the entire length of Lebanon. In a country that is only some four thousand square miles, the range can be seen from nearly every house and village. Below it, a persistent flow of cultures, religions, and languages streamed by throughout the millennia. But Mount Lebanon provided a protective constant—remote and bright with the snows that cover its summits six months of the year, with the sedimentary rock that shimmers in a perpetually white horizon. It was in Bsharri, Mount Lebanon, in 1883 that Gibran Khalil Gibran was born.

~

"The date of my birth is unknown," Gibran once said. No documents that attest to his date of birth have been found. But journal entries and letters written in 1903 confirm that January 6, 1883, was his preference.[2] Information about the birth dates of relatives suggests that official dates were based somewhat on creative choice. His choice of January 6 coincided with the Feast of the Epiphany; his cousin Rose's[3] was on August 15, observed as the birthday of Mary, the mother of Jesus. Dates

3

were imprinted in the memories of those who recalled—or embroidered—facts, unfettered by concern for documentation. For this has long been a region where history has been forced to resort to myth in order to explain itself, and where the two could not always be easily distinguished.

In the last decade of the nineteenth century, only seven or eight Gibran families lived in Bsharri, and they were not known for either industry or leadership. The root of the name Gibran, *jebr*, has been linked to the word *al-gebra*, based on the introduction to a thesis on equations by the ninth-century Arab mathematician, Al-Khwarizmi. A nineteenth-century missionary, discussing the origins of proper names, reinforced this linguistic deduction with the mention of a boy called "Jebr or Al-Jebra."[4] Time has a way of lending substance to such theories. Khalil himself traced his name to the same source.

The few scanty records mentioning the Gibrans indicate that they arrived in Bsharri toward the end of the seventeenth century. Where they came from is unclear. One family myth links them to Chaldean sources, a Semitic people who were a dominant presence in Babylonia. Another story relates that the men named Gibran came from Syria in the sixteenth century, settling on a farm near Baalbek and moving to Beshelah, in 1672. Somewhere in their history, a brother was condemned to death for religious reasons and died in Tripoli, twenty-five miles from Bsharri. Yet another version places the Gibran family originally in Acre, Palestine, and then traces their migration in 1300 to Beshelah. There, a document exists that quotes a patriarch, Boulos Massaid: "Those people called Gibrans are from Beshelah and at the end of the seventeenth century moved to Bsharri."[5]

There was enough evidence, in any event, to allow the poet, as an adult, to tell of distinguished origins. Yet in his own immediate past, the Gibran family story was pervaded with difficulty. His great-grandfather's name appears in a petition from the townspeople of Bsharri seeking protection from the Turks during the bloody Druze and Christian massacres of 1860. Tannous, Issa, and Said Gibran all signed it. It was Said—his great-grandfather—who fathered Michael, who in turn fathered the poet's own father Khalil.

This Khalil was handsome, drank and gambled, had a mercurial temper and an appealing charm. A man whose status symbol was an amber cigarette holder, he owned a walnut grove on Gibran land near Baalbek, some thirty-five miles from Bsharri. He had a resistance to hard work, preferring gambling at *damma* (backgammon) to the exhausting manual labor of peasants.

As a young person, Khalil viewed his father as proud and imperious, a large man with a domineering manner who came from a "lofty" background. His mother

Kamila, who came from a family of Maronite priests, brought a sense of aspiration to her family and an enduring strength of character of her own.

~

Bsharri was a refuge and stronghold of Maronite Christians who had fled there. Maronites traced their origins to the fifth century, when the early Christians of Syria pledged their allegiance to a legendary monk, St. Maroun, whose memory is perpetuated in a monastery at the source of the Orontes River. Despite an alliance with the Church of Rome, the Maronites always preserved the right for priests to marry. As Khalil would recall, "Half the population of North Lebanon are priests and clergy, and the other half are the offspring of the descendants of priests…It would be quite a task to count the number of priests and clergy there." He explained his mother Kamila's closeness to the Church:

> I am the son of a Maronite priest's daughter…my maternal grandfather was…very fond of church music and music other than that of the church, and for that reason I have forgiven his being a priest. My mother was the most beloved of his children and the one most like him.[6]

One story of Khalil's maternal grandfather settling in Bsharri reflects the intermingling that could be found then among Christians and Muslims, an openness that would be reflected in the poet's own expansive vision. Two horsemen supposedly entered Bsharri one day and, liking what they found, settled in the town. The two brothers, 'Abd al-Qadir and 'Abd al-Salaam, married into the Rahme clan and, converting from Islam to Christianity, both took the name of Rahme. The Rahme clan was large and, as a result, influential in Bsharri, a town of two thousand. The male child of 'Abd al-Qadir—Istifan 'Abd al-Qadir Rahme—grew up to be a Maronite priest. Kahlil's mother, Kamila, was Istifan's youngest and favorite daughter.

Istifan was an independent-minded cleric, unafraid to challenge authoritarianism within the Church or hypocritical embroilments in clan politics, an independence of spirit reflected in his strong-willed daughter Kamila. Historian Tanys Ludescher writes:

> Istfan was excommunicated for officiating at the marriage of a young woman from the pro-Ottoman al-Dahir clan and a young man from the politically-opposed al-Khoury clan. The marriage, which was witnessed by the eighteen-year-old Kamila, was quickly annulled by the church. Following the event, a breach developed between Istfan and the ruling clerics. In retaliation for the Church's actions, Istfan prevented his daughter, an intensely religious woman, from entering the convent… Thus at an early age, Gibran was made aware of the injury done to his family and the

hypocrisy of the Church. Moreover, in the figure of his beloved grandfather, he was presented with a model of a man who was both deeply religious and…anticlerical.[7]

Kamila would transmit her strong but self-directed spirituality, inherited from her father, to her son. Later, describing his mother's desire to become a nun, Gibran acknowledged the extent of Kamila's early influence.

> Strange that she should have resolved and prepared herself while in the prime of her life to enter the Nunnery of Saint Simon in the north of Lebanon. Ninety per cent of my character and inclinations were inherited from my mother…and although I do feel some antipathy towards monks, I love nuns and give them my heart's blessing. My love for them may stem from those…dreams which pervaded my mother's imagination in her youth.[8]

When Kamila reached marriageable age, she was betrothed to her cousin Hanna, the son of her father's brother 'Abd al-Salaam. Such interfamily alliances were a norm in villages like Bsharri, where for generations bloodlines crossed and strengthened insular clans. It was considered better to marry "one of us" than "one of them," even if "they" were neighbors from a nearby town.[9]

But Hanna 'Abd al-Salaam Rahme proved to be an undependable spouse and a restless man. In Bsharri, he had little to sustain him and his bride but empty dreams of glory. Kamila bore him a son, Peter, before he left to venture in Brazil, motivated by a lack of prospects and a hope for something better. But like so many other pioneer emigrants whose immunity to disease in new surroundings was fragile, he died in the alien climate, leaving Kamila and Peter in Bsharri.[10]

~

When Hanna died, Kamila was still in her late twenties. One day, needing to buy some ointment for an infected finger, she entered Isaac Gibran's herb shop. There she met Isaac's nephew, Khalil. Isaac introduced them, and Kamila attracted the interest of this handsome man with the amber cigarette holder. Sometime between 1879 and 1882, they were married, and in 1883 Kamila bore her second son. In accordance with the tradition of naming a boy by prefacing his father's name with the surname of his father's father, the child was called Gibran Khalil Gibran.

The man Kamila met in the apothecary's shop, for all his wayward charm, proved no more reliable a spouse than her first. In the four years following Khalil's birth, she bore two daughters, Marianna and Sultana. But growing responsibilities did not spur their father to earn a living wage. His lack of ambition and his habit of seeking to solve his financial problems at the *damma* table rather than in the fields were familiar to many. Even the family's simple stone house with its mud roof proved too burdensome for Khalil's father to keep up, and when the neglected home began collapsing around them, he found another place for them in one level of a four-story house on publicly owned land near the center of town. There, the overseer—an Ottoman official named Raji Beyk—gave the Gibrans free living quarters in exchange for Khalil's adeptness in local politics.

It was in this precarious situation that the family's shaky foundations began to break apart. To be poor in Bsharri was not unusual. But to be destitute and without pride, abandoning the last remaining shreds of respectability, was shameful. Through her attitude, Kamila's diminished position conveyed a sense of inferiority to her growing family. The children also felt the incompatibilities of the marriage. "There was a subtle, silent gap in understanding between the two," Gibran remembered later, when as a young man he reminisced about his childhood. "My father had a very imperious temper and was not a loving person."[11]

Khalil's father lived beyond his means, unable to provide for the family, and Kamila, while she lacked formal education, was worldly enough to resist her expected dependent role. She was aware of her qualities and refused to accept the vulnerability of the family's situation. If her behavior soured him, he retaliated in kind. Far from satisfying the needs of a growing family, he increasingly squandered the profits from his walnut grove at the gambling table. He and his alcoholic brother Eid became legendary subjects of local gossip, as they drank and caroused. Years later, Bsharri villagers still recalled stories about both brothers, tending to combine the two personalities into one.

~

While his family lacked the sense of security essential to the well-being of a young child, Khalil's circumstances offered wellsprings of strength upon which he could draw. Foremost was his mother, whose "sweetness, gentleness, and magnanimity" provided a lifeline for him.[12] Once he recalled an early time as a child when his mother spoke to him of Jesus.

> She said, "He was the greatest of all great poets. He who wrote not one single line save that line upon the sand." And in my perplexed ignorance I asked her…"But how can any man be a great poet without writing lines?"…With a smile…she said, "Who knows, my child? Perhaps, even we ourselves are the lines He wrote."

Kahlil's pen and ink drawing of the Gibran family tree, done at around age eight, with the names of family members on each leaf. (Courtesy Museo Soumaya.)

Another source was the magnificence of the countryside. Inspiring to Khalil were the nearby cliffs, split by yawning gorges, along with the clear and gushing torrents of the town's four rivers and cascading waterfalls. All his life, he would remember their vivid beauty and evocative names: *Wadi Qadisha*, the Blessed Valley; *Nahr Qadisha*, the Blessed River; *Nahr Nabaat*, the River of the Springs; *Nahr Ruwayyis*, the River of the Leader; *Nahr Simon*, the River of Simon. He reveled in the lore of his birthplace and sensed the sanctity of the crystal waters and the verdant forests. As an adult, he would constantly look back on the natural environment's perfection.

At the heart of Khalil's youthful world were the Cedars of Lebanon, monumental testimonials to vanished civilizations. Since biblical times they had been casting their shadows on the mountain snows, and though they were diminishing, they seemed as eternal as Mount Lebanon. The cedars linked isolated towns like Bsharri with the wider world beyond and the sea. For centuries, they had attracted travelers to the Holy Land who brought with them intimations of other civilizations and cultures. During the eighteenth and nineteenth centuries, Europeans made ritual pilgrimages to the giant groves. The notes of one pilgrim, writing in 1836 of how deeply moved he was by the cedars, reflected the meaning that the cedars held for many.

Watercolor of the Cedars of Lebanon, from twelve-year-old Kahlil's sketchbook. (Courtesy Museo Soumaya.)

The trunks of the old trees are covered with the names of travellers and other persons who have visited them…They are difficult to approach, and are surrounded with deep snow, which is not passable until the middle of summer when it begins to melt away…Their position, on the brow of the mountain, surrounded on every side by deep and solemn valleys, rocky and almost perpendicular descents, waterfalls and dreary dells, has something sacred and awful in it; they seem as if placed in their splendid and perilous site, like sentinels between time and eternity…[13]

Retreating from parental tirades at home, young Khalil found shelter and solace in his surroundings and, as he grew, came to identify with the timeless spirit of the places in which he could worship his own childlike sense of the divine. Much later, he recalled his impressions.

The first great moment that I remember was when I was three years old—a storm—I tore my clothes and ran out in it…And there were other great moments of new perception [as a] child…I was eight when I first saw [the sea]…My mother was on a horse, and my father and I were on a very beautiful, large Cyprian donkey—white. We rode up the mountain pass, and as we came over the brow, the sea was before us. The day was one of those when the sea and the sky are of one color.

There was no horizon visible—and the water was full of the large Eastern sailing vessels—four- and five-masters with sails all set. As we passed across the mountain, suddenly I saw what looked like an immeasurable heaven…and the ships sailing in it. I cannot describe what I felt…[14]

How did Khalil first develop the ability to later express his sense of the land as a sanctuary? Where did he learn the basic skills of reading and writing? In villages like Bsharri at the end of the nineteenth century, public schooling was nonexistent. The only education to be had came from priests, who taught a select few to read and write Arabic, along with elementary calculations. But this limited learning was offered essentially for one purpose: for young boys to become familiar with the Scriptures and the liturgy, and to assist during masses and religious services. Many of his friends and relatives attended these classes, but Khalil did not. So for his first twelve years, formal schooling was unavailable to him.

In later years, when explaining his early education he would refer to "tutors." The concept of a personal tutor for a boy in the straitened circumstances of the Gibrans' existence may seem incongruous, perhaps an effort to enhance the drab facts of an impoverished childhood. Yet if a tutor can be seen as an older, wiser, and significant person to whom a child turns for knowledge and guidance, then Khalil did have a tutor who was an important influence in his formative years.

It is unclear how Selim Dahir came into the boy's life, but he was a man who noticed the young boy's loneliness and felt his curiosity and thirst for knowledge. Even as a somewhat remote child, Khalil may have accepted his friendship gratefully and with some awareness of what it meant, for in his later years he remembered Selim Dahir in terms that glowed with love and admiration for his attentive creativity.

> Some people are so wonderful that I wonder whether their life isn't creation after all. …Selim Dahir…was a poet, a doctor, a painter, a teacher, yet he never would write or paint as an artist. But he lives in other lives. Everybody was different for knowing him. All Becharry was different. I'm different. Everybody loved him so much. I loved him very much, and he made me feel very free to talk to him. Once I asked him, in great confidence, whether if a company of the learned physicians came together, they couldn't find means to graft the human head on the horse and make centaurs. I may have been about seven years old then.[15]

Years later, Khalil's series of centaur drawings and paintings enabled him to create a language to express elemental links of humans to creatures and to nature—and the underlying unity of the Creation itself—intimations that Dahir's interest in Khalil helped him as a youth to imagine.

From Selim Dahir, Khalil learned the rudiments of the alphabet and language. The older man also opened him to the wider world and showed the boy how he could discover it through history books, through atlases that described the shape of continents and the spread of seas, and with scientific instruments that measured the universe. The debt the poet owed his friend was remembered and acknowledged when, in 1913, he wrote an elegy memorializing Dahir's passing.

> The son of the Cedars has died.
> Arise, o youth of the Cedars.
> …
> The son of the Mountain has died.
> Gird him with his father's sword.
> …
> Your sage, o youth, has died.
> Do not lament him.
> Do not flood his corpse with tears.
> Recall the words of his days and nights.
> Repeat the memory of his virtues.
> For every man there will be a day.
> In that day the design of his life
> Is reflected on the faces of his people.[16]

~

To a teacher concerned with his development, Khalil must have seemed complex and compelling. He was lonely, thoughtful, and seldom smiled. But his inner resources

Gibran's later painting,
Spirit of the Centaurs, 1913.
(Courtesy Museo Soumaya.)

abounded, and he drew upon them. Unsatisfied with mere dreams, he wanted them to be true. An aspect of this is seen in his almost compulsive drive to fill his days creating toys. Absent from his environment, toys were made with whatever could be found, and sometimes reached far beyond a young boy's ability. He remembered them with affection.

As a child I did not know I was sad. I just knew I was longing to be alone, making things. And they could never get me to play.

When I was…five or six or seven, I had a room all my own, filled with things I collected…It was a perfect junk shop…old frames and bits of clear stone and rings, and plants…and pencils—I had hundreds of pencils—and little ones that I wouldn't throw away. Later it became colored pencils. I drew swiftly and covered dozens of sheets of paper. And when there were no more sheets I drew on the walls of the room…And I wrote compositions. I remember one on an old man, poor and miserable—I said over and over again how old and cold and miserable he was—and then how another man came and helped him and did him good—a real Good Samaritan story.

Casting was my greatest delight when I was about eight years old, in the simplest and easiest of metals—lead. I would use sardine cans and sand…I wasn't always successful…But I made gods and goddesses in this way, and I loved it.

When I had finished a thing, I'd bring it down to be shown. But I liked them to look at it while I was not there. The pleasure was while I was doing the thing. The result was never what I wanted…It was always that way from the time I was nine or ten—and so I was never happy.

Once I planned a…garden, 14 or 15 yards square…all laid out and planted…I was going to carve all the gods and goddesses—in wood—for it…and each was going to make an appropriate gesture. Then when all was ready, I was going to pull the string, and every god at the same time would make his or her gesture…I was deeply interested in flying. And [I] bought yards and yards of stout cloth and rope and made a big thing to fly off the roof with. They let me finish it and then they wouldn't let me try it…But wheels were my chief joy. I made them myself—and waterwheels were the greatest. I made a big wheel that ran many little wheels by belts. But I was always unhappy because my vision was so far beyond anything I could do.[17]

Manipulated gods and goddesses, mechanical devices, vehicles of escape—all manifested his desire to imagine a universe he could help create. But they also show another aspect of his character: he was no idle dreamer, but a child who equated labor with love. This appetite to build worlds and earn respect for his work remained with him and was probably instrumental in driving him, once in America, toward the element of society that recognized even more innovative forms of talent and creativity.

Meanwhile, other events left indelible impressions on him. An especially significant one was an accident that occurred shortly before the family sailed for America.

> When I was ten or eleven years old, I was in a monastery one day with another boy, a cousin, a little older. We were walking along a very high place that fell off more than a thousand feet…The path had a hand rail, but it had weakened—and path and rail and all fell with us—and we rolled probably one hundred and fifty yards in the landslide. My cousin fractured his leg, and I got several wounds and cuts in the head down to the skull, and injured my shoulder. The shoulder healed—but healed crooked—too high and too far forward. So after it was well and sound, they pulled it apart again and strapped me to a real cross with thirty yards of strap and I stayed wrapped to that cross forty days. I slept and all sitting up. I was not strong enough to take ether when they broke the shoulder again. If it had hurt less, I should probably have cried out. But it hurt too much for me to cry. My father and mother were with me talking to me and that helped.[18]

The cousin, N'oula Gibran, remembered details of the prolonged mending of Khalil's shoulder. The painful incident contained a rare moment of truce, when both parents could set aside their differences, in order to calm and reassure their son. In Khalil's mind, the event acquired other associations. An ordinary splint became a cross, and the painful period of convalescence stretched out to forty days—the period Christ spent in the wilderness. The transposition illustrates the degree to which biblical legend imbued his thinking.

~

Religious awareness has long permeated the lives of the people of Mount Lebanon. Since they first banded together in the fifth century, Christians of Syria, united by their allegiance to Saint Maroun, had learned to live introspectively and protectively within the values of their religious thought. In 685, already known as rebels, they defied the Third Council of the Byzantine Church in Constantinople, setting themselves up as a separate body headed by their first patriarch, John Maron. The step was decisive and one that has lasted to this day.

While this schism was tearing apart the Catholics of the Byzantine Empire, the forces of Islam were invading the Holy Land. Large numbers of Christians readily accepted the Islamic faith, but a majority chose to resist, pay tribute, and retreat to Mount Lebanon. Throughout the period of Muslim ascendancy, physical remoteness, an indomitable spirit, and a warlike reputation protected these pockets of Maronite Christians and allowed them to preserve their distinct creed. Although Arabic replaced

The former Mar Sarkis (Saint Sergius) Monastery in Bsharri, in the seventh century a grotto for monks seeking refuge. (Courtesy Gibran Museum.)

the native Aramaic and Syriac among Maronites, even those who would never read the Scriptures used the sayings and symbols of Christ. Legends, tales, and songs perpetuated the stories of saints and holy figures from generation to generation. To a child in nineteenth-century Lebanon, stories about the asceticism of St. Maroun, the visits of Saint Anthony to Mount Lebanon, and the feasts of Saint George were ever-present contemporary events. Strengthening this spirituality was the mysticism that imbued local landmarks—inscribed stones, refuge-like caves, and prayerful grottos.

Thus, when the poet Khalil recalled his painful accident and its aftermath, he associated it with Jesus' forty days in the wilderness and suffering on the Cross. Throughout his life, when searching for a suitable simile or metaphor, he would turn to biblical traditions of his childhood. His early experiences, steeped as they were in Aramaic-inflected Arabic and the Gospels, connected his poetry to both the East and West, and remained for him a source of creative identity.

~

Politically, Lebanon in the late nineteenth century was the most modern of the Turkish provinces under the Ottoman Empire. In 1516, Turkish expansion beyond their Anatolian borders intensified a sense of isolation among the Maronites of Mount Lebanon. Since their first contact with the Roman Papal See in 1201, the Maronites had been strongly influenced by the West. Gradual rapprochement with the Roman Church culminated in 1736 with Maronite allegiance to Rome, while acknowledging their right to the Syriac liturgy and a tradition of noncelibate priesthood. Ties to Rome became stronger with the establishment of Franciscan, Carmelite, and Lazarist monasteries in the most remote areas of the country.

The Maronites continued to flourish under the reigns of two powerful leaders who attempted to unite the country against foreign domination. In 1590, Fakhr ad-Din II, a feudal lord of the Druze sect, was the first emir of Lebanon to command a united front of Christian and Druze leaders. Combining elements of Christian, Islamic, and Jewish thought, the Druze were open to Western persuasions, particularly since their leader, Fakhr ad-Din, had spent five years of exile at the Tuscany court of Cosimo II, where he observed firsthand the crafts of Western diplomacy, economics, and administration. Upon his return, he entrusted state offices, land grants, and military commands to enterprising Maronites, and he opened Lebanon to the Westernizing agents of missionaries, traders, and teachers.

A century and a half later, a second period of Westernization was launched by the emir Bashir II, who ruled Lebanon from 1788 to 1842. Breaking up the old patterns of feudalism and undermining Ottoman authority wherever possible, Bashir introduced modern Western machinery and other engineering achievements, and strengthened his authority by dispensing swift and impartial justice. Bashir's rule was like a long-delayed flowering of Lebanese culture. But in 1830, the old threat of foreign interference once again brought strife and dissension to Mount Lebanon. Imbued with a new sense of nationalism and outraged by Bashir's increasing domination, Druze, Christians, and Muslims united to depose him. Although he eventually proved to be a tyrant, Bashir II became a genuine national hero to many Lebanese. The young Khalil was profoundly influenced by tales about him, and as his feelings for his native country grew, he associated qualities of the heroic emir with his own father. Such feelings grew even stronger as events imperiled the Lebanese after Bashir's downfall.

With colonialism in full surge after Bashir II's deposition and exile, European powers intruded directly into Lebanese affairs. The brief alliance between Lebanese factions failed. Where Druze and Christians had shared Mount Lebanon under a carefully observed, symbiotic understanding, they now once again viewed each other with distrust. By 1845, unrest had given way to open hostility and a series of atrocities finally shattered their hard-won cooperation. In Constantinople, Turkish authorities secretly encouraged the violence, which benefitted Ottoman rule. Offstage, the English were unacknowledged allies of the Druze, while the French—also seeking to capitalize on the religious schism—were outspoken protectors of the Maronites.

15

For the next twenty years, ambush, slaughter, and pillaging beset the country-side. Scores of Christian villages were laid waste, while the Christian world watched in horror and blamed the Muslim population for acts of vengeance perpetrated by a few. In 1860, France openly intervened, supported weakly by the other European powers. French troops occupied Beirut for ten months and helped to shape a con-stitution for Lebanon, but the peace it was supposed to produce never materialized. Meanwhile, Bsharri—rife with intrigue, plotting, and destruction—reverted once again to its survival instincts. The town drew in upon itself, shunned outsiders, and sought only to protect itself in the steep hills shadowed by Mount Lebanon. In so doing, Bsharrians also raised a wall against a new invader from the Western world: the American Protestant missionary.

The heyday of these proselytizers, who sought to "revive pure Christianity among the Eastern Christians and to make 'spiritual conquests' among the Muslims," was beginning.[19] Based in Boston, they espoused a policy of "disinterested benevolence." This zealous band, products of New England divinity schools, fanned out globally, and the closed boundaries of the Levant only provided further incentive to their work. Their early attempts to settle in Palestine were frustrated by disease, death, and native hostility. Finally, they chose Beirut as the center of their missionary efforts and managed to lure a few Eastern Catholics to their first rudimentary schools. For years they limited their spiritual aims to establishing schools, providing medical aid, and publishing and distributing Arabic Bibles and religious tracts, aware that their efforts were punishable by death to both Muslim and Christian converts.

But in towns like Bsharri, Protestants from faraway America never gained a foot-hold. Mindful of an 1826 Maronite encyclical that forbade transactions with the atheist "Biblishiyyun," and remembering the fate of Asaad Shidiaq—an early Syrian Protestant who was imprisoned in a monastery near Bsharri, tortured, defiled, and fi-nally killed for his heretical beliefs—Bsharri aggressively resisted Protestant intrusion. Frustrated in their attempts to bring enlightenment to the hinterland, the missionar-ies contemptuously blamed resistance on native stupidity: "Bsharri, near the Cedars of Lebanon," the dean of the mission wrote home in 1874, "is one of the places where the people are so ignorant that the other villages laugh at them."[20]

~

For the young Khalil, religious persecution, atrocities, and such instances of biased snobbery had formed his parents' generation. All around him was evidence of sectar-ian enmity, and even though Maronite Christians no longer were forced to wear black, denied by Muslims the privilege of testimony in court, or forbidden to own horses, the memory of these offenses and the terrors of bygone violence haunted them. In his later search for some meaning to the deep antagonisms that divided his country's various sects, Khalil finally departed from all expressions of orthodoxy that stood in the way of freedom or growth.

Impoverishment entrapped many families in Bsharri. The meager soil of the rocky Lebanese hillsides no longer produced enough for the growing population. The fledgling economy fostered by Bashir II had slipped into severe depression: the Suez Canal diverted shipping from Lebanese ports; competition from Asia undermined the silk industry; a disastrous fungus destroyed wine production.

For the first time, many from Mount Lebanon considered emigration as a way out of their difficulties. Kamila's first husband, Peter's father, had been among the earliest to seek opportunity abroad through peddling. Others from Bsharri followed him, and by 1890, a small Gibran caravan headed by Khalil's cousin, Melham Gibran, had ventured to Boston, where they settled.

The departure of Khalil's own family was prompted by a final blow that led to its collapse. Although particular details remain unclear, an outline of events is apparent. Khalil's father, at least to some extent from his own lack of judgment, became involved in a small-town political racket. It came about because the powerful Raji Beyk, of the Hanna Dahir clan, had introduced a scheme of petty graft and extortion. It finally became intolerable, and a committee of outraged villagers turned to the patriarch and demanded Beyk's removal from office. The patriarch, beset in other areas by challenges to his authority, reviewed the case and ousted Beyk.

Khalil's father inevitably was caught up in the consequences of the scandal. He had long since undertaken certain duties for Beyk, and he was not liked in the town. Possibly he had misused taxes collected on Beyk's behalf. Whatever the case, he was accused of embezzlement, arrested, and arraigned for trial. For Kamila, proud daughter of a respected family, this was more than she could bear.

Long afterwards, Khalil would recall the event.

> The morning when the summons was served on my father—how the crowd rode into the courtyard of the big old house and how my mother stood bravely smiling. At the end of three years, [he] was found guilty and all his property was confiscated except the clothes on our backs…so that [we] became guests of the government in our own house.[21]

At the time of his father's arrest, Khalil was eight years old. His youth and innate sense of pride may have prevented him from learning the details of his father's downfall—whether or not he was subsequently jailed is still unknown. The boy's

The last portrait of the Gibran family together, just before their departure to America in the spring of 1895.
(Courtesy Museo Soumaya.)

strong-willed mother became his center. Her family suggested America as the best avenue of escape. Later, Khalil would protest that before she accepted emigration, she tried "to move heaven and earth to absolve her innocent husband from the crime of which he was accused."[22]

~

Shortly before the family left, a photograph showed them together for a last time. At his father's left is Kamila. In front of them sits the older of the two daughters, Marianna, clutching a bouquet of flowers. Beside her is an unfortunate gap that perhaps showed her sister Sultana. Behind the mother stands Peter, alert and alive to what may come next. Khalil, in a stalwart stance, clutches in his left hand a pencil, in his right a scroll. It is a touching photograph, one that mirrors the mingled loss and hope of a moment of transition known to so many others as well.

But the Gibran family's hope, however fragile, had memories to sustain it, considering the history of their lives and of the homeland they were leaving. Fortifying them were dreams of *al-mahjar*, destinations to which Phoenicians had traveled when cities dotting the Mediterranean were beacons for their quests. In 1895, New York was the mahjar for an ever-widening flow of emigrants from Mount Lebanon and Greater Syria. That spring, Kamila and her children embarked there, on a voyage of some five thousand miles.[23]

Point of departure, the Port of Beirut. Photo by the American Colony Photographic Division in Jerusalem. (Courtesy Library of Congress.)

Photo by Jacob Riis of an alley playground reminiscent of the Gibran family's Oliver Place neighborhood in Boston in 1895. Documenting urban tenement life, Riis used the term "Street Arabs" to describe often homeless children who panhandled in immigrant districts. (Courtesy Jacob A. Riis/Archive Photos/Getty Images.)

2

A CITY WILDERNESS

"When we left Syria," Khalil would recall, "we waited for my father in Egypt. Then we went on to France and waited there, and then we were going to Belgium to wait." But when the opportunity arose to save some of the family's property, his father remained behind.[1] So the Gibran family departed from the French port city of Boulogne aboard the Holland Line's SS *Spaarndam* on the final leg of their journey. On June 17, 1895, they arrived at Ellis Island.

The Gibrans were part of the Great Migration from the Near East that took place from the late 1870s until 1924, when severe restrictions on immigrants from that region would be imposed in the U.S. They and their fellow travelers were usually identified as Syrian or Turkish, given that the province of Mount Lebanon was part of Greater Syria and the Turkish Ottoman Empire. Greater Syria encompassed the historic lands of Lebanon, Syria, Jordan, and Palestine. Lebanon would not become a state until forty-eight years later, in 1943. Beleaguered immigration officials sorting through this boatload of newcomers identified the family of four steerage passengers as Rahmé—not Gibran. Probably because Boutros, or Peter, was the eldest male of the group, his name was entered—misspelled—as "Poutros Rhamé, 20 y." Kamila was entered as "Came Rhamé, 40 y"; young Khalil as "Jubran Rhamé, 11 y"; Marianna as "Marianne Rhame, 9 y"; and Sultana as "Sultani Rahmé, 7 y." Marianna recalled that after spending their first night at Ellis Island, the next day they began their journey north to Boston.[2]

~

Boston was the natural choice of place for the family to settle, since it was home to Melham Gibran and his family, as well as many other cousins and friends who had emigrated from Bsharri. Economically as well as ethnically and racially diverse,

Oliver Place, Boston, where the Gibran family first settled. (Courtesy Private Collection.)

Boston's South End was also home to South Cove, an area next to South Station where many immigrants from Greater Syria settled.

Arriving in Boston, the Gibrans moved into the same building with Melham and family at Oliver Place. Now mostly razed and renamed Ping On Alley, part of Boston's Chinatown, it was in 1895 a major Syrian enclave in the city's South Cove. Protected on four sides by brick row houses, it was reached by a narrow entrance that tunneled between two tall buildings facing toward Beach Street. To what extent immigrants chose the security of this self-enclosed retreat, or were simply shunted there by officials, is uncertain. But here Kamila could hear her native Arabic language spoken, feel comforted by familiar customs, and seek the understanding of other immigrants like herself.

To many in Boston at the time, the teeming South End was at once too close to the center of the city to ignore and too complicated in its cultural diversity to make sense of. The chosen home of immigrants from many countries and religions, it lacked the solidity and identity of older neighborhoods like the North End, or the aspiring middle-class values of residents in outlying Charlestown or Dorchester. By 1892, its social problems were compared unfavorably to East London's notorious slums. "But the picturesque features which light up the gloom of East London are wanting in the South End where life is characterized by a pathetic monotony," commented a report of the *Wellesley Prelude*.[3] City natives feared the diseases—tuberculosis, typhus, cholera, trachoma—that newcomers might carry. They also feared that poor immigrants, unable to support or care for themselves, would drain the resources of the state or the charity of neighbors.[4]

In the 1890s, pioneering social scientists were examining the indignities of the South End that awaited thousands like the Gibrans—crowded housing, disease, and poverty. One of them, Robert Woods, in his book *The City Wilderness,* left a description that reveals the attitudes of early social workers and a vivid picture of the South End and its forty thousand inhabitants.

> The nearness of the district to the city's throng, together with remoteness from its best life, allows the irresponsible class of people to come and go, who throw aside the ordinary restraints and give reins to their worst impulses...This South End which once rose out of the water, as it were, to become a refuge for the older American families, has now become a common resort for all nationalities...In this wide variety, however, a comparatively small number of nationalities make up the greater part of the population. The Irish, Jews, British Americans, Americans, and Negroes are its chief constituents; but the English, Germans, Scotch, French, Swedes, Norwegians, Italians, Greeks, Armenians, Austrians, and a few other nationalities are represented, though in considerably smaller numbers. And if we add to these, Chinatown and the Syrian settlement in Oliver Place, both on the outskirts of the district, we supply an appropriate finishing touch to the group, a population as complicated as it is inharmonious.[5]

The Syrian community, mentioned by Woods almost as an afterthought, was an incomprehensible presence. Social surveyors could more easily describe Irish and Middle European ways than account for the behavior of swarthy Levantines who called themselves Christians, held their prayer beads tightly, and showed a suspicious resistance to becoming Americans. Oliver Place was a territory equally alien to the overseers of the Associated Charities of Boston, who observed:

> The Syrians are nearly all peddlers if they are anything. Some are persistent candidates for charity. There are very few of them in the South End outside of Oliver Place. Next to the Chinese, who can never be in any real sense American, they are the most foreign of all our foreigners. Whether on the streets in their oriental costumes, or in their rooms gathered about the Turkish pipe, they are always apart from us. They are hospitable in their homes, but they are also deceitful, and out of all the nationalities would be distinguished for nothing whatsoever excepting as curiosities.[6]

Kamila began to earn a living in the expected way. Carrying fifty pounds of laces and linens, she trudged back and forth to the grand houses of the Back Bay, and even worked her way to the suburbs of Brookline and Cambridge. Peddling was a way of life for many immigrants from Ottoman Syria. Except for some sporadic, missionary-sponsored visits in the 1850s and 1860s, Syrian immigration to America was negligible until the well-documented 1878 arrival of a Protestant family to New York. In the next decade, a widening trickle of merchants from Greater Syria came and hawked olivewood trinkets and colorfully embroidered native handiwork, popular for their Holy Land associations. These wayfarers found a market for their colorful wares at country fairs and expositions, and slowly traveled westward until, perhaps, they took up homesteading along the frontier or settled down in midwestern farming towns. In time, they eventually assimilated. Not so with those who followed.

In the 1890s, small "Syrian colonies" began to form in cities, from where they fanned out into surrounding areas and pedaled their growing selection of dry goods, laces, hardware, or whatever would satisfy the household needs of the American public. More than their dress, speech, or religion, it was their seeming avoidance of wage labor for an employer—the expected path to salvation—that set them apart and made them incomprehensible to even charitably inclined social workers.

> They come…thinking to sweep up money in the street…They have little idea how to work, for they have never had to stick to anything at home. They have worked when it pleased or when the crops demanded it. Work in our sense of the word they have never done. Regular hours throughout the year is a thing unknown to them. Even those who start in at factory work often prefer peddling… They peddle in nearly all the suburbs of Boston…Who has not seen these dark-complexioned women with black kerchiefs over their heads and baskets under their arms, getting in or out of electric cars? How many families of Boston have not had them at their doors, peddling so-called Syrian silk and Oriental goods (which are usually made in Paris or Constantinople), or with their baskets filled with needles, pins and other small wares?…They seem to need money, are thinly clad, and footsore.[7]

Perhaps most outrageous and repellent to Puritan New Englanders was the practice of mothers leaving their children "to be looked after by their idle husbands" and going out to work. A woman who was little more than a drummer or packhorse—although, like Kamila, probably the financial support of her family—could not have been more foreign to Yankee understanding of an industrious woman.

The idle husbands can be seen at almost any hour of the day by going into Oliver Place and looking around. It is not the custom in this country to let the women work and have the men remain idle at home. When girls and young men go out on the streets to peddle, they fall into bad company, and, as one who understands his people well, says: "They often end by going to houses of ill repute." And all this is encouraged by buying of and aiding these people.[8]

Thus, many of Boston's Syrians were visibly different in appearance and attitudes, prompting stereotypes. "Every time a kind-hearted individual buys of a Syrian something he does not want—or gives food, clothing, or money for doctors' bills without investigating the case—he encourages begging, lying, idleness, neglect, exposure, and a future increase of 'Syrians to sweep up money from our streets,'" said an Associated Charities report.[9] Even the wretched living conditions of Oliver Place were blamed on moral depravity: "The desire to appear poor encourages a mode of living which is alike unhealthful physically and morally…They overcrowd tenements to avoid high rents, and dirt and squalor are their companions. Things are permitted in Oliver Place, which if it were a public way, could not exist."[10]

~

It was within this setting that twelve-year-old Khalil, ever sensitive to the slightest affront toward him or his family, soon became aware of the scorn that accompanied the charitable distribution of food, clothing, and medicine. What he thought of the nascent social reforms is unclear because he rarely spoke of it in later years. Instead, he looked past the hardships of Oliver Place, clouding our understanding of the social forces and early influences that shaped him. Amid the squalid surroundings of his early immigrant years began a protectiveness of his private life and thoughts, one that continued throughout his life. Perhaps because the indignities were so difficult to accept, he overrode the filth and stench of Oliver Place with a sense of pride and privilege. Early on he found a way of removing himself, noted by a friend who observed that all his life he has been "remote."[11]

One avenue that would lead Khalil—and many other immigrant children—out of their "offensive conditions" was the public school system. For every foreign enclave, there existed a nearby school ready to immerse youngsters into the indoctrinating waters of the American dream. Close to Oliver Place on Tyler Street was the Quincy School, a boys' school whose ethnic makeup was becoming as diversified as that of the South End. One-third of its pupils were Irish, one-third American, and the remaining third consisted of Jews and "other foreigners." Among the latter was a mixture of Central and Eastern Europeans, along with a scattering of Chinese children. It was in this polyglot environment, brief records tell us, that Gibran Khalil Gibran first went to school.[12]

The experience marked him indelibly. Due either to impersonal registration procedures or to clerical impatience, his name was misspelled and shortened to "Kahlil" Gibran. And so, except for a few attempts to continue calling himself Gibran Khalil Gibran, the ac-

Tyler Street, Boston. From *right*: two wings of the Quincy School, adjacent to the building housing Our Lady of the Cedars Maronite Church. (Courtesy Schlesinger Library, Radcliffe Institute, Harvard University.)

culturation of the little boy to America began with his acceptance of an abbreviated name, one more time-saving and compatible to the American bureaucratic ear and eye. After his death, efforts to realign his name to a transliteration acceptable to Arabic scholars failed, frustrated by the simple reality of turn–of–the–century decisions that anglicized not only names but attitudes and manners. These surgically swift gestures penetrated more deeply than the perpetrators or their unwary victims realized.

When he entered school on September 30, 1895, Kahlil had been in the U.S. just a little more than two months. He was placed in the ungraded class reserved for immigrant children who were to be immersed in English-language classes. In this no man's land where pupils might chatter in half a dozen different languages, a child could progress as fast as his "admirable traits" would allow; that is, if he were "ambitious, quick witted, and imitative."[13] Kahlil apparently reached the expected levels of achievement and further impressed his teachers by the confidence with which he sketched and drew. Marianna always remembered her brother's drawing as outstanding. Whether the family story of his interrupting a chalkboard lesson and showing the teacher how a figure should be drawn is true or not, the Yankee and Irish women who remained to teach another generation of Gibrans recalled Kahlil vividly.

Kahlil's own thoughts about Quincy School, and the teachers who helped him adjust during his first months in America, were later expressed when once he was asked what was the most difficult period in his lifetime. He replied:

> The two years when I was first in Boston. They were my most miserable. I had only the teachers in the school. And they were so loving to me, so kind. When I was in college, I had letters from all of them. You see, I had gone through so many of the grades while I was there. And they really loved me. And I felt it. But we had nothing in common.[14]

School was an opportunity offered by his family only to Kahlil. Marianna and Sultana were not allowed to attend. Tradition and precedent, as well as economic need, prevented their going, and neither ever learned to read or write. Instead, they became part of a new family enterprise: they joined their older half-brother Peter in operating his store. This expansion of the family's commercial activities was entirely the result of Kamila's hard work, perseverance, and thrift. Within a year she had saved enough money to enable Peter to open a small dry goods store at 61 Beach Street. Marianna and Sultana worked as salesgirls, and Marianna later remembered it as fun—particularly when Peter was occupied and she would reach into the cash box and filch a penny for her and her sister to squander on a Syrian sweet or sherbet. But despite a flurry of effort and activity, Peter's business never thrived.

Harrison Avenue and Beach Street, Boston, where the Gibran family's dry goods store run by Kahlil's brother Peter was located. (Courtesy Rickards Collections, Boston Athenaeum.)

Yet, if ever a child of Kamila's was to prosper financially, Peter seemed destined to be the one. Of all the children, he was regarded as the most personable and socially talented, even the most handsome. He played the oud—or lute—with feeling and had a large repertoire of songs. People liked him for his charm and easy attitude. Marianna and Sultana adored him; it was no secret that they, and others, preferred Peter's outgoingness to Kahlil's introspection. Years later, Marianna fondly recalled Peter's verve and loved to tell how proud she had been to walk through the South End streets with her dashing older brother.

Kahlil, especially, recognized and respected Peter's popularity. "Father loved Peter, his stepson, very much, much more than me," he once said. "He had a good head…And everybody loved him. He was so courteous, and sweet and upright and gentle."[15] Peter's worldly ease was somewhat shared by the youngest daughter, Sultana, whose own beauty and personality were emerging. Marianna's reminiscence of the childhood alliances within the family was that she and Kahlil "used to be together against Sultana because everything was 'Sultana, Sultana.' She was so lovely, and she and my mother had such lovely voices."[16]

Despite the poverty and occasional despair about making it in America, it was a good and close family. Kamila's energy was unflagging, and her courage seldom faltered. She had an intuitive respect for her children's spiritual development, and for Kahlil's in particular. His fragmented impressions and memories of this period point to an increasing sense of withdrawal, looking for some interior route that would compensate for the abrupt change from a rural refuge to this city wilderness. Kamila must have protected her introverted son, for later he often recalled her sympathetic understanding of his need to be alone. "My mother understood…When I was a boy, say from nine to thirteen, sometimes she would smile at someone who came in and look at me and lay her finger on her lip and say, '…He's not here.'"[17]

At the same time, Kamila conveyed to Kahlil a spirit of independence and fostered in him a will to develop outside the family's pressing mercantile existence. Her open-minded attitude encouraged him to meet strangers and form acquaintanceships beyond tightly knit Oliver Place. The sequence of events that would facilitate Kahlil's early access to the Boston world of art and letters was only possible for a self-directed boy who felt free to explore the adjacent neighborhood. Later he remembered his mother's wisdom with gratitude and love.

> My mother was a most remarkable being…she was always doing little things that put me on the way to love others besides myself—always, as it were, pushing me away or out a little. She freed me from herself. And she said things to me when I

was twelve years old that I'm just realizing now—prophetic things. She knew things very wonderfully.[18]

~

The emerging South End street culture must have fascinated Kahlil, as well as the benevolent social scientists. To them, the omnipresence of unsupervised children, gutter-fast and alley-wise, signaled family breakdown. Preoccupied with youthful gangs, they observed:

> The term "street children" is used advisedly, for as a matter of fact, most of the children of this locality live on the street when they are not asleep. The streets educate with fatal precision…In this promiscuous street life, there is often every sort of license that can evade police authority. Juvenile rowdyism thrives.[19]

While overestimating the percentage of "incorrigible truants" with "criminal tendencies," the social scientists finally conceded that "a small minority of these children manage to keep an obedient, law-abiding spirit, in spite of 'street education,' although one does not know how."[20] The Gibran children, if noticed, would probably have been classified within this latter group. Kahlil later recalled once trying to fly a kite in a crowded South End street and being stopped by a policeman, an offense unlikely to qualify as "promiscuous street life."

Around him, all the time, the city was expanding even as he grew. Attractions of all kinds flourished in the South End. There was Washington Street where the Grand Dime featured lurid melodramas, while its rival, the Grand Opera House, advertised vaudeville shows as "expressly suited for women and children…every day a bargain day." The Columbia catered to an audience that demanded Irish comedy. Along with varied and cheap theater, close to Oliver Place there were numerous public dance halls and "a variety of minor attractions…of a catch-penny character"—shooting galleries, a poorly stocked aquarium, a flourishing series of merry-go-rounds on a vacant lot, waxwork shows, and the sidewalk fantasy of "Barnum's What Is It?" As one contemporary account described it, "the noise of discordant music, the glare of electric lights, and the gaudy decorations of tents and booths" contrasted with "the dimly lit, squalid neighborhood."[21] Just a few blocks away from this colorful sidewalk world was the self-consciously uplifting culture of Brahmin Boston.

Invisible barriers preventing social interaction between the South End and neighboring Back Bay were more impenetrable than the railroad that physically divided them. The chief contact between the two areas came from South End servants working in Beacon Street and Commonwealth Avenue mansions. Robert Woods described the breach between these geographically close yet culturally distant worlds.

> Though the lack of friendly association between the Back Bay and the South End is so complete that there is no direct street car communication, yet it must not be said that the two sections have no dealings with each other. The Back Bay which sometimes "investigates" the South End would probably be surprised to know how constantly it is being in turn investigated by means of back-door and below-stairs points of approach.[22]

Still, Back Bay residents did not completely ignore their less fortunate neighbors. The record of Boston's charity-minded citizens was already long and generous. The Associated Charities of Boston, founded in 1879, had been strongly supported by the "fiery inspiration" of Phillips Brooks, a distinguished Episcopalian minister. In the 1890s, the illuminating stewardship of the great reformer Robert Treat Paine guided the association's efforts toward a "new charity." Socially conscious leaders like Paine were finally recognizing themselves in Emerson's words about the "foolish philanthropist" and were beginning to understand that in "miscellaneous popular charities… men do what is called a good action, as some piece of courage or charity, much as they would pay a fine in expiation of daily nonappearance on parade…Their virtues are penances."[23] By the 1890s, social reformers were demanding more than money to relieve human distress.

Parts of the South End by this time could already be described by Edward Everett Hale as "the most charited region in Christendom." The "new charity," by contrast,

Municipal playground on Tyler Street, one block from Denison House.

was based on "reconstructive" principles that aimed "to build up a better life for the district out of its own material and by means of its own reserve of vitality."[24] This call to neighborhood pride and self-sufficiency was designed to erase the earlier images of outdoor work relief and the degrading poorhouses. It demanded individual involvement on the part of the charity-minded, who were to "endeavor by personal friendship and counsel and co-operation to help them upward and onward."[25] In short, Back Bay Boston was about to enter the South End slums and work side by side with the immigrant population to improve their lot. The consequences for Kahlil would be far-reaching.

~

Enabling this new approach were "settlement houses." Established within needy neighborhoods, these domiciles served to "lighten the burdens of discouraged fathers and mothers, so that it shall be possible for them to have homes as bright and happy as our own."[26] In 1891, a group of dedicated men began an experiment in social living at 20 Union Park and founded the South End House. A year later, another settlement house followed when a four-story brick house on Tyler Street, across from the Quincy School, was converted for service. Sponsored by the College Settlement Association, Denison House was managed by a group of college-educated women, who in years to come were to set a distinguished example of dedicated, practical, and positive reform.

Denison House soon became a South End landmark. Children were encouraged to visit and play in its backyard; mothers were invited to tea; even the parish priest,

(Courtesy Schlesinger Library, Radcliffe Institute, Harvard University.)

anxious lest these Protestant women evangelize his parishioners, became involved in the dialogue. In the next two years, the Denison House "family," under the guidance of headworker Helena Stuart Dudley, made significant inroads into the community's social life, and their South End neighbors began to trust these well-bred, educated social workers, and even to seek their aid.

Kahlil discovered Denison House sometime in the winter of 1895. At that time, its social workers were endeavoring to entice neighborhood children with a variety of diversions based on their genteel notions about culture. Poetry readings, dramas, and recitals attracted children in from the streets. Arts and crafts classes, social studies groups, and Shakespeare clubs were also introduced. Wellesley College students, who contributed to the settlement's financial resources, volunteered their services, soon establishing a pattern of shared musicals and plays with their newly found audience. Before long, young boys and girls, barely familiar with English, were performing in *As You Like It*, *Twelfth Night*, and *Julius Caesar*.

Kahlil may have been one of the first Syrian visitors. The chief concern of the Denison House women at the time were Irish Catholics, and judging from the carefully kept notes in the house's daybook, the presence of a Syrian child was unusual. Not until the turn of the century does the daybook show evidence of growing Syrian attendance. Kahlil was unique also for his draftsmanship, which the Denison House women recognized. As he sketched in classes there and at Quincy School, his skill grew, and he began to seek out other places where he could enrich his knowledge. In doing so, he was unexpectedly thrust into a highly publicized end-of-the century controversy.

Boston's latest contribution to the cultural enrichment of its citizens was its imposing public library, designed by the New York firm of McKim, Mead and White, and completed in 1892. Not only did the exterior of this imposing edifice rival that of any other American library, but its interior—decorated

Bacchante statue, by Frederick MacMonnies, at the Boston Public Library. (Courtesy Daderot, Wikimedia Commons.)

with works by Puvis de Chavannes, Edwin Austin Abbey, and John Singer Sargent—proclaimed the city's determination to lead in "the great movement toward popularizing art culture."[27] Along with the impressive frescoes decorating its halls, architect Stanford White contributed in 1895 what he thought would further enhance the library's aesthetic position: Frederick MacMonnies' life-sized statue of a bacchante, which stood in the courtyard as a fountain ornament.

The Bacchante proved to be a controversial beauty. Clasping a lively babe in one arm and holding aloft a bunch of grapes with the other, the dancing nymph was an immediate and sensational attraction. Her heel-kicking posture and general air of abandonment became a cause célèbre for the Boston censors—the whole city took sides on whether her provocative nudity was a fit subject for public exhibition. The publicity brought thousands to the library's courtyard. "The Bacchante continues to draw great throngs," one article read. "Suburbans are now coming in battalions, and Bacchante special trains are shunting the regular theater trains onto the sidings."[28]

Thirteen-year-old Kahlil was also smitten by the bronze figure. Sometime during the winter of 1896, he drew her likeness. The sketchbook containing this rendering surfaced in the late 1970s, its contents attesting to Kahlil's remembrances of his

Kahlil's sketchbook drawing at age twelve of the same Bacchante statue. (Courtesy Museo Soumaya.)

early Boston years. However, illustrations of his beloved cedars and of himself as a shepherd confirm his precociousness. Especially arresting is a drawing of "Death Staying the Hand of the Sculptor," Daniel Chester French's memorial to sculptors Martin and James Milmore, and dedicated at Forest Hills Cemetery in 1893. His preoccupation with newly installed art testifies to the adolescent's resolve. It is one thing to walk from Oliver Place to a newly built library in nearby Copley Square. But leaving central Boston and venturing three miles to what was then a sanctuary in suburban Jamaica Plain demonstrates determination.[29]

It was fortunate that Kahlil drew Bacchante early on, because late that year a phalanx of outraged citizens petitioned for her removal, and she was exiled to the more libertine corridors of New York's Metropolitan Museum. With this perspective on the figure who, to Victorian eyes, was "the incarnation of drunkenness and lewdness, a goddess of shame,"[30] Kahlil's interest in the statue seems significant, as he must have been aware of the controversy surrounding it. This early encounter with museum art was made possible by the rise of American public institutions, despite the tinge of Victorian prudery that still inhibited these cultural efforts. The well-publicized censorship of a major American art work and its removal from the library doubtlessly impressed the thirteen-year-old artist.

~

Starting in 1887, there was another effort to help Boston's immigrant children: the distribution of books throughout the city. Jessie Fremont Beale, a social worker at the Children's Aid Society, had devised and guided the project known as "home libraries." Its aim was to develop local stations in the homes of the poor, each one consisting of a "neat little bookcase filled with fifteen carefully selected juvenile books and five bound collections of suitable magazines."[31] Along with instilling a love for the care of books, it was hoped that home libraries would give poor children a chance to act as their own librarians. The plan included an interested outsider, or "friendly visitor," who would meet the children weekly, lead them in group discussions, initiate games, and sponsor outings. By 1896 there were sixty-seven home libraries scattered throughout Boston, and their success in keeping children off the streets was spreading.

In discovering new ways to bring refinement and literature to poor and immigrant children, Miss Beale organized a formidable group of volunteers. She also used her position as librarian of the Children's Aid Society to enlist members of the Boston establishment—those from among the wealthy and artistic, literary, and academic circles—who were invited to help the poor. Miss Beale would introduce Kahlil to a patron whose literary tastes and aesthetic sense would energize and provide focus to his artistic interests. The link to this introduction was Kahlil's art teacher at Denison House.

Florence Peirce was a Denison House resident from 1894 to the spring of 1896. Her role included attendance at meetings, visits with families in the Tyler Street area, and helping the ailing get to hospitals. It is not known whether she was a college student interested in social science or an artistically inclined volunteer. But she belonged to that growing clan of self-effacing women who were "distressed" and "made restless" by a "sense of privilege unshared."[32] Her early presence in Kahlil's life, and the important role she played in it, foreshadowed the female prototype with whom he would often be associated with in later life. Liberated and liberating, interested and interesting, the emerging type of emancipated women whom Florence Peirce represented would help Kahlil throughout his career.

Recognizing the thirteen-year-old boy's ability, Florence Peirce brought him to Jessie Fremont Beale's attention, whereupon Miss Beale wrote to a gifted photographer and publisher whom she believed could guide a child with artistic promise.

November 25, 1896

My dear Mr. Day:

...I am wondering if you may happen to have an artist friend who would care to become interested in a little Assyrian boy Kahlil G—. He is not connected with any society, so any one befriending the little chap would be entirely free to do with him what would seem in their judgment wise. He strolled into a drawing class at the College Settlement on Tyler Street last winter and showed a sufficient ability to make Miss Peirce feel that he was capable of some day earning his living in a better way, than by selling matches or newspapers on the street, if someone would only help him to get an artistic education.

His future will certainly be that of a street fakir if something is not done for him at once. The family are horribly poor, living on Oliver Place, and will insist upon having some financial assistance from this little boy just as soon as the law will allow unless he is on the road to something better. Next year he will be fourteen, beyond the school age, so we are specially interested to start the little fellow this year in his drawing, if such a thing is at all possible.

A drawing which he made in the cloisters, at the library, of the Bacchante made quite a sensation.

I fear you will feel this request in regard to Kahlil almost an intrusion, but I am so interested in the little fellow myself, and yet so utterly helpless, that I feel as if I must try to find someone else who can be of real use to him.

Wednesday

Very cordially yours, Jessie Fremont Beale[33]

Beale's letter reveals attitudes common to the social milieu that Kahlil was about to enter, a complex mix of good intentions and cultural blinders. But her belief in, and generosity on behalf of, the "little Assyrian boy" would prove well-founded and be rewarded by his achievement of an artistry that would gracefully accommodate such complexities as the ones that mark her letter to the singular Mr. Day.

One of his early bookbindings, Kahlil's cover for *Omar the Tentmaker*, by Nathan Haskell Dole.
(Reprint: Boston Photo Imaging.)

3

BOOKMAKING AND
BOHEMIA

Fred Holland Day, the potential mentor to whom Jessie Fremont Beale had
addressed her letter, was one of Boston's end-of-the-century flashpoints. A
financially independent literary maverick, photographer, and supporter of the
avant-garde, he was at that time engaged in a venture as partner of the publishing
firm Copeland & Day. In this capacity he had not only supplied Jessie Beale's home
libraries with many donations of richly illustrated books, but also played the role
of weekly "friendly visitor," reading aloud to children from the slums, introducing
them to classics of Western literature, and generally acting as a teacher.[1]

Born in 1864, Day was the only son of a prosperous tannery owner in suburban Norwood and a mother who was associated with a post-abolitionist group
that worked to offer educational opportunities to African Americans. By the 1880s,
Day had managed to head for Boston. Though he struggled at expressing himself
verbally, he possessed an instinct for the magic of words and a keen sense of beauty
and aesthetic judgment. Coveting rare first editions by renowned figures such as
Shakespeare, Keats, and Balzac, he also looked for the new and controversial, like
Oscar Wilde. Bohemian Boston became mostly forgotten before the new century
was very old. But for a brief decade, it enabled Day to thrive.

Day's involvement with immigrant street kids appears not to have stemmed
from the usual feelings of guilt shared by other do-gooders, like his mother. Instead,
he was attracted to the vivid drama found on the South End's bazaar-like streets. He
enjoyed the dizzying range of sights and sounds, and the varied faces and features of
Chinese, African, Italian and other Mediterranean children inspired him to experiment with the new art of pictorial photography. Just as Jessie Beale's letter plunged

Kahlil Gibran into the Boston art world, it also provided Day with a subject who would become widely recognized.

~

Portrait of F. H. Day, 1899, by seminal American photographer Gertrude Käsebier. (Courtesy Library of Congress.)

When Miss Beale wrote him about Kahlil, Day was thirty-two and had already toured Europe, where he collected all manner of materials about his favorite writers and visual artists.[2] He captured in photographs the homes and countryside haunts of his literary idols and used these prints in search of literary souvenirs. Before long, editors and academics began to consider him an independent scholar of sorts and an artistic bridge between American and English letters, thus allowing him to play an important role in shaping a renaissance in poetry.

Day's closest friend in his literary adventures was poet Louise Imogen Guiney, daughter of an Irish immigrant named Patrick Guiney who during the Civil War rose from the ranks of private to become one of Lincoln's generals. Her natural eloquence and well-turned phrases balanced Day's awkwardness; her single-minded devotion to literature offset his haphazard passions; and her pragmatism, based on a threadbare poverty, counterbalanced his overflowing purse. In their youth, they followed a wayfaring life trekking the English countryside. He became attracted to the thoughts and trappings of aestheticism. She lived to perpetuate the memory of writers out of fashion, especially the poets of the seventeenth century.

Fred Holland Day's bookmaking background stemmed from the 1880s, when he worked in the Boston office of the New York publishing firm A. S. Barnes. By the nineties, he had become a moving spirit in the crusade by Boston's intellectual elite to stamp out mediocrity, mammonism, and hypocrisy. "Little magazines" and new literature about to thrive in the U.S. included Herbert Stone and Ingalls Kimball of *Chapbook*; Herbert Small of Small, Maynard & Co.;, Herbert Copeland and Fred Holland Day. The revolt was embodied in the birth of two new magazines: *The Mahogany Tree* and *The Knight Errant*. Day was an important force in each of them.

Louise Guiney and Day, probably at Five Islands, Maine. (From the former collection Norwood Historical Society.)

The Mahogany Tree, first appearing in January 1892, included an editorial staff of Harvard graduates and the youthful Herbert Copeland. Day contributed articles under the pseudonym of "Bibliophile." Its philosophy was defined as "the deeper side of American life...away from the narrowing rush of business; away from all shallow trivialities."[3] Lasting from January to July 1892, *The Mahogany Tree* appeared in twenty-six weekly issues, and shortly before its demise, Day was already collaborating on a new magazine called *The Knight Errant*. Financed by Day, it was created by the talented Bertram Grosvenor Goodhue, architect and designer; Ralph Adams Cram, architect and critic; Francis Watts Lee of the Elzevir Press; along with Herbert Copeland. A quarterly magazine, it lasted only for four issues—from April 1892 to July 1893—its brief life fulfilling Louise Guiney's words in her dedicatory poem: "A short life in the saddle, Lord! / Not long life by the fire!"[4]

Such failures left Fred Holland Day undaunted. Recognizing that American audiences yearned for the new English talent, and that the 1891 Copyright Act signed by the U.S. and Britain permitted joint publishing in its countries, Day undertook his most meaningful and lasting endeavor. Copeland & Day was born when Day again chose as his business partner Herbert Copeland, then on the staff of *Youth's Companion* magazine. Located in an "aesthetic little office"[5] at 69 Cornhill, known for its bookstall associations, it became a serious and successful publishing house, respected for "a higher standard of integrity in craftsmanship and in commercial standing as well as in the character of the literature issued."[6] Embellished with the symbolic imprint of lilies and roses, recalling the sixteenth-century printer marks of Richard Day and Robert Copeland, the ninety-eight books issued in its five and a half years of existence pioneered the way for modern typography and bookmaking. A colleague later described Day as being among "those artist-publishers and artist-printers who by their work and influence have restored printing to its rightful place among the Fine Arts."[7]

First appearing in December 1893, the firm's initial offerings included several co-editions originating from London's Elkin, Mathews and John Lane. Most notable were Oscar Wilde's *Salome*, illustrated by Aubrey Beardsley; Francis Thompson's *Poems*, and Dante Gabriel Rossetti's *The House of Life*. Its first American contribution was Architect Ralph Adams Cram's *The Decadent*.[8] Set in an opium and wine-drenched estate called Vita Nuova, the booklet, printed on handmade paper, discussed socialism, art, and even the "clash" between an "exotic East" and a "practical West."

By 1895, the firm was well established and publishing new works. Copeland induced many of his Harvard colleagues

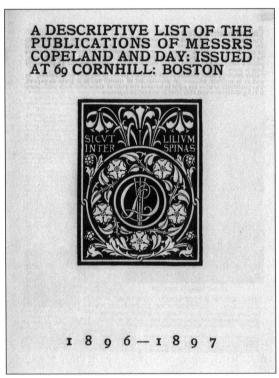

Copeland & Day colophon and publisher's list, by noted American architect and typeface designer Bertram Grosvenor Goodhue. (Courtesy Boston Athenaeum.)

to submit their manuscripts. Louise Guiney unabashedly championed her own and her good friend Alice Brown's works. A lively juvenile series called "The Yellow

Hair Library" was successfully launched. Gertrude Smith's Arabella and Araminta stories were embellished by Ethel Reed's saucy and surprising illustrations.

One barely known writer who gained influence after his Copeland & Day introduction was Stephen Crane. Seeing merit in his starkly agnostic protests, Day published *The Black Riders and Other Lines* in 1895. Significantly affecting the shape and style of free verse by a generation to come, these poems also profoundly affected young Kahlil. Day—like other bright, dissatisfied young people around him—was searching for relevant movements and causes at the "sick little end of the century." After exploring Jacobism, spiritualism, and decadence, and after dressing young poets' words in fine new packages, he would explore one more art form—pictorial photography. It was here that the "potential street fakir" would perhaps inspire him. He, in turn, would challenge and encourage Kahlil, through his carefully acquired background in poetry and art, leading toward results that Jessie Beale is unlikely to have imagined. The artistic circles into which Kahlil was about to enter seemed far removed from his childhood in Mount Lebanon and his adolescence in the South End. Kahlil's self-image first would be pressed to germinate beneath Day's complex gaze.

~

After Jessie Beale requested Fred Holland Day's help with Kahlil's education, Florence Peirce worked hard to locate the elusive boy. Finally she wrote, "Through the ministrations of Denison House, Kahlil has been seen and promises to come to us Thursday evening. I trust we may not be disappointed."[9] Kahlil did come, and he brought along a selection of his drawings. He had been working hard and had begun to see the advantages of the opportunity being offered to him. As he waited, Miss Peirce leafed through the drawings. A few days later she penned another note to Day: "Kahlil has brought his sketches which I send you. Unfortunately he has given many of them away. The boy is here now and if you can see him, I hope you will do so."[10]

That Day liked the drawings is evident from the context of Miss Peirce's next note to him and from the uncharacteristic promptness with which he expressed a willingness to meet Kahlil. The two met on December 9, 1896, and the encounter appears to have stimulated them both, because soon after the holiday season, Day requested Kahlil's address from Miss Peirce. "Kahlil Gibran's address is 9 Oliver Place," she replied. "Have you heard anything concerning his future? I am anxious to know if a decision has been reached. It will be most interesting to hear the boy's comments. May I be there too?"[11] Within weeks, Kahlil was before the camera of his newfound mentor.

Photography was by this time Day's primary concern, taking precedence even over Copeland & Day's publishing activities. Where he had begun by using photography to capture literary scenes, he now sought a painterly style, inspired by his knowledge of "composition, of light and shade, of proportion, of outline, of the intermediate links."[12] The result—called "coal mine" effects by some—was a sharp image surrounded by misty tones.[13] A Boston firm fashioned for him a special lens that was "deliberately uncorrected," rendering photos similar to that of a wet lens. The image was sharp with a halo surrounding the light tones.[14] With the resulting images, his models and their poses complemented an unusual effect.

Day derided the shallowness of contemporary "art photographic" and the current vogue of "hideous caricatures of the human figure…disarrayed in all states of nakedness, postured in impossible attitudes against commercial backgrounds, and surrounded by papier-mâché columns, fruit, or trees." Simultaneously, he sought "the most striking, unusual, and weirdly picturesque set of models…black, white and yellow, that ever posed before a camera."[15]

Kahlil's initial reaction to Day's world is unclear. The publisher Elbert Hubbard once described visiting Day, who "wore a fez and turned-up Turkish slippers…and wrote only by the light of thirteen candles."[16] The critic Sadakichi Hartmann told an anecdote about Day's posturings.

The stranger knocked and heard a most cheerful "Come in," but entering found to his great astonishment nobody present. He looked around everywhere, but could find no trace of Mr. Day…then suddenly he heard a clucking sound, he looked up and saw Mr. Day sitting on a shelf right under the ceiling, wrapped in an oriental costume, smoking a water pipe![17]

Photo of F. H. Day by Frederick Evans. (Courtesy F. Holland Day Collection from Norwood Historical Society, now at Library of Congress.)

Day's early photo of Kahlil in "Eastern" attire, with leopard skin and staff. (Courtesy Library of Congress.)

Such accessories—water pipes, fezzes, and incense—may have seemed commonplace to Kahlil. But how did he view the fact that an affluent, well-educated American enthusiastically responded to such familiar belongings? What did he make of being asked to contribute to his patron's fanciful imaginings of others—of whom he was one? While some Bostonians may have believed that these fantastic props were all imported at great cost from faraway lands, they more likely were found locally at places like Peter Rahme's "Fancy Goods" store on Beach Street in the heart of Boston.

Kahlil was entering adolescence, and his recollections of the sessions spent before Day's intrusive lens allude to a prevailing sadness. "Mr. Day made a great many photographs of me," he once said. But he also recalled that once "Mrs. Day said to her son, 'I like that young man very much, but I don't want to be with him because he never smiles.'"[18] Day's countless photographs clearly show this; the pictures portray a serious, unsmiling, proudly dignified, almost defiant boy.

In considering Kahlil's introduction to what would become a far-reaching apprenticeship, it is important to remember his—and his family's—circumstances. Recommended to Day by social workers, here was a thirteen-year-old boy from a poor, immigrant Syrian family, living in a fatherless household and South End

43

tenement. With no formal education before coming to America, and not yet fully fluent in English, he had no real prospects. But in seeking a sense of direction, he had found an interest and talent in draftsmanship. His response to the wealthy, accomplished, and eccentric Mr. Day would involve a complex negotiation of social attitudes, privilege, power, and trust. From this exchange, Kahlil would acquire a sense of freedom and openness to others, exposure to Euro-American writers and visual artists, and to bookmaking as a craft, enabling him to develop a beginning sense of confidence as an artist. Yet he would also take away from this exchange a lifelong need to reconcile these new creative sources with those of his origins in Mount Lebanon.

Day was steering Kahlil—along with the other African, Armenian, and Chinese children who posed for him—to echo *his* moods, imaginings, and self-searches. The resulting images, with their mysterious tones, were beginning to stamp Day as a "veritable Rembrandt of the camera." Already, British and American photographic journals were linking him with another innovator, Alfred Stieglitz. The two were characterized as "artistic photographers [who] like the true artist…only depict what pleases."[19]

If photography critics had cared to write about where he got his models, they might have reported an interesting story. Day's concern for the fate of underprivileged children had remade him into a veritable Pied Piper of the South End, a role tempered by his own artistic agenda. Dressed in a dashing cape and a broad-brimmed hat, he took children by the streetcar-load on country outings or to cultural entertainments, selecting from their ranks the precise "type" he sought for a particular picture.[20] Refusing to discriminate, he saw only what he wanted for his camera. "You're no reflector of color," a cousin once said to him. "Remember the night at Symphony Hall we heard 'em say, 'Let's see who he's got *this* week; last week he had a Chinaman!'"[21]

Day's methods were as patient as they were somewhat bizarre. A year after he met Kahlil, he wrote:

> I once knew an enthusiast who, after discovering in the scantily-clad figure of a street urchin what he supposed to be almost the unattainable perfection for the subject he was at work upon, waited six weeks while the little fellow was letting his hair grow into the required condition, being all the time paid by my friend for the concession he was required to make, that he might become more nearly the classic ideal. In this case all proved well and the results more than justified the means.[22]

Day was in fact referring to himself in the third person. He was the "friend" who paid and waited for his subject's hair to grow.

Kahlil may well have been the boy; photographs show that he let his hair grow. Day posed him in mysterious Arab burnooses, just as he dressed Armenians in turbans, Africans in Ethiopian regalia, Chinese with flutes, Japanese in kimonos. Through Day's lens, ghetto waifs became "Armenian Princes," "Ethiopian Chiefs," and "Young Sheiks." Despite their contrived fantasies, these titles and images somehow also managed to convey a sense of pride and dignity. For a teenager needing to find and fortify his own self-image, and to overcome an impoverished childhood, these portrait sessions and pictures were compelling. No longer a slum child from a dark alley, these images testified to the possibility of far more, but at a long-term price. Fred Holland Day's fascination with immigrant subjects costumed to reflect his fantasies about their cultures both empowered and sentenced them—and Day himself—to uneasy worlds of mutual self-invention. Kahlil's involvement in Day's agenda, at the same time that it opened doors to achievement, entangled the youth in what then was not yet called "orientalizing," an entanglement with which he would struggle for years to come.[23]

The Young Sheik by F. H.Day. From Day's article, "Portraiture and the Camera," in the *American Annual of Photography and Photographic Times Almanac,* 1899. (Reprint: Private Collection.)

~

Spring came, and Florence Peirce, satisfied that Day was providing young Kahlil with some opportunity and security, wrote Day that she was going to Europe and thanked him for his gift: "Kahlil's photograph was most acceptable."[24] With his integration underway, the social planners turned their attention to his sisters. On June 10, 1897, Jessie Beale announced a plan to take the three children to the country. Her letter shows the delicacy and care required of sensitive settlement house workers attempting to allay a foreign family's fears and distrust of outsiders. She wrote,

> My dear Mr. Day, Miss Johnson, the lady who has charge of the country week outings, tells me that Kahlil and his two sisters are to go for their visit about July

first. Shall she not send the invitation to you? It seems that it will seem a little more personal coming that way. The Christian Union is specially anxious to have them seem to the children like any other invitation. It was kind of her to arrange for them all to go together. This is unusual but being foreigners she feared they might be homesick if separated.[25]

The gentle conspiracy of having Day extend the invitation did not work. In spite of personal sponsorship, Kahlil, Marianna, and Sultana did not go to camp that year. Kamila knew that Oliver Place held no joy, but she considered the separation of children from family to be unnatural. Beale tried again. On July 9, she wrote to Day, "I have just heard indirectly that Kahlil and his little sisters did not get off on the sixth. Is this true I wonder? And if so can we do anything about getting Miss Johnson to arrange a second outing."[26]

The Gibrans had disappeared, and Day may have combed the Syrian neighborhood for word or sight of Kahlil. Vanishing suddenly, then surfacing again just as unexpectedly, they were typical of the mobile poor who dropped in and out of life in the tenements, and by mid-September, the family appeared once again. On September 22, Jessie Beale wrote,

> My dear Mr. Day, I am so much obliged to you for your trouble and interest in Kahlil's behalf, but I am exceedingly sorry that I caused you the bother when investigation proves there was no need of such anxiety…These people are so apt to suddenly disappear from our sight, that I feared Mrs. Gibran might be one of those quiet mortals, who tell their plans to no one, but silently move off and are lost sight of.[27]

Obviously, Day did finally find the boy and managed to win the family's permission. For the next few months, his studio was a whirlpool of activity, with Kahlil observing it all. He eagerly absorbed the exhibitions, book productions, literary discoveries, and general antics. Alert, open, and hungry to learn to read fluently, he was an apt pupil.

In the fall of 1897, new interests began to intrigue the fourteen-year-old. Under the guidance of Day, who often read to him, he began to discover literature. *The Treasure of the Humble*, a new work by Maurice Maeterlinck—one of Day's favorite authors—had just been translated into English. This series of brooding Neoplatonic essays fed soul-searching Americans with hope, for "we are on the verge of a wonderful spiritual awakening which will come near to laying bare the soul of one man to another."[28] A poet friend related in her journal Day's account of how he introduced the young Kahlil to the thoughts of the Belgian symbolist.

Mr. Day read to him out of the newly translated *Trésor des Humbles* of Maeterlinck one day, and the boy would not let him go till he had read the whole volume at a sitting. Then he borrowed it. Then he had to own it himself…One day Kahlil Gibran came back with a copy of Lemprière which Mr. Day had lent him and said: "I am no longer a Catholic: I am a pagan."[29]

The book that inspired the young Maronite Christian to question his own religious identity was the *Classical Dictionary* by the English scholar John Lemprière. Published in 1788, and widely used as a reference work in the nineteenth century, it outlined classical mythology and history. Perhaps Kahlil's infatuation with Olympian gods and goddesses was predictable, but his simultaneous response to Maeterlinck was surely unusual. As the same poet-diarist observed: "His aptitude for literature is like his drawing: his mind is in every way marvelous."[30]

In this last decade of the nineteenth century, Maeterlinck—often called "the Belgian Shakespeare"—believed in the "oneness of the individual with the absolute." His idealistic concerns often were compared to those of Boston's own Ralph Waldo Emerson. Those Bostonians, in particular, who were conscious of the transcendental legacy bequeathed to them by Emerson, recognized and respected Maeterlinck's parallel beliefs. Kahlil, by this time, already had some of Boston in him and was a child of his time. As a teen, Kahlil idolized Maeterlinck's work, especially *The Treasure of the Humble*—"his masterpiece."[31]

Maeterlinck's preoccupation with "death that is the guide of our life," his conviction that "a spiritual epoch is perhaps upon us," and his allusions to a predestined love deeply affected young Kahlil. Throughout his career, he never completely abandoned the Belgian writer's attempts to penetrate into the "souls of all our brethren… ever hovering about us, craving for a caress, and only waiting for the signal."[32]

Kahlil was also exposed to the North American contemporary literary scene through Copeland & Day. In 1896, capitalizing on the popularity of Bliss Carman and Richard Hovey's *Songs from Vagabondia*, the firm published a sequel. The first two poems in *More Songs from Vagabondia* alluded to remote regions with which Kahlil could identify. In "Jongleurs" the images evoked immigrants who "Wandered at noon / In the valleys of Van / Tented in Lebanon, tarried in Ophir." These romantic pictures portrayed his homeland. If American poets sang about the land where he was born, did not his personal origins then offer him a way of belonging in this new country? Did not his childhood in the Qadisha Valley provide him with a cherished religious heritage? Instead of abandoning his origins, as so many first-generation immigrant children did, he began to understand that his background could further his artistic growth.

Another influence on Kahlil's development was the "Decadent" movement, as the emerging literary and artistic movement was dismissively dubbed by its critics. In an article entitled "Decadence—or Renascence," Richard Hovey attempted to explain the crimes of "decadence" with which the contemporary poets were being charged, lucidly spelling out the "gospel-crusade" that characterized the "children of one mother—Today."[33] "The younger poets," Hovey wrote, "are not, strictly speaking, a school at all…They cannot be catalogued under one formula…Their greatest unity lies in the stress of individuality." Analyzing the beliefs held by his contemporaries, Hovey stated, "The right to live involves the right to love, and the freedom of man must include the freedom of woman." Referring to the strong influence of Emerson on the new poets, he noted, "Materialism seems almost without a representative, the tendency being to the other extreme of mysticism as in the native symbolism of Carman or Maeterlinck's strange new development of Neo-Platonic thought." Day agreed with this closely reasoned and farsighted analysis. He especially appreciated America's poet of democracy, Walt Whitman, and his English counterpart, the liberal socialist Edward Carpenter, both of whom were included in Hovey's discussion of free verse poets.

The impression made on young Kahlil is clear. In years to come, he would include all prototypes discussed by Hovey among those whom he had admired and trusted in his youth. The boy recognized a common chord on which to build, and from his new country, he adopted anything and everything with which he could identify.

Nevertheless, reading contemporary literature was less important to Kahlil than making pictures. The sketches saved from this period show his ravenous appetite for copying anything he saw. On the blank backs of public library call cards, he drew countless heads and figures derived from Blake, Beardsley, and Burne-Jones.[34] He also laboriously printed the new Roman alphabet he was learning, trying to perfect the letters by copying the most ordinary forms and

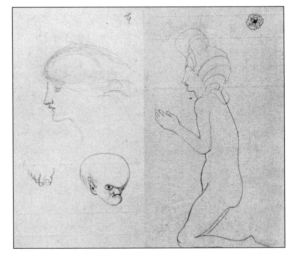

Kahlil's pencil doodles on the backs of library call cards.
(Courtesy Museo Soumaya.)

titles. "I promise to return this book to the Public Library," he spelled out again and again, interspersing the words with Beardsley-like heads of gnomes and Blake-like dancing figures. In his student notebook are carefully wrought letters copying the titles of Copeland & Day books. Once, looking over these early attempts in later years when he was a mature artist, Gibran remarked on his stylistic indebtedness, asking, "Wasn't I having a good time with Blake then?"[35]

The Copley Square Library was a grand studio, for the modern art that decorated its halls was the talk of artist circles in Boston. In 1897–1898, Kahlil also took advantage of the weekly exhibits organized by the library's active fine arts department. Fred Holland Day frequently lent the library new issues from Copeland & Day, and from his own Kelmscott Press editions. In the spring of 1897, the library sponsored a showing of William Morris's medievalizing works, mostly from Day's collection. A year later an exhibition of American and European book and magazine covers included contemporary work by Maxfield Parrish, Edward Penfield, and Will Bradley. The growing availability of photographic reproductions allowed the library to acquire Hollyer platinotypes of the English Pre-Raphaelite school,[36] as well as prints of Assyrian, Egyptian, Greek, and Roman sculpture from the British Museum.

Inspired by these images, Kahlil began to develop his own design technique and point of view. Not only did Day encourage this, but he eventually permitted Kahlil to work on covers for some of the firm's publications—unlikely as this might seem for a publisher who was commissioning illustrations from artists like Will Bradley, Ethel Reed, and John Sloan. That Kahlil was actually involved in

Drawings by Kahlil (*left*) in a dummy copy of Gertrude Smith's *The Arabella and Araminta Stories*, with Ethel Reed's illustrations for the book (*right*). (Courtesy Museo Soumaya.)

Copeland & Day's publishing program by 1898, at age fifteen, is proven by a pen-and-ink illustration he drew for a book of poems published that December. It was one of the boy's first attempts to make an original cover illustration, and although it was never used, it shows the progress he had made in the three years since he had been introduced to Day.

Earlier that year, he had made a pictorial representation of Duncan Campbell Scott's long title poem from his volume, *Labor and the Angel*. Kahlil picked out every detail of the pastoral scene described by the Canadian poet: "The angel that watches o'er work," while "Down in the sodden field / A blind man is gathering his roots / Guided and led by a girl." The girl who "touches his arm with her hand" is there, radiant and golden, and so are the "dark colored beets in the barrow" and the angel, a full-winged Pre-Raphaelite female embracing the peasant couple. Tight in execution and detail, this drawing shows knowledge of composition and perspective, and much familiarity with the Pre-Raphaelites. Its printer's marks indicate that it was prepared for reproduction.

Fifteen-year-old Kahlil's illustration of the title poem from Canadian writer Duncan Campbell Scott's *Labor and the Angel*, 1898. (Courtesy Museo Soumaya.)

Day did not keep his protégé under artistic wraps. Convinced of the boy's talent, he referred Kahlil to other artists who needed a model and could, in return, offer Kahlil guidance. With this interchange, Kahlil was able to enter Back Bay front doors, ordinarily accessible only through an elaborate maze of protocols and introductions.

One of the generous and benevolent individuals he met was Lilla Cabot Perry, a versatile painter who had studied with Pissarro and Monet, and a poet whose book, *Impressions*, would soon be published by Copeland & Day. Her husband, Thomas Sergeant Perry, was descended on his father's side from the two commodores Oliver Perry and Matthew Perry, and he was related on his mother's side to Benjamin Franklin. Everything surrounding the Perrys—his former careers as instructor of literature at Harvard and editor of the *North American Review*, her translation of Turgenev's poetry, the family's extended tours throughout Europe—was rich with the heaviest cream of privileged Boston and Cambridge. But Kahlil entered 312 Marlborough Street with self-assurance. Lilla Perry's affection for her young model, and her interest in his career, began with his first day's posing. She later gave him gifts, including perhaps his first set of paints, writing to Day: "I only gave Kahlil a part of the paints I had for him the other day, and I send the remainder in this little box with your things. I also send him the robe he posed in, as I thought he would like to own it and that you might like to photograph him in it."[37]

Portrait of Kahlil by Lilla Cabot Perry. Oil on canvas, around 1898. (Courtesy Telfair Museum of Art.)

Essentially asking Kahlil to portray himself as she imagined him, Perry painted the fifteen-year-old as a Bedouin, dressed in a voluminous white robe with elaborate sleeves and a *kaffiyeh* headdress. Even for someone from Mount Lebanon, this was an extraordinary costume. Standing and holding what appears to be a sword, the young man's demeanor evokes confidence and dignity, along with faint disdain. Surely this portrait, handsome in style and content, impressed the model and its viewers in complex ways. As he became acquainted with the cultural elite, Kahlil began to be valued and admired. It is clear that Kahlil's status as a stranger—an attractive, cultural "other"—added to his charm. His half-learned English—laden with romantic images—intrigued and pleased people. And he soon learned the manners and deportment expected of any Back Bay visitor.

Within a year, the Perrys had departed for Japan, where Thomas Perry was to lecture on English literature. But Kahlil maintained his acquaintanceship with

Back Bay society. In the winter of 1898, Day's photographic work was featured in an exhibition at the New York Camera Club, and soon after, the exhibition opened on March 8, 1898, at the Boston Camera Club. A highly successful showing, three hundred prints were acclaimed not only for their unusual presentation, but also for their subject matter.

"Mr. Day has displayed exquisite taste in the selection of his mats and his backgrounds," wrote critic Charles Peabody. Noteworthy was the fact that the photographer showed nude studies of males and females along with his diverse models. "The photographs pass over the merely pictorial and become almost as sculpture. Myron would have delighted in them, and Michael Angelo would have made many compliments."[38] The *Transcript* critic described the models in a way that presaged the photographs Day would make a few years later of Kamila, Sultana, and Marianna: "Give Mr. Day a girl or two with long chins and almond eyes and an expression of anxious long-suffering and hunger, and he can make a better pastiche of an Italian primitive altar-piece than most of the English Pre-Raphaelites."[39]

Kahlil was featured in a number of Day's pictures, and he and his family attended the opening. No effort was spared to show him off to his best advantage, as he later recalled.

> I was invited to his exhibition of course. There I met a great many fine people. It was an event and mother dressed me with especial care. She had wonderful taste and she always chose the richest and best of everything. I was all velvet—knicker-bockers—with silk stockings; my hair was longish. Mr. Day introduced me to Mrs. [Joshua] Montgomery Sears, who took photographs herself, and she carried me home after the exhibit. I met Miss Peabody, too, and she said to me, "I see you everywhere," for to my surprise, I had found seven or eight studies of myself, mounted and framed on the walls. "But you look so sad…why are you sad?" she said.[40]

Perceptive and spirited Josephine Peabody was asking a question that would follow Kahlil. Amid all the excitement, attention, and early success, where was the unfettered joy of childhood in the talented youth? What were the consequences of being asked by others to model a romanticized version of himself as the price of achievement and self-worth?

Even so, and despite the fact that fine clothes meant sacrifices for the whole family, Kamila and her daughters viewed the exhibit as Kahlil's very own triumph. And it was, for through it he met more "fine people." Artist and collector Sarah Choate Sears, the talented widow of Joshua Montgomery Sears, one of the city's wealthiest real estate men, liked the portraits of Kahlil well enough to buy one, and she was to invest in Kahlil's own art as he grew older. Poet Josephine Preston Peabody was to become a friend whose insightful loyalty would deeply affect him.

~

Later in his life recalling his early Boston years, while acknowledging a loss of childhood, Kahlil pointed to the importance of the design craftsmanship he gained.

> Most men would gladly repeat at least their boyhood and youth from six to eighteen; they had such a good time playing and running and enjoying themselves. I think I was first made to realize this by other people. When I was thirteen or fourteen, there were articles in papers and pamphlets about my work, my drawings and designs.[41]

Elsewhere he referred to public recognition of his earliest designs. Recalling a binding that he created when he was fourteen years old, he pointed out, "The Maeterlinck books all have that binding—I did several of them—but I've never been able to trace any of the others. Probably they were used on books that passed and were forgotten."[42] These statements align with a journal entry written by Josephine Peabody, four months after Kahlil would leave for Beirut to complete his schooling.

> Mr. Day told me of a lovely thing that happened. In New York, just before he sailed, the boy tried to sell some of his designs for book covers. He sold many, not knowing what [books] they were to be used for. Only a fortnight ago, there came to Mr. Day from Macmillan, I think, the new volume of essays—*Wisdom and Destiny* by Maeterlinck—with one of the boy's designs for a cover. "That," said Mr. Day—and I would have hugged him for it—"is one of the pleasantest things that ever happened to me."[43]

That Kahlil had sold his designs to a New York publishing house is also acknowledged by a letter from Lilla Cabot Perry, then living in Japan. On March 2, 1899, she wrote Day to acknowledge a package which contained

> your wonderfully beautiful photograph of "It is finished," the Maeterlinck with its delightful inscription, and the first copies I have seen of my book [*Impressions*]… Mr. Perry, who is as you know a great book lover, is delighted with the form which you have given to my fugitive fancies and agrees with me in liking also Kahlil's cover very much…Please tell him this with my affectionate remembrances…I wish I knew what Kahlil is doing and that I could be where I could take a look at his work from time to time, especially if he has begun to work at oil painting when my advice might be of some use to him.[44]

The fullest reference to Kahlil's book designs appeared in the April 2, 1898 issue of *The Critic*, a New York weekly review of literature and art.

IMPRESSIONS
LILLA CABOT PERRY

Kahlil's cover design for Lilla Cabot Perry's poetry collection, *Impressions*. (Courtesy Boston Athenaeum.)

> Some days ago a Syrian youth not more than sixteen years of age walked into the office of Mr. S. W. Marvin of Messrs. Scribner's. He carried a letter of introduction in his hand and a portfolio of drawings under his arm. In very good English, he asked Mr. Marvin to read the one and glance over the contents of the other. Mr. Marvin did as requested. The appearance of the boy interested him. His large dark eyes and olive skin made him remarkable amid his American surroundings. The boy sat modestly by while his portfolio was being examined. It was found to contain a collection of the most striking Oriental designs for book covers. When Mr. Marvin had run his critical eye over them, the boy asked him if there were any that he might find worth using. "Have you any more?" inquired Mr. Marvin, to which the boy replied that all he had were there.
>
> "I will take them all," said Mr. Marvin, "and when you have any more, bring them along and I will take them also."
>
> I happened in some time after, and was shown the designs. They are certainly striking, and remind one, not unnaturally, of the designs of Oriental stuffs. Only one was Americanized, and that was the least successful. Now I wonder why more Syrians, Turks, and other Orientals with whom New York abounds have not tried their hands at this sort of work before. This particular Syrian said that he had never studied the art of design but had simply picked it up.[45]

A Boston bookshop discovered another of his early bookbindings in the early 1980s, this one the work of respected editor and translator Nathan Haskell Dole. *The Rubaiyat of Omar Khayyam* was an L. C. Page publication and bore an image of the serenely seated Persian poet-astronomer. The name "KGibran" was perfectly imprinted on the multicolored hardboard cover. Dole's inscription was addressed to the treasurer of Boston's Khayyam Club, Charles Dana Burrage, "Genuine Omar Khayyamic-culturist."

The journal excerpt, Lilla Perry's letter, and the anecdote in *The Critic* all point to Kahlil's precocious entrance as a teen into the fine art of bookmaking via his apprenticeship at Copeland & Day, a key step in his development. Working at 69 Cornhill placed him at the center of the city's thriving bookstore and publishing district. It offered him an extraordinary opportunity to study firsthand the outstanding work of Will Bradley, Bertram Goodhue, and Ethel Reed, along with noted works like Aubrey Beardsley's *Yellow Book* and Stephen Crane's *Black Riders*.

But more important was his exposure to fundamental principles of typography, page layout, design, and decoration. Beyond illustrating covers, Kahlil gained the skills and understanding to later design the artistic look of Arabic magazines like *Al-Funun* or to decorate his English books with ornamental breaks. His relationship with Copeland & Day amplified his natural talent, so that when he was ready to publish his own works, the look and the heft of a book, its binding, and presswork became just as vital as its contents, and clearly contributed to the overwhelming success of what would eventually become his most significant work.

The spring of 1898 foreshadowed Gibran's lifelong ability to negotiate American intellectual and artistic circles. It also reveals a charisma that he seemed to possess, along with innate talent, personal appeal, verbal ease, modesty of manners, and a will to succeed.

~

In March 1898, Aubrey Beardsley died of consumption. Louise Guiney and Fred Holland Day mourned this self-taught prodigy and felt that a few of his admirers, "select Bostonians," should commemorate his efforts. Just before he died, Beardsley had converted to Catholicism, and so they arranged for a requiem low mass to be celebrated. This event embarrassed Irish Catholics and papal-wary Yankees alike. Beardsley remained associated with decadence and Oscar Wilde, and a posthumous mantle of Christianity did not fit him.

It is unclear whether Kahlil attended the mass. But the fact that Louise Guiney and Day had arranged for it testified to how they and other Boston bohemians tried to rid America of the respectable trappings that for so long had mummified liberal forces and thought. Being close to Day and his works better equipped Kahlil to contend with popular censorship and prudishness. "Today there are self-appointed rulers the world over who attempt the handcuffing of Art," Day wrote in 1898.

"Here in America the censors of art and letters are flourishing as the proverbial green bay tree."[46] Kahlil's apprenticeship offered him lessons in the role of the artist as iconoclast.

But with these lessons and small successes came problems. Kamila and Peter worried about his gravitation toward the outside world, far beyond their family, and the old specter of heresy and Protestantism. Kahlil himself naturally missed Bsharri and the presence of his father, intimidating as it could be. The family decided that he would return to Lebanon and finish his education there.[47]

Before his long journey, Kahlil benefited again from Day's efforts. To supplement a meager income, Louise Guiney had been acting as postmistress for the town of Auburndale, Massachusetts. In 1897, seeking escape from the job's bureaucratic rigors, she had bought a spit of bayberry-covered land far up on the Maine coast, Five Islands, near Bath. In July 1898, she invited Kahlil and some other young city boys to visit her, a rare opportunity for any resident of Boston's poor, immigrant districts. The arrangements were made through Day. To ensure that the unsupervised boys would not wander off or miss train connections, the boys traveled on an old sailing vessel called *The Headchance*. The fresh air and healthy living that Kahlil had been denied the previous summer were now his. The benevolent Louise Guiney assured Day that "everything was OK" with the boys. Then she mentioned that Kahlil had told her of his coming departure. "Is he really going for *good*? I hope not," she wrote.[48]

Miss Guiney was not the only one who was upset by the family's unexpected decision. Clearly, Day had also notified Florence Peirce, and from her comment, it seems that Day was also collecting money to help pay for the boy's trip. "Will you let me contribute the enclosed cheque toward Kahlil's expenses?" she wrote. "Can you not dine with us tomorrow at six o'clock? I have asked Kahlil to come at that hour, and you·can then have an opportunity to get the desired information from Miss Beale."[49]

Thus it was that Kahlil enjoyed a farewell supper given by his earliest, most perceptive, and generous sponsors. We know that at age fifteen he sailed from New York to Lebanon sometime before September 4, 1898, for on that day Louise Guiney conveyed a message to him in gratitude for a farewell drawing: "When you write Kahlil," she asked Day, "pray thank him for me…Is the boy not coming back at all?"[50]

Writing later in September from the Adirondacks, where she was staying for a "troublesome cough," Miss Peirce expressed a similar concern about Kahlil's departure from the U.S. "Kahlil, I suppose, is on his way to Syria. I fear his going is a mistake but possibly now since he has recognized his artistic tendencies, he may renew the local coloring and return to us benefited by a visit to his nation."[51]

~

When Kahlil first saw Josephine Preston Peabody at Fred Holland Day's photographic opening, she was "twenty-three: and not grown-up yet." "Why should I be?" she wrote then.[52] Fifteen-year-old Kahlil had remembered her and tried to capture in a drawing her radiant diminutiveness, ruffles of dark hair piled above her heart-shaped face, and bright brown eyes. He showed this attempt to Day who, provocateur that he was, probably urged the boy to inscribe it to her and leave it as a memento from him. Kahlil had composed his dedication in Arabic, a gesture that may have

Kahlil's pencil drawing of Josephine Preston Peabody. (Courtesy Private Collection.)

conveyed more mystery than his written English. It read, "August 23, 1898, to the dear and esteemed Lady Josephine Peabody."[53]

In late September, Josephine was waiting eagerly for her first book to appear under the Copeland & Day imprint. She noted in her journal:

Cheered by the mail which brings me the third proof of *The Wayfarers* and a note from F. H. Day with a delicate little drawing which he says was left for me by a little Syrian boy (a protégé of his whom I saw for a few moments last winter at the photograph view)—Kahlil Gibran. Says FHD, "He is now on his way to—where he will study Arabic literature and philosophy. He always kept a bright memory of you and wished that you would not forget him."[54]

Sahat al-Burj, or Tower Square, as it appeared in 1898 as an Ottoman showcase during Kahlil's school days in Beirut. It was renamed Martyrs' Square, in honor of Lebanese nationalists executed for their opposition to Ottoman rule. Photo by the American Colony Photographic Division in Jerusalem. (Courtesy Library of Congress.)

4
BEIRUT

When Kahlil returned to his homeland in 1898 at age fifteen, he spoke Arabic fluently, read it well, but could barely write it. Day gave him a copy of Bulfinch's *Age of Fable* for his voyage. Inside it Kahlil wrote in colloquial Arabic, "This book I studied between Nairik [New York] and Beirut and all the studying I did was with great zeal." On the last page he practiced his Arabic script again: "I arrived on Beirut in good health. Nothing is missing."[1]

Kahlil chose Madrasat al-Hikma, École de la Sagesse, as the school at which he wished to complete his secondary education. Founded in 1875 by pioneering educator Yusuf al-Dibs, the Maronite archbishop of Beirut, the school was open to students from all religious sects and offered a curriculum emphasizing nationalism, as well as church writings, history, and liturgy. Among Dibs' own extensive writings were an eight-volume history of Syria. His forward thinking motto for the school was, "Your fellow citizen in the nation is worth more than your coreligionist."[2]

Kahlil tried to convince those in charge that he was ready to study at the upper level. Even though his Arabic was so poor that he could not arrange his courses without help, he complained to Father Yusuf Haddad, a resident teacher, about having been put into the most elementary class of the school because of his weakness in Arabic grammar. Father Haddad explained that learning was like climbing a ladder; one must climb each rung, one at a time. Birds, replied Kahlil, did not need ladders to fly. He insisted that he had just completed English lessons in America and that since he—not his parents—was responsible for his tuition, he should also be responsible for his own studies. If he could not choose his own curriculum, he would go instead to the American University of Beirut.[3]

The Maronite school was vigorously competing with the Protestant-run AUB for Lebanese students, and Kahlil's American upbringing lent weight to his promise. Father Haddad made a special effort on his behalf and secured the headmaster's

Bishop Yusuf al-Dibs, Maronite archbishop of Beirut, pioneering educator, and founder of Madrasat al-Hikma in Beirut. Photo from the *Golden Book for Madrasat al-Hikma: 1876-1926* (Kuzhma Printing Press.)

agreement that Kahlil's curriculum be tailored more to his needs. Impressed by the youth's sense of purpose and confidence, he also agreed that Kahlil could audit lectures and read the assigned literature for three months before being called on for answers. The result was a seminar-like course, created in no small part by Kahlil's powers of persuasion. As a result, his oral fluency in Arabic and his rootedness in the language developed rapidly. Father Haddad encouraged his creative efforts at writing and assigned him Arabic literature that would fill in the significant gaps. Selections emphasized the Arabic-language Bible, especially the Gospels, in whose style and cadence Kahlil immersed himself.

Teachers would remember him distinctly. He wore his hair long and told colorful stories, lacing his conversations with references to American and English writers, and plays that he had seen. If he

Madrasat al-Hikma (École de la Sagesse), Kahlil's school in Beirut. Photo from the school's *Golden Book*. (Kuzhma Printing Press.)

was candid enough to accurately describe his Boston experiences, his unconventional patron, the American poets he had personally known, and his bookbinding designs, it would not be surprising that these stories were only half-believed.

~

As Kahlil tried to reconcile his experiences in America with his immersion in Arabic studies, back in Boston the poems of "dear and esteemed lady" Josephine Peabody were about to bring her into partnership with Day and, through him, a deep friendship with Kahlil.

For Josephine Preston Peabody, life had been a paradox of surplus and denial. Her earliest memories were of a perfect and privileged childhood in New York. Her Boston-bred parents, Charles Kilham Peabody and Susan Morrill Peabody, shared their devotion to good literature and the theater with their three daughters. It was a singing household that encouraged the girls to express themselves

Kahlil while a student in Beirut.
(Courtesy Museo Soumaya.)

through pageantry, tableaux, and poetry writing. Grimm, Hawthorne, and Dickens were daily fare. The whole family recited Shakespeare's speeches, just for the pure delight of it.

The idyll was broken in 1882 when the youngest of the three girls died. Two years later, Josephine was ten and the fairy tale ended forever with her father's sudden death. Her mother was left without the means to sustain the life they had known, and the Peabodys gradually descended into genteel poverty. Adapting their graceful style of living to the reality of meager finances, they moved to Massachusetts, where they settled in with Mrs. Peabody's mother. Cramped though Mrs. Peabody's circumstances suddenly were, they allowed her to build a modest house in the Dorchester section of Boston.[4]

Poet and playwright Josephine Preston Peabody.
(Courtesy Private Collection.)

Coping with the unaccustomed pressures of public schools and adjusting to a fatherless household, Josephine withdrew into a private world of words, which she spun into countless stories, plays, and poems. By fourteen, she was sending her sonnets to editors in New York and Boston. Several poems had been published by the time she was about to complete the rigorous, classical curriculum of the Boston Girls' Latin School. However, a chronically weak constitution forced her to leave school in her junior year. Abandoning neither Greek nor literature, she read voraciously—six hundred books between 1888 and 1893.

Her journal was, quite literally, her best friend. Here she made up for all the giggling, gossiping, and confiding she yearned for.

May 1894. I want some fun, some fun, and there is none to be had; good times I have, reading. But oh! I want young people and gaiety and something droll…I go in town full of the May feeling, wanting to laugh and talk, and there is nobody at all to laugh and talk with; and I just have to sit and read all by myself, and I can't always do that in comfort; and then I come home again and feel like crying out of sheer caged-up youth…The sky is so blue and the trees are budding—and I want somebody to PLAY WITH![5]

When she was nearly twenty, Josephine's verses attracted Horace E. Scudder, editor of the *Atlantic Monthly*. Scudder not only agreed to publish "The Shepherd Girl," but he arranged that she study at Radcliffe College as a special student. She felt welcome in Cambridge, a city that offered her far more than she had ever dreamed. She was able to indulge her thirst for music at the Boston Symphony, where "people of my age will walk in, Friday afternoons, and buy apotheosis for twenty-five cents." Her professors—William Vaughn Moody, Lewis Gates, Francis

Child—found her refreshing, and their regard for her enabled her to experience "a strange new-made Spring of occasional comradeship, of several genuine 'Good Times.'" She observed, "I have met with almost unvarying kindliness and affection… and I have been patted on the head to excess."[6]

Although she read Homer in the original language and soaked up Whitman, Rossetti, Leopardi, de Musset, and Verlaine in their own languages, Josephine was the antithesis of the blue-stockinged, female scholar. She charmed scholars with guileless gestures: "*April 1896.* Yesterday Professor Child read at the open meeting of the English Club. We talked to him in the parlor for a few moments before the reading and I put some of my trailing arbutus in his buttonhole."[7] These impulses, coupled with her sincere frenzy in seeking the "winged thing" that prompted art, identified Josephine Peabody even then as a catalytic personality. It is not surprising that her high spirits were countered from time to time by bouts of discouragement. Radcliffe buoyed her for two years. But then, as if stricken with a sudden awareness of the uselessness of it all, her thoughts turned. "The things we have been reading have become almost a bore, under the present *regime*," she wrote. Even the noted lectures of Charles Eliot Norton began to pall.

> *October 1895.* I wonder if these dear and reverend people realize what an impression they give the younger ones when they beg them to believe that there is nothing high and lovely in this country or this age…Professor Norton expounds the pitiful degeneracy of things and the hopeless unloveliness of our country.[8]

In June 1896, Josephine left Radcliffe. "I desire above all…to deal with things that concern all people. I don't want to be a 'literary' poet."[9] Returning to Dorchester, she reentered the daily routine of a female household, where her ailing grandmother, mother, and older art student sister Marion were enduring the privations of rapidly dwindling funds. Her circumstances depressed her; a feeling of guilt at being a financial burden dogged her. Nevertheless, she was able to produce a continuing stream of stories and poems, and a retelling of the classical myths, *Old Greek Folk Stories.* Her suburban refuge outside Boston's center became a sort of salon, accessible by trolley car, for Cambridge intellectuals.

Fast becoming a favorite within literary circles, Josephine held out for more than that. She genuinely wanted a different and more satisfactory relationship between the sexes than existed in turn-of-the-century America. Wanting to establish and maintain warm friendships with men, she mourned the artificial barriers that prevented communication between men and women.

We cannot seem to befriend each other. I never felt the piteous helplessness of it more than I did the other evening—nor the possibility of a true affection for a man-friend as for a woman-friend, the will to be sympathetic and comradely in vital, unworldly childish ways if you like; and anxiously tender of temperamental trials and sadness. Yet people insist that all this is impossible for men and women…I *do not see*, and I *will not believe* that there is nothing for men and women between Love and the purely intellectual impersonalities that we are forced to call friendship.[10]

Defiantly mercurial and impulsive, she made herself known. Within a year, she was mingling with older female poets who flourished in Boston's several authors' clubs and poetry societies. Louise Guiney, her friend Alice Brown, Louise Chandler Moulton, even Julia Ward Howe and Annie S. Fields welcomed her. When finally she summoned up enough courage to submit *The Wayfarers*, a collection of her own favorites, to Copeland & Day, Herbert Copeland assured her that, as editor of *Youth's Companion*, he had admired her juvenile work for years. In fact, he and Day had been about to invite her to publish these early poems and committed to do so.

But as the year passed, Josephine distressed over Copeland & Day's languid pace. Suddenly she was perplexed by the premature publicity in October 1898, front-page headlines proclaiming, "Boston has a new poetess."[11] On December 3, Josephine visited 69 Cornhill to discuss the publishers' apparent laxity in distributing her book. For half an hour, Day showed her "a whole sheaf of drawings of the Syrian boy, Kahlil Gibran," that captured her attention. At a loss for words, she acknowledged, "I can hardly tell of them."[12] Seeing how visibly moved she was, Day then told her all about Kahlil—about his responses to Maeterlinck and Lemprière, about the designs he had created and sold, about his return to his homeland in the Biblical Levant. When Josephine left the office, her anxiety had vanished.

She recounted in her journal her responses to the conversation with Day.

December 12, 1898. Today I mean to write a letter to Kahlil Gibran! The very idea of him is like a wellspring and locusts and wild honey…His father is a sheik, a tax collector, says Mr. Day…He is only fifteen years old…His drawings say it clearlier than anything else could. There is no avoiding that young personality. You are filled with recognition and radiant delight…These you can see in every sketch and a perception, a native-born wisdom that is second sight. I bless the day I saw these things, for there is nothing that so warms one's heart and cheers the thoughts that are growing down in the dark as to meet one of these creatures who are dear to God.[13]

Two months later in Beirut, Kahlil received a decorative letter from Josephine.

12 December 1898

My Dear little Friend:

A lovely surprise came to me, some time ago in the shape of the drawing that you left for me, before you sailed away. At first I found it hard to believe that it really was for me, or that you could have kept me in mind so long. But since the picture is in my hands, be very sure that I mean to keep it.

It lies before me as I write; and, if I can, I am going to find somebody wise enough to tell me what the inscription means. I have not hurried to find that out, because the face itself says so much to me: my ears can hear a lovely voice from it, whenever I stop and listen.

Very lately I saw and talked with your friend Mr. Day. We spoke of you; and he let me see many more of the drawings that you had left with him. I wish to tell you that they made me feel quite happy for the rest of the day. Why? Because I seemed to understand you through them clearly: and I felt sure that you will always have within yourself, a rich happiness to share with other people. You have eyes to see and ears to hear. After you have pointed out the beautiful inwardness of things, other people less fortunate may be able to see too, and to be cheered with that vision. I think that your spirit lives in a beautiful place: and to believe that of anyone always makes me happy.—May it always live there.

To my mind, it is thus with people who can truly make lovely things, whether pictures or pottery or music or anything else: whoever they are, they are sure of a daily bread which is nothing less than the Bread of Life: and they have the perfect happiness of giving that Bread away to others, poorer than themselves, who might go hungry and unbefriended.

I wonder what your country is like, and whether you have some quiet place to grow in. I am sometimes so perplexed with the noises and crowded sights of the city, that I feel like a lost child hunting after my own true self. I remember how many prophets have grown up in solitude, even perhaps tending the sheep (like Apollo in the story, keeping the flocks of King Admetus!) and I wish that all people who *must* be in a lonely country-place for a time, could know how to find the blessing in solitude, like spring hidden in the desert. (Have you ever seen the Desert? I have wished to know what it is like.)

You know what Maeterlinck says of silence in *The Treasure of the Humble*. Well I think you listen to silences: and I hope that you will come back someday and tell us what you have heard.

If you should ever tell me something of your life in a country far and strange to me, how gladly will I listen! And if you want news of anything that goes on here, ask me, and I will tell you all I know. This is but a little of my thanks for the drawing.

Your very sincere friend,
Josephine Peabody[14]

Josephine's message, with its references to her own work ("Daily Bread" became the title of a poem that would be published in 1900 in her *Fortune and Men's Eyes*), was speaking to him as a fellow artist. Day had sent him a copy of *The Wayfarers,* but this letter was in her own hand. Striving to live up to Josephine's belief in him—and to her expectations—while unaware of predictions about him, Kahlil replied, drawing resourcefully on the English he had learned.

My dear Josephine,

It seems that if I have gained you for a friend after all, "Have I?" the hope of that was near the side of its graive.

Of course I was so pleased when I saw your picture and what they says about it but not so much if it was just little letter from you to me which will open the door of our friendship. And as I says that the hope of getting a letter from you was allmost dead, till your letter arrived which did tell me great more that was what was in it of words. O, how hapy I was? How glad? So hapy that the tongue of poor pen can not put my joy in words.

You can see that I allway feel disconted when I come to write English because I know not how to translate my thought as I want, but perhaps you won't mind that, and I think I know enough to tell you (that I will keep your friendship in middest of my heart, and over that many many milles of land and sea I will allways have a certane love for you and will keep the thought of you near my heart and will be no sepperation between you and my mind)...if I know better English or if you know Arabic it will be great pleasure to us still I will prommis that I will write to you all what I know and do, hoping that you will write to me sometime telling me about you, andall what you write will give me pleasure.

Yes, I did kept you in mind so long, as you said in your letter "for I allways keep things of that sort" and for a certane thing I am just like a camera and my heart is the plate, why? I kept you because your face seems to tell me somethings when I ever thinks of it, not that I will forget when you spoke with me by your own self that night in Mr. Day's exhibition. At the same night I asked Mr. Day who is the lady in black he said "She is Miss Beabody a young poet and her sister is an artist" "What a hapy family" said I, "I love to know them." And after that time, days past so readily that I did not seen you to know you more, untell the love of wisdom caryed me over that long distance and put me in Byrouth in a college studying Arabic and French and many things beside.

Syria is very nice country so old ruen [ruins] found in many places it so defrance to America it is very silence more in the country in the villages like mine where people are all of one kinde of heart they love eachother and they dont do very much work like the people in America for they only work in their ground, Rich and poor are seems to be very happy.

I wonder what make you know that I love silence and quite pleaces, why, yes I do and I realy could hear its beautiful music, I wonder do you ever set in a dark silence room lessening to the music of the rain so calm that is (won't you write me?? I will tell you many thing in my next litter)

From your far far friend
Kahlil Gibran

Kahlil's improvised spelling and punctuation was enough to appeal to rebel Josephine. And substituting the letter *b* for *p*, which is nonexistent in Arabic, he called her 'Miss Beabody,' another plus. His need and determination to express himself figuratively transcended the obstacles of learning to write in two languages.

When his answer reached her in March 1899, Josephine was thrilled. This young woman who had memorized twenty-one Shakespeare sonnets, "sundry Italian things," plus a "number of English lyrics" so that she would never be alone, who read Dante for relaxation and took Herodotus with her to read in the bath, was overjoyed at the attempts of her youthful, newly literate artist-admirer. Fortunately, she carefully copied this "marvel of a letter" in her journal, "to keep it safe."[15]

So "hapy" was "Miss Beabody" with this adventure in writing by a spirit unfettered by grammar, spelling, or conventional style, that on March 25 she wrote to Day: "This last week brought me a letter from Kahlil Gibran: English as broken and sense as perfect as I have ever seen. It was a great pleasure. I wonder if you would mind showing his drawings to my friend Mrs. Prescott and me, if we should come to Cornhill some day after Easter."[16]

Josephine had been studying clay modeling with Kate Prescott, as a "desperate effort at self-help,"[17] and her early efforts to get her teacher interested in Kahlil's work were predictive of things to come. When Kahlil returned to Boston three years later, Josephine's quest for her own voice would be more secure, and she would take it upon herself to seek a niche for him. Thus, while Kahlil was struggling to master fundamentals of classical Arabic, Josephine was already praising his range of view. Long before he was able to present his perceptions in *any* language, an audience was being prepared to receive to them.

~

In Beirut, Kahlil had accelerated his studies, pushing himself to fit into the creative role that he wished to fill, a role that others had begun to expect him to play. Adjusting to the strict discipline at school was difficult at first. He later recalled:

The first two years in college were hard, because of difficulty with the authorities. The college was strict—they keep a far more rigid hand on the students than colleges do [in America]—and I didn't believe in their requirements and I wouldn't obey them. I was less punished than any other student would have been, however, because I made it up in other ways—I studied so hard. And the last year was good—because of the magazine that Hawayek and I were getting out, and the many occasions for poems—and they made me the college poet.[18]

Youssef Howayek represented to Kahlil an embodiment of culture and prestige. Nephew of the Maronite patriarch of Antioch—Elias Peter Howayek, who would become a founder of the Lebanese Republic—Youssef enjoyed privileges accorded to a relative of an influential religious figure. Easygoing and sophisticated, he was open and responsive to the intense spirit of the youth from Bsharri. Together the two started a magazine called *Al-Manarah*, or *The Beacon*.[19] This venture, to which Kahlil contributed creative leadership drawing from his experience at Copeland & Day, enabled him to offset his inferior economic and social position with talent and skill. His later account of how Howayek supported and admired his skills shows that from early on he valued experimenting in media.

Sculptor Youssef Howayek, whose long friendship with Kahlil began during their student days in Beirut. (Courtesy Dar An-Nahar.)

In college…I first got [Howayek] to draw. He thought I was wonderful because I could draw a cat & a tree—We published a paper together: he was manager and I was editor. At first we printed it on one of those metal and gelatin machines and in our senior year the president let us use the college presses.[20]

Howayek's later memories of Kahlil included a description of their magazine, for which Kahlil also wrote and illustrated. He also recalled Kahlil as "lonely, obstinate

A Beirut vegetable market. Photo by the American Colony Photographic Division in Jerusalem.
(Courtesy Library of Congress.)

and strange in appearance."[21] Resisting as he did the routines pressed upon students by the priests, Kahlil's resistance took many forms. He skipped classes; filled his school notebooks with drawings and satirical sketches of his teachers; avoided religious duties; and, when forced to receive communion, would forgo the obligatory confession. It is a measure of Father Haddad's sympathetic understanding that he recognized the ambitious boy's behavior as more than just defiance or disrespect.

The recognition that Kahlil sought came in his final year when his poetry was selected for merit. Later he described how important this award was to him.

> The year before I finished college I was trying very hard in the poetry contest. That is a great thing in the college life, because the successful man is the college poet for his last year and a great many honors are shown him. I was very much excited and very eager to get the prize. About ten o'clock I was in my room and one of my teachers came by and knocked at the door.
>
> "Gibran Effendi," said he, "are you still awake?"
>
> "Yes," said I, "I don't want to sleep."
>
> "Now," said he, "you go to bed, and go to sleep, and dream good dreams."

I knew they were even then holding a meeting in the prefect's room and probably deciding about the poems. "Probably," I said to myself, "probably he just came by to give me that knock and that word"—and it made my hopes firmer, and I went to bed, and to sleep.

In my dream I was in a little garden. Near the wall—the wall is of marble and you know how strange beautiful colors come in marble with time…the soft red and the blue lines. Well, instead of looking outward towards the flowers as I usually did, I found myself looking towards the wall. Then Christ was there. There was no way for him to come—at the wall—but he was there. And he said the very words of my teacher, "Go to sleep and dream good dreams." I did not wake then—but in the morning I remembered I was successful in the poem—and very very happy. It was ecstasy. I suppose in all my life I shall never know such an uplift again.

[The poem was] a description—of a place—we were all given the same subject. It was just school work—but it meant a great deal to a boy.[22]

The satisfaction Kahlil received at school in Beirut contrasted starkly with the reception he found in Bsharri. He returned to his hometown during summer vacations, only to encounter his father's stubbornness. Still proud despite his damaged reputation, still indifferent to his son's educational and artistic pursuits, Gibran's personal indulgences and disregard for others were, if anything, worse than before. Kahlil felt torn. He could not help admiring his father's resilience and strength of will, but he resented the antagonism his father set between them.

I admired him for his power, his outspokenness & refusal to yield—that got him into trouble eventually. But if hundreds were about him he could command them with a word. He could overpower any number by any expression of himself…

My father hurt me often. I remember once especially. I had just written a

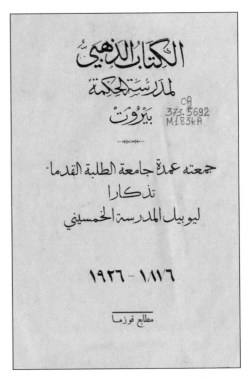

The *Madrasat al-Hikma Golden Book: 1876-1926,* compiled by alumni as a memorial for the school's fiftieth jubilee.

poem—I was in college—about sixteen or seventeen. And it had been published—and I was very proud and very conceited and thought everybody would be so interested and would speak to me about it when I went home. Well my father gave a dinner party—& one of the guests was Salima [Selim Dahir] a literary man I was very anxious to see. I longed to appear well in his eyes. During the dinner one of the ladies told me she had read my poem—and liked it so much—and then several spoke and praised it. The lady said, as a woman of 50 would to a boy, to encourage him, "And shall you write more, Kahlil?"

"Yes. In fact, I wrote one last night"—glad to say it in the happiness of her commendation.

"Oh! how interesting. I'd like very much to hear it. Won't you read it to us after dinner?" Then the others joined in & said, "yes, Kahlil—Read us your poem."

I looked at my father, & he made a face—of contempt for it all.

After dinner when we went out into the hall where coffee was served, presently one of the men asked me to read my poems—& the lady said, "Especially the one you wrote last night." My father said, "I don't believe, Kahlil, that our friends will find such things interesting"—

Then they insisted & I said to myself that I would *be* myself & I got the poem & read it.

They all listened—& I shall never forget it—They liked it—it touched them—they all looked kindly at me—It was my first reading ever to a selected audience—I cannot describe what it was to me. But they all were with me—they were loving me. And my father said—"I hope we shall never have any more of this stuff—this sick-mindedness."[23]

With the widening estrangement, Kahlil left his father's house. Still, when in Bsharri, he shared a room with N'oula Gibran, the cousin who had been with him when he had his childhood accident, and who was now apprenticed to the village carpenter. In later years, N'oula remembered those long summers when he and Kahlil, who was penniless but full of stories about life in Boston, lived simply in a shabby room in the house of Kahlil's earliest childhood days—the house that was still managed by Raji Beyk. For Kahlil, the condition of that room represented a part of the darker side of his life that he rarely mentioned in his later descriptions of Bsharri. Its shabby dilapidation symbolized the grim reality he always wished to forget. But N'oula in later years did not hesitate to recall the damp, vermin-infested quarters, and the unease that he and Kahlil always felt upon entering. When they opened the door, hordes of bedbugs clinging to a rope hanging from the ceiling would drop and scuttle to their beds. And Kahlil, fastidious about personal cleanliness, would curse the poverty that forced them to endure such degradation.[24]

In contrast to the indoor squalor was the outdoor splendor. Just as when he was a child, Kahlil found solace along the cliffs, in the gorges, and in the dark shadows of the cedars. His friendship with the poet-physician Selim Dahir also sustained him, more than ever. In his improving calligraphy, he began to record Dahir's stories and poems. The older man's knowledge of young Kahlil's traditional aphorisms, local history, and memorable personalities filled in Kahlil's understanding of his background and taught him colloquial vocabulary he would use when he himself began to write.

In Bsharri, Kahlil was dependent on the hospitality of friends and relatives for food, and he often visited the home of an influential family related to both Raji Beyk, who belonged to the Dahir clan, and Selim Dahir. Here, in the house of Tannous Asad Hanna Dahir, warmth and material comfort offered him a pleasant refuge. In return, he began to help the Dahir daughters with their chores. He was attracted to the oldest sister, Hala Dahir. She responded to solitary Kahlil, walking with and listening to him. Their friendship blossomed and was noticed. Gossipers began to speculate on the possibilities of a betrothal—which was impossible. Not only was Hala older than Kahlil, but her brother Alexander, legal scribe and town official, strongly discouraged the "son of the goat tax farmer." He made it clear that Hala could do much better.

Ten years after Kahlil's forest hikes with Hala, he published *The Broken Wings*, a story about a Lebanese student's unrequited love for an unhappily married woman. The book led readers to speculate about the sources of heroine Selma Karema's identity. Clearly his time in Bsharri had reawakened him to his origins, and in portraying Selma he may have tenderly recalled Hala Dahir. Thinking of her, Kahlil could compose a portrait of a woman from rural Mount Lebanon, her qualities and the constraints she faced.

Once, while cousin N'oula and Kahlil rested on a riverbank, Kahlil drew a picture of a sleeping angel lying in a meadow filled with flowers. "What are those flowers?" N'oula asked. "They are the flowers that put you to sleep," he replied. Kahlil based the winged figure lying in a poppy field on images of Greek mythology. It was also perhaps an echo of Fred Holland Day's photo, "Hypnos."[25]

Kahlil carefully saved the drawings he made in Bsharri and sent a package of them to Day. If N'oula had been incredulous about Kahlil's stories of a friend who took hundreds of photographs of him, brought him to concerts, and gave him books, he and others in the village became believers with Day's response from Boston. It not only acknowledged receipt of the drawings but it contained a check for fifty dollars.

Fifty dollars—nobody in town could cash that unbelievable sum. So Kahlil set out for Tripoli, twenty-five miles away, to convert his patron's payment into cash.

Sleeping angel, from Kahlil's pencil drawings made when he returned to Bsharri, around 1900.
(Courtesy Peter A. Juley / Smithsonian.)

While he was there, he bought a tan suit with pearl buttons and a splendid pair of high leather boots. When he returned, many envied him for his opulence, his success, and his mysterious rich friend. N'oula resolved that he, too, would emigrate.

~

Fred Holland Day was becoming increasingly involved with photography. He decided to retire from publishing, and by June 1899 Copeland & Day was nothing more than a list of remainders, acquired by the Boston firm of Small, Maynard & Co. Day threw his energies into making photographs and writing about photography as art. His articles were in demand, and in 1899 the *American Annual of Photography* published his essay, "Portraiture and the Camera," illustrated by his portrait of young Kahlil, probably in the first year that they met.[26]

Then, after a controversial series of "sacred studies," Day invaded England with a collection of his own and other American photographers' art. His membership in the Linked Ring, a splinter group of the Royal Photographic Society, devoted to the advancement of photography as fine art, influenced British photographic societies. By the fall of 1900, he had organized two London shows. Under his influence, the Eighth Photographic London Salon, sponsored by the Linked Ring, committed one-third of its exhibit to American photography.

The second show, held at the Royal Photographic Society's gallery on South Russell Square, featured the works of forty-one artists from the exhibit, entitled "The New School of American Photography."[27] Although Day's work predominated, the notably successful exhibition included works by Alvin Langdon Coburn, Frank Eugene, Gertrude Käsebier, Eduard Steichen, and Clarence White.

Day's pictures included portraits of fellow artists and South End models. At least three photographs of Kahlil were shown.[28] Also shown was "Portrait of Miss S. G.," one of Day's efforts to capture Sultana Gibran's solemn beauty. The surviving Day portraits of Sultana, Marianna, and Kamila attest that the photographer remembered the Gibran family during Kahlil's absence.[29]

Left to right, Kamila, Sultana, and Marianna as photographed by F. H. Day, 1901
(Courtesy Museo Soumaya.)

Following his London success, Day moved to Paris, where he stayed at the Montparnasse studio of the young painter-photographer Edward Steichen. Response in Paris was favorable to his and Steichen's mission to show that a photograph was a work of art. But restless, Day gave in to his longtime yearning for travel in the Middle East. On April 23, 1901, he wrote to Louise Guiney from Algiers: "Here I am…in the anti-room of the East, bewildered, enchanted, hypnotized by the strange beauty of architecture, the radiance of the atmosphere and the ever changing… [k]aleidoscopic quality of costume which everywhere and at all times of day and night confronts one."[30]

~

In the spring of 1904, Kahlil's father received a letter from Boston saying that Sultana was ill. From Beirut, Kahlil wrote his father about his plans and also tried to reassure him that his sister was fine.

> During the last seven months I have received five letters from Mr. [Day] who assures me that both of my sisters Marianna and Sultana are in excellent health. He extols their fine characters, marking Sultana's refined manners, and speaks of the resemblance between her and me both in physique and character.

Yet Sultana was more gravely ill than anyone realized. Twelve years later, Marianna recounted her sister's passing to a friend.

> When Sultana was twelve, glandular swellings came on both sides of her neck. The doctor gave her medicines. He said she would not live long anyhow, therefore he would not operate, since she might die under the operation. Peter had taken Sultana to the hospital, for our mother spoke no English. He did not tell her or our mother what the doctor said, but simply followed instructions as to treatment.
>
> Consumption of the bowel set in, and after seven months in bed Sultana died. Two months before her death, when I came home one day, Sultana showed her feet and legs, swollen to the knee, and said with bitter tears, "Now I can never get up at all." And she never did again. It was a terrible illness in every possible way, and felt in every possible way by the child and all who loved her and nursed her…
>
> The night before Sultana died had been very bad. We had been up all night. In the morning Peter went upstairs to rest. I asked Miss Teahan when I got to work [as a seamstress at the dressmaking shop], not to keep me but to let me go back home. And Miss Teahan did. When I came in again, Sultana said, "Why aren't you going to work?" I said, "You know we were up all night, so I thought I'd rather sleep this morning." Sultana said, "All right." Then she said to call Peter, and I did.

Our Aunt M'ssahia was in the room. Peter tried to make Sultana take a little hot beef wine, and after a great deal of coaxing she did. Then she asked for Mother, and I went to her. She was helping a woman who had come in to wash, and she told me to hang out the basket of wet clothes while she went to Sultana. In little more than a minute I heard my aunt scream. I ran back to the room. Sultana, who had been resting on my Aunt M'ssahia's arm, was dead. I started to scream like my aunt. I had never seen anyone dead before. My mother said to hush. "That is not a right thing to do." Then I cried quietly, like my mother.

Peter had gone into the little room. For three days and nights, he cried. He couldn't eat nor sleep.[31]

~

Sultana died on April 4, 1902. She was fourteen years old. On the death certificate the name of Sultana Gibran, whose solemn face just two months before had graced a display of Day's photos in his Boston studio, was changed to "Annie Gobran." The official cause of death was noted as "chronic diarrhea and interstitial nephritis." But her illness was like others that commonly afflicted the South End's Syrian district, and other immigrant neighborhoods.

On his way home to see Sultana, who he believed to be ill, Kahlil found out in Paris that she had died. He arrived on the SS *Saint Paul* from Cherbourg on May 10, 1902. Marianna described her brother's homecoming.

Kahlil was away at college. He knew Sultana was ill, but not how ill. Shortly before her death, he wrote to my mother that he had finished at [school] and wanted to come back. She answered, "Come." He started at once—we had not expected that—and in Paris he read in a paper of Sultana's death. We had written him the news, but to Beirut. For some time before her death, Sultana had said she longed only to see Kahlil and our father, and then to go...

It was the second Sunday afternoon after her death when a telegram came for Peter, at about four. He was out walking, till six. Then he got it. "Mother!" he cried, "Kahlil's coming!" and for very joy wept as if his heart would break. And my mother didn't speak for two hours, she was crying so for joy Kahlil was coming, and for sorrow that Sultana's not here.

Kahlil was coming by boat. That morning at four, we were all up. I wanted to stay at home from work, but my mother said, "You'll have plenty of time to see your brother at noon—and maybe Miss Teahan can let you stay at home for the afternoon." But Miss Teahan was too busy and gave me only a whole hour at home at noon.

Lots of company were there to see Kahlil, just come home, when I got in. Mother was getting dinner, our Aunt M'ssahia was with us. Company were invited to stay for dinner, but did not. Peter could not control himself, but all through dinner was running out to dry his tears.

Kahlil…did not mention Sultana—not at any time of that homecoming. Because he knew if he began to cry, he couldn't stop. Two or three weeks later, I said to him, as children will say, talking to one another, "Kahlil, I think it was awfully hard, you did not even ask about our sister that day." "Why should I?" he said. "I knew she was dead. I knew my mother loved her and my brother loved her, and you. I knew all our hearts were aching. And you knew I loved her, and my heart was aching. I didn't want to make it just harder for Mother."[32]

But Kahlil did observe the conventional gestures of bereavement. Marianna remembered,

He got a black suit and a black hat and black shoes for mourning…for all the clothes he brought back from college were light, with a brown hat and tan shoes.[33]

No one suspected how necessary his mourning apparel would become, or the losses that would continue to overshadow the Gibran household.

Kahlil's sister Sultana, photographed by F. H. Day.
(Courtesy Museo Soumaya.)

Compassion, from Kahlil's centaur series. Oil on canvass, around 1916. (Courtesy Peter A. Juley / Smithsonian. Reprint: Boston Photo Imaging.)

5

"PEGASUS HARNESSED TO AN ASH-WAGON"

By the fall of 1902, almost four years since Josephine had copied Kahlil's letter, she had published two books: *In the Silence*, a self-published poem, and *Fortune and Men's Eyes*, a one-act play centered on an Elizabethan tavern scene involving Shakespeare. In 1901, *Marlowe*, her first full-length play, appeared.

But in the spring of 1899, the King Street home of Josephine's family had been publicly auctioned. Josephine hid behind the shutters and overheard the proceedings from her room. As she listened to "Going, going—gone at fifty-five hundred, that's settled," she had had second thoughts about moving. But she and her sister Marion wanted to be part of social circles in Cambridge. So the family rented a house at 36 Linnaean Street. "Appearances, appearances!…We must cling together…look thoroughly presentable, and answer all Philistine demands, while the moneys grow less."[1]

Knowing and helping other poets was Josephine's way of defining herself. That same spring of 1899 she had met Edwin Arlington Robinson. She wrote to a friend that Robinson "affects me with the sense of almost pathos that any creature does who seems fated to wait for an interpreter…"[2]

The kind of struggle that Robinson endured early in his career turned Josephine into an empathetic creature and made her drawing room a shelter for vagabond poets. In September 1900, she could count eight friends who were publishing books, including William Vaughn Moody, Gelett Burgess, poet Lewis Gates, and Daniel Gregory Mason.[3] Mason, who became a composer and taught music at Columbia, remembered Josephine: "Whenever Josephine could forget herself enough not to be a bird…or a flower…she rose to heights of loyalty, both as friend and as artist."[4]

In September 1900, she started lecturing at Wellesley College, where she taught two courses: "Victorian and Georgian Poets" and "Modern Masterpieces." Except for "the thrilling experience—to be a wage-earner *and* to get your wage"—she regarded teaching as a chore. Her yearning for a reprieve at the end of the first year was satisfied when a generous patron, Lillian Shuman Dreyfus, sent her to Europe, where she visited with Wilfrid and Alice Meynell, Swinburne, and John Singer Sargent; toured Oxford with Louise Guiney; and journeyed to Stratford, including Anne Hathaway's garden.[5]

For all her new maturity and acquired sophistication, she clung to her perpetual search for self-knowledge. Writing her friend Mary Mason, the wife of Daniel Gregory Mason, she touched on this, confiding, "I regard Kahlil Gibran's drawing, above this desk: and last night I transferred it to a little peg beside my bed, where I should see it as soon as I woke up: and perhaps it will help me to grasp on my Identity (which is to say—'what God meant when he made' Posy Peabody)."[6] A few months later, she again reflected on her own altruistic intentions.

> I have just found out what I am and why I am so funny. (And why did I never see it before?)…*I am a bankrupt Fairy Godmother.* I have nothing much to give; but I have the giving mania, and I go about trying to make people be Up and Doing on an illimitable capital of Faery Gold…Yes, and when they understand, I feel as if I appeared suddenly in all my glory.[7]

~

Kahlil waited until November of 1902, half a year after his return, to contact Josephine. She answered his note the day after she received it. Two weeks later, she invited him to an evening at her Sunday salon.

> Our Sundays, now, are very different from our Sundays in the dark ages…Mr. Gordon and Mr. Michael [who] is coming back in the evening…after staying the afternoon; and with Semitic-Swiss Fleischer dropping in between seven and eight—and Scotch Gordon and German Denghausen and Syrian Kahlil Gibran…I have thought so many things about that boy's drawing and the beautiful letter, that it was wonderful to hear him, back from his own country, "touch a foreign country," saying these things to me. Spiritual substance again.[8]

The backgrounds of Josephine's guests reflected her fondness for cultures beyond her own. But in fact, Charles Fleischer, the popular rabbi at Boston's Temple Israel, had immigrated to New York City from Germany. After graduating from the Hebrew Union College of Cincinnati, he arrived in Boston in 1894, where he was greeted at the train station by the respected Unitarian minister Dr. Edward Everett

Hale. Welcoming Rabbi Fleischer as "one of the preachers of New England," Hale presaged Fleischer's fascinating career.

His buoyant energy, liberal stances, and brilliant oratory made Fleischer a favorite not only among his Jewish congregation but among parishioners of all persuasions, women's groups, and free thinkers up and down the East Coast. Josephine's reference marked the first time that Gibran and Fleischer met. But given the trajectory of their lives, and Fleischer's later description of his friendship with Gibran, the rabbi and the poet appear to have continued to meet and exchange ideas for several decades.

In her journal, Josephine wrote of her time with Kahlil that evening at the salon. He had asked her if she even remembered him, since they had met only once, five years ago. For her part, she had wondered if his drawing was meant for her, or if he had confused her name with someone else's. He told her that he had received her two letters and that he had sent her three, of which two were lost in the mail ("Talk of lost treasures," she commented). He was so glad for her letters and remembrance, for although he had met her only that once, when he looked at her, it seemed that they had known each other "long many years before."

Popular freethinker and orator, Rabbi Charles Fleischer, drawn by John Singer Sargent, 1903. (Courtesy Adelson Galleries, New York.)

Thinking back to that earlier time five years ago made her smile.

> He being then fifteen years old—this was rather comical…But I knew what he
> meant, and I was filled with comfort, because of the realness of these things to
> children of a certain consciousness—and I am blessed to be such a one—and
> knowing what the boy's consciousness was…I felt it as a shining honor…

Kahlil apologized for his hesitant English: "I felt when I wrote you…I sent you
my wrong self." But she reassured him that his English was "as close as possible" to
her…"much clearer than most spoken English." She added, "When in speaking to a
foreigner, we use our own common daily words more freshly, more reverently…and
we go to the simplest truth of things."

After Josephine had bolstered a wary Kahlil, whom she realized was still a youth,
she playfully introduced her learned circle. "There's Scotch Mr. Gordon who digs
up things in Mexico and Central America—mummies and palaces, you know. And
here's Mr. Denghausen, who knows all about music and sings like an angel too…
And Mr. Michaelis who finds out everything anybody wants to know…and *my*
sister who designs." She adroitly included the Syrian in the entourage: "—and you
who are writing and drawing all the time."

Unfazed by the group's apparent status, he turned his attention back to Josephine.
"And you. What shall we say of you?" This reply, with its implied allusion to Josephine's
own talent, "pleased [her] inexpressibly." The fact that he was at ease contributing to
the conversation also delighted her, and she noted that he "has read my books, even
Marlowe, and was not at all upset by the old English things in the latter because he had
read a great deal of Shakespeare. He knew something about everything that we mentioned from the script of the Book of Kells to Duse and to the Slugger [murder] case."

Kahlil's welcome into "Posy" Peabody's world was illuminating. Here he was
able to be with her and understand her in her own milieu. As for Josephine, her
comments convey a sense of renewal.

> If [his drawings] have developed in any proportion at all to the early ones, he will
> shake up the world. I do not in the least believe that his writing can be anyway as
> remarkable. How can it? I told him, last night, something…of the impression that
> his drawings had left me. And he was surprised with that much and deeply pleased.
> But his surprise was as nothing to mine when I found that he had delighted in my
> poetry…
>
> The knowledge of his beautiful heart of a young prophet has been a comfort to
> me all these years; and how beautiful to know again that all the things I desire to be,
> have taken shape and gone about with a foreign soul to comfort it likewise. I cannot

doubt now from the boy's drawing, this letter, and his story, that it was given me to be remembered as something beautiful…And indeed it was a draught of wine to me, J.P.P., who has felt of late her identity fading from her in a kind of bewilderment of dying. He reminds me of that old fresh assurance I used to have, like a boy David, that I was somehow dear to God; and that He cared about my singing, if no one else did.

A week later, Kahlil returned with a portfolio of his latest drawings. "Here is the Syrian back again, whom I hardly expected to see in this life," she wrote.[9] This time they were mostly alone and "talked and looked at the drawings and talked again with much quietude." Her artist-sister Marion was sick in bed, and Josephine sent the drawings upstairs to her for comment. The whole household was impressed, with Mrs. Peabody reporting Marion's approval—"Do you know you're entertaining an angel?"

Encouraged, Kahlil became more confident. When Josephine tried "to make Gibran say what things my face had seemed always to be telling," he proposed drawing her, explaining that "his English was not equal to some things." This time he promised to make it a portrait of her mind, although, he added, "The best portrait of you is your books." Before he left, it was understood that they would meet soon.

That night Josephine realized what their mutual affinity was and what it might be. She imagined the relationship that she, a twenty-eight-year-old recognized poet, and he, a nineteen-year-old immigrant artist of promise, would share for the next four years.

> There were other remarks of this young mystic that set me thinking much: What ever-lasting symbols women are! I know so well, now, when these beautiful moments happen, that it is none of it for me. I know so well that I am a symbol for somebody; I am a prism that catches the light a moment. It is the light that gladdens, not the prism. And yet for that moment, the prism, the symbol, the bringer of tidings, the accidental woman, becomes perforce an αγγλος, a messenger of God, an angel truly, wonderfully, most humbly. And if she stops to know it, she knows how and why and for how long, and she must choose between the humbleness of real angelhood or the bitter pride of self-love that is bound to hurt sooner or later.[10]

Just as she considered herself a muse for Kahlil, so was he a source for her own writing. "Return," written that November, appears to be related to their first two meetings.

> This word from long ago, can it be true?
> For you have told me that I gave you bread,
> Even as I would, in that young joy, have fed
> All souls and hungers with the joy I knew.[11]

~

Josephine had been out of contact with Fred Holland Day since the publishing firm's demise. Now, spurred by Kahlil's interest, she was again following news of exhibits. In December, she and Day met and talked at a show in Day's Irvington Street studio.[12] Soon after, she finished the first draft of an eleven-stanza poem initially entitled "His Boyhood," later retitled "The Prophet." It referred to Kahlil's life in Bsharri, as she imagined it. It was eventually included in her collection *The Singing Man* (1911).

The Prophet
All day long he kept the sheep:—
Far and early, from the crowd,
On the hills from steep to steep,
Where the silence cried aloud;
And the shadow of the cloud
Wrapt him in a noonday sleep...
Last he reached his arms to sleep,
Where the Vision waited, dim,
Still beyond some deep-on-deep,
And the darkness folded him,
Eager heart and weary limb...

Sketchbook self-portrait of Kahlil, herding sheep in Lebanon, late 1890s. (Courtesy Museo Soumaya.).

Twenty years later, when Kahlil was about to publish his signature work, *The Prophet*, he could recall a caring poet's tenderness and respect.

That December, Kahlil offered her presents of drawings and letters. More mature in appearance than in years, he no longer appeared a boy to her. "This time he was yet another three years older than last week." Even his periods of silence enlivened her. "We two had some twenty minutes of...quiet and cryptic conversation, and again I was not amazed and...not appalled at the boy's way of assuming that I know all things, and that it isn't necessary to tell me things in English, or even to talk at all."[13]

Josephine was beginning to identify with Kahlil. Although he was only nineteen, he had seen the world from another side, which she knew existed but could never explore. He had been born in the Holy Land, had faced the poverty of the South End, and had known family tragedy. Perhaps at this time she needed his experience and he needed her confident articulateness. Her facility in English, along with her understanding of literature, strengthened his own expression.

Still questioning his effect on her, and the unusual nature of their growing friendship, she wrote:

> But it was strange enough, in one way to have the boy tell me quite simply his rela-
> tion with this world, as I have very often thought of mine (when we were alone).
> It made me feel more than ever the inescapable identity of an αγγλος Κυρίον [angel
> or messenger of God]. It does not look quite simple either. But I will do my best.

Later she added, "What is my best going to be, I wonder? This is the most unprec-
edented of all things…"[14]

On one occasion, Kahlil met Josephine and her sister at Marion's Boston studio on Boylston Street. There Josephine read her poems aloud to him while he drew her and told her "some of the thoughts that came to him," for he had promised that the drawing would mirror her mind.

> It was wonderful, the things we talked about. And to hear of the cedars of Lebanon
> that have been sweet in my mind ever since I was born…I must sleep and learn
> how to disentangle twentieth-century responsibilities from deserts and date palms
> and…cedars.[15]

A year later, her poem "The Cedars" appeared in her *The Singing Leaves*. Imagining these trees through Kahlil's eyes was a special tribute for which he was grateful. Her first letter had opened to him the "bigness of things," and now he was more sure of himself. He knew "what he wanted to do and to be."[16]

On Christmas Eve he sent her a shepherd's flute, and on Christmas night he visited her. Two days later, he drew her again at Marion's studio. Then, on New Year's, "Evening brought in…a drawing! ٤٨٥ Inspiration—all colors of pale flame and lines of music." Magic names and secret symbols had always embellished her diaries. Now, she adopted Kahlil's own design of his initials G. K. G. in Arabic, the mono-gram with which he had signed the pastel drawing, *Inspiration*. Soon her attempts at copying it were flawless.[17]

On January 5, 1903, Kahlil spent the eve of his twentieth birthday with Josephine, and she told him about a plan she had thought of for him.[18] One of her friends at Wellesley, Margarethe Müller, was a well-liked German teacher and faculty adviser to Tau Zeta Epsilon. This Greek-letter society was dedicated to aesthetics, "whether in realms of painting, sculpture, architecture, music, or literature." She wanted to ask her friend "Tante" Müller to include some of his drawings in the society's annual spring exhibition. Kahlil quickly agreed to submit his work, saying, "Nothing would please me more than to give your friend some pleasure if I could."[19]

~

Kahlil's friendship with Josephine offered him relief from family and economic pressures in the South End. Living conditions there had not improved much since the Gibrans' arrival eight years before. In 1902, the Associated Charities reported, "Sickness was the 'chief cause' [of referral] in about forty-two per cent of our families and one-third of all the sick were consumptive."[20] The Gibrans were moving from tenement to tenement within the Syrian district, almost as though they were trying to elude the diseases stalking them. Peter was trying to hold together the dry goods business. Kamila, so ambitious when she had first arrived, felt her strength waning.

When Day made portraits of Sultana and Marianna early in 1902, he also photographed their mother. She no longer canvassed the streets with her pack. Even the period of mourning for her youngest child was cut short by the dreadful sickness that was invading Peter and her. Years later, Marianna recalled details of the months after Kahlil's return.

> Peter had been consumptive for some months at the time of Sultana's death, but he had been taking care of himself and building up…He was wonderful about guarding others from the contagion. Now he got worse and in the fall the doctor told him to go to Syria. Instead, he decided on Cuba, where he had friends in business, took some samples and left on Dec. 13.

Said Marianna:

> In two days he was ill, and he was never well again. He kept losing and losing, and all the time he wrote to my mother…and to me that he was gaining, and to Kahlil that he was gaining. Only to the fellow that worked for us he wrote how sick he was.

Throughout it all, Kahlil was growing closer to Josephine. During January, he did not reveal his bleak home conditions. The chasm between her cultivated salon and his own disease-ravaged home was almost unbridgeable. But the drawings that let him enter this world were a passport to survival.

Her diary revealed the extent to which their lives had become entwined. "*Jan. 15, 1903. A.M.* Late train to Wellesley, studying Arabic alphabet on the way.

Class. P.M. To see M. Müller and show her drawings. *Jan. 19.* 10° below. ⚹⚹⚹ &
Mr. Denghausen. Songs and drawings."[21]

The temperature that Josephine recorded on the nineteenth describes that
winter of 1903. Along with the tuberculosis that was plaguing crowded South End
tenements, the exceptionally bitter cold and a crippling shortage of coal and other
fuel caused unexpected hardships. Whether or not the Gibrans were relieved by
the Denison House or any official agency, the outstanding provisioner of solace
and warmth for Kahlil was clearly Josephine. Throughout that frigid winter she
welcomed him, and he in turn welcomed this chance to find some respite.

Unaware of his troubles, she did notice his remoteness. During January, unaware
that Kamila was hospitalized, she wrote, "I noticed last evening that whenever I
spoke to the boy, I seemed…in spite of my candor, to be willfully assuming alien
speech and hard to understand. And I am wondering if it is not true that when
people understand each other intimately, they [cannot] speak at all without suffering
some sort of disguise."[22]

Despite such misgivings, their companionship thrived. The inclusion of Kahlil
in the Wellesley exhibit was developing. On January 25, Miss Müller met him at
Marion's studio, where "he pinned the drawings up one by one and two by two, on
the big dark green screen." Miss Müller's comments supported his claim that all of his
drawings of faces were inspired by Josephine. Both artist and poet greeted her opinion with a naive glee. "Didn't you have her in mind when you drew 'Consolation'?"
she asked. "Why yes, of course," he remarked. And in her diary Josephine added,
"But yet this thing he drew last summer before I had come home from Europe; and
he had not seen me for four years!"[23]

Now that she was reassured in her judgment, Josephine began to more widely
disclose her faith in her latest discovery. She wrote to Mary Mason, "He is a Syrian
boy. He writes Arabic poetry all night; and he draws (much better than William Blake)
all day. And if E. A. Robinson will come to Boston, he shall see that I speak truly."[24]

During February, Kahlil and Josephine became publicly identified with each
other. She took him out to suburban Milton, where he met Mrs. Barnard, a former sponsor. They also attended concerts together. And so, guiding her diminutive
figure, he learned how to be a proper escort. Not much taller than she, he was still
perceived as foreign. The appearance of this uniquely matched couple would have
drawn attention as they strolled through Back Bay streets.

While Josephine's diaries reflect the exuberance of their midwinter companionship, Kahlil's surviving copybooks testify to his distress. Still using dummy copies of

Copeland & Day books, he crowded pages with random thoughts in English and Arabic. As he strained to find the proper vehicle to express himself, he described in Arabic the advantages of the mountains—as opposed to city life—for tuberculosis victims, and wrote about his experiences in Maine, probably at Five Islands. The most significant passage was set down soon after Peter's return from Cuba. Written in Arabic, it reflects both his despair over his brother's health and a tentative belief in the value of his own thoughts.

> I write strange thoughts. Ideas pass like flocks of birds. This is my life. Who would buy it?…All these are great hopes, a lot of books and strange drawings. What is this learning that walks with me? And I do not know where I stand. What is this earth with gaping mouth and bared chest demanding more?

Two pages later he described a premonition he had concerning Peter.

> Wednesday night I heard a bodyless voice which came…and the truth I felt is that the soul of my brother Peter would take to its God and Creator in eternity after five days.[25]

Kahlil's dream did not occur. However, within five days, he admitted to Josephine his situation at home.

> I learn from him—only by asking—that his mother and his half-brother are dying, undoubtedly of two different illnesses beyond hope; and he "has not drawn at all lately" and "written very little," because he has been nursing the two, writing business letters, and keeping watch over them at night. A terrible ordeal…and one that makes my mind dizzy.[26]

A few days later she heard by mail from him. He had left the city and was staying with relatives at the seaside town of Gloucester, forty miles north of Boston. But he soon returned to Boston and saw her on February 25. To revive his spirits, she let him read her old journals, which she had never before shared. Revealing to him the chronicle of her oldest joys and sorrows seemed to help. The next day, they went to a concert, and the day after that they met at Day's studio.

By the first week in March, Kahlil had taken over Peter's business at 61 Beach Street. The decision had not been an easy one.

> *March 7.* ﻛﻬﺠ was here yesterday and most unhappy. But he had done a very fine thing—entirely against his strongest inclinations—to save the business honor of his brother who is hopelessly ill. He thought it would be dishonorable—or at least "very easy" to fail (in the business his brother had started with several loans)

so he made up his mind to work up the business if he could, till those men at least could get their money back; and he has persuaded the chief creditor to be his partner…I know with all my heart, the anguish it will be to him…Win out of it—he must and then soon; and when 'tis over how sevenfold realer he will feel and be.

Feeling personally triumphant over a hundred-dollar check received that day from *Harper's* for six poems, the money allowed Josephine to stay at the Wellesley Inn for a few days instead of repeating the trolley car journey back and forth to Cambridge. Before leaving, she confided to Mary Mason:

The Syrian ‏حبيبي‎ is…watching his mother and elder brother die, slowly, of different incurable diseases, himself forced to step into his brother's little business (importations) because he does not think it would be honorable to go bankrupt… Pegasus harnessed to an ash-wagon would suffer less. It's enough to make angels weep; but the timely grasp of the bitter old nettle by this visionary creature… does my heart good to see. I wonder why we should all have to suffer so that most hideous anguish, a grinding service of work for the base privilege of food and raiment—when you don't care a D…about living to eat or be clothed—if you can't be yourself and make your own work. But I am much wiser…by all that wretchedness of last year…and I comfort the poor prophet with such living witness— song of the Bondages, so to say. He will win out splendidly, and that before long, in some manner, I feel sure.[27]

Josephine Peabody, dressed "old Egyptian" style. (Courtesy Private Collection.)

Josephine's image of the artist as an altruistic "giver," and of the resilient spirit of creativity, appears to have become a credo shared with Kahlil, one that would help him to endure the coming months. But her fantasizing of his origins and talent may also have reinforced the same kinds of expectations being directed at Kahlil by Fred Holland Day or Lilla Perry. The legend in which Kahlil was being cast—and casting himself—would both strand him between, and force him to seek to reconcile, his different worlds.

Marianna, photo by F. H. Day, around 1901. (Courtesy Museo Soumaya.)

~

Peter's last days as recalled by Marianna were indeed as difficult as Josephine had foreseen. He arrived from Cuba around the beginning of February, a week after Kamila's return from the hospital.

> It was six o'clock in the morning. The cabman rang the bell, and my mother said to me, "You'd better go to the door." O how Peter had fallen away! I didn't know him. I said to the cabman, "What do you want?" He said, "This man wants to get in." I said, "We don't have any furnished rooms," and I shut the door. Then the cabman rang the bell again, and when I opened the door Peter said, "I'm your brother, dear. Don't you know me? Tell Kahlil to come help me upstairs," for he was so weak he couldn't walk up by himself. So I ran up and got Kahlil out of bed, he came down in his nightgown and slippers, and he and the cabman got Peter upstairs…
>
> Peter went to mother's room and said, "Mother will you get up and let me stay in your bed till sister can get mine ready?" Then I said, "Mother can't get up, Peter dear." He said, "Why? Is she ill?" "Yes," I said, "she's ill," and I explained to him. So he got in my bed till I fixed his. Peter was in the front room, and mother

Peter Rahme, probably by Day, sometime before 1903. (Museo Soumaya)

was in the back room. I put my bed between the two, so that I could hear if either of them moved.

Peter lived four weeks. And every morning and noon and evening when I'd take him his food he'd say, "Marianna, have you had your breakfast?"…"Marianna, have you had your dinner?"…"Marianna, have you had your supper? You know you must take care of yourself now, Marianna, because you are all we have to take care of us…"

The night before Peter died was anxious and fearful. Sultana had not changed in appearance before death, but Peter's look grew different. His eyes were larger, his face had a dead look, and he looked at me differently…I said, "What's the matter?" Peter said, "Only a little pain, dear…it will pass. Don't be afraid. Just go and try to get a little rest." My Aunt M'ssahia was there, and she said…about three a.m., "Get your brother's clothes out, and his black suit." I…did not realize he was dying and thought it absurd to get out his clothes when he could not dress and get up. So [my] aunt took his closet key and got his suit herself. Several of Peter's friends were there, in a friendly way, and they and Kahlil were in the room when he died.

All through this double illness, Kahlil was in the store.[28]

Later that day, Kahlil sent a note to Josephine at Wellesley. Then to Day he wrote, "The dear brother went home, at 3 o'clock this morning, leaving us in the dept of sorrow, wounded hearted. I am to console…poor sick mother…She is as [Marianna] and I, looking on the darkness of the future."[29] The signing of the death certificate—official acknowledgment that "Peter Rahmeh" of 35 Edinboro Street, twenty-five years old, a salesman, had died of congested lungs and exhaustion, March 12, 1903—and the burial at Mt. Benedict Cemetery were hurriedly observed.

~

Josephine expressed her sympathy and wrote of her inadequacy during this sorrowful time. "I suppose the poor mother can hardly live longer now. And what to do for him I am helpless to know."[30] Four days later, Kahlil visited her in Cambridge, breaking with the tradition of mourning at home for at least a week. Ferris Greenslet, Josephine's editor at Houghton Mifflin, and a Mr. Boynton were also there. She secluded him in another room while she met with them. "ↂↈↂ rests in my study while I see them all evening."[31]

A week later, he visited her again, "looking somehow older and with sad cheerfulness in his eyes and his black tie and his more foreign look." This time the two of them were able to speak undisturbed the whole evening. They reminded themselves of ways in which they were blessed. "All over my soul as soft as snow, as soft as a rain of cherry petals on the pass," was how she described feeling when she saw him. Tenderly she held his hand in hers. "When we sit down, all is changed. I do not understand it: nor does he…I am an [alms giver] somehow; and glad and grateful and filled with wonder above all that life lets me know these things."

Josephine relinquished her properly worded world of language to more directly express her feelings to him. Every pain of which Kahlil spoke touched her, and her understanding comforted him. "I feel his bondage…and I…know what it is to be parted from one's own soul and sent to the galleys."[32]

Even if Day could not provide such instinctive warmth, he too offered his support. Thanking him, on April 13, Kahlil wrote, "Mother blesses you for the refreshing gift, dear Brother." The note shows that the Gibrans were not forgotten in their last days together. Small, sympathetic gestures from people beyond their community, as well, helped the family understand that they were not alone.

To lift his spirits, and to relieve him from his long hours at the store, Day also invited Kahlil to hear music at Symphony Hall or to see a performance of *Hamlet*. Kahlil's insistence on maintaining contact with his American friends during this agonizing time may be viewed as thoughtless. Marianna had no comparable escape valve. But no matter how much they conflicted with propriety, these choices may also be seen as reflecting a deepening sense of trust and creative will.

~

In April, Josephine was invited to Chicago to lecture and read at poetry groups and women's clubs. To read during her trip, Kahlil gave her *Towards Democracy* by Edward Carpenter, a leader of England's Sheffield socialists. Carpenter's prose poems, close to Walt Whitman in style and feeling, were more spiritual than polemical in tone, envisioning a world freed from selfish human hypocrisy.

When Josephine returned, exhausted from two weeks of lecturing, she immediately learned that the Peabody family was moving—they could no longer afford the monthly rent. She tried to react as Kahlil had: "I must learn of ٦٨٠ to take misfortune on trust."[33] Actually she stayed in bed for a week, blaming the flu, and brooded. By May 8, she was able to sit up, and her first visitor was a "disproportionately anxious" Kahlil. This time it was he who encouraged Posy. "He was very old and wise; and I was very young and docile and pleased to be revived with news of how great…I am. We were almost funnier than ever."

Her description of this wooing of a convalescent poet by her "Syrian genius" evokes Edwardian romance. While talking, she twirled a large pink daisy. Then she "got tired" and "handed it to ٦٨٠." He took her coquetry seriously, remarking, "It came off your dress," and matched it with the tracery of pink on her "flowered white empire." "With a benign air" they held hands. He worried about how pale hers were. Then he drew a picture. The evening ended with a farewell gift: "And then after much more talk we look at the vase of white roses that had been sent to me—critically. And I give him one, and he goes home."[34] A page in English from one of Kahlil's notebooks reads, "I have just said good morning to the rose which you gave last night and I kissed its lips, you kissed them too."[35]

~

With the academic year at Wellesley coming to an end, Tau Zeta Epsilon's exhibition and reception took place in mid-May. Josephine's scheme had worked, and Kahlil's drawings were included. It was his official debut as an artist. On May 21, 1903, they attended the reception. A brief critique appearing in *The Iris*, the society's annual publication, was gently encouraging: "Mr. Gibran's work shows a wonderful originality in conception and an exquisite delicacy and fineness in execution."[36]

Kahlil enjoyed more kindness at Wellesley that spring. May 30, Whitsun Eve—or the Eve of the Pentecost, seven weeks following Easter—was Josephine's birthday. That evening she invited him, Marion, and her mother out to the college for a series of open-air plays. "With joss-stick fire-flies, and stars overhead," they sat with Margarethe Müller and watched the play *The Sad Shepherd*.[37]

But the happy circumstances of the exhibit and the distracting hours of theater marked an end to their halcyon hours. The events of June would crush Josephine and Kahlil simultaneously. Still working at the store, selling dry goods and imported merchandise, he was preparing for another vigil, and she was too depressed to rally to his cause. She had rashly decided to give up teaching. How her family would survive without her regular stipend terrified her, and she cursed their growing financial tangle.[38]

"Dark within and without," packing and preparing to leave the house, she even derided herself for her former naiveté and eagerness, "that bundle of unconsidered energies, that feathered monkey." Her gloom was only temporarily relieved by a visit. "*June 24.* Yesterday evening ᘓᘔᘓ came out… We had a wood fire in the grate, for bitter chill it was." After some interruptions [we were] "able to talk as we used to do."

She gave him "a little old keepsake," which she called a charm in her diary. Said Posy, "[I] told him something of the things it made me think of and remember, when I looked at it."[39] Three days later, they walked through her neighborhood. By now the household was broken up. Josephine and Marion planned to visit friends, while their mother and grandmother boarded in the suburbs.

~

Kamila died the next day, June 28, 1903.

Kahlil notified Day, "Mother suffer[s] no longer, but we poor children are suffering and longing for our loving Mother. Write to me and bless me dear Brother."[40] Once again, Marianna provided the most detailed account.

> Mother lingered till June 28. That day she was…restless. "Marianna, lift my head. Marianna, turn me this way. Marianna, turn my foot. Marianna, fix my arm." She had not tasted food or water for a week. Now, she asked for something. I always had chicken broth ready for her, and I brought some. But when I put a spoonful in her mouth, she said, "Marianna, take it out." She couldn't swallow it, and she couldn't get it out by herself. I was frightened, and after I had helped her I ran for the doctor. I told him how restless she was…and I suppose he knew it was the end. He gave me

some things to give her, and then she was quiet and went to sleep.

Kahlil was going out to dinner, and he said to me, "Marianna do you think I ought to go?" And I said, "Yes, Kahlil. Nothing will happen to mother. You see she's sleeping now. Go but don't stay late. Come back at six." Neither of us had any idea she would die soon now. So Kahlil went.

My aunt was there...And late in the afternoon, two friends came in to help with Mother—and they were so glad to see her asleep. They said, "How nice to see your mother better"...I was glad, and I was telling them about her day and how the doctor had given me something to quiet her. My aunt said, "I shouldn't think you'd be talking now. Look at your mother." Mother was [breathing] so very quietly...

Then she was gone, and I felt I didn't have anything in the world.

About five minutes after that, Kahlil came in. There he saw his mother dead, and he fainted away. And the blood came out at his nose and mouth.[41]

II

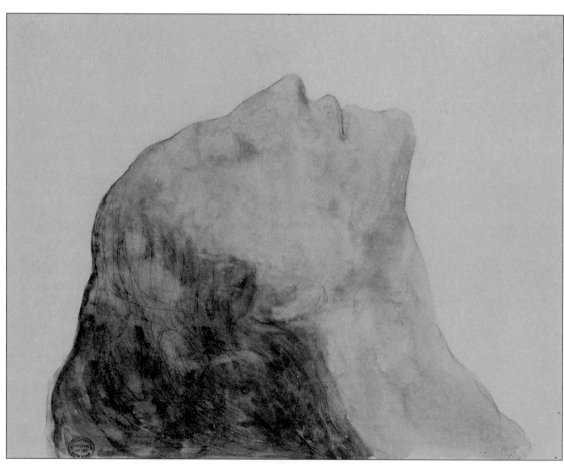

Towards the Infinite, Kahlil's graphite and watercolor portrait of his mother Kamila, 1916. In 1920 he wrote to poet May Ziade, "It portrays her at the last moment of her life over here and the first moment of her life over there." (Courtesy © Metropolitan Museum of Art. Gift of Mrs. Mary H. Minis, 1932. Image source: Art Resource.)

6

"A GALLERY OF GRACIOUS AND NOVEL HEADS"

"Do you remember the Syrean boy Kahlil Gibran?" Josephine wrote to her friend, poet Louise Guiney, sometime after she heard of Kamila's death. "He is back again…and drawing more than ever…left all alone with one younger sister…his imagination…as shiningly unspotted from the world as ever it was."[1] While Josephine's comment acknowledged the insistency of creative work in Kahlil's nature and the restorative role it played in his life, the loss of his sister, brother—and now his mother—had taken a toll.

Kamila had been the persistent presence who, despite her own lack of formal education, had believed in the possibility of something more for her children. She had nourished Kahlil's imagination with legends of Mount Lebanon and tales from the Bible; introduced him to the Syriac-Christian traditions of the Qadisha Valley; inspired in him greater self-reliance.

In fact, Kahlil had been ill since his mother's death. From then on, the slightest cough or fever would terrify both Kahlil and his sister Marianna,[2] as would worries about the elevated railroad in the South End, which was choking off air and sunlight from the already densely packed neighborhood. Describing the health trials that Kahlil and his family faced, Rosina Hassoun places them in the larger context of immigration to America at the time.

> In Kahlil Gibran's immediate family, the burden of their way of life is evident. Gibran's fourteen-year-old sister, Sultana, died in 1902 of "chronic diarrhea and interstitial nephritis." While his mother was hospitalized on one occasion, a small-pox epidemic swept through the hospital. Gibran's mother died of cancer. Gibran's brother, Peter, died of "consumption" (possibly tuberculosis). The famous author

and poet suffered heart pains of an unknown nature, eating and sleep disorders, a thyroid problem, and chronic fatigue. The information from a single family is anecdotal, but it points to the kinds of serious health problems that haunted immigrants to the United States at the turn of the century.[3]

Louise Guiney wrote back to Josephine, in the summer of 1903 "I am so grieved to hear how [badly] things go with him. Can it be possible that that shining talent can go under for long, in a place like Boston, where there are many of the generous and appreciative who are able to help?" In early August at Day's behest, Kahlil left for a week's rest stay at Five Islands, Maine, Guniey's seaside property, where he could regain lost weight and strength.[4]

~

At the end of August, Josephine Peabody learned that her family had lost "practically everything." Poverty now sat on the doorstep of the Peabody household. Kahlil's powerlessness to help her affected him deeply. Her story had "upset his trust in things," he wrote.[5] Despite her reassurances, it was with sorrow and frustration that he watched her sell her gold jewelry for $7.50, and then her study table. She was even forced to part with her books. On September 17, the family moved to a cheaper apartment in North Cambridge, on the "the wrong side" of Massachusetts Avenue. When Kahlil visited her at 20 Forest Street, he found his muse staining floors, painting walls, and doing "all the repairs…that Landlord wouldn't do."[6]

Her overly hasty resignation from Wellesley had left her with a bank balance totaling $105, plus $10 in her pocketbook, and she desperately needed a regular stipend. So she agreed with her old friend Agnes Irwin, the dean of Radcliffe, to tutor a young girl in literature and composition. On September 27, she met her pupil, Frances Gibbs, and the girl's teacher, Mary Haskell.

Seeing Mary Haskell reminded Josephine of her association with Mary's sister Louise during their Radcliffe days. The two Haskell sisters had traveled from Columbia, South Carolina, to gain the benefits of education in New England. Although their original purpose for coming North—Louise to Radcliffe, and two years later, Mary to Wellesley—was to return to South Carolina and educate working people there, they remained in Boston-Cambridge, drawn by its powerful magnet of intellectual life. After graduating, Louise founded Miss Haskell's School for Girls at 314 Marlborough Street, Boston, where Mary joined her in 1901. By 1903, Louise had met and married Reginald Daly, a promising young geologist, and Mary became headmistress. Josephine's renewed friendship with the Haskell sisters prefaced a series of circumstances and alliances that within three years would realign her, and Kahlil's, careers.

For almost a year, Kahlil's relationship with Josephine had radiated gentle warmth.[7] But amid the strains and uncertainties facing her and her family, the mood inevitably was changing. Early in October 1903, a rupture surfaced, sparked by a letter Kahlil had sent to her. By November, each had retreated into his or her private world, and they never would again meet with their previous closeness, even though Kahlil still cared for Josephine more than ever.[8]

At the same time, Kahlil spoke in his notebook of his disentanglement from his role in the family's dry goods store. "The firm of P. Rahmeh & Co. is no more. I placed it in the hand of an assigner, so you can see that I am in trouble, which I hope will be the end of troubles," he wrote. He was still attempting to write in both Arabic and English, creating accompanying drawings. Following these losses of family, and

One of Kahlil's drawings for Josephine. (Courtesy Josephine Preston Peabody Papers, Houghton Library, Harvard University.)

then Josephine, he addressed in his native Arabic his soul as his last refuge.

There is nothing left except you, soul—so please judge me with justice—which is your glory—or call death upon me. You have burdened me with love I cannot handle…She lying on the throne—on the mountain—showed me happiness.

Then in English, he confided to an unnamed listener how bewildered he felt.

What shall I call you? Learn me your name…and save me…There was a cup of wine, a poem, and your sad eyes—one pain in three formless forms; one tale in three chapters—three sad flowers in a vase—So when I came to write that same evening, I found how little one can say. For who can speak of the soul—Who can reduce the infinite into five lines?[9]

Kahlil's graphite sketch in a dummy copy for *Lyrics of Earth* by Canadian poet Archibald Lampman, published by Copeland & Day, 1895. (Courtesy Museo Soumaya.)

Despite the turn in their relationship, he continued to escort Josephine to cultural events. Her book *The Singing Leaves* had just been published, and he showed her a review of it in the Arabic press. Her homage, "The Cedars," was included, and it is possible that he had brought her poems to the attention of the immigrant Arabic press in America. That he showed her a review offers an early reference to his new preoccupation with the writings of Arab émigrés.

In Josephine's eyes, Kahlil's growth up until that November had been that of a talented foreigner—albeit an idealized one—onto whom Euro-American cultural influences could be grafted. But over the next year, he would turn away from trying to express his feelings in English, a language he still had not mastered, and write almost solely in Arabic. In this way, he could clarify his thoughts and transmit them to an audience of some twenty thousand or more Arabic-speaking immigrants, like himself. For the next ten years, 1903 to 1913, from the age of twenty to thirty, Kahlil would seek to balance the pushes and pulls of these two linguistic and artistic worlds, as he and fellow émigré writers found themselves poised at a confluence of cross-currents between "East" and "West."

It was a time when the spiritual offspring of the transcendentalists—Whitman, Emerson, and Thoreau—were drawn to ideas of "psycho-physics" and "mental chemistry," and Boston Brahmins sought to enter "the mystic atmosphere of the Oriental Circle" by attending private lectures by Siddi Mohammed Tabier on *The Book of the Dead*. To the nucleus of responsive Americans who had recognized and encouraged his early artistic interests, Kahlil would continue to be perceived as a talented visionary who could draw like an angel, not as the son of an impoverished immigrant woman peddler.

From their viewpoint, the young Syrian artist's Eastern Christian mysticism seemed to mesh with the transcultural atmosphere. The city that had recently spawned the spiritual movements of Christian Science, the Society of Psychical Research, and Theosophy welcomed such voices as Kahlil's. When Josephine observed that this silent boy seemed to meditate in her presence, she was reflecting the temper of her times, which recognized the value of "going into the silence."[10] This hunger was fueled in part by a deepening dissatisfaction with American materialism, as well as a growing awareness of, and genuine interest in, the spiritual and religious traditions of older, colonized cultures in the East. At the same time, rebellion against Ottoman rule and other political and religious strictures in their region were turning Kahlil and other émigré writers toward the transcendental voices, and other voices in the West.

Fred Holland Day's patronage and faith in Kahlil would also continue to provide a platform for his artistic growth over this period. The youth's evocative perceptions, his life in Lebanon, and his loss of family seemed to deepen Day's personal commitment. One early indication that Day was introducing Kahlil's work to the public comes from a letter written to him by Gertrude Smith, a Copeland & Day author. "I have some friends who want to see your Syrian genius pictures. Are they at your studio? One may be of real aid to him?"[11] Josephine's faith in Kahlil's promise also reinforced Day's belief in him.

For the next ten years, Kahlil worked hard to live up to the belief that Day, Josephine, and others had placed in him. In Boston during the 1890s, the immigrant teenager, with little formal education, had been exposed to portrait photography and painting, bookmaking and design, along with voices such as the English romantic poets, the Boston decadents, Maeterlinck, Carpenter, and Yeats. As he returned to his native language and culture, these voices would converse with his own Syriac-inflected Bible and the colloquial oral poetry of his origins. He would begin to address his own immigrant community in America and readers in the Middle East. Later, as he sorted through various influences and gained in fluency, he would prepare to write in English. But while responsive to his first sponsors, ultimately he would not write for a cultural elite. Instead, the accessible, rhythmically fluid free verse of his prose poetry, that marked his rebellion against all limitations on the human spirit, would be written for readers everywhere, including the modest community from which he came.

~

For Christmas 1903, Josephine invited Kahlil to spend some time with her, as in the past. But this time he refused and explained that he should be in the South End with Marianna: "On Christmas day most of the Syrians will come and visit the [ones] who lost…mother, brother, and sister in one year. It is the custom among us to go and comfort the friend. I will tell you all about it."[12] For the holiday, he sent her a pot of white cyclamens native to Lebanon, and Josephine, always pleased by flowers, happily recorded his gesture, along with mention of another, more romantic and surprising floral tribute, "some edelweiss in a box from Mr. Marks who gathered it in Switzerland himself."[13]

English born and educated at the University of London and Cornell, Lionel Marks was then an associate professor in mechanical engineering at Harvard. During the Christmas holidays, he had traveled with Mary Haskell to Ottawa to visit his best friend and colleague, Reginald Daly. Louise Haskell Daly was delighted that her husband's closest associate found Mary attractive.

Back in Boston, Kahlil gave "a little old, old Eastern ring of silver" to Josephine. She described it a week later.

> For almost two hundred years it was on the hand of a certain image of the Virgin in a little old church of hers in Bisherri of Mt. Lebanon. And it was there with scores of other rings and votive offerings. And when جبران was born and taken to be christened there, his great grandfather, then a pontiff, took this little gift from the Madonna, to bless the baby with (choosing silver as luckier for a baby) and tied it on his finger for a few hours. It was laid way for him till he was seven: and he wore it then till he was fourteen. And now he gives it to me. The ring part of it is battered but not worn. The stone and the setting are worn down with the kisses of pilgrims. No wonder I think it is a blessed ring.[14]

Despite her delight over the ring and its story, her relationship with Kahlil, who was now twenty-one, remained stalemated. But he still came and entertained her as usual and tried valiantly to pull her out of her discouragement.

Although her state disturbed him, he was able to observe firsthand the predicament of the American artist, unprotected and unsponsored in a heedless world.

He himself was preparing to enter that unstable arena in the spring of 1904 under the sponsorship of Day, who offered him an introductory show in the photographer's Harcourt studio, along with paintings by Langrel Harris, an idiosyncratic artist who had died three years earlier.[15]

But Day's space in his Irvington Street studio, located in an area known as St. Botolph and bordering Back Bay and the South End, was increasingly devoted to exhibits of American and English photographers. His influence within the school of pictorial photography was beginning to wane. In 1901, still full of plans for cooperative efforts among art photographers, he had approached his New York rival, Alfred Stieglitz, with a plan for a show at Boston's Museum of Fine Arts. To procure the museum facilities, he sought the influence of art patron Sarah Choate Sears, also known as Mrs. Joshua Montgomery Sears, wife of Boston's reputed richest man. She exhibited her watercolors widely, studied photography with Day, and was known as a major collector of contemporary, especially French, paintings. Stieglitz, however, always cautious about Day's enthusiastic excesses, rejected his plan for the American Association of Artistic Photography. A year later, when Stieglitz was ready to form a New York-based group, Day refused to ally himself with it.

This decision not to join the Photo-Secessionists was the beginning of Day's international decline. All his friends and students—Gertrude Käsebier, Alvin Langdon Coburn, Clarence White, Edward Steichen—and even his Boston disciples, including Mrs. Sears, jumped on the New York bandwagon. Day began to retreat into his peculiarly Boston shell.

But in 1904, Day was still active locally, and in March, he showed an exhibit of works by Gertrude Käsebier, whose photos of Native Americans and women, and whose advocacy for women in the field of photography, would make her one of America's seminal photographers of the period.[16] Including photos of several Boston women, such as artist Beatrice Baxter Rüyl, Käsebier's work appealed to both Kahlil and Josephine, who attended the opening reception together. "We had a good time," Josephine wrote in her diary, acknowledging that she and Kahlil still could enjoy their friendship at a convivial, artistic event.[17]

~

That winter Kahlil worked furiously to prepare for his projected show. Several notes to his patron indicate that he made regular trips to Day's studio to check reactions to the drawings he was producing. "I am very sorry, dear brother, for being unable to come Saturday to hear music. I have an engagement and there is no possible way of breaking it. But I shall come Monday and perhaps with a drawing under my arm." In the same letter he also described the kind of grippe-like malaise he would often experience. "I have not been well for days—very little sleep and less food—but I am not in bed."

Day was inviting interested patrons to the show. First he secured the blessing of Mrs. Sears. Because she had purchased a Gibran drawing, *The Past: The Present: The Future*, her name was prominently included in the catalogue. Day sent out an elegantly simple invitation, in which Kahlil was introduced as Gibran Kahlil Gibran.

Y OUR company with friends is requested at an exhibition of drawings studies & designs by Mr GIBRAN KAHLIL GIBRAN together with a small collection of miniatures and sketches by the late Mr LANGREL HARRIS to be held at the studio of Mr F. HOLLAND DAY 29 Harcourt Building 23 Irvington Street Boston on the afternoons of April 30th to May 10th inclusive from one until five o'clock

Invitation to the first exhibit of Kahlil's work, at the Harcourt Studios, Boston. (Courtesy Museo Soumaya.)

In April 1904, Josephine—who lent five of her works by Kahlil to the exhibit—went twice to Day's studio to help mount and hang pictures. She offered to send announcements to her many friends. Although her feelings toward Kahlil were diminishing, still she tried to attract as many viewers as possible, and on May 2, she begged Lionel Marks that Mary Haskell see the show. He relayed Josephine's message the following night.

That same evening, a review of the drawings appeared in the *Boston Evening Transcript*. This first major critical attention, praising a "gallery of gracious and novel heads," was more than a twenty-one-year-old artist might hope for.

Mr. Gibran is a young Syrian, who, in his drawings, manifests the poetical and imaginative temperament of his race, and a remarkable vein of individual invention. The ponderous beauty and nobility of certain of his pictorial fancies are wonderful; and the tragic import of other conceptions is dreadful. All told, his drawings make a profound impression, and, considering his age, the qualities shown in them are extraordinary for originality and depth of symbolic significance. The series of drawings entitled "Towards God," recently executed, is perhaps as remarkable as any of the works in the exhibition. In spite of some crudity in the draughtsmanship, the drawing called "Earth Takes Her Own," in this series, is fairly majestic in its meaning and expression. It reminds one of William Blake's mystical works. Similar qualities are to be remarked in "The Souls of Men," "The Past: the Present: the

Future," loaned by Mrs. J. Montgomery Sears, "Memory," loaned by Mr. Day, "The Lost Mind," "The Dream of Life," "The Descent of Wisdom to India," "One of the Worlds," loaned by Miss Josephine Preston Peabody, and "Light" and "Darkness."

All these drawings are, as their titles imply, spiritual allegories of the most solemn character and import. The earnest desire to give expression to metaphysical ideas has triumphantly prevailed over technical limitations to the extent that the imagination is greatly stirred by the abstract or moral beauty of the thought.

There are faces here which haunt the memory with something of the spell cast upon the fancy by the visions of dreamland; and, mingled with some almost grotesque and repulsive types, incomplete realizations of the artist's conceptions, wherein the hand has not been able to answer to the idea, there is a whole gallery of gracious and novel heads which express the purest aspirations and the most subtle shades of moral moods.[18]

A predictable flurry of interest followed this publicity. Day's longtime friend and Pinckney Street neighbor, William Bustin, purchased a drawing, and Mrs. Sears bought another one. On May 8, Dr. Charles Peabody (not related to Josephine) saw

Two drawings (graphite) from Kahlil's first exhibit, 1904. *Left, Good Friday.* (Courtesy Josephine Preston Peabody Papers, Houghton Library, Harvard University.) *Right,* untitled.
(Courtesy Peter A. Juley / Smithsonian.)

107

Portrait of an angel. Graphite, ink, and charcoal, 1903. (Courtesy Josephine Preston Peabody Papers, Houghton Library, Harvard University.)

The Vision of Adam and Eve. Colored chalk, 1903. (Courtesy Telfair Museum of Art.)

and expressed enthusiasm over the work. Trained in classical philology and archaeology, Charles Peabody was also interested in the fine arts and had for a time served as a critic for the influential Boston weekly *Time and the Hour.* Both he and his wife Jeannette were amateur photographers; he had joined the Photo-Secessionists and, like Mrs. Sears, was greatly influenced by Day's ideas. By 1904, he was at Harvard as assistant professor in European archaeology. On the day he came to the Harcourt Studios, he bought a drawing later described as a "man and a woman with closed eyes hand in hand and a bambino 'in nimbus.'"[19]

The next day Lionel Marks again encouraged Mary Haskell to attend: "Tomorrow is the last day of that exhibit. You must go." Josephine too was making last-minute efforts on Kahlil's behalf. On May 10, she brought a distinguished Harvard professor, Hugo Munsterberg, from the German and psychology departments. Kahlil and Day were there, and she also saw Mary, who had finally found time to take from girls' basketball games, teacher recruitment, and the women's labor movement. In her diary, Josephine simply noted the headmistress's presence: "Tuesday I took Mr. Munsterberg to see drawings…also Miss Haskell and E. Puffer there."[20]

Mary, likewise, made the following matter-of-fact observation: "Carried school circular to Foster. Mr. Gibran's pictures and Mr. Harris's—young man died in Paris. Mr. Day had both exhibits at his studio." Six years later she would recall the day in greater detail. "I went and was deeply interested. I looked slowly—and while I lingered before a red pencil drawing, a little dark young man came up and said in a very gentle voice, 'Are you interested in that picture?' When I said I was indeed, he offered to explain them all to me and did."[21]

Kahlil's own version of this scene came much later and, with the benefit of hindsight, reflected the way he saw himself and his situation as the focus of an elite circle in Boston. He would write Mary:

> I was drawn to you in a special way the very first time I saw you. It was at the exhibition of my drawings in Mr. Day's studio. You were wearing black—and it was very becoming to you—and a silver something around your waist—I loved talking to you that day…I knew many people in Boston at that time—some of them among the very finest there were…The others found me interesting. They liked to get me talking, because I was unusual for them. I said, they liked to watch the monkey. And they would have people meet me, as someone who was interesting. But you really wanted to hear what was in me—and you weren't even content to hear what I had to say—you kept making me dig for more.[22]

Mary at this time was the particular friend of Lionel, the man who had sent edelweiss to Josephine at Christmas. Soon the involvements of the two women and two men would be reversed. Kahlil—encouraged by a sophisticated artistic circle and nurtured by Josephine's special romanticism—had perhaps tired of his "monkey-on-a-string" role and sought the clarity and friendship of a pragmatic soul such as Mary Elizabeth Haskell. As Mary's interest in the "little dark young man" grew, Lionel, her man of intellect, moved away from her, just as Josephine, an instinctual artist, moved away from Kahlil. These uncanny, undercurrent shifts in sensibility of feeling and reason progressed for two years, leading to Josephine's and Lionel's marriage. With that, Kahlil and Mary were drawn together closely for the remainder of their lives.

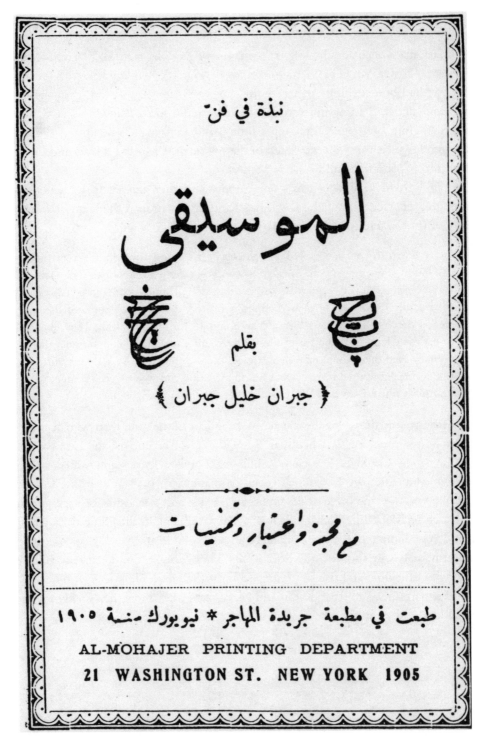

نبذة في فنّ

الموسيقى

بقلم

﴿ جبران خليل جبران ﴾

مع مجموعة واعتبار وتمنيات

طبعت في مطبعة جريدة المهاجر ٭ نيويورك سنة ١٩٠٥

AL-MOHAJER PRINTING DEPARTMENT
21 WASHINGTON ST. NEW YORK 1905

Kahlil's booklet, *Al-Musiqa, About the Art of Music*, printed and distributed through the support of the newspaper *Al-Mohajer*. (Courtesy Houghton Library, Harvard University.)

7

AL-MUSIQA

"Strange music mixed with the voice of my beloved...
I listened when she spoke with flowing words
...and again with...words half uttered."[1]

Four days after he met Mary Haskell, Kahlil was invited to see her at the School for Girls on Marlborough Street in Boston. Always trying to enliven the curiosity of her teenage students, Mary thought that showing them a young artist's works fostered her philosophy of experiential learning. The art teacher, Alicia Keyes, also encouraged her to bring Kahlil's exhibit to the school "because it would be good for the girls to see the work of a man of promise before he won recognition."[2]

Kahlil's first impression, that Miss Haskell was different from the native Bostonians he had known, was essentially accurate. She was the first American he had encountered who was not Yankee born and bred. Although outwardly at home in Boston, she too was in ways an alien. Her father, Alexander Cheves Haskell, had been an outstanding cavalry officer in the Confederate Army.[3] At twenty-eight, he surrendered the Confederate Cavalry at Appomattox. After the war, he enjoyed political success in South Carolina.

After his marriage to Alice Alexander, sister of respected Confederate General E. P. Alexander, Colonel Haskell taught law at the University of South Carolina. Mary, their third child, was born on December 11, 1873, during the period when the South—especially her father's beloved South Carolina—was suffering the humiliation and rigors of a conquered nation. Her early years were spent living frugally on a large farm near Columbia. The family grew rapidly to four boys and six girls, while her father played a major role in assuring the economic and political rebirth of his state.

Mary's regard for her father also grew as he methodically and prudently worked to repair the ruptures of war and occupation. She saw the family's fortune evolve from postwar poverty to a comfortable prosperity. At the time when she met Kahlil, her mother had been deceased for two years, but her father—then vice-president of a bank in Columbia—was an esteemed progressive figure in the South. Within this context, Mary emerged a strong and selfless personality. From her father she inherited a reasoned sense of reality and a passionate yearning for justice.

Mary saw herself as part of a "new breed" of women. Although she had lived near Boston during its frivolous fin-de-siècle years, the decadent and decorative did not interest her. At age thirty, she pursued a regimen of fresh air, exercise, and cold brisk showers. Pulling back her light brown hair in the style most suitable for her profession, she did not pretend to have feminine allure, preferring candor and purpose. Indeed, she had always considered herself plain and awkward.

A more athletic type of naturalist, Mary viewed the outdoors as a physical challenge. She spent summers camping with the Sierra Club in the White Mountains of New Hampshire and preferred long, hard hikes. Within the limits imposed by long skirts and stays, her active stance might have been regarded as awkward. But Kahlil would come to admire her hurried stride and flung-back shoulders. Observing her guiding students, entertaining visiting relatives, and explaining social causes clearly made an impression on him.

At Wellesley College, she had stated that her desire to learn to write was motivated by a wish to "do something for the South, by collecting such materials of history, localities, ideas as might be available for others to use in a work that should tell and should be a help to our people."[4] Associate editor of *The Wellesley Magazine* and organizer of "The Free Press" column in which students criticized school policy, she encouraged classmates to "live a larger life." She contended that the school was "peculiarly out of touch with the rest of the world" and spoke of "the deplorable conditions in our country" at a Republican rally in 1896. Calling for a spirit of reform, she joined the Agora Society, which publicized "the political questions of the day" and held that "woman must be broad enough to have a place in her heart and in her life, not only for her home but for her country and for the world."[5]

Ever inhibited when it came to her own feelings, in 1894 Mary had started a diary inspired by the example of Colonel Thomas Wentworth Higginson, abolitionist, minister, and diarist who fought with the first black regiment in the Civil War, and who became a noted women's and civil rights advocate, as well as a mentor to Emily Dickinson. Mary defined her diary's purpose: "The idea of writing something that might serve years hence to furnish me with a setting of the customs and circumstances and ideas of my youth, if such a setting should ever be sought by some writer or chronicler." Then she vowed that her chronicle would not be a repository for pure emotion. "As for the record of my innermost self: If I write my deeds, it will be folded up within them, the spirit prompting and informing them. For I am not one thing, and my deeds something apart; but my life is the truest expression of myself."[6] By 1904, ten years later, her habits of daily record keeping had not changed. She factually noted the racing pace of her days and her first brief meetings with Kahlil, as well as his first visit and several more during the week of his exhibition.

~

Apparently Mary invited outsiders to the show; twenty-five to forty-five visitors attended each day, despite some days of "pouring rain."[7] On Wednesday, she dined with Kahlil and a friend, Henry

Miss Haskell's School for Girls, at 314 Marlborough Street in Boston. (Courtesy Museo Soumaya.)

Schofield. On Thursday, she again invited Kahlil to dinner, along with her brother, Adam, and three other friends. Afterward he entertained everyone. "Gibran drew *Melancholy* and *The Voice of Love*," she wrote.

Although her students, faculty, and at least a hundred acquaintances saw the exhibit, Kahlil did not sell anything. Margarethe Müller, probably coaxed by Josephine and Mary, decided to support the young artist whom she had met the year before at Wellesley. She reserved a pastel entitled *The Dream of Life*, priced at $150. But her interest in just one of his works did not cheer him. On the following Monday, Josephine went to Fred Holland Day's studio and found Kahlil "in a low state of mind," the sinking letdown so common to artists after interest in their work fades.[8] Then, a few days later, Josephine told him that Miss Müller had confessed to her that she could not afford *The Dream of Life*.

Later that month, after she had returned from a New York trip to recruit teachers, Mary's schedule was less hectic. On June 17, Kahlil came to see her. They walked down Marlborough Street toward the Public Gardens and were able to talk uninterruptedly for the first time since they had met in early May. He told her about life in his native country. When she returned home that night, she wrote, "Kahlil at 8. Sat by Swan Pond. Difference between Syria and America."[9]

Two days later, they stayed into the evening at the school, which was being redecorated. She had painted the kitchen and hall earlier that week, and he helped her make a "screen for kitchen out of clothes [rack] and burlap." She made a note of his summer addresses: "Kahlil Gibran through July c/o Mr. Field [Day's caretaker], Five Islands, Maine. Then back to 35 Edinboro."[10] A day later, always the sightseer, she was traveling west toward the latest in expositions, the St. Louis World's Fair.

Kahlil, however, did not immediately go to Maine. On July 5, he saw Josephine at Forest Street, where they sat on the piazza and argued in the midsummer heat. A few nights before, she had listened to a similar message from "Il Signor Marks." Chastising her for her "foolish or New England ways or Cambridge ways," Lionel had exhorted her about her negligence in building a sensible career. She "rallied" through that unpleasant scene in which he "wished her some kind of awakening." But when Kahlil similarly questioned her, she was completely abashed and confessed how deeply his words had cut her. "I hear some more harsh sayings and know not what to do…And the third disquieting interview…reduced me to tears. But that was about other things; or rather the same thing from another point of view."[11]

If Kahlil and Lionel were vying to pull Josephine out of depression, she admitted her gloom: "Some person is undoubtedly roasting a waxen image of me." But just as she had given Kahlil a crystal the previous year, Josephine bestowed a token upon Lionel before his summer vacation. "I gave him a moon-stone for a safeguard, with some exhortations for him."[12]

~

During this time, one visitor to Day's studio described an encounter with Kahlil.

> I arrived at the studio of Mr. Day about 3:15 and expected to stay until four. While walking in the work room, I chanced to come across a piece of brown paper which I took and started to sketch a girl's head, but a young fellow of Syrian nationality who was looking over my shoulder beheld the sketch and said it wasn't just right. He took the paper and started to draw a sketch of my head…which he did first rate.[13]

While continuing to assist Day with his photography, Kahlil was looking for another outlet for his art, something that would supplement the meager income Marianna earned at Miss Teahan's shop. He was by then more assertive when it came to his career. When the editor of a New York Arabic émigré newspaper visited Boston's Syrian community that spring, he quickly made himself known.

Ameen Ghorayeb had started his newspaper in 1903. Its title, *Al-Mohajer,* or *The Emigrant*, was significant to Arabic-speaking Americans. Containing the root *hegira*, meaning journey, *mohajer* evoked the emotional implications associated with Syrian traders' journeys since the days of the Phoenicians. *Mohajer* was also synonymous with New York City, the mecca of the New World. Early in the twentieth century, competition among Arab publishers for readers was intense, especially in New York where at least three newspapers provided political and social forums for more than five thousand immigrants.[14]

When he first met Kahlil, Ghorayeb was impressed by his literary background and articulate presence. Kahlil showed him reviews of his exhibitions, and the editor recalled later that he was especially intrigued to read that "the drawings were admired in the newspapers of Boston, the esteemed city of arts and sciences."[15] Kahlil invited Ghorayeb to his Edinboro Street tenement and showed him his notebooks. Although the editor admired the talent shown in the sketches, he was more interested in the possibility of publishing some of Kahlil's poems.

Sometime between the summer of 1904 and spring of 1905, Kahlil saw his writing published in *Al-Mohajer*. Typical of the romantic essays that followed, "Vision" portrayed disillusionment. Its symbol was a caged bird, "in the midst of a field on the banks of a limpid stream," dying for lack of food and water "like a rich man locked in his treasury who dies of hunger in the midst of his gold." As the image sharpened, the cage became "the dry skeleton of a man, with the dead bird transformed into a human heart." Resembling "a deep wound," the heart spoke and proclaimed that "this cage of laws fashioned by men" was responsible for its imprisonment and death. "I am the human heart which is imprisoned in the darkness of the multitude's edicts and fettered by illusion until I am arrived at death's point."[16]

~

By mid-August, Kahlil and Josephine had returned from their summer vacations, during which they had continued to write to each other, and in the fall he visited her. Although her diary shows that the two continued to quarrel, she was at the same time apparently helping him write. "*Oct. 11.* Arabic poem from ᴄᵂᴅ *Oct. 15.* Evening ᴄᵂᴅ here with a poem in Arabic. LSM [Lionel] here also. Me stupid likewise dismal."[17]

While Josephine could respond to content and idea, she could not evaluate his use of language. His school experience in Beirut had not fully enabled him to perfect his Arabic, and there is no record of friendship with a local instructor to whom he turned. When transcribing his thoughts, he relied upon his own ear for spoken Arabic. Rather than writing in classical Arabic, he began to develop a style rooted in the everyday language of his rural childhood in Mount Lebanon, the Syriac of his Maronite faith, and the colloquial mix he heard as an adolescent among Arab immigrants in the South End. His accessible style appealed to Arab immigrants, who identified with, and responded positively to, its simplicity and familiarity. Often barely literate in Arabic, his readers enjoyed this instinctual, improvised reimagining of their native language.

Kahlil also continued to receive counsel and support from Fred Holland Day. The photographer's invitations to the Boston Symphony helped Kahlil begin to form his own thoughts about classical Western concert music.

> The fourth symphony of Beethoven is very wonderful, and I even thought that I could understand the work of the "miracle of man" until last Saturday when every note of his sought its echo from the innersmost of me.[18]

When Mary returned from her whirlwind tour of the Midwest and South, she again threw herself into a full schedule. In October, she entertained her father at the school and was actively involved in the Women's Trade Union League. Her diary continued to note visits from Lionel, attending the theater, reunions with members of the Sierra Club, and visits to the Wellesley Agora Society.

On November 7, Mary's sister Louise Daly invited Josephine to Ottawa. The invitation was prompted by the forthcoming production of Josephine's *Pan, A Choric Idyl*, which had been set to music and was to be produced on November 15 at a state farewell concert for Canada's retiring governor general. Josephine decided to attend the elegant function, even though it would strain her budget, and on Saturday, November 12, she departed.

~

That same Saturday morning, the Boston headlines read: "Fire! Loss $200,000 in Harcourt Studios." The four-alarm fire started at seven o'clock on Friday evening, turned into a devastating series of explosions during the night, and smoldered on well into Saturday. Threatening nearby St. Botolph area structures and hindering the progress of trains on the adjacent railroad track, the fire attracted hundreds of onlookers. Kahlil may have heard about the disaster sometime Friday night or Saturday morning, and gone to the building where all of his drawings were stored.

The *Boston Herald*'s front-page coverage of the devastating fire at the Harcourt artists' studio building, November 12, 1904, when Kahlil was twenty-one.

The total destruction of work by a young and relatively unknown immigrant was far less consequential to Boston's art world than the loss of "one thousand paintings by famous artists." The morning papers listed the forty artists who had studios in the gutted building; Kahlil's name was not mentioned. That morning, tenants assembled to watch the fire, "which clung stubbornly in the basement of the ruined building." According to the *Boston Herald*, "All Bohemia was there," and Kahlil may have stood with "other artists who…gazed unhappily at the smoking ruin and wondered when they would get together again, where the inspiration for another picture would ever come."[19]

Day talked to reporters about his lost pictures and prints beyond value. "It was practically the work of twenty-five years," he grieved. "And I have not the slightest conception of the value of the collection." He referred to other well-known exhibitors like William Paxton, Edmund Tarbell, and Joseph De Camp, those "who were like myself, without insurance and…must have suffered a great loss."[20] Two days later, after the fire had been extinguished, nothing was salvageable, and Day was ordered to vacate the condemned building. The publisher-turned-photographer never completely recovered from the loss. Kahlil—whose bereavement of a sister, a brother, and a mother was less than two years old—retained his stability throughout this latest shock.

Josephine received Kahlil's news of the fire on the day of her Ottawa production. Four days later, she answered and also wrote Margarethe Müller, begging her to "help out something that is being patiently borne" by sending Kahlil a "written word from you." But only when Josephine returned did she reluctantly face the news.

> *November 26.* I did not want to write it down; it is such a dreadful thing...The Harcourt Studios here burned to the ground...including F. H. Day's works and, in some ways the most poignant loss of all, Kahlil's great portfolio with all his best drawings—yes, *Consolation,* that whole record of an inspired childhood, that picture of the divine heart of Youth...I cannot tell what I felt and still feel about it. But he replied to my letter with such fortitude and sweetness, that I was amazed and reassured.

She conveyed her sympathy to Day, her friend and the first publisher of her poetry.

> I know, too, that according to your beautiful hospitality of spirit, you will doubtless be grieving even more over the loss to your friends—of the work which has always had house-room with your own. But I hope you will comfort yourself with the knowledge that everyone appreciates poignantly the sharpness of that special circumstance, and must feel keenly that it is a burden brought upon you, strangely enough, by your most generous interest in others.

Mary, who had dined with Lionel the night of the fire, in time sent Day a note of regret, adding,

> I am almost a complete stranger to you—perhaps quite so by this time—but the memory is still bright and grateful with me of an afternoon in your studio last spring when the work of Mr. Gibran and of your young friend Harris was on exhibition—when you kindly took pains to illuminate to me out of your own friendship the sketches of the man who was gone.

She also wrote to Kahlil, whom she had not seen that fall. She kept his answer, which is possibly the first letter he ever wrote her, and the first one she saved.

> My dear Miss Haskell. It is the sympathy of friends that makes grief a sweet sorrow. And after all, the perishing of my drawings...must be for a beautiful reason unknown to us. Few days ago I thought of seeing you but I had not the strength, but

I shall try to come sometime soon. I do not know what to do with my coloured pencils at present; perhaps they will be kept in the chest of forgetfulness. But I am writing. Your sweet letter is indeed a consolation. Your friend, Kahlil.[21]

His promised visit to Mary did not take place that winter. But he still kept in contact with Josephine. On Christmas Eve he brought her some Syrian sweets, and on January 6 celebrated his twenty-second birthday with her.

"After the Harcourt Studios fire…I set to work," Kahlil told Mary in 1916. Josephine's comments on his visits during the winter of 1905 echo his immersion in work. When Edwin Arlington Robinson came to her house in February, she enthusiastically showed him Kahlil's latest drawings. Four days later "ﺟﺮﺝ here with poetry to read and pictures to show and I read aloud to him somewhat." On March 1 it was "English translation of a poem by ﺟﺮﺝ."[22]

~

The Arabic essays that Kahlil was submitting to Ghorayeb's newspaper were earning him a weekly sum of two dollars. He wrote to Ghorayeb, "Until now I did not understand what you want. If it is a must, then I would write two articles or more a week for two dollars."[23]

Perhaps in recognition of indebtedness to Day, he called one of these early pieces "Letters of Fire" and began with the lines inscribed on Keats's grave in Rome: "Here lies one whose name was writ in water." He went on to question the fragility of man's worldly efforts: "Shall death destroy that which we build / And the winds scatter our words / And darkness hide our deeds?" Reversing Keats's premise of the impermanence of man's deeds, Kahlil ventured,

> The air bears every smile and every sign arising from our hearts and stores away the voice of every kiss whose source and spring is love…If that sweet singer Keats had known that his songs would never cease to plant the love of beauty in men's hearts, surely he had said: "Write upon my gravestone: Here lies the remains of him who wrote his name on heaven's face in letters of fire."[24]

With his essays, Kahlil was creating for his émigré readers a bridge to English writers. In the spring of 1905, his articles from a column entitled "Reflections" conveyed the theme of love. Often gently erotic, they expressed the joys of physical and mental union. "The Life of Love," published on April 1, 1905, depicted the four seasons of love. In it the poet yielded to separation from his beloved only by the "icy breath" of death and winter.[25]

Kahlil's contributions to "Reflections" often depicted a generous muse. At times she personified the rapture of dreams, as in "The Queen of Fantasy," where the "mistress of regions of fantasy" caused "the earth to open and the firmament to tremble." She also loomed importantly in "A Visit from Wisdom," when she gazed upon the poet "like a tender mother and wiped away his tears." She answered his confused despair by pointing "to the wild places" and beseeching him "to learn pity through sadness, and knowledge by way of darkness." Similarly, her understanding emerged in "Before the Throne of Beauty," where she became a "nymph of paradise…on her lips was the smile of a flower and in her eyes the hidden things of life." She defined beauty as "that which draws your spirit…that which you see and makes you to give rather than to receive."[26] This figure became the mirage who entered his dreams and spoke through his consciousness.

Early that summer of 1905, at the age of twenty-two, Kahlil's first book was published thanks to the support of Ameen Ghorayeb and *Al-Mohajer*. Entitled *Nubthah fi Fan Al-Musiqa (On Music)*, the book focused on the divine sources of music and its role in the civilizations of the past, describing and paying special homage to the musical modalities of music of the Middle East. He begins by likening music to the sound of the voice and speech of his beloved.

> I sat by the one I love listening to her conversation. I was speechless and felt her voice was a force that moved my heart. My soul was electrified and swam in a boundless atmosphere—seeing the world as a dream and the body as a prison. Strange music mixed with the voice of my beloved and so involved was I with her conversation that I was struck dumb. When my beloved sighs, o people, I hear music. I listened when she spoke with halting speech and again with flowing sentences and again with her words half uttered between her lips.[27]

The poetic essay turns to the history of music and its role in ancient Chaldean, Egyptian, Persian, Greek, Hebrew, and Hindu cultures. "Music is like poetry and photography—representing the conditions of man," he continues, then describing the tone-poem qualities of four technical Persian modes. In the end, he called upon listeners to glorify Orpheus, David, Beethoven, Wagner, and Mozart, and especially urged his fellow Syrians to remember the great musical traditions embodied in the Arab composers.

~

During the spring of 1905, Josephine had delivered six lectures on "Symbolism of the Present," which included readings and reflections from Ibsen, Maeterlinck, and Yeats. Her play *Marlowe* was produced at Radcliffe in honor of the opening of Agassiz House. Public acceptance reenergized her, and she was able to finish *Chameleon*, a play based on the follies of marriage.

For her birthday on May 30, Kahlil wished to create a special gift, something that perhaps would halt their gradual drift apart. So he wrote a story, a parable that contrasted lavish treasures presented to a victorious king with the simple homage of a beggar: "I come from a distant land to offer you a feeling from my heart."

The monarch was moved to tears and said that the "poor one's" gift was the more meaningful tribute. It ended with a customary kiss of the monarch's hand by the beggar and was dated "1905 A.D.—on the thirtieth of May."[28]

He dressed this fable in an illuminated double page of Arabic calligraphy, dedicated to Josephine. "May the gods bring back this day many times with much happiness and joy so that you may take from this beautiful

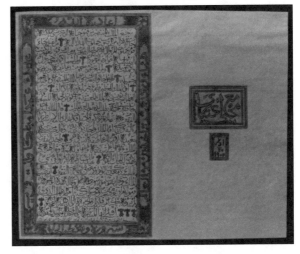

Twenty-two-year-old Kahlil's ink and watercolor card to Josephine Peabody on her thirty-first birthday, May 30, 1905. (Courtesy Private Collection.)

world as much beauty as you give it. ⏜." Josephine loved the present and message, but whenever he voiced his fantasy of a serious relationship with her, she was quick to point out "mistaken talk." The disparity in their age and background, and the sad similarity of their poverty, ruled out plans for a future together.

In July he brought a special copy of *Al-Musiqa* to Josephine. She listened as he read to her a translation of the introduction, interrupted twice by other visitors. Later they spoke together "contentedly on the piazza."[29] But throughout the ensuing fall and winter, Kahlil's presence in Josephine's diary, and life, diminished as a "Grand Duke" appeared. Before long she was able to express her growing feelings for Lionel, by now her open suitor: "But everything has sailed into new regions of the air. The stars are different; and so is he; and so am I. Everything slow appears to be going fast and I am a me I never met before."[30]

Mary Haskell (*right*) and friend on Sierra Club outing, around 1910. (Courtesy Wilson Library, University of North Carolina, Chapel Hill.)

If these developments left a void in Kahlil's life, so was Mary's life affected by Lionel's courtship of Josephine. That autumn, Kahlil and Mary renewed their acquaintance. He visited her during the first week of October and listened to her tell of her summer adventures in California, where she had explored Yosemite Park with the Sierra Club. She told him about being arrested in Illinois, "for fast driving," and about a notorious escapade in nearby Cohasset, where in front of a good-sized crowd she had dared to ride a horse bareback and walk in tightrope fashion across some playground equipment. In later years, she would attribute the resistance of many Brookline mothers toward her school to this lack of decorum. Still, she continued to defy the customary notion of the proper schoolmistress. That fall she "celebrated Russia's being given a constitution by hanging out the flag." Then she "gathered the girls into the library, told them about Russia, read the Czar's proclamation and sang America."[31]

A month later, over dinner at Marlborough Street, Kahlil shared with Mary his favorite writers. Josephine's and Mary's diaries reveal that in November he visited Josephine only once, just as Lionel saw Mary only once. In December, Mary traveled to South Carolina for a family reunion. While she was there, she refused a suitor, the second within a year. She enjoyed the company of men until faced with their serious intent. She still described dancing until 2:30 A.M. as "blissful."[32]

On Christmas Day, Kahlil sent Mary a note: "My beloved Godmother: May all your days be birthdays of songs and all your years be new as the newly strung harp." With the new year, Josephine rejoiced: "It has all come true. I feel still as if I were walking in my sleep."[33] At Sudbury's Wayside Inn, Josephine and Lionel—with

Margarethe Müller as chaperone—openly toasted the year 1906 and drank to their unannounced engagement. Slowly Josephine's and Lionel's secret was disclosed. "Glorious," exclaimed Mary to Josephine: "There is no other man I know so close to the deepest life of the human heart as Lionel."[34]

Now twenty-three years old, Kahlil did not officially hear about it until February 20, three days before the public announcement. Five days later he sent best wishes: "I rejoice with you and I bless you always…"[35] Two days after Josephine received Kahlil's note, she told Lionel how close she had been to the young artist. "I tell him about ﺣﺐ."[36] By then he was so far removed from their social world that he was absent from the several dinners and dances honoring the couple.

Suddenly everything was blossoming for Josephine. On April 17, her one-act play *Wings*, a subtle piece mourning the thralldom of womanhood and starkly set in Anglo-Saxon times, was performed at the Colonial Theater. Audiences in Boston loved the performance, and for the first time in her adult life, she was experiencing the material and emotional abundance that she had known as a child, while wedding gifts poured in.

On May 2, Kahlil visited her. Once again he showed her some "new pictures" and lingered for a while to listen to the sound of the voice that had inspired his youthful dreams. He followed this final "good talk" with a birthday note on May 30, and then, unwilling to play the well-bred game required of rejected admirers, retreated from her life and, for a while, from Mary's circle as well.[37]

On June 21, Josephine and Lionel were married at Harvard's Appleton Chapel. Marion Peabody and Mary Haskell were bridesmaids. The ceremony was simple, with no "obeys." Before Mary sailed to Europe and the newlyweds departed for Italy and Germany, over three hundred of the Boston-Cambridge artistic and literary elite gathered for the reception, held at the Colonial Club. Absent was "Mr. G. Kahlil Gibran of 55 Beach Street."[38]

From Kahlil's self-portrait with Mary. (Courtesy Telfair Museum of Art.)

8

"THE PRESENCE OF
A SHE-ANGEL"

Following the loss of family, the closest friends of Kahlil's Boston days also were retreating from his life—Josephine forever, Mary for a while, and Fred Holland Day more and more, as he suffered from deteriorating health. Increasingly isolated, Kahlil sought companionship and support from his Syrian community. He spent time during the summer of 1906 at Five Islands, but then, determined to write about his growing sense of estrangement, returned to Boston.

Marianna and Kahlil had lived for the past three years in various apartments among fellow Syrian immigrants in the South Cove. Only a year apart in age, his sister by now was twenty-one. Associating the dreaded tuberculosis with dirt and squalor, she had become an immaculate housekeeper, and he was grateful for her efforts to maintain quarters where they could entertain relatives and friends. From their mother Kamila, and later from older women in the community, she had learned secrets and shortcuts in preparing favorite dishes, and she was gaining a reputation for her cooking and hospitality. More important, her wages now supported their small household. Marianna's deftness with a needle made her Miss Teahan's favorite. She created hats and sewed fine seams during the day, and at night she fashioned clothes and shirts for her brother and for herself. This enabled Kahlil to stay at home and work.

But Marianna depended entirely upon Kahlil for her own social life. Only he could tell jokes and stories that allowed her to forget the losses that were still fresh in her memory. Afraid of the world outside their neighborhood, she let him venture beyond and waited for him to return and tell her about Americans he had met.

Despite all of her accomplishments, Kahlil was frustrated with one limitation— she still could not read, and she persistently refused to attend the Denison House classes. Over time her illiteracy gradually had assumed more importance as she tried to cope with subway and street signs, identify products in stores, or make sense of letters addressed to her or to her brother.

Kahlil alternately begged her to try and teased her for her reluctance. He bribed her with a dollar to learn to write her name, which she did. But when he offered to pay her fifty cents for every page she read to him, she balked. For the rest of his life, Kahlil, who so admired the educational and other opportunities available to women in America, was distraught by her stubbornness, which became a point of contention. It rankled him, too, that she could not read his work in any language. She, in turn, became silently protective of this shortcoming and tried to conceal it.

He was equally concerned that N'oula, his cousin and childhood companion from Bsharri, should succeed in learning the language so needed to survive in American society. When N'oula was first due to arrive in New York in 1905, Kahlil tried to arrange for him to be met when disembarking. But N'oula arrived in Mexico and then settled in Scranton, Pennsylvania, for a year before coming to Boston. Kahlil wrote to advise him on how to find his way in America and offered to help him raise some cash.

> About work in Boston, like any other place in the U.S.A., there are lots of shoe factories, also lots of men who are unemployed. Be aware of this fact if you come, because that is a big complaint, and I do ask you not to give up, but be brave and work hard so that you can speak the language. After that you will find America is the best place on earth. You are young and should look to the future. If a year goes by with no results, have no regrets, because gains are available for those who use their brains…I am still heavy with the costs so I can continue to write, and I beg you to care for your health. I know by experience because my health is no good and hinders my studying…Keep the antiques with you and maybe they will be of some value. When a friend comes back from Europe, I will show them.[1]

As his role changed from one who received help to one who could help others, Kahlil assumed a respected position within the Syrian community. Historical feuds between Maronite and Orthodox Christians had followed members of the sects to America, especially in New York. These divisions significantly affected the social and business lives of Syrian immigrants, and even became news. "Assailants Said Syrian Paper Slandered Them: Shooting result of a church feud," read the *New York Times* headline of February 1, 1906, reporting on one especially violent incident. Gunmen representing a rival religious faction had entered the office of *Al-Hoda* (*The Guidance*)—one of the first Arabic language daily newspapers serving Syrian immigrants and based primarily in the Maronite community—and accused Salloum Mokarzel, brother of the editor, Naum Mokarzel, of printing false or misleading stories. The scene continued, with the gang retreating to a restaurant, killing the brother of the Syrian Catholic archbishop and accidentally wounding another.[2] Attempting to mediate the dispute, the editors of *Al-Mohajer* (*The Emigrant*) newspaper ran a front-page drawing by Kahlil, showing an angel extending both hands to the contending factions. The illustration was supplemented by an article written by another young immigrant from Mount Lebanon, Ameen Rihani, who also decried the strife and the clerical dependence that divided the Syrian immigrant community.

In Ameen Rihani, who was seven years older, Kahlil had found an ally and future colleague. Kahlil responded by writing "The Poets of *al-Mohajer*," an essay on contemporary Arab writers, in which he chastised fellow writers for mimicking the traditional Arab poets and for using poetry solely for financial gain. The article was interpreted as a personal attack by several older poets in America and Syria, and its rather shaky literary analysis was criticized as linguistically weak and artificial. However, the ensuing notoriety lent prominence to the young iconoclast from Boston. Soon his column, "Tears and Laughter," was being read by leading Arabic language literary figures in America.[3]

Kahlil's portrait of his friend and colleague, writer Ameen Rihani. Charcoal, 1910. (Courtesy Peter A. Juley / Smithsonian.)

~

In his writings, Kahlil began to fashion a more complex Garden of Eden—one choked with painful thorns, in contrast to the earlier blooming roses. Irony tinged with bitterness appeared in his work; life and love became double edged. Often his stories were built around a simple hierarchy of a society peopled by the forces of good and evil, in which poets and simple folk were arrayed against the rich and powerful. Nature remained the constant truth and death the final liberator. In the tale "Vision," a poet, mired in the "fields of perplexity," encountered Melpomene, the goddess of tragedy, who showed him "the world and its sorrows, for who has not seen sorrow cannot see joy." In this story, Kahlil depicted "an earth strangled by priests, sly like foxes, and false messiahs…lawmakers trading their garbled speech in the market of shame and deceit," a domain where "the wretched poor sowed" and the "powerful rich" harvested.[4]

In "The Poet's Death is His Life," the title character waits for his "hour of deliverance from the bonds of existence." Death becomes the ultimate love affair, a longed-for-release, and in the end a triumph for the neglected creator when people erect a statue to his memory in the town center.[5]

Along with these brief imagistic flights to domains where people "knew the manner of the flower's breathing and the meaning of the songs of the thrush,"[6] Kahlil was organizing his thoughts into a trilogy of longer, more realistic stories set in northern Lebanon. The first two, "Martha" and "Yuhanna the Mad," portrayed the title characters as victims of those in society who oppress others. An orphan, Martha, is seduced from her isolated village to Beirut, "wherein the air was leavened with the breath of death." There she falls into a life of prostitution and squalor. Finally, as she lay dying, Kahlil, as the first-person narrator, tries to ease her sense of shame: "It were better that a person should be the oppressed than…the oppressor…fitter that he should be a victim to the frailty of human instincts than…be powerful and crush the flowers of life." Consoled, Martha finds death's ecstasy. Kahlil helps her son and his friend, "whom the adversaries of existence had taught compassion," bury Martha "in a deserted field…for the priests would not pray over her remains, neither would they let her bones rest in the cemetery."[7]

In "Yuhanna the Mad," madness becomes a refuge for the hero. Tyrannical priests torment a poor herder whose calves have strayed into a monastery's pastures. Pleading for mercy from the monks, who demand payment for trespassing, Yuhanna desperately resorts to his Bible: "Thus do you make a mockery of the teachings of this Book," he cries.

Yuhanna's secret reading and use of the Bible to defend himself, his subsequent imprisonment, and brutal beating by sadistic monks, all paralleled the life of the Lebanese religious martyr Assad Shidiaq. In 1829 Shidiaq, an early convert to Protestantism, was captured and brutally murdered in a monastery not far from Bsharri. Kahlil had grown up aware of this story and knew that the message of the Scriptures was still being ignored by local religious orders in Lebanon's mountain towns. But Yuhanna's fate differed from that of his real-life model. The governor, condemning his Christ-like sermons as words from someone deranged, finally pardoned him, and he lived out his days as a madman beleaguered by jeering village hypocrites.[8]

The last story in the trilogy, "Dust of the Ages and the Eternal Fire," dealt with reincarnation and preordained love. The hero appears first as Nathan, the son of a Phoenician priest in Baalbek, and then as Ali al-Husaini, a Bedouin nomad. Nathan's dying beloved had promised that she would return to the world. Nineteen centuries later, the vow is fulfilled when, amid the ruins of Baalbek, the shepherd Ali experiences "distant remembrances" of life there as it was in Nathan's time. "He remembered those pillars standing upright in greatness and pride...He felt the impressions of sleeping things stirring in the silences of depths." Taken by this memory, Ali returns to his sheep and momentarily envisions a girl. She seems to share his sense of memory, and their reunion is "the act of one who finds an acquaintance who has been lost." Kahlil's innocent message was one of love conquering the onslaught of time, and finally consummated.[9]

Ameen Ghorayeb wrote an afterword to the three stories and published them in 1906. The original title *Ara'is al-Muruj*, or *Spirit Brides*, became *Nymphs of the Valley* when translated years later. The fresh approach of the tales—ironic and anticlerical in tone, realistic, and portraying lower-class heroes—contrasted sharply with the mannered Arab writing of the day, and they immediately appealed to émigré writers in New York. Although living in relative obscurity in Boston, Kahlil was becoming recognized for his fascinating drawings and rebellious stories.

Shortly after *Ara'is al-Muruj* appeared, Kahlil visited New York. While getting to know people in the Syrian community, he was asked to be the godfather of an Orthodox Christian child. Upon learning that the poet was a Maronite, the bishop raised objections. In the end, it was agreed that he could share honorary parenthood with an Orthodox member, and both men took part in the christening.[10] To Kahlil the incident strengthened his dream of an enlarged sense of the human family. He believed that the readers of *Al-Mohajer* needed someone who could say: "For the earth in its all is my land...And all mankind my countrymen."[11] And he began to believe that his role was to be a voice of a unifying message.

As he identified more with his own ethnic, cultural, and literary roots, Kahlil—who four months before her marriage had promised Josephine that he would always be indebted to her—no longer kept in contact with her. She and Lionel had spent a blissful winter in Germany. There, for the first time, she was able independently to devote herself to her writing. She took advantage of this freedom to compose a play about the Pied Piper of Hamelin and faithfully corresponded with everyone left behind.

Kahlil did not answer any letter she sent him. Finally, in May 1907, Josephine wrote to Day, asking if he could arrange a letter of introduction to Maeterlinck. But something else was troubling her. "The other thing is: where is Kahlil Gibran? And is he well?—And working? I have written several times to him in the summer, and since, with no reply whatever, which is quite unlike the boy. It would be most kind of you to send me word."[12]

~

When or where Kahlil and musician Gertrude Barrie first met is unclear. Letters suggest that editor Salim Sarkis, who had corresponded with Barrie from the New York offices of *Mirat al-Gharb* (*Mirror of the West*), may have been responsible for introducing them.[13] Musician Gertrude Barrie was four years younger than Kahlil. The Boston-born daughter of Henry Barrie, an Irish Protestant writer who was educated at Queen's College in Dublin and who contributed to one of the oldest Roman Catholic newspapers in the U.S. (*The Pilot*), Gertrude was a highly trained and accomplished pianist. Her New England Conservatory diploma stated that her concentration was in "Piano-forte Playing as Soloist," with additional study in "Theory, Harmony and History of Music."[14]

Kahlil's earliest postcard to Gertrude, sent from Five Islands, Maine, bears no message. A letter postmarked October 3, 1906, suggests that their friendship began around four months after Josephine's marriage.[15] By that time, Gertrude had previously taught music at a girl's school in Tacoma, Washington.[16] One review called her "an interpreter of the modern school of composers," describing her playing as "sympathetic and emotional in the best sense of the word."[17] By 1905, giving private piano lessons had become her main livelihood and would sustain her throughout her long life.

Gertrude's second-floor studio apartment in a five-story row house at 552 Tremont Street was just a five-minute walk from Kahlil's South Cove neighborhood, on a busy thoroughfare in the city's South End, directly opposite the National

Theater and the Cyclorama, a popular exhibit hall. In her studio, Gertrude kept symbols of Goddess Diana and a magical moon lamp. "Of passion," Kahlil wrote Gertrude in 1907 when he was twenty-four, "I can say nothing now. I only know that it is within my soul."[18] Another note confided:

> I wish I could talk to you of these things…Once we spoke of things beyond this world, and we used to find a comfort in them. Things are quite different now and my heart is struggling for more space and more aire.[19]

Pianist Gertrude Barrie, in 1907. (Courtesy Museo Soumaya.)

Gertrude carefully saved their correspondence. How did she affect Kahlil's perceptions of his new country and of how some young people handled their daily expressions of love and choice? Here was a talented musician in her early twenties, living alone as a single woman; a female artist unafraid to socialize with male friends in her studio; a romantic whose choices were not controlled by what neighbors, or even relatives, might think about her relationships. Even Mary Haskell, for all her outspoken positions, guarded her reputation more closely. For Kahlil, his enduring friendship and correspondence with Gertrude appears to have marked a crucial turning point and transition, leading to passion and maturity.[20]

~

Life for Mary Haskell during 1906 and 1907 was full of dreams for her popular girls' school and for helping talented young women and men. When she returned from her European tour that year, she brought Sarah M. Dean into the school to join her as a new partner. For the next six years, the Haskell-Dean School pioneered educational reform. Concerned with the insular atmosphere of classrooms, it sponsored experiential learning and field trips, such as visits to nearby Massachusetts General Hospital to see X-rays being taken or to the Boston Navy Yard's rope factory. Girls were encouraged to develop "self-government meetings." In a more controversial move, the concept of sex education became part of the curriculum.

Dr. Richard Cabot and Ella Lyman Cabot played major roles in these teaching experiments. Dr. Cabot, who had introduced a social service program to Massachusetts General Hospital as early as 1905, advised Mary on her hygiene courses. Ella Cabot, a member of the state board of education, was a prominent educator and author of books, including *Everyday Ethics* (1906). When Mary first became principal, she frequently visited the couple's Cohasset summer house. There she studied anatomy and ethics with the Cabots.

As early as her freshman days at Wellesley, Mary had admitted that she was no longer "an orthodox Evangelical Christian."[21] Organized church services offered no appeal to her. However, she remained committed to the moral responsibility of the individual, and her deep, long-lived friendship with the Cabots greatly influenced her personal philosophy. She devoted more time to preparing "sermons" for assemblies. Covering a wide range of moral issues, these talks often stressed the importance of honesty, charity, and tolerance in daily life.

Yet another friend who guided Mary was Sarah Armstrong, a school principal who had retired to New Hampshire. How dependent she had become on the older woman is illustrated in letters that she wrote her from Scotland and England during the summer of 1906. This contemplative pilgrimage, inspired by Armstrong, changed Mary's attitude toward life. After years of neglecting spiritual concerns, Mary acknowledged to herself the necessity of "religious devotion." She described this reawakening to Miss Armstrong.

…How after a lapse of several prayerless years, I first began once more to turn pretty often to God, and of how gradually…I came back to constant thought of Him, so that it was not until a year ago I began to speak of Him to my girls.[22]

In October 1906, Sarah Armstrong died unexpectedly. Mary, who had so matter-of-factly recorded family and school deaths, fell into a deep depression. Openly mourning her mentor for two years, she wrote a series of letters to her deceased friend.[23] Gradually she withdrew from her outside interests—the women's labor movement, Wellesley activities, and waning family responsibilities. Most of her friends were by now married, and her independent personality made her cautious about any possible intrusion into their domestic lives.

At thirty-four she was at a crossroads. Ready for new acquaintances and interests, she restored her stamina by gathering about her an unlikely trio of characters. They included a worldly divorcee trying to succeed as a playwright, a French teacher aspiring to be an actress, and Kahlil.

~

In 1904, Mary became friends with Charlotte Teller, a freelance writer, through her brother-in-law Reginald Daly. Separated from her husband Richard Johnson, a civil engineer, Charlotte actively supported labor and women's suffrage. Daughter of James B. Teller, who eventually became the attorney general of Colorado, and niece of U.S. Senator Henry Teller, she had traveled east to pursue her education. At the University of Chicago she had been a favorite of John Dewey, who once accused her of hypnotizing her pupils instead of teaching them.

In the winter of 1906, Charlotte and her grandmother moved to New York City and settled in a cooperative home called the A Club, at 3 Fifth Avenue. She once explained that the residents there

Feminist and writer Charlotte Teller, 1911. (Courtesy Wilson Library, University of North Carolina, Chapel Hill.)

lived ordinary lives, even if their views were mostly "radical."[24] Also residing at the A Club when in New York was William English Walling, Mary Haskell's good friend and her sister's brother-in-law. A journalist, married to the activist Anna Strunsky, Walling was recognized for his coverage of the 1905 Russian Revolution and for his role in founding both the National Women's Trade Union League and the National Association for the Advancement of Colored People (NAACP). He and his books on socialism became topics of conversation between Kahlil and Mary throughout the years.

That spring, Charlotte arranged a meeting between Samuel Clemens and several Russian activists recently arrived in New York. The writer lived a few steps away, at 21 Fifth Avenue, and Charlotte organized a meeting between Clemens and Nikolai Tchaikovsky, who paved the way for the arrival of his fellow Marxist, writer Maxim Gorky. On April 12, A Club members paid tribute to Gorky, with Clemens addressing an enthusiastic audience, and Charlotte gained an ally in Clemens.[25] After a six-month period of correspondence and conversation between them, a falling out ensued. But

Portrait of Samuel Clemens by Kahlil. Charcoal, around 1907. (Courtesy Museo Soumaya.)

an unsigned and untitled portrait of Clemens was among Kahlil's Boston portfolio. Charlotte Teller's close association with a range of American Social reformers centered around Greenwich Village nurtured a receptive Kahlil when he eventually moved there. The stories she told, and the people he met through her, introduced him to labor, women's rights, and cultural activists, at the same time that he was deepening his ties with emigrant writers and reformers from the Middle East. This confluence of populist American and diaspora activism would form the cradle of Kahlil's social thought.[26]

By 1907, Charlotte was becoming known for her articles on contemporary issues and personalities. National magazines—*The*

Crisis, The Independent, The Arena, Everybody's Magazine—liked her forthrightness in tackling progressive issues, whether at Jane Adams's Hull House, in the Colorado labor wars, or in the Chicago sweatshops. *The Cage*, her first novel, published in 1907, was set in Chicago lumberyards. A reviewer who described its heroine could have applied his words to its author: "The right heroine of the new order...has an epic sense of what is happening about her...is enchantingly feminine with a new kind of archery fitted better to that life which shall come after *The Cage* ["the tyranny of the law"] has been broke."[27]

Charlotte's ebullience contrasted with Mary's pragmatism, but they became close confidantes. Soon she was fascinating the high-minded schoolteacher with accounts of her urban adventures. Slowly the women's correspondence grew into a deeper relationship. Charlotte was convinced that the theater needed a woman playwright to interpret the new society. Mary promised money to support her aspirations, so Charlotte tried to settle down to write.

Charlotte's New York letters did not completely satisfy Mary's yearning to know the world beyond Boston. And so when Emilie Michel, a young French teacher whom she had interviewed for a teaching position in June 1906, arrived at the school that fall, she found another companion. Little is known about Emilie Michel's background, but by the beginning of 1908 she was the highest-paid teacher on the school staff. Even so, she confided to the headmistress that she wanted to be an actress.

~

Kahlil did not see Mary again until early in 1907. Their first meeting took place on his birthday, when he was invited to tea and stayed until ten. He brought her a copy of *Ara'is al-Muruj* (*Spirit Brides*), respectfully inscribed, "With the love of a strong child to Mary Elizabeth Haskell, from Kahlil, January 6, 1907." Although she saved the volume, she did not record it in her diary. That evening he drew two sketches for her. She called them *The Blessed Seed* and *Love, the Giant*. He did not visit the school again for eleven months, when she invited him to supper on December 7. Afterward he "drew his own picture from the looking glass" on her desk.[28]

Mary began to cultivate individually the friendships of her three protégés—Charlotte, Emilie, and Kahlil—until it was time, she realized, to introduce the three to each other. "They clicked," she later recalled about her first dinner for them. They all drank porter, and Kahlil's first effort to draw Charlotte was well received. "Very good," noted Mary. "Girls delighted with picture."[29]

Mary was also organizing another reunion. She had seen Josephine and Lionel Marks a few times since their return from Europe in the fall of 1907, and knowing of Kahlil's previous friendship with Josephine, she planned a dinner for them. Kahlil responded cautiously to her invitation for dinner on January 30: "I shall be delighted to come Thursday and meet the Markses. I say 'meet' because I have not seen them as man and wife yet…I too must fulfil an engagement after 7:30 on Thursday. A thousand goodnight[s] from Kahlil."[30]

This evening was not a success. In her diary, Mary did not mention his presence, merely noting, "Lionel and Josephine to dine and took me to 'The Great Divide.'" But Josephine, still radiant and now joyously anticipating the birth of her first child, was more candid: "We take a holiday now…Then to dinner with Mary (who has 𝄞𝄫𝄢 there and a rather dissatisfying time with him)."[31] Never again did Mary arrange such an event including both Kahlil and Josephine. In fact, her growing association with Kahlil seemed to preclude further socializing with the Markses, and they began to drift apart.

Within a week, Mary had observed two sides of Kahlil—a charming and confident artist, and a self-conscious, uncomfortable young man.[32] Four years, later he would admit to her that, until she had concerned herself with his future, he had been lost in himself and naive. "Why didn't I know you at fourteen—or someone like you?" he complained. "I ought to have been painting in oil all these years. I stayed naïf so long…after I was a man in writing." Mary replied that she understood that he had refused to study painting formally, when he returned from Lebanon, to retain his individuality. Kahlil agreed. "Yes…because that idea had been drilled into me. Mr. Day and the other friends who seemed wonderful people then told me not to study…that I would be spoiled."

When he claimed that "no one told him his drawing was bad," she suggested that he "might have been unready to hear" criticism. "Perhaps," he said, and went on to explain:

> [The] whole stress of my environment was not for training but for self admiration. Mr. Day's exhibit of my work in 1904 was the worst thing that ever happened to me…Some really big people actually bought things: Mr. Buxton [Bustin], Mr. Charles Peabody, Mrs. Montgomery Sears—and of course I thought I was big too, and all right.[33]

By 1908, Kahlil's boyish artistic promise was fading. At twenty-five, no longer an adolescent prodigy, he was not maturing as an artist. Timid with oils, he was beginning to recognize the necessity of learning anatomy and working with live models.

Mary—who had recently learned from her administrative partner, Sarah Dean, that Brookline mothers were avoiding the school because the headmistress was "opinionated and imposed [her] views on them"—was well aware of her tendency to intrude.[34] Yet she could not resist a worthy cause. Both Kahlil and his career were stalled, and she was confident that he needed her. On February 2, she wrote him, suggesting that he draw from life at the school at least once a week. She also began actively to solicit critical appraisals from those who saw his work. He appeared at a life class four days later. The model was Emilie Michel, and although his first attempt was "not good of her…will try again," both artist and model enjoyed the experience. Mary described their encounter: "Wonderful to see these two; each just what other needs now." When he returned to draw Emilie on February

Kahlil's portrait of his friend Emilie Michel ("Micheline"). Graphite, around 1908. (Courtesy Telfair Museum of Art.)

11, she again followed their interaction with interest. "Kahlil and Mlle. again. Result much better. She read French poetry aloud. Exquisite."[35]

Sometime during those first two weeks in February, Kahlil and Mary reached an understanding about his future. He agreed with her evaluation that his artistic development was stalemated. Furthermore, he gratefully accepted her offer to send him to Paris for at least a year. On February 12, he exultantly wrote Ameen Ghorayeb, the publisher at *Al-Mohajer*, about this prospective journey, and he referred to the woman who was making it possible.

I am going to Paris…in the late part of the coming spring, and I shall remain there one whole year…The time which I will spend in the City of Light will be, with the help of God, the beginning of a new chapter in the story of my life…

I never dreamed of this voyage…for the expense of the trip would make it impossible for a man like me…But heaven, my dear Ameen, has arranged for this trip, without my being aware of it, and opened before me the way to Paris…

Know that my stay in Boston is…due to the presence of a she-angel who is ushering me towards a splendid future and paving for me the path to intellectual and financial success. But it makes no difference whether I am in Boston or in Paris…[Al-Mohajer] will remain the paradise in which my soul dwells and the stage upon which my heart dances.

My trip to Paris will offer me an opportunity to write about things which I cannot find or imagine in this mechanical and commercial country whose skies are replete with clamor and noise. I shall be enlightened by the social studies which I will undertake in the capital of capitals of the world where Rousseau, Lamartine, and Hugo lived; and where the people love art as much as the Americans adore the Almighty Dollar.[36]

That February, Kahlil expressed to Mary his gratitude and thanks for the extraordinary opportunity: "This is more than happiness. I am indeed a child of Light."[37]

~

Mary enjoyed supervising the evening art sessions with Kahlil and Emilie more and more. She offered one hundred dollars for two of his drawings, *Dance of Thoughts* and *Fountain of Pain*, and one night she invited her sister Louise to watch. Kahlil was becoming the resident entertainer who told stories while sketching, a role reminiscent of earlier days in Cambridge. Meanwhile, in New York, Charlotte learned that he thought her to be "indeed a strangely beautiful woman…one of the blessed few to whome is given the joy of looking into the eyes of things." She wrote to Mary that she sympathized with his theories of reincarnation.

He seems like an early-age brother of mine—as though if I were often with him I might recall actual scenes in those Egyptian times in which I *know* I lived…Some day we will understand these things: I expect to after death—don't you.[38]

Charlotte was somehow able to combine "battling wordily the Wall Street fortress" with an inward search "in the most scientific sense." Mary was intrigued by this "new Socialism—an actual Socialism of the spirit."[39] By March, Mary's diary revealed that while school still mattered to her, growing relationships mattered more. She began to introduce Kahlil to other friends. The first person she brought to Marlborough Street was an old acquaintance of his, Margarethe Müller. He drew her while Mary corrected a manuscript for her. Two weeks later, he returned and made a portrait of another friend. This time he brought Mary a "little bronze Osiris" sent him by an acquaintance in Egypt.[40]

He continued to express gratitude for her growing attention and support. On March 21, he brought her his three published books, inscribing and signing them with Arabic characters "Gibran Kahlil Gibran." In *Al-Musiqa* (*Music*), which he had not given her when it was published, he wrote, "To Mary Elizabeth Haskell, who inspired the muses to fill my soul with songs." In a second copy of *Ara'is al-Muruj* (*Spirit Brides*), this one adorned with a hand-decorated jacket, he acknowledged her patronage: "To Mary Elizabeth Haskell, who wants to make me closer to the world now through her love and generosity and who wants me to see myself and bring it out to the people." Finally, he gave her his just-published *Al-Arwah al-Mutamarrida* (*Spirits Rebellious*): "...to Mary Elizabeth Haskell, who has initiated and will initiate life in myself."[41]

Frustrated by her inability to read in Arabic these books or their dedications, she contented herself by rereading his favorite book, Maeterlinck's *The Treasure of the Humble*. Four days later, she was thrilled to receive an ecstatic letter from him.

> ...Last night I dreamt of Him who gave the Kingdom of heaven to man...if I could only tell you of the sad joy in His eyes...I sat near Him and talked to Him as if I had always lived with Him...
>
> The hunger of my heart today is greater and deeper than all days...My soul is thirsty for that which is...beautiful. And yet I cannot write nor draw nor read. I can only sit alone in silence...[42]

The events following his gifts, together with his letter, triggered for Mary an expression of emotion not previously expressed in her writings, not even upon Miss Armstrong's death. For the past ten years, she had carefully adhered to reason and objectivity in her journal entries. But she now released that restraint. On March 27, they visited Emilie Michel's apartment. The evening moved Mary to reflect on the French teacher's appearance—"she in tan wrapper, with red velvet stripes"—the "exquisite white wine," and the conversation. Kahlil walked her home from Copley Square to Marlborough Street under "angel tower, bare trees, flushed city sky."[43] Her romantic mood continued the following evening. After dining together, they visited Mary's sister Louise Daly and her husband, now back in Cambridge. She attempted to convey her growing impression of him.

> I never felt him so vividly before. But much more vividly on Sat. when he dined here. He spoke of his sense of being...and his work...Kahlil is quietly and calmly usurping a place in my thoughts and consciousness and my dreams. It is only by *slow* degrees that I have come to feel a sense of companionship with him in little ordinary details, jokes, etc.—as in the big ones.[44]

Mary continued to encourage Kahlil to meet regularly with Micheline. He had access to the Chestnut Street studio of the young artist Leslie Thompson, and Emilie may have sat for him there. The two were plainly falling in love. By now, Kahlil had met Mary's relatives in the Boston area, as well as most of her local friends. But his portraits of them that she had commissioned did not matter to her as much as seeing him and Emilie together.

On Sunday, April 26, the day after he had finally drawn Mary at Thompson's studio "with half success," Kahlil brought his sister Marianna to Marlborough Street for supper. The enthusiastic headmistress called her "Mary" and wrote—"She is dear."[45]

Considering Kahlil's exposure to Mary's relatives, along with his unexpected introduction of his sister, how did he view his relationship with this woman ten years older than himself? Letters clearly suggest that he looked to her as a dependent son toward a giving mother. In one he asked, "Do you know what it is to feel like a found child?…Perhaps someday I will be able to bring to you the flowers and the fruit of your motherly love and tenderness. Today my hands are empty." And in another, "I work with desire much like that of a lost child for his mother. I believe now that the desire of revealing the *Self* is stronger than all hungers and deeper than any thirst."[46]

In turn, Mary nurtured the interplay between him and Micheline. By May, her comments reflected a candor and receptivity on the part of her three friends toward the closeness that was involving them. One night, he confided some of his life's most vivid experiences: "K's becalming in boat on lake into the night…the woman who left him letters etc. while student," and he gave her some photos of the early days in Boston when Day had photographed him.[47]

Three days later, Mary invited Emilie to dinner. Because they talked until one, Micheline spent the night. The following Sunday, Mary noted their conversation. For the first time she needed a larger notebook, one that she continued to use whenever a passage about Kahlil demanded it.

> Micheline came to dinner…She told me of his depression because his former friend and professor at Beyrout has called him a "false prophet"…
>
> Micheline: "That boy is so easily hurt…and I want to prepare him if I can for some of what he must meet in the world. Here he is surrounded by love. He has near friends. But he will not always find people to love him this way—tenderly and truly and for himself. They will love him for what they can get out of him. He has many illusions—and they are very beautiful. But they cannot last. Life will crush them—and then I tremble for him. He will suffer so—and what may he not lose with his illusions?

"K. has many sides. He has a very strong side—and a side not so strong. He thinks he is invulnerable—and I would not try to undeceive him, because that belief lends him strength. But he is vulnerable. He is very much influenced by the atmosphere around him—and that student life in Paris is terrible. It breaks the health of some strong men—and what will it do with him? He is not strong, and that life can burn him up.

"We have talked frankly about the changes that may come. Two years—one year—from now, there may be only a memory between us. But I have said to him, 'Kahlil, there is one thing I want you to keep about Micheline. You may forget everything else, but remember, that I give you my affection because you merit it. Guard those qualities that were worthy of Micheline's heart, so that in the future you may merit the hearts of other women.'"[48]

Mary thrived on the excitement of that period. One Saturday, she and Kahlil went to see *Countess Coquette*, and then he stayed at Marlborough Street until one in the morning. They decided that she was to be his business agent while he was in Paris. "He will send his pictures here and I am to sell them or not, as I see fit and he suggests." Then she spoke of her inability to recall the faces that she loved best. She wrote, "He seemed moved and presently said: 'I will tell you something in my life…that will remain with you.'" The story that he told was of his school days in Lebanon and a woman he had known, named Sultana Tabit.

A widow of twenty-two…beautiful, accomplished, poetic, charming. She seemed wonderful to him. He thought much about her. Four months they knew each other. They exchanged books and notes. Her notes were brief, to the point, cool, impersonal. Then she died. Her friend sent for Kahlil and gave him, unopened, a silken scarf, some bits of jewelry, and a packet of seventeen letters, sealed and addressed to him by the dead woman. Those were love letters—tender, near-beautiful. "And cannot you imagine what a sorrow that was to me?" [he said.] "What a pity? Why did she not send them before? It was…months before that ceased to fill my mind."

When Mary asked him to draw a picture of Sultana Tabit from memory, he did, saying that her eyes were the longest he had ever seen and that he had "got them well when it was done…I'd like to put in a white rose just above the ear—she used to wear one."

He mentioned how uncomfortable the American collar and tie made him feel. "In America everyone has to wear certain things—but at home I never wear one." "Take them off," Mary suggested. "I'd like to see you without them." "Yes I'm glad to," he responded.[49] They talked about his settling in a Paris studio, possibly going

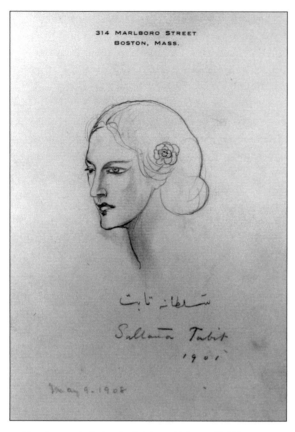

Graphite and ink sketch of Sultana Tabit, as Kahlil remembered her in 1908. (Courtesy Telfair Museum of Art.)

to Italy. Then she urged him to do a portrait from memory of Micheline. But he was unable to.

On May 14, Kahlil brought Mary his poem, "Death Beautiful," composed in Arabic. Together they worked on an English version of it. Mary had helped other friends with translations and manuscripts, but this was her first collaboration with Kahlil. The shaky result, full of alternative phrases and ambivalences, bore little resemblance to the English translation made some years later, in which he pictured "Death's bride standing as a pillar of light" between his "bed and the void."[50] However, it marked the beginning of a new and enduring commitment. He dedicated the version published that spring in *Al-Mohajer* to "MEH."

In June, Mary was arranging last-minute details for his trip to Paris, as well as her own. She and her father also were anticipating a European adventure, along with Micheline who was booking passage for a visit with her parents. When Kahlil came to the school for a final dinner on June 9, the farewells were brief. He left his portfolio with Mary, and knowing they all would meet soon in Paris, they simply exchanged goodbyes.

The next day, Mary traveled south for her sister Marion's wedding. Kahlil waited in Boston until June 25. While preparing for his journey, he wrote his old friend and mentor Fred Holland Day, who was slowly disappearing from the Boston art world. Kahlil was no longer close to Day but wrote him out of respect.

I leave Boston on the twenty fifth of this month, dear Brother. My steamer sails on the first of July from New York. I hope I will be able to see you…I have so many things to say and so many questions to ask…But if it is not possible, just send your blessings to your little brother. Kahlil.[51]

Charcoal and ink illustration on the dust jacket of the 1948 Knopf edition of *Spirits Rebellious*.
(Courtesy Alfred A. Knopf, Inc.; Reprint: F. Frank Isik)

9

REBELLIOUS SPIRITS IN PARIS

"And if it is a despot you would dethrone,
see first that his throne erected within you is destroyed."[1]

On July 1, 1908, at age twenty-five, Kahlil sailed from New York for Paris. Although he didn't want to travel alone, he enjoyed the prestigious social surroundings and the good company on the Holland American Line's popular SS *Rotterdam*. A few hours before the boat docked, he sat and described the trip to Mary.

> The ocean and the heaven were good friends, and I enjoyed them both…I made many studies of fine faces during the journey…a Greek [woman] born in France… knows Micheline very well. I made a drawing of her head…She is sad…and thoughtful…that, of course, adds something to her beauty.[2]

Mary and her father were by now traveling throughout Ireland. On July 13, they sailed to England. That same day, Kahlil finally settled in Paris—"the heart of the world." He wrote of how Micheline had helped him find a temporary fifth-floor room on Avenue Carnot. He admitted to Mary his dependence upon his young French friend and how much he would miss her when she left to visit her family in Nevers. "But if she is going to find herself on the stage, as I am finding myself in Paris, then…[she] must not stay and I must not ask her to."[3]

Micheline also assured Mary that all was well in a letter that became a spontaneous joint effort. Her greeting began, "Mary dear…Kahlil is here with me looking very fine! He has just shaved!" Kahlil interrupted, "And yet he is serious and his soul dwells in an unknown island." Then another friend chimed in, and Micheline begged Mary to hurry to Paris and share in the fun.

By the end of July, their exuberance hadn't faded. Kahlil had moved to Montparnasse, where he had found a small studio at 14 Avenue du Maine. He was

145

even learning how to prepare his own meals. More important, he had enrolled in the noted Academy Julian, where he worked every afternoon. He wrote Mary,

> I have already seen the two sides of Paris, the beautiful and the ugly. I am here to study both sides…Yes, the spirit of decay is stealing [its] way through this wonderful city: but we are apt to forget the existence of a hideous worm in the heart of a lovely apple…My heart is full of wingged things: I shall keep them there untill you come.[4]

After using wings as a symbol with which he signed their communal letter, it became a custom he would often follow for many years.

When he saw Mary on July 31, and again four days later, her anticipated arrival was a letdown. She had become so involved with sightseeing and meeting old friends that she was unable to stroll through the streets with him as he had hoped. On August 4, the last morning of her stay, she and her father visited him at Avenue du Maine, and she simply recorded the visit as one of the day's several activities. Her neglect of her protégé was understandable in the press of travel. Kahlil always expressed wistful awe of the entire Haskell clan. But whenever he saw her away from school, phalanxed by her distinguished father or other admirers, their growing rapport diminished. For Mary, too, the reunion was an uncomfortable one. Differences in their backgrounds and cultures became magnified when she was observed by those closest to her.

~

Even amid the uncomfortable circumstances, Kahlil's creative life seemed to thrive. He had been in Paris only a short time when his recently published book, *Al-Arwah al-Mutamarida*, or *Spirits Rebellious*, received considerable attention, raising his position in American and Arab literary circles. The book was a collection of four narratives that had originally appeared in *Al-Mohajer*.[5] Like *Ara'is al-Muruj* (*Spirit Brides*), the tales dealt with oppressive social conditions in Lebanon. This time, Kahlil imagined different fates for his rebellious characters. In "Wardé Al-Rani," a married woman abandons her wealthy husband for "a youth who walked the highway of life alone and who dwelt alone among his books and papers." Unlike Martha, who paid with her life for defying convention, Wardé openly expressed emancipation from man's "corrupt laws." Not only did her act allow her happiness, but she could say, "Woe to them who would judge and weigh! I was a harlot and a faithless woman in the house of Rashid Nu'man because he made me the sharer of his bed by virtue of tradition and custom…But now I am pure and clean, for the law of love has set me free."[6]

Similarly, he created a triumphant fate for the protagonist of "Khalil the Heretic." Instead of suffering madness as did his prototype, Yuhanna, he retaliates when maltreated by monks. The villagers heed his bold exhortations and stage a bloodless revolution against evil clerics and politicians. This utopian community embodied Gibran's own hopes. He was becoming a reformer who, with his words, was seeking to create paths toward liberation and justice.

In the third story, "The Bridal Couch," a desperate bride slays her lover—and herself—on the night of her forced marriage to a man she never loved. But even these bloody consequences are not treated as defeat. As the suicidal bride challenges a frantic wedding guest, the deaths symbolize release.

> You shall not come near us, reproachful ones, neither shall you separate us lest the spirit hovering above your heads seize you by the throat and put an end to you. Let this hungry earth consume our bodies in one mouthful. Let it conceal and protect us within its heart.[7]

In the fourth allegory, Kahlil recalled the ruthless injustices of nineteenth-century Lebanon. The narrator in "The Cry of the Graves" bears witness to the wrongful death sentences of three prisoners by a malevolent emir—reminiscent of Emir Bashir II. As the background of each prisoner is revealed, their offenses are shown to be consequences of societal failure. The murderer condemned to decapitation is a man who had protected a woman's honor by killing a lustful tax collector; the adulteress destined to be stoned is revealed as a woman wrongfully accused; the thief sent to the gallows is a poor farmer who had snatched two sacks of flour from the monks' swollen granaries. The unfortunate trio are executed and left for carrion. But later they are surreptitiously buried, and above their graves a sheathed sword, flowers, and a cross appear—symbols of courage, love, and the "words of the Nazarene."

In contemplating the inequities of crime and punishment, Kahlil, who had grown up believing that his father was unjustly accused by corrupt authorities, was vehemently challenging the law. "What is the law? Who has seen it descend with the sunlight from the heavens?…In what age have angels walked among men, saying: 'Deny to the weak the light of existence and destroy the fallen with the edge of the sword and trample upon the sinner with feet of iron'?"[8] But throughout these stories runs a continuous yearning for spiritual renewal. Years later, Kahlil mused about the dark period when *Al-Arwah al-Mutamaridah* (*Spirits Rebellious*) was written.

At that time life was full of terrible things for me. It seemed as if everything was piled up—illness and death and loss—and things that don't seem part of the inevitable lot of man—but just extra…I'm thankful for all of it…But that doesn't change the fact that it was hard.[9]

Early in 1908, Ameen Ghorayeb wrote a long introduction to the book, justifying its "new ideas" and the aims of its "social philosophy." Describing Kahil as a person who "heard and saw complaints and was affected and then complained," the publisher defended the morality of the book's iconoclastic characters: "Everyone has the right to search for what he sees as his happiness as long as he doesn't harm others…" Kahlil's audience was new to this discussion of individual rights in social and moral conduct. Already he had been criticized by members of the Maronite clergy, who challenged as exaggerated and distorted the clerical posture implicit in "The Bridal Couch." Ghorayeb reminded readers, "It is hard for the youth of our days to understand the oppression of priests in the older nations and that this still flourishes in the twentieth century." Summarizing the aims of the twenty-five-year-old author, he observed:

This book is the second wall of the house which Gibran is building. The writer combines knowledge of Lebanon with work in the United States and the thought of a philosopher. He tries to depict and contrast the feelings of different classes of people—from the poor to the princely—from the atheist to the priest.

The introduction pleased Kahlil "because it was free from personal comment."[10] In March, Kahlil wrote to a cousin in Brazil.

The people in Syria are calling me heretic, and the intelligentsia in Egypt villifies me, saying, "he is the enemy of just laws, of family ties, and of old traditions." Those writers are telling the truth, because I do not love man-made laws and I abhor the traditions that our ancestors left us. This hatred is the fruit of my love for the sacred and spiritual kindness which should be the source of every law upon the earth, for kindness is the shadow of God in man. I know that the principles upon which I base my writings are echoes of the spirit of the great majority of the people of the world, because the tendency toward a spiritual independence is to our life as the heart is to the body…

Will my teaching ever be received by the Arab world or will it die away and disappear like a shadow?[11]

Later he wrote Ghorayeb, traveling in the Middle East, about promoting his work in Lebanon and Egypt. He interpreted an unfavorable review of "Wardé Al-Hani" as an encouraging sign: "I was well pleased with the criticism because I feel that such persecution is a diet for new principles, especially when it comes from a learned man like [the writer, Lufti] al-Manfaluti."[12]

The dedication to *Arwah al-Mutamarida* read: "To the spirit that did embrace my spirit. To the heart that did pour out its secrets into my heart. To the hand that did kindle the flame of my love."[13] Also appearing in the book was his first self-portrait to appear in any of his Arabic books. Done in pen-and-ink, it resembled in expression and posture a photograph that Fred Holland Day had taken of him years before. Perhaps it expressed a sense of the youthful commitment to spiritual independence at the core of his emerging sense of direction.

To Mary, however, he admitted his own lack of formal training: "When I came to Paris I...knew nothing of the technical side of painting. I did things instinctively without knowing how or why. I was in darkness, and now I feel that I am walking in twilight towards light."[14]

Self-portrait from *Spirits Rebellious*, published by *Al-Mohajer* in 1906. (Courtesy Private Collection.)

His choice of the Academy Julian was a natural one. Its late director, Rudolph Julian, had long attracted artists from Boston and elsewhere to the popular atelier on the Rue du Cherche-Midi. Associated with Academy Julian were several Boston artists: Lilla Cabot Perry, Edmund Tarbell, and Maurice Prendergast, along with symbolist-influenced painters Maurice Denis and Paul Sérusier, and the Nabis post-impressionists Pierre Bonnard and Edouard Vuillard.[15] By the fall, Kahlil recorded a brief observation of his own progress.

> I am painting, or I am learning how to paint. It will take me a long time to paint as I want to, but it is so beautiful to feel the growth of one's own vision of things. There are times when I leave work with the feelings of a child who is put to bed rather early...I understand people and things through my sense of hearing...I am beginning to understand things and people through my eyes.[16]

But by November the luster of Paris was beginning to fade, and he was both homesick and uncertain about his work.

> When I am unhappy, dear Mary, I read your letters. When the mist overwhelms the "I" in me, I take two or three letters out of the little box and reread them…And now I am wrestling with colour…The professors in the academy are always saying to me "do not make the model more beautiful than she is." And my soul is always whispering "O if you could only paint the model as beautiful as she *realy* is."[17]

He had also been ill and had recuperated with some Syrian friends, the Rahaims, in Le Rainey. The comforting suburb was "like a great garden divided into little gardens by narrow paths," its red tiled roofs "like a handfull of corals scattered on a piece of green velvet." He gratefully promised that he would make a portrait of Hasiba Rahaim, "the noble Syrian lady" who had helped him.[18]

Something else was also on his mind. He wanted Mary to feel that he was worthy of her largesse.

> And now while I am in perfect helth, both physically and mentally, I wish to say that the few pictures and drawings which you have now, are all yours if I should die sudenly here in Paris…I also wish to say that all the pictures and studies found after my death in my studio here in Paris are yours, and that you are free to do whatever you wish with them.
>
> …I hope I will be able to live long and be able to do somethings that are realy worthy of giving to you who is giving so much to me. I hope that the day will come when I shall be able to say "I became an artist through Mary Haskell."[19]

At this time, Micheline had returned to the U.S. That September, before she left Boston for the theater in New York, she had seen Mary every day. With the relationship between Kahlil and Micheline cooling, the strongest bond between them remained Mary, who continued to support him in Paris and began to send checks to Micheline in New York.

Kahlil also depended on Mary as a link between himself and his sister Marianna. In her journal, Mary wrote:

> *November 20.* Marianna Gibran found me in at 7:10 when she came to supper. She is almost ill for sheer loneliness since Kahlil left. Has had pleurisy, but is better now. Working with Miss Teahan again. Shall she visit her father? *November 27.* Long letter to Kahlil about what to do for Marianna. Keep her here or send to Syria on a visit.[20]

Lonely and depressed by the damp and chill of the city, when he received this word of Marianna from Mary, Kahlil became distressed.

> I am so very anxious about my sister. I think of nothing ells but her. She must be very ill. I dream such dreadful dreams of her. She appears to me so thin and so pale…Is she very ill dear Mary? Is she dead? Will you not tell me something about her?…I am working as before. I work with the same feeling of one who talks in his sleep.

But the imagined crisis dissipated. In depending on Mary to watch over Marianna, he had not told Mary that his sister could not read or write, and that her illiteracy made it difficult for her to communicate the pain of being left alone. But by mid-December, an Arabic speaker had been found to help Marianna herself write directly to her brother. Kahlil's relief was immediate.

> Few days ago I had a letter from my sister. She said nothing about her health but I gathered that she is not ill; and I feel less anxious about her than I did before. You have no idea, beloved friend, how unhappy I feel whenever I think of her as a sick child. She, beside being a good sister, is a very near friend. We suffered so much together.[21]

~

The new year of 1909 brought with it new involvements. He had discovered another teacher, Pierre Marcel-Béronneau, whose methods Kahlil found more sympathetic than those at the Academy Julian. Béronneau was a visionary painter and disciple of Gustave Moreau.[22]

> He is a great artist and a wonderful painter—and a mystic. The State has bought many of his pictures: and he is known in the artistic world as the "Painter of Salome"…I took one or two little things to show him the other day. He looked at them for a long time; and after saying few encouraging words about them, he gave me a long personal talk. He said "You must forget yourself for the time being—Do not try to give an expression to your thoughts and ideas *Now*. Wait until you have gone through the *Dictionary* of painting."

In February, Kahlil reported,

I am working now with Berinau only, and I have stopped working at the Julian. It is useless to divide myself between two defrent schools. M. Berinau has a smal class of 10 or 12 people. We have sometimes the nude and sometimes the draped figure. M. Berineu works with us. He wants me to see everything in values and not in lines. He said he likes my work because I am not trying to be a *small Berinau* like the others.[23]

The studio of Marcel-Béronneau (standing, *left*), 1909. Kahlil is in the front row, second from *left*.
(Courtesy Private Collection.)

Ever practical, Mary was concerned over his leaving the Academy Julian and losing tuition fees. "Make no long engagement ahead with Berinau as you did with Julian. We never know…when the moment may arrive when we shall…have learned our lesson that it lies in him to teach." Kahlil replied, "I did not leave Julian untill the three months term was finished, so the school owes me nothing. And as to Berinau, I pay him about fifty francs a month and so much for colours and canvases and other things. But I am paying this out of the 375 francs without any difficulties at all. So I really do not need more."[24]

But constantly contending with loneliness, he wrote Gertrude Barrie on April 18, 1909, "Think of me a little when you are gazing at Diana."[25]

~

Throughout this period, his contact with the Arab literary world continued to flourish. On February 13, 1909, *Al-Mohajer* printed a prose poem that he had written the year before on his twenty-fifth birthday. A month earlier, on January 6, 1909, he had sent Mary a birthday greeting. His message to her, of desire and life struggling to push past discouragement and death, revealed in English the substance of the longer poem in Arabic.

> On this same day twenty-six years ago I was born.
> I have already made twenty-six journeys around the Sun—and I do not know how many times the Moon has journeyed around me—and yet I do not understand the mystery of Light.
> During the twenty-six years—
> "Many a time
> I have been half in love with easeful Death,
> Call'd him soft names in [many] a mused rhyme."
> And now, dear Mary, I have not outgrown my love for Death, but I am half in love with Life. Life and Death has become equally beautiful to me. And I am beginning to look upon each day as a birthday.[26]

Mary was delighted when she saw the poem in *Al-Mohajer*. Below the words in Arabic, she found the dedication: to *MEH*.

> I am sending you a prose-poem "On my birthday" which I wrote thinking of you. The soul of this poem is yours. The body belongs to other peoples of other land and of deferent language. It was published in New York and then copied by many other Arabic papers and magazines.

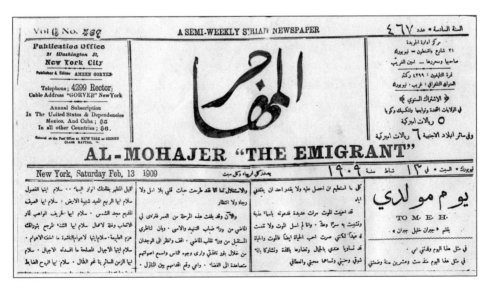

(*Lower right*) The beginning of Kahlil's birthday poem to Mary, in a February 1909 issue of *Al-Mohajer*. (Courtesy Wilson Library, University of North Carolina, Chapel Hill.)

In response, she relayed the happiness and faith given to her by words, these written in Arabic, which she was unable to read: "I loved the poem you sent me—loved it eyeless and earless so to speak. I am like a German having faith in Keats!"[27]

~

The tempo of his life was accelerating. He even was able to meet Auguste Rodin, once in the sculptor's studio and later briefly at an exhibition.

> He was indeed very kind to me and to the friend who took me to him. He showed us many wonderful things both in marble and in plaster…I am sure, that you remember my telling you once of an Arab who went to Italy from the desert and saw the work of Michel-Angelo and was so moved by its power that he wrote a beautiful poem called "The Smiling Marble." When I came home from Rodin's studio I had the same feeling of that Arab, and I too wrote a sonnet on "Man the Creator"…
>
> April is a month of Salons and Exhibitions in Paris. One of the great Salons was open few days ago and of course I went to see it. (All the Artists of Paris were there looking with hungry eyes on the shadows of Souls of Men)…Great Rodin was there. He recognized me and spoke to me about the work of a Russian sculptor, saying, "This man understands the beauty of form." I would have given anything to have that Russian hear what the great master said of his work. A word from Rodin [is] worth great deal to an artist.[28]

Encouraged by his acceptance into artistic circles in Paris, and aware of her role as business agent, Mary was working on a plan to promote his work by means of a second showing at Wellesley College's Tau Zeta Epsilon Society. For help, she once again turned to Margarethe Müller, who had exhibited his drawings there six years before. "I hope you will only let her take…those that are less imperfect!"[29]

But by the time of the show, Mary was too preoccupied to worry about its details except for managing delivery. Within one April week, both her nephew, the two-year-old son of Reginald and Louise Daly, and Reginald's mother, died. Suddenly, her outside activities were curtailed, and a few weeks later she decided to accompany the Dalys to Hawaii where Reginald would carry out geological field studies and where her sister Louise could recover from the loss of her only child.

A review in the college newspaper conveys reaction to Kahlil's second Wellesley show.

> The exhibition of Mr. Kahhl Gilran's [sic] studies…was one of peculiar interest. The color studies were nearly all uniform…purple of evening shadows shading

Colored chalk and ink drawing, *The Souls of Men Flying before the Face of the Inevitable,* 1909.
(Courtesy Telfair Museum of Art.)

into green and lit with tiny yellows of isolated flowers. There is one picture which differed somewhat in spirit—a slight woman's figure in an orchard of blossoming apple trees…The other studies were pessimistic and almost Gothic in their weird expression of pessimism…

The "Souls of Men Flying before the Face of the Inevitable" was one of the most curious of the compositions…The "Inevitable" is a huge gray head, before whose expressionless, sightless face a flock of tiny white birds are borne irresistibly. The contrast of the might of eternal laws and the puny weakness of human effort is one on which he delights to dwell. Usually the Immortal is represented by a huge figure, and the mortal by a pygmy…The characteristic of his treatment of the human form in the color work is truth with the greatest simplicity; it is almost pure outline work and yet the impression is rounded softness. The imaginary portraits are interesting… they are still romantic but with Pre-Raphaelite rather than Gothic romanticism…

The "Lost Mind" was the one most talked of on account of its horror: a face without a mind, more vaguely suggestive than idiocy, more haunting than madness.

Margarethe Müller, an early supporter of Kahlil, who arranged for his drawings to be exhibited at Wellesly College. Graphite, 1908. (Courtesy Museo Soumaya.)

This face was also remarkable for the delicacy of treatment about the eyes rendered with the utmost simplicity. Of course the college was particularly interested in the portrait of Fraulein Müller, a piece of work remarkable as a piece of technique but doubly interesting in its subject.[30]

That summer, Charlotte visited Paris to find a French producer interested in her plays. When she and Kahlil met in June, some rivalry for Mary's sponsorship surfaced. These feelings only gradually became clear to Mary over the next few years. Indeed, Charlotte sent Mary, now en route to Hawaii to be with her sister, a glowing report about Kahlil's progress.[31] In trying to please Mary, to show her that those whom she loved could care for each other, the two spent much time together. Charlotte and Kahlil vacationed for a week at Versailles, and he started a portrait of her but could not finish it because, he complained, "Charlotte has so many ideas and scheams and dreams and she is always running—running—running after her own shadow…[and] dose not rest anywhere."[32]

~

But that June, Kahlil received sudden word of his father's death. He wept bitterly whenever he read the last notes from him. Hearing that his father had blessed him before he passed, Kahlil agonized over memories of the proud man who had alienated his family, the father who did not quite understand his young son, and who was alone when he died in the "old house where he was born sixty-five years ago." Inevitably, Kahlil recalled earlier times.

I know now, dear Mary that he rests in the bosom of God...I cannot but see the dim, sad shadows of the bygone days when he and my mother and my brother and my young sister lived and smiled before the face of the sun...Where are they now?...They are nearer to God than we are...They no longer play hide and seek with the spirit, because they understand. I feel all this...and yet I cannot but feel the pains of sorrow and regret.[33]

In less than a year, when Mary's own father passed away, Kahlil wrote her, "Will the time ever come when all the children of God shall see the Absolute which is hiden behinde these masks and these veils?"[34] His preoccupation with life's passages would continue, from which Kahlil—always recalling the deaths of his brother, sister, mother, and now father—would produce words of comfort and consolation for others to read.

Kahlil's father, who died in June 1909 when Kahlil was twenty-six. (Courtesy Museo Soumaya.)

~

But his father also had "called out the fighter" in him; and now when Kahlil was again being tested by grief, this time over the loss of a father who had so often been absent, resilience was needed. That July, Kahlil "threw himself into his work."[35] Already cited at two artistic competitions since he had been at Béronneau's, his painting now received a silver medal. Moreover, he had met up with Youssef Howayek, his friend from their school days in Beirut. Although he had come to Paris to study art, this gifted sculptor and nephew of the Maronite patriarch was also interested in Montparnasse café life. Howayek remembered Kahlil at this time as a man possessed, concerned about his reputation, his limited finances, and his role as a reformer. Still, the two found comfort in their companionship. "We are both trying to do

Youssef Howayek. (Formerly, Wilson Library, University of North Carolina, Chapel Hill.)

something," Kahlil wrote, but we do it in two deferent ways. My friend is seeking himself in nature, and I am trying to find myself *through* nature."[36] Confused by the aesthetic revolution taking place around them, and trying to take in the ideas of the cubists and the colors of the fauvists, Kahlil suggested that they make an effort to understand everything and then choose whatever style they wished.

Kahlil himself was not attracted to these emerging artistic styles and instinctively sought the ideation of the symbolist painters. His greatest treat was to walk with Howayek to the Panthéon and admire Puvis de Chavannes' mural, *The Life of St. Genevieve*, on the patron saint of Paris. He recalled his own childhood in Boston, when the de Chavannes murals decorated the new Public Library and modern art meant successfully translating emotion and poetry into a picture. He still pursued this ideal, which he told Mary was "being able to give a *good* expression to a beautiful *Idea* or a high *thought*."[37]

At this time he also discovered Eugène Carrière, who had painted in a subtle style with which he identified.

> I feel now that the work of Carier [*sic*] is the nearest to my heart. His figures, sitting or standing behind the mist say more to me than anything ells except the work of Lionardo da Vinci. Carier understood faces and hands more than any other painter…And Carier's life is not less beautiful than his work. He suffered so much, but he knew the mystery of pain: he knew that tears make all things shine.

But the days of Kahlil's immersion in new influences were coming to a close. De Chavannes and Moreau had died in 1898. Three years before Kahlil discovered his work, Carrière died in 1906. Nevertheless, Kahlil committed himself to an atmospheric dream world, to Carrière's "love of the manifestations of Nature," and to the "mysterious haze that hung over his painting."[38] Over time, "mist" would become for Kahlil a focal image of his life and art.

~

During the fall of 1909, Kahlil and Youssef Howayek were working alone and sharing the costs of models. Kahlil had left both Béronneau's atelier and the Avenue du Maine studio, where he was never happy because of the cold, and was staying in a hotel. Again, settling down was difficult.

> I did not go back to Berinau because I feel and my friends feel that I have taken from the man all he can give. I must find someone who works more directly…and who is less of a dreamer…I am realy tired of all fantastical lies which people call pleasures…Even the idea of living in a hotel for few days is rather hateful to me.[39]

In November, a studio promised to him was still not available. But he was working with new models and finishing a painting called *The Young Poet*. He had also met Marie Doro, an American actress, and had received permission from her aunt to draw her. He teasingly described her to Mary. "She has a great soul and a clear mind, and she believes she has been in the Orient for many ages. I feel that too. People take us for brother and sister…But Mis Dora dose not feed my heart nor I hers!…Now you are smiling, my dear Mary; I can see you smiling."[40]

Within a month Kahlil was in a Rue du Cherche-Midi studio—high, dry, warm, and light—and was supplementing Mary's monthly checks with a part-time job teaching drawing and composition to five pupils, twice a week for one hundred francs a month. "It is hard work, but I like it because it makes me sure of the few little things I know about art."[41]

He was also about to undertake a far more ambitious project. He had recently drawn the American sculptor, Paul Bartlett, whose equestrian statue entitled *Lafayette* stood before the Louvre and who was working on the allegorical figures that would enhance the New York Public Library. Bartlett's reaction to the portrait was so favorable that he was inspired to begin a "wonderful scheam"—a series of "drawings of the great artists of our time—the pillars of modern art and culture: I only ask thirty minutes from each…Of course I must have the great women like Sarah Bernhardt and Ellen Terry."

Included in his list, along with his favorites Maeterlinck and Rodin, were the dramatist Edmond Rostand and the popular novelist Pierre Loti.[42] As with Puvis

Kahlil's portrait of sculptor Auguste Rodin. Graphite and charcoal, 1910. (Courtesy Gibran Museum.)

de Chavannes, Loti's popularity was waning, but his delicately rendered travel novels were described by Henry James as "flowers of reminiscence and imagination" in their depictions of the Middle East.[43] Day had praised Loti as early as 1892 in the literary magazine *The Mahogany Tree*. Loti's immortalization of his Circassian mistress, the sloe-eyed Aziyadé, paralleled Kahlil's interests, and his sorties—as an outsider—into the secluded courtyards of Levantine life prompted Kahlil to consider his own portrayals of his native Lebanese world.

Kahlil's growing interest in new currents in the Middle East went deeper than Loti's romances. After the 1908 revolution of the Young Turks against the Ottoman regime of Abd al-Hamid II, Paris was alive with small pockets of dissidents from Greater Syria. Secret societies were advancing nationalism and home rule in Ottoman-occupied countries, and among its leaders was Shukri Ghanim, a writer and journalist from Mount Lebanon who had spent his adult life in Paris. Known for his opera *Antar*, Ghanim produced both poetry and essays. Although Kahlil's association with these nascent groups was peripheral, he was conscious of them, and of Ghanim. A month before Ghanim published a statement on Arab self-determination, Kahlil was writing Mary about the older writer: "I have a Syrian poet friend. His name is Ganim. He writes bothe Arabic and French. One of his plays has been given here this winter and it was a great success. He is about fifty years old but the flame of youth is still burning in his soul."[44]

In the same letter, he described his growing list of acquaintances, for which Howayek was most likely responsible: "I have several congenial friends: Syrian and French poets, English and American painters, German and Italian musicians. We meet sometimes in public places, other times in the private houses of good people who like to entertain artists."[45]

Howayek's vivid memories of that winter of 1910 include a parade of international students and artists, who lend life to Kahlil's brief note to Mary. These people remained vividly alive for Howayek. Forty years later, in his recollection of this time in Paris, he remembered the Belgian doctor who invited Kahlil and himself to tour the Pasteur Institute and argued with them about the ascendancy of science over religion. He described the print store where its Romanian entrepreneur, Monsieur Kalmy, and his two nieces—Susanne and Leah—befriended them. Recalling the great January flood of 1910, he described the rampaging Seine inundating first-floor studios. He told about sharing his studio with Olga, a Russian student committed to Tolstoy and revolution, and how he and Gibran listened to her play Beethoven sonatas and drank endless cups of tea from the samovar.

Howayek remembered Kahlil as a young man liked and admired by this group. Olga gifted him with a Russian cap. Leah and Susanne were curious about his love life. But even Youssef Howayek, who had become close enough to Kahlil to care for him during one of his recurrent illnesses, wondered about his impenetrability.[46]

On one occasion, Howayek did glimpse Kahlil's shy playfulness. Kahlil never danced when he visited a café, because he had never learned. So just before the July 14 national holiday, Howayek persuaded Kahlil to attend a celebration and to try a dance lesson. Demonstrating how to approach your partner, bow politely, and ask for a dance, Howayek placed one hand around his friend's waist, and then, holding hands, with Kahlil's other hand on his shoulder, guided him through some steps. They tried this out to music, with Kahlil objecting but giving his best. On the night of the party, Howayek signaled when it was time. With labored dignity, Kahlil stood and walked toward his chosen partner Leah; Howayek requested the hand of Martine; and the two friends danced with their partners in honor of Bastille Day.

But Kahlil's purposefulness, single-mindedness, and absorption in his painting and writing preoccupied him. An absence of small talk in his letters reflects this. Even after he returned to Boston, his conversations about how Paris had affected his life were general in nature. Only inadvertently did some particular details creep into his stories, as when he told Mary about discovering his tolerance for wine.

> In Paris when I had to give a cafe party as new students all do, I drank as much as anybody. I was…having a good time. And everyone of the rest was affected; some fell asleep. Some were sick—some were foolish…I didn't feel it then—and next day I was fresh and ready for work as ever in my life.[47]

One scene that he did recall vividly concerned the church's attitude toward his works. Mary Haskell's later account of an exchange between Kahlil and a bishop reveals clerical Maronite views toward his books at the time.

> *Spirits Rebellious*, published while [Kahlil] was in Paris, was suppressed by the Syrian government—only 200 copies got into Syria, secretly…But the church considered excommunicating Kahlil. Practically he was excommunicated, but the sentence was never actually pronounced… When…two representatives of the Patriarch, however, came to Paris they invited Kahlil with other Syrians…and when [Kahlil] came to take leave asked him to stay and dine alone with them. He did not want to—but urged, he stayed.
>
> One bishop had a sense of humor—the other none. Humorous, I believe, was kin to Kahlil. Nonhumorous took him aside: "You…are making a grave mistake. Your gifts you are using against your people, against your country, against your church. The holy Patriarch realizes this. But he does not condemn you. He sends you a special message and loving offer of friendship…And now—seek out every copy of the book—destroy them all—and let me take word from you back to Syria and the Church and to the holy Patriarch."

Then Kahlil let himself go—furiously…He told his Holiness he had heard all that had been said…before it was uttered. Nothing in it had surprised him. Far from "returning," he was working then on a book to be called *Broken Wings*. He hoped his Holiness would read it—he hoped the holy Patriarch would read it…They would see in it how entirely he disagreed with them and how he was advancing as he had begun. And he said Goodnight—did not stay for dinner.

As he passed through the outer room where the reception was still not over… the humorous bishop said, "Well, Effendi, have you had a good talk with his Highness?"…"Yes, your grace," said Kahlil, "delightful. But I am only sorry I was not able to convince him." The bishop laughed. He understood the case was hopeless. The others all understood too—that there had been a battle.[48]

Even without other accounts to shed light on this incident, clearly Kahlil was garnering "critical attention." By the spring of 1910, he was able to offer Mary more evidence of his progress. First, the Société Nationale des Beaux-Arts had accepted his painting *Autumn* for its spring exhibit. Of this showing Kahlil wrote, "I never saw such a crowd in my life, nor…such enthusiasm."[49] Howayek's recollection was

The Autumn. Oil on canvas, around 1910. (Courtesy Gibran Museum.)

more subdued, but evidently the reception was so large that Kahlil felt lost in the press of artists and critics. Worst, the painting looked dwarfed, and he was dissatisfied with its location. Perhaps for that reason he wrote Mary afterward, telling her that the painting no longer pleased him.

The second achievement was that Mary finally would be able to read a published story by him. "Martha La Banaise" appeared in the November 1909 issue of *Les Mille Nouvelle Nouvelles* (*A Thousand New Stories*), as part of a collection of short stories in various languages. He was disappointed because the translators had taken the liberty of deleting the final scene, in which Martha is buried in unconsecrated ground. Even so, his writing was being published with that of such writers as Anton Chekhov and Arthur Schnitzler. The biographical description of the "young Arab writer" that preceded the story stated:

> …J. K. Joubrane writes less to tell a story than to plead reform. Among the social problems which he addresses…is the emancipation of the Oriental woman from her unjust mistreatment by man: reform of marriage in the last analysis would be left to the young girl and not her family. He would also like to break the religious yoke in Lebanon. J. K. Joubrane is read, commented on, and discussed. His novella *Wardé Al-Hani* has inspired 237 newspaper articles or reviews.[50]

~

In June 1910, Kahlil met—probably for the first time—Ameen Rihani. His fellow expatriate writer was returning to America after a five-year stay in Lebanon. A leading figure of Arab and immigrant literature in America, his work had received considerable exposure, and he had been regularly sending articles about his travels back to American publications. One of his favorite forums was Michael Monahan's intrepid little magazine *Papyrus*, a combination of socialist tract and assorted curiosities, which catered to the early-twentieth-century interest in writers like Carpenter, Ernest Renan, Whitman, Wilde, Lafcadio Hearn, and Poe. Rihani, who admired Walt Whitman, sought to facilitate creative exchange between the Middle East and America. Of the influence of the American transcendentalists—Whitman, Emerson, Thoreau—in Syria, he wrote in February 1908:

> I bring with me from…across the Atlantic nothing more than a pair of walking shoes, a bathrobe, and three books published respectively in Philadelphia, Boston, and New York. The good Gray Poet of America, the Sage of Concord, and the Recluse of Walden are my only American companions in this grand congé.[51]

In addition to their shared belief in the possibility of a "grand congé"—or "great exchange"—across cultures, their responses to their Maronite backgrounds also connected Kahlil and Rihani. Although both were Maronites rooted in the culture of Mount Lebanon and the Near East, they had come of age in Boston and New York, aided and influenced by ideals of social reform and progress. This infusion of American culture into their outlooks lent a new, and as yet untested, quality to their style and approach to issues facing the people of their native region.

Early in the summer of 1910, Kahlil and Rihani set off for England. In London they divided their time between

Writer Ameen Rihani. Graphite, charcoal, and colored chalk. (Courtesy Peter A. Juley / Smithsonian.)

tourist attractions and the art galleries, where Kahlil fell in love with the paintings of romanticist Joseph Turner at the Tate Gallery. Their concern with home rule for the people of Ottoman Syria led them to Thomas Power O'Connor, the Irish nationalist leader, through whom they were able to visit the Houses of Parliament. Kahlil also told Mary about going to a costume dinner and recital at the Poetry Society, where he and Rihani dressed in Arab attire.

By the end of July, Rihani had left for New York, and Howayek was traveling in Italy. Kahlil, too, may have visited Italy, as well as Spain and Germany. When he finally returned to Paris, he sought out "sweet and very dear" Micheline, who was back in Paris after a challenging time in New York. But as Micheline had predicted two years before, their initial attraction had faded. Kahlil wrote Mary, "Do you know, that I do not find one word to say to her." Her attempts to work in theater had been unsuccessful. She was ill and Kahlil promised that he would take care of her. Within five weeks, he reported to Mary that she had left the city to visit her parents. "Indeed, she suffered a great deal, but she was very brave and very calm. She is yet thinking of the stage and its glory, but she knows too well the darker side of it. I hope she will get over it."[52]

Once again, he felt isolated. He was still recoiling from the loss of his father. He missed hearing from Mary, who was in Yosemite; his friends had left Paris, and mentally he too was preparing to leave. An honor that he was awaiting finally arrived when the Union Internationale des Beaux-Arts et des Lettres invited him to send six paintings to its salon, which would open on October 1. Reluctantly he decided against the exhibit, since he did not want to stay in Paris "homeless with no place to work." He proudly sent Mary an invitation to the salon, which she kept.[53]

Kahlil's invitation to exhibit his work at the October 1910 salon of the Union Internationale des Beaux-Arts et des Lettres. (Courtesy Wilson Library, University of North Carolina, Chapel Hill.)

On October 22, Kahlil sailed for New York. His time in Paris had nourished him and renewed his self-confidence. But he was looking forward to Boston. "I can allmost see myself in a...little place working on that mystic series 'towards God' which you liked," he wrote Mary.

> I feel, beloved friend, that I must go back to Boston and find a quiet corner in which I can work...And perhaps in few years I shall be able to come back and see Italy...Syria and Italy are the two countries I love. I feel that I will be able to see Italy many times but not Syria. The songs of Lebanon will never reach my ears again except in dreams. I...am exiled by...my work..."[54]

One may wonder, as Kahlil docked in New York on October 31, 1910, how exile was remaking his very sense of homeland. But with his Parisian adventures, his travels abroad had ended. What remained ahead was the body of his work.

Sketch of Mary and Kahlil, 1912. (Courtesy Wilson Library, University of North Carolina, Chapel Hill.)

10

FRONTIERS OF FRIENDSHIP

Kahlil met Mary, back from Hawaii, for supper the day after he landed, but their visit lacked the spontaneity of earlier times. Lonely, he missed close friends. The next day he began to think about suitable living arrangements. He wanted a studio where his sister could live with him, and this posed challenges.

Marianna had subsisted in an Oliver Place rooming house for the past two and a half years, and she was yearning to set up a home for them. For Marianna, too, the news of their father's death had reawakened the pain of earlier losses, and she again mourned for her entire family. Her brother's return renewed her faith in the only immediate Gibran family member left for her to love. As soon as she saw him again, she told him that she was determined to devote the rest of her life to him. But no matter how tenderly he felt toward her, he realized that this dedication could become complicated.

Knowing Marianna's need to be near him, Kahlil also needed to decide on the best location for a studio. For the first time since 1896, he was determined to leave the South Cove. But by choosing to leave his Syrian neighborhood, he would be going against his sister's wishes. Moreover, refusing to live in a spacious studio, Marianna wanted to be able "to touch the walls."[1] Kahlil wrote Gertrude Barrie, "I...do not know what to do first...I am homeless in Boston and we are looking for a studio and a home..."[2]

Finally he found an apartment at 18 West Cedar Street. Near the studio where he had drawn Micheline and a minute's walk away from Fred Holland Day's town apartment on Pinckney Street, the address was right for an aspiring artist. The two rooms approximated Marianna's idea of what an apartment should be, and the rent was within their limited budget.

During the second week of November, they moved in. From the start, things were difficult. No matter how he tried to help Marianna adjust to her new surroundings,

Kahlil could not help her reconcile the differences between the South End and sedate Beacon Hill. The orderly provisions stores and genteel tearooms did not nourish her. She missed the sounds of their language, the open-air stands, the grape leaves, puffs of wafer-thin bread, and the nighttime stoop sitting of her familiar enclave. This new world was just a ten-minute walk across the Boston Common from Oliver Place, but her daily symbols of security and survival were missing—the new address was not home. Even with her brother in the studio, she felt isolated. One room was set aside for his work, and they waged a silent battle over who was responsible for it. She believed it should be spotless and followed him around with a cleaning rag. If papers or books became disarrayed, she rearranged them; if paint spilled, she rushed to wipe it up. For Kahlil the room was not a studio, and it lacked privacy. He also felt inhibited by Marianna's silent but growing concern over Mary's presence in their lives. Although she respected the schoolteacher, her unspoken question was, "Would you leave me for her?" It was one that he could not answer, even though he was spending more time at Marlborough Street.

~

As soon as Kahlil started to paint, he formed the habit of bringing his results to Mary's school. Five years later, he expressed how much Mary's reaction meant to him. "You were interested in my work—but I was bringing you my heart with it all the time. I'd work in that little room and then hurry to you...those two evenings a week...I just waited the days between for those evenings to come."[3]

His studies finally arrived from Paris. "With quick, ardent movements," he opened the crate in the school's kitchen. As he showed her the paintings, Mary crowed. "Great fun," she wrote in her diary that night.[4] He was proudest of his Temple of Art series. Besides the sculptor Bartlett, he had drawn portraits of Debussy, Rostand, Rodin, and the editor and critic Henri Rochefort. He and Mary began planning whom to add.

Gradually, she included him in the weekly parties she gave. Every Sunday evening, she encouraged teachers and visitors to entertain their male friends at the school. After dining lightly, they drew the curtains and danced, in defiance of prevailing blue laws. "But one teacher told of it as a good story," Mary remembered later, "so the dancing was given up. Boston would not have stood for it—Yet the Sunday parties kept on." She showed Kahlil's paintings, and sometimes he came to sketch a visiting relative or join in the fun and games.[5]

He escaped none of her subtle efforts to enlighten. She initiated reading sessions—lessons, really—during which he read aloud to her. They began with Swinburne, whom he had told her he considered the greatest living English poet. On November 9, they read "A Leave-Taking," a poem which dealt with death. Her father, Alexander Cheves Haskell, had died that spring; both of her parents now were gone. As the oral reading exercises continued, Swinburne became her favorite poet too, and Kahlil perfected his spoken English by reciting from "Laus Veneris," "Atalanta in Calydon," and "By the North Sea." Mary observed his reacclimation to her world. She noted his interaction at supper with two teachers: "A little hard to mingle—but his courtesy was lovely." Once, while visiting friends, the conversation turned to Parisian morality, and how men and women in "bohemian circles" lived together. Kahlil's views ran counter to the general opinion that such men were irresponsible. Although he was "uncomfortable" and "didn't want to talk about it"—as "their points of view were so far apart"—she was impressed by his open-mindedness.[6]

By December, Kahlil and Mary frequently were seen together publicly. They visited Dr. Richard and Ella Cabot, toured the Museum of Fine Arts, and attended the theater. Then, for the first time since he had known her, he brought up with her the topic of his family background. Often she had asked him about it, but he had always refrained from answering directly.

> …There is hardly a smile in those years…I have loved a great deal—and I have always seen the beautiful: and between love and beauty I was and always shall be, a lost, hungry child of the Unknown. I must tell you more in detail…some day.[7]

He was aware that these allusions could not satisfy her curiosity. On December 7, he began to tell her about his family and his early years. His colorful portraits of the Gibrans—filled with pride, boasts, and daring—are perhaps best summarized by a message that his paternal grandfather sent to a Turkish overlord: "Tell him Syria is the best province of the Turkish Empire, Mt. Lebanon is the most magnificent part of Syria, Bechary is the most beautiful village in Lebanon, the Gibrans are the most distinguished family of Bechary—and I am the head of that damned family." Describing his father as "magnetic and a man of tastes," Kahlil told how his father had been wrongly accused of embezzlement, tried, and found guilty. As time passed, it seems that Mary understood her protégé's need to compensate for an impoverished background and that she gently overlooked what she perceived as his more fanciful claims.

However confusing his story may have seemed to her, within a month of his return Mary saw Kahlil as deserving of her continued patronage and as a permanent figure in her life. Her interest in sponsoring other talents like Charlotte and Micheline would continue, and she would add other students to her personal scholarship list. But her interest in Kahlil went beyond charity, and beginning on December 7, 1910, she would devote her journal and many remaining years of her life to his. Her ambition "of writing something that might serve years hence" was being realized. Her subject— a restless, aspiring painter and poet who was neither comfortable in her language nor secure in his artistic expression—was a risk, but one that she had decided to take.

~

Even as he was settling into West Cedar Street and developing a close relationship with Mary, Kahlil could not resist the pull of his homeland. By the end of November, he began to send Najib Diab, editor *Mirat al-Gharb* (*Mirror of the West*) in New York, a series of articles that would land him in the midst of political debate among Syrian factions, an episode recovered by Tanyss Carol Ludescher.[8] She describes how, starting with his controversial poem, "Ila Suriyeen" (To Syrians),[9] Kahlil challenged himself and his compatriots for their collective failure to overthrow the Ottoman yoke or to create religious, governmental, and religious reform. International response from Syrian intellectuals and students filled Diab's Letters to the Editor columns, sparking intense debates between "extremists and reformers in the Syrian-American community for years to come," she writes.[10]

Kahlil's desire not only to be part of this ongoing dialogue but to be actively involved with publishers, editors, and writers from the several Syrian-owned New York publishing houses motivated him to look beyond Boston. Despite his contentment with the new studio, his devotion to Marianna, and even his attachment to Mary, he began to yearn for more. He was drawn to the activity that was happening in the multiple presses of New York's Little Syria. Only that bustling area in Lower Manhattan, embracing Washington Street to Battery Park, could satisfy his need to be working near the center of an incipient Arab-American journalism. By spring he was visiting New York and investigating the community that would produce countless newspapers and magazines in the early twentieth century. Within less than a year, he would be living nearby the familiar neighborhood that would fuel his literary ambitions and nourish his artistic vision.

~

On December 10, 1910, now almost twenty-eight years old, and six years after meeting her, Kahlil proposed to Mary, then turning thirty-seven. They had spent that Saturday at the Museum of Fine Arts and had planned an evening at the Symphony. But there was no concert, so they returned to Marlborough Street. It was then that he told her that he "loved" her and "would marry" her—"if he could." As though prepared to answer him, she replied that her "age made it out of the question." Her objectivity, he later recalled to Mary, cut deeply into his pride.

> I came back from Paris full of this. I went and gave you my heart so simply…so sincerely…I was just a boy putting all I was and all I had into your hands. And you met me so coldly…All the while I was in Paris I felt your faith and your warmth. And when I came back to Boston you were the same sweet, kind, wonderful spirit—Then the very day after I spoke to you of marriage you began to hurt me."[11]

On a Saturday one year before, Mary had turned down another ardent suitor, shedding tears and agonizing over her decision. This time her response was so matter-of-fact that the following day's events surprised him. December 11 was Mary's thirty-seventh birthday, and just before her party, he visited—whereupon, she simply changed her mind: "I told him yes."[12]

His immediate response went unrecorded by her, but over the next weeks her consent lulled him into a new sense of security. Although she fretted about his habits—"Coffee six times a day—smoking—late hours—little exercise—all nerves"—they enjoyed a placid December. He felt comfortable enough to discuss candidly and at length his waning friendship with Micheline. His painting was going well. Besides using Marianna and two younger cousins, Rosie and Amelia, as models, he turned to Denison House for potential sitters. Through Mary's ministrations, he drew Dr. Cabot, about to be appointed chief of staff of Massachusetts General Hospital. A week later, Charles Eliot, president of Harvard, agreed to pose for him, and they talked about Kahlil's favorite

Charles W. Eliot, president emeritus of Harvard College. Graphite, 1910. (Courtesy Museo Soumaya.)

subjects: art and the Middle East.[13] As she observed his growing ability to establish rapport with men whom she deeply respected, Mary began to consider sharing a life together. On December 28, they walked through the snow to see Ruth St. Denis in her Egyptian dances. Two days later, he was so excited by the play *Madame X* that he borrowed three drama books and "went off in high spirits" to write.[14]

In observation of his twenty-eighth birthday he presented Mary with a prose poem published January 6, 1911, in the newspaper *Mirat al-Gharb*. *Al-Mohajer* was no longer an outlet for his work, since Ameen Ghorayeb had left New York for Lebanon in the summer of 1909, but Najib Diab, editor of *Mirat al-Gharb*, had eagerly accepted his writings. Like his birthday poem of 1909, "We and You" was dedicated to "MEH," and typically it contained overtones of social protest. It was a litany in contrasts between "we"—"the sons of sorrow and oppression"—and "you"—"the sons of idleness and vanity of the world."[15]

Mary and Kahlil tried unsuccessfully to render it into English. She felt challenged to learn Arabic, and their January evenings became filled with discussions of Semitic languages and the intricacies of the Arabic alphabet. This led inevitably to the problems of the Middle East. He sketched a brief history of the Arab peoples, told her about St. Maroun, the founder of the Maronite church, described the motivations of the Young Turks, and speculated about reports of the latest efforts of people to win their liberty in the 1911 Yemen revolution. Because of their voracious appetites for listening to each other, their teacher-student roles constantly alternated.

That month he made another effort to legitimatize his claim as a worthy husband by offering to become a naturalized citizen. But his belief that Mary might prefer him if he were an American was ill-founded, and the subject was dropped.

Mary, who usually refrained from expressions of sentiment, began to experience a flood of feeling. "*January 4*. K. in after supper refreshing me utterly. *January 7*. To lunch Tante Müller and K. who drew her. I come to care much more." On January 24 she was reading Francis Thompson's poetry in search of suitable love poems for her students. "In a strange, dreamy nap on floor by fire" she imagined Charlotte, who appeared to her and said, "Kahlil making strides in my being."[16] It was ironic that Mary's intuition should insist on her friend's approval of Kahlil, since Charlotte's letters were expressing the fullest enthusiasm for him. Yet Mary was aware of a potential rivalry between the two people she loved so much.

Four days after the dream, she told Kahlil about supporting Charlotte. She revealed that she had originally sent him to Paris as a "test" of his stability and of their relationship, and that she felt "bound" to continue that test for at least two more years. He protested that he was "absolutely sure." "For the first time in my life," Mary went on, "I have had an impulse of deepest desire after money in order to endow Charlotte with $1,500 annually." He volunteered to share her commitment: "[He] could probably get work on a paper at forty or fifty dollars a month, could perhaps at once do picture work cheap which would be commercially profitable." She hurriedly rejected his offer. "No, not for a month—a day—an hour."[17]

She explained that for the past few years, she had been contributing to the education of two other young men. One was a Greek boy whom Sarah Armstrong had met working at a soda fountain run by a "callous Levantine shopman," and who was now enrolled at Mount Hermon, a boys' school in western Massachusetts. Her other protégé was a twenty-three-year-old senior at Harvard. Aristides Evangelus Phoutrides, also a Greek immigrant, had attended and graduated from Mount Hermon. His promising future as a classicist prompted Mary's financial and intellectual involvement. Kahlil realized that her commitments meant postponing their marriage. "I knew there were other 'children' though you never said it," he admitted. "But it is not forty or fifty a month that would be felt. That makes little matter. It is a case of four or five thousand dollars."[18]

The financial question was the first obstacle to their union. Even with this change in their relationship, Kahlil was cheerful. "In the relation of husband and wife," he said, "as in the case of most else…if the big thing is right—and this big thing I call understanding—all the rest can be worked out…Let us trust in [God] and feel quiet assurance that all will be…well. If you say to me, 'Kahlil I think it is not wise for us to marry,' I will accept absolutely what you say—and believe."[19]

In years to come he admitted how her equivocation affected him. Already, he had felt pressured by her demands that he prove himself. Undeniably, she was encouraging him to develop a strong self-image. One night she pressured him to acknowledge that in the Arab world his writing was highly appreciated and could be compared with Gabriele D'Annunzio's. Kahlil appeared unconvinced: "I am sure—that if I died tomorrow some things I have said will live. But nothing I have ever done satisfies me even a short while after it is done." He was dissatisfied with this probationary period. "Every time I left your house I was all filled up. That was the most unproductive year of my life. I've almost nothing of any account even in writing to show for that winter."[20]

There was another side to Mary's test. Said she, "My 'disillusionment series' of camp snapshots…failed. I had collected all the old snapshots of myself that I had—some are ghastly—to show K. and give him a distaste for me…and he was interested but utterly unmoved." She tried the same tactic when she told him stories of all her former suitors and showed him a picture of her "first beloved." She notes: "K. surprised but not changed."[21]

In February, Charlotte visited Boston. Her presence at the school lessened the tension building between Kahlil and Mary. For two weeks Mary, relieved by a school vacation, appreciated the nonstop dialogue with her. Mornings she spent listening to Charlotte interpret dreams and Near Eastern symbols. Charlotte urged Mary to calm herself and to "put on coral earrings." She told her that the barrier between herself and Kahlil would be removed if only Mary would recognize her "Oriental self."[22]

Afternoons, Charlotte posed for Kahlil, and this time after seven hour-long sessions he managed to finish a satisfactory portrait. Mary's admiration was based not only on her critical judgment but on the fact that it was a portrait of Charlotte by him. "I told him anew how I love Charlotte's picture…that I long intensely for him."[23] Accompanying Charlotte for a sitting at 18 West Cedar Street on February 18, Mary saw the studio for the first time and carefully noted its every aspect.[24]

> The room was so immaculate that I wondered whether there'd been a Marianna's housecleaning for us…The yellow tapestry—one large gleam and shine…the death mask of the beautiful young woman found dead in the Seine…the red silk piece with a beautiful Japanese print…the two or three old bits of deep cut gilded wood carving…Beethoven's death mask against an oriental linen with embroidered ends.

She carefully examined the contents of his small bookcase, which included the conspicuously bound Masters in Art series and the Copeland & Day edition of Rossetti's *The House of Life*. The workroom filled her with joy—"I felt as if I had seen it all before it was so characteristic."

Between sittings, Kahlil made them coffee—"delicious, but devilish stuff"—and served them a salted mixture of pistachio nuts, melon seeds, and chickpeas. Often Mary read aloud as he painted. Once she chose selections from his copy of Josephine's early poems, *The Singing Leaves,* and made Charlotte guess who had written them. As they strolled home after the second sitting, Mary confided to Charlotte, "Kahlil and I want to be married when we can." Charlotte wholeheartedly approved; she had "hoped since she saw him in Paris that it might be."[25]

The evenings were spent at Marlborough Street, where Charlotte tried out her plays on Mary and Kahlil. She declared that if they were ever produced, he was to help with the color schemes and costumes. Sometimes the three of them invented games. Mary read their hands or just lay on the floor watching them. They talked about reincarnation. Mary's theory about Kahlil was simple: "Blake died in 1827, and Rossetti was born in 1828; Rossetti died in 1882 and Gibran was born in 1883." Other times they talked about spiritual messages. Mary was sure she had seen a vision while looking at a Kahlil drawing, and Charlotte was always interpreting significant dreams. Kahlil offered tales about his "trance-experiences." Then Charlotte left Boston, and the discussions ended.

~

Something else was ending: Kahlil's happiness with Boston as a place to live and work. Aware of his growing dissatisfaction, Mary asked how he felt: "I often wish for something else than library or museum." Neither were his friendships as meaningful as in the past. Day, impressed by the Temple of Art series, suggested that it be broadened to include Andrew Carnegie and other figures outside the humanities. But his enthusiasms no longer drew Kahlil's interest. He found it difficult to communicate with his old mentor. "When I came back from Paris, I found him...still just where he had been ten years before."[26]

He saw nothing of Josephine. The previous year had been a successful one for the Markses. Their second child was born on the same day that she learned she had won first prize in an international playwriting competition at Stratford-on-Avon. Her reputation rose with the 1910 London production of *The Piper* and its successful New York run. Cut off from former friendships such as the Rüyls, interaction with colleagues, and opportunity, Kahlil found Boston limiting.

> Everything in Boston is very beautiful—except there's no art life here. Everything seems dead...Even my artist friends...seem to belong in the eighteenth century. Nothing that has been doing within the last forty or fifty years seems to be known or to meet sympathy...And there's another thing that's hell—if you'll excuse my mentioning it—The people...such faces—it's terrible. So cold—so far away—so hard...
>
> There are people here who used to feed my very soul...And I have blamed myself because tho' I care for them I no longer find it the same to talk with them...it has always seemed to me we ought not to need inspiration from outside ourselves. Yet I keep on being conscious of...a desire for the life I do not find...I always thought [Boston] was one of the best and most beautiful and desirable cities in the world.[27]

Mary was sure that New York would promise more, while Charlotte agreed.

"Should Kahlil come to New York," she wrote, "he must live near enough to me to take his meals here—his dinners. It will *be* home-like for both."[28]

By this time, Mary, frequently visiting the West Cedar Street studio, was arranging for female friends to pose. No wonder speculation was growing about the artist and the headmistress. When Louise Daly, understanding her sister Mary's intense feeling for the artist, began to closely question her, Mary tried "to shake off discussion by confession." But the couple chose "to finally to let conjecture die instead of tackling it." For his part, Kahlil was concerned about Marianna's growing suspicions. "I've told no one," he said. "I do not tell my sister because while she would say something very kind and sweet to me, afterwards I know she would go into her room and say to herself, 'Alone.'"[29]

On the other hand, Mary's boldness often worked to his advantage. By April she was organizing two plans. She asked Charlotte to help find a studio in New York for him, and she began trying to contact those in Boston who could lead him to the most powerful art patron in that city—Isabella Stewart Gardner. The Cabots suggested the Copley Greenes, who belonged to the St. Botolph Club, an art association that sponsored influential exhibits. And so Mary invited her friends Mr. and Mrs. Copley Greene to dine with her and Kahlil on April 14.

> They really loved the work…And when he said he wrote during the morning they asked about that and cried that Mrs. Joe Smith [wife of Joseph Smith, then an illustrator and Egyptologist at the Museum of Fine Arts] knows Arabic and he must know Mrs. Joe Smith. So they took his address and phone number and next Friday at luncheon or supper tis Mrs. Joe Smith he shall meet! The three went off together a little after nine—finding each other a joyful discovery and the Greenes saying they wanted him to paint their Francesca.

So confident was Mary that she added, "It was the moment of the opening of the door between K. and the world that shall love him…I *think* his future is not far away now."[30]

Mary then made her decision:

> And so I made up my mind to follow what seems to me the final finger of God—I put definitely from myself the possibility of being his wife…My age is simply the barrier raised between us…the blunder of our marrying, not my age constitutes the objection—but the fact that for K. there waits a very different love from that he bears me…and that shall be his marriage…Towards the woman of that love, I am but a step.[31]

The next day, April 15, she prepared to speak to him. She "wanted so much to think" that all morning she sat at the piano and "practiced hard new hymns," and then walked up and down the Back Bay streets, rehearsing how she would tell him. He arrived at the school after the Symphony, and they "swapped news." When they were sitting on the library sofa and she "could command her voice," she began.

> Everything in me protests against my saying it, except the one thing that makes me say it. But I know the one thing is right. You will acquiesce in what I say—but my heart longs to be overpersuaded. Still I know in the end, I should not be persuaded.[32]

She told him how, since December, whenever she visualized their marriage she felt "obscurely" it was wrong. Her "great passion for him" had grown slowly. Her age remained "insuperable." Although she knew that she still possessed "a certain youthfulness and great vigor," she would be "soon on the downward path" while he was "still long climbing upwards." While she talked, he wept. "Mary, you know I cannot say things when I am this way."

When she finished, they held one another, and when it grew late she kissed his hand—"as I have often longed to do, but as I have not before." At the door she cried again, and it was Kahlil's turn to wipe her tears. "And as he went, he said as well as he could, 'You've given me a new heart tonight.'"[33]

Both of them remembered that scene for many years. Mary interpreted Kahlil's immediate acquiescence as proof that "he never wanted marriage…And through his silence I think I hear that K. knows I'm right." He argued that her vacillation had destroyed their marriage plans: "What hurt me so was that you couldn't see *me*. You couldn't believe in me. You were interested in my work, but a man's work isn't the man…You stood off from the real me like an indifferent spectator."[34]

A day passed, and he avoided the Sunday night gathering. When she found an excuse to visit on Monday, he was working on a study that he called *Chaos*. They refrained from alluding to Saturday night. Then Marianna arrived "with the big black bag she carries everywhere." She was rarely around when Mary visited, and now the schoolteacher eagerly seized the opportunity to make her drop the formal title "Miss Haskell." She got the shy young woman to whisper "Mary" until she felt relaxed enough to call her by her first name. As she studied her, she concluded that Marianna looked thin, "but not badly…" She also noticed that her voice was "still melancholy itself—the seat of tears" and realized that the thought of Kahlil's going away represented "a terror to her."

"When Kahlil goes to New York I'll see much of you," she promised. "Ah! When Kahlil goes to New York! Shall you go with him?" "What do you think?"

Marianna hesitated. "Well, I'm sure he'd like it." And then the phone rang. Miss Teahan wanted her, and although she was weary, Kahlil's sister prepared to walk back to the shop. Said Mary, "For the first time I realized how like his her eyes are."[35]

The next day Mary contrived another reason to go to the studio. For *Broken Wings*, a painting he was doing of Marianna, Kahlil had mentioned his need to study some birds. She hurried to the market, bought two doves, and walked over to West Cedar Street. No one was home so she hung them on the door. The implications of her recent decision overwhelmed her: "Gradually realizing life without living with Kahlil in its future outlook—I in Boston or California—he abroad—It hurts!"[36]

Kahlil went to the Copley Greenes that night. Mary's prediction about his future being settled as a result of meeting them was sadly exaggerated. At dinner he managed to conduct himself pleasantly; he met Mr. and Mrs. Joseph Smith and exchanged amenities. Kahlil did learn of the Greenes' interest in Eugène Carrière and borrowed some reproductions of his work to take to Mary the next night. As he showed them to her, they discussed Charlotte's latest theater project. She had accepted an offer to travel with a repertory group, The Lyceum Players. She had a minor part as Lady Parchester in Alfred Sutro's *The Walls of Jericho*. She also invited Kahlil to use her Greenwich Village apartment while she was on tour. He wavered—"if she were a man I shouldn't hesitate—but a woman—it seems like intrusion." At last Mary persuaded him to take advantage of the offer.[37] On April 26, 1911, Kahlil took the Joy Line boat from Boston to New York and arrived at 164 Waverly Place early the next morning.

~

April and May in New York were "alltogether too good...New York is not the place where one finds rest." But, he asked Mary, "Did I come here for rest? I am so glad to be able to run." He especially reveled in the Metropolitan Museum: "America is far greater than what superficial people think."[38] Preventing him from working at Waverly Place were "too many friends and too many callers and too many things to see." He immediately reidentified himself with the New York Syrian community, and the activists there rekindled his passion for the nationalist struggle. Within a week he had met the Turkish ambassador at a dinner given by Naum Mokarzel, an editor of the émigré newspaper *Al-Hoda* (*The Guidance*). "The ambassador was trying all the time to be *sweet* and *gentle*. We talked about art, and he even invited me to go and see him in Washington. That is the Turkish way of leveling and smoothing down the things that stay in the way!"[39]

Ameen Rihani's presence in New York was another important reason for Kahlil's relocation there, and reestablishing their friendship became one of his main interests. He saw the other writer every day and proudly related his achievements: "Read Rihani's poem 'The Song of Siva' in May number of *The Atlantic Monthly*...I want to bring Charlotte and Rihani together. They will like each other."[40]

All through May, Kahlil balanced his contacts and friendships in his two separate worlds. With Mary's letter of introduction, he reached her old friend, composer and musicologist Arthur Farwell, and drew him on May 5. In turn, Farwell took him around New York galleries. As a result, he met William Macbeth, the art dealer who specialized in contemporary American painters.

Deciding that the Lyceum Players was a "dry experience," Charlotte returned to New York on May 15. She at once made sure that Kahlil met everyone in her Greenwich Village circle. She wrote Mary that the minute she arrived at Waverly Place, she had contacted him and another freelance writer—"and we three *with you so present!* spent the evening, as I felt on the threshold of a new life for all of us." She also mentioned how much Kahlil had changed and become "full of reposeful power."[41] Although she had heard of their broken engagement, she was convinced that it was only temporary. She remained sure that if only Mary would relax, Kahlil would take the initiative and insist upon marriage.

He moved into a rooming house at 28 West Ninth Street, where Rihani was staying. The quarters were cramped, but he painted in the larger room. Every morning he walked to Charlotte's for breakfast. Despite finding no sponsors for her own work, she did possess amazing catalytic powers. He met her close friend Charles Edward Russell, the defeated Socialist candidate for governor of New York. Knowing how much Mary respected this man's reform politics, Kahlil immediately shared the news.

Rihani also introduced Kahlil to his friends, American as well as Syrian: the poet Edwin Markham whom Kahlil drew; Michael Monahan, the editor and publisher of *Papyrus* ("he is Irish and possesses rare charms"); and Richard Le Gallienne, the critic and chronicler of the Yellow Decade when Wilde and Beardsley had shocked English and American censors. Then, Le Gallienne sat for Kahlil who reported that his study was "so real that it made him sad."[42]

Back in Boston, after school commencement on May 26, Mary turned her attention toward New York. But first she had Micheline for a visit. Now teaching at the Ely School in Greenwich, Connecticut, she had seen Kahlil in New York that month, and after catching up on Micheline's life, Mary loved hearing about him.

"We talked K. for hours. It is very fresh still and she [envisages] him just the same as always." Micheline also met Marianna that weekend. True to her word, Mary conscientiously met up with Marianna at least once a week and treated her to plays, operas, and concerts. Marianna had responded by giving her "the best" of Kamila's bangle bracelets, the proud possession of any Syrian matriarch. Thereafter, the schoolmistress proudly wore this symbol of her affection. Micheline found Marianna so much like Kahlil that she made friends with her at once, and Marianna responded fully.[43]

Arriving in New York on June 1 for a twelve-day visit, Mary rushed to Waverly Place. Kahlil had started another painting of Charlotte, and she could hardly wait to see it. Envisioning a female cupbearer, or "Sakia," he posed Charlotte nude amid swirling "green, apricot and orange veils" and holding "a brazen jewelled bowl of incense." In his words she was "a goddess, an image…so many prayers have risen to her that at last she is coming to life." When he had begun the painting two weeks earlier, Charlotte had told Mary how much they had wanted her there: "Kahlil said beautifully that he never began his work in here before he had summoned you. And yet I feel we need that wonderful eye of yours, to see critically and creatively." Now for the next three days their world revolved around the picture. "Charlotte trips about in her veils, stepping on the ends, lifting them again—wrapping them intervalwise about her."[44]

On Saturday June 3, Kahlil brought Rihani for dinner. Charlotte had met him two nights before, but this was the first time Kahlil had introduced Mary to his Syrian colleagues. At Charlotte's instigation, the two women wore costumes, Mary an alluring black satin dress and Charlotte her Lady Parchester costume with "puffs and night gown." Rihani wore traditional Middle Eastern dress. He good-naturedly scribbled bits of Arabic and English so Mary could read his hand. They burned incense and listened to his poetry.[45]

Once during the evening Kahlil gave Mary a lengthy, piercing look. She remembered it for a long time for what she felt was its painful quality. When over the next few

Kahlil's sketch of Ameen Rihani.
(Courtesy Museo Soumaya.)

years they analyzed the turning points in their relationship, he always recalled "the night they painted up" as a fiasco.[46] What had annoyed him most were Charlotte's mischievous efforts at matchmaking, and the penetrating look turned out to be only his expression of uneasiness.

Two days later, Charlotte left for Denver. For the next five days, twelve hours a day, Mary and Kahlil roamed unencumbered through New York. They visited the Cathedral of St. John the Divine and Columbia University, the Metropolitan Museum and the Brooklyn Museum. In Prospect Park they watched President Taft review a children's assembly.

> When the crowd pressed suddenly to the bandstand…to see Taft enter his auto, the vibration was so wonderful that K. said, "Chaos that's what it means to me…chaos out of which anything may come."[47]

They ate at blue-collar lunch counters; went to Ferard's, a meeting place for artists; ate goulash at a little Romanian place; and found their favorite restaurant on Eighth Street—Gonfarone's, where the waiters sang and the fixed price with wine was fifty cents.

Their "feast of experiences" also included reading from *Thus Spake Zarathustra*, borrowed from Rihani.[48] One day it rained, and they stayed in the apartment. Kahlil drew a series of motifs of how various poets seemed to him visually:

> Swinburne—rising alone in great simple curves from the sea…Keats in the blue lighted groves, deep yet clear—Shelley treading the fields as if they were air—Rodin a simple massive harmony of line—Dante loneliness with serpent—Shakespeare colossus, the heavens passing by his head, and mankind clustered about his feet and knees—Michelangelo, a big sculptor head holding an image…And a wee rectangle 'K.G' in the corner.[49]

After Mary returned, Kahlil visited Boston before her annual trip west, on June 18. She proposed that she replace monthly checks with five thousand dollars, the amount bequeathed him in her will. He could invest the money as he chose (she suggested her own brokers Moors and Cabot, whose investments were yielding a healthy eight percent). After settling these details, they sat down and made out his will. Earlier that month he had said,

> Speaking of wills, I want to do something that will stand in law about my pictures. If I should die, I don't want anyone else to touch my work or have anything to say about it, but you. I want it all in your hands. How can I do this? And how can I go about returning the money I have used?[50]

Mary saved the first draft for her journal, and Kahlil copied it. On the first page were the names of nine persons who would receive a memento. With the exception of William Hunt Diederich (a grandson of William Morris Hunt and a sculptor Kahlil had known in Boston), all were people instrumental in his development. First was Fred Holland Day, followed by Charlotte Teller, Ameen Rihani, Diederich, Emilie R. Michel, Mrs. Louis (Beatrice) Rüyl, Mr. and Mrs. Joseph Rahaim, and Youssef Howayek. Although simple in form, the terms thoughtfully outlined provisions for his artistic and literary legacy.

Dated in Mary's diary June 7, 1911, and written when he was twenty-eight, it reads:

> I, Kahlil Gibran being in sound mind and body, do herein make my last will and testament, and this will shall render void any previous wills, testaments or memoranda. All pictures, drawings, and studies made by me I leave to Mary E. Haskell as her sole property. If before my death I become insane they shall thereupon be at once her property.
>
> I leave my literary manuscripts to my sister Marianna Gibran, advising her to consult about their publication with Ameen Rihani, N. Diab, and Ameen Ghorayeb, Beirout Syria. My manuscripts on politics and sociology I leave in the hands of Ameen Ghorayeb. Whatever money remains to me I leave to Mary E. Haskell. To her I leave all the letters written in English to me. All letters written to me in Arabic or French I desire my sister to keep unread for five years after my death—and during that time to allow the writers of them to claim any or all of their own if they wish. At the end of the five years I desire her to put those which have not been claimed into the hands of Joseph Hawaik [sic].
>
> If Mary Haskell is living I desire the heart to be taken from my body and given to her, and my body to be sent to Bechary Syria to be buried in Mar (St.) Mema. If she is not living, my heart shall not be removed from my body and the body shall be buried in Mar Mema.
>
> I leave my books that are in Bechary to the Bechary Society's Reading Room. I leave my books in America to the Golden Links Society, Boston—with the exception of books concerning art; these I leave to Mary Haskell, with all prints.
>
> I leave all my personal effects to my sister Marianna, except my two smaller Chinese silver rings: these to Mary Haskell.
>
> If Mary E. Haskell is not living at the time of my death, I desire my friend Fred Holland Day to take charge of all pictures, drawings and studies made by me. My wish is that in this case they shall become eventually the property of the public in a museum—and that they shall be kept together as far as is possible; but also that by means of them my sister Marianna shall be provided for. I should, Mary Haskell

being dead, be willing to let them become the property of any museum or society which would undertake for their sake to provide for my sister.[51]

Then they talked about summer. While Mary was away, he planned to work in Boston. First he wanted to revise *The Broken Wings*, a book he had started in 1906. "It is how I felt five years ago—I don't feel that now. But it is well done and I don't want to discard it." He was also beginning a series of essays about a "madman" and had promised to illustrate Rihani's *The Book of Khalid*. When Mary worried about what he would do for a vacation, he answered, "Lie on the grass." "How long?" she laughed. "About two minutes."[52]

The next morning she almost missed her train for Chicago. As she boarded, she spotted an artist with an obviously older wife. The train sped west, and she recorded in her journal the lengthy entries for the past month. The task was not finished until she reached Salt Lake City, where she contentedly summed up her feelings: "Wholly at peace with our situation—especially when I see fading wives on train!"[53]

The Tenth Street Studio Building in New York City, at 51 West 10th Street. The first structure of its kind, designed to provide work and gallery space to artists, the building became a hub of visual art activity in the city, and nationally. Kahlil found a studio there, which he called "the Hermitage." (Courtesy the New York Historical Society.)

11

FROM BOSTON TO NEW YORK

The summer of 1911 in Boston was a productive one for Kahlil. Dodd, Mead and Company paid him fifty dollars for illustrating Rihani's forthcoming *The Book of Khalid*. Having finished Charlotte's portrait, now entitled *Isis*, he worked on four more paintings. But his most extensive work was revising *Al-Ajniha al-Mutakassira* (*The Broken Wings*).

Focusing on the alienating effects of corrupt power, in his longest novella in Arabic he once again made use of melodramatic plot and characterization. Platonic love between a poor young visionary and the beautiful Selma Karema is thwarted by her forced marriage to the nephew of a villainous bishop. Her fate, although relieved by forbidden meetings with her poet-lover, is doomed. The story ends with her death in childbirth and with the grief-stricken narrator burying his heart in her grave.

Kahlil called *The Broken Wings* a spiritual autobiography. The lovers' meeting place, in the chapter "Between Christ and Ishtar," depicted by the symbolic walls of a secluded temple, was considered sacrilegious by Arab critics. On one side, "speaking wordlessly of past generations and the evolution of religions," was a Byzantine bas-relief of the agonized Christ, with his sorrowing mother and Mary Magdalene. The other wall showed a Phoenician carving of Ishtar, the queen of Assyrian goddesses.[1]

These images of character and place suggest that on some level, Kahlil was paying homage to Kamila, his own courageous and resolute mother. He wrote, "The mother is every thing—she is our consolation in sorrow, our hope in misery, and our strength in weakness. She is the source of love, mercy, sympathy, and forgiveness."[2] Telling this story seemed to be a way to acknowledge and repay the debt he owed her.

The ghosts haunting him since 1906 were disappearing, and he began to pay more attention to his health. He even spoke of taking a course in economics. After climbing mountains in California with Sierra Club companions, Mary learned of these changes while in Wenatchee, Washington, where she was working farmland that she owned with her brother Tom. Later she noted,

> All his life his deepest desire had been to give pleasure to people…bring joy… happiness—show it, create it; but himself has never laid hold on it; he shrank from evil…feared it…longed to escape it—wept at the world's woes…One day last summer he was alone in the country with a book—and suddenly…thought…why should he go on always pointing others to joy and himself not enjoy it? Then his fear went and he laid hold on Reality as the goal of life—and life itself as the greater art.[3]

When Mary returned to Boston, they met on September 16 in the Italian North End and ate at the Hotel Napoli. To her, Kahlil appeared "better than ever—young, carefree, assured, happy." He wore a new light brown suit "from Hollander's—the nicest thing they had, $25…and a tie to match—15 cents."[4] Over two days they met. He brought her his story "Slavery," recently published in *Mirat al-Gharb*. A narrator tells of roaming the "East and West" to discover the faces of enslaved people and nations. After walking in "the Valley of the Shadow of Life where the past attempts to conceal itself in guilt," he arrives at the Blood and Tears River, where he listens to "whispers of the ghosts of slaves." Finally, he meets a spectral image of Liberty, who describes her children: "One died crucified; the other died mad; the other is not yet born."[5]

This kind of protest was marking twenty-eight-year-old Kahlil as a passionate voice among emigré artists. M. M. Badawi writes that his "rebellion against outworn social customs and religious tyranny, no less than his total rejection of outmoded literary modes and values, made him an inspiration for the younger generation of writers."[6] And although Mary delighted in every sketch and painting that he shared with her, she continued to express her disappointment that she was forced to depend on his oral translations: "…Longing to read you. Not in a different tongue–but in the Arabic."[7]

~

After the animated conversations of their two-day reunion, Kahlil left for New York to renew his search for a studio. Arriving in the city on the Joy Line, he stayed at Rihani's West Ninth Street rooming house. Within a few days, he reported he had found a place at 51 West Tenth Street, one with good light and low rent, "only twenty dollars."[8] The historic Tenth Street Studio building, designed by Richard Morris Hunt, had served for fifty years as home, studio, and gallery for many leading American artists. In celebration, he sent news of his new place to his friend Gertrude Barrie in Boston: "I have found a studio which…is more like the studios in Paris and it has a little balcony and very high windows. I know that you will like it…Two kisses for your blue eyes and two more for your hands." Another undated letter to Gertrude recalls an earlier moment in their lives.

> My life in New York is quite full—but I hunger
> for other places other regions and other things.
> I love New York because there is a great, powerful spirit
> dwelling in it: there is a positive element in New York
> an element which is unknown in Boston. And yet
> I am longing for an undiscovered land. Perhaps I will
> always be longing—even when the undiscovered land is discovered.
>
> Please…tell me soon that you are well again.
>
> Tell me that you are smiling and even laughing at things as you did long ago –
> long ago when you and the moon were
> such good friends.
>
> May the breath of God be your garment, sweet, dear Gertrude.
>
> Kahlil[9]

Even amid complex relationships with Mary and her other protégés, he hadn't lost track of his work. Just before leaving his new studio for Boston to pack and vacate the West Cedar Street apartment, he made sure to settle with his publisher, Najib Diab. *The Broken Wings* was to appear that winter, and he had to attend to details of its publication.

Returning to Boston in late September, Kahlil brought Mary his latest picture saying, "This painting is the parting of the ways in my life." The image was of a solitary nude figure, turning away from a bleak and cavernous landscape, cautiously stepping forward with his arms raised behind his head. The pose is strikingly similar to Michelangelo's marble sculpture, *Dying Slave*, a figure Kahlil knew well. For years, a copy of the famous statue had stood in Day's Five Islands camp in Maine. After sitting up with it all night, Mary christened it *The Beholder* and agreed that "it was his best so far." Earlier that month, she had asked him to paint Nietzsche's Zarathustra. Now, she could write, "Here is Zarathustra—here is the hand hungry and wearying to give."[10]

For the next two weeks, Kahlil and Mary were relieved of some of the uncertainty that previously had clouded their time together. "He is handling every human and social activity…" she noted. "No man talking with him now would find him sentimental…or unpractical—but full of actuality—alert—and critical, wary,

The Beholder, oil on canvas, 1911. (Courtesy Peter A. Juley / Smithsonian. Formerly collection of Telfair Museum, Savannah, Georgia.)

judgmatical." They saw "the Irish Players under Yeats" perform John Millington Synge's *The Well of the Saints* and Lady Gregory's *The Workhouse Ward*.[11] Afterward, they visited Kahlil's studio and looked at his summer's work. Still euphoric over *The Beholder*, which renewed their hopes for a Boston show, they stopped to see the Copley Greenes. The next day they heard Yeats address the Drama League at the Plymouth Theater. Kahlil went backstage, saw George Pierce Baker, then professor of drama at Harvard, and made an appointment to draw Yeats.

The meeting with Yeats on October 1, at the Hotel Touraine, reinforced his new mood. The drawing took under an hour, but the two men talked for three. Yeats confided that Boston bored him. "He can't work here," Kahlil related. "Lady Gregory can…But he can't and he wants to get away." According to Mary, Kahlil caught in his portrait the "homely, spirituelle, real" qualities of the Irish poet. Although the encounter did not lead to a sustained friendship, it deeply impressed Kahlil. He was convinced that Yeats would "do work of absolute worth" and identified with the Irish writer's struggle to resolve in his life and work the tension between politics and art: "One very bad thing is spoiling Yeats' work. He is a patriot—and he ought to be simply an artist. He knows it."[12]

Similar forces were pulling at Kahlil. Ever since his return from Paris, he had belonged to the Golden Links Society, a group of young Syrians brought to his attention by Gertrude Tebbutt, a Denison House social worker. Formed in 1910, the Boston branch—Gemaat Surea Americanea (Syrian American Society)—was similar to many groups organized in cities throughout the world.[13] The club's purpose was to improve the lives of Syrian citizens. As he became involved, Kahlil gradually adopted a view favoring national

Irish poet and playwright William Butler Yeats. Charcoal, 1911. (Courtesy Gibran Museum.)

and individual self-reliance. Not only did he believe "the Syrian looks in vain to Turkey for help," but he applied this concern to the Syrian immigrant's position in American society: "He errs to look to any government in any country to solve his problem—for he must help himself."[14]

One of the ongoing debates of the Golden Links Society[15] was "whether tis better for Syrians who are living in other countries to settle into Syrian colonies or to mix with the foreigners." Denison House dedicated itself to a healthy exchange of culture and customs: "The hearty co-operation of Syrians and Americans in this colony certainly shows that each nationality appreciates the other, and that each is grateful for what the other brings to the common pleasure and common education."[16] From his own closeness to Western culture, Kahlil agreed with this call for integration. Yet in trying to realize his artwork, his final decision was to maintain an autonomous distance from partisan causes, saying, "I have known each [world] well enough to stand now outside of both at will."[17]

Kahlil's insistence on maintaining his autonomy as an artist struggling to express "the Absolute" was difficult to sustain, for he was intensely patriotic. His passionate

Denison House participants at their performance of a mystery play.
Zakia Gibran, biographer Kahlil G. Gibran's maternal aunt, is in the second row, fifth from *left*.
(Courtesy Schlesinger Library, Radcliffe Institute, Harvard University.)

stance for an independent Syria and for his fellow immigrants to strive for self-reliance is evident in a speech addressed to members of Boston's Golden Links Society in 1911. Kahlil described how his fellow Syrians might seek freedom for themselves and their children.

> …What, then, can the Syrian do if you rob him of his hope of a reformed future in the lands of his birth and childhood? Does he become a naturalized citizen of the country to which he immigrated? Or does he seek help from foreign countries throwing his weakness [at the mercy of] European powers—the Druze clinging to England, the Orthodox [Christians] to Russia, and the Maronite to the French—as our fathers did?
>
> He who empties his heart from the illusions and false dreams of the Ottoman state only to fill it with the promises and ambitions of the foreign states resembles one who runs from fire to hell. The Syrian only has self-reliance and his talents, intelligence and excellence to rely on.
>
> The money earned by a solitary peddler is money earned by all Syrians. Every word a pupil learns in the American schools is a word learned by all Syrians…Free your children from the slavery traditions and old customs, and they will remain free even in chains and jails.[18]

During the last week of September 1911, Italy declared war on Turkey to gain colonies in North Africa, and hope revived for home rule in Turkish-occupied countries. Despite his questioning of Yeats's political involvement, Kahlil was likewise entrapped. Mary recognized the dilemma. After he spent an entire night talking about the Italian-Turkish conflict, she observed, "More and more I see him ceasing to be remote even while his remoteness grows."[19]

~

Perhaps because they were anticipating separation and his permanent move to New York, their time together during the beginning of October was peaceful. One night as they were looking through a stack of magazines, a poem by Louise Imogen Guiney caused him to reminisce, recalling the days when she had helped and encouraged him. Then they saw a picture of Josephine Peabody Marks. According to Mary, "[This] led K. into saying…that if something different had been her environment she might have done work with a touch of the Absolute. To his mind, the promise of her first achievements is unfulfilled—tho' her craftsmanship is improved." Following their discussion, she wrote more about their talk that night.

I was aware that K. had made a stride in loving, when in discussing Jos., he spoke of the love in such simple tenderness—and then [said]: "next after that came a good love that is friendship mixed with passion." Something seems added to him—wide, restful and enduring—as if he had *attained* in loving as in painting.[20]

On Friday, October 6, the Greenes, the Cabots, and two women friends were to join Kahlil and Mary for dinner. Because the Cabots and Mrs. Greene were ill and unable to attend, only Mr. Greene came, with the two friends. "It was the devil of an evening." Mary reproached herself for Kahlil failing to score any points, socially or professionally. Noting how his "remoteness" revealed the distance between his world and that of others he was so often pressed to accommodate, she brooded.

> Poor management!…K. and they seemed of such different worlds—and I of his, rather than of theirs—But the remoteness was so much completer than I had expected, that I was unprepared to meet it. K. is used to it: he handles it better. But I've realized only so recently the…gulf between him and most other minds…An illuminating experience for me at his cost.[21]

Seemingly unconcerned about the evening, a few days later Kahlil brought her three more paintings, which they titled *Pain, Where the Dead Gods Lie,* and *The Two Crosses*. He told her that the "wide billowing mountains and far mist" to which she responded in *Dead Gods* was conceived after he had heard about her "mountain summer."[22] As their days together grew shorter, they both became apprehensive about the year ahead. On October 10, Mary was "swallowing lumps all the time because…of K.'s near departure. He was so conscious of it all last evening." They finished organizing her "world-soul" course in literature and included selections from the Egyptian Book of the Dead, Job, Aeschylus, Sophocles, Euripides, the Qur'an, Dante, Shakespeare, *Faust,* Balzac, Nietzsche, Ibsen, and Whitman, despite Miss Dean's admonishments that inclusion of the last four writers would "damn" both Mary and the school.[23] Kahlil held out for a medieval miracle or mystery play and Swinburne, but finally agreed that neither fit the concept.

Including Kahlil in her curriculum planning, their reading-aloud sessions required him to think and express himself in English. If he disagreed with her, he had to search for vocabulary to express his arguments. He covered the blackboard with diagrams and illustrations, and before erasing them for morning classes, she carefully copied them into the burgeoning journal.

Lady Gregory had been impressed with the Yeats portrait and sat for him on October 13, Kahlil's last day in Boston. While he drew her at the Hotel Touraine, admirers flocked to her side. "Mrs. Gardner came in and recognized me," he told Mary that night. He described how she was "like a bee…talking with Lady Gregory and reading her a letter—emphatically and with much animation." Also present was Ezra Pound, whom Mary had met at Charlotte's apartment earlier that year. When she and Kahlil had discussed his work then, Kahlil had felt a "lack of music in it—especially since E. P. is young and youth is preeminently singing time."[24] Their last evening together again was spent at the Irish Players, since Lady Gregory, "pleased with her portrait," had given Kahlil two tickets. They saw her own *The Image* and

Irish playwright Lady Gregory. Charcoal and watercolor, 1911. (Courtesy Peter A. Juley / Smithsonian.)

Shaw's *The Shewing Up of Blanco Posnet*. Then they parted. "I'll send you sketches of everything I do in New York," he promised.

~

After Kahlil left for New York, Mary became determined to arrange a show of his recent work at Boston's St. Botolph Club. To this end, Kahlil had left behind all his paintings, drawings, and sketchbooks. Unfortunately, the Greenes' interest in his latest work was wavering, and for the rest of the month she bustled to solicit other responses to *Where the Dead Gods Lie* and *The Two Crosses*. They were not encouraging. "Dead Gods!" one woman shuddered. "No wonder it is terrible. Dead humans are bad enough—but dead Gods!" Such attitudes only intensified her resolve. She invited Alicia Keyes, the art teacher who had originally suggested Kahlil's first show at the school and who was now the confidante of the elusive Mrs. Gardner. "She will know whether Mrs. Gardner might be interested," she wrote Kahlil. "If Mrs. G. would be, and would come on Miss K.'s suggestion, and if she approved, the exhibit could almost surely be at the St. Botolph."[25]

On October 23, Miss Keyes arrived and proceeded to deliver a "solar-plexal swatting," Mary later recalled. "She ripped them all to pieces technically—no color in shadows—further outlines always meaningless—no care taken of edges of his work—unevenly studied." As painful as it was, Mary recorded every devastating word. Two friends accompanying Miss Keyes were mortified and tried to make polite amends. But Mary accepted no sympathetic noises. Her plan for securing Mrs. Gardner as an ally was ruined. "I didn't mention Mrs. Gardner—felt it would be useless, especially since Mrs. G. saw K. at Lady Gregory's and could have followed up his work had she been interested."[26]

She delayed for the next three days, and then she wrote him a fifteen-page letter. After writing it, she noted, "I miss him continually—and never felt lonelier than I do when I look at his pictures with someone indifferent to them—deaf to the imaginative call in them." But Kahlil's response was clear.

> All artists think that severe, unsympathetic critics are absolutely wrong. Now I do not think that Miss Keyes is wrong…She is a *slave* of the old accepted forms of expression—and slavery is not a vice; it is only a misfortune. She and I belong to two different worlds and we see art and life from two different points of view…I know…well what is wrong with my work and I am to trying to make it right—but Miss Keyes dose not know—and she thinks it is the technique. But I am almost sure that even when my style or technique becomes perfect Miss Keyes will not like my work. She is too old in flesh and too young in spirit to accept new forms and new thoughts…
>
> If I was a *famous* artist and Miss Keyes had read much about me and my work, she would not have dared to criticize the last three pictures and the series of drawings. Her fear of other people's opinion would have made her swallow her own thoughts! But I am unknown in this land, and people like Miss Keyes *must* try their wits on me…And as to exhibiting, you know I really have no body of work to show. I wanted to exhibit because there is always a chance of selling a picture or two. I am anxious to make my living one way or the other.[27]

Meanwhile Mary had asked Day to advise her on arranging an exhibit. But by then he was far removed from the art world, and her inquiry went unanswered. When she received Kahlil's letter, she was delighted by his response. However, she cautioned him about objective criticism and the value of a loyal soul who could respond to a work as a kind of devil's advocate.

> Miss Keyes is a Concord Soul—If the world think one thing, their unanimity makes the Concord Soul suspect this thing: and when the Concord soul differs from the world, the more it may suffer from expressing the difference, the more bound it

feels to express it. There is a noble side to this conceit—and Miss K. would criticize you not less loudly if you were famous, but more loudly. Believe this or not, at your will—it is true. Concords are rare—Miss Keyes is one of them.[28]

Mary had characterized Alicia Keyes as a "Concord Soul" because of her family's position in that historic town and their close ties with notable families there. As a child, Miss Keyes had lived with the Emerson family, had studied art with May Alcott, and her sister was Mrs. Edward Waldo Emerson. Coming from a homeland where contending with the views of notable families was daily fare, Kahlil's reply was undaunted.

I did not know that Miss Keyes paints. She never seemed like a painter to me—but if she realy insist on cutting out burnt siena, umbers, and ochers, I, too, will insist on saying that she never had a real pallete in her hand! And as to her being a Concord soul—Well—have I not known all the *Concord* souls in the Arabic world? Have I not fought them for the last seven years?[29]

That he at times could be proud and stubborn, or that he perceived her meanings in ways she did not intend, Mary could not deny. Even so, because of her partisan commitment to his future, she strove as best she could to become for him a level self and honest appraiser; in truth, his "Concord Soul."

~

The night before she departed for Thanksgiving in New York, Mary treated Marianna to dinner and the theater. Since Kahlil left, she had seen his sister at least once a week. This kind of caring made Marianna trust her, even to the point of letting Mary see where she lived. At the expiration of the West Cedar Street lease, Marianna had moved back to 15 Oliver Place. There she tried to forget her loneliness by sharing a tenement with her cousin Maroon and her husband Assaf George, and—spurred by Kahlil and Mary—by enrolling in classes at the Denison House. But the settlement house could not satisfy her. She complained that the "talk was trivial and stale that is meant to be elevating for the Syrian Club," and even Mary realized that what mattered to this woman—"so sincere, and so mediocre but *real*"—was simple survival.

I never knew a woman so passionately and consciously longing for the age-long woman work. "I have to take somebody to the hospital," she says…"to go to them when they're sick…and make their bed and wash them and fix their room and nightgown and cook for them. Oh I just love to do that."

Mary somehow was shocked when she finally saw Oliver Place: "It is a regular shabby slum." Marianna saw Mary off on the midnight train to New York with "tears raining from her eyes at Miss Teahan's brutality—heart wrung with longing to see Kahlil—and inexpressible messages to him. Her last words were resolutions to leave Miss Teahan—but I was not to tell Kahlil."[30]

That Mary perceived Kahlil's sister as so "*real*" but "mediocre," that she could be shocked by the conditions of poverty the Gibran family faced reveals inner distances concealed from the intimacy among them. It perhaps points to the price of opportunity and patronage that Kahlil had been pressed—and chosen—to pay.

~

In New York for four days, Mary stayed with Charlotte. Before Thanksgiving dinner, the two women eagerly visited the Tenth Street Studio—"such a personal old simple building with its low-arched wide black windows and the irregular reliefs in the white air-shaft." To try to understand Kahlil in his new setting, Mary naturally inspected everything: the "four candlesticks that light seems to melt upon…his tapestries from the Paris rag fair for a few francs…a hanging lamp—marvels of old iridescent Syrian glass—one plate of it hanging up and three small shelves of smaller pieces…[Oriental rugs] sent and lent by Mme. Kuri from Atlantic City."[31]

Marie el-Khoury—gem dealer, noted hostess, and sometime sponsor of Arabic literary efforts—was, along with Ameen Rihani, one of "a growing circle of friends." Thought to be the first Syrian woman in the U.S. to graduate from a university and to work as journalist, Marie contributed to the immigrant press. In 1902, at age nineteen, she married Esau el-Khoury, a journalist and publisher of *Al Da'ira al Adabiya* (*The Literary Circle*), who died two years later. Marie went to work in her father's Atlantic City jewelry shop, The Little Shop of T. Azeez, taking over the business after his death and rebuilding it despite fire and burglary. Eventually moving her boutique to Fifth Avenue, she was about to become one of the city's noted gem dealers, while she gained a reputation for her parties and sponsorship of Arabic literary efforts. Kahlil's early friendship with her continued throughout their careers.[32]

Mary hardly slept that weekend. They visited the Metropolitan Museum twice, she read the faces and hands of Charlotte's visitors, and they all went to the Hippodrome and watched "a wonderful Oriental world" of acrobats, elephants, and dancers. Drumming time to the music on her "contented arm," Kahlil mentioned how proud he was to see the Syrian dancers—"It could be done only in America." Then they went back to Charlotte's and sat up till three listening to her read her latest play.

Back in Boston, Mary became aware of a new dimension in their delicately balanced relationship when she received Charlotte's eleven-page letter devoted to Kahlil's friend, Rihani. He had recently returned from six months in Lebanon, bringing her a copy of his just-published *The Book of Khalid*, a long autobiographical tale of a Syrian antihero's wanderings in New York City and the Near East. From the moment Charlotte read the breezy picaresque adventures, she was taken by the author's work, which made her "*feel* Syria."

Kahlil, I think, will hardly reassure him on his work as I do, for one reason— Kahlil has not the lash of humor…and he will take Rihani for flippant when he is

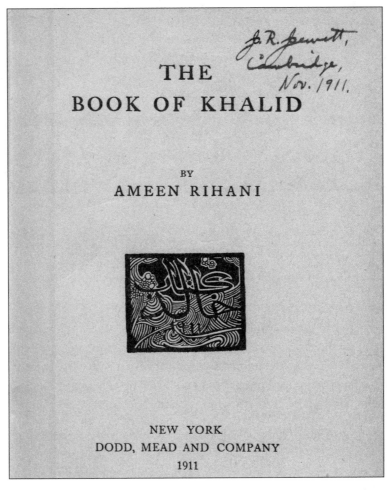

Kahlil's design for the title page of Ameen Rihani's *The Book of Khalid*. (Courtesy Houghton Library, Harvard University.)

Ink illustration by Kahlil from Rihani's *The Book of Khalid.*
(Courtesy Houghton Library, Harvard University.)

throwing his tortured body into a pool of mockery…He will probably never do the limpid work of Kahlil—although it is for clearness and simplicity I shall drive him along one trail, *Satire!!* If anyone knew how I believed in its destructiveness![33]

A century after Dodd, Mead and Company first published *The Book of Khalid,* Melville House Books reissued Rihani's book in 2011, calling attention to the scope and richness of Rihani's complex, sprawling, forward-looking saga—the book's hybrid mixture of "classical Arabic literary forms" and "Western literary conventions," its critical picture of immigration and of relations between the Middle East and the West, and its reflections on religious unity and conflict.

Told with great good humor and worldly compassion, and with illustrations by Kahlil Gibran, *The Book of Khalid* recounts the adventures of two young men, Khalid and Shakib, who leave Lebanon for the United States to seek their fortune in turn-of-the century New York. Together, they face all the difficulties of poor immigrants—the passage by ship, admittance through Ellis Island and the rough immigrant life. Khalid, always the dreamer, tries to participate in the political and cultural life of the teeming city—to often humiliating and comic result.

Tiring of their sojourn, he convinces Shakib they should return to Lebanon. But their heads are now full of New World ideas. And Khalid, trying to improve his brethren, turns his understanding of Western thought into a call for political progress, and religious unity and tolerance in the Arab world. A call that has him, accidentally, almost founding a new religion—and almost becoming its first martyr, when his ideas incite the faithful to riot.[34]

~

In Boston for the holidays, Kahlil and Mary, instead of talking about his work, mostly talked about the deepening relationship between Charlotte and Rihani. By early January 1912, however, Charlotte was already complaining that Rihani's attentions were draining her and that she had not been able to work. "There may be some great glorious fights ahead of those two yet," predicted Kahlil.

While Kahlil worked and sent dutiful notes on his progress, Charlotte became more involved with Ameen and sent rambling letters. Each letter from Charlotte, describing the intimacy between herself and Rihani, shook Mary's rational decisions against marriage, "I love K. yet age and homeliness would make me fearful to marry him even if he had means and desired it. I who have wept not during the struggle of these months to put marriage from my thoughts, showered tears last night."[35] On January 26, he sent her a copy of *The Broken Wings*, in which he had translated the chapter titles and his dedication to her. But other messages reflected unrest in New York. Kahlil, whose polite reserve prohibited "indiscretion," was beginning to resent the teetering Charlotte-Ameen relationship and the increasingly messy dynamic between friends that it created. He wrote, "In fact I don't see much of anybody. I feel rather funny with other people—even those whom I care for…Charlotte and Rihani are coming to see me this afternoon. I hope they will bring a different spirit with them…"[36] To Mary, Charlotte expressed conflicting emotions, colored by her perceptions of "Oriental reserve," an apparent dishonesty and lack of trust.

> Kahlil is openly disappointed tho' he is doing nobly to conceal the true human qualities of envy and criticalness…Kahlil feels…that I am not being true to my 'own true self'…Rihani is perfectly honest and outspoken but what Oriental is *frank*…Their reserves have, at times, the appearance of mendacity. And the unconsciously mendacious do not trust anyone…I only hope they won't ball each other up, for their friendship will have great value for each—and serve the world.[37]

Soon afterward "the inevitable misunderstanding" occurred. It led to Charlotte's rejection of Ameen, to outbursts on both sides, and to her vow to abandon writing and return to her family in Denver.

Mary hurried to New York and eventually turned her thoughts to her own relationship with Kahlil, which prompted an argument about who took the initiative in their friendship. Back at school the "upheaving talk" tore at Mary's nerves. Charlotte finally wrote, "Romance is throttled…I am giving up even the pretense of friendship with Rihani." Kahlil, who had tried to be loyal to both, also lost favor in Charlotte's eyes, and she urged Mary to reconsider her relationship with him.

In early March, Mary suggested to Kahlil a complete break. A break would imperil both their friendship and partnership, and Kahlil reassured Mary of his commitment to her. For the rest of the month he instead spoke with her of new acquaintances of his own. Artist Adele Watson, the collector Mrs. Alexander Morten, sculptor Ronald Hinton Perry, "Mrs. Benette, a society lady who writes poetry,"[38] and a Spanish count in the diplomatic service all came to his studio.

On April 3, Kahlil came to Boston intent on repairing the damages of the past months. Two days later they walked to the Public Garden and sat on a bench facing the pond. "We sat till after six—and our vital talk was on Kahlil's mind and habits in sex things." For the past two years she had stored a long list of impressions, capped by Charlotte's warning of his "inflammability," coupled with her scathing lumping together of him and Rihani as untrustworthy "Mohammedans." She confessed that she had never been able to reconcile rumors, given his "unifiedness and stability and fastidious reserve." He described his "physical reserve."[39] She was relieved. "I believe as he does that sex-relations except as regards health and scourge of children, are properly the affairs of the persons concerned—not of society."[40] For her, the dialogue "had changed the world." Mary introspectively concluded: "It wasn't marriage I had been longing for—but nearness."[41]

They came back to the school the next night after the Saturday symphony. There followed a scene which bothered Mary briefly but which continued to affect Kahlil for some time. He later told Mary:

> While we were spending the evening at Marlborough Street, the bell rang—It was your brother and his wife. You hesitated about letting them in—but decided to do so. There was a peculiar feeling about their finding me there and you felt very uncomfortable. When we met two days later you were still a good deal upset—And you said something about your brother's attitude toward me—that he would consider me in the light of such foreigners as you call dagos.

That finished me—And the very *next* time we met you were your very sweetest self—just as if nothing had happened. But with me something had happened. The man in me towards you had to change for self protection. But until I learned that, I couldn't work. I couldn't see friends normally—I couldn't be sane and keep going through what you continually were putting me through. And after awhile, I said to myself, "On any personal, intimate daily plane, relations with this woman are impossible. They must be restricted to the spirit…"[42]

When Kahlil returned to New York, his letters reflected this shift. He wrote Mary about meeting and drawing Abdul Baha and acting as an interpreter between the Persian religious visionary and some of his visitors.[43] Juliet Thompson, a portrait painter who lived directly opposite Kahlil's West Tenth Studio and knew him as a neighbor for many years, arranged the sitting for early in the morning of April 19. He drew Baha before a small group that grew to twenty-five or thirty people. Like others who watched the portrait take shape, Juliet Thomson was deeply moved by the way it revealed Baha's presence.[44] Decades later, Thomson remembered Kahlil as "very modest and retiring in his personal life" and as often with Baha in Boston.[45]

Kahlil's charcoal and graphite portrait of Abdul Baha, 1912. Facsimile reproduction. (Courtesy Private Collection.)

Work prevented Kahlil from coming to Boston on May 23 for Baha's speech to nine hundred people in a Greek-Syrian Relief Society gathering at the Denison House. He also regretted missing Baha's presence the next day as the honored speaker at an international conference sponsored by the Free Religious Association of America. Then on July 25, Baha again spoke in Boston, at the Victoria Hotel. Involved with these events were leaders with whom Kahlil would interact for the rest of his life.[46]

One speaker was Abraham Mitrie Rihbany, like Gibran and Rihani a Lebanese immigrant, who in his early years in the U.S. edited the Arabic language newspaper, *Kawkab Amirka* (*Star of America*). By 1911 he had settled in Boston as minister at Boston's Unitarian Church of the Disciples. A prolific writer, he became known for his autobiography *A Far Journey*, published in 1913, and for *The Syrian Christ*, published three years later.

Chairing the Boston symposium for Abdul Baha was John Haynes Holmes, then a prominent Unitarian minister who, like Baha, was a faith-based peace and social justice advocate. The eventual leader of New York City's Community Church, Holmes would become an enthusiastic supporter of Kahlil's work.

Also speaking on state and church in America at the Free Religious Association Conference was Dr. Charles Fleischer, whom Kahlil had met twelve years earlier through Josephine Peabody. Recognized at the Baha summer symposium as an "advocate of religious and political liberty," Fleischer left Temple Israel in 1911 to lead the Sunday Commons. His weekly sermons at Boston's Majestic Theater on Tremont Street, just two blocks from the Syrian South Cove enclave, attracted large audiences, and he would publish a provocative collection of his essays on faith and democracy, entitled *American Aspirations*.[47]

Meanwhile, Charlotte's interests had led her to the work of Carl Jung through her contact with Dr. Beatrice Moses Hinkle, recognized for her contributions to the field of public health. As early as 1904, Hinkle was publishing articles on psychoanalysis, and in 1908 she co-founded the first American psychotherapeutic clinic at Cornell Medical College. A widow of thirty-eight, she had just returned from Europe where she had met Carl Jung and attended the 1911 historic Weimar Congress. Although Charlotte would not remain in Kahlil's circle of friends, her friendships with intellectuals like Hinkle would continue to influence him in years to come.

~

When Kahlil and Mary saw each other in New York on September 7, 1912, the strains of the past months were fading. Physical intimacy was no longer a possibility between them. "When K. came there was no question even…and made me feel a thousand times more loved than ever before. He has shamed me out of my self-protectiveness."[48] For his part, he was learning how to cope with her intrusions, however well-intended. She chastised him for smoking too much and eating too little, and spoke of her plan for him to travel out west to recover his health. He refused. He was beginning to understand just how much closeness he could tolerate.

Charlotte's absence from Waverly Place forced Mary to rent a room near the studio at 25 West Eighth Street. When Kahlil and Mary had dinner at Charlotte's new place, they met her new friend, Gilbert Hirsch, a Harvard graduate and journalist eleven years younger than she. Then, after meeting Jung in New York and writing a long article about him for the *New York Times*,[49] Charlotte and Gilbert quietly married on October 16. They left for Europe the next day.

Kahlil would retain his closeness to both Mary and Rihani. But never again would he involve his New York colleagues and friends with Mary. As the relationship among the four broke up, Kahlil's life in New York was no longer dominated by the volatile friendship and rivalry among young artists. The intrigue and jealousy rising to such heights the past year had been dispelled.

Kahlil's distinctive hand and flame colophon, gold embossed on black cloth covers, would become his signature icon on his Borzoi Books published by Alfred A. Knopf. (Courtesy Alfred A. Knopf, Inc.; Reprint: George Lynde/Art Imaging.)

12

GROWING PARTNERSHIPS

As Kahlil began to recognize the decisive role that social contacts played in New York's art world, he struggled to adapt to his new environment. He wrote to Mary:

> New York is a strange place…It has its own technique in bringing a man out. It is to begin him socially and end him professionally. I want to begin professionally. But I can't change New York technique, and I don't feel the strength to combat it besides doing my work. So to a certain extent I accept it and am being known in the New York way.[1]

At issue was his financial dependence, which he perceived as being rooted in his émigré status. "Were I in Syria, my poetry would ensure notice to my pictures, were I an English poet, it would ensure them English notice. But I am between the two—and the waiting is heavy. I want to be independent—to have enough to fulfill my work—to help my sister and to entertain a friend."[2] Mary understood, but believed this dependence should be seen within a larger view.

> …Long after, looking back, one will see sweetness in this relation of guest and host, and know its core was good…realizing that he is choosing dependence for his work's sake which is dearer than independence…[3]

Mutual recognition and acceptance of their interdependence had taken eight years to realize. For their twelve remaining years, Mary not only sought to lessen Kahlil's discomfort over her patronage but encouraged him to bridge his disparate linguistic and intellectual worlds. Within four years, he would publish in English; within ten he would compose most of his work in it.

But even though she tried to act as his agent and to introduce his work to Americans, Mary was never quite successful. She was too instructive a personality—too unbending—to play matchmaker to artist and audience. Charlotte, with her instinct for the right introduction, was in fact responsible for his initial contacts in New York. But Charlotte was also aware of Mary's key role in his development. "Kahlil…has a big writer's work to show in concept and visions, but [it] has not grown in *vigor* as it should. How I long for your nurturing eye upon it…You *sustain*—your whole being is sustenance and maintenance!"[4]

French novelist Pierre Loti questioned Kahlil's dual pulls as an émigré artist. In the fall of 1912, he was in New York for the production of his play *The Daughter of Heaven*, written for actress Sarah Bernhardt. Kahlil described to Mary his reencounter with the writer whose work inspired Marcel Proust.

> Pierre Loti is here and I had a charming hour with him on Thursday. We talked about the East, "his beloved East." He said he saw my "Broken Wings" and other things and he ended by saying "You are becoming more brutal and less oriental—and it is too bad…"
>
> I told him that I loved my country too well to be like her other children. But he dose not see that…he is too delicate…He has all the *beautiful* Oriental diseases in his artistic soul…It makes me feel *good* to see such a dreamer of shadowy dreams. It makes me feel real to be with such an orientalized occidental.[5]

Loti's visit to the U.S. foundered. Within a month Kahlil wrote, "Pierre Loti is gone back to live in the shadow of some temple in the East…His last words to me were 'Now, Gibran, let me tell you in behalf of Syria that you must *save your soul* by going back to the East. America is no place for you!'"[6]

Mary would have financed a trip to France, or even to Lebanon, if Kahlil had asked. But work—not travel—satisfied him. After he had six teeth pulled in the fall of 1912, he declined her plans for him to recuperate in Vermont. A year later, sure that he was "a candidate for consumption," she carefully plotted a winter vacation in Bermuda for both him and Marianna. Although she took care of schedules, hotel reservations, and insurance, he again refused. "Please do not be angry with me," he wrote.

> When winter comes one wants to think and work—regardless of how one feels. And besides, I am naturally stupid about going to a *different place*. I always feel as though I am leaving my reality behind me. Even in the summer I love to stay where my pictures and books are.[7]

Slowly they worked out a formula: Boston, for holidays; New York, for the beginning and end of Mary's summer trips and for the Headmistress Association's November meetings. As this pattern became clearly defined, Mary rededicated herself to the school. The Haskell-Dean partnership had been dissolved in the spring of 1912, and she relished "the new freedom in having the reins again" in her hand. Said Mary, "My interest has come all to life again."

At first she contemplated buying a larger building to house a Montessori program for younger children. But she settled for remaining on Marlborough Street and broadening her philosophical goals. She evolved her own innovative approach to learning history, literature, and art through experience and weekly trips to local museums. "I think no school has done this before—using a real live museum. Watercolors, clay, embroidery: the children can use all these—Think how they will love it!"[8]

She saw her own contribution to progressive education as paralleling Kahlil's creative endeavors, and she tried to spell out their separate but equal roles in their partnership. They worked apart, but with special acknowledgment to each other. After she gave a speech to about a thousand public school children, she wrote, "A fourteen-year old boy yesterday reminded me of you—and we made friends straightway, with looking at each other and with my showing him once or twice that he knew what he thought he didn't know."

~

Their first visit after Charlotte's marriage came on November 9, when Mary journeyed to New York for the annual headmistress meeting. She spent a morning at the studio, noticing "the hum of the building and the movement" but also its inconveniences—the cramped quarters, the lack of central heating, the inadequate plumbing—"no hot water and twenty-five cents a bath."

> Today I caught…more vivid realization of how the twenty-four hours sound and feel…His rugs are never shaken…and the place looks dingier as months pass—but its spirit is so noble in the spare setting and so masculine and clear and labor filled. I feel a home likeness and a bachelordom at once—bareness, quietness, intense thought, life rubbed to the bone and loneliness.[9]

To Mary it seemed that Kahlil, nearing thirty, was losing his resilient, boyish looks. "K. ages very quickly. His face shows now so much strain and stress—shows privation and loneliness and burden and intensest concentrated effort." Each time they met they reviewed the events in their lives. Mary began by reciting school problems or what was happening to her family; he followed with accounts of his latest acquaintances in New York.

But since the spring of 1912, when Micheline had taken him to the Mortens' party, he had been learning to socialize more. Friendship with Alexander and Marjorie Morten was an important start. Later that year Charlotte observed, "Last night I dined at Mrs. Morten's and some of Kahlil's incense was burned, so I knew he had been there…Mrs. M. has money and taste and ought to be a good friend to him."[10] The Mortens were pioneering patrons of contemporary American art. Among their favorites were Arthur B. Davies, Albert Pinkham Ryder, and Childe Hassam.

Early in 1913, just before the Armory Show, Alexander Morten arranged for Arthur Davies to visit Kahlil's studio. As founder and president of the Association of American Painters and Sculptors, and prime organizer of that transformational exhibit, he was one of New York's most influential art patrons. Kahlil, who in Boston had been introduced to his work by the Rüyls, immediately sent Mary a joyful report.

> Mr. Davies kept repeating the word "wonderful" as he gazed at the paintings and drawings, then he said to Mr. Morten, "This man is going to surprise the world as he surprised me." And then he told me how sorry he is that he did not see my work a month ago—he said he would have asked me to send half a dozen pictures to the large exhibition which will open tomorrow…
>
> "But," he said, "I will see to your having an exhibition by yourself. I shall speak to Mr. MacBeth about it."
>
> Mr. Morten, who owns more of Davies' pictures than any other man in New York, said that he, too, will see MacBeth.
>
> Mr. Davies said, as he was leaving, "I want to see these things again and I hope you will come and see me—I am sure we are going to be great friends—In the meanwhile do not be anxious about exhibiting—that is quite secondary—the thing is to keep on working. And do not be like me—Here I am at the age of fifty and I have not done much—I have lost so much time fooling around!" The next day Mr. Morten said to me over the phone "I have never heard Davies speaking of anybody's work as he did of yours—you should feel very happy."[11]

That year Kahlil also got to know others through Charlotte. In the spring he met Carl Jung, who was visiting the city. Encouraged by Dr. Beatrice Hinkle, Jung visited his studio, where Kahlil drew a pencil portrait of him. Kahlil met several times with Jung, who invited him to Zurich. Jung's secretary also became interested in Kahlil's drawings, such as *The Valley of Delightful Dreams*. The philosopher Henri Bergson also agreed to have his portrait done if Kahlil were ever in Paris. Remaining close to Dr. Hinkle, he drew her portrait also, describing to Mary "her vitality, power and magnetism," adding, "She admires Jung immensely, and so do I."[12]

His own circle of friends and supporters was growing, as well. Meeting the Mortens led to his acceptance in the art world, and friendship with Dr. Hinkle introduced him to admirers of Jungian psychology. At the same time, Julia Ellsworth Ford, wife of hotel owner Simeon Ford, began to invite him to her Friday night literary dinners. Known for her children's books, and for her advocacy for global peace and the abolition of the opium trade, Ford provided a gathering point for poets and artists. Kahlil formed endur-

Charcoal and watercolor portrait of Carl Jung, around 1913. (Courtesy C. G. Jung Foundation for Analytical Psychology, New York. Reprint: George Lynde/Art Imaging.)

ing friendships with several American writers at her dinners, among them Witter Bynner, former editor of *McClure's Magazine* and peripatetic poet, who would play an important role in his career.

Yet he told Mary that no one knew him as well as she did, and in terms of his origins, clearly this was so. Oliver Place and its privations were far from the image perceived and encouraged by admirers. His identity among his friends in New York was based less on his personal history as an immigrant adolescent, who advanced through practice, training, along with apprenticeship, patron interest, and the good faith and support of caring colleagues. Instead, perceptions of him sprang from his arrival in New York as a Levantine newcomer with an unknown past, cosmopolite, fluent in Arabic, English, and French, artistically precocious, and intent on building a future.

When speculation arose about his source of income, he would tell Mary about people's conjectures. Mrs. Ford's comments were typical. "I'd like to help that young man," she said. "Has he any money? Where does he get it from? I'm afraid of him. I don't even dare ask him the price of a picture."[13] To be the secret source of his support appealed to Mary, and in February 1913, a letter from him caused her to contribute even more solidly.

> There is a chance of my getting a fine, large studio here in this building [51 West Tenth Street]. It is three times as large as mine and it has north light, south light (sunshine) and skylight—very cheerful and very good for work. The rent is forty-five dollars! Now I have been debating with myself for the last few days and I do not know what to do! I shall have to spend some money to make the place look nice and clean—about fifty dollars. May I take it if they would let me have it?

His words pained her, and she deliberated her next move. "May I take it?...That made me think with fire and sword in my heart...K. would never fulfill himself until he could be free at last."[14]

Thus she proposed an "arrangement," an advance to Kahlil of one thousand dollars toward what they would call the Haskell-Gibran Collection. With this newest gift, she proposed that all her former "loans" to him be canceled. In turn, she would receive ten of his paintings (by June he suggested that the total be fourteen). These pictures were to be chosen "according to intrinsic merit and to representativeness of development." Taking into account the amount of canceled loans and the frugal measures required of her to help Kahlil and her other protégés, this arrangement confirmed Mary's confidence in her talented friend. She also decided to transfer some securities to him to "carry him through until he is independent."[15]

Kahlil was relieved and grateful to move to the larger living and work space.

> Putting aside the physical comfort, I know it will mean very great deal to the work.[16] Humanity is afraid of the work of a starving artist who lives in a "dark little hole." *Respectable* people, and it does not matter how broad they are, can never really be themselves save in respectable places! To be a victim of the respectability of people is a fine thing from the *artistic* point of view—but somehow, Mary, it is not in me to be a victim of anything or anybody.

Mary's savings were constantly strained to accommodate her generosity. That year she estimated her share of the income from her and her brother Tom's Washington State orchards to be between $2,000 and $3,000, but with Miss Dean's departure, profits from the current school year were lean. A modest bequest from her father's estate supplemented her income but in no way justified her largesse. A year before, at Charlotte's suggestion, Mary began to send another immigrant teenager—Jacob Giller, a Russian-Jewish youth from New York City—to Mount Hermon. By 1913, though her payments to Charlotte and Micheline had ceased, she was responsible for two tuitions at Mount Hermon, was continuing to aid Aristides Phoutrides, and had just endowed Kahlil with a stock portfolio. Their newest financial arrangement allowed Kahlil to increase his production not only of paintings and portraits but of his written work.

~

Ongoing was his commitment to his Temple of Art series. In September 1912, he had drawn playwright Alice Bradley, and six months later, Sarah Bernhardt.

French stage and film actress Sarah Bernhardt. Charcoal, 1913. (Courtesy Peter A. Juley / Smithsonian.)

> The drawing which I made of her yesterday, though it does not show her *real age*, is a great success. But if I am to go through the same process with the rest of the great men and women, I might as well give up art and become a diplomate! She wanted me to sit at a distance so that I may not see the *details* of her face. But I *did* see them. She made me take off some of the wrinkles. She even asked me to change the shape of her…mouth!…I think I understood her yesterday—and I behaved accordingly, and perhaps that is the reason why she liked me a little![17]

Another subject in the series was Giuseppe Garibaldi II. Kahlil had discussed the idea of Garibaldi leading a regiment of Syrian emigrants to overthrow the Turkish yoke. In the spring of 1912, he met and drew the grandson of the Italian general and nationalist at Mrs. Ford's. A figure much admired in the mahjar press, Garibaldi was praised by editor and publisher 'Afifa Karam, of *Al-Aam al Jadid al-Nis'i* (*The New World for Women*) for his participation in the First Balkan War against the Ottomans.

Karam, who arrived to the United States as a young bride, had established herself as a talented novelist. From 1906 to 1910, *Al-Hoda* published three of her

Italian revolutionary Giuseppe Garibaldi II (1879–1950) was admired in the Syrian immigrant press for volunteering to support popular uprisings around the world. Charcoal, 1912. (Courtesy Peter A. Juley / Smithsonian.)

'Afifa Karam, pioneering Lebanese-American journalist, novelist, translator, and publisher/editor of Al-Aam al-Jadid al-Nis'i (The New World for Women). Photo from The Noble Sentiments, 1924. (Courtesy Khayrallah Center for Lebanese Diaspora Studies.)

novels: *Badi'a wa Fu'ad* (*Badi'a and Fu'ad*); *Fatima al-Badawiyya* (*Fatima the Bedouin*), 1908; and *Ghadat 'Amhseet* (*The Girl of 'Amsheet*). They soon were heralded in Near Eastern literary circles as among the first modern Arabic novels. Like Kahlil's early work, 'Afifa railed against governmental and religious oppression. Central to her message was a call to liberate women from the yoke of subservience through education and dialogue. She coupled this spirit with a willingness to entertain her Arab readers by translating popular American best sellers, and even a French romance. Because of her productivity, New York became among Syrians a "center of female literary production."[18]

Kahlil's own output was dampened by his desire to actively serve his homeland, as reports of war and unrest in the Middle East grew. Still he balanced work with dreams of an independent Syria.

~

During the busy spring of 1913, he urged Mary to see the Armory Show—or, as it was officially called, the International Exhibition of Modern Art. After its sensational reception in New York and Chicago, it had traveled to Boston, abbreviated to include only European selections. Mary identified with the new spirit and immediately wrote Kahlil about her visit to Copley Society's Hall where she was inspired by the work of European artists like Redon, Brancusi, and Gauguin. Although she complained about Boston's weak reception of the avant-garde show, she assured Kahlil that she was planning to introduce him to the New York artists associated with it. By the end of the day, she had made friends with the show's principal organizer, Walter Pach, an art historian publicly acknowledged as a respected adviser to collectors of modern art. Inviting Pach back to the school for supper, she and the critic established a rapport. Later that week, she joined him in a visit to the Mount Vernon Street studio of Maurice Prendergast, whose paintings had been included in the Armory's American exhibit but had not traveled to Chicago and Boston.[19]

Partially in defiance of Alicia Keyes's rejection of his work, and hoping to involve him in this exciting movement, she shared with Kahlil her enthusiasm.

> And how indignant the Modern Exhibit makes me with the art teachers here!…
> But truly…after my experience with people there this afternoon, I believe I could
> go daily into that exhibit, and single-handed start a tide that would in time rise
> above the heads of…Keyes and Co., and save Boston several years of waiting to see
> the human value of this work.[20]

"I am so glad you liked the International Exhibition of Modern Art," he replied.

> It is a revolt, a protest, a *declaration of Independence*…The pictures, individually, are
> not great: in fact very few of them are beautiful. But the Spirit of the Exhibition
> as a whole is both beautiful and great. Cubism, Impressionism, Post Impressionism
> and Futurism will pass away. The world will forget them because the world is always
> forgetting minor details. But the spirit of the movement will never pass away, for it
> is real—as real as the human hunger for freedom.[21]

When they met in New York the third week in June 1913, he explained his interests in the new painters.

> Matisse knew he could not do anything beyond mediocre in the great current of
> painting—too intelligent to hope against hope about it—so worked out for himself
> a self-expression in the decorative way which has much excellence. That was a big
> thing to do…the Cubists too cannot satisfy themselves in the great current of paint-
> ing…they have had the cleverness, the acumen to work out a new expression which
> is independent of grades as pictures are not. Pictures are good, poor, or mediocre.
> The *Nude Descending the Staircase* is neither poor, mediocre nor good; it is different.

Of his favorites, he thought that Davies was "in a beautiful garden, full of strange forms, beautiful forms, exquisite and delicate and strong forms." Redon "has a mind and has greatness—he grasps widely, inclusively—but not completely—lacks earth the mineral." Gauguin he considered "the most interesting of the others…(other than Redon)." He liked best "his 'golden panel'…and the *Tahitians on the Rosy Sand*."[22]

Mary determinedly followed this talk with a call to Walter Pach, who invited her to lunch the following day. She met all the members of the Association of American Painters and Sculptors, and toured Davies's studio. "All these men are wrapped up in what they are doing and the love of every detail of their work. I think they will not care for K.'s—it will seem too 'simple' and 'undeveloped,' 'thin,' *to them*(!)."[23]

Two days later, she brought Pach to Gibran's studio. Neither man was particularly impressed with the other. When Pach left and she berated Kahlil for his "air of superiority," he refused to accept her criticism. Observed Mary, "If it was childish and contemptuous, he would still stand for it; it was his. Once or twice he answered me as he had answered Pach…he seemed unable to stick to the exact issue—excited and troubled." She had never heard him this way before, and they argued until she became aware of his extreme tension. "K. had seemed so nervous…And I had the roughness to tell that to K. in the course of our talk."[24] Finally, she relented.

~

By the time Mary next visited New York on August 29, 1913, he had escaped the city three times, visiting friends in Vermont and Marianna in Boston. A week spent at the Japanese-style estate of the Alexander Tisons in Denning, New York, left an impression. Tison was a lawyer who had taught for several years at the Imperial University in Tokyo. The house and gardens were Kahlil's first taste of luxurious American country living. Although Mary thought he looked older, "his first holiday for years" had exhilarated him. "One can live a hundred years in one moment of life in certain lovely places," he told her.[25]

But within two days, Mary began again to question him about making contacts with wealthy people. "I spoke out in irritation…said the rich had a chance at all artists through riches; the poor and the professional had no chance for lack of riches… It was through money, I said, that I too had happened to be able to keep connection with him." The ensuing scene nearly ended their arrangement. According to Mary, Kahlil wanted her to tell him why she had given him the money so that he could know where he stood. Was it a gift…a loan? Was it intended to create a bond between them? Either way, he would adjust. Whatever her expectations, he would try gladly to meet them. But he couldn't stand the uncertainty and not knowing. Mary had "said opposite things with equal earnestness," and he couldn't tell which one she really meant. It had been "one of the hardest things of [his] life."[26]

After dinner, Mary apologized.

If ever I trouble you again as I did about money—just cut me off. You've given me chances enough. If I'm so dense and so careless and can so hurt you, it is not worthwhile to stick to me…And I shan't complain if you tell me. I know justice when I see it and I'm willing for justice. And I know mercy too—when it is shown me.

She was sure that he would forgive and forget. "I believe he has no hanging to a past grief or injury."[27]

But just as he had continued to recall the night when Adam and Nattie Haskell had surprised them and commented about his Middle Eastern background, he brooded about this scene for almost a decade. Nine years later, he acknowledged to Mary that their arguments about money had troubled him a lot.

When you were in New York another time, and we were walking home from Gonfarone's one night you said it was the fact that you had given me money that kept the bond between us. That night I made up my mind to raise the full sum of money that I'd received from you and send it to you and I set about it the next day—and the matter was going nicely—you had meanwhile gone back to Boston when I had a letter from you. It was the loveliest letter, so dear, so near…that I felt again, "how can you receive such kindness from a soul and then make such a return as you are planning to make her?"[28]

If Mary had recognized the degree of Kahlil's concern with the dynamics of her sponsorship, the upheaval of the next two days may have been averted. She went the following day to be drawn by Davies. At his studio, he unexpectedly asked her to pose nude. She was surprised, but not shocked. "It seemed wholly impersonal… we arranged that I should bring Kahlil at three the next afternoon, and I went."[29] When she told Kahlil about posing, he reacted protectively. "In some ways you are very ignorant about the world," he told her."[30] Although they did visit Davies the next day, Mary's plans for the older artist to continue endorsing Kahlil's work were mostly unsuccessful. Not only was Davies "brusque," but he refused to sit for the Temple of Art series.[31]

~

Mary's tenuous role of supportive sponsor and close friend would shift to that of collaborative assistant, hastening Kahlil's commitment to the use of the English language for his work. The turning point came when, three weeks after their latest skirmish, he sent her some lines he had composed in English.

From "The Diary of a Madman"—Last night I invented a new pleasure. And as I was giving it the first trial, an Angel and a Devil came rushing toward my house. They met at my door and fought with one another over my newly created pleasure. The one crying "It is a sin," the other "It is a vertue." Now, Mary, will you not translate this into English![32]

Ever since his return from Paris, she had heard about *The Madman*. In June 1911, she had noted, "K. G. is writing the 'Madman' in English." A year later she inserted into her journal some lines from Stephen Crane's *The Black Riders*.

In the desert I saw a man, naked, bestial, crouching upon the ground—who held his heart in his hand and ate of it. "Is it good?" I said to him. "It's bitter," he said, "bitter, but I like it because it is bitter—and because it is my heart."[33]

First published by Copeland & Day in 1895, it is possible that the poem had haunted Kahlil for years.

If Crane's lines were for Kahlil an early literary source on madness, his personal concern sprang from witnessing the cruel, medieval treatment of the insane in Lebanon. As late as the twentieth century, the *mejnun*—"possessed by a jinn"—were considered to be the Church's responsibility. Priests were in charge of exorcising evils from troubled minds and hearts. Kahlil's memory of visiting a monastery madhouse had led him to appreciate the innate wisdom of society's outcasts.

In Syria, madness is frequent. There has been much contemplative life there for… hundreds of years—and it results…sometimes in extreme nervousness; sometimes in madness; sometimes in just apparent idleness; sometimes in wonderful wisdom…

At a monastery in Syria…[they] had a little madhouse there and…people were brought from even far away in the country. They treated them badly—but somehow they made them well. One day I was at this monastery and the monk who was talking with me said they had a madman from the mountains…As we came near we heard chains and then he appeared. He came straight to us—and he had one of the most remarkable human faces I ever saw.

Just about that time there was a great dispute going on in that part of the world about the Song of Songs. The Church held that it was a mystic symbol of Christ and that the Church was the beloved. And others held that the Song was pure poetry. As the Madman came up to us he called out: "Kahlil Gibran! Go and tell…that Solomon loved a real woman as you and I would—I myself know the Shulamite very well."

Then he went away and did not come back.

Again, in another incident, Kahlil expressed his identification with the insane.

> Once when I was riding with a companion we came upon [someone] who was well known in all the country round as mad but harmless. It was the time of year when all the people were busy, getting in the harvests. But he was standing on a rock—twenty or thirty feet above the road—where we were riding…I called out, "What are you doing there?" "I'm watching Life," he said. "Is that all?" said my companion. "Isn't that enough?" said he. "Could you do better? I am extremely busy. I have spoken." I was thrilled through and through.[34]

With those few lines in English, Kahlil had ventured into territory that Mary had hoped for. As much as she admired his Arabic writings, she was unable to be part of that aspect of his creativity. Together, they had occasionally tried to translate his poems, but the results were never publishable. For a while she had thought that the problem would be solved if she learned Arabic in order to translate his work, but by 1913 she realized this was impossible. Her goals of studying alone in the mountains or of traveling someday to Turkey or Syria were equally unrealistic. Laboring to learn English, he had progressed through many stages. Although his speech and writing were less flawed than when he had first met her in 1904, he still needed assistance with pronunciation, fluency, and colloquial vocabulary.[35]

Mary prepared a tutorial program that worked two ways. First, she helped him compose, in English, letters to artists and performers for potential sittings. Gradually, most of the serious spelling and grammatical errors almost disappeared, but she felt that even his brief letters to her were stilted in expression. "He is a silent person and has the masculine desire to write little—his expression in letters is so meager compared to his speech. He is a *talker* on general art subjects with me but not a *writer* on anything."[36]

But perhaps Mary's more important contribution was discussing literature with him. Because he had always been a voracious reader, it was easy to interest him in her favorites. One was Nietzsche. Kahlil's affinity for him had developed ever since he was a youth of twelve or thirteen, and he was infatuated with the philosopher's style rather than every aspect of his thought. "[He] agrees with Nietzsche's conception of returning cycle[s] of identical experience…The return will be always in different form." As Kahlil put it, "Spring returns but no two springs are alike."[37]

Pulling Kahlil away from themes and contemplations of his childhood and forebears were complex Western influences.

> Wagner, Nietzsche, Ibsen, Strindberg, Dostoyevsky, Andreyev, Tolstoy ("though personally his work is not agreeable to me…")—Maeterlinck, Renan, Anatole France,

Rodin and Carrière of course, and the greatest, Carpenter ("though I can't read him any longer"), Walt Whitman ("though there is a great deal in Whitman that I don't care for") and William James.[38]

With Mary he began to share in her intellectual discoveries. "Montessori is epochal," he stated. Mary sent him Symonds's translation of Michelangelo's sonnets, to which he gratefully responded, "There is something in these sonnets of Michael Angelo— something that moves me as no other thing does. Perhaps they would have moved me much less if they [were] writen by someone else: but this is a case where it is so hard to divide between the man and his work."

If she was unable to send him an especially inspiring book, she would sit up till dawn copying lines of poetry. She did this in April 1913, when she wrote out six pages of poems by the metaphysical poet Thomas Traherne. This devotion to Kahlil's education triggered her own creative spirit. "Personally, I've no impulse to creative expression—but to appreciative expression—Yes! I long to make known my joy to its sources—to God and you—I want your hand and His on my heart, that you may hear its extremity of speech."[39]

Kahlil's period of intensive English-language study was coming to a close when he asked Mary to "translate" his lines on "a new pleasure." The couple would continue to talk about writers and writings, but their conversations would not be so purposefully directed to his education. At the same time, her suggestions were moving more toward contemporary authors, such as the *Song Offerings* of Rabindranath Tagore. In November 1913, she asked him to read William English Walling. This old and brilliant friend, the brother-in-law of her sister Frederika Walling, was to her the ideal of the complete thinker. Social reformer and historian of Russia before the revolution, he was "a spirit like the North Star and honester than day or the surgeon's knife." Kahlil enjoyed his book *Larger Aspects of Socialism*, especially the chapter on "Nietzsche and the New Morality," and wrote Mary, "I, too, have been reading a good deal about socialism. To me it is the most interesting human movement in modern times…It is a mighty thing and I believe it will go through many changes before it becomes a form of government."[40]

Mary had been instrumental in Kahlil's survival on many different levels.

We talked more frankly and fully than ever before about the suffering of our lesser selves in the money relation—mine because it is a barrier to the sort of love I want, his because he is not sure I shall have enough in my years to come and is sure I deprive myself now…We both see that apropos to the collection, our course is absurd commercially for we change so constantly…*I think* money heartaches are probably nearly over for us…for it *is* simply just the working out of our inner partnership, which we discover more and more fully as we grow towards our larger selves that are so at one."[41]

If their physical and social relationships had failed, their partnership of ideas had been renewed. Mary's journal reflected this change. In October 1913, she abruptly ended her more intimate diary. Perhaps she stopped recording the personal events of her day because she was weary of details, or perhaps during an attack of painful neuritis that fall she was tired. The closing lines were wistful and sad: "*Back* in *school*—Everybody so *Lovely*—lay down in P.M. No energy or strength."[42]

~

In the midst of his growing involvement with the art and literary scene in a rapidly changing New York City, the first issue of *Al-Funun* (*The Arts*) was published in April 1913. Its presence in New York reflected a collective effort by Syrian emigrant writers to create and publish an inclusive, nonsectarian periodical devoted to both

Key figures in the Arab immigrant press and literary field in America: (from *left*) Nasib Arida, Kahlil Gibran, Abd al-Massih Haddad, and Mikhail Naimy. (Courtesy Museo Soumaya.)

Eastern and Euro-American literature and art. Jumpstarting a key period in Kahlil's growth, it was edited by the poet Nasib Arida, whose scholarly background included Russian language and literature. *Al-Funun* also enjoyed the editorial assistance of Nazmi Nasim, Raghib Mitraj, and eventually Mikhail Naimy.

A feature of *Al-Funun* was its publication in Arabic of works by Russian authors, such as Leonid Andreyev, Anton Chekhov, and Maxim Gorky, along with Arabic translations of pieces by other prominent writers, including Heinrich Heine, Victor Hugo, Maurice Maeterlinck, Friedrich Nietzsche, Rabindranath Tagore, Walt Whitman, and Oscar Wilde. Although many of these translations were unsigned, it seems likely that Kahlil suggested, and perhaps translated, works by several of his favorites.

Linoleum block for printing Kahlil's hand and flame colophon, around 1913. (Reprint: George Lynde/Art Imaging.)

Kahlil's thirty-eight literary works and seventeen signed drawings, along with several unsigned decorations, resulted in his unofficial designation as "resident artist."[43] The inclusion in *Al-Funun* of paintings by George Watts, Arnold Böcklin, Eugene Carrière, and Albert Ryder, though not credited to Gibran, reflects his interests and style. Often appearing on the magazine's title page and cover was a version of the distinctive hand and flame that would eventually become Kahlil's signature icon.

Along with Kahlil's frequent drawings, *Al-Funun* published several illustrations and designs by Ephraim Moses Lilien, a Polish artist whose art-nouveau approach echoed Kahlil's. Lilien's drawings and prints, often depicting Jewish scribes and prophets in traditional Middle Eastern dress, were associated with his several trips to Palestine during the early twentieth century.[44]

Kahlil's contributions to *Al-Funun* fueled his work and raised his profile as a writer, artist, and thinker. Several of his pieces became the nucleus for his "Madman" writings. The magazine faced three interruptions due to paper shortages, the inability of immigrant readers to pay for subscriptions, and labor shortages over its life span of twenty-nine issues between 1913 and 1918.[45] But Kahlil's role decisively affected his reputation within the emerging Arab-American intellectual community.

~

Ironically, it was this "Easternness" that seemed to fascinate many in New York and that gained him proximity to successful partnerships in the art world. He attended the opening of Percy MacKaye's play *A Thousand Years Ago* as a guest of the Fords. Among the party in the box were Ruth St. Denis and the MacKayes. Within weeks, he added the dancer and the playwright to his Temple of Art series.

> I made a few little drawings of her while she was moving…in her fine, large studio…Miss St. Denis is *many persons* besides a wonderful dancer. She knows how to listen and she knows how to receive. People do not like her because she does not tolerate their stupidity. They call her queer because she lives her own life.[46]

Gradually the people he met at Julia Ellsworth Ford's Friday night gatherings began to recognize his talent. Percy MacKaye, known for his popular pageants, used his portrait as the frontispiece to a special edition of his masque, *St. Louis*. Kahlil's favorite among this group was Judge Thomas Lynch Raymond, a bibliophile and art-minded scholar who soon would be elected mayor of Newark, New Jersey. While drawing Raymond in 1914, Kahlil was fascinated as he listened to him describe the problems of a fast-growing city. That spring, Raymond began to invite Kahlil to his Newark home, and he suggested that since Kahlil was having trouble finding a New York gallery, he could arrange a

Graphite sketch of American modern dance innovator Ruth St. Denis, 1914. (Courtesy Peter A. Juley / Smithsonian.)

Portrait of Thomas L. Raymond, mayor of Newark, New Jersey. Graphite, 1919. (Courtesy Collection of the Newark Museum 32.160. Gift of Mary Haskell Minis, 1932.)

show for him at the Newark Library-Museum. It was not to be, but the news buoyed Mary.

Even old friends and acquaintances turned up at Mrs. Ford's that spring. Kahlil encountered W. B. Yeats, still with that "sad, sad look in his dim eyes."[47] He was happy that Yeats had remembered their earlier Boston talk, and this time they talked about Tagore. At the end of February, he saw a far more familiar face— Josephine Peabody Marks, now the proud mother of two, who had come to New York for literary and poetry events. They saw each other at Percy MacKaye's production of *A Bird Masque* at the Hotel Astor.

Ties with Charlotte and Micheline were not yet completely broken, either. By 1914, Charlotte and her husband had shared an exciting year and a half in England, Germany, and France. They had spent time with Yeats, and in Paris had learned of Leo and Gertrude Stein and Marsden Hartley. Micheline had continued her romance with the lawyer Lamar Hardy. In 1914, he was appointed special counsel to the recently elected Mayor John Mitchell of New York, and she also became friends with the Mitchells. By April, Kahlil had visited her twice. "A recent evening with Micheline...She kept on talking of the Mitchells. Told me how to make money—to draw this big man—and then his friends will want to be drawn."[48] A few months before her marriage to Hardy, Micheline wrote to Mary:

> How changed he is—his face has no longer that indefinable expression made of illusions, of longings and hopes for a radiant future...that only belong to Youth! He is a man now, a man that life has touched with a little cynicism, or rather bitterness. The boy in him appealed to me tremendously, Mary, the man in him brings to my heart a vague feeling of fear. How foolish, is it not?[49]

~

Gradually Kahlil became expert at balancing his several worlds. In January 1914, hopes for a New York show of Kahlil's work were raised when Alexander Morten brought William Macbeth to his studio. But although the work greatly interested the art dealer, the verdict that Kahlil relayed to Mary was disappointing. "Mr. Mackbeth will not exhibit my pictures…he cannot see his way to showing so many nude figures to the public." A bout with depression accompanied the rejection. "No, beloved Mary, I am not ill. I am simply tired out…But it will not last long. I think the end of this winter will bring the beginning of calmer and freer life…I shall try to live my own life and not that of 'an interesting young man from the East.'"[50]

By June of 1914, Kahlil's progress with his painting and drawing was eclipsing his previous work in Boston. He had continued to write for *Al-Funun*, but the magazine temporarily ceased publication. His latest book, *Dam'a wa Ibtisama* (*Tears and Laughter*), a retrospective anthology of his youthful poems, parables, and stories— "the first zephyr of my life's tempests"—was published by Nasib Arida. In August, he gave the initial copy to Mary, "the noble spirit who loves the zephyrs and runs with tempests." But he had begun to feel distant from his earlier writings. "Love and Death and Beauty…it's all full of that…I don't like this book now."[51]

What interested him more was that his faithful friend Alexander Morten had at last brought to the studio art dealer N. E. Montross, who promised him a show in his gallery on Fifth Avenue. When he saw Mary on her way west that June, he was able to tell her that their financial arrangement appeared finally to be paying off. Morten had suggested that Kahlil's work could be priced at fifteen hundred dollars, or twice the value that Kahlil and Mary had agreed upon for each painting. With the exhibit set for December, Kahlil and Mary now spent their time together planning for it, and working on *The Madman*.

Charcoal and graphite drawing for Montross Gallery exhibition, 1914. (Courtesy Peter A. Juley / Smithsonian.)

13

WORK MADE VISIBLE

Kahlil had read some of *The Madman* in English at Judge Raymond's, where Rose O'Neill especially had been moved by it. Formerly married to Harry Leon Wilson, novelist and editor of the humor and political satire magazine *Puck*,[1] the talented artist was at the apex of her career as one of the world's highest paid magazine illustrators and the designer of the Kewpie doll. That whimsical figure was sweeping the country and making a fortune for its creator. Rose and her sister Callista welcomed Kahlil to their Greenwich Village salon in Washington Square, and later to the Carabas Castle in Westport, Connecticut.

An ardent feminist, Rose's true love was painting. Along with marching in women's suffrage rallies and designing ads of Kewpies sampling Jell-O, she studied painting and considered Kahlil's work important to her Pre-Raphaelite style. Years later, she recalled his paintings that "seemed in twilight; nude figures representing strange things, lovers leaning together...a centaur carrying off a woman...His black-and-white drawings were most thrilling—exquisite faces with delicate shadows running to the corner of the curved lip such as Leonardo dreamed about."[2] That summer she created a wash drawing of Gibran with a shock of unruly hair and brooding stare. Her 62 Washington Street studio was "his favorite house for a time," along with Leonora Speyer's place nearby.[3] As well as entertaining painters, O'Neill also mingled with poets like Witter Bynner, Edward Arlington Robinson, and Amy Lowell. It was no coincidence that by 1922, her first book of poetry, *The Master-Mistress*, illustrated with her "Sweet Monsters," appeared in New York under the imprint of up-and-coming young publisher Alfred Knopf.

Although Mary noted Kahlil's friendship with O'Neill, her journal did not reflect the colorful personalities of his growing circles, but mentioned them to chronicle his continuing progress with his art and writing. The journal now was more devoted to their own collaboration on *The Madman*. She liked his latest

Portrait of artist, illustrator, and creative catalyst Rose O'Neill, by noted American photographer Gertrude Käsebier, 1907. (Courtesy Library of Congress.)

Rose O'Neill's portrait of Kahlil, from her "Sweet Monsters" series. Graphite and wash watercolor, 1914. (Courtesy Smithsonian American Art Museum, Renwick Gallery. Gift of the Smithsonian Women's Committee, in memory of Adelyn Dohme Breeskin.)

pieces even more than the earlier ones. Remarked Kahlil,

I am always doing the same thing in my Madman, from many points of view. He is destroying veils and masks and laughing at absurdities, and exposing folly and falseness and stupidity and cowardice—and always saying I am here, I am there, I am everywhere, I am now. I am life.[4]

Sometimes he saved special problems for them to solve together. About the parable that would become "The Greater Sea," he sought her advice.

"I want to add another type of foolishness to the people in the Madman and Soul seeking a place to bathe," said K. "I have six and I want seven— the saint, the realist, the philosopher, the scholar—somebody. I think I'll take the saint." Then he…chose the realist…he should be listening to the conch shells and calling it the sea.[5]

They evolved a system. "He dictates and I write, because my spelling is quicker and surer," noted Mary. "When we are not satisfied with an expression, we make tries at it until we get it…He gets it oftener, I think, than I. But when he has completed a thing before I hear it, there is little or no change needed." Mary acknowledged:

K.'s English is remarkable—has a final quality that I for instance could

Kahlil at work in his studio on West Tenth Street in New York. (Courtesy Private Collection.)

not get if I were translating from his original—Simply a structure occasionally wrong. And this three pages of Night and The Madman he wrote off in less than an hour…It will not be long before he will be so a master of English that he need look nothing over with anybody…And his English prose is poetry-prose—"the voice of a voice" is in it…he does not mind the English seeming as if a foreigner did it.[6]

They decided to wait until after the upcoming Montross exhibition to find a publisher for *The Madman*. Kahlil finished three large drawings, four paintings, and added a drawing of Marjorie Morten to the portrait series. In a letter, Mary exclaimed to him, "And now!—New York—and so much more, already!"[7] Yet while overwhelmed by the upcoming exhibit and the possibility of significant publicity, Kahlil was looking forward to starting new work. Just before the opening, he was addressing invitations and wrote her:

I have finished those pictures…They belong to my past. I shall only use them as a means. My whole being is directed toward a fresh start. This exhibition is the end of a chapter.[8]

Kahlil's show at the Montross Gallery on Fifth Avenue opened on Monday, December 14, 1914. The day before the opening, an article in *The Buffalo Times* did not review the Montross exhibit but instead published a major article on Kahlil's views on the women's movement. Marguerite Mooers Marshall, who had once reviewed Ameen Rihani's *The Book of Khalid*[9] and was soon to become known for her "The Woman of It" columns, was the author. She led her interview with three humorous cartoons, his photo, and an image of his painting captioned, "Gibran's 'The Great Solitude' symbolic of the 'oneness' of mankind."

> An interesting figure in the Western world of arts and letters…as versatile as a Renaissance genius…We were talking in the corner of Mr. Gibran's deep workman-like studio. He is not one of the artists who prefer atmosphere to easel space. Even he himself refuses to look obtrusively picturesque…a slight, graceful, courteous man in a conventional sack suit, with silkily black hair and mustache, olive skin and excellent if somewhat slow-spoken English. "A man's

Buffalo Times cartoon illustration of Kahlil's views on the women's movement, December 15, 1914.
(Courtesy Buffalo History Museum Research Library. Reprint: George Lynde/Art Imaging.)

mind goes this way," and he thrust five supple fingers forward in an uncertain zig-zag gesture. "A woman's mind goes like this," and the hand moved in a swift, straight line, to its imaginary goal. "The man usually gets there in the end, but it takes so much longer...[10]

Mary came to New York five days later. As Kahlil escorted her through the gallery, Mary observed his demeanor. "I feel him sensitive at every pore, with people—as if raw edges were being touched...I understand why he says it takes him three hours to get back to himself and his own 'quiet life' after one hour with people." After reviewing the familiar series of portraits—Rodin, Debussy, Rochefort, Rostand, Abdul Baha, Lady Gregory, Richard Le Gallienne, Paul Bartlett, Percy MacKaye, Judge Raymond, Ruth St. Denis, and Sarah Bernhardt—she looked at the latest drawings. "The new ones clashed like a great orchestra in my ears—Fourteen in ten days! I felt weak in the knees and glad of my umbrella to lean on. I can't get over them." Later she denied that she still found his drawings more interesting than his paintings, while admitting, "It seems to me you have gone farther in the use of that medium!" "I have," he responded. "I've always drawn." She insisted, "I *never* found your drawings more interesting than your paintings, after you began really to paint...But I do think that you've done something new, even for you, in these latest drawings."

Sales, too, were encouraging. Of the forty-four paintings and drawings, five paintings had been purchased: *Nebula* by the Mortens, *Ghosts* by Cecilia Beaux (the popular portrait painter whom Kahlil had met earlier that year), *Silence* by Julia Ellsworth Ford, *The Elements* by a Mrs. Gibson, and *The Great Solitude* by Rose O'Neill.

After viewing the gallery, they had lunch at Child's ("wee lamb chops for thirty cents and coffee") and then she returned alone to the drawings. Again, she met people from Kahlil's new world.

> In the gallery Mr. Montross soon came and talked. From time to time he went to look after a guest. Then he would come back. About 3:30 I heard a lady say, "Has Miss Haskell from Boston come?"
>
> I turned and caught M.'s eye and laid my finger on my lips. Soon he came up and said, "It is Mrs. Morten. Shall I introduce her?" I was glad to meet her. She is direct and real and sensitive—in her early thirties...We talked about the pictures and about her portrait. I told her why I liked it so much.
>
> "It is my potential self," she said.

French composer Claude Debussy. Charcoal and graphite, around 1910. (Courtesy Peter A. Juley / Smithsonian.)

Edmund Rostand, French poet and playwright, author of *Cyrano de Bergerac*. Charcoal and graphite, around 1910. (Courtesy Peter A. Juley / Smithsonian.)

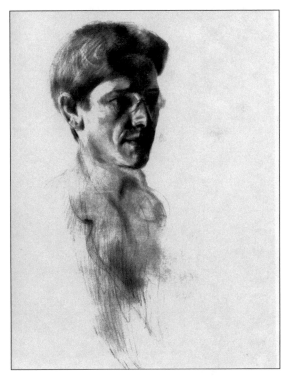

Percy MacKaye, civic theater innovator and poet. Charcoal and graphite, around 1913. (Courtesy Peter A. Juley / Smithsonian.)

French intellectual and politician, Henri Rochefort. Charcoal and graphite, around 1910. (Courtesy Peter A. Juley / Smithsonian.)

Mother and Child. Oil on canvas.
(Courtesy Gibran Museum.)

American modern dance pioneer, Ruth St. Denis. Graphite
and watercolor, 1914. (Courtesy Private Collection.)

Medusa. Pastel, around 1905-1908. (Courtesy Telfair Museum of Art.)

At the studio that evening, Kahlil and Mary talked about their "master-passion for the Great Reality," which, they believed, transcended being "in-love." But their uniquely defined relationship carried with it both fears and a sense of loss from un-fulfilled hopes and wishes. Mary's journal entries revealed her apprehensions about aging and both his and her concern with outsiders' opinions.

> How I used to wish people might know he loved me because it was the greatest honor I had and I wanted credit for it—wanted the fame of his loving me. He wants it known that I had faith in him—and made his start possible—that I backed him financially—And he has no desire to conceal our friendship. But he does not want it to be called a mistress and lover affair.

A week later they met in Boston. So that he could avoid the distractions of Oliver Place, she found Newbury Street lodgings. Their project was to find a gallery that would show his paintings, and they spent hours going up and down Back Bay streets. She was unusually preoccupied—"chilled and barren and sad"—and tried to evade his questions. Finally she told him

> how the lack of freedom kept raising protest in me—how the other night in New York and every sex-stirring made me feel more what I missed; how I had

thought of saying, "Let us be free" and had finally settled it again in my mind and was all right…

"But…[w]e can't…because the risk is too great."

"Yes, and we've always been saying it in many more words."

However, gallery interest could not be found. Even Lilla Cabot Perry, who may have viewed their closeness when they were touring the Guild of Boston Artists, did not acknowledge Mary, who was her next door Marlborough Street neighbor, or Kahlil, her former model and illustrator of her poetry book. Finally, The Boston Art Club agreed to exhibit his work in May, but that promise was inexplicably canceled. Some secretly may have wished that Miss Haskell would curtail her championing of him. Not only were a number of Boston patrons less interested in Kahlil's work, but Mary was confronted with implicit criticism from other sources.

Earlier she had asked Montross to arrange an anonymous gift of a painting to the Metropolitan Museum, and now she learned from him that the museum had turned down the offer. Two days after Christmas, she received a letter from Charlotte. The Hirsches, returned from Europe, had attended the Montross opening, and from their fleeting encounter with Kahlil, Mary learned that recent motherhood agreed with her old friend. But when Mary pressed him for more details, he declined comment: "Well I saw them for such a moment only—there were so many people. I can't say." In her outspoken way, Charlotte now wrote that she had turned away from "the East."

> Orientalism is the sleeping sickness of the Universe—it is the soft, sweet-scented night. No one can deny its beauty—nor the beauty of death. That is what we found in Kahlil's pictures the other day. They would be very dangerous if they were a little stronger: They are like Yeats' poetry and Debussy's music, but lack a certain clear-cut something which those two have; for that reason they may be more perfect in their way, the Orient Way…He came West for the spirit of the West—but he is the East as it works upon us. If I wrote an art criticism for him—I could make him famous.[11]

When Mary read the letter to Kahlil, she laughed, "Still explaining the Universe." But the promise of a splendid review must have seemed cruel, knowing that several critics were not sympathetic. Kahlil had already warned Mary to expect this reaction. "This is how my work stands: I am an excellent draughtsman; I cannot draw at all; I am early Italian—and modern French; I am obscure and childishly imitative; and I am a pupil of Rodin, of Davies, of Miller."[12]

Three newspaper articles were mostly negative. "Cloudy visions of striving and unhappy humanity with literary suggestions," wrote the anonymous critic of the *Times*. The *Tribune* characterized him as influenced by Rodin, "a kind of feeble Arthur Davies," and the *Evening Post* reviewer confessed that the pictures "wrapped in foggy symbolism" produced "a feeling of irritation—something like trying to read in a room where the lights are turned down."[13]

Joseph Edgar Chamberlain of the *Evening Mail* was kinder. Formerly associated with the Boston *Evening Transcript*, he had written two books for Copeland & Day, and had followed Kahlil's career. Along with a favorable review, he sent him a personal note congratulating him on his steady growth. "Your pictures interest and delight me very much, and it has been a matter of great pleasure to see you getting along so well, and 'arriving' so serenely among the great." Even more encouraging was Charles H. Caffin's article in the *American*. Calling the exhibit "very unusual and highly interesting," he gave the "dreamscapes" special consideration.[14]

> It is a world of original creation that unfolds itself, a world mostly composed of mountains, vegetation, and sky…It is remarkable, as showing how an artist, influenced by the modern tendency to revert to the primitive and elemental, can direct it, if he have high capacity of imagination, into channels of deep significance.

The *Evening Sun* found Kahlil of sufficient interest to feature an interview on the women's page. Reporter Jean Hamilton was mostly concerned with his comments on woman, love, and marriage. "Women's influence," Kahlil said,

> is to be found somewhere behind all the creations of man throughout the centuries…palpable throughout history…The world is stuffed with romance…little can be hoped of marriage based on the sentimental idea of love…A [successful] marriage has its foundation on comradeship not romance…it is the attraction of complement and supplement, invariably the coming together of two great natures for whom there is no other choice but marriage…[15]

What intrigued the interviewer and so many like her was not Kahlil's paintings or his role as a writer from the Middle East, but his simple and direct conversation about the rites of life—birth, marriage, and death.

The art critic for the *Sun*, Henry McBride, was less impressed with the message of the paintings. "The style has been greatly influenced by that of the late Eugene Carrière. The work on display is certainly sufficiently earnest to make all visitors sympathize with the artist in his pursuit." But McBride deplored "the pessimism" symbolized by "the crushed mortal striving for he doesn't know what; pushing on for an unknown destination, and leaning in his bitterest moments upon a female as blind and as hopeless as himself."[16]

Shortly afterward McBride again visited the Montross Gallery and unexpectedly found Albert Pinkham Ryder standing alone in front of one of Kahlil's pictures. McBride, who admired the elusive sixty-seven-year-old painter and had tried unsuccessfully to meet him, introduced himself. Ryder apologized for having broken appointments—"Explanations," McBride later recalled, "that were like the Gibran paintings, rather vague." McBride waved to the paintings. "How do you like these? He seems to be after something mysterious. All of them are the same." Replied Ryder, "He seems to mean it at any rate. That's the main thing."[17]

~

Ryder's attendance at his show touched Kahlil more than any review. Eight months before, he had told Mary how eager he was to meet the painter.

> The big person in this country is Ryder. He has painted little and nothing new for a long time. But there is so much *in* what he has done. And the *man* is the great thing. He is very hard to see. If he says you may see him next Thursday, he will be a week preparing for the visit—he is so sensitive—preparing himself, preparing his place…I do hope to get him for my series—but I have to approach him carefully.[18]

Kahlil hesitated to approach Ryder, but early in January 1915 he decided to write a prose poem to him as a sort of tribute and thanks to the older man who had taken the time to see the work of a younger artist. He sent it to Mary, promising, "If you like the poem I will publish it separately on Japanese paper and send it to him."[19] Staying up most of the night to go over the two pages, she immediately returned them. She followed her praise with seven pages of suggestions, several of which Kahlil included.[20]

The two-page poem was privately printed by the Fifth Avenue firm of Cosmus & Washburn two weeks later. On January 28, he sent her the rough sheets, embellished simply with brown lettering and orange motifs. "The Poem to Ryder delights me in every way," she responded. The poem closes:

> Son of the New World, who has loved thee but those who know thy burning love?…we whose bread is hunger and whose wine is thirst…

~

Kahlil's growing career did satisfy Mary more than her own unfulfilled promise. In early 1915, she wrote him.

TO
ALBERT PINKHAM RYDER

POET, who has heard thee but the spirits that follow thy solitary path? Prophet, who has known thee but those who are driven by the Great Tempest to thy lonely grove?

The beginning of Kahlil's poem honoring Ryder. (Courtesy Museo Soumaya.)

Your own treasured letter tells me again that it is not my fancy, but reality, that this life of ours is together…I long with all my soul to see you—but I understand so well that we had better wait…But tell me how you are—And what more about Ryder. That was such a wonderful hour with him. I fairly eat up all you told me of it.

Kahlil replied, with word of Ryder's response to the poem.

One of the most creative hours in my life was…with Ryder the other day. I found him on a cold day in a half heated room in one of the most poor houses on 16th street. He lives the life of Diogeneus, a life so wreched and so unclean that it is hard for me to discribe. But it is the only life he wants. He has money, but he does not think of that. He is no longer on this planet. He is beyond his own dreams…And he read the poem. Oh what a thrilling moment. His face changed, and there were tears in his old eyes. Then he said, "It is a great poem. It is too much for me. I am not worthy of it…then after a long silence, he said, "I did not know that you were a poet as well as a painter…" He promised to sit for a drawing. I shall go to him tomorrow. And if I do not find him I shall go again and again untill I make a drawing. It must be done. His head is wonderful—very much like that of Rodin—only it is unkept.

Later he described how he managed to arrange a Ryder sitting for the Temple of Art series.

I don't try to make appointments with him because if he has an appointment it keeps him anxious for days beforehand. I just start when I am ready to try for him—and take my chances. This day I put my portfolio under my arm, and started—Near 16th street I saw him on the street, walking along very slowly—you know he takes steps about two inches long. I waited to see what he would do. He went into a restaurant, and ordered lunch. He ordered corn beef and cabbage and ate it very slowly—

It took him till quarter past four to eat his lunch—his hands are so feeble. I waited till he was through Then he came out. And he said, "O Mr. Gibran. I saw you through the window. Have you been waiting all this time for me?" I said I had, and I walked along with him. In a step or two we passed by a saloon and he said, "Will you have a drink?"

I said no but I would be glad to wait for him in his studio. He went in and took one. He went into two on his way home…

I have made two drawings of Ryder. To me they are finer than anything I have done. One of them is not finished yet and I must go to him again. But, oh, Mary, how tired and weary he is—and how aloof. He told me the last time I saw him that he is painting pictures in his mind. He can use his hands no more.

When Mary came to New York in April, Kahlil told her more about the older painter.

He is sixty to sixty-four and seems eighty to ninety…K. says Ryder used to be a beautiful creature and rather a dandy, used to wear white a great deal, and was a conspicuous figure on Fifth Avenue. But he loved a woman whom his friends thought not worthy of him, and they planned to part him from her and her influence. They got him to go abroad and when he came back she had disappeared. Ryder was never himself again.

"Probably he hasn't bathed since," said K.

He has two rooms—one on 14th and one on 16th street—but he received K. in the room of an old English lady of eighty—because his own room was too cold. He sleeps at 16th street on three chairs with old clothes on them—of money he has quite enough, but seems lost to comforts.

"He made me ashamed of being clean," Kahlil confessed. "He is so gentle and courteous—'May I take it for you?' he said when he saw my portfolio, though he uses his hands with such difficulty…has no will of his own…no skill for contact with people."

When K. had finished drawing him, he took the picture and looked at it. "So carefully," K. recounted, "it was a great revelation to me—such looking—as if he were looking to see what life was in it."

Then he said, "Wonderful work. You've drawn what's inside me—the bones and brain."

Portrait of Albert Pinkham Ryder. Graphine, 1915. (Courtesy © Metropolitan Museum of Art. Gift of Mrs. Mary H. Minis, 1932. Image source: Art Resource.)

"He hadn't been to an exhibition for eight years when he went to mine," Kahlil said. "Mrs. Morten sent him—the Mortens have several of his pictures."

"Your pictures have imagination," Ryder said, "and imagination is art. Art is nothing else…"

"Ryder has been a great lesson to me," concluded Kahlil. "He is full of wonder—of that wonder that is the mark of the real and great ones."[21]

He mailed the Ryder poem to friends, and it attracted the attention of those who had previously considered Kahlil only a painter and an interesting conversationalist. That spring Percy Grant, an old friend of Charlotte's and the liberal vicar of the nearby West Tenth Street Church of the Ascension, read it from his pulpit. "This is the second time Doctor Grant spoke of me and my work," Kahlil said. He also reported that two of the long poems in *The Madman* were read to the Poetry Society of America. Reaction to these pieces was mixed, but it was significant that American poets were criticizing his English work, despite the fact that it had never been published in a magazine. One of his first supporters in the Poetry Society was Mrs. Douglas Robinson, the sister of Theodore Roosevelt. Corinne Roosevelt Robinson first thought his work "diabolical stuff—contrary to all our forms of morality and true beauty."[22] However, her initial reaction was soon replaced by admiration, and she became another influential supporter.

In June, Kahlil went to Boston, again staying at Miss DeWolfe's rooms at 9 Newbury Street. He settled into a pattern of alternating evening visits between Marianna and Mary. Most of the time with Mary was now spent in polishing his English work. On this visit she captured the essence of the subtle change in their relationship. "Pale and burned out he looked…" On the third night she gave him two bronze laurel leaves. Her annual ritual of sending him a fresh laurel branch from the Sierras was now incorporated into the school's honors program: the small unsigned leaves based on his designs had become the school's scholastic awards. Like the school pin he had drawn earlier, the bronze shield bearing honor students' names, and his sketch for the class ring (an open hand holding a rose), the leaves symbolized Kahlil's contributions to the school. She turned to him for advice whenever educational concerns pressed too deeply. At three o'clock one morning, she wrote to him about her conflicted loyalties.

> I am defying bed in the interests of M. E. H.—mine is life like a submarine's—in the day, I come to the surface and cruise actively in school waters. At night I go into the depths whose fascination *makes* me a submarine…And life like an aeroplane's: all day in the hangar—after sunset in the sky…These two waking lives are as far apart as awakeness and dreams are.[23]

When he read his latest poem, "The Perfect World," she identified with it. "And the English of it is superb…we hardly touched it—it was so perfect." What made it different from his earlier efforts was his process "I *wrote* this in English," he said. "It is the first thing I have written in English instead of translating it from Arabic…But I tell you, this writing in English is *very hard* for me…I've been finding out that the English is a very wonderful language if I can learn how to use it."[24] He showed her a large notebook in which he had started another series of English poems, which would eventually become *The Earth Gods*.

Bronze laurel leaf that Kahlil designed for students at Miss Haskell's School for Girls. (Courtesy Private Collection.)

Mary then edited with him material from two unfinished works. "We worked at the passages not yet final in the Prologue…We must have spent three hours on it…K. had long been tired but he kept on and on—and I was the one to stop him at last. He called it his 'lesson'—though it assuredly was mine." That week they also added several poems to *The Madman*. The more they removed themselves from personal matters, the more productive were their evenings.

From drawing the face, Kahlil went straight into writing the story of the man with the valley full of needles ["On Giving and Taking"]. When we had done that, he wrote about the cat who said that for prayer it would rain mice and the dog who despised their superstition, knowing it would rain bones ["The Wise Dog"]. And then the story of the two hermits and the earthen bowl ["The Two Hermits"].[25]

Mary followed Kahlil to New York, first spending two days with Charlotte and her family. Without a work schedule, these times seemed to be marred by recrimina-

Ink and graphite sketch of a hermit. (Courtesy Peter A. Juley / Smithsonian.)

tions and accusations. That summer she reversed her usual schedule by spending July with her brother Tom in Washington and then traveling south to Little Yosemite. The turbulence of the past five years haunted her, and from Wenatchee she sent Kahlil a message, castigating herself for inhibiting his personal life.

Never in all these years have I let you be yourself, save as by one of these hopes, whose shattering meant more pain…I said I wanted you to be free with me. But if, ever you were free, I hit you. With your Self I was like one in a room in the dark, who knocks everything down.[26]

Acknowledging her admission, he predicted a new era for them both.

All is well now, beloved Mary…Indeed, we have had five long years of great pain. But those years were extremely creative. We grew through them and though we came out of them covered with deep wounds, yet we came out with stronger and simpler souls.

…Each and every human relation is divided into seasons of thoughts and feelings and conduct. The past five years were a season in our friendship. Now we are at the beginning of a new season, a season less cloudy and perhaps more creative and more eager to simplify us.

And who can say, "This season is good and that season is bad?" All seasons are natural to life. Death itself is part of life. And though I have died many times during the past five years yet I feel now that the marks of death are not upon me and my heart is without bitterness. The past five years taught me how to work and now I am beginning to use the power of work as an instrument.

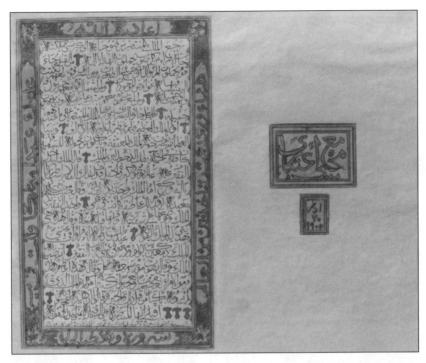

Young Kahlil's ink and watercolor birthday card to Josephine Preston Peabody, 1905. (Courtesy Private Collection.)

Untitled. Watercolor, around 1924. (Courtesy Gibran Museum.)

Tree of Life, from *Jesus the Son of Man*. Watercolor, around 1925. (Formerly at Telfair Museum of Art, Savannah, Georgia. Gift of Mary Haskell Minis. Reprint: George Lynde/Art Imaging.)

Ages of Women. Oil on canvas, 1910. (Courtesy Museo Soumaya.)

Blessed Mountain, from *Sand and Foam*. Watercolor, 1926.
(Courtesy Telfair Museum of Art.)

Anguish. Oil on canvas. (Courtesy Gibran Museum.)

From *The Prophet*. Watercolor. (Courtesy Gibran Museum.)

Three Stages of Being. Watercolor, around 1922. (Courtesy Gibran Museum.)

From *The Prophet.* Watercolor, around 1922. (Courtesy Gibran Museum.)

The Archer, from The Prophet. *(Courtesy Gibran Museum.)*

The Burden, from Twenty Drawings *(Knopf edition).
Watercolor and graphite. (Courtesy Brooklyn Museum. Gift
of Mrs. Frank Babbott.)*

Family Scene. Oil on canvas. (Courtesy Gibran Museum.)

The Greater Self, from *Twenty Drawings*. Watercolor and graphite, 1916. (Courtesy Telfair Museum of Art.)

The Dawn. Oil on canvas. (Courtesy Gibran Museum.)

Centaur and Child, wash drawing, from *Twenty Drawings*. (Courtesy Peter A. Juley / Smithsonian.)

14

WAR AND FAMINE

"My heart burns for Syria. Fate has been most cruel to her...
Her Gods are dead, her children left her to seek bread in far away lands...
and yet she is still alive—and that is the most painful thing."[1]

A rising artist entering his thirties, Kahlil did not conceal his nationalistic feelings. As early as the fall of 1912, with the Balkan states challenging the Ottoman Empire, he was convinced that Turkey's hold on Lebanon and Syria could be broken only by an allied attack. "Treat poetically with the Turkish government!" he once told Mary. "You might as well sing the songs of Keats to...Standard Oil!" His support for war as a means of gaining his country's freedom caused him to guard closely his Near Eastern ties and friendships, at a time when he was forming deeper commitments within the New York art world and literary community. The distance between his Syrian nationalist and American pacifist friends was to him a "gulf that had to be crossed every day."[2]

From its outbreak in July 1914, World War I dominated Kahlil and Mary's thoughts. Both came to see the horrific conflict—which claimed the lives of some sixteen million combatants and civilians—as part of an evolutionary process. As Mary noted, they shared the view that narrow nationalism would eventually lead to global awareness of "collective national personalities as members of the world personality...like family members—each different and separate—yet with *the* stamp and bond."[3]

In 1912, not long after his meetings with Abdul Baha and friends, including the Mortens, who were Bahaist pacifists, a large reception for Abdul Baha prompted Kahlil to question some of the assumptions underlying the growing peace movement in the U.S. "Why should man speak of Peace when there is so much of *ill-at-easiness* in his system that *must go out* one way or another?" In the fall of 1912, he had told Mary how much he opposed nonalignment. Referring to the cruelty of Europe's dissociation from the suffering of the peoples of the Balkan states and Syria, he said,

> I have been made *sick* and *tired* by those passionless statesmen of Europe. Because they are free and tranquil they think that the whole world should be satisfied. Mary, there is a sort of cruelty in the optimism of happy people. Rich and happy people protest against the young Balkan States because they fear that they might "break the peace of the world"—And why should they not break the hypocritical peace of the world? They have suffered enough under that one-sided peace, and I pray to God that this war may bring about the dismemberment of the Turkish Empire, so that the poor crushed nations of the Near East may live again...I am not patriotic...I am too much of an Absolutist, and Absolutism has no country—but my heart burns for Syria...[4]

In June 1913, his friends Najib Diab and Ameen Rihani represented emigrant Lebanese at the First Arab Congress. Kahlil had conflicting feelings about not participating in this historic event.

> During the last week of this month a conference will take place in Paris. More than 30 Syrians will meet and discuss Home Rule in Syria...Diab and myself were asked by a committee of Syrians to go as two representatives. The idea is fine—but after talking the thing over with these good people, I found that they do not agree with me on any point, nor I with them. They were to pay my expenses and I was to speak [their] minds—not mine! And since [their] minds and my mind are so different, there is no way of representing them without being insincere and cowardly.[5]

Two weeks later, he again brought up with her the difference between "the old school of dealing with Turkish problems" and his sense of political renewal. "They would appeal to the Powers of Europe and by diplomacy seek Home Rule...But their very asking for it diplomatically obliges them to accept Turkey's consent diplomatically given. And Turkey *will* consent; will promise; and will not keep the promise." That night Mary noted, "K. wants Revolution. He feels that even if it fails, Home Rule will result." She chided him for not asking her to send him to Paris when she saw how he brooded in New York while his friends attended the conference. "This battle with his own people, his sense of their waste of time, his *not* going to Paris—have made it a time of great anguish, sleepless...solitary."[6] But on July 10, the limitations of the conference became clear. He wrote,

> I think the conference of Paris is a failure. Those patriots are altogether too wise and too considerate...I have made up my mind to be alone. I can't agree with anyone on anything unless I swallow nine tenth of my thoughts—and just now I am not in

the mood of swallowing anything. In order to work in harmony with those men, one must be as patient as they are—and patience, Mary, has been, and *is* now the curse of all the Oriental races. Oriental people in general are fatalists—they believe in an inevitable necessity overruling their fortune and their misfortune…They resist passion and think by resisting passion they become victorious over themselves. And they *do* become victorious over themselves—[but] not over the others! Passion, Mary, is the only thing that creates a nation.[7]

He redirected some of his sense of urgency into his writing. Five months after the conference, he published in *Al-Funun* "An Open Letter to Islam," addressed "To Muslims from a Christian Poet."[8] Calling for an alliance of religious factions in Ottoman-occupied countries, the prose poem stressed the commonalities between readers of the Qur'an and those of the Bible.

> I am Lebanese and I'm proud of that,
> And I'm not an Ottoman and I'm also proud of that.
> I have a beautiful homeland of which I'm proud,
> And I have a nation with a past—
> But there is no state which protects me.
> No matter how many days I stay away
> I shall remain an Easterner—Eastern in my manners,
> Syrian in my desires, Lebanese in my feelings—
> No matter how much I admire Western progress.

Implicit in his "open letter" was a caution to both Christians and Muslims that unless they linked forces to defeat the Ottoman Empire, "the yellow-haired blue eyes" would conquer them, and the Middle East would be controlled by new European masters. Kahlil's next broadside against the Ottomans appeared in March 1914. This time he chose a dramatic form in which two intellectuals—a Muslim and a Christian—meet in a Beirut coffeehouse and discuss the never-ending Ottoman occupation of their country and the need for cooperation between their religions. Calling this unsigned piece "The Beginning of Revolution," he overestimated its political influence.

> My 'Open Letter to Islam' created the feeling which I wanted to create…It was that short letter which I kept in my pocket for two years before publishing it. But there are some friends in the East who think that in publishing that two page letter I have signed my death warrant with my own hand! *I do not care!*[9]

In August, reflecting further on the disposition of the Middle East by the Western powers, he conjectured:

If Turkey joins Germany, a protectorate of Syria will come, by France and England—England taking the lower part, because she wants both ends of the Canal and France the upper...And twenty to twenty-five years of such government will be a governing school for Syria and she will learn to govern herself and become free...Syria has so many close bonds with France, and French protection will be very acceptable to the Syrians as a whole.

The war haunted him—"I'm always drawing lines about the fighting in my head"—and Mary identified with his partisanship, but its atrocities shocked her. "Sometimes it drives me up and down the floor...till daylight comes," she wrote him in October, "and more and more the pains suffered by women and children and by soldiers mutilated on the field live in me. Something in me weeps all the time and makes me want to stop everything." He responded,

Man is part of nature. Each and every year the elements in nature declare war on each other...Man is elemental. He must fight and he must die for what he does not fully understand. And it is the fight and the death of any seed in the fields...Man fights for a thought or a dream. Who can say that thoughts and dreams are not a part of the elements that once came together to make up this planet?[10]

A month later, as he was preparing for the Montross Gallery exhibition, she realized the extent to which his political involvement was affecting his artistic output. His Syrian compatriots were constantly seeking his attention, and she wondered how he managed his time to allow for this double life. "I've got used to it now—to adjusting my mind to one thing quickly after another," he said.

Although he expressed his desire to support an uprising against Ottoman rule in Syria, he acknowledged to Mary that even if "his death for Syria...would effect something, the something would be very small: smaller than his *living* can effect." He argued with himself, "Syria is not the purpose of my life...perhaps I shall find myself as much an alien there as anywhere else. But I should be glad to know whether this is the case or not."[11]

During the weekend of the show, Mary asked, "Now that Turkey is in the war, do any leaders appear in Syria?" "No," he answered. "Then...will the *possible* quickening of her freedom...be worth...being your job?"[12] He was not to go; in the end, they both understood that. But he tried to compensate by sending small sums of money to Syria and promised to contribute the royalties from his latest book in Arabic, *Dam'a wa Ibtisama* (*A Tear and a Smile*), to the effort.

By 1915, communication between Lebanon and the rest of the world had become increasingly cut off. A successful French blockade of the Syrian coast and

Turkish military occupation, with its strict censorship, made wary emigrants fearful for those left behind. Added to the political uncertainty was the specter of famine and disease. Early in 1915, rumors of widespread atrocities by the Turks had reached the Syrian emigrant communities. Under a reign of terror, religious leaders were being deported, while those suspected of anti-Turkish sentiments were subject to arrest and imprisonment. Six men, including Dr. Ayub Tabet, organizer of the First Arab Congress, had been charged with treason and sentenced to death in absentia. Dr. Tabet, one of Kahlil's best school friends, was a physician and the brother of Sultana, with whom Kahlil had been infatuated while in Beirut. Dr. Tabet had managed to escape to New York, and now they met together daily, as he rallied Syrian-Lebanese immigrants around a pro-French position. Kahlil observed the confusion, fear, and disunity among the community and its leadership.[13] Yet he persisted in using his art to advocate for conversation beyond old divisions and mistrust.

Four months later, *As-Sayeh* reported on Kahlil's speech on Islam at the conference of the American Academy of Religion in New York. Beginning with the Muslim Declaration of Faith, he emphasized the universality of the Prophet's voice. Frequently interrupted by applause, *As-Sayeh* described Kahlil's talk as "wine for minds."[14] Reflecting on Islamic influences in literature, science, and mathematics, especially during the Andalusian period in Spain, he addressed the Ottoman Empire's current control of Islamic culture. "Faith settles in the heart, is confirmed in the tongue." He warned, "Sometimes it is [that] two-faced people lie and make promises they cannot keep." Kahlil received a standing ovation and was thanked by the academy's president, Charles Foster Kent. *As-Sayeh* reported, "The one thing that must be said of Gibran, New York's Arabic poet, Jesus is in half his soul and Muhammad, in the other half…He is loyal to his Arab roots as much as he is loyal to himself, and he sacrifices all he has to for his nation and people." Kahlil's message of universality and respect was reaching wider audiences.[15]

In May 1916, Kahlil was actively soliciting funds for his beleaguered homeland. He wrote Mary,

> My people, the people of Mount Lebanon, are perishing through a famine which has been planned by the Turkish government. 80,000 already died. Thousands are dying every day. The same things that happened in Armenia are happening in Syria. Mt. Lebanon being a Christian country, is suffering the most.[16]

This plea elicited a generous check for four hundred dollars from Mary. But Kahlil wrote back that the donation was too extravagant. "I want the Syrians here to feel that they must unite and help themselves before others can help them." On June 29, he wrote that he had given in her name one hundred fifty dollars to the Syrian-Mount Lebanon Relief Committee. "It is the largest contribution from an American so far."[17]

Kahlil was seeking help from others to raise funds for the Syrian crisis. In June 1916, an article in the *Washington Times*, entitled "Washington Asked to Give Syrians Aid," noted that his friend and neighbor Juliet Thompson was leading "an effort to form a committee to secure relief for hundreds of thousands of starving women and children in Syria." Describing letters testifying to the conditions in Syria, the article revealed that the information source was Kahlil Gibra[n] "prominent Syrian, exiled from his own country, now in New York."[18]

As secretary of the Relief Committee, of which Rihani was assistant chairman, Kahlil was now an official spokesperson. Earlier that year he had received a personal tribute. Several Arab-American writers and editors—Nasib Arida, Abd al-Massih Haddad, Najib Diab, Elias Sabagh, Wadi Bahout—had presented him with a ruby ring, which he wore proudly on his index finger.

~

That spring of 1916, *Al-Funun*—having suspended publication for the past two and a half years—was revived. Even with its hiatus, the journal, along with its sister publication, *As-Sayeh*, had served as incubators for the gradual coalescence of immigrant poets from Greater Syria—the Mahjar writers. For years, *Al-Funun* editor Nasib Arida and his colleague at *As-Sayeh*, editor Abd al-Massih Haddad, had called for a writers' union to advance the modernization of the Arabic language and protect the rights of diaspora writers, while offering opportunity for dialogue across sectarian lines.[19] Kahlil had often spoken of forming "a little society" through which writers could meet and discuss what was happening in their creative worlds.[20] Now several contributors to *Al-Funun* and *As-Sayeh* began to identify themselves as members of a literary group.

In the May 4, 1916, edition of *As-Sayeh*, Ilyas Ata Allah became the first author to sign his work "Udu fi al-Rabitah al-Qalamiyah," or "a member of the Pen Bond." Following suit in *As-Sayeh*'s May issues were Nasib Arida, William Catzeflis, Nadra Haddad, Amin Mushriq, and Ameen Rihani. In the June 1916 issue of *Al-Funun*, the names of Kahlil Gibran and Rashid Ayoub were added, while Abd al-Massih Haddad completed the list of contributors in the journal's July edition, signaling the inception of a literary society of Arab immigrant writers.

In June 1916, the youngest member of the group, eighteen-year-old Amin Mushriq, published in *As-Sayeh* a statement of purpose explaining the society's orientation and aims. Seeking to revive the Arabic language—both in style and content—they would reject stultifying rules in favor of finding ways to infuse their native language with new forms of free verse, vernacular vocabulary, and colloquial dialect to better express their voices and ideas. Mushriq promised to answer questions about the group and its members. "If I had a mustache I'd twirl it to swear to other organizations that we're not crowding them out and to tell those in politics we're not taking their places." Recalling honored Syrian poets of the past who "belong to eternity," his hope was that the group would "seize the opportunity to establish a new life…preserve the remains of Arabic literature, feed it with new and beneficial literature, and establish a reinforced position of authors who will create a real bond."[21]

But it was not until 1920, four years later, following Mikhail Naimy's return from service in the U.S. Army, that the group would be formally organized into a functioning literary society with designated leaders and planned publications. And over time, members of the Pen League would become recognized as key contributors from within the Arab diaspora to the the Nahda movement, or "the awakening," of Arabic letters and culture.[22]

~

At the same time, a short play by Kahlil appeared in *As-Sayeh*, in an April 1916 edition devoted to his work.[23] Unlike his poetic prose, the one-act *Al-Wujuh 'Al-Mulawana* (*The Two-Faced Characters*) was written entirely in a realistic style.[24]

In an ostentatious setting, a group of well-to-do Syrians are socializing. A sharp-tongued hostess rudely instructs a recently hired maid to prepare coffee for everyone. This servant is an elderly Lebanese woman, new to America and unsure of herself in her role as "hired help." Questioned about her, the hostess says that, although distinguished looking, the new servant is unsatisfactory and was hired only as an act of charity.

An outspoken young woman—clearly unlike others present—brings to the group's attention a newspaper article interviewing a fellow Syrian immigrant painter and poet about his views on women and marriage.[25] The group resents the artist's progressive attitudes and growing popularity. Scorning the penny press newspaper's "yellow journalism," they demean the Boston poet, accusing him not only of attacking the church but of embracing both Western and Eastern thinking, and abandoning their heritage, attire, and customs. Dismissing him as a grasshopper that merely hops back and forth between Eastern and Western thought, they ridicule his long hair and "empty dreams," excoriating him for being a "disbeliever."[26] The young woman defends the poet, accusing the group of being envious and materialistic, and clinging to their accustomed privileges. She defends her own outspokenness, even as an unmarried woman who supposedly should remain "silent as the grave and still as a rock."[27]

Suddenly the bell rings and the poet himself appears. Introducing himself, he explains that he has a message for the newly arrived servant. The maid is called for, and she immediately recognizes the guest, bursting into tears of joy. He delivers a note to her from expatriate friends in Brazil—along with a money order from them—and she and he fondly recall their homeland. Admitting to him that in her old age she has been forced by poverty to become a servant, the poet replies, "We all are servants."[28]

The group invites their unexpected guest to coffee, and even a cigar. They watch as he enjoys their hospitality with charm and dignity, and then leaves. The young woman suddenly accuses them all of lying and behaving like chameleons. "We all have many faces," she exclaims. "In the blue hour, we put on our blue faces. In the yellow hour, we put on our yellow faces. In the red, we put on our red faces." After she too leaves—"like someone running away from hell"—the guilt-ridden bunch remains, sitting and staring at the ceiling, while they silently imagine that a ghost had written their earlier tirades.[29]

The play's views are illuminated by *Al-Hoda* editor Salloum Mokarzel's recollection of an episode that took place during the community's fundraising efforts. Committee members were stalemated in agreeing on a name for the group, "with some opting to name it the Syrian Relief Committee and others holding out for the Syrian Lebanese Relief Committee." At one particularly difficult meeting of "leading figures of the community," things were not working and hope was fading. Mokarzel recalled that Kahlil then spoke up.

> He stood for sometime motionless, then managed…only the single sentence: "My brothers, shall we let them die?" And Gibran could not control his tears…as he delivered his…appeal…Gibran's tears won the day."[30]

Mokarzel's recollection revealed Kahlil's conflicted feelings about how, even at times of crisis, people elevate vanity and self-interest above the suffering of those in need. As well as being torn between supporting the conflict along with fellow Syrian immigrants or opposing it nonviolently with his American friends, divisions within the community took a toll.

~

Anxious to see Kahlil, Mary stayed in New York for three days in July before traveling south to visit a cousin, "Aunt Loulie" Minis. She tried to sort out his confusion
and despair over the latest reports. Fourteen people—Christian and Muslim—had
been hanged in Beirut that May, and although details were confusing, the dangers
of being a Syrian nationalist were clear. Kahlil linked the Turkish atrocities to recent
British retaliations against the Irish Home Rule movement.

> [At] the conference in Paris…they drew up a proclamation, signed it and would have
> presented it to the French Government. But France then was [close] with Turkey.
> The proclamation was not published…A copy of the Proclamation was given to the
> French Consul at Beirut. War broke out…The Turkish Government took the papers
> and the signers of the Proclamation were killed—about fifty of them were known to
> me personally. Doctor Tabet…feels terribly because of these deaths.[31]

Kahlil's reports on the war news seemed to reach a crisis in the summer and fall of
1916.

> Turkish spies are of course watching everything that is done here. But Doctor Tabet
> comes in a great deal, gives his ideas, which are invaluable, and writes a few letters.
> I can't get away from Syria, I never shall, I am a Syrian…and yet this work is almost
> more than I can bear. Rihani—and all the others—they understand one another
> so well…but I don't understand them and they don't understand me…they say, "O,
> you just come down there and sit, and all will be well"—they are taking care, as
> it were, of the bird that lays golden eggs…I can get money when no one else can.
> Because the work of Turkey has been to divide those she governs—the Syrians do
> not trust one another. They fear that if they give money to the Committee the
> money won't reach those who are suffering in Syria…I have to talk to all these
> people to explain, to convince them…Spies watched the Committee's every move-
> ment in New York and if *any* Syrian in U.S. displeases Turkey, his relatives are killed.
> That is why the U.S. Syrians are so infinitely cautious and watchful.[32]

A special edition of *Al-Funun*—"The Syrian Crisis Issue"—appeared in October
1916. Contributions to the issue included Kahlil's illustrations and his poem "Dead
Are My People," with designs by German illustrator Heinrich Vogeler; Naimy's
"Festival of Death," describing a starving woman's unsuccessful plea to a wealthy
landowner; Rihani's piece entitled "Hunger"; and a profile of Kamila by Kahlil,
captioned "My Mother's Face, My Nation's Face," accompanied by an editorial
statement that read: "For us the drawing means that every Syrian must follow it as a
guiding principle for his actions and goals in these days of bitterness and hardness."
The issue was completed with a series of poems, "Night" by Abu Maadi and "A

Complaint and an Appeal" by Rashid Ayyub, along with a translated excerpt from the novel *Hunger* by Norwegian writer, and eventual Nobel Prize winner, Knut Hamsum.[33]

Kahlil's elegy, "Dead Are My People," dedicated to the victims of Syria's horrific famine of 1916, appealing to his fellow exiles for support, was an indictment of his own helplessness and of the wider malaise in the Near East.

> The knolls of my country are submerged
> By tears and blood...
>
> What can an exiled son do for his
> Starving people, and of what value
> Unto them is the lamentation of an
> Absent poet?...
>
> This is my disaster, and this is my
> Mute calamity which brings humiliation
> Before my soul and before the phantoms
> Of the night...
>
> Yes, but the death of my people is
> A silent accusation...
> And if my People had attacked the despots
> And oppressors and died as rebels, I would have said, "Dying for
> Freedom is nobler than living in
> The shadow of weak submission..."
>
> But my people did not die as rebels;
> Death was their only rescuer, and
> Starvation their only spoils...
>
> ...Remember, my brother,
> That the coin which you drop into
> The withered hand stretching toward
> You is the only golden chain that
> Binds your rich heart to the
> Loving heart of God...[34]

Kahlil's illustration that appeared with Mikhail Naimy's story, "Festival of Death," in the Syrian Crisis issue of *Al-Funun*, October 1916. (Reprint: F. Frank Isik.)

~

In September of that fall of 1916, Kahlil had left New York and the pressures of the Relief Committee to spend time with Marianna. The year before, they had found a small cottage in Cohasset, a seaside village twenty-five miles south of Boston. There, brother and sister, along with visiting relatives, had enjoyed their first vacation together, a family gathering they would repeat annually for the rest of his life. His letters from New York to Marianna reveal the comfort he felt from being with relatives.

> Wish I could stay for a whole year so I could take pleasure in your delicious food, drink and Shesh Besh [backgammon], whether I win or lose. This is just a brief note but full of regards, thanks and gratitude to Shayeb, Mrs. Adel, Assaf, Maroon, N'oula, Rosa and your great self. Do me a favor, tell them I left them by force.[35]

When he escaped the city later that fall, he returned to the house on Jerusalem Road. In a letter to Witter Bynner, he acknowledged his poor health:

Marianna, Kahlil, and cousin Maroon George, Cohasset, Massachusetts, summer of 1916. (Courtesy Museo Soumaya.)

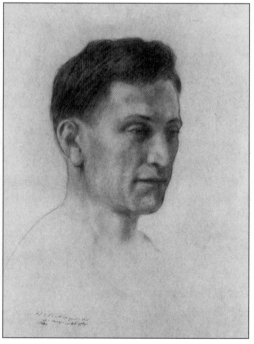

Kahlil's cousin, N'oula Gibran. Graphite and charcoal. Inscribed, "In memory of a a week spent between the forest and the sea—Cohasset on Jerusalem Road, August 1917." (Courtesy Private Collection.)

266

I am ill in bed. I came to Cohasset about two weeks ago with a wingless body and a weary soul—and now my sister and a good doctor are taking care of me. This house is between the deep woods and the deep sea; but I have not been strong enough to sit in the green shadows or dip my pale self in the blue water. I fear, Witter, that I shall remain a songless thing for a long while.

Several days later, he again wrote Bynner, describing his state in more detail.

Bless you for the wonderful letter. It did so much good. It is a nervous breakdown. Overwork and the tragedy of my country have brought a cold, dull pain to my left side, face, arm and leg. It will pass away, Witter, and I shall be well again. Here I sit in the sun all day turning the left side of my body to its warm, healing rays. And the left side of my face is darker, much darker, than the [right] side. The effect is strangely queer—not unlike the jesters of the xvth Century![36]

When Mary saw Kahlil at her school in Boston on October 5, she was shocked.

More than forty years are graven now into his 33-year-old face. Even his hands look older than he is—and this time he has gained no flesh…In his run-down state, his left side, always susceptible, from his childhood injury, had been almost paralyzed—and he has given it sun treatment. In New York he had taken some electrical treatments—but the rest has done more for him.

To distract him from the stressful work for the Relief Committee, that night she introduced several topics of conversation. They talked about his growing interest in astronomy, which led them to their mutual interest in extraterrestrial life. "Suppose fish should believe that above the water is no life," he conjectured, "because they don't know such life: that would be as natural, and no more reasonable, than for us to believe there is no life in elements impossible to human existence." A magazine article about Amy Lowell prompted Mary to deliver to him a short lecture on psychiatry and modern literature. "Then we read 'The Opal' and another little poem of hers. I showed him how the psychoanalysts find sex and masturbation in them. Kahlil was not entirely convinced. 'I think psychoanalysis is a wonderful thing but why call everything *sex*? Everything *may be* sex—but I can't feel that it is.'" Later she asked him to draw her "vision of a far-winged soul impeded by a clinging small-winged soul." He complied by filling four of her journal pages with winged figures, until he grew bored. The long disjointed session ended with Mary's wistful vigil as he left the school.

He took Jung's *Psychology of the Unconscious* to read. And he ate a slice of pineapple and two wee ginger-snaps—and smoked four or five cigarettes—and between

12:00 and 1:00 started for—I don't know where he was staying. I watched him down the street, as always—through the window—his walk so unchanged—but no cigarette lighted, as it usually is, as long as he was in sight. He walks with a peculiar little rocking—a sort of swing and dip—very springy.[37]

The reason for his borrowing *On the Psychology of the Unconscious* was that the text had been translated by psychiatrist Beatrice Hinkle. She and Kahlil had remained friends ever since she introduced him to the young writer James Oppenheim.

~

Early in 1916, Oppenheim had become a regular visitor to Kahlil's Tenth Street studio and was impressed with portions of *The Madman*. Despite their different backgrounds, Kahlil found a common bond with him. Born in 1882 in St. Paul, Minnesota, Oppenheim's father had died when James was six, and his early years had been difficult ones. His education—high school and two years as a special student at Columbia University—had been spotty. His entrance into the intellectual mainstream had been nurtured in New York settlement houses, working as assistant headworker at the Hudson Guild Settlement and as a teacher at the Hebrew Technical School for Girls. To make a living, he turned to hack journalism and magazine fiction. By 1914 he had published eight books of poetry and prose. Infused with fervent social idealism, his most popular poem—"Bread and Roses"—had become associated with the 1912 textile workers' strike for "bread and roses" in Lawrence, Massachusetts.

When Kahlil met him, he was in analysis with Dr. Hinkle and was preparing to publish a magazine that would embrace the visions of a new American literary movement. To Oppenheim, Kahlil's unorthodox approach to literature, the very fact that passion rather than reason moved him to self-expression, was enormously appealing. What mattered was not Kahlil's misspelling of simple words, but that he possessed a forceful and intuitive sense of musicality and emotion. When Oppenheim, encouraged by Dr. Hinkle and sponsored by Mrs. A. K. Rankine, a wealthy patron, founded *The Seven Arts*, he chose as associate editors Waldo Frank and Van Wyck Brooks, and included Kahlil on the advisory board along with Robert Frost, Louis Untermeyer, Robert Edmond Jones, Edna Kenton, and David Mannes. The only immigrant on the staff was Kahlil.

Kahlil first mentioned *The Seven Arts* to Mary in July 1916, when he gave her a copy of the magazine's prospectus. Its message sent out a spirited challenge to young American writers.

It is our faith and the faith of many, that we are living in the first days of a renascent period, a time which means for America the coming of that national self-consciousness which is the beginning of greatness...We have no tradition to continue; we have no school of style to build up. What we ask of the writer is simply self-expression without regard to current magazine standards. We should prefer that portion of his work which is done through a joyous necessity of the writer himself.

Kahlil did not know any of the other writers except Oppenheim. "He likes the things I do—and I like his ideas...He wants to publish all I've written in English... And some of the Syrians are angry because I have given him my name."[38] Even before it was launched, Kahlil knew that his association with a potentially pacifist-leaning venture would raise concerns among his Syrian colleagues, some of whom were challenging Ottoman authority at great personal risk.

One future contributor to *Seven Arts* whose views on culture were closer to those of Kahlil and his Syrian colleagues was Randolph Bourne. Although a fierce opponent of the war, Bourne's outspoken writings on transnationalism echoed the thinking of immigrant reformers. His views are likely to have influenced Kahlil's cosmopolitan views. During a period when fears of, or hostilities toward, non-Anglo-Saxon immigrants could be used to stir up anti-immigrant sentiment, Bourne rejected uncritical "assimilation," which often reinforced the dominance— economic, social, and cultural—of Anglo-Saxon Americans. Instead, he advocated a cosmopolitanism in which immigrants retained their linguistic and cultural identities, as well as active ties to their homelands of origin, while embracing, building, and helping to shape the future of their adoptive countries. These transnational links, Bourne argued, could enrich the social fabric of nations, and foster integration—both within and among them. This vision of generationally rooted personal ties crisscrossing national borders could lead toward a more globalized, peaceable view of the wider human family—the "beloved community."[39]

Despite the potential resistance from colleagues, Kahlil continued actively to support Oppenheim and even requested copies of the prospectus to send to the Near East. In August, he worked with Oppenheim on a possible design for the magazine's cover. Similar in concept to his hand and flame motif for *Al-Funun*, it was never used. But he cheerfully accepted the rejection and assured Oppenheim, "You are quite right. The hand was not strong enough in the first design, and the flame did not look like a flame...I am more than glad I can be of some use to 'The Seven Arts.' I am very much interested and I want to see that everything in it is right."[40]

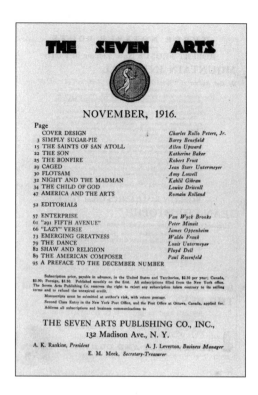

THE SEVEN ARTS

NOVEMBER, 1916.

Page
COVER DESIGN .... *Charles Rollo Peters, Jr.*
3 SIMPLY SUGAR-PIE .... *Barry Benefield*
15 THE SAINTS OF SAN ATOLL .... *Allen Upward*
22 THE SON .... *Katherine Baker*
25 THE BONFIRE .... *Robert Frost*
29 CAGED .... *Jean Starr Untermeyer*
30 FLOTSAM .... *Amy Lowell*
32 NIGHT AND THE MADMAN .... *Kahlil Gibran*
34 THE CHILD OF GOD .... *Louise Driscoll*
47 AMERICA AND THE ARTS .... *Romain Rolland*

52 EDITORIALS

57 ENTERPRISE .... *Van Wyck Brooks*
61 "291 FIFTH AVENUE" .... *Peter Minuit*
66 "LAZY" VERSE .... *James Oppenheim*
73 EMERGING GREATNESS .... *Waldo Frank*
79 THE DANCE .... *Louis Untermeyer*
82 SHAW AND RELIGION .... *Floyd Dell*
89 THE AMERICAN COMPOSER .... *Paul Rosenfeld*
95 A PREFACE TO THE DECEMBER NUMBER

Subscription price, payable in advance, in the United States and Territories, $2.50 per year; Canada, $3.00; Foreign, $3.50. Published monthly on the first. All subscriptions filled from the New York office. The Seven Arts Publishing Co. reserves the right to reject any subscription taken contrary to its selling terms and to refund the unexpired credit.

Manuscripts must be submitted at author's risk, with return postage.

Second Class Entry in the New York Post Office, and the Post Office at Ottawa, Canada, applied for.

Address all subscriptions and business communications to

THE SEVEN ARTS PUBLISHING CO., INC.,
132 Madison Ave., N. Y.

A. K. Rankine, *President*   A. J. Leverton, *Business Manager*
E. M. Meek, *Secretary-Treasurer*

AN EXPRESSION OF ARTISTS FOR THE COMMUNITY

James Oppenheim, *Editor*   Waldo Frank, *Associate Editor*
Advisory Board
Kahlil Gibran   Robert Frost
Louis Untermeyer   Edna Kenton
Van Wyck Brooks   David Mannes
Robert Edmond Jones

DURING the summer months, we sent out the following statement to American authors:

It is our faith and the faith of many, that we are living in the first days of a renascent period, a time which means for America the coming of that national self-consciousness which is the beginning of greatness. In all such epochs the arts cease to be private matters; they become not only the expression of the national life but a means to its enhancement. Our arts shown signs of this change. It is the aim of *The Seven Arts* to become a channel for the flow of these new tendencies: an expression of our Amer-

[52]

The first issue of *The Seven Arts*, November 1916. Part of the little-magazine movement, it became a seedbed for a new generation of American writers. (Courtesy Houghton Library, Harvard University.)

The first issue appeared in November 1916, and for Mary, the inclusion of Kahlil's work in it was his most significant accomplishment. "The Seven Arts has come—and for 'Night and the Madman' I prize it. Give something to each issue, do please, if you can K. G."[41] Here Kahlil's work was being presented among voices that would influence American letters for a generation. Along with Lowell and Frost, they included Eugene O'Neill, D. H. Lawrence, Sherwood Anderson, Theodore Dreiser, John Dos Passos, and H. L. Mencken, all of whom contributed to the new effort.

The success that Kahlil would soon enjoy when he began publishing his books in English was clearly related to his identification with this movement, as he himself realized early on.[42] His next piece, "The Greater Sea," appeared in the December issue, and two shorter pieces, "The Astronomer" and "On Giving and Taking," in January 1917.

~

Once again, disappearing into his work seemed to have relieved him of stress and side effects related to his activity on behalf of his homeland. When Mary saw him in November she noted, "He looked well as his handwriting had led me to expect." Indeed, because of his relaxed attitude, they both enjoyed their time together. She had seen the Hardys and the Hirsches, and she told him of "Micheline's fine Beatrice...and of Charlotte's dainty boy, and how Charlotte and Gilbert had earned $3,000 in the past year." Even Charlotte's news sounded "splendid" to him. "We talked on most comfortably and warmly at dinner and I can't remember what we said—save that K. too loves the Russian music."[43]

Mary learned that he was preoccupied not with the Near East but with preparing a show at M. Knoedler & Co. early the next year. She helped him choose the forty wash drawings for it. "Knoedler's is the biggest art dealer in the world," he observed. "Everybody is astonished at Knoedler's exhibiting my drawings. 'Why should they?' they wonder."[44] The impetus had come from Mrs. Albert Sterner, a gallery employee, who had visited his Hermitage studio and had liked his work.

The sketches represented a departure in style and objective from the earlier pastels and paintings. Freer in form and more vibrant in color, they bore more resemblance to Rodin's watercolors than to his earlier symbolist attempts. He had made most of them during the past two summer vacations.

> At Cohasset I did 75...Sometimes I'd come in from the woods at 5 o'clock and do 3 or 4 before dinner—and I didn't know beforehand what they would be...while I worked I hardly knew what I was doing. I'd go to sleep...the next morning I would sometimes not remember their look—and they would surprise me when I saw them.

The entire series was built around three motifs—centaurs, mothers and children, and dancers. "I want this [exhibit] to be just the human form in its relation to other forms—trees, rocks—other forms of life—that peculiar wiry something," he said describing the emergence of this expression of an elemental unity of people and nature.[45] For the first time in six years, Kahlil did not see Mary during Christmas holidays. For a while, he had stopped sending her poems in English, but by the new year, his letters reflected a resurgence in literary, as well as artistic, production.

> Beloved Mary, I am having a hard time with the frames and some of the drawings. But I think I can get everything ready by the 29th. And I am in a working mood. My heart is full of moving forms...I am sending you this with a poem which I wrote a few days ago ["God," *The Madman*]. Will you not look it over...and correct its English?
>
> I am sending you another little thing—a parable—["The Three Ants," from *The Madman*] to read and correct its English—when you have the time...But I must learn a great deal more before I can give form to my thoughts in this wonderful language. The poem on God which I have sent you is the key to all my

feeling and thinking. And if need be I will change its present form, because I want it to be simple and clear. This little parable…too, belongs to what I have been going through during the past year. But these short glimpses are not enough. Large thoughts must be expressed in a large way before they are felt by others. My English is still very limited but I can learn.[46]

~

M. Knoedler & Co., in New York City, would become one of America's oldest and most prestigious art galleries. Photo of the interior shows artwork displayed salon style. (Photo by Blauvelt and Co. Courtesy the New York Public Library.)

The show opened on Monday, January 29, 1917. Kahlil's note inviting Mary to it reflected his high spirits. "*The Seven Arts* and this exhibition are making my dayly life as full and as rapid as I want it to be…It is all so wonderful—even when I am not working: and it is even wonderful when I am so physically tired. Life is sweetly rich—not less rich when it is painful." A final request reflected his growing independence: "Will you not telephone me on Friday or Saturday? I have my own telephone now and I do not have to run up and down those stairs all day long!"[47]

Avoiding the opening of the Fifth Avenue gallery, Mary visited the exhibit alone. She was able to observe reactions of Syrian visitors, and later that day she described people she had seen. "He identified one of them as Mme. El-Khoury...They had said he was the 'greatest thing we have here,' that he 'had the divine in him,' that he and Rihani were 'rivals,' but in different veins." Promising sales and favorable reviews had softened him. "This exhibition has done a great deal for...my own life... The Seven Arts publication...has given me something."[48]

Earlier that year, through Witter Bynner, Kahlil had met and drawn British poet laureate John Masefield and Laurence Housman, the brother of A. E. Housman. Now Mary learned that he had dined with Frederick MacMonnies, the sculptor of the *Bacchante* statue, which Kahlil had encountered twenty-one years earlier at the Boston Public Library.

She learned more about his experiences in New York. "Mrs. Ford telephoned... Oppenheim called up too—and they talked of [literary entrepreneur William Marion Reedy] of the *St. Louis Mirror* whom they both liked very much. Reedy wants to have K.'s drawings in St. Louis and it has been suggested that K. publish a dozen of his drawings with Mrs. E.'s article." She stressed that his highest priority should be a show in Boston, and he agreed to speak to Knoedler about the possibility.[49]

"Mrs. E."—Alice Raphael Eckstein—had written an article about Kahlil for *The Seven Arts*. Oppenheim's generosity in championing his work continued to encourage him. Said Kahlil, "He's growing all the time in his work and he comes to talk things over constantly with me." New York reviewers had been kind to the exhibit, but it was Mrs. Eckstein, a Goethe scholar and also Dr. Hinkle's close friend, who called out the implications of his work.

> It is at the dividing line of East and West, of symbolism and representation, of sculptor and painter, that the work of Mr. Kahlil Gibran...presents itself as an arresting force in our modern conception of painting...We see the body of a woman who rises out of the vast forms of the *Erdgeist* carrying in her arms man and woman...Erda, Amida, Ceres, Mary, it is a matter of choice and of temperament. The meaning is universal... His centaurs and horses have a charm utterly apart from their natures, so that they are never wholly animal in character...so in these centaurs we sense the beast that is yet man and again that in man which is and must be animal, that evolution upward which is in itself a miracle but which will forever prevent us from clutching the stars.[50]

FROM KAHLIL'S KNOEDLER GALLERY EXHIBIT, JANUARY 1917

CATALOGUE

1 Reclining Figure
2 A Group
3 Nude with Blue Drapery
4 Centaur
5 Seated Figure
6 Two Centaurs
7 Three Figures
8 Crouching Figure
9 Centaur, Woman and Child
10 Two Figures
11 Study of a Head
12 Centaur and Child
13 Running Horse
14 She-Centaur and Man
15 Mother and Child
16 Head with Red Cap
17 Dancing Figure
18 Dancer with Veils
19 Rock Group
20 Study of a Face
21 Veiled Head
22 Man with Red Drapery
23 Leaping Figure
24 Captive Centaur
25 Lifted Figure
26 Another Study of Lifted Figure
27 Two Masks
28 Lovers
29 Stooping Figure
30 Girl with Red Drapery
31 Falling Figures
32 Sleep
33 Flight
34 Man Dancing
35 The Greater Self
36 Serenity
37 Man and Child
38 The Kiss
39 Man and Woman
40 Nude and Rock

List of works exhibited. (Courtesy Private Collection.)

EXHIBITION OF FORTY WASH-DRAWINGS
BY KAHLIL GIBRAN, AT THE GALLERIES OF
M. KNOEDLER & CO., 556-558 FIFTH AVENUE,
FROM JANUARY THE TWENTY-NINTH UNTIL
FEBRUARY THE TENTH INCLUSIVE, MCMXVII.
UNDER THE DIRECTION OF MRS. ALBERT STERNER.

Knoedler Gallery exhibition announcement. (Courtesy Private Collection.)

From centaur series. (Courtesy Peter A. Juley / Smithsonian.)

Mother and Child. (Courtesy Peter A. Juley / Smithsonian.)

Flight. (Courtesy Private Collection.)

277

Uplifted, from *Twenty Drawings*. (Courtesy Private Collection.)

278

~

In March, Joseph Dudley Richards, owner of the Boston gallery Doll and Richards, agreed to exhibit the wash drawings. Before the opening, however, Kahlil learned on March 28 of the death of painter Albert Pinkham Ryder. He had kept in contact with the elderly artist since meeting him in 1915. When Ryder was seriously ill in St. Vincent's Hospital, Kahlil visited him almost daily and movingly described his appearance to Mary: "He looked so beautiful in the hospital, all gone away here (cheekbones) so that the bony structure showed through the thin flesh—and the hands were so beautiful—he talked slowly, but clearly. His memory is feeble so that he tells you a thing and then repeats it." Mary noted how much Ryder loved K's poem to him, the elder artist musing about Kahlil, "he had to come way from Mt. Lebanon and I am here—and we found each other. Nobody introduced us." However, "The truth was that I went to him," said Kahlil.

The comfort that he found in their friendship fed Kahlil's self-identity. Ryder's alienation from society seemed to mirror Kahlil's own isolation, and in acknowledging his reverence for the older, reclusive artist, he confided, "I count my knowing him one of the great things of my life—that I was able to get through to his real life and have him in my real life."

> I stopped going to see him in the last months because of the effort it was to him…about twenty years ago, or so, he was in the world…But I seem to know why he left it—I understand the course of Ryder's life. It is such a struggle to meet the world—to pull the mind and the heart away from their own objects in order to answer the words that are meaningless…He just gave it up…left the society of gentlemen and ladies, and he sought the low life of New York that made no demand on him. That was a refreshment—a rest from the effort. And since his mind had stopped the struggle, his body went too…No one else had such a vision of the earth.[51]

In his memorial article, critic Henry McBride mentioned meeting Ryder at the Montross Gallery and concluded with Kahlil's tribute to him. "The following is the first poem addressed to Albert Pinkham Ryder that I have seen. It is by Kahlil Gibran, a Syrian artist and writer. It is too bad that we have to go all the way to Syria to sing the praises of Ryder." National publications picked up the poem. Mary mentioned that its lines were quoted in the Toledo *Blade*, in a Chicago newspaper, and in three other newspapers. *Current Opinion* not only included an excerpt, but also reproduced the portrait. "We are indebted to Mr.

Kahlil Gibran, the Syrian poet, mystic and artist, for this striking portrait study," the caption read.[52]

Amid this recognition, Kahlil's show in Boston opened on April 16. He did not go to see it, but waited for Mary's reports. "Doll and Richards have hung the wash-drawings in their small room between the gallery at the back and the large front room…The light is good—the space too small, and the hanging order fair only." Of the people whom he knew, Mary's sister Louise had been most appreciative, saying, "To me they were most wonderful as presenting Man as a work of Earth's, an earth-product or many earth-products—Man the root, man the rock, man the vine, the flower, man the animal." Another interested commentator was Charles Peabody, who had bought a pastel from Day's 1904 show. He and his wife Jeannette were Mary's good friends, their daughters attended her school, and he had photographed her a few years earlier. "Mr. Peabody didn't care for the form, but thought the color glorious…perfect. It made him think of 'the finest old Pompeian.'"[53]

Boston reviews were heavily influenced by Alice Raphael Eckstein's article. But one article in the *Boston Sunday Herald*, by F. W. Coburn, entitled "Syriac Suggestions," selectively recalled the artist at the turn-of-the-century, without noting what was surfacing in this latest work.

> This Syrian artist, who came to Boston in 1903 [*sic*] is favorably recalled as assistant at the Harcourt Street studio of F. Holland Day. Of late years he has worked in New York. More than perhaps any of the then group of symbolists he has carried forward the sort of vague, mystical expression that was the beau ideal of advanced Boston in the days when white roses were worn on the birthday of Charles the Martyr and when wealthy ladies scrubbed church steps. Into a super-refined atmosphere of revolt from the prosaic and literal came the young Arab and found himself breathing congenially.
>
> Mr. Gibran in literary New York has run true to the quest of the inchoate. Still, as of yore, he pulls a pencil point around and round in sweeping lines and then fills in the shaggy contours with nearly flat washes of dull color. A faint gleam here of red and blue: the least bit of accenting to indicate construction; but for the rest, all is flow and flux, is rhythm and mystery…Art conceived in a sublimated ether…this of Gibran's surely is.

Mary called the review "stupid," irritated by its tone.[54] Slowly the facts of Kahlil's origins and artistic beginnings were being submerged. Replacing the realities of Mount Lebanon, South End immigrants and settlement houses, or Bohemian Boston was the image of a vaguely Eastern purveyor of artistic spiritualties; one who had neither struggled nor suffered, and who essentially was detached from the defining imprints or cruelties of history.

Another significant figure from his past also saw the show. Josephine Peabody Marks went on April 24. Her diary remarks did not record her reaction. But according to Haskell, several Boston admirers preferred his earlier style; as expressed by an unnamed friend who regretted that he had departed from the "purely and exclusively ideal."

~

America's long-awaited entrance into World War I in the spring of 1917 overtook Kahlil's concern for reactions to his Boston work. On April 20, he wrote,

> Since the day America made a common cause of the Allied Governments, the Syrians and the Lebanese in this country have decided to join the French Army which is almost ready to enter Syria. With the help of some Syrians in the city, I have been able to organize a "Syrian-Mount Lebanon Volunteer Committee." *I had to do it*, Mary. The moral side of this movement is what the French Government sees and cares for.[55]

The League of Liberation actively encouraged young Lebanese and Syrians to bear arms against Turkey. Woodrow Wilson's message adorned its letterhead. "No People must be forced under sovereignty under which it does not wish to live."[56] Affiliated with similar groups in Paris, London, and Egypt, the American movement openly advocated autonomy and self-rule for peoples of the region. Editors of leading Syrian papers—Elia D. Madey and Najib Diab from *Mirat al-Gharb* (*Mirror of the West*), Abd al-Massih Haddad from *As-Sayeh* (*The Traveler*), Nasib Arida of *Al-Funun*—were on the executive committee. Dr. Ayoub Tabet was president, Ameen Rihani, vice-president, and Mikhail Naimy, secretary of Arabic correspondence. Kahlil was chosen secretary of English correspondence.

Kahlil's renewed commitment again conflicted with his involvement with *The Seven Arts*. By the summer of 1917, the magazine had become a passionate forum where Oppenheim, John Reed, and Randolph Bourne were denouncing the war. Caught in a crisis of conscience, he tried to justify his position when he saw Mary in July.

> You know I like Oppenheim—though I feel so oppositely to him about what to do in this war…I'm anti-war—but for that very reason I use this war. It is my weapon. I'm for justice—and so I make use of this great injustice…And Oppenheim knows

how I feel. He's come to me—you know he always comes to talk things over and I've told him. I don't want to hurt the magazine and they want to keep my name. I can't, somehow, hurt them—so I think perhaps it is better to let things drift.

Countless Americans shared his dilemma that summer. The differing positions held by Charlotte, a staunch pacifist, and Mary, an ardent patriot, widened the rift between these old friends. Mary's relief efforts, at first personal, were by now directed at the entire school. On April 22, she had written, "[The] school has sent more than $1,000 so far since October—to various needs in Syria, France, Belgium—and I think we shall reach $1,500 before the year ends." Charlotte was unsympathetic: "And you, I fear, like Aunt Rose, glory in Red Cross, service badges, thrift—and the whole subtle armament which war begets for the enthusiastics."[57]

Another lively exchange between Amy Lowell and James Oppenheim occurred in the summer of 1917. The poet resented the editor's insistence "to keep snarling at the war."[58] The Sedition Act of 1918, passed under the Wilson administration, had criminalized criticism of "the Constitution, government, the military, or the flag."[59] Under fire from all sides, he eventually agreed with his backers Mrs. Rankine and Miss Lowell to subdue his pacifist ardor. But despite Lowell's pledge of two hundred dollars to support the magazine in its financial plight, rallying support for *The Seven Arts* was too late. In the issue of October 1917, Oppenheim announced the demise of his bright venture. Another publication, *The Dial*, inherited its literary vigor, but in its brief life, *The Seven Arts* served as a vital springboard for Kahlil.

Again he felt torn. "I can't do any regular work with this war going on—work of my own...And if it all ends, and I'm still here, you know what my life will be then—just trying to do things."[60]

In December he visited Boston, where Marianna finally had found an apartment at 76 Tyler Street, a clean and warm building next to the Maronite church. When Mary saw him the day after Christmas, she deplored his appearance—"His face in repose has no laugh beneath it. A deep restless suffering underlies it—and the cause is Syria...more specifically, Mt. Lebanon." For the next two nights his conversation centered on the war. "It is this constant sense of Syria and her uncertain fate—that has leached his face again of its good color and given it that look of unquiet burning." The terrors that had subsided for a while were resurfacing.

I know I'm of use because a new price has been set on my head—not that I mind that...The other day a letter was sent me—anonymous—and a similar one to Doctor Tabet in English. "Turkey is not dead—and she has a long arm—if you do not stop what you are doing—"...Of course...I know that if the agents of Turkey were really planning to kill me in New York they wouldn't say anything about it—but just the same I made use of that letter, I telephoned straight to the Department of Justice.

What was Gibran's dream of a nation? Where might the centaur and the child in his drawing find refuge? Adel Beshara portrays Gibran's nationalism as one that embraced the lands and people of "Greater Syria," including present-day Syria, Lebanon, Jordan, and historic Palestine. It expressed an elemental sense that these lands and people, while distinct, were also intrinsically indivisible. His was an expansive, inclusive idea of nation.

While honoring and asserting the beauty and richness of Arabic language and culture, Kahlil's forward-looking perspective as an increasingly globalized citizen-artist rejected conditions of belonging defined or restricted by race or ethnicity, religious creed, gender, privilege, or circumstance of birth. Instead, individuals should be encouraged to unfold and exercise their talents as a community of citizens, intimately tied to land and place, informed by heritage, and united by a shared commitment to justice, sovereignty and home rule, and fundamental rights and freedoms. [61] But the possibility of liberation and renewal of Greater Syria, for Kahlil, revolved on whether her people could recognize and build self-reliantly upon their own most creative qualities, breaking free from a legacy of subjugation, dependence, and defeat.

"No, I haven't always faith," he answered when Mary asked his opinion of the outcome of the fighting. "Sometimes I think Syria may quite perish. Sometimes I see the coast of America bombarded with submarines and zeppelins." Gradually, she drew him away from his terrors. "K. seems only one-third living in his conscious; two-thirds in his subconscious. This war dethrones all life except its own and it holds him captive."[62]

~

Because of a bitter cold spell, he did not return to New York until January 12, and all during his visit she coaxed him to write and draw. Toward the end, they began to collaborate. They finished an elegy to Rodin, who had died the past November, and worked on four parables: "The Pomegranate," "Ambition," "The Eye," and "Other Seas."

By the time he left, Kahlil had regained his composure and his will to work. "K. loves everything lovable and everything and everybody—loves all life that is alive," she wrote after their final meeting. "Poverty of spirit on the left never blinds him to what rich things may be on the right…He looks much better for the three weeks of removal from his working scenes, in the comfort Marianna knows how to make." The evenings spent with Mary had produced many drawings, for which she told him she was "rich." "I can no more help drawing them than I can help breathing," he replied.

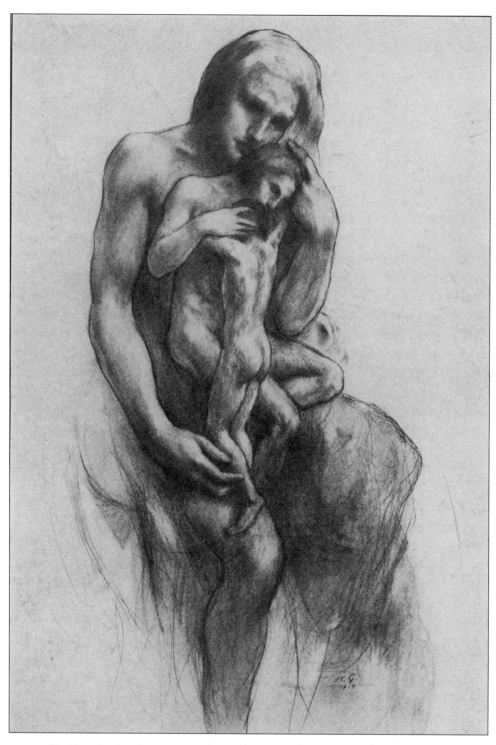

The Three Are One, frontispiece to *The Madman*, 1918. (Courtesy Telfair Museum of Art.)

15

A PEOPLE'S POET

By the end of January 1918, opportunities for Kahlil to read at literary gatherings and events in New York were increasing. That month, he spoke about Syria to a group in Newark at the request of Mayor Raymond. He had read at the Poetry Society of America and was promised an entire evening there. He accepted an invitation to read again at the home of Corinne Roosevelt Robinson. "Music and poetry," he said, "are the only two elements that can remind us of [a] calmer yesterday and kinder tomorrow."[1]

With growing recognition of his writing, his sense of disorientation lessened. Thirty-five now, he attributed this change to new opportunities for sharing his work with others. "Talking to people about poetry and reading to them give me a great deal of real pleasure," he wrote Mary on February 5, 1918. "It seems that human beings…are hungry for beauty…truth and for…that other thing which lies beneath and beyond beauty and truth."[2]

Still, hardships related to the war reached home, and Mary fretted about his drafty studio. "May you get enough coal to keep warm! I think of you all through the bitter days—and wonder how it feels in the studio—doubtless there'd be 'plenty' of coal if the government had allowed us all to be stuck $20 a ton for it!" But inflation and profiteering did not discourage him.

> These are hard days…But we are learning so much about Life and about ourselves—and we are learning about clothes and food and fuel. And when better days come…the things we have learned will be of great value to us all…Life…is altogether too kind and too gracious to me…I am often unhappy because…others…millions…are handled so roughly. And I am quite conscious that this…form of unhappiness is not free from self-glorification.[3]

No longer anticipating a bleak endgame to the war, he saw hopeful signs of a shift in attitudes toward more global ways of viewing and approaching the world.

I believe the end will be good, though just now all looks darker than ever before… In all these years, man has been thinking locally—in terms of himself, of his family, of town, of country, of continent. Now he is beginning to think in terms of the planet…speech has become planetary—in telegraph and telephone and movie.[4]

Witter Bynner. Graphite and charcoal, 1913. (Courtesy Witter Bynner Letters, Houghton Library, Harvard College.)

When Mary visited New York in March to see a memorial exhibition of Albert Pinkham Ryder's work, she saw how Kahlil's reputation was spreading. He showed her his latest portrait drawings of Pierre de Lanux and Witter Bynner. De Lanux, attached to the French embassy in Washington, D.C., was a writer interested in nationalistic movements. He had just published a book on Serbia and a study of the new wave of American poets, both of which were attracting attention. Kahlil's drawing of Witter Bynner was not the first. Shortly after his arrival in New York in 1913, he had drawn a sketch of the poet.[5]

The fact that Howard Willard Cook had dedicated his anthology, *Our Poets of Today*, to "his good friends" Julia Ellsworth Ford, Witter Bynner, Kahlil Gibran, and Percy MacKaye was promising news to Mary.[6] But the best news was that for the first time he had submitted a manuscript, *The Madman*, to an American publisher, William Morrow. A partner at Frederick A Stokes, Morrow published Witter Bynner's *Greenstone poems*.[7]

One morning, Kahlil read Mary an embryonic poem in English, which she called "Passage to Men and Women."

Love each other—and
Let your love be as a sea between
The shores of yourselves—
Fill each other's cup—but drink not from
One cup—Give bread to each other—

But share not the same loaf—
Be each alone in your togetherness—

This passage would become a central one in *The Prophet's* celebrated counsel, "On Marriage." Moved by it, she confessed a feeling of fatigue toward her work at school. Kahlil reassured her.

> There's just one thing our work needs—and that's Love. That's what pupils want, what friends want, what strangers want, what an audience wants—what we all want…I mean just freedom and welcome and want and being all there with all of one's self. Not with a philosophy and lots of ideas…but just with ourselves—the dearest thing we have—but the thing we don't give. And it's the only thing people want…We are not very loving beings…we Humans."[8]

Everywhere they walked, his high spirits were apparent. And this euphoric mood was helping his productivity. He continued to work on a long, lyrical Arabic poem begun in Cohasset the previous summer. "Processions" was a contrast in two voices—"one of the woods…the other more mental, more philosophical." He also showed Mary new drawings and talked about a work he had often described: "My island man has changed a great deal in these years. I'm not so sure as I was about some things!"[9]

~

The first reference to Kahlil's "island man" had appeared in Mary's journal six years earlier.

> *June 12, 1912.* Today K. got the first line…or first motif…for his Island God. For he has finally decided that his Promethean exile shall be an island one—instead of a mountain one.
>
> "I can put a mountain on the island—but I couldn't put an island on the mountain. And an island gives so many possibilities—especially if it is near enough the mainland for a city to be visible"…At the end of seven thousand years…from the shore near the city he puts off in his boat alone—and we learn why he had left the Gods to be an exile among men, and why now he leaves men as an exile to solitude: because he must await a new race that shall be able to accept the fire. K. has done a good day's work on it.

In a marginal note, apparently at a later date, she added the name of the god: "Almustafa of *The Prophet*." Three months later he again mentioned the project. "It will probably be five years more—but it is complete now in structure in my mind.

I shall probably get out two or three other books in the interim."[10] Over time, Mary intermittently referred to both the Island God and a new work that was being called *Commonwealth*.

April 6, 1913. Three chapters are added to Mustafa.

September 4, 1914, New York. He had been all night…sleeping not at all but making notes [about] "the big aspects of human life. Birth, education, marriage, death—and the other big details though not the biggest, like expression which is art, and labor, which is construction—these are in it."

She recorded their conversation about it.

"Have you any personalities or characters as mouthpieces in it?"

"No. It is the prophetic form. That is the really great form…what I said about punishment was very simple. Let a man restore to the world as much life as his crime destroyed…Let a man who kills a farmer add to his own work what the farmer would have produced if he had lived—or an equivalent. This is simple, and it is really a solution. I have taken other aspects of life, and reduced each to its simple reality. And just as to be simple and real as in an individual, is called madness, so simple reality in the state will be called madness."

"Your Commonwealth is the Mad State then…Do you treat of interstate relations or is it all of internal affairs?"

"…It seems to me it is not complete without relations between different states. But treated briefly. Everything will be short…the realest books *are* short. How short *Job* is!"

On November 14, 1914, he sent her an update on his progress: "I've written more than I've drawn and painted—in Arabic—some on my War—some on my Commonwealth, and some separate pieces."[11] Then on April 11, 1915, she observed that he was treating the theme of marriage "as he treats of all big things in common life—The Commonwealth is to be…like his Mustafa…one of the things he wants to leave behind as life work."[12]

After April 1915, no mention of the *Commonwealth* or Almustafa appeared in Mary's journal until April 21, 1916, when he finally decided to combine the two works.

Perhaps I shan't ever publish the Commonwealth, but…put all that is in [it] into the mouth of Mustafa…I am not a thinker. I am a creator of forms. The Commonwealth is not in my language. Only what I say in that language…is what I want to say—And only what I say in that language is going at last to matter to other people…There is absolute language, just as there is absolute form—An expression may be absolute just as a triangle is absolute…People may add this and that—but the eye will perceive in it the triangle. I am always seeking the Absolute in language. And I shall find it. There is nothing to do but wait. It will come. I am finding it more than I used to.[13]

While searching for a quality of "the Absolute" in language, through which to express his signature work, he was also trying to achieve greater mastery of English. Mary showed him a copy of *Lights of Dawn*, the recently published poetry of Greek classicist Aristides Phoutrides, whose studies Mary had supported. While Kahlil "was much interested in Phoutrides' book," Mary wrote, he still questioned whether any poet could successfully use a second language. "After all, foreigners can't write English poetry…Yet I keep on trying."

She described Kahlil's style as "a sort of universal English—the simplest structure, 'pure line' English…the Bible style." Explaining his attraction to this style, he said,

The Bible is Syriac literature in English words. It is the child of a sort of marriage. There's nothing in any other tongue to correspond to the English Bible. And the Chaldo-Syriac is the most beautiful language that man has made—though it is no longer used.[14]

Also affecting his decision to write this Almustafa-Commonwealth project in English was the support he was getting from his American friends. *The Madman* had been turned down by one publisher, but he submitted it to a second. He wrote Bynner, still a faithful champion of his work.

I am sending you some of the parables you like. But you have heard them so often that I should think you must be quite weary of them. The Poetry Society gave me a most generous reception and everybody was really more than kind. Yet our friend Mr. Morrow does not want to publish the little collection. He does not think the book will sell enough! I have turned the mss. to the MacMillan Company.[15]

~

During the spring of 1918, Kahlil accepted an invitation for a retreat at the farm of Boston writer Marie Tudor Garland, where he would be able to work in a cottage of his own. Marie divided her time between a Greenwich Village house, a place in New Hampshire, and her rambling Bay End Farm in Buzzards Bay,

Massachusetts. A widow for ten years, this ardent feminist approached bringing up six children as an adventure. Her homes were open to her family, their friends, and to many artists—Rose O'Neill and her friends especially enjoyed Marie's love of entertainment. A collection of her poems, *The Potter's Clay*, had been published in 1917. Her writings on education were rooted in Hindu philosophy.[16] Her charismatic son Charles Garland would found the philanthropic organization, the Garland Foundation, also known as the American Fund for Public Service, which supported radical and labor activism. Others in the colorful Garland family were pioneers of environmentalism and organic farming.[17]

When he wrote Mary about Marie Garland's farm, he described his next work: "One *large thought* is filling my mind and my heart; and I want so much to give it form before you and I meet. It is to be in English—and how can anything of mine be really English without your help?"[18] During the twenty-four days he spent at Bay End Farm, he outlined and finished most of the first draft of that "large thought." It was renamed *The Counsels*, and by June 1919, it had evolved into its final form—*The Prophet*.

Letters from this April retreat show how content he was amid the family and farm life. For a while, Rose O'Neill, dressed in her Grecian robes, came with her sister Callista, Indian activist and writer Dhan Gopal Mukerji, and his spouse, artist and painter Ethel Dugan. Kahlil felt free to wander by the seashore and freshwater pond, or watch the Welsh ponies, sheep, and forest animals. Each guest was encouraged to search out solitary places. Meanwhile, the presence of Marie Garland's family of six, and her eight adopted children, created a lively, festive atmosphere. Hope, the fourteen-year-old daughter, later recalled that Kahlil made a roseleaf cake with the children and spent time discussing and looking at their artistic efforts.[19]

Although Kahlil accomplished a lot, the weeks were like a vacation and flew by. "Regards from the trees and the flowers," he wrote Marianna. "I am a royal guest in a royal house in a royal countryside. I can work here, ride horses and can drive the auto whenever I want…Please send me two pounds of halvah and two hundred cigarettes." To Mary he exclaimed, "I would like to stay here forever…because I am free to be what I want and to do as I like. And I feel that I shall be able to do some good work." She answered him with a long-felt wish of her own. "Some of your pictures…and some of your English things would be dear to the soldiers in a pocket-sized book. I think, for instance, of 'God' and of the 'Hand in the Cloud' you showed me in March. They would be like God's reserves in a man's heart. And I wish the prisoners of war could have them, for love and light and space."[20]

~

On May 6, he returned to Boston with the work he had done. "I've had a glorious time. I felt like work and was able to do it." He found refreshing Mrs. Garland's attitude toward her children, one of respect and self-definition. "That's one of the things I admire most...the freedom she gives others. With the boys, for instance, she tells them that she learns from them instead of teaching them."

Of his new work, he said:

> ...the big piece of English work...has been brooding in me for eighteen months or more, but I've had the feeling that I wasn't big enough yet to do it...but in the past few months it has been...growing in me and I began it. It is to have 21 parts—and I've written 16 of them.

He described the prologue.

> In a city between the plains and the sea, where ships come in, and where flocks graze in the fields behind the city—there lives and wanders about the fields and somewhat among the people, a man—poet...prophet—who loves them, and whom they love—but there is an aloneness, an aloofness, after all, about him. They are glad to hear him talk—they feel in him a beauty and a sweetness—but in their love of him they never come very close—even the young women who are attracted by his gentleness do not quite venture to fall in love with him. And while the people count him as a part of the city, and like it that he is there, and that he talks with their children in the fields, there is a consciousness...that this is all temporary. And one day...comes a ship towards the city—and somehow everyone knows...that the ship is for the hermit-poet. And now that they are going to lose him—the feeling of what he is in their life comes to them—and they all crowd down to the shore, and he stands and talks with them.
>
> And one says, "Tell us about Children," and another, "Speak to us of Friendship"—and he speaks of these things...It is what he says about them that I've been writing. There are 21 or maybe 24 parts—And when he has ended—he enters into the ship—and the ship sails away...[21]

He read Mary the parts on children, friends, clothes, eating and drinking, talking, pain, men and women, death, time, buying and selling, teaching and self-knowledge, houses, and art. "And at the end," she wrote in her journal, "one says to the poet, 'Tell us about God,' and he says, 'of Him I have been speaking in everything.'"[22]

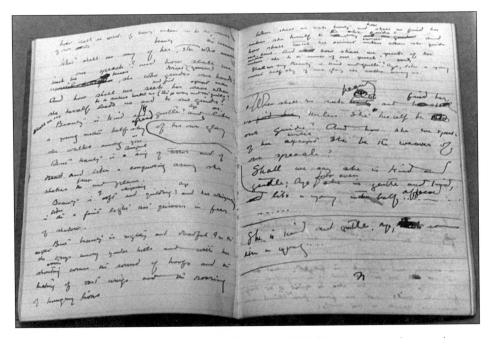

Pages from Kahlil's notebook for *The Prophet*, around 1920. (Courtesy Museo Soumaya.)

They began to make "very slight needed changes" in seven parts. "I'm not trying to write poetry in these," he said. "I'm trying to express thoughts—but I want the rhythm and the words right so that they shan't be noticed, but shall just sink in, like water into cloth—and the thought be the thing that registers."

Although he did not at first read the part on love, when he did begin—"When love beckons to you, follow him, Though his ways are hard and steep"—she responded that there was "none more beautiful." Asked Kahlil,

> Do you notice how full these things are of what we have said in talking together sometimes years ago?…Talking about them with you has made them clear to me. And one writes these things in order to find in them his own higher self. This poem…has made me better.

That night they called the work *The Counsels.* After he left, borrowing a book and a black rubber coat against the rain, she mused, "And when he described the Hermit poet of the Counsels and the relation of the people of the city to him—it was a description, to the very heart, of the way people are towards himself. And he expressed it with an accuracy, a mastery, complete—the words fitted as close as light…"[23]

The next working session occurred on May 11. She felt that six parts were complete but had reservations about the language in others. He confided,

> I oughtn't really to be writing English, anyhow…But I talk English so much—and all my friends…write all the time. It's all around me. But I still think in Arabic… when I've been writing in Arabic, English is…so far away. I have to think out how to spell even the slightest word.

Partially to dispel his doubts, but more to clarify her own aims, she outlined her own approach to responding to his use of language.

> When you read your things, I'm always listening with three ears—1. of my own soul. 2. of the ordinary man—and others—of today who might read it or to whom it might be read. 3. of the simple man generations hereafter…I don't report on 1. …I only say "I love it," or "It is beautiful"…I report on 2 and 3… Will it say to [the ordinary man] what you mean it to say?…Will it be solid still to [the simple man of generations hereafter]…and is there anything in it that time will discard?

While confessing to "sledge-hammer" tactics, she acknowledged that there must be a better way of criticism—"and truer to a larger reality."[24]

Back in New York, Kahlil's creative output continued, and he mailed five packets of poems and pieces to Mary at 314 Marlborough Street. "I hope that you do not mind my sending you these things, now that you are so busy," he apologized. "Please do not give them a thought until you have nothing else to do."[25]

~

Mary's life had never been so full, for she was closing the school. For the past few years, she questioned its direction and her role as an educator. After one headmistress meeting, she worried,

> I spoke a different language from all but the *young* women in the association… we at 314 are doing a different work because we here have to meet To-Day and be worth while to girls of To-Day only—whereas the fashionable schools can live with less vital work, because of the social desirability of their clientele.[26]

She blamed herself for failing to win support of the elite of Boston society. One night she showed Kahlil an outfit that she thought would allow her the freedom her active life demanded. When he speculated about parental reaction to its "different" look, she retorted,

Boston has already sized me up and turned me down, so I need not hope for advantage in Boston through any conformity...I am ranked next to Miss Winsor [headmistress of The Winsor School]—with her by some—in spirit and in some gifts—but they don't want to send their children to me because I am different—and they don't want their girls to be different and they do want to know just what they are sending them to...But I queered myself with the Back Bay in 1903 when I rode the bare-backed horse and walked the trapeze-top in the Lees' yard at Cohasset—They enjoyed watching these things in me, but they didn't want their girls to do them.[27]

In April, she had accepted an opportunity to more fully realize her vision of what a school should be. She was asked to head the Cambridge School, founded in 1886 by Arthur and Stella Gilman. Pioneers in women's education, they had also founded the Cambridge Society for Collegiate Instruction, which eventually became Radcliffe College. Kahlil thought it was a good move. She described the school's wanting her as "like a request, 'Come and love us. We want to be loved.'"[28]

Mary Haskell at a Cambridge School graduation, 1912.
(Courtesy Private Collection.)

And so she left Boston and her school—a place smothered by narrow brick buildings, a detested back alley, and busy street, for the Cambridge School, at 36 Concord Avenue—a sprawling Victorian mansion surrounded by flowering trees and broad lawns. Her final letter to Kahlil from Marlborough Street summarized the years since 1903.

This is our last night in this old house...and for what is best and farthest and deepest in the change I...bless and thank God for our friendship more than for all the other things...When I think of it as a whole—fifteen years... the same period as my life in this house and this school...for we met, my first winter—it has been like a single moment.[29]

He replied:

I have blessed you a thousand times for that letter, the last from 314 and the first from Cambridge. It tells me so many wonderfully sweet things about the past fifteen years…314 was indeed the stream from which I drank the water of life, and I shall always think of that large room as the birthplace of all that is worth while in me and in my life. But, Mary, wherever you are is 314. It is the spirit of the house not the house.[30]

~

At the same time that Mary was beginning life anew, so in a way was he. In the spring of 1918, he was introduced to Alfred A. Knopf, a young publisher whose reputation was attracting talented writers. James Oppenheim, whose *The Book of Self* had recently come out under the Knopf imprint, arranged a luncheon in Greenwich Village. Also present were Witter Bynner and Pierre de Lanux, who offered to translate *The Madman* into French. Prior to the meeting, Kahlil had reported, "Alfred Knopf, the publisher, wishes to bring out my 'Parables.' It is a good house and more interested in placing a book before the public than the other firms." Mary approved: "Knopf…is getting out many interesting books by people of other countries, and I shall be much interested to know if he is solid and desirable." Within a month, on the same day that Mary moved to the Cambridge School, Knopf's commitment to Kahlil had become clearer.

Mr. Knopf and I have gone over almost everything concerning my little book "The Madman—His Parables and Poems." The contract was signed yesterday, and the frontispiece was given to the engraver while I was there. The book will come out sometime in mid October. The more I see of Mr. Knopf the more I like him. He is young and has an eye for the beautiful, and though he is no philanthropist! yet he is honest—he does not leave anything unsaid. Of course I want the book to be a success commercially, for both Mr. Knopfs sake and for the sake of my next book, "The Counsels." But I think we can make it a success. There will be three drawings in the book, the frontispiece and two others, and they should make the book more interesting.[31]

Throughout July he continued to push ahead with his work on "the Counsels," energized by country retreats with the Fords in Rye, the Baynes on Long Island, and the Mortens in Connecticut.[32]

Mary continued to look after Marianna. When Kahlil's sister finally moved into the three-room apartment at 76 Tyler Street, both he and Mary began to encourage her to leave Miss Teahan's establishment. Mary had once summarized its drabness by noting how "soured and bilious and disappointed with all memories Miss Teahan looked." But it was difficult for Marianna, then thirty-three, to tear herself away from the only life she had known. Finally, Kahlil threatened not to visit anymore. Mary insisted that sewing seams for others was "not dignified," and she was forced to retire. Mary still guided the younger woman, supervised important purchases, and regularly reported on her health. "Marianna Gibran has a winter coat!" she wrote that summer. "Our dream come true—and she is going to have an Oxford grey suit made, and don't mention it—but we're taking treatment with a fine woman osteopath who is straightening the spinal rotation that keeps her from her native vigor."[33]

Kahlil left New York for his Cohasset vacation, and he and Mary did not see each other that summer. Said Mary, "I'm just so glad you won't stop in Boston or Cambridge, for I am myself such a desert of solitude…but I will see you before you go back to New York, anyhow."[34] He finished his long Arabic poem, now entitled *The Processions*, scheduled for a fall publication by Nasib Arida, editor of the again defunct *Al-Funun*. Leaving Cohasset hurriedly—"both the Syrian committee and Mr. Knopf seemed to think I am very much needed"—he contacted Mary about seeing her in New York the following weekend. Of his vacation he said, "I have added seven new processions to the original Arabic poem. But each one of the new

Reproductions from ink illustrations in *Al-Mawakib* (*The Processions*), Marat Al-Gharb edition, 1919. (Courtesy Houghton Library, Harvard University.)

processions calls for a new drawing…I am not only hard pressed by things outside myself but also by things inside."[35]

Wrote Mary:

> The processions are aspects of life as seen by Man in two selves—the self of civilization…and the spontaneous simple self…or man as he accepts and chimes in with life, not analyzing, doubting, debating, or defining. The two meet where their two worlds also meet—on a ridge of land just outside the city and at the edge of the forest… and each says what the given thing is in his experience…There are three processions of love: one of summer lust; one of great and overwhelming passion; and one of understanding.

Portrait of Blanche Knopf. Graphite and charcoal, 1920. (Courtesy Harry Ransom Center, University of Texas at Austin.)

Both Kahlil and Mary had anticipated the coming fall when he would simultaneously publish one work in English and one in Arabic. However, a paper shortage delayed *The Processions*. He was anxious that this poem, his first serious attempt to write a traditionally rhymed and metered work in Arabic, would succeed as well-crafted bookmaking, and he decided to wait for Arida to locate good paper stock. As for his American publisher, he told Mary, "Knopf is such a sweet being and he wears well. He is very beautiful in his openness to suggestions, too, when you are working with him. He's twenty-five—married…and they have a dear little child."

ALFRED A. KNOPF
Drawing by Kahlil Gibran

Alfred Knopf. Graphite and charcoal, from *The Borzoi 1925*. (Courtesy Alfred A. Knopf, Inc.)

Another mark of Kahlil's growing confidence in his English writing was the publication of "Defeat, my Defeat." The poem appeared in 1918, in a pamphlet advocating self-determination for the fragmented Eastern European countries. It was sponsored by Franklin Nicola, a Pittsburgh financier and friend of Marie Garland, whom Kahlil had met through poet Haniel Long. Mary had never seen it before its distribution. "I am sending you two copies which I hope you will like," he wrote. "And if you should find any faults in the English, please let me know them. It is never too late to know mistakes." But later, when he had decided to include it in *The Madman* and she volunteered to work on it, he refused her offer. "It's all printed now, and can't be changed."[36]

Pamphlet for Serbia, 1918, commemorating the country's defeat by the Ottoman Empire at Kosovo field in 1389. (Courtesy Museo Soumaya.)

The poem also marked a new kind of role in which he was finding himself among his pacifist American friends, as earlier rifts became reconciled. It was a role that acknowledged his keen sense of empathetic understanding. He wrote it, he explained, to express encouragement to people who thought they were failures.

The following poem has been written for Serbia by Kahlil Gibran, Syrian poet and leader who lives in this country. It is given here as a token of all that brotherhood which unites oppressed nations in their sufferings.

Defeat, my Defeat, my solitude and my aloofness
You are dearer to me than a thousand triumphs,
And sweeter to my heart than all world-glory.

Defeat, my Defeat, my self-knowledge and my defiance,
Through you I know that I am yet young and swift of foot
And not to be trapped by withering laurels.
And in you I have found aloneness
And the joy of being shunned and scorned.

Defeat, my Defeat, my shining sword and shield,
In your eyes I have read
That to be enthroned is to be enslaved,
And to be understood is to be levelled down,
And to be grasped is but to reach one's fullness
And like a ripe fruit to fall and be consumed.

Defeat, my Defeat, my bold companion,
You shall hear my songs and my cries and my silences,
And none but you shall speak to me of the beating of wings,
And urging of seas,
And of mountains that burn in the night,
And you alone shall climb my steep and rocky soul.

Defeat, my Defeat, my deathless courage,
You and I shall laugh together with the storm,
And together we shall dig graves for all that die in us,
And we shall stand in the sun with a will,
And we shall be dangerous.

"I've heard more from that poem than from any of the others," Kahlil said.

> People are so lonely. Of the hundreds who weep on my shoulder, so to speak, and tell me their life histories, almost all say, "I'm a failure, and I'm alone," whether they are married and successful and beloved at home…They've found the truth. That each one of us is eternally alone—and alone with imaginative life—and they don't know what to do with their imaginative life. They shrink from the vagueness and the labor of thinking into it and feeling into it. They just wish they could change things so that its presence wouldn't make itself felt. They haven't got in touch with the whole so that they can dwell with it. They are baffled and puzzled.

On October 2, 1918, Kahlil sent Mary a copy of *The Madman*. The handwritten inscription was simple: "To M.E.H. This also I owe to you. K.G."

Two weeks later he sent word of an event more splendid than any personal victory.

> Thursday—the seveneth Day of November. One Thousand nine hundred and Eighteen.
> Mary. Out of the dark mist a new world is born. It is indeed a holy day—The most holy since the birth of Jesus.
> The air is crowded with the sound of rushing waters and the beating of Mighty Wings. The voice of God is in the wind.

His joy, sparked by news of the false Armistice on November 7, 1918, was misplaced. But on November 17, six days after the real Armistice, he was still euphoric.

> Long ago, Mary, I said to myself, "God dwells within a thousand veils of light," and now I am saying, "The world has passed through one of the thousand veils of light and is nearer to God." Everything is different. Everybody is different. The faces on the streets and in shops and on cars and trains are different.[37]

They had long waited for this armistice, as well as for this peace between them. The publication of *The Madman* that same month made both all the sweeter.

Kahlil's illustrations for the covers of *As-Sayeh*. (*Left*) Special issue for Armistice Day, November 1918. "This is the free Syria...
On the rubble of the past, we shall build our true glory... trembling with the memory of five thousand years." (*Right*) "Victory
over Savagery," January 1919. (Courtesy Private Collection. Reprints: George Lynde/Art Imaging.)

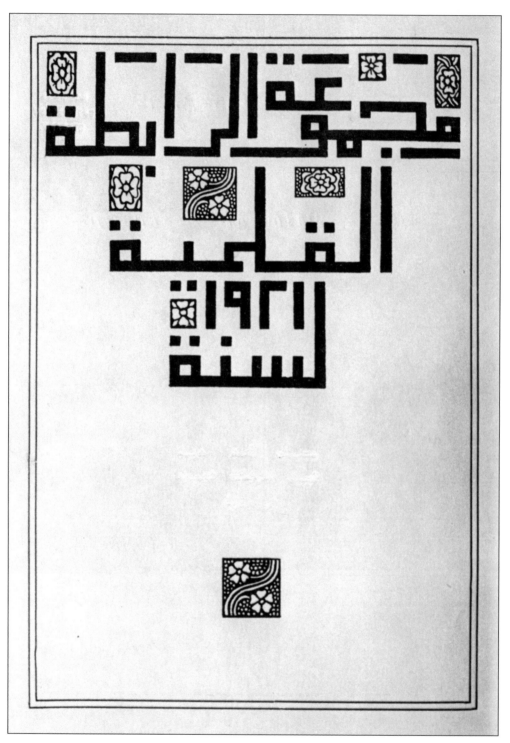

Kahlil's cover design for a collection of poems and essays by members of Al-Rabitah—the Pen League, the first Arab-American literary society. From the Pen League Collection, 1921. (Courtesy Museo Soumaya.)

16

AWAKENINGS IN THE IMMIGRANT PRESS

"W eren't you going to send me some leaflets about *The Madman?*" asked Mary. "I could easily use one hundred."[1] The leaflet read: "Auguste Rodin said of Kahlil Gibran, 'He is the William Blake of the Twentieth Century.'" As early as 1904, reviewers were likening his work to Blake's, although Kahlil himself had never mentioned those words of Rodin during his time in Paris. The quote appears to have been used in the spirit of promotion, but even so, Mary—known for her candor—approved the statement.

Two years earlier, Kahlil had submitted a biographical note to *Al-Funun,* "Gibran was born in the year 1883 in Besharri, Lebanon (and more precisely, it is said, Bombay, India)."[2] When editor Blanche Knopf asked about it, Kahlil explained: "Dear Blanche…I was born…on the sixth day of January in the year 1883…birth, like death, is a myth. Yet we are strangely held by myths, even as we are held by words and symbols."[3]

He and Mary had talked about creative versus dead truth.

> The Arabs distinguish between the two kinds…They dislike impertinent questions and the trivial. Ask one what he had at a supper, and he may tell you nectar and birds of heaven—and you may find it was really potatoes, mushrooms and beans. But he's not lying; he's refusing to answer—what he doesn't like is your asking.

Kahlil had often expressed his discomfort with a kind of inquisitiveness that he sensed when interacting with some Americans. In conversation with people, he resisted being pressured to supply facile answers.

> I meet curiosity a great deal—and I hate it. There isn't anything about me that can't be seen—in my work—in my face, in me. But people don't want to find

it out—they want me to tell them in words. They don't want to work for it... There are many things in me that I don't want any human being to know. They are mine—and no one else's...There is a gulf between each soul and other souls... it is not meant to be bridged. I feel nearer to people who are a little remote—who have in themselves that aloofness. Curiosity is one of the most hateful qualities of the human mind. And the pleasant mask it assumes is Sympathy.[4]

When *The Madman* was reviewed, Kahlil often was portrayed as a mysterious hero, ready-made genius, and Near Eastern counterpart of Indian poet Rabindranath Tagore. His impoverished origins in Bsharri, adolescent days in the South End, and cultural apprenticeship in Boston were overlooked. "This book introduces to English readers the work of the greatest poet of Arabia," wrote the reviewer for the socialist daily newspaper, the *New York Call*. "In the opinion of many critics, he is a far greater poet than Tagore." At the same time, Howard Willard Cook from the conservative *New York Sun* and Julia Ford's Friday dinner group, added to this perception. "It is proper that out of Lebanon in Syria should come a new psalmist and writer of fables, who gives to us of the Western world a note too seldom found in the writings of our own poets." The *Evening Post* reviewed *The Madman*, together with a translation of Chinese poetry by another young writer, Maxwell Bodenheim.

> Kahlil Gibran's volume, exquisitely embellished by three symbolic drawings by the author, reflects beauty of an entirely different calibre. It is the power of the parable that Gibran uses, and he employs it with great skill...It seems like a blend of Tagore, La Fontaine, Nietzsche, and Dr. Sigmund Freud—a blend which, in *The Madman*, is surprisingly successful. Gibran, the publisher assures us, is as much read in his native Arabia as Tagore is in India. This seems rather improbable, for where Tagore furnishes his readers pleasant and palatable sweetmeats...Gibran offers them strong and often acrid doses of disillusion and truth, a tonic enjoyed by but few.[5]

A month later, on March 29, 1919, the *Evening Post*'s Joseph Gollomb interviewed Kahlil and likened him to Tagore in terms of popularity, non-Western origins, and use of the parable. "But there resemblance ends, and differences appear."

> Tagore...is a figure from some canvas Sir Frederic Leighton might have painted of a religious mystic. Gibran is Broadway or Copley Square or The Strand or the Avenue de L'Opera—a correctly dressed cosmopolitan of the Western world.
>
> His dark brows and moustache and somewhat curly hair above a good forehead; the clear brown eyes, thoughtful but never abstracted in expression; the sensibly tailored clothes, smart but not conspicuous—there seemed to me a chameleon-like ease of adaptiveness about him. In his studio in West Tenth Street he looked a

sensible denizen of Greenwich Village—for such there be. But had I seen him at a congress of economists, or in a Viennese cafe, or in his native Syria, I feel sure he would look equally in the picture in each instance.

Notwithstanding his citizenship in the world as a whole, Mr. Gibran feels himself a Syrian. To him there is no contradiction here. He is working to bring about a world in which there is a great fellowship of mutual understanding and sympathy. "But in that great process the task of each people will be not to do away with the national character, but to contribute to it," he said.

Gollomb continued:

[His influence on the] "English-reading people…remains to be seen. But he has come to stay, if one is to judge by the impression created by his first work…He is emerging into the citizenship of the whole new world. Is it Kahlil Gibran, the individual, who is thus emerging? Or is it the voice and genius of the Arabic people?"[6]

The idea that Kahlil's artistry might reflect the strengths of Near Eastern culture, as much as individual talent, invited new ways of viewing his work and creative resources. By contrast, a piece in *The Nation* questioned *The Madman*'s lasting appeal, due largely to the assumed inherent inferiority of Eastern culture.

Disciples of the modern cult of things Eastern will possibly welcome the specimen of the work of the Arab sage, Kahil [*sic*] Gibran…We think, however, that most Westerners will find the work repellent in its exotic perversity, and will lay it aside with an uncomprehending shake of the head, for East is East and West is still West, and Tagore has not really succeeded in bridging the chasm between them, nor do we think Gibran will do so.[7]

Harriet Monroe, the editor of *Poetry*, questioned the credibility of the promotional copy.

If Auguste Rodin actually called this Syrian poet "the William Blake of the Twentieth Century" as the slip cover reports, I can only smile in remembering from personal acquaintance with the great Frenchman, his serene amiability toward all fellow-artists; and in this case it was the fellow-artist—the [painter], not the poet—that Rodin's alleged remark must have referred to.[8]

But even mixed reactions reinforced the legend. A writer for *The Dial* observed:

It is not strange that Rodin should have hoped much of this Arabian poet. For in those parables and poems which Gibran has given us in English he curiously seems to express what Rodin did with marble and clay.[9]

Regardless of the response, Kahlil remained motivated by the intrinsic rewards of his work and the way it lifted his spirit. In reply to Gertrude Barrie's thanks to Kahlil for sending her sister a copy, he wrote:

> Dear Gertrude, You ask me if I know what there is anywhere that is worth pursuing. And I answer that work—any work is the only thing worth pursuing…the only path to knowledge and understanding and love: and it is the only key to the house of dreams. Through work one can get over wanting people, if one does not want wanting people: and through work also one can get nearer to people if one should desire nearness. It is like magic. I am so glad that your Elaine liked the little book. She is such a sweet soul. I shall come to Boston sometimes in January, and of course I want to see you and your pretty house. And may God bless you always, Kahlil.[10]

Another Boston link was distributing Gibran's first book in English. Fred Holland Day, who by 1918 had abandoned not only art photography but quite literally the world, still followed publishing events. A general malaise, attributed to the war or to his mother's failing health, had driven him from active life. Permanently retreating from Boston, he spent the remaining fourteen years of his life at his family's Norwood estate. Contacts with the outside world included family retainers, faithful friends, and correspondence with a select few. In December, he sent a copy of *The Madman* to his former partner, Herbert Copeland, whose literary activity had also deteriorated. After their partnership, Copeland edited Booker T. Washington's *The Future of the American Negro*, but then he drifted through minor posts in publishing houses and was currently working as a clerk at Boston City Hospital. His letter thanking Day reflects apparent surprise at Kahlil's artistic growth.

> I am glad to have Kahlil's book. Thank you. I disagree with you about it. I think it really clever, surprisingly so. I should hardly say "The William Blake of the Twentieth Century" for it is so utterly lacking in simplicity; but I honestly think it is very good indeed, really good in the abnormal way which seldom attains to greatness, but of its kind I think remarkably good and "smart." I would not have said he had it in him, though I have not seen him for years, of course. Where is he nowadays? In this part of the world? Do you ever hear from him? It has quite aroused my interest—and enthusiasm.

What Day himself thought of the book is unclear. But he knew that his former apprentice's work was gaining recognition beyond the world to which he had introduced him.

That same Christmas, Mary received a response to the book from Charlotte Teller, now living in Washington, D.C. The last word from Charlotte, six months before, had conveyed her fear of an impending earthquake and the news that, as an "act of sacrifice" toward the war and society, she had burned two hundred fifty pounds of her manuscripts. After describing her growing practice as a lay psychoanalyst, she wrote:

> When I saw your handwriting on the announcement of "The Madman" I was so glad—and then so disappointed when I found no slightest note of you—except your implied pleasure and interest in K.'s success…The War has changed my feeling about fiction and drama…[Allegory is] permissible—so would Kahlil's be in form, were not the content so dangerously Oriental, perfectly done I admit—but so full of the autoerotic—I take it with [Ralph Adams] Cram that the Gothic is the only Christian form we have had—in living and in expression—the spire, the alert, the eager, not the bent head and nerveless hand and satire. All this at one time held me as it holds you. But now I am afraid of it.[11]

With this exchange, contact with Mary's closest friend—and Kahlil's artistic advocate—ended. Charlotte's disparaging comments and views of "dangerously Oriental" culture had incurred Mary's distrust.

Along with Charlotte's exit, Kahlil would also lose close ties with his old friend Ameen Rihani, who married the American impressionist painter Bertha Case in 1916. An intrepid traveler, Rihani would roam the continents, especially the Near East region, where he would chronicle the life of the region, its issues and leaders. In distancing himself—first from Josephine, then Day, Charlotte, and even Rihani—Kahlil seemed to be shedding old identities, or "masks." In the words of *The Madman*, "I woke from a deep sleep and found all my masks were stolen…I cried, 'Blessed, blessed are the thieves who stole my masks.'"[12]

~

Early in 1919, while he was visiting Marianna in Boston, Kahlil read from *The Madman* and from the unpublished "Counsels" to students at Mary's school. She observed:

> Before we went in, four of the tiny ones were in the hall…and I let them shake his hand. "Hello!" he said, quite delightedly, to them…He read very charmingly—just exactly as he reads when in his studio…The girls were amused, and delighted, and moved, by turn. He began very directly when he was before his audience—and at the close simply vanished—no chance to speak with him—and waited in the office… "That was the sweetest audience I ever had," he said.[13]

Alfred Hoernlé, then at Harvard's philosophy department, liked Kahlil's first book in English but objected to the figure in the drawing of the soul moving upward. Supporters of the new Imagism admired the poetry's construction. "Kahlil Gibran is writing poems and parables that have an individual music, a naive charm and distinction and a structural symmetry based on symbol, contrast, repetition and parallelism," wrote Marguerite Wilkinson in an anthology of contemporary poetry. "[It] is almost entirely a poetry of symbolism. His poems are parables, not designs in rhyme, rhythm or imagery, although his rhythms are clear and pleasing. In... *The Madman*, we have the best parables that can be found in contemporary poetry."[14]

Perhaps the suggestive power of his writing was a key to his varied readership. Social reformers also liked the book. One in particular was Rose Pastor Stokes, the nonconformist activist whose commitment to economic revolution was as secure as Kahlil's was to change from within. Although she acknowledged the necessity of the use of force to produce needed change, while he held out for the exercise of thoughtful devotion, they established a rapport. He began to understand and appreciate socialism as a method "for more justice in the conditions of life—for a better distribution of opportunity." One of his then unpublished parables, "The Capitalist," depicted "a man-headed, iron-hoofed monster who ate of the earth and drank of the sea incessantly." A year later, when he gave a reading of it "there was a dead silence—except for a single person who applauded...Rose Pastor Stokes." Kahlil renamed the piece "The Plutocrat."[15]

Kahlil remained close to Stokes, who at the time was involved in a federal case for violating the Espionage Act. Estranged from her affluent, activist husband, Graham Phelps Stokes, and living in Greenwich Village, she sponsored a blind, young baritone named Vladimir Resnikoff, whom Kahlil also knew. The Russian immigrant had arrived at Ellis Island at age fourteen. Eventually, the young singer became recognized for his performances of native folk songs. By 1917, Stokes and her Grove Street circle "women influential and understanding" organized a recital for him. Featured prominently on the flyer was a notice by Kahlil, praising Resnikoff's talent, while emphasizing the spiritual qualities of his singing. Two years later, *Unity*, a magazine published by the Free Religious Association of America and edited by John Haynes Holmes, published an enthusiastic review of *The Madman*. The two-column article included Resnikoff's praise: "*The Madman* is the greatest of books. No one can have any idea...how much Gibran means to me—his work, his spirit, his beautiful measures of song." Echoing the motto of *Unity* magazine— "He Hath Made of One All Nations of Men"—Kahlil's Greenwich Village circle of friends was expanding.[16]

By 1919, his ties to socialist activists had grown. Early that year, *The Liberator*, in an enthusiastic review of *The Madman*, said of Kahlil's writing, "He has breathed the spirit of the East on our cold and indifferent souls."[17] Signed H.P.S., the article's complimentary tone suggests it may have been written by a friend of Kahlil's. Since Rose Pastor Stokes was under indictment for her pacifist views, it is possible that she used her middle name Harriet to author this review. From his exposure to Charlotte Teller's early days at the A Club, to his friendship with Stokes, he was growing closer to the social movements in Greenwich Village, and to American writers and artists engaged with issues of progressive reform.[18] Kahlil expressed particular affinities with Percy Grant and John Holmes. Interacting with progressive thinkers, both of these religious leaders were trying to link social and economic reform to spiritual freedom in a faith-based vision, an effort to which Kahlil was drawn.

About the Rose Pastor Stokes's method, Kahlil commented, "She's always saying we must have a revolution in this country…it's easier to kill than to reason, and so the Bolshevists kill."[19] In the end, his commitment to renewed economic democracy was tempered: "Socialism is really just a desire for more justice in the conditions of life—for a better distribution of opportunity." Ultimately, nothing deterred him from his search for "the Absolute," and he negotiated relationships with dedicated reformers and activists with harmonious parables and cautious optimism.

~

Occasionally in 1919, Mary would see him with his associates in New York. She treasured these glimpses.

We saw Oppenheim in the little French restaurant on Sixth Avenue and Ninth Street—such a lovely face! K.'s look as they greeted was so lively and affectionate that I knew he must be speaking to a real friend. O…has infinite gentleness and sensitiveness and receptivity and lovingness and earnestness…He simply turned a hose of sunshine on Kahlil when he looked at him.

As we were walking to supper, a big automobile full of people suddenly whirled round and drew up to the sidewalk with the apparent intention of asking a question. But instead the uniformed naval man at the wheel called out, "Hello Darling! Hello little Darling!" to K. And they all laughed and K. laughed and stepped out to shake hands with them. "That's Birger," he said to me afterwards, "a Norwegian and a fine composer. And the woman on the front seat is Rose O'Neill."

It was a nice crowd, and the atmosphere of their greeting was delicious—like the atmosphere one feels among the groups of young friends in Shakespeare's plays.[20]

Kahlil's ongoing friendship with Rose O'Neill may have prompted him to tell Mary, "I am more interested in people than ever before and I like them better," whereupon she added, "I see plainly the change within the last eighteen months. Life hurts him less and gives him more. He is freer with his kind and from his kind." Conjoined with work and solitude, friendship in its many guises would remain for Kahlil—whose name in Arabic means friend—a lifeline.

Evenings at Rose O'Neill's Washington Square studio were a kind of theatrical utopia, called Zanzos, where the password was playful creativity and where poets ruled. "Kahlil Gibran was of the court, telling legends of Syria," Rose O'Neill re- called in her unpublished autobiography. "The Syrian poet-painter took me to his countrymen for rugs, lanterns, large decorated brass trays and carved taborets to set them on." Her letters revealed the symbolic role of each performer. "Come back to Zanzos, where you cannot tell the woman from the nightingales," she wrote Birger and Matta Lie.

> Could we have made a Zanzos out of this New York! With a princely stab of intel- ligence, a "sweet musician," a court fool or two, a dark gleaming from the East, a fairy child, a little elephant, a smouldering flame of an architect, Syria to proclaim it, and poetry to *convince it*! More immediately! More Zanzos! Let there be no geography but Zanzos![21]

Escape to Zanzos was a release for Kahlil. Here he could step back from personal involvements, yet still enjoy the warmth of companionship. Rose's sister Callista was dubbed "the little elephant" because of a small stone Ganesha—the Hindu god of wisdom—that he gave her. At these parties he first encountered the artists whom he began to describe to Mary—Irish Revivalist Padraic Colum, Irish fantasist Lord Dunsany, and violinist and author Leonora Speyer and her husband financier and arts patron Edgar Speyer, who also lived close by in Washington Square. In Zanzos, the most serious demand on him was the commissioning of a poem: "Darling Prince, here is Kahlil's poem to the Princess [Matta Lie]. I think the first three stanzas are very lovely with 'all things gentle,' 'all things sweet,' and 'all things golden.'"[22]

In November 1919, Mary observed still another facet of his growing social world when the Reverend William Norman Guthrie, former editor of *The Drama*, displayed Kahlil's wash drawings at St. Mark's Church-in-the-Bowery. "I've talked and read at his church," said Kahlil, "and I like him and his work." Receptive ministers in New York, many of whom belonged to poetry societies, heard Kahlil read, and eventually became solid sources of his popularity. Although this reception sometimes embarrassed him—"I am going now to a church to read to a large group of people. May God forgive me for talking and reading so often!"—he clearly thrived on attention and thought from these open-minded congregations.[23]

~

Al-Mawakib (*The Processions*) was published by *Mirat al-Gharb* in March 1919, with an introduction by Nasib Arida. Featuring rhyming quatrains in the traditional Arabic style, the two-hundred-line poem became a beloved lyric sung by Arab vocalists ("Give me the nay [flute] and sing, for singing is the secret of life").[24] While its English translations never achieved similar popularity, some critics agree with Suheil Bushrui's claim that it "will remain as the most original and influential poem of the school of romanticism in Arabic literature."[25]

As well as experimenting with classical Arabic verse, Kahlil mentioned another reason for trying to contribute to what he called "modern Arabic poetry." In a letter to Emile Zaidan, then editor of the Egyptian journal *Al-Hilal* (*The Crescent*), he described why he so carefully designed and oversaw every detail of the handsomely illustrated edition of *Al-Mawakib*, inevitably drawing upon his early years of apprenticeship in book craft with Copeland & Day.

> My intention in bringing out this in a form different from most Arabic books is to awaken the efforts of Arabic publishers and to show them the appearance of Western books…In my opinion, printing is an important art and should concern us these days when we are moving from one period to another. I know that beautiful poetry will remain beautiful even if it is written with charcoal on a wall. But don't you see that we regret the bodies of all our anthologies because they lack external beauty and perfection. *The Processions* as a poem comes from my dream of a forest…I pictured myself as a carver trying to make a statue with sea mist. How would the poet express his dreams with only metaphor and meter—that only shackle him to chains?[26]

Nine months later, in December 1919, Knopf brought out its handsome edition of *Twenty Drawings*—for which Kahlil designed a borzoi colophon—prefaced by Alice Raphael Eckstein's *Dial* article. Comparing this edition with *The Madman's* simple design, it is clear that both author and publisher successfully produced a unique edition. Its half-brown cloth and paper boards, with the impressed gilt-stamped title and author's name appearing above the circular golden palm and flaming figures, recalled the finest qualities of bookmaking. Housed in a custom chemise and clamshell box, *Twenty Drawings* also introduced the artist's own borzoi. Unlike

Knopf's usual colophon of a running wolfhound, Kahlil's stood solidly on four slim legs amid a darkened woods and flying birds. This rectangular design would adorn most every title page of Kahlil's twelve Borzoi Books.

Borzoi colophon, designed by Kahlil for Alfred Knopf Publishers.
(Courtesy Alfred A. Knopf, Inc.; Reprint: F. Frank Isik.)

~

Work on *The Counsels*, however, was not progressing, although in April Kahlil was still confident that the book would soon be published. "I'm going really to work at the Prophet (Counsels), brood over it and get it in shape during the summer and it will be published next winter."[27] This statement is the first appearance of the new title, though Mary preferred and continued to use the title *The Counsels*.

Coming to Boston in July, he still hoped to meet the deadline: "The Prophet to come out in October." But two factors impeded progress. First were his commitments to Arabic-language publications. His publisher in Egypt, Emile Zaidan of *Al-Hilal*, was pressing him for an anthology of the prose poems that he had written during the war, which meant revisions. He had also agreed to contribute to a semiweekly newspaper published for Syrians in Boston between 1914 and 1922 called *Fatat Boston*, for which he wrote an article encouraging children of first-generation Arabs to preserve their heritage, along with their citizenship.

Second, increased interest in his writings was distracting him from doing his work.

Kahlil's title design for the Syrian immigrant newspaper, *Fatat Boston.* (Courtesy Museo Soumaya.)

From the making of my bed in the morning…to going to bed at night…my life has ceased to be anything but labor. And most of it is not the labor that I am longing to do and must get out of my system if I am not actually to explode… It's come all of a sudden—with the Madman and the Arabic world, also—where I used to get six letters—I now get thirty-six—and I answer them all…I need time, say six more months or so, before I can adjust to the tempo of this new life.[28]

Throughout August, he and Mary met in Cambridge at least once a week. Instead of working on *The Prophet,* he started a new set of parables in English, which would become *The Forerunner.* Together they finished "The Dying Man and the Vulture," "The Small Nations and the War," "God's Fool," "Values," and "Knowledge and Half Knowledge." But at one meeting he retraced the development of his major effort, *The Prophet,* now temporarily set aside.

I found the other day a composition of mine when I was sixteen, that is an embryo of the Prophet…It is the work of sixteen but it has a faint hint of style… not at all in the classical style…I always rebelled against the classical. A group of people are at an inn and they talk about all sorts of things and one man in particular disagrees with the rest and gives his philosophy about the food and various things. Then they depart…and I linger with this man to draw him out. And we walk out into the fields and meet a company of peasants. And he delivers little sermons. You see the idea is there that I have now in the Prophet. And there is my island man Mustafa—he too is a development of the same thing.

When she saw him in November, he had decided first to finish the other book of poems and parables, and possibly another volume of drawings.

And after those I'll publish The Prophet. You know The Prophet means a great deal in my life. All these thirty-seven years have been making it—and I have the Arabic original of it, in elementary form. It is full of what is the sweetness of my inner life…I began it, and it's always been in me. But I couldn't hurry it. I couldn't do it earlier.[29]

In Boston at Christmas, he had made a drawing for Mary's newly renovated school, and he seemed to enjoy the teachers and pupils who came in to watch him. Speaking at length with Mary, he recited and explained one parable, that of the Lark and the Serpent ("The Poet and the Scholar") that would appear in *The Forerunner*. "There are two great classes of people in the world—the Life Seekers and the Truth Seekers—those who would live more and those who would understand more—the poet (you know I don't mean only the man who writes poetry) and the scholar."

Silence followed his return to New York. Then he wrote Mary, "It has been the most terrible winter that I have known—terrible in many ways," he admitted. "But somehow, when I feel like a little, helpless fish in a muddy lake I cannot help but say to myself, 'The air, which is above the water, is not muddy. I cannot lose my faith in the God-Element.'"[30]

During her visit that spring of 1920, he had a "glorious piece of news" for her.

You know how the housing situation has become…Twenty-five thousand families in New York are living on the streets—in tents and in the open—well, I've pretty nearly been turned out of this building. A group came along to buy the building and our rent was to be put up 300%—so we bought it ourselves—the twelve artists who live here. Now we are safe. The Jacobses who live below me and I will put in bathrooms and share the expense of plumbing—and we shall do the few things we want to make the whole place livable.

The Forerunner, with its five accompanying drawings, was at Knopf, ready for press, and he had more news. "I've accepted Pond's [the lecture bureau] offer to make a lecture tour next winter. And I've given five readings…three of them I was paid for—but I gave the money back for one—my reading in the Public Library—for them to buy more Arabic books with." *The Dial* had reproduced two drawings, "Mountain and Cloud" and "Study," in its April issue. *Twenty Drawings* had received a penetrating review in *The Nation*. Previously having found his work to be "repellent to Westerners," their article observed in part, "Gibran's message is not one of arcane transcendencies, but one of graceful emotional exposition of form. There his work is valuable and secure."[31]

Mary also heard about his portrait of Johan Bojer, the popular Norwegian writer, who portrayed the lives of the country's poor. The session, described later by Howard Willard Cook, had delighted the artist: "Bojer says it is the first thing of himself he really likes." Bojer's novels, with their themes of spiritual realization, were becoming popular in America, and Cook's comparison of the two of them was enormously satisfying to Kahlil.

As I sat in [Gibran's] studio one day last April, on the occasion of Bojer's first visit to America, and saw him dip into the soul of the man who had written *The Great Hunger*…I knew that Gibran's genius was two-fold—the poet and artist were insepa-rable…Bojer was manifestly nervous. He folded and un-folded his hands as he talked and his talk was mostly about fairy tales, tales of his own saga that declared his kinship with Hans Andersen…The sitting lasted more than an hour, and when it was over Bojer stood before the drawing with his hands behind his back, bal-ancing himself upon his toes. Turning to Gibran, he said: "You are a sculptor. Your work should be in marble! Your drawing resembles works by Michelangelo and Rodin."[32]

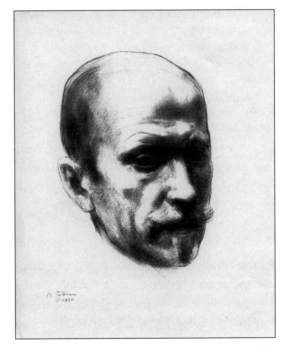

Kahlil's portrait of Johan Bojer, from the frontispiece of the Norwegian author's biography. (Courtesy Private Collection.)

This flurry of interest strengthened Kahlil's resolve. After Mary had reviewed the illustrations for *The Forerunner*, she listened to its epilogue, which he had named "The Last Watch." The need for her corrections was diminishing.

> Now he read it all—how he had loved Man…loved them absolutely—and none heard his love or saw it or felt it or understood it—and he had neither one to love, nor many, but loved alone. Only this I had not known: that when he upbraided men and denounced them, then they had begun to love him…
>
> When I was dictating from K.'s ms. of the "Last Watch"…I cried—and when I said, "Don't mind my crying," K. answered, "Mary, don't think I mind your crying…I cry a great deal, here alone, and you see I can give free rein to tears because I *am* here alone…"
>
> It needed hardly a word changed. K.'s English is the finest I know for it is creative and marvelously simple. And now he rarely misspells a word—though he still uses the dictionary as aid—and rarely misses an idiom.

Kahlil was unifying not only his linguistic and artistic fluencies through this work but his life with his art, as well, using his art to express ideals he wished to live out.

> …And now my whole being is going into The Prophet. Everything that I have done is already over for me. And they have all been just my schooling. But in The Prophet I have imprisoned certain ideals—and it is my desire to live these ideals. It is not writing them that is my interest. Just writing them would seem to me false. I can only receive them by living them.

At their April meeting, in discussing the chapter "Crime and Punishment," he said, "I can never divorce myself from the Criminal. When I read of a forgery, I feel that I am the forger—and of the murderer, that I too have committed murder. If one of us does a thing, we all do it—and what collective humanity does, is done by each of us."[33]

~

At the same time that he was attempting to articulate his understanding of a "world consciousness," he was trying to establish a voice for emerging artists of the Arabic-language diaspora. At the height of his success in American letters, he confronted unexpected success in the Arab world, as well. This was due largely to the critical ability and organizational efforts of Mikhail Naimy, who had recently returned from a year of U.S. military service in France.

Naimy was first mentioned in Mary's journal in 1914, when Kahlil described him as a new critic who "praises to Heavens and damns to Hell." Although she did not mention the title of his review, it may have been "The Dawn of Hope after the Night of Despair," published in *Al-Funun*. Naimy, a recent immigrant and then Washington State University law student, had analyzed Kahlil's influence on Arabic literature. Naimy's own literary background, including his studies at the Greek Orthodox Russian Teachers' Institute in Nazareth, in Palestine, and four years at Russian theological seminaries, was more scholarly than Kahlil's. In Naimy's twenty-page analysis, he refrained from raising Kahlil "to the level of Shakespeare as some have done" or "throwing him into

Portrait of Mikhail Naimy. Graphite and charcoal, 1920. "His face radiated with the joy of work," Naimy recalled, watching Kahlil draw. From *Kahlil Gibran: A Biography*. (Courtesy Peter A. Juley / Smithsonian.)

the first circle of Dante's Hells." He was the first critic to treat the author of *The Broken Wings* as something more than simply a cause célèbre. Pointing out Kahlil's role in the émigré newspapers, he identified him as the first authentic voice of his exiled countrymen and the first Arab novelist to employ successfully native names, customs, and backgrounds. He perceived, however, an external use of national characteristics. For Naimy, the heroine of *The Broken Wings* was not "Syrian in mind or heart." Stripped of the jasmine blossoms and lemon scents, Selma Karema could easily have been "French, English, Russian, Italian or Austrian." But Naimy welcomed Kahlil's attempts, "though incomplete and deformed," as the beginning of a dawn of Arabic literature.[34]

Having settled in New York in 1916, Naimy had met Kahlil at *Al-Funun*'s offices. Partially as a result of Naimy's opinion, Kahlil had become an acknowledged leader among Syrian immigrant poets and writers. In the spring of 1920, building on efforts begun in 1916, this group moved formally to create a writers union. Naimy reported on a gathering hosted by Abd al-Massih Haddad, the editor of *Al-Funun*'s partner newspaper, *As-Sayeh*, and his brother Nadra Haddad, on the evening of April 20, 1920.

> The discussion arose as to what the Syrian writers in New York could do to lift Arabic literature from the quagmire of stagnation and imitation, and to infuse a new life into its veins so as to make of it an active force in the building up of the Arab nations. It was suggested that an organization be created to band the writers together and to unify their efforts in the service of the Arabic language and its literature. The suggestion was met with warm approval by all the poets and writers present.

According to Naimy's notes, the group discussed and unanimously agreed upon points to found a literary organization. They agreed to adopt the same organizational name used to identify writers when the group first came together in 1916. It would be called in Arabic Al-Rabitah al-Qalamiyah—the Pen Bond, or Pen League; in English publications, Al-Rabitah. It would have three officers: Kahlil as president ("chieftain"), Naimy as secretary ("counselor"), and William Catzeflis as treasurer. There would be three categories of membership: active ("workers"), supporters ("partisans"), and correspondents. Its aims would be: "to publish the works of its own members and other Arab writers it may consider worthy, as well as to encourage the translation of world literature masterpieces" and "to foster new talent by offering prizes for the best in poetry and prose." Mikhail Naimy would draft the bylaws.[35]

Years later, Catzeflis, a frequent contributor to immigrant publications, recalled Kahlil's key influence in this venture, the first Arab American literary society.

> Ar-Rabitah was not a society, not a literary club in the accepted sense of the word, but rather, a small round-table gathering of kindred souls and minds whose aim was to help reform the then stagnant Arabic literature and who aided and encouraged one another towards that goal. Arabic literature had fallen into the depths of stagnation. With the fall of their Empire its culture remained stationary, shackled by rigid and obsolete rules and regulations. Purism was the god of the writers and poets. Steeped in traditionalism of the narrower sort, there were hundreds of versifiers but few poets. They sacrificed substance to form and no one dared to deviate from the trodden path.

318

Members of Al-Rabitah. Top row (from *left*): Abd al-Massih Haddad, William Catzeflis, Amin Rihani, Wadi Bahout, Nadra Haddad. Bottom row: Nasib Arida, Raschid Ayoub, Mikhail Naimy, Elia D. Madey, Kahlil Gibran. Missing from the original 1916 group are Attah Allah Ilias and Amin Mushriq. (Courtesy Museo Soumaya.)

Into this spiritual morass, Ar-Rabitah, with Gibran in the lead, threw a bomb-shell by saying, "If the meaning or beauty of a thought requires the breaking of a rule, break it…If there is no known word to express your idea, borrow or invent one…If syntax stands in the way of a needed or useful expression, away with syntax."

Gibran was never a purist, although he took extreme care in furbishing and refurbishing his phrases. His Arabic was never orthodox and he broke the rules right and left: however, this beautiful and fecund Arabic was the right vehicle for his winged words.[36]

For the next few years, each member signed his work with the phrase "a worker in Al-Rabitah," the Pen League, next to his name. Kahlil designed the society's logo—an open book inscribed in a circle and bearing a saying by Prophet Muhammad: "How wonderful the treasures beneath God's throne which only poets' tongues can unlock."

Pen League logo design, from the January 1921 issue of *As-Sayeh*. (Reprint: George Lynde/Art Imaging.)

~

September 9, 1917, cover of *Al-Funun* (*The Arts*), with Kahlil's hand and flame design. (Courtesy Private Collection. Reprint: George Lynde/Art Imaging.)

The key roles that the newspapers *As-Sayeh* and *Al-Funun* played in the coalescing of the Mahjar writers and the Pen League reflects the papers' importance in the evolution of Kahlil's ideas and output. Earlier, in 1916, Kahlil's search for more globalized views of the world and *Al-Funun*'s mission to "promote a sense of cultural identity" and "depict the best of Arabic culture" had intersected in a major project. To encourage in *Al-Funun*'s mostly Christian Arab readers a greater appreciation for the interwoven richness of Christian and Islamic cultural heritage, and strengthen ties between the two faiths, Kahlil composed a series of short essays and imaginative drawings about pre-Islamic and Islamic poets and philosophers: Ibn-Sina, Al-Ghazali, Umar Ibn al-Farid, Abu al-Nawwas, Ibn-Khaldun, Ibn al-Muqaffa, and Al-Maarri. He paid tribute to the Persian physician and scholar Ibn Sina (Avicenna), the ancient poet to whom he felt a close affinity. He described how Ibn Sina's poem "al-Nafs" ("The Self") proved that knowledge is the life of the mind and ascends from physical matter to a spiritual sense of God.[37] Kahlil called attention to the spiritual unity between the thinking of Al-Ghazali and St. Augustine, referring to Al-Ghazali as the link between the Indian mysticism that preceded him and the deism that followed;[38] and he paid homage to the devotional character of the poetry of Umar al-Faird,

IMAGINING PLURALISM: PRE-ISLAMIC AND ISLAMIC POETS AND PHILOSOPHERS

Kahlil's series of drawings and essays, 1916–1917, sought to cultivate among *Al-Funun*'s Christian readership a greater appreciation for the interwovenness of Islamic and Christian heritage, and to strengthen ties between people of the two faiths.

Islamic scholar, physician, and poet Ibn Sina (Avicenna).

Al-Ghazali, Islamic philosopher and theologian, likened by Kahlil to St. Augustine.

Poet Umar Ibn al-Farid, author of "The Poem of the Sufi Way."

"The philosopher of historians," Ibn Khaldun.

Classical Arab poet Abu Nuwas, who appears in *One Thousand and One Nights*.

Qays, who becomes lost in madness for love of Layla, from the epic love story *Layla and Majnun*.

Al-Mu'tamid ibn Abbad, the Andalucian Poet-King of Seville.

All drawings graphite and charcoal. Series from *Al-Funun*, June 1916–November 1917. (Reprints: George Lynde/Art Imaging.)

Kahlil's portrait of *Al-Funun* editor Nasib Arida, who in 1916 first published and promoted writers as members of the Pen League. (Courtesy Private Collection.)

author of "The Poem of the Sufi Way."[39] He also contributed drawings and stories of the poet Abu al-Nawwas, who so often appeared in the tales of *One Thousand and One Nights*, and historian Ibn Khaldun.[40]

More personally, Kahlil and other writers were encouraged by the presence and leadership of the much admired Nasib Arida. Known affectionately by his colleagues as "the Arab Encyclopedia,"[41] Arida—along with publishing *Al-Funun*—contributed his own poetry and articles to *As-Sayeh,* the semiweekly newspaper edited by his brothers-in-law Abd al-Massih Haddad and Nadra Haddad. So close was the relationship between the two papers that Arida took over *As-Sayeh*'s editorship when the Haddads were away. Because of Arida's gentle demeanor, compatibility, and expertise in classical Arabic and modern Russian, the writers in this network surrounding the journal began to identify with one another. They socialized and enjoyed sessions of "drinking, playing cards and even writing poetry together," with Kahlil often hosting them at his West Tenth Street studio.[42]

~

A month after Al-Rabitah's launching, Kahlil visited Boston and mentioned to Mary that work on *The Prophet* was still stalemated. She thought this was due to the work of refinishing his studio and small, unfinished tasks. He expressed the sense of responsibility he felt toward his culture: "Something is going to come out of that Mountain (Lebanon) that will surprise the world… And it's up to me to organize a body of work. I'm doing some of the folk songs of Lebanon into English for two women."

Back in New York, he explained his continued silence.

> Yes, indeed, I am coming to Boston this summer but not before I put this studio in order…My sister and I cannot get the rooms at Cohasset…But it does not matter. I shall come to Boston and we will make the best of it. I can always do more work in the city than the country. And I *must* do a great deal of work this summer or else be snowed under."[43]

On August 20, he finally appeared at Mary's school. In their next four visits, he and Mary spent some time on *The Prophet*, but they mostly talked about recent activities. He told her about his latest long prose poem, one he had written for *Al-Hilal* (*The Crescent*) in Egypt.

> My political farewell—the meaning of it was, your Syria is not my Syria and my Syria is not your Syria. The sheep-tending shepherd in Lebanon is more to me than the deep laid scheming of men in the government. I love the Syria that was real generations ago and will be real ages from now.

He showed her another drawing, "Breath on a Windowpane," which *The Dial* had reproduced. They looked at *Al-Awasif* (*The Tempests*), his anthology that had just arrived from Egypt. "Naimy has written a very beautiful thing on that book. I think no one else could have done what he has done."[44]

He introduced an idea for yet another book. "I have about 500 short sayings—too short for *The Madman*—most of them in Arabic, but I can put 300 or 350 of them into English; and they would make a very nice little volume." Mary began randomly to record them and referred to them as "The Way of the Seven Days." He read to her some short sayings. "Once I saw at the gate of the temple a dog biting a dead lion. Then I lost my fear of the dead and my respect for the living." Said Kahlil, "That was written about six years ago—and I was bitter then. But there's no bitterness in me now." She listened again to the counsels on "Good and Evil" and "Crime and Punishment" and questioned an apparent disparity.

> In "Good and Evil" K. used the word 'your giant self' wherein in "Crime and Punishment" he had used 'God-self.' I was talking of the English use of 'giant' as so different from the sense in which K. uses it—and the use of 'God'…As to what word I shall use when I mean God—I shall use God—not 'Life' or 'Law' or 'Love,' even

though those all mean the same thing. If in my consciousness the word is God I shall say 'God.'[45]

Three days later he arrived excitedly at the school.

I've a perfectly good idea for these sayings…these bitter things are very distant from me now—they aren't myself at all, but if I throw away everything I outgrow, I'll throw away a very great deal. And all these things were real to me when I wrote them. Well I've thought of a form that will hold them all—in a setting that would use them for just what they are: the story of a consciousness—I am on a journey to the Holy City. In the morning I overtake a stranger…and we naturally fall into a conversation. He is sad and bitter and all day we talk. He says the bitterest things. The next day he is a little less bitter—and we are a little nearer to the Holy City—and so he changes—on to the fourth, the fifth and the sixth—and on the seventh he is saying the planetary things…and we arrive to the Holy City. As we come near to the Kaabah, I lose sight of him—in the evening, I see him dead, near the wall of the temple.

The aphorisms poured out, and Mary continued to edit them: "I closed my hand and when I opened it, in it was a soft mist. I closed it again and opened it—and lo it was a worm." "I desire eternity because there I shall meet my unpainted pictures and read my unwritten poems." This exercise broke his year-long silence about *The Prophet*. On September 7, she was able to sum up its opening.

And so today, though he is still almost in fragments bodily—he had brought the beginning of The Prophet—how Almustafa had waited twelve years for the ship of purple sails and when he saw it come, how he spoke to himself of the dearness with which his pain had clothed the city in his heart—so that he sorrowed to depart.

When she questioned the repetition of the pronoun "he" for the Prophet, Gibran replied,

I thought that I would use [Almustafa] once only in the book—at the very beginning—and through all of the rest of it say 'he.' Almustafa in Arabic means something very special—the Chosen and the Beloved too—really between them both—there is no name in English with any such significance.

He then debated whether to add "the Chosen and Beloved" after the name.[46]

He explained the meaning of "land of your memories," the phrase used by Almitra. "All that is written here is written with many things in mind. Each thing is a symbol of man's life as a whole—and the 'land of his memories' is all our historic past—Life bears us from our great past towards our greater future."

After they had analyzed the introduction, he returned to his collection of sayings.

> I don't know what date to set for either The Prophet or The Way of The Seven Days, I can't publish anything later than The Prophet which shall be any way less than The Prophet. This would mean that if the Sayings come later, a good many of them would have to be left out…I won't hurry about either of these books. It doesn't matter how long they take.[47]

On September 14, Mary reviewed the visit.

> Never before has he written so systematically on an English book while in Boston—nor has he paid Marianna so long a visit. So we are doing more than usual. It is the pressure of The Prophet to be finished this autumn…Our method is: first, K. reads it through aloud to me. Then we look together at the text—from the beginning of the new part or from an earlier section; and if we come to a bit that I question, we stop then and there until the question is settled. K. uses me as the reader embodiment of his English speaking audience. When he waits, to read me only the final draft, it is rare that the English ear would dream of desiring any change.

Their productive collaboration had kept him in Boston longer than usual. Yet he worried about his Arab colleagues. For the first time, he described The Pen League to her.

> We founded what is practically an academy of Arabic in New York—and in Boston too—and probably it will get branches in the Arabic world also—at Beirut or Damascus or Cairo. It will publish in Arabic yearly the best that has been published in the other languages of Europe…[48]

When he left on September 17, he planned to return to Boston within a month to finish *The Prophet*. But *The Forerunner* appeared in October. W.S.B. or William Stanley Braithwaite, the *Boston Evening Transcript*'s popular African American literary editor, who was a consistent admirer of Kahlil's work, wrote: "There is a great deal of beauty and imaginative power in Mr. Gibran's pages which sink into the consciousness with a kind of Oriental hush that is captivating."[49] Harriet Monroe's *Poetry* magazine had never responded favorably to Kahlil's work. The noted journal described his parables as having "all the unpopularity of sermons outside the pulpit." In writing about *The Forerunner*, however, the reviewer did mention that the "accompanying drawings, in dim shadow-shape and vague lines, give a fine touch of completeness to the book, supplying a somewhat needed justification for the text."

It went on to say, "Incidentally, this volume should be praised as a specimen of bookmaking. Mr. Knopf has been conscientious in making out his list; and he has been careful, as other progressive publishers have not, to give each book an appropriate format."[50] Slowly, with Alfred and Blanche Knopf's approval and support, Kahlil was able to pursue his dream of bringing a higher level of craft to the design of his books, intended for the hands of ordinary readers.

When in December he once again saw Mary, he was involved with producing the Pen League's New Year's issue of *As-Sayeh*. "Of late I have been lost in my own mist," he wrote her. "And whenever I feel lost I turn to writing Arabic poetry... to...finding another dawn."[51]

⁂ وجه أمي وجه أمني ⁂

جبران خليل جبران

هذه كلمة ولدت في قلب جبران   وعندنا انهُ يجبُ على كل سوري ان يتخذهُ دستورا

ــ لاميله ومقاصده في هذه الايام المفعمة بالمرارة والشدائد

Kahlil's drawing, *The Face of My Mother, the Face of My Nation*, from *Al-Funun's* Crisis in Syria issue, October 16, 1921.
"These words were born in Gibran's heart...Each and every Syrian must follow them as their guiding principle...in these times
of strife and hardship." (Reprint: George Lynde/Art Imaging.)

17

NO LONGER APART

Kahlil had become a poet of two often conflicting worlds—his native world and his adopted one. He saw himself as a voice for each, roles he kept trying to reconcile. When Mary visited him in December 1920, he mentioned a recent meeting with Rabindranath Tagore: "[He] has talked about America as a money-grabbing land without a vision—he talks as so much of the East talks about the West. I tried to say…that spirit may be manifest in machinery…and in everything."[1]

He described his latest writings in Arabic, especially a play about "the city of imagination," *Iram, City of Lofty Pillars*, and its characters—a Persian mystic, a Lebanese scholar, and Amina, a seer. He also told her about the reception of his work in the Near East. "The Political Farewell," in particular, was receiving increased attention, but his stance as an advocate for independence was also clearly recognized by his opponents. He recalled a piece he had written for *Al-Hilal*, "You Have Your Lebanon, and I Have Mine."

> Your Lebanon is factions and political parties.
> My Lebanon is young boys climbing rocks and running with the streams…
> Your Lebanon is a chess game between a religious leader and a military leader.
> My Lebanon is the temple that I enter with my soul…
> Your Lebanon is delegations and committees.
> My Lebanon is gathering around stoves on stormy nights
> that are cloaked with the purity of snow.
> Your Lebanon is speeches and lectures and discussions.
> My Lebanon is bird sounds…and the rustle of branches of oak trees and poplars.[2]

Kahlil explained that the piece had been removed from publication.

> Well, the censorship in Syria cut it out of the magazine and out of the Syrian papers that printed it, and out of the papers coming into Syria from New York

and Cairo and South America…But they didn't cut my name and the title out of the table of contents so now everybody knows the piece was there—and they are determined to get it—and it will do more than if the government had let it alone.[3]

In a letter to Emile Zaidan he apologized for the controversy over the poem.

I didn't know that censorship in Syria has become so bad…It makes me laugh and cry at the same time—I feel that those who have extracted that article out of *Al-Hilal* have praised me and I don't deserve their praise. They insulted themselves and they don't deserve the insults…In the twenty years I've spent until now, I've really done nothing that deserves to remain eternal. My vine has only yielded sour grapes and my net is still covered with water. Please ask my friends to give me more time.[4]

To Mary he confided a similar inadequacy.

I want some day not to write or paint but simply to live what I would say, and talk to people. I want to be a Teacher…I want to wake their consciousness to what I know it can know. Because I have been so lonely, I want to talk to those who are lonely—and so many are lonely…I've moved very slowly. I ought to have been ten years ago where I am now. But there are certain streaks in me that held me back—a certain inheritance. In my father's people is much temper, and restlessness, and vainness. And I have all these and they held me back for long: The caring for fame and what people said and thought. But they will not hold me back longer.[5]

In Boston for Christmas, he was preoccupied with the challenges facing new countries in his homeland. For *Al-Hilal* he was writing an article on "the two consciousnesses in the Near East: the creative consciousness, simple, direct, that everyone, workmen and all, can have, and the other consciousness—complex, often political or economic or social—that is a thing of the moment and not creative." Soviet Russia and America seemed to represent the "new consciousness" of seeking "goodness and reality." He wanted to influence emerging nations' ideals and goals: "A young country can produce a new form of self…this new consciousness, new desire, new vision—that is my business."[6]

Kahlil stayed in Boston long after the holidays. He wrote Mikhail Naimy that he would miss the next Pen League meeting and also that he would not be part of the Syrian delegation to the White House.[7] On January 24, 1921, Mikhail Naimy, along with editor Nasib Arida, writer Abd al-Massih Haddad, and two Lebanese financial leaders, met with President Woodrow Wilson. On behalf of fellow Syrians in Brazil, they presented the president with an elegantly carved box with a golden cover surrounded by thirteen diamonds that represented America's thirteen original states. The design included columns on which were inscribed the words "Mount Lebanon and Syria"; the number fourteen, referencing Wilson's Fourteen Points speech at the 1916 Paris Peace Conference; a lamb's head symbolizing Syria's vulnerability during its Ottoman occupation; and an American eagle above the English inscription, "From the Syrians of Brazil to the President and the United States."[8]

Naimy addressed the president simply: "We are pleased to present to you in the name of a sector of the Syrian nation—in the name of our fellow Syrians in Brazil—this small gift." In return, Wilson graciously expressed his gratitude.

> What I did and what the United States of America has done for Syria is only one of the duties that we are called upon by humanity to do. I wish you and your country all the success and progress…I will cherish this as a beautiful memory of the gratitude of Syria and the Syrians.[9]

The next day, newspapers throughout the country, including *The New York Times*, described the plaque given to the president as a "token of gratitude…for his 'efforts in behalf of small nations and for helping the Syrians during the war.'"

Although Kahlil didn't attend this ceremony, he may have discussed it with close associates of the president.[10] Shortly before the ceremony, perhaps resulting from his friendship with violinist and poet Leonora Speyer and her husband Edgar Speyer, Kahlil had met Wilson's secretary of state, Bainbridge Colby, and his wife Nathalie Sedgwick Colby. The friendship began with Kahlil signing his books for them. Subsequently, the couple purchased two of his drawings, and Mrs. Colby—a writer—began to invite Kahlil to parties they hosted. Through these gatherings, he met writers and artists from her broad international literary circle.

In her memoir, Nathalie Sedgwick Colby described Kahlil as a "Syrian painter and poet" with "immense tragic eyes he had to pity the world with, and a laugh… in the corner of his mouth." She wrote, "An Arabic rasp edged the soft depth of his voice when he got annoyed. He got annoyed at America's slapdash ways, for he demanded a ceremonious give-take in his friendships." She also recalled his persistent immersion in his work.

> Scholars and poets came. But not Kahlil Gibran. He liked to stay unjostled in his own studio, reading unpublished manuscripts in his white robes. The little smile the West put on the corner of his lips never once touched the prophetic blaze of his eyes. We wrote the same things—only the clothes were different—he always said.[11]

What mattered to Kahlil was to pay attention to and follow an elemental sense of belonging, from which an unbounded picture of his world was forming. In March 1921, he wrote Mary:

> I have a sense of being a mist of movement…beginning in the mist and the mist solidifying and becoming hot…and burning…and suns coming off…and the sun throwing off little planets…and upon the planets little bodies peeping up…and in these bodies something of the mist also. And this sense too a language by which I mirror reality to myself.[12]

When Kahlil returned to New York, following the White House ceremony, he continued to try to articulate his views of a global universality that placed humanity above blind self-interest. He incorporated some of his ideas in the remarkable article "The New Era," also translated as "The New Frontier," which appeared in April 1921.

> In the East there is an awakening.
> In Eastern fields there is a young man who calls the inhabitants of the grove
> To stand up and walk.
> The East has two Masters.
> One is an old dying man.
> The other is silent and ready to talk.
> Which one are you?…
>
> Are you a politician who says, secretly, in his heart,
> "I want to benefit from my nation"?
> Or are you a patriotic and passionate person who says,
> "I long to benefit my nation"?
> If you are a man of yesterday,
> Then you are a parasite.
> If you are a man of tomorrow,
> You are an oasis in the desert.
>
> Are you a merchant who uses people's needs to profit greatly,
> Monopolizing necessity to sell for a penny?
> Or are you a man of hard work
> Who uses his experience as a tailor or farmer
> To link the person desiring and the person supplying.
> If you are the former, you are a criminal who lives in castles.
> If you are the latter, you are benevolent…
> Whether people are grateful or ungrateful to you.

Are you a head of a religion who weaves from people's naiveté
A luxurious robe for his body,
Who crafts from simplicity
A crown for his head
And claims he lives on his own earnings?
Or are you a God-fearing man
Who sees the virtue in an individual's beliefs
For the nation's glory
Seeking secrets of his soul on a ladder to the Absolute.
If you are the former, you are a disbeliever
Whether you fast during the day
And pray during night.
If you are the latter, you are
A lily in the garden of truth...

Are you a journalist who sells his principles in the market
And flourishes and feeds
On calamity that society produces
Like a vulture landing on a carcass.
Or are you a teacher standing before a dais
and takes from the day's lesson, sharing it with his students
After he heeds the advice himself...[13]

Although his writings in Arabic were delaying *The Prophet*, by now three-quarters finished, he could at last say that his lifelong ambivalence, his painful search for identity, was giving way to a more unified sense of direction.

> I used to think I was a fragment of something else—something different from the rest of Life—and in everything I wrote was something that expressed, directly or indirectly, aloneness. But that was really false...I know now that I am a part of the whole...Now I've found where I fit...Feeling myself always different and alone, I was self-centered. You know, if one is in a room, one can either dig into one corner of the room—or can project himself to fill the room. Filling the room is harder, but it is realer...and when one really *accepts* the whole room, or accepts all of life, with its suffering and its pain, and its relations with other peoples—then one finds one's place in the whole.[14]

This affirmation demonstrated Kahlil's talent for the aphorism. *The Dial* published some sayings that Mary and he had worked on the summer before. But he still hedged when it came to working on *The Prophet*. This was due to his recurring general malaise, this time described as heart trouble. Mary addressed this exhaustion

The Traveler, from the January 1921 cover of *As-Sayeh*. (Courtesy Museo Soumaya.)

Kahlil's illustration for Mikhail Naimy's poem "If Thorns but Realized," in *As-Sayeh*, January 1921.

the first week in February. He kept up dictating three or four hours' worth of material for Arab newspapers and journals, but he complained that his "personal life seems absolutely still…I've lost even my dreams when I sleep…I don't want to do anything. I'm tired, played out—I need six months' rest."[15]

When he showed Mary the Pen League's first annual issue, he described the cover: "For 'The Great Traveler, God,' I invented letters beneath [squared Arabic letters]. I like it but I haven't got quite enough in the movement of what I wanted…I wanted absolute evenness." Mary took note of two other pictures: "One of two faces in a mountain…a wash drawing, blue, which Mme. El-Khoury bought a few years ago; and another…a youth with his back turned to crouching figures hedged with thorn-vine bonds, himself beholding a lily that grows up beside him." Kahlil said that the thorn-vine image illustrated Mikhail Naimy's "If Thorns But Realized the Secret of Flowers," in praise of solitude, which Kahlil believed to be "one of the great poems." It appeared in 1921 in a special edition of *As-Sayeh*.[16]

Kahlil's health concerns persisted, along with pressures to

complete the book. James Pond had recently asked him if he was ready to launch a lecture tour with a public reading in New York. When Mary advised that she "wouldn't for a moment consider doing it," he replied, "I'm so glad to hear you say that…I *could* 'order' a Farewell to the Prophet…But nothing in me wants either to end the Prophet to order, or to do that kind of reading."[17]

Knopf wanted to publish it in the fall. "I told him no," Kahlil said.

> I want to read it next winter—and then it can be published the next fall—Knopf says, "Mr. Gibran, you don't go about enough. People ask you here and ask you there. You ought to accept. It would increase the sale of the book."…They are all the same way. The young woman in the office says, "Mr. Gibran, if you'd give an exhibit of pictures and drawings, it would make the book sell yet better." And they say it in kindness.[18]

That June, Kahlil found a measure of relief at a Catskills hamlet called Cahoonzie, in upstate New York, with three other Pen League members. Mikhail Naimy recalled, "Gibran, Arida, Haddad and myself decided to spend a short vacation in the country…We put up at a large two-story farmhouse, located on the top of a most pleasant hill. In that solitude…we spent ten days which passed like ten minutes." One day they hiked to a waterfall. Afterward, inspired by the majesty of the forest—along with the *arak* they drank—they sang folksongs, which led to their composing Arabic verses. Heading back, Kahlil and Naimy fell behind. "We walked a distance to the time beat of our silent thoughts," said Naimy.

> Suddenly Gibran stopped, struck the road with his cane, and called aloud, "Mischa!" I, too, stopped. Looking at my companion I was abashed to see the change in his face. The glowing picture of the waterfall and the hours we spent with it had entirely evaporated from his eyes. Instead there was a cloud of bitter sadness. "Mischa!" he called again, "I'm a false alarm." Saying that, he bent his head and fell silent.

Naimy regarded this scene as "the most touching…of all the moments I had with Gibran during the fifteen years of our comradeship."[19] He soon responded to his friend's expression of anxiety with lavish praise in a letter that may have reassured Kahlil.

> Dear Brother Gibran: O Lamb of Christ at heart, O Jupiter of mind, My heart is sad because I didn't see you before [a trip]. I felt in a vacuum that night when the brothers wished me farewell, because the main link of the chain was not there…

Michel Naimy and Kahlil, in the Catskill Mountains in upstate New York. (Courtesy Museo Soumaya.)

Hoping that I will see you safe and sound, creating pearls and spreading them before people...[20]

~

Through July, August, and September of 1921, Kahlil spent time with Marianna and visited Mary on numerous occasions. "I've come to Boston to finish that book and finish The Prophet," he explained to Mary. "That book," or "that awful book," was another anthology in Arabic that Zaidan and another publisher, Yusuf Bustani, were preparing. Kahlil had agreed to edit it, and the details were burdensome and complex. "Never again will I give my word to finish a thing by a certain date!" he fumed.[21] But the commitment had been made, and he spent half of July polishing his most recent articles and finishing "A Ship in the Mist," his latest story in Arabic, which dealt with a man's love for an invisible companion.

During their frequent meetings in Cambridge, he drew something for Mary. Often he voiced dissatisfaction with his earlier oil paintings and described plans for a new series:

I haven't been painting now for a long time…I can't paint again now until I am free from writing…When I was younger I used to do them both together—would just draw at any time; but now I can't do that…I have been learning about putting form and color together…I knew there was something radically wrong with my work…It didn't say what I wanted it to say and that something was color…When I have painted these [new] pictures, I will destroy everything else that didn't lead up to them.[22]

On August 8, she filled two notebooks on Ouspensky's *Tertium Organum*, H. G. Wells's *Outline of History*, and the natures of Christ, Buddha, and Muhammad. Kahlil turned again to *The Prophet*. "'Man's needs change: but not his love, nor his desire that his love shall satisfy his needs.' That's from the Farewell. Do you like it? It's not written yet." She copied it down for him and another aphorism that appealed to her, "Teach never what you know—but always how the child may find a path for himself."[23]

On his next visit she confessed to a longtime anxiety. At forty-eight she feared old age and the prospect of inactivity. Kahlil tried to ease her fears with another view.

When people dread age, they are thinking in a very local way. If elderly people seem less alive to *you*, there's something wrong with your way of consciousness…I sometimes imagine myself…after death, lying in the earth and returning to the elements of earth: the great loosening, the change everywhere, the opening into simpler things—the widening out into those things from which anything may be built up again—the Great Return—such deep quietness and a passing into the substance of things…It is the autumn of the body—that leads to the winter…and this winter is necessary to another spring…

He also relieved her doubts about her administrative skills. "It is the *being* that teaches, not the ideas, and not the organizations we create…Plato organized nothing—yet he lives, and lives among people who actually know none of his ideas."[24]

Mary's sympathetic criticism again gave him impetus. For the last three weeks in August, he cloistered himself at Tyler Street and finally returned to school.

Kahlil was looking lovely in every one of his thousand aspects when I came in a little late today and found him waiting in the office. The day was hot. *He* was doubtless hot and his skin was soft and transparent—his eyes shining—and he was full of that radiant smile of his—

He has written the Farewell of The Prophet and read it to me. His same message—of the Greater Self and the Oneness of Life and the lovingness of the Greater

Self—put again in words and figures that reach where one has thought words and figures could not reach.

"If its general structure is right, I can change any detail in it," said K. when he had ended. "If it isn't right, I'll rewrite the whole thing…" But it was the very soul of rightness and such a mirror of the prophet's soul. And how absolutely the Prophet is Kahlil—although Kahlil has several times said, "This is not I but the Prophet."

They spent two more afternoons polishing "The Farewell." On September 6, she dictated from the "exceedingly careful and accurate and clear" manuscript, and he copied it.[25] Three days later they reviewed the manuscript because he was concerned about the "quantity-proportions" of the book. "I may have said this or that very badly," he admitted, "but I feel that the *amount* in this opening ought to be kept…The beginning, middle, and the end has each its proper weight, and if we misjudge any one of them, a certain harmony is lost." Then he spoke of Nietzsche and his Zarathustra.

The mistake of making too short a beginning has been often made. Take Zarathustra, for instance—probably I sound almost sacrilegious, for Zarathustra has much beautiful poetry, and I *love* it and love the book—But Zarathustra comes down from the mountain. He talks two or three minutes to an old hermit on the way—that is all—Then he finds the townspeople waiting to see a tight-rope dancer, and to this crowd in their present mood he begins to talk—like a god or a superman. Of course they couldn't hear his real meaning. And there's a certain *twist* in his doing it that way. There *was* a twist in Nietzsche—a lack of balance in him as an artist. He had an analytical mind…And the analytical mind always says too much.

Because it was his last visit to the school that summer, Mary recorded seventeen pages and still apologized to her future readers for its brevity. "And more than ever does he express realities wonderfully in talking—But I retain less vividly and fully than of old—even though I record as promptly as possible." She noted his version of two important names in *The Prophet*.

Almitra's name has in it the ancient Mithras-root—that is in the name Mitras, or Mithraic—a very early religion, about which we know little. And the city of Orphalese has in it the Orpheus-root. Apparently there were two Orpheuses—a musician, one—and a really great prophet, the other—We have lost the actual details of him but he must have told profoundly upon man's life at one time.

Both of them were unaware of how changes in her life would alter the course of their friendship. But during that session, he digressed and in a few phrases offered his sense of life's ambiguity: "There is no mystery; there is no lie; there is no truth; in a certain sense we may say that. Unless a tree is a truth."[26]

That November, she missed the annual headmistresses meeting. Her older cousin Louise Gilmer Minis, known as "Aunt Loulie," had died on November 16. Mary traveled to Savannah for the funeral and returned south during Christmas vacation to visit the widower, Jacob Florance Minis. In Cambridge on January 5, 1922, she saw Kahlil, who had spent the past ten days with Marianna. He appeared restless; he spoke of traveling but seemed unable to pull himself away from everyday commitments. "I shall have many things to do in England and France and Italy," he told her. "Perhaps after those countries, I might go to the East—certainly not earlier!" "When he spoke of the East," she wrote, "there was the look of real trouble in his face, of real suffering."

~

Perhaps Mary's increasingly infrequent journal entries reflected the turning point she was facing. Florance Minis, then sixty-nine years old, had asked her to come live with him as his companion and hostess. Formerly president of the Southwestern Railroad and the Savannah Cotton Exchange, he was a landowner and enjoyed a luxurious life. Tempted to escape her general weariness and school responsibilities, Mary told Kahlil of her indecision. His reaction was "Wait. You will know presently...Perhaps you won't have to sacrifice school to uncle or uncle to school. You may be able to harmonize them and keep both...just don't feel you have to hurry your decision—and it will come."[27]

Ten months before, even two months before, they would have discussed the show of his wash drawings, which was to open at the Women's City Club on Beacon Street four days later. But indecision clouded her attention. The day before the opening, Mary hung his drawings with the help of Jeanette Peabody, and that afternoon he and Mary viewed the exhibit. They were both disappointed with the rooms, but Kahlil was philosophical about it, so they went for a walk along the Esplanade and then back to Park Street where she picked up her car.

By the first of the year, the Women's City Club had arranged for Mary to discuss Kahlil's work and read from *The Forerunner*. Whenever they met, she concentrated on her "inner debate" rather than discussing the event. She wanted Kahlil to meet Minis. "Yes," he said, "I'd like to see your uncle too—but if you like him there is no question about my liking him too." Quietly he began to answer her arguments against living with someone who did not fully "understand" her. "You'll never find congenial people to live with—never the one in a million to whom you can always say everything…And what is ordinarily called being understood does enslave something in us…what does being understood really matter? The great thing is increase of realization."

The importance of her decision seemed to have freed the communication between them, and unexpectedly he told her why he had broken with Charlotte when she had come to the Montross exhibition in 1914.

> C. said, "Kahlil, I could write something about you that would make you famous in 24 hours from one end of the country to the other"—and instead of answering her sweetly, chiming in with her, I answered her with just what was in my mind. I said, "C.—there is only one way to fame—and that is to do work worthy of it. And when one does that, the fame matters little"…Well C. didn't like it because she wasn't ready for the steady effort of real work, and she wasn't ready to confess her unwillingness.[28]

Mary's irresolution became the topic of their meetings that month. In describing Minis, she spared none of his faults and confided that she hoped to change some attitudes of his that she found irritating. She had been angered at Christmas, when she criticized him for comparing the prices of presents. Kahlil gently tried to curb her reforming zeal and draw attention to the older man's positive qualities.

> If I went to live with a person like that—one thing I'd never do. I'd never criticize. But I'd show by doing and perhaps by doing with a bit of overemphasis. I'd trust that to teach him, but I believe criticism won't teach him. The man who faces his age so squarely, and who writes to you as he does, and who loved his wife so genuinely, who did so good a part by his parents, and adds to servants' wages secretly because he thinks them too low, must be fundamentally kindly. Talking about prices may be a very superficial thing. The people he is talking to may think just as much about them, without mentioning them.

Aware that he was no longer contributing to her life as he once had, Kahlil encouraged her to leave the school. She professed still to have the energy and commitment necessary to develop an ideal learning environment. For several years, however, she had become more aware of her shortcomings. He tried to persuade her of how unimportant it was to succeed in meaningless administrative duties. In turn, he expressed his own attitude toward institutions.

I am an individualist of the Eastern type…I believe every living organization is… made by one individual whom the others follow. The fault I find with the mammoth organization is that it has only one head and too many tails, too many ins and outs, hands and feet. Many of those tails should be heads. They should develop as individuals. The work of life is to make individuals.[29]

Only eighteen months before, he had urged her to yield to concerns when some mothers and teachers had objected that his nude figures "might feed undesirable impulses or thoughts—and that girls cannot feel the 'spiritual' quality of the drawings." He begged her to take down every drawing of which she had heard the slightest unfavorable remark, but the censorship disturbed her. "The effect of these drawings on girls seems to me just a part of the very complicated and fear-beset and harassed mind toward life that people are giving me glimpses of," she wrote to him at that time. "But what I do not quite know is how fully to meet it—or when to disregard it—when school is concerned."[30]

Kahlil made it easier for her to abandon her lifelong work. "I can't have an opinion about your going to live with your uncle," he said to her on January 14, 1922. "I can only say, 'don't hurry.' I know the school work doesn't hold you. You've outgrown it." Again he showed her how to use praise instead of criticism when trying to influence Minis.

I've tried the same thing with my Syrian friends. There is a group of really creative men [in New York] now…But when these men first came to N.Y. they were all separated. I made up my mind to get them to meet at least once in two weeks— apart from the Society—to talk and read together…At first they used to criticize one another's work—just as the Americans did—just as we all do—by pointing out the flaws…

Well—I deliberately do this: when a man reads a poem, I pick out the best thing in it—it may be only a line—and I talk about that line…And presently the man himself *feels* that line as his best…After a year and a half with these men it has come to this: A man will say "I've written a poem—but there is only a line or two that matters." He's become his own critic.[31]

After his last visit, she watched him, now approaching forty, as he walked away from the school. "It was seven when K. left—he missed a car—didn't run hard for it…He does not run hard for things now—because he is determined to be fit for his work and to get his heart in good shape." In February, she wrote him that she was coming to New York for a committee meeting and asked if she could visit for an evening. "Precious Kahlil. When I see you this time, let's look at a good many of your pictures. Wear your rags—so that we shan't mind dust—and keep a sheet or a towel out of the laundry to cover me with too."[32] At his insistence, they saw each other three times during her stay. The retrospective showing she had planned was put aside for three nights of retrospective talk. On March 12 she wrote,

> Our third evening from 5:30 to 3:45 A.M.—and K. said, "This has been the most wonderful of all our evenings—and I thank God for it. We have made many things clear to each other."
>
> …K. told me the whole story of our relation from his side—because something led me, I forgot what, to confess I had thought that he must have cared for me because over here he had not found many people he could be near to, despite his army of friends…and that near, personal love for me had been killed in him by me, and that he had such patience with me always because he felt—as he said to me once years ago—"I want to die your friend, Mary."[33]

He recalled his self-discovery in Paris and return to Boston. "Many people thought I was in Paris for a political purpose…because I wrote political articles…The only thing I was really caring about was the unknown in [me]."

> But it was only the lesser thing in me that changed toward you. The deepest thing of all never was moved. That deepest thing, that recognition, that knowledge, that sense of kinship began the first time I saw you, and it is the same now…I shall love you to eternity and I know I loved you long before we met in this flesh.
>
> …Sex things are temporary—always. And if we had had a so-called sex relation, it would have parted us by this time. For we would certainly have outgrown it. And marriage would have parted us too…If we had married, you wouldn't have put up with my wanting solitude for ten days at a time…
>
> I can't ever visualize it when you tell me…that nobody loved you as a child…I hear people call you lovable almost as often as I hear you spoken of at all and by people who don't know that I know you well…[34]

This led to discussion of topics outside their relationship, and Kahlil even mentioned Day—a figure who had been conspicuously absent from the journal for many years.

> Mr. Day is one of the sweetest men living…my not seeing him is largely a matter of temperament…He does beautiful photographs. He is practically the father of the so-called art photography. And he published some very fine books when he was in Copeland and Day. And he loves fine things and beauty. His Keats collection is one of the finest in America. And he has a wonderful place out in Norton [sic]. I must go to see him when I come to Boston again, soon.[35]

The conversation was so decisive for Mary's future that her usual consideration of his health did not appear until the end of the entry. "He's tired much—and has pain often—especially about the heart. Stays in bed regularly till about noon. Interested in Berman's new book *The Glands Regulating Personality*. I got him one and he was glad."[36]

A month later his failing health drove him from New York to Cambridge. As he approached the school, Mary noticed that "he walked slowly—and when we met at the door, he was dark and thin, and his face full of shadows. He is not so well—his heart a constant trouble—and his nerves feeling shattered." He had made up his mind to get away from New York and with Marianna to find a little place in the country. He agreed to see a specialist Mary recommended, but while she was making inquiries he interrupted her, "…I'd rather talk with you."

Because he was planning to stay in Boston for several months, he urged her to accompany Minis to Europe that summer. Already he had postponed his book for another year. "Knopf says The Prophet is too late for next fall; that it can't come out before spring…It's not ready yet, and I won't hurry it—and I like the fall best for publishing."[37]

It had been years since she had interfered with his personal habits. They both had outgrown her regimens of lotions, Turkish baths, and nasal douches, but now she sent him some thyroid medicine, which he declared made him sleep better than he had for two months. For a while the dosage seemed to work. After his physical examination on April 25, she reported, "Dr. William H. Smith…had found nothing organically wrong—no enlargement, no valvular trouble—Had called it a nervous heart and had asked K. to go to the Mass. General for some further examination." Said Kahlil of the visit, "He gave me a little dissertation on the artistic temperament…and said I might be paying now for irregular eating and sleeping during all my long working life. The thing he didn't tell me was why I'm so nervous. I don't know myself why I am."[38]

~

Kahlil felt the need to stop working for a year "and learn just how to live," but *The Prophet* was then in typescript and the final polishing weighed heavily on him. On April 21, he told Mary, "We've an awful thing soon to do—to go over all *The Prophet* and paragraph the typewritten sheets. I want the paragraphs as short as they can be made—Some even one line only. The appeal to the eye and to the spirit is so much simpler and more direct."[39]

A year and a half earlier, Mary had reported, "Kahlil hasn't decided whether to have any quotation marks in the book or not. Indenting may be used instead—and the whole thing may be in capitals."[40] He had admired the all-uppercase typography in the Copeland & Day edition of *The Black Riders*. Now he decided to reject both quotation marks, a natural deletion, since they are not used in Arabic, and the capitalization of all words. On May 5, he brought the typed manuscript to Cambridge. Before working on the spacing, he and Mary reviewed each passage. He stated:

> Let us make the divisions by ideas so that each division, whether it is one line or several, shall be in itself a complete thought and can be taken alone...I want the division to be a natural one—not according to rule—but just the actual pauses of the thing itself—the freedom of free verse without its eccentricities...Let's not copy the Bible but we can bear it in mind.[41]

They met six times more that month, and along with reviewing phrases in the manuscript they discussed her dilemma and his health. After Dr. Smith's second examination revealed nothing, Kahlil acknowledged that his discomfort was not solely physical.

> Neither he nor any other doctor seems to notice much the pain that I have in my heart. The dull sort of pain. But my greatest pain is not physical. There's something big in me...I've always known it, and I can't get it out. It's a silent greater self, sitting and watching a smaller somebody in me do all sorts of things. But none of those things are what the greater self would say. All the things I do seem false to me.

Mary observed, "K. was walking up and down and talking in bits—His face was moved—It was dark between the brows—He had never spoken before so directly and avowedly of the pain of his long waiting." He conceded, "All that I can say and do say is foreign to the real thing that I would say and cannot. Only this one book, The Prophet, has as it were a shadow of that thing—a bit every now and then."[42]

Despite their progress, throughout the month of May, his uneasiness continued. "I've worked so much on The Prophet," he said on the nineteenth, "that I can't hear it any longer." The same day he found some distraction in making a small sculpture. Wrote Mary, "He was carving two small faces in wood—with the little white knife he had found—a bearded man, and a face—like mine...he found the wood in the Arboretum."[43]

344

On May 30, Mary finally could report: "We worked on the line-spacing of the Counsels and finished it." In acknowledgment of its completion, he reflected on the book's theme: "The whole Prophet is saying just one thing: 'you are far, far greater than you know—and All is well.'"[44]

One of Kahlil's small woodcarvings. (Courtesy Museo Soumaya.)

~

Mary's anguish over leaving Cambridge strained them both. Over and over, he told her not to hurry and to follow her own feelings. Sometimes it seemed that if he had uttered one word of restraint, one indication that he himself needed her, she would have discarded all plans of moving. Once she showed him a letter from Minis, hurt by her procrastination. "When I said, 'I'm rough sometimes' K. looked me straight in the eye for just a second's pause and then said, 'Yes,' and laughed."[45]

On June 16, he again brought up his ambivalence about traveling to the Near East.

> The East is in sad need of everything and of men most of all...but I know that if I do go I can't stand it physically...and the East isn't really my work. Movements of all kinds—political, literary, artistic even—do not concern me. I want to make things... things that will be seen by people who will never hear my name. I have to be alone. The slightest presence of another mind destroys things for me. I am most worth while alone. One is near to everyone by being near to no one.

As he left, Mary observed, "[He] looked badly still. When he boarded his car on leaving, his shoulders looked 40 years old, for the first time. An unutterable pain and sadness filled my heart all through our visit."[46]

~

Mary's trip to Europe trip was her first since 1908, when she had seen Kahlil in Paris. She who had so carefully saved pennies was about to savor first-class indulgence. Kahlil seemed relieved and told her how much it meant to him. Within two months she returned, excited by the ease of luxury and laden with gifts for him. He and Marianna had spent the summer in a spacious house in Scituate, south of Boston.

By mid-September he arrived at the school with "an expression as if his mind were elate with incessant creation," and with twenty-six watercolors under his arm, recorded Mary.

> Yes, the people at the beach must have known I wanted solitude, for the grown ones have hardly come at all. There are ninety-seven children on that hill…and I must have made sixty or seventy kites for them…And the other day they came to me and said, "We've left you alone all summer. But won't you come now and be a judge at the Children's Parade?" So I was a judge—and the children paraded—and they gave me quite a little ovation![47]

The Archer, from The Prophet. "You are the bows from which your children as living arrows are set forth." Watercolor, 1922. (Courtesy Gibran Museum.)

Mary felt that his latest drawings were "as far beyond all his previous work as that most recently previous is beyond the work of his boyhood." One picture he had made in pencil for the end of *The Prophet*. "[He] showed me the ring of wings, around the hand in whose palm is an open eye-and the celestial equator of souls engirdling," said Mary." Others he would save for poems yet unwritten, in addition to the one "On Children." Kahlil explained, "And this is the Tree of Heaven, that man feeds [on] as does the lamb and the fruit [*Jesus, Son of Man*]; and Joy and Sorrow. Here is "the archer with the parents who are the bow in his hand" [*The Prophet*].

Then it was Mary's turn. She gave him overcoats, ties, a tooled leather book cover from Paris, a cigarette case, a leather box, and lastly "our jewel—the opal chain and pendant. 'Why Mary—glorious…but you must wear it. Wear it for me. Of course I'll accept it—and call it really mine. But you must wear it for me.'" He reciprocated by offering her the original drawings of *The Prophet* "to do what you wish with."

In the midst of this exchange of presents, she shared with him her future plans. "I told him about my decision to go to live with my uncle. He is glad because I am glad to do it." He assured her that he didn't consider this a betrayal. "When I said F. was always asking whether I loved him better than anyone else in the world—best of all—K. said, 'Every love is the best in the world, and the dearest. Love isn't like a pie that we can cut pieces of, large or small. It's all one…Of course, you can say he is the dearest thing in the world to you…' And he laughed—so serenely."[48]

~

By October 7, they were choosing the illustrations for *The Prophet*.

> We fastened a string along the wall, so as to stand the pictures in a row grouped according to color—the ones with purple in the long row—and three of the blue-green colors only on the big candlestick…We assigned different pictures to different Counsels…using about fifteen of them…of all of them, Kahlil liked "Pain" the best— "the woman form with hands outstretched as [if] crucified against the breast of two men." He conceded that the Archer would be the most popular picture ("objective people like objective things"), thought the composition of Death most successful, and criticized his winged hand as being "too large, too definite, too limited."[49]

Mary had decided to leave her school during Christmas vacation. In November, faithfully attending the annual meeting of headmistresses, she saw him twice in New York. The freedom and solitude of Scituate still lingered with him.

Those three months were the best I've ever had in my life…Everything came easy and it's still coming easily. I get up and have my coffee, and then I go right to work without effort and stick at it for four or five hours—and what I produce is what I want. The mistake I used to make was that…I kept myself busy every moment—until activity became a disease.[50]

He also continued to enjoy making small sculptures.

His carvings were on the table—all in settings of his making also. A circular portico of columns, Greek, carved from wood, held one; another had a square curtain-like background of grained wood put together in a design of tree stems and clouds. The head lay in a soapstone tomb, with a setting cut out to show it—and a raised entablature—and he has made two most beautiful settings from stones found on his beach at Rosecliff.

They went to the Metropolitan Museum "to see the Chinese collection—especially the room with the black head and the [bronze] hand and the bodhisattva that is so simple and supreme." Mary did not admit it, but she was deeply fatigued. Upon her return to Cambridge, she faced packing and distributing twenty years of accumulations. Many precious objects—the familiar decorations of Marlborough Street and a large selection of books—she sent Kahlil. As he thanked her a week before Christmas, he admitted, "And now, with your last letter before me, I no longer feel like a loved guest, but rather like a child in my mother's house."[51]

He had already hoped she would come once more to New York. She could not stay away, and so before beginning her new life, she spent three days with him. The day of New Year's Eve, 1922, was "a wonderful twelve hours that seemed not five hours." That afternoon they enjoyed a pilgrimage to one of their favorite spots, the Museum of Natural History. From her passionate recital of the minerals and fossils, she inventoried the wonders they had shared. They spent the evening in the studio, silently reading *The Prophet*—"to see if anywhere it sounded preachy." But they only changed an occasional spacing."[52]

Again Kahlil begged her to take anything she wanted from the studio, and on the final day, she noted his features. "I looked long at that wonderful face of his—and the mouth—the mouth of patience and of all feeling—that changes almost as the pupil of the eye changes—so different is it at one time and another…I think all the tides of human life and planetary life flow through the mind that informs that face."

Her parting gesture was to reassure him about his English when he confessed, "For years I have wondered about this, but I have not said it to you. Is my English, modern English, Mary, or is it the English of the past? For English is still to me a foreign language. I still think in Arabic only. And I know English only from Shakespeare and the Bible and you." Her reply was that "like his Arabic, his English too is creative. It is not of any one period. It is his own."[53]

Then she left.

They had both agreed to write, and he had promised to visit her in Savannah. That winter they kept in close touch, and on March 19 he sent her the galley proofs of *The Prophet*. "I have gone through them and made a few corrections, but with the feeling that they need your keener eye for punctuations and other *niceties*...The frontispiece—the face of Almustafa—is also finished. I have a feeling, Mary, that you will like it more than any other face I [have] drawn."[54]

They met in New York for three days at the end of May, and then twice in June. The first night they had supper together, went for a bus ride, and returned to the studio. Mary was full of talk about her new life, but Kahlil also had news. Portrait commissions were producing income. One couple was interested in commissioning him to do a stained-glass window based on his watercolor *The Tree of Life*. He also showed her his "partly unauthorized" latest Arabic anthology, *Al-Badai wa Al-Taraif* (*Best Things and Masterpieces*). But because so much friction existed between the publishers, *Al-Hilal* and Bustani, he had lost interest in the book and treated it as an unwanted stepchild. In a sense nothing that he had written in Arabic or English concerned him now except *The Prophet*, his "first real book."[55]

What excited him most was the opportunity to work on the book's production. Adapting a type design from an eighteenth-century font by the seminal type founder Pierre Simon Fournier (le jeune) created an accessibility that welcomed readers. Gibran and Alfred Knopf made sure that the warm, cream-colored paper stock from W. F. Etherington & Co. also reflected the text's tone. Kahlil closely supervised the photography and engraving of the twelve drawings that appeared in the book. Engravers from New York's distinguished Beck Engraving firm were "really interested in these pictures," said Kahlil. "When I went there to see them, they crowded around...said they'd never seen such pictures and they loved having them to work with...couldn't believe I'd done them without models." The black cloth cover featured the gilt title and author's name along with his embossed decoration of a golden extended hand with flaming figures. Centered on both the frontispiece and the dust jacket was the image of a spectral face gazing simply at the reader. Beneath the heading, "Books by Kahlil Gibran" on the dust jacket's reverse were review excerpts, including *The Liberator*'s description of *The Madman* as a "breath of an intense beauty" and the *Detroit Free Press*'s assessment of *Twenty Drawings*: "He has sensed a relation between man and the universe."

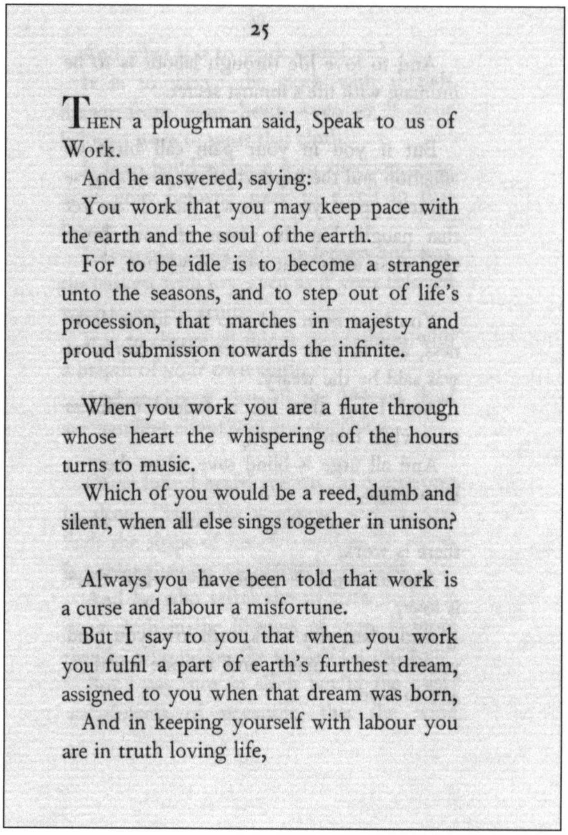

25

THEN a ploughman said, Speak to us of Work.

And he answered, saying:

You work that you may keep pace with the earth and the soul of the earth.

For to be idle is to become a stranger unto the seasons, and to step out of life's procession, that marches in majesty and proud submission towards the infinite.

When you work you are a flute through whose heart the whispering of the hours turns to music.

Which of you would be a reed, dumb and silent, when all else sings together in unison?

Always you have been told that work is a curse and labour a misfortune.

But I say to you that when you work you fulfil a part of earth's furthest dream, assigned to you when that dream was born,

And in keeping yourself with labour you are in truth loving life,

Final typography for *The Prophet*, 1923. (Courtesy Private Collection.)

"I don't see how I could ask better for a book," said Kahlil, "that is not to cost more than $2.25." Knopf's integrity continued to reassure him. "The big publishers don't publish their books and Knopf does publish. So does Mosher in Maine."[56]

~

As Mary was planning to travel to Egypt with Minis, Kahlil was planning his next books: "the second part of *The Prophet* will be between the Prophet and his disciples—and the third part will be between the Prophet and God." On May 30, she caught a chance glimpse of him at the theater, at a performance of Chekhov's *The Cherry Orchard*, ironically a play regarded as iconic of moments of transition and change.

I [saw] K….sitting with Sir [Edgar] Speyer and two ladies in the fifth row orchestra. He did not see me—but I stood in the first balcony *near* him—and saw him for the first time since youth with a group—and for the first time ever, followed his reaction to a fine play when he was full in my eye. Between acts one of the women would ask him a question and that would start him and then he'd talk right along… they were a very quiet group, yet the busiest and most animated in the house…and once, at a very touching moment, in the last act, K. leaned way over and put his head down in his hands—in the most spontaneous gesture of the understanding of sorrow and despair…He has not a bit of self-consciousness. Once or twice between acts, too, he illustrated some point by sketching or diagramming on a program in his ardent way. I was happy beyond words watching him.[57]

Inevitably, Kahlil and Mary were drawing apart, just as the book whose creation reflected the enduring bond between them was reaching the hands of the typesetters.

Mary Elizabeth Haskell. Graphite and charcoal, 1910.
(Courtesy Telfair Museum of Art, Savannah, Georgia. Gift
of Mary Haskell Minis.)

Untitled early pastel, around 1906. (Courtesy Peter A. Juley / Smithsonian.)

18

"O MIST, MY SISTER"

The Near East has a disease...of imitation, of the cheaper things of the West...They have taken to heart that if the greatest philosopher in the world and the smallest gun...are pitted against each other, the philosopher has no chance...They want to be safe. I want to show them that such safety is destruction...[1]

During the eight remaining years of his life, not only did immigrants to America from the Near East claim Kahlil as a voice, but those in South America, Africa, and Australia identified with him, as well. His writings could be found most widely in the U.S., Syria, and Egypt. Cherished among other writers with whom he corresponded during this period was May Ziade, known to leading Arab intellectuals and artists as "Miss May."

Born in Nazareth, Palestine, in 1886, May attended Roman Catholic convent schools and in 1908 moved with her family to Cairo. There her Lebanese father, Elias Ziade, had started the daily newspaper *El-Mahrousah* (*The Protected*). Exposed to an active literary life at home, she became fluent in French, English, and Arabic. In 1911, she published a book of her poetry, *Fleurs de Rêve* (*Dream Flowers*), under the pseudonym Isis Copia. That year, too, she published in her father's paper essays on what would become her lifelong concern: the rights of women in the Near East. Ziade wrote biographies of Christian and Muslim Arab women writers, researched women in world history, and constantly addressed their role in society. Attending Egyptian National University in Cairo, she joined reform groups founded by early twentieth-century women activists. They included Bahithat al-Badiyah, the pen name of Malak Hifni Nasif, who published her early articles on the status of women in Egypt in a book entitled *Nisaiyat* (*Feminist Pieces*); Nabawiyyah Musa, a renowned, pioneering educator; and Huda Sharawi, a social reformist and philanthropist who championed Egyptian nationalism and founded the Egyptian Feminist Union. Along with May, they participated in the Women's Refinement Union, which encouraged Egyptian and European women to meet together and discuss issues affecting their entrance into the public world of careers and professions. They also joined together in the Egyptian Ladies Literary Improvement Society, whose lecture series often focused on pathways to women's rights.[2]

May's Tuesday salon, which would become a leading one in the region, brought together a wide variety of people, both women and men, and was known for its far-ranging conversations exploring new directions in Arab literature and its support for *al-Nahda*, the Arab awakening. Antje Ziegler writes about May that "her position as a woman and Syrian-Christian immigrant in Egyptian-Muslim society… was strongly dependant on integration and throughout her life [she] advocated the reconciliation of conflicting views. A direct result of this commitment was her literary salon, in which an Azhari sheikh conversed with a Darwinian thinker."[3]

Reading *The Broken Wings* in 1912 prompted May to write to Kahlil for the first time. Although she questioned aspects of the story's portrayal of Selma Karema, she shared Kahlil's commitment to reimagining women's roles in the culture. A year later, at the request of publisher Salim Sarkis, Kahlil composed a poem honoring the Lebanese-Egyptian journalist, translator, and poet, Khalil Mutran. May read the poem, "The Poet from Baalbek," at a gathering held for Mutran at the Egyptian National University. Positive response to her reading led her to champion Kahlil's writings. Their correspondence was interrupted during the war, but by 1919, she had written a long and penetrating criticism of *The Processions* for *Al-Hilal*.

Spiritually and intellectually, Ziade's background enabled her to understand many of the influences that had shaped Kahlil's life, while the distance between them created a unique sense of trust. Perhaps theirs was the kind of bond that he described in the following draft of a letter found among his papers.

> Strangely I felt many times the existence of your noble self in this room talking to me and arguing, expressing your opinion on my work and how it relates to my life…
>
> You said once, "Isn't there between minds a recorder, between ideas, an exchanger that is not realized by reason but which cannot be denied by people of the same homeland?"
>
> …Lately I have come to realize the existence of a strange bond which differs in motive, characteristic, and influence from every other…It is stronger than blood and racial bond…it can exist between two people who have not been together in the past or the present and whom the future will not bring together.[4]

May Ziade. (Courtesy Wikimedia Commons)

With the passing years, Kahlil playfully embellished the details of their imagined times together. Once she apologized for missing his art show, but he reminded her that she had enjoyed it. "…We strolled round that vast hall, searching, criticizing and exploring what lay behind the lines and colours of those symbols and meanings and purposes…"[5] Although they never met in person, their letters became a delightful companionship filled with serious reflections and fanciful inventions. They joked and teased, asked and answered questions, argued and made up.

~

As Kahlil found himself turning more and more to writing in English, May remained a touchstone who grounded and encouraged him to remain close to political and cultural events in Cairo and his homeland. After the October 1918 landing of a French naval division in Beirut, a series of armistices and treaties led to French authority throughout Greater Syria. Lebanon was gradually achieving autonomy through the League of Nations mandate. One of Kahlil's final works addressing the machinations of the European powers in the Middle East appeared soon after the Allied landing in Lebanon. Like so many of his political pieces, it was ignored by English readers and seldom remembered in Arabic criticism. The play features five characters imprisoned in a Beirut jail. They argue all night about the fate of Syria. By morning, with the arrival of liberating soldiers, the prisoners escape. Amid sounds and scenes of jubilation, the protagonist, despite his poetic speeches, remains anxious and powerless to solve the unsettled condition of his country—Kahlil's frame of mind throughout the endless disagreements and unsuccessful conferences that characterized his compatriots' conflicts during and after the war.[6]

His published messages to readers in the Middle East and its diaspora became more philosophical. "But whatever the nations agree upon, the Syrians themselves must make or unmake the future of Syria," he told Mary Haskell in February 1919, at the time of the Peace Conference. "No matter what happens in Paris...I, among many Syrians, shall go on fighting for my country. Perhaps the best form of fighting is in painting pictures and writing poetry."[7]

Following the 1920 publication of "You Have Your Lebanon and I Have Mine," Kahlil's thoughts on the rebirth of Arab culture through its language, writing, and creative growth appeared in *Al-Hilal*. His prevailing theme was that emerging nations should adopt only constructive aspects of Western society and reject others.

> The Near East has a disease...of imitation, of the cheaper things of the West—especially of America—but not of your railroads, and your fine sanitation, and your educational system—but of your dress and your guns. They have taken to heart that if the greatest philosopher in the world and the smallest gun in the world are pitted against each other, the philosopher has no chance. And so Syria and Armenia and Mesopotamia and Persia want to combine in one great federation and be strong with army and navy like those of a Western power. They want to be safe. I want to show them that such safety is destruction for them. For it is not their real life, their creative life, their natural contribution.
>
> The Near East has been conquered...and so they were turned to a more contemplative life. And they developed a consciousness of life, and of self, and of God...[8]

But many in the region remained unconvinced of Kahlil's views on their safety, or spiritual heritage. Ever since the appearance of *The Broken Wings*, the influential Lebanese literary journal *Al-Mashriq* had attacked his books. In 1912, the Jesuit publication labeled his antagonism toward the Church hierarchy as "dirty sayings that belittled the sayer." Even by 1923, the journal's tone had not softened. "Who can imagine this poet?" wrote critic Louis Cheikho. "Is he a poet or an idiot? He seems childish, empty like his Great Sea...In his heart is the irreligious microbe."

This polemic provoked Pen League members to respond, and soon the two camps were contending with one another. Defending Cheikho, *Al-Mashriq* warned that Gibran's ideas were "lustful and cheap" and his influence pernicious. "Stop reading him!" they urged their readers.[9]

Kahlil seemed undaunted by the controversy. But when his poem *The Processions*, a work so important to him, was attacked not only for its "corrupt images" but for its linguistic and metrical weaknesses, he began to concentrate more on his writing in English. He decided as well to narrow the scope of his art. No longer creating paintings, he focused his draftsmanship on pencil portraits and wash drawings. At the same time, he further limited his writing to self-contained passages, soulful and satisfying to people in need of spiritual solace. By building on these strengths, he could create work that was both refined in idea and appearance, and accessible in scale and form. As he once described his intent to Mary, "I feel ideally a book should be small...I want you to be able to read it at a sitting—before you go to sleep at night—or to put it in your pocket and take it out on an afternoon walk."[10]

His vision of a well-crafted book that is brief, as well as visually evocative, became a key to its appeal, and by 1923 he had few doubts that *The Prophet* would find its readers. Years later, when asked to account for the ever-multiplying sales of the slim volume, Alfred Knopf recalled, "*The Prophet* is another one of those books the appeal of which seemed to be well known to its author before it was published."[11]

Kahlil's expectations echoed Mary's predictions, made upon receiving her copy at the Minis country home in Clarkesville, Georgia. On October 2, 1923, she wrote:

> *The Prophet* came today and it did more than realize my hopes. For it seemed in its compacted form, to open yet new doors of desire and imagination in me...
>
> This book will be held as one of the treasures of English Literature, and in our darkness and in our weakness we will open it to find ourselves again and the heaven and earth within ourselves.
>
> Generations will not exhaust it—but instead, generation after generation [will] find in the book what they would feign be—and it will be...better loved as men grow riper...as years go by...long after your body is dust. They will find you in your work...[12]

Mary had foreseen that it would become a global favorite. Within a month, the first edition of thirteen hundred copies of *The Prophet* sold out. When Kahlil showed her a favorable review in the *Chicago Post*, he shared his reaction to its reception.

> I have been actually overwhelmed with letters about it, and many of the letters from people I never heard of...Twenty days after the book appeared, some Syrian

publishers tried to buy a number of copies and there was not one left...I read from it at the Poets' Club...And it was read in a church—St. Mark's—first of all by [Butler] Davenport. To my regret he read the whole book...but his spirit was ever so good...You know, I had wanted it first read in a church.[13]

A key to its success was that spontaneous popular response was overshadowing literary approval from postwar elite intellectual circles. *The Prophet* received much less literary attention than had *The Madman* or *The Forerunner*. It was his only book in English that the *New York Times* did not review. Typical of waning interest among literary circles was the review in *Poetry* by poet Marjorie Allen Seiffert, which conveyed some of the insular but powerfully entrenched perceptions with which Kahlil had contended.

> Kahlil Gibran has written a third book, *The Prophet*, following two others of the same genre, a book that will have a deep appeal for some readers and leave many others cold. It is a bit of Syrian philosophy, a mode alien to our culture and yet one in which many restless and unsatisfied spirits of our race and generation find a curious release...
>
> The discourse on beauty ends with the following lines:
> *Beauty is eternity gazing at itself in the mirror.*
> *But you are eternity, and you are the mirror.*
>
> This seems to relapse into the sheerly mystical, and as the poem curves on to its end, one feels that it could never be a satisfying interpretation of our world. Moreover, the book lacks vigor...One feels that the poem could be a sort of decoration for us, like a faded Buddhist painting, that it could hang on our walls, but it would never be part and parcel of our house...Doubtless this book will awake response in many readers, for it is not without beauty, but the essence of the book, which is its spiritual significance, cannot satisfy the robust hunger of the occidental spirit.

But the book had touched thousands of readers beyond the reach of American literary circles, and from the beginning, they sent letters expressing gratitude for its publication. At one point, Knopf planned—and then cancelled—a flyer with quotations from readers' correspondence. Instead, the firm depended on word-of-mouth recommendations or on favorable articles from small town papers across the country. Six months after its publication, Kahlil described to Mary a type of person who was enjoying his book.

> "I've received a beautiful Letter," and he showed me one from a woman in Michigan—just saying he was blessed *for* having written...The Prophet—and

thanking him "in the name of thousands of children."

"I have answered it of course," said K.—"and I think I can see almost the very face of that woman, from her letter. She is not intellectual, but she feels deeply—and she is genuinely religious, and a very sweet being."[14]

A year after publication, the book continued steadily to build interest.

~

During this same time that *The Prophet* was gaining its first generation of readers, immigrants from Greater Syria were facing restrictive laws when applying for citizenship. Kahlil had expressed willingness to become naturalized when he and Mary discussed marriage, but afterwards citizenship was never again mentioned in her diary. In well-publicized court cases, Syrians were denied naturalization because they were not designated "white." Kahlil referred to his own appearance as "swarthy." Describing his parents, his father's family—the Gibrans—were "a fair race, slight and tall who look like English people tho they are Chaldeans."[15] He accounted for his looks by saying that he took after his mother's family—the Rahmes—whose hair and features were dark.

Beyond nativist racial discrimination toward Syrians, U.S. governmental exclusion was formally imposed with passage of the Immigration Act of 1924, or Johnson-Reed Quota Act. This repressive measure, like ones before it and directed toward groups from other global regions, allowed only one hundred immigrants from the Near East annually to enter the United States. The bill was cosponsored by Washington State Congressman Albert Johnson and Senator from Pennsylvania David Reed who, referring to the "hordes of aliens that fill our jails and asylums," characterized Syrians and groups from the Balkan Peninsula and southeastern Europe as "the trash of the Mediterranean."[16] The Immigration Act of 1924 effectively closed the door to the U.S. to peoples from the Near East, ending the Great Migration from Greater Syria—Lebanon, Syria, Jordan, Palestine—to Little Syrias in Boston, Detroit, and Lower Manhattan that had begun in the late 1870s, cutting off generations from one another.

Syrian immigrants and their press reacted passionately to the new restriction. In Massachusetts, sixty thousand Syrians protested to Senators Walsh and Gillett in response to Reed's remarks.[17] Two years after the bill's passage, Salloum Mokarzel founded *The Syrian World*, an English-language monthly review. Recognized for his nationalist views that often appeared in the Arabic daily *Al-Hoda* (*The Guidance*), and edited by his brother Naum, Salloum continued to educate readers about their heritage and to promote religious tolerance.[18]

Gibran's Message
To Young Americans of Syrian Origin

By G. K. GIBRAN

Author of *"The Prophet,"*
"Jesus the Son of Man,"
etc.

(Written Especially for
The Syrian World)

Reprinted from the First Issue of
The Syrian World, July, 1926

I believe in you, and I believe in your destiny.

I believe that you are contributors to this new civilization.

I believe that you have inherited from your forefathers an ancient dream, a song, a prophecy, which you can proudly lay as a gift of gratitude upon the lap of America.

I believe you can say to the founders of this great nation, "Here I am, a youth, a young tree, whose roots were plucked from the hills of Lebanon, yet I am deeply rooted here, and I would be fruitful."

And I believe that you can say to Abraham Lincoln, the blessed, "Jesus of Nazareth touched your lips when you spoke, and guided your hand when you wrote; and I shall uphold all that you have said and all that you have written."

I believe that you can say to Emerson and Whitman and James, "In my veins runs the blood of the poets and wise men of old, and it is my desire to come to you and receive, but I shall not come with empty hands."

I believe that even as your fathers came to this land to produce riches, you were born here to produce riches by intelligence, by labor.

And I believe that it is in you to be good citizens.

And what is it to be a good citizen?

It is to acknowledge the other person's rights before asserting your own, but always to be conscious of your own.

It is to be free in thought and deed, but it is also to know that your freedom is subject to the other person's freedom.

It is to create the useful and the beautiful with your own hands, and to admire what others have created in love and with faith.

It is to produce wealth by labor and *only* by labor, and to spend less than you have produced that your children may not be dependent on the state for support when you are no more.

It is to stand before the towers of New York, Washington, Chicago and San Francisco saying in your heart, "I am the descendant of a people that builded Damascus, and Biblus, and Tyre and Sidon, and Antioch, and now I am here to build with you, and with a will."

It is to be proud of being an American, but it is also to be proud that your fathers and mothers came from a land upon which God laid His gracious hand and raised His messengers.

Young Americans of Syrian origin, I believe in you.

Gibran's message to young Syrian immigrants, which first appeared in the inaugural issue of *The Syrian World,* July 1926. (Courtesy Eric Sommer & Partners, Washington, D.C.)

The first issue of *The Syrian World* featured Kahlil's text, "To Young Americans of Syrian Origin." Its message praised, and expressed his faith in, his younger compatriots.[19] One reader response to it stated: "That this Credo should appear on the very first page of *The Syrian World* is gratifying...This serves as a pleasant reaction to us, who have been decried and denounced too often.—E.K.S., from Bridgeport, Connecticut." Within a year, its author Edna K. Salomey began to gain recognition as a young poet. Although pioneering author and editor 'Afifa Karam had died a year before the startup of *The Syrian World*, Salloum Mokarzel continued the tradition of publishing the work of women writers, such as Labeebee Hanna, a young Boston writer—and the first Syrian-Lebanese teacher in the city's schools—whose stories and poems appeared in the magazine from 1929 to 1931, as well as several articles and poems by Barbara Young.[20]

Kahlil's poem to young Syrian Americans would continue to attract readers. By 1928, the Foreign Language Information Service included it in the June edition of their newsletter, *The Interpreter*, with a note explaining that there "could be no more fitting recognition of the noble sentiment expressed in the message than to reprint it as an indication of the true motives actuating Americans of foreign extraction."[21] So popular was it among readers that the magazine offered every subscriber a copy of this "beautiful message by Gibran, printed in large type on heavy paper with an ornamental border."[22] Although *The Syrian World* would cease publishing in 1932, in part a casualty of the Depression, the poem survived the twentieth century and continues to remind subsequent generations of Middle Eastern immigrants of their heritage.

~

Despite the passage of the 1924 Immigration Act, Syrian immigrants and *The Prophet* continued to extend their roots, often to welcoming soil. In November 1924, the *Sunday Herald* featured a lengthy portrait of Boston's Syrian community. A local tourism diary of sorts, the article revealed how the artistry of Kahlil's poetic prose could be seen as reflecting not only the individual talent of its author but also the richness and tenacity of the culture from which it sprang, echoing Joseph Gollomb's observation five years earlier in the *Evening Post*. Reflecting how neighboring ethnic communities might be encouraged to learn about—and from—one another, the story presented glimpses of the ancient pluralism, as well as age-old divisions, that immigrants embodied.[23]

Herald writer Katherine Crosby's excursion through Boston's own Little Syria in South Cove included passages on socializing, food, faith, and poetry. Delighting in

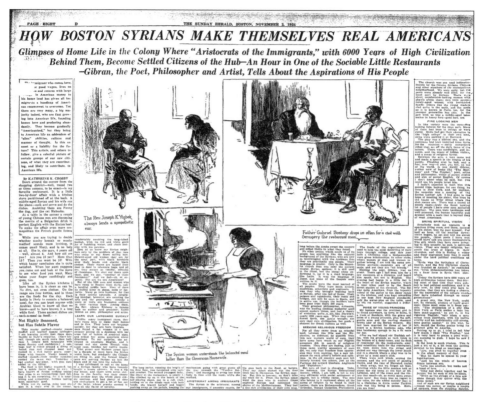

The Boston Sunday Herald, November 2, 1924.

her favorite Syrian restaurant, while deciding between *koosa mihshee* or *mulfoof mih-shee* (stuffed squash or stuffed cabbage) she enthusiastically described her visit to the Maronite Church at 79 Tyler Street, praising how it was attended by "Greeks, Syrians, Chinese and other members of the cosmopolitan neighborhood." She watched the first act of a biblical play, noting the "softly sumptuous" costumes against the actors' faces amid the candlelight, incense, and music.

> Between acts a man came out and made a speech in the tongue of his people. Flashing eyes he had, and a fine free way—a poet you felt on top of the world. It was Kahlil Gibran, author now of the books, *The Madman* and *The Prophet*, poet, artist, and philosopher…you could see his people loved him.

Afterward, Crosby interviewed Kahlil in Marianna's apartment next door and listened to stories about Mount Lebanon and Syria, noting that "most poets would have talked about themselves." Kahlil spoke with Crosby about the earliest Christian church, founded in Antioch, and about Islam in Syria. She heard from Kahlil that in South Cove, seeking religious freedom, immigrants were finding relief from oppressive conditions and "a new tolerance for each other's beliefs and opinions." Most important, he described in "vigorous English" the attributes that allow immigrants to infuse their adopted country with new life: "Only when a man comes from elsewhere, with his native vitality and individuality still strong, does genius appear." For "genius," it could be inferred, stems in part from the richness and tenacity of culture itself.

Leaving, she tried to tell him how much she liked *The Prophet*. "It is very hard to praise a poet without seeming to gush," she mused. "I hope he saw I meant it." Then, after she recited to him several of her favorite lines from his new work—"Even as the strings of the lute are alone though they quiver with the same music"—the reporter left Tyler Street. "Such are our Syrian neighbors—around the corner, maybe a couple of corners from our shopping district."

~

For Mary, life in Georgia had altered her daily activities and commitments. She used her still abundant energies to oversee a Savannah mansion and a country estate. Her propensity for guiding young men and women remained strong. But instead of helping promising students and creators, she became involved with the lives of her several nieces and nephews, and especially with the lives of her servants. With the exception of Kahlil, time and tragedy had removed the other most promising protégés from her view. Micheline Hardy was happily married and maintained friendly but purely social contact from New York. Aristides Phoutrides had been appointed assistant professor of classical literature at Yale University, but tragically drowned in an accident in August 1923. That November, when Kahlil asked if she had received any word from Charlotte, she answered that she had not.[24]

Another death marked the end of an era for both Kahlil and Mary. After two years of an agonizingly slow deterioration of body and spirit, Josephine Peabody Marks died on December 4, 1922, at the age of forty-eight. Her premature and painful death had occurred at a time when a new generation of poets was displacing the earlier twentieth-century romantics.[25]

During this time period, Mary's descriptions of Kahlil mentioned that his favorite working outfit was a long, loose garment similar to his native dress, and she noted new studio additions: the hanging Byzantine tapestry of a crucifixion that he had bought from the recently widowed Mrs. Morten and a carved screen made by cousin N'oula, who then was living in Boston with his growing family.[26] She also noted Kahlil's comment on friendship and solitude: "I'm the most social human being in the world but the most unsociety person."

~

Following publication of *The Prophet*, Kahlil continued to work on what would be entitled *The Garden of the Prophet*. Mary kept track of its progress.

> The Second Book is in the Garden of the Prophet and the Third is the Death of the Prophet…he has gone to his island—and there he goes to his mother's house—and he spends a great deal of his time in his mother's garden. And he has nine disciples, who come from time to time to talk with him…And what he talks about…is how the small things and the great things are connected—of man's kinship with—his actual sharing in the other things of the universe. He talks of the Dewdrop and the Ocean, the Sun and Fireflies, of the Air and Ways and Space, of the Seasons, of Day and Night, of Light and Darkness…And it ends with not a farewell like *The Prophet* but in a closing part which expresses Peace…In the third book he returns from his island—and talks with various groups as they come to him…The Prophet is put into prison. When he is freed again, he goes into the marketplace and they stone him.[27]

Over the years, both in his painting and writing, Kahlil had conveyed death as a passage: "Death changes nothing but the masks that cover our faces."[28] In composing Almustafa's message in *The Garden of the Prophet*, he chose mist as its central metaphor. Mist signaled a state of being that is free from fears and boundaries. This metaphor ran persistently throughout his previous works: in *The Madman*, the introduction to *The Forerunner*, and *The Prophet*; then it would appear in *Sand and Foam* and again in *The Wanderer*. But nowhere did Kahlil describe the mist of freedom and poetic expression more evocatively than in *The Garden of the Prophet*.

He waited to publish these last writings, understanding that they represented his concluding message on friendship and solitude, life and death. While working on other publications, he continued to describe the singularity of mist that culminated in his final work, which appeared two years after his death.

The prose poem begins when Almustafa arrives at the island of his birth and tells his listeners, "If you would freedom, you must needs turn to mist." When they question him, he repeats, "Did I not speak of freedom, and of the mist which is our greater freedom?" After days of silence and discourse, a follower admits his fear of solitude. Almustafa replies, "Alone! And what of it? You came alone, and alone shall you pass into the mist." Finally, as he reaches the hills and steps toward the mist, he welcomes her as his sister and offers thanks that he is at peace.

"O Mist, my sister, white breath not yet held in a mould,
I return to you, a breath white and voiceless,
A word not yet uttered...

"O Mist, my sister, I come back, a heart listening in its depths,
Even as your heart,
A desire throbbing and aimless even as your desire,
A thought not yet gathered, even as your thought.

"O Mist, my sister, first-born of my mother,
My hands still hold the green seeds you bade me scatter,
And my lips are sealed upon the song you bade me sing;
And I bring you no fruit, and I bring you no echoes
For my hands were blind, and my lips unyielding.

"O Mist, my sister, much did I love the world, and the world loved me,
For all my smiles were upon her lips, and all her tears were in my eyes.
Yet there was between us a gulf of silence which she would not abridge
And I could not overstep.

"O Mist, my sister, my deathless sister Mist,
I sang the ancient songs unto my little children,
And they listened, and there was wondering upon their face;
But tomorrow perchance they will forget the song,
And I know not to whom the wind will carry the song.
And though it was not mine own, yet it came to my heart
And dwelt for a moment upon my lips.

"O Mist, my sister, though all this came to pass,
I am at peace.
It was enough to sing to those already born.
And though the singing is indeed not mine,
Yet it is of my heart's deepest desire.

"O Mist, my sister, my sister Mist,
I am one with you now.
No longer am I a self.
The walls have fallen,
And the chains have broken;
I rise to you, a mist,
And together we shall float upon the sea until life's second day,
When dawn shall lay you, dewdrops in a garden,
And me a babe upon the breast of a woman."[29]

From "On Prayer," *The Prophet*. Wash drawing, around 1920. (Reprint: Interlink.)

The closing lines of *The Garden of the Prophet* invoking "life's second day" echo those of *The Prophet*—"and another woman will bear me." Both reflect a belief that our return to the earth frees the self, while proclaiming the bounty of aimless desire and formless thought.

~

Reading Gibran's poetry through the lens of global security and conflict, Costas Constantinou suggests that we consider these passages not as "naïve nostalgia of infancy, but…passionate reunion with what is close and there, but from which one is egotistically separated…Mist, then, is our greater, formless multiversal security."[30] For Gibran, Constantinou asserts, "our greater freedom outside self-centered care is our greater security."[31] From this view, real safety lies in a benign, expansive sense of belonging, in building trust in our shared humanity and respect for the Creation that supports life. And poetry may be seen as a naturalization process, a path to this elemental, borderless citizenship. Kahlil wrote to May Ziade:

> You tell me, "You are an artist and a poet, and you should be happy being an artist and a poet." But I am neither an artist nor a poet, May. I have spent my days and my nights drawing and writing, but the "I" [that is my Self] lies neither in my days nor in my nights. I am mist, May. I am mist that cloaks things, but never unites them. I am mist unchanged into rain water. I am mist, and mist is my loneliness and my being alone, and in this is my hunger and my thirst…
>
> Tell me, my friend, is there anyone in this world who would be able or willing to say to me: "I am another mist, O mist, so let us cloak the mountains and the valleys, let us wander among and over the trees, let us cover over the high rocks, let us together penetrate the heart and the pores of all creation, and let us roam, through those faraway places, impregnable and undiscovered…"[32]

In *The Garden of the Prophet*, Almustafa urges his listeners to seek the face of God in all beings.

> Again I bid you to speak not so freely of God, who is you ALL, but speak rather and understand one another, neighbour unto neighbour, a god unto a god…It is only when you are lost in your smaller selves that you seek the sky which you call God. Would that you might find paths into your vast selves…it were wiser to speak less of God, whom we cannot understand and more of each other, whom we may understand…Yet I would have you know that we are the breath and the fragrance of God. We are God, in leaf, in flower, and oftentimes in fruit.[33]

The creative capacity to "find paths into your vast selves," Kahlil believes, is innate.

> By poet, I mean every inventor, be he big or small, every discoverer, be he strong or weak, every creator, be he great or humble, every lover of pure life, be he a master or a pauper, and everyone who stands in awe before the day and the night.[34]

The theme of continually moving toward a "greater self" runs throughout Kahlil's life and art. In *The Garden of the Prophet*, it becomes insistent. But sustaining a sense of "awe before the day and the night" in the face of history's destructive forces requires commitment, persistence, and courage. It requires a faith in the benign, in a "unity of being," for which there is often little or no evidence. "My comrades and my beloved, be bold and not meek; be spacious and not confined."[35] Through his meditations on "mist," Kahlil defied the assumption that, when the poet and the gun are pitted against each other, the trust and innocence of the poet in each of us stand no chance. Collective self-destruction, fueled by the presumed ultimate safety of borders and weapons, need not inevitably be our fate.

Scales of Justice, from *A Tear and a Smile*, 1950. Mikhail Naimy wrote, "Around the main figure with the scales is a stream of human forms representing men and women seeking justice, only to find that uneven-handedness which the more powerful of the world always mete out to the less powerful." (Courtesy Alfred A. Knopf, Inc.)

19

"AFTER ALL THE DEBTS ARE PAID"

"Yet unless the exchange be in love and kindly justice,
it will lead some to greed and others to hunger."[1]

Practical advice between Kahlil and Mary had long been reciprocal. Since 1911, they had consulted about health and financial matters, always sources of uncertainty. At first she had advised him about investment, and he had used her stockbroker. But gradually he started to invest any limited extra cash with his Lebanese friends in Boston. Most of his colleagues there had become small businessmen, and as early as 1912, he began to lend money to the local baker, Adolph Nahass, or to the community tobacconist, Dimitri al-Khoury. Mary approved of, and even assisted with, this plan. It was upon her suggestion that he used the resulting interest to endow Marianna with some regular income.

After the war, as income from portrait sales increased and Knopf royalties—however small—began, Mary had suggested that real estate was the only safe investment during times of rampant inflation. Increasingly aware of his weakening health and concerned about Marianna's financial security, Kahlil launched into an investment project. On May 21, 1924, he told her that he and a partner, Faris Malouf, had bought a building, twin brownstones at 409-411 Marlborough Street. It was a time of heightened real estate speculation, and with a shared capital outlay of about $24,000, he and Malouf acquired seven stories of prime real estate on Marlborough Street and Massachusetts Avenue—one of the city's busiest corners. Run by Boston businesswomen, it may have seemed both a safe and worthwhile investment of much hard-earned savings.

The row houses were mostly empty and needed renovation. The partners scraped and borrowed every available bit of cash for plumbing, electricity, and elevators, but by midsummer Kahlil was sending Mary warning signals. Forced to spend much time in Boston, he asked urgently to see her. "I have many things to tell you and many questions to ask you. You are the only one in the world who could advise me about 'me.'" Early in September he gave her more details about the "Marlborough Chambers Co." A fledgling attempt at social entrepreneurship, the building would support the activity of businesswomen in Boston.

> We have leased the building…for ten years to Miss Josephine M. Quimby and Miss Harriette M. Fowler. These two ladies conduct the Fenway Business Women's Club. The 150 rooms in our building will eventually be occupied by business women only.
>
> I am sending you a copy of the lease. The alterations and repairs, detailed on the first page, will cost us from ten to twelve thousand dollars…My partner, Mr. Malouf, rebels against such a high rate, and I too feel it is too much. So we are trying to raise as much money on the basis of 6% interest as we possibly can.

In October, faced with unpaid insurance bills, taxes, and mortgage payments, he again sought her help.

> We have no securities for the rent of our lessees. Miss Quimby and Miss Fowler cannot give any. And because the lease is not secured we have not been able to raise any money for repairs and alterations…We have contracted for all sorts of things, and men are now working…
>
> I realize now our error. It is the error of small people trying to do big things… and I am very sorry…
>
> Do you know of any banking institution that would be willing to lend us ten or fifteen thousand dollars on the strength of the good future of the building? Or do you know someone who would trust us enough to take a fourth mortgage?
>
> Please tell me what to do, Mary. I know I am involved in something quite foreign to whatever intelligence I have. I have made a mistake, a grave mistake…But it seems to me that I should not be utterly crushed by that mistake.[2]

Mary advised him to refrain from further involvement, sent him a personal check to cover the most outstanding demands, and asked him for an accounting of unpaid bills to review. This rescue placed her in an awkward position. Mary never admitted to Minis the full extent of her generosity toward Kahlil. She warned Kahlil to keep confidential her support and began to use the agreed-upon initials "C. J." when noting payments to him.[3]

Similarly, Kahlil was struggling to maintain confidentiality about this social investment experiment gone awry. He felt forced to cancel a long-promised appearance at the dedication of a Lebanese orphanage in Albany. He was unable to enjoy the success of *The Prophet*, except for a banquet given by Lebanese and Americans in Detroit, an event he could not cancel since it had been made much earlier.[4]

When he returned from Detroit in October, Mary was in Boston reviewing the situation. His share of outstanding bills was $6,045. She juggled assets and finally figured that by recovering personal loans, she could meet the cost of the debts. They saw each other in New York on November 16. Letters acknowledging the stream of checks reveal that Kahlil appeared deeply affected, anxious to draw up a will that would assure her of repayment and yet hopeful that the businesswomen's promised occupancy would save the property. But Misses Quimby and Fowler defaulted, the partners were overextended, and in February 1925 the banks began to foreclose. When she heard the news, Mary responded with understanding.

> Beloved Kahlil, I'm just as sorry as sorry can be, for the loss—And my heart just aches for you—there is not the strange sort of nourishing quality and strength in money troubles that there is in other and deeper troubles…
>
> But that is all there is to this—a mistake…And money loss leaves the soul intact after all…I've nothing to forgive—nothing. When you're in trouble I'm just a thousand times more standing by you.

He answered her two weeks later.

> After all the debts are paid I shall get about three thousand back. This sum I shall put in a savings bank in my sister's name. Other money, lent or invested here and in Boston, is still where it was before the unfortunate affair started…I am trying to return to my own world so that I may be able to do some work. I have forgiven everyone who made me pay so much for being what I am. May God help them all.

To Marianna, he was even more laconic. He had always sent her brief notes expressing concern for her comfort, which Maroon or Assaf George or N'oula Gibran would read to her. But by January 1925, he was forced to restrain even her small indulgences. "Enclosed is money order for six hundred dollars," he wrote at Easter. "I send it as pocket money for your needs. I will not come for the holidays for many reasons. I am at present drowning in a sea of work…I should do the work I was created for. Everything else is bad."[5]

Later that year, he wrote Mary about the difficulty of maintaining privacy with his American associates about the failed venture and how he wished to be identified with his work.

Kahlil's watercolor box. (Courtesy Museo Soumaya.)

Even if I go to Boston [in August] and spend my days in Franklin Park, it will be better than staying here or visiting my formal friends. Most of my friends are most loving and most considerate; but they do not know what I have gone through, and I do not want them to know. It is better that they should think of my work rather than thinking of me or my problems.[6]

~

Myths surrounding the popularity and success that Gibran's work—particularly *The Prophet*—has achieved since his death can mask the actual circumstances of his life as an innovative, working immigrant artist in the early decades of the twentieth century. This is especially so as it pertains to Kahlil's and Mary's views of artistic sponsorship, the role of money, and the material sacrifices Mary made to enable his art.

Kahlil mostly subsisted on the progressive social margins of the times. Throughout his life, he was an outlier who, in a unique partnership with Mary Haskell, created work that was shaped by her reform-minded ideas of art and societal change. He described how her views had influenced him.

> You looked at money so wonderfully—and you said something about money then that I've remembered ever since…You said money was impersonal, that it belongs to none of us, but simply passes through our hands; a responsibility not a possession; and that our right relation to it is to put it to rightness.

How Mary managed can be explained in part by her scrupulous attention to her budget and by her self-denial. She scrimped on clothes ("My spring hat cost

Kahlil's letter opener.
(Courtesy Museo Soumaya.)

me half a nineteen-cent bottle of colorite—clothes nothing") and saved on food. One economy was her devoted cook Katy's habit of preparing leftovers from the well-provided kitchen of a nearby Back Bay mansion. Noted Mary,

> After supper. I wonder what the rich old lady across the alley would think if she knew that…I had her asparagus for lunch today and more of it for supper, with her fried chicken, mushrooms, rice and ice cream? On Tuesday a fry of her pineapple?…I sin with an open eye—for I know all that's bought in this house and recognize the Avenue Superior brands!…Cooks commonly feed their friends—but I know of no other case of feeding their ladies![7]

When Mary's philanthropy toward Kahlil was revealed, she was written off as wealthy. Unrecognized were the self-imposed sacrifices supporting her generosity. Recalling her history of supporting young immigrant students, like Jacob Giller and Aristides Phoutrides, as well as financially enabling Charlotte to write and promote her plays, it is not surprising that Mary would cut corners to assist Kahlil in this failed venture.

For years Kahlil had recognized the extent of her personal sacrifice, how she scrimped and saved so that she could help not only him but other promising artists and intellectuals. Their candid discussions—and arguments—about her altruistic mentorship had deeply colored their relationship. As early as 1909, when she sponsored his stay in Paris, he had included her in his will and offered art in return for her support. When faced with disposing his own material assets, his values reflected her philanthropic philosophy.

Kahlil's oil lamp.
(Courtesy Museo Soumaya.)

Mary's support for Kahlil in 1924 during the real estate episode demonstrated the continuing nature of that partnership. In return, the studio artwork, including the early paintings and hundreds of drawings, were partially hers—they always had been and would be. In all, her monthly stipends, supplemented with her gift of securities two years later, totaled approximately $14,000 over a period of eight years. But as they had once agreed, the "Haskell Gibran collection" she would

(Above and facing page) Interior of the Hermitage, Kahlil's living and studio space on West Tenth Street in New York City. (Courtesy Museo Soumaya.)

inherit was worth significantly more, and Mary, ever pragmatic, probably convinced herself that she was richer for being part of it.

Surviving on interest from her subsidies, his occasional art sales, and portrait commissions, along with slim royalties from Arabic language publications allowed Kahlil a meager lifestyle. Elias Shamon, the Boston lawyer who helped him resolve his Marlborough Chambers obligations, who acted as a spokesperson for Syrians of Boston protesting restrictive immigration quotas, and who in 1944 would be appointed one of the earliest Syrian-Lebanese judges in America, once described how Kahlil fared.

> A true idealist, he disregarded utterly material wealth. The royalties from his books could have made him a rich man, but his attitude [was] expressed in the following words, "I don't work for material purposes. If there is any profit from my books, I'll be the last one to have it." His sympathy with the poor and unfortunate, his generous spirit in bestowing gifts upon his friends, combined to make a wealthy state impossible…He never left his studio for any length of time without providing a certain mouse who was his fellow tenant, with a morsel of cheese…But after all,

he had no need of wealth; his tastes were simple, his only luxuries being music and the theater. Besides, those having the greatest of all gifts, the capacity for loving life and those who live, have no need of mundane possessions. Perhaps Gibran realized his opulence.[8]

With the arrival of royalties from his Knopf publications, Kahlil settled into a fairly secluded pattern at 51 West Tenth Street. Mikhail Naimy pictured the well-named third floor studio as remote and modest: "The 'hermitage' was a room of about nine yards in length and six in width…It spoke more eloquently of Gibran's poverty and his magnificent struggle against it than his love for austerity and self-denial."[9]

Even with *The Prophet*'s steady sales, Kahlil merely got by. As Alfred Knopf explained, "Gibran died in 1931 before the big money started to come in."[10] Just after the real estate loss, Kahlil did ask his publisher for a two thousand dollar advance toward *Jesus the Son of Man*. In his reminiscences, Knopf acknowledged this. "We paid it cheerfully enough and naturally went on to offer it for his next book, only to have him refuse it. He explained that when he asked for it he was only testing our belief in him and was now quite satisfied."[11] Considering the proximate dates of the real estate debts and the *Jesus the Son of Man* contract, Kahlil probably desperately needed the advance. Whatever the reason, he spent his final years carefully planning the division of what he thought was a negligible estate. Helping his cousins Assaf George and wife Maroon purchase what would be a home for them ensured that they would care for Marianna if she ever needed help. His eventual renting of a second floor apartment across from Boston's Franklin Park represented a solution that made certain of his sister's independence and comfort. Entrusting Mary with the studio contents repaid his debts to her and created a means of making contributions to his birthplace. Providing his sister with all his cash and the ownership of the studio secured her future. Finally, with the royalties from his English books donated to Bsharri, the home village he yearned for, meant a dream fulfilled. This gift, as unexpected and unassuming as it initially appeared, represented a fortune—figuratively and literally. And, despite the ensuing chaos described by Knopf as "a terrible time,"[12] his birthplace continued to prosper and grow as a result of its native son's generosity.

Money box from Peter Rahme's dry goods store in Boston, which helpred support the Gibran family. (Courtesy Museo Soumaya.)

~

Still, debts other than financial remained to be paid, and he would pay for them with a long, painful, and solitary illness. Kahlil had always contended with uncertain health, characterized by an "ongoing malaise," often mentioned by Mary Haskell in her diary entries. This malaise calls to mind the sense of dislocation and loss that marked his life from an early age: displacement from his homeland; his lifelong estrangement from his gambling and heavy-drinking father; the separation of his parents; and the early deaths of his sister, brother, and mother, from illnesses afflicting many immigrants.

As well, it recalls ways in which Kahlil as a teen became entangled in, and resisted, the myths of those who sought to "rescue" him, or who discovered or acclaimed his talent: Fred Holland Day, who first portrayed the "young sheik" from the South End in oriental robes of "greatness"; Josephine Preston Peabody, who showered praise and projections upon her young "prophet"; Charlotte Teller, his close friend and artistic rival, who recognized Kahlil's promise, while deriding his "oriental" sensibility; members of New York's cultural elite, who extolled his talent as a newcomer from "the East," as he attempted to establish himself as a working artist. Friends and allies such as these played into susceptibilities in Kahlil created by his precocity, precarious family supports, and immigrant status.

At the same time, Kahlil had resisted cultural norms and patterns in the Near East and its diaspora. Through his early stories, poems, and essays in Arabic, and his drawings, he had challenged religious and social hypocrisy and corruption in the Arab world, incurring denunciation and censure. Overcoming his early meager literacy, as part of a literary renaissance he had helped to renew Arabic poetry, while drawing on the richness of his native language to recast the beauty of his adoptive English in evocative works of poetic prose. In his paintings, the central presence of the nude human form, iconic of transparency, had been condemned by many, in the U.S. as well as the Near East. As a leader of the Arabic-speaking communities in the Americas, he had sought to overcome sectarian divisions and to foster a proud but pluralistic and cosmopolitan identity. And he had advocated for the peoples of Greater Syria, suffering under Ottoman rule, while he formed ties with reformers from artistic, social, and political movements that challenged the militarism, profit motives, and cultural norms of American society.

Kahlil's remarkable capacity to embrace—and struggle to reconcile—his differing worlds led him to recreate his sense of homeland. But his attempts to unify these worlds exacted a toll and, along with the Marlborough Street real estate failure, triggered a downward spiral in his health. His friend Mikhail Naimy believed that, in pulling Kahlil away from the sources of his work and health, the real estate incident "quickened the march of the disease in his body."[13] Kahlil at forty-two unobtrusively had already turned to alcohol as medication for the illness to which it was tied. After that incident, he more frequently began to rely on what he had once enjoyed in moderation.

From good times with Youssef Howayek in Paris cafes, to convivial sessions with Pen League colleagues, or the Prohibition whiskey he offered an abstaining Naimy,[14] Gibran had always enjoyed a drink. But from now on, this preference began to be noticed even by well-meaning colleagues. His Boston friends and community, concerned for and protective of the public image of someone in whom they could take pride, worried about and monitored his hesitant speech or unsteady gait when addressing local events. Observant compatriots who drank and played cards at the local Syrian-Lebanese social club related stories of his drinking well into the night. But he had always made good on his debts. He would make payment in full for the mythologizing in which he had played a role, which had facilitated his rise, and which ultimately would erode his health, but from which through his art he would continue to extricate himself, up until his death.

Earlier, in his poem for Serbia, he had spoken to Defeat, his beloved, of the redemption he had found in the acknowledgment of failure.

> Through you I know that I am…not to be trapped by withering laurels.
> …In your eyes I have read that to be enthroned is to be enslaved.

Underlying his "universality" were Kahlil's ties with those who have been defeated or vanquished; his recognition of lost homelands and of the costs of a divided self and human family. But he had transformed defeat, displacement, and division into glimpses of a unifying, beatific sense of belonging, which steadily would continue to be recognized by increasing numbers of readers.

~

In response to the real estate incident, Kahlil found refuge once again in his work. Throughout this time, he continued to correspond with May Ziade and sent her a series of postcards describing his favorite art. Three were of the Puvis de Chavannes murals in the Boston Public Library: "He had the simplest heart, the simplest thought…among painters he resembles Spinoza among philosophers."[15] One was of Leonardo da Vinci's *Saint Anne*: "I was a boy when I first came across the drawings of this incredible man…a moment I shall never forget as long as I live."[16] Another was of *St. George* by Andrea Mantegna: "In my opinion every painting by him is a beautiful lyric poem."[17]

The strategy may have helped. The way in which Kahlil's art brought focus to his life is perhaps reflected in an article by Konrad Bercovici, a Romanian-born writer living in New York. Featuring the city's Syrian district, the piece included a description of time Bercovici spent with Kahlil during the worst of the business venture.

> I have passed many hours with the poet and artist, listening to his musical voice, which makes English as sonorous as if it were Italian as he read me his poems. Faultlessly attired, Kahlil Gibran looks more like a cultured Frenchman than a Syrian.

But at home, in his large studio on Tenth Street, discussing with me the Orient, he instinctively bends his knees under him as he sits down on the divan to sip the thick coffee, the preparation of which is his particular pride, when he makes his guests feel at home. Everything Occidental is forgotten on entering his room and facing him. Instantly all feeling of hurry is banished. The day seems to be longer; the hours seem to be slower; even the rumbling below, in the street, the noise coming through the heavily shuttered windows, seems to be more distant than it actually is.[18]

Kahlil had nearly abandoned his Temple of Art portrait series, but he still enjoyed drawing his friends and illustrating their books. He offered to illustrate Witter Bynner's latest volume of poetry. In 1922 he had decorated *Companions*, an anthology which included poems by Le Gallienne, and was printed by the Assyrian Samuel Aiwaz Jacobs. He had illustrated a book of verse by a young writer, Madeline Mason Manheim, who would translate *The Prophet* for a French publication. Shortly after he met Blanche and Alfred Knopf, he had drawn portraits of them, and now the violinist-turned-poet Leonora Speyer also sat for him.[19] The resulting portrait appeared on

Portrait of a woman and nudes, inscribed to poet Leonora Speyer, 1921. (Courtesy Museo Soumaya.)

the dust jacket of Knopf's edition of her *Fiddler's Farewell*, which earned a Pulitzer Prize in 1927. No longer trying to draw the likenesses of noted figures, Kahlil settled into the more relaxed practice of sketching friends and colleagues whom he liked and admired.

In June of 1925, Suleiman al-Bustani, a leading Arabic scholar and writer known for his translations of the Greek classics, died while in New York. Kahlil, who had entertained him in Boston a year earlier, drew a series of posthumous sketches. *As-Sayeh* featured one of them in its issue devoted to Bustani, and several members of the Pen League, including Kahlil, wrote tributes. The group had been unable to sustain its professional goals, and except for such formalities the organization—and Kahlil's role within it—had become almost entirely social.

In 1925, the divide between his Arab and American circles seemed to widen. Perhaps his business experiment had left him more self-protective. When Mary visited him in the spring, it was clear that her role of confidante had changed, as well. At the beginning of the year she had begun an abbreviated diary, and her brief notes revealed how her new life allowed for few personal observations. Referring to Kahlil as C.J., she wrote in her diary: "*July 11, 1925.* Letter to C.J. while F. slept."

In early September, Mary met with Kahlil briefly upon her return and received his two gifts, figures of a Madonna and a Christ. Wherever they saw each other—in Pennsylvania Station or at a Thompson's Spa—the substance of their talk was no longer noted. In Europe, she had decided to marry Minis, and a sense of propriety forbade her from openly chronicling another man's life. Her own days were quietly spent shopping, reading, and caring for her future husband. And yet for the next six years she would continue quietly to record news of Kahlil and his work.

What Kahlil especially enjoyed, though, was his annual trip to Henderson House, writer Corinne Roosevelt Robinson's summer home in Herkimer, New York. "I think that the genius of the Roosevelt family is in its simple and wholesome *family* life," he wrote Mary. "They are very clannish and strangely devoted to one another. And they know so much, and they are interested in so many things." Another couple whose hospitality he enjoyed was Frederick and Margaret Lee Crofts. A publisher of textbooks, Crofts had purchased that division from Alfred Knopf. Kahlil drew several portraits of the ebullient Mrs. Crofts. It was at places like their summer home in Stamford, Connecticut, and the Robinsons' that he felt most wanted and could retrieve the comforting impressions of his childhood days. "I was recently in the country visiting friends," he once told Mary.

And in the morning about six o'clock I got up and looked out of my window. The trees were budding, the birds were singing, the grass was wet—the whole earth was shining. And suddenly I was the trees and the flowers and the birds and the grass. I was all of it…and there was no I at all.[20]

Stills from a 16-millimeter motion picture clip taken in 1929 by Alfred Knopf, entitled *A Publisher Is Known by the Company He Keeps.* (Courtesy Alfred A. Knopf, Inc.) [Produced by Louis DeRochemont Associates, distributed by McGraw-Hill.]

20

THE FINAL YEARS

Kahlil had translated many of his own works for Arabic-language periodicals. But in 1925, he accepted an offer to entrust the task to a young Antiochian Orthodox priest, scholar, and translator from Douma, Lebanon. Antony Bashir had taught Arabic literature at the American University of Beirut. He eventually would become archbishop of the Diocese of New York and by 1936, Metropolitan of North America. As the church's leading official in that region, he was recognized for helping reconcile ecclesiastic divisions within the church's Syrian community, introducing English to services, and diversifying the church's immigrant base by welcoming parishioners of all backgrounds.[1]

This fascinating collaboration between Gibran, a controversial poet who had often incurred the wrath of Maronite officials, and Bashir, a rising Orthodox cleric and scholar, steeped in Arab literature and the aesthetics of Eastern Christianity, offers another glimpse into Kahlil's creative spirit. The partnership between them was one that may have raised eyebrows. But to those who questioned Kahlil's faith, Antony Bashir replied:

> If we confined ourselves to merely the external appearance of religion, then one could call Gibran an atheist, and in that case I would be mistaken in translating [*The Prophet*] into Arabic. But this translator is not an atheist, and he examines the essence of religion and not merely its exterior. If we approach Gibran and his works in this way, then it becomes clear that he stands at the head of the most faithful, but at the same time seeks the eternal truth without fear or delusion and without the bustle and vanity of the world.[2]

Though Kahlil was creating his artwork within the context of a secular marketplace, Bashir could also understand and appreciate it in relation to the historic tradition of Eastern Christian liturgical art of the poet's early formative years.

The young priest's defense of Kahlil defined the role of the artist as an instrument for making "eternal truth" visible via the artist's inner life and faith, as in the aesthetics of Eastern chant and iconography. This role is echoed in Kahlil's search for "the Absolute," in both his writing and his visual art. Kahlil's writings often reflected aspects of oral tradition, both prophetic and colloquial. In *The Prophet*, Almitra asks of Almustafa, "Speak to us of Children," "Speak to us of Giving," suggesting that the book's counsels are spoken and casting the reader in the role of listener. Kahlil alsorelied upon the spoken word to hone the book's language and phrasing, reading the text aloud to Mary and gauging from her responses as a listener.

Antony Bashir's background made him perhaps an ideal translator for introducing Kahlil's writings to many Arabic readers. In addition to *The Prophet*, Bashir would translate *Sand and Foam*, *The Forerunner*, *Jesus the Son of Man*, *The Earth Gods*,

Father Antony Bashir, Antiochian Orthodox priest, scholar, and eventual Metropolitan of North America, who translated Kahlil's works into Arabic. (Courtesy Antiochian Heritage Museum and Library.)

and *The Words of Gibran*, playing an informed and encouraging role in support of Kahlil's writing, for which Gibran would be indebted. "Your translation of *The Prophet* is an act of kindness towards me that I will gratefully remember as long as I live," Kahlil wrote to Bashir in November 1925.[3]

Along with their correspondence about the intricacies of conveying *The Prophet* from English to Arabic, and issues that Arab immigrants faced, Kahlil wrote to Bashir about other titles to consider translating, from among his favorite works by Western writers. Topping his list was the symbolist classic *The Treasure of the Humble* by Maurice Maeterlinck, still cherished in his personal library. Then came *Tertium Organum* by P. D. Ouspensky, introducing the work of George Gurdijeff and translated by Kahlil's friend, architect Claude Bragdon. Next was *Folklore in the Old Testament* by James George Frazier, analyzing beliefs across cultures; and finally Havelock Ellis's *The Dance of Life*, on the relation of art and life.

~

While Bashir was translating *The Prophet* into Arabic, another author was translating it into Yiddish. Isaac Horowitz's version, *Der Novi*, was published in 1929 by Yatshkovski's Biblyotek in New York. Born in Romania, Horowitz had come to New York in 1909. The Yiddish writer may have been introduced to the Arabic one through Konrad Bercovici, another Romanian who spoke Yiddish. Bercovici, author of *Around the World in New York*, had interviewed Kahlil in his studio and had become familiar with local authors. He had praised the magazine *Al-Funun*, writing, "No other magazine in the country is so beautifully got up as this one." It seems likely that, with his eye for detail, Bercovici was acquainted with writers from New York's diverse neighborhoods.[4]

Meanwhile, Kahlil gathered his short sayings—many of which had already been published in Arabic or English—into a ready-made book for his American readers. It was at the time of this compilation of *Sand and Foam* that he met Henrietta Boughton, who would lighten the burden of organizing, transcribing, and typing during his remaining years of productivity. When she first heard Butler Davenport read *The Prophet* at St. Mark's Church in the fall of 1923, she was forty-five years old. Like so many others who responded powerfully to Kahlil's writings, she was an idealist and pacifist. Originally from Albany, New York, she had taught English in private schools before moving to Manhattan, where she pursued work as a writer. "Netta" had survived an unhappy marriage, raised her only child, and was able to catch a foothold in publishing by contributing steadily to the *New York*

Times poetry page. A special talent was her adaptability: upon demand she could compose a Shakespearean sonnet, a bit of doggerel, or modern verse. She wrote under several pseudonyms, among them Ben Brigham and Barbara Young—the name she adopted as her own.

When she first heard *The Prophet* read aloud, she was deeply moved and began to include her favorite counsels in her own poetry readings, which supplemented the meager stipend she received from newspaper poetry pages. In March 1925, she learned that Kahlil was not a recluse secluded in Mount Lebanon, but a writer living and working in his studio on West Tenth Street in New York. She wrote him a letter praising his work and asking to meet with him.

Barbara Young was not affluent, like a number of Kahlil's social acquaintances, nor glamorous. She was impressionable, reliable, fiercely loyal, qualified, and eager to help, without being closely involved in his personal life. In the autumn of 1925, he started to organize the aphorisms, and her role as secretary began. Over the next three years, she not only published a book of her own poetry, *The Keys of Heaven*, and opened the Poetry House bookshop on 12 East Tenth Street, but she promoted Kahlil by sponsoring a public reading of his poetry at the Brevoort Hotel and arranging for him to read before a meeting of the Fifth Avenue Bookstores Association.

~

In 1924, Kahlil was honored with a position on the board of directors of the Orient Society in New York. Syud Hossain, the Indian-born editor of the society's magazine, *The New Orient*, was a lineal descendant of the Prophet Muhammad, as well as an international writer and lecturer for Indian independence, fervent Gandhi supporter, and outspoken advocate for Hindu-Muslim friendship.

Subtitled "a journal of international friendship," the magazine was global in outlook and cosmopolitan in readership. An early editorial defined its purpose: "The moment then would seem to be opportune for the sharing of a new synthesis: for the East and the West each to bring its quota of inspiration and aspiration to the common service of an indivisible humanity."[5] Kahlil had found a fitting platform. Similarly, in his "Between Ourselves" column, Hossain commented on the Lebanese board member: "There is no more sincere and authentic or more highly gifted representative of the East functioning today in the West than Kahlil Gibran."[6]

Among others serving on the editorial board were Julia Ellsworth Ford and the noted art historian Arthur Upham Pope. Articles and poems by Claude Bragdon, Witter Bynner, John Haynes Holmes, Alma Reed, and Barbara Young pointed to Kahlil's editorial influence. Included in the distinguished list were Annie Besant, Ananda Coomaraswamy, John Dewey, Yone Noguchi, Bertrand Russell, and H. G. Wells—all of whom were dedicated to working internationally on issues of peace and social justice.

Sarojini Naidu's presence in the magazine was another boost for Kahlil. The Indian activist and poet quoted Gibran when writing to Jawaharlal Nehru.[7] Also contributing was Dr. Charles Fleischer, the former rabbi who, after seven years of preaching to progressives at Boston's Sunday Commons, was in New York as editor of *The New York American*. Well-suited among these advocates of transcultural exchange, he had reviewed the

Syud Hossain, Julia Ellsworth Ford, and Kahlil. (Courtesy Museo Soumaya.)

recently published *Teachings of Buddha in Biblical Hebrew* by George (Goetzel) Selikovitsch. Fleischer praised this "rare event in publishing annals," as he described "the transcendent teachings of Gautama in the crystalline language of the Hebrew Scriptures."[8]

The New Orient also paid serious attention to Abdul Baha and his call for "the federation of faiths."[9] Its most beloved voice came from board member Mahatma Gandhi. His words remain as provocative today as they were in December 1924: "There is no escape for man or woman, black or white or for the East or the West except through innocence (nonviolence) and truth."[10] Kahlil said of Gandhi, "He teaches nonresistance. He says 'accept nothing from the English—neither office nor title, and do no commerce with them; neither resist if they kill or abuse you.'"[11]

The New Orient lasted only three years, but its influence persisted. Sometime during or just after its demise, Kahlil met writer and teacher Jiddu Krishnamurti. Biographies reveal that Krishnamurti visited New York several times during the

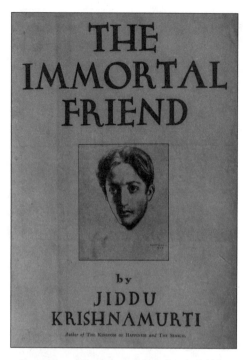

Dust jacket of *The Immortal Friend*, with Kahlil's
drawing of its author, Jiddu Krishnamurti, 1927.
(Reprint: F. Frank Isik.)

1920s. The dust jacket portrait of his poetry book *The Immortal Friend* was dated 1927 and signed by Kahlil. He and Krishnamurti shared several defining experiences in common: their discovery and grooming as prodigies; losses of beloved family members to tuberculosis; the role that solitude played in their creative lives and thinking; their global appeal to readers; even their mutual decisions to remain unattached. Moreover, they both were considered by many in their homelands to be leading voices.

~

The year before *The New Orient's* demise, in 1926, Kahlil at age forty-three had reached a professional plateau. His writing and publishing were being facilitated by Barbara Young's secretarial assistance; his reputation was steadily developing; and by Christmas of 1926 he was producing new work in Boston, where he stayed long after his holiday vacation. Along with finishing a few pieces for *The Garden of the Prophet*, he was writing two plays in English. As with most of his later works, the seeds of *Lazarus and His Beloved* had been sown much earlier. In an entry dated April 26, 1914, Mary described the title poem of the volume of four long poems.

> It is the Lazarus of the Bible and the 3 days during which he was dead. He went then into his own soul world. There he met the woman he loved and lived with her. But the power of the world-god compelled him back to earth.

Kahlil had chosen, instead of prose poetry, a straightforward dramatic form for Lazarus's quest. In *The Blind*, the second one-act play, he attempted to create a piece without relying on imagery associated with literary motifs of the Near East, to speak to a more international audience.

Kahlil's collaboration with Mary was also changing. Recently married, Mary and Florance Minis came to New York in May of 1926. On May 10, Mary was able to meet with Kahlil at his studio.

> F. went downtown to see about passports…he stayed for lunch in Wall Street—I returned to lunch with Micheline and then saw J. Grinch. Much moved—almost tears—showed "Sand and Foam," a few of 300 aphorisms—"I have more than a 1000: chiefly Arabic"—and picture of the blind poet and the bit on Dew for *The Garden of The Prophet*.

Three days later, he read "Lazarus" to her. Florance appears to have agreed to Mary's visit to Kahlil's studio: "F. had…to lunch while I saw Gibran. F. alright about it now. G. read me his 'Lazarus'…and told me about 'Blind Man'…and 'Snow' for 'The Garden of The Prophet.'"[12] Then Mary and Florance left for Europe, and Kahlil finished the remaining details on *Sand and Foam* in Boston. He enjoyed overseeing every design detail in his books and told his editor, "I would like the book…to be printed in the same manner as the manuscript, that is in regard to the number of aphorisms on *one* page and the number of pages it should contain."[13] He then turned to what would become his most ambitious work in English. Without his usual prolonged inner deliberation, and with an advance of two thousand dollars, he set aside *The Garden of the Prophet* and settled down for a year to work on a life of Jesus.

~

For nearly twenty years, Kahlil had thought about creating a story of Jesus. Since 1908, Mary's journal had devoted pages to his dreams about it. As a youth, Kahlil had written from Paris, "My greatest hope now is to be able to paint the life of Jesus as no one did before. My life can [find] no better resting place than the personality of Jesus." He read whatever he could find: "Everything about him I could ever lay hands on. And I have been all through his country from Syria to Lower Palestine. And all my life the wonder of him has grown on me." Ernest Renan's *Life of Jesus* contributed to his conception of Jesus as "the greatest of all artists in as much as he was the greatest of poets…To call him God makes so light of him. Because as God's his wonderful sayings would be small but as man's they are most perfect poetry."

The appearance of Jesus as a human being in everyday surroundings characterized Kahlil's dreams. Far from visions, they abounded in details of his homeland in Mount Lebanon. In 1911, when he reported having several of these dreams, he told Mary that they usually occurred in three settings—"a slope near Besharri where there are many big stones and pieces of columns," "near a big spring, where a river rises up quietly out of the rock," or "in a little garden near Beirut, full of flowers—with a wall and a gate where I used to study."

In one dream, he encountered Jesus at a Phoenician tomb outside Bsharri. "The walnuts and weeping willows arched over the road, and I could see the patches of sunlight falling through on his face." Sitting and talking on a large carved stone in front of the tomb, they could hear an old Franciscan monk, a friend of Kahlil's grandfather, chopping trees with a "tremendous sound that filled all the valley...like a great hell—as if the tree were of metal." Sometimes he would recall the words of Jesus, always simple and ordinary.

> I was sitting on a log near the pool. He came along and sat down too...His skin had the look of the petals of those very dark roses—so clear and soft and living—with that strange olive green color. And dust lay on it as you've seen—a sort of gold on a butterfly's wing. Then he half lay down on the ground, with his staff...I said to him: "Is your staff of fig?" "No," he said. "It's shahbi." Shahbi is a hard wood common in Mt. Lebanon.[14]

Over the years he shared stories about Jesus that had been told in Lebanon for centuries. "There are enough of such stories," he said, "to make a large book and it will be a very wonderful book. They ought to be collected."[15]

According to Barbara Young, Kahlil began to record with her the first of seventy monologues about Jesus on November 12, 1926. After eighteen months, "when it was finished...it was as though both the poet and the one whose hand had transcribed the record had come through a mighty and terrible struggle."[16] During this period, Kahlil was spending more and more time in Boston, where he had written much of the first draft.

As well as working on *Jesus the Son of Man*, Kahlil was helping to design a new hardcover edition of *The Prophet*. He was encouraged that his signature work was steadily appealing to a wider range of readers and that his other works in English were continuing to sell. Even the "little magazines," which catered to more select readerships, were predicting the new edition's success, as reflected in the mention that the poetry magazine *Palms*[17] gave it that spring.

> Knopf sends THE PROPHET by Kahlil Gibran bound for the holiday season... Gibran's austere truths are saved from the severity of prose by the rose and gold of his covers, his sentences are living and moving, and his imagery is magical. It is a book worth reading, worth buying and possessing.[18]

~

By 1927 Kahlil had become a respected and popular figure in the Boston Syrian community. When he came to town, Marianna's apartment was always smoke-filled, as visitors constantly stopped by. Next to 76 Tyler Street was Our Lady of the Cedars Maronite Church, and although Kahlil never attended its services, he and its pastor, Stephen el-Douaihy, were close friends. The pastor could easily visit the adjoining house by climbing onto the adjacent roof and walking down the stairwell to the second-floor studio, rather than coming in the street entrance.

Another institution that kept an eye out for Kahlil's return was the Denison House. By the twenties it had become Boston's most important social agency for Syrian children, as well as for the growing Chinese community. In 1919, because of Kahlil's reputation, Marianna was selected as one of four neighborhood representatives to serve on the board of directors. He rarely came to Boston without paying respects to that building diagonally across from her apartment. In the spring of 1926, Louisa McCrady—then the headworker and an old labor union friend of Mary Haskell's—gave a dinner in honor of him.[19]

Still, he remained ambivalent about the role of social workers and their intrusion into the lives of Syrian immigrants. In 1922, he complained to Mary:

> You know I don't love the sort of thing—settlements. I don't love missions—and I think the approach made to the Syrians is stupid. The Americanization of the Syrians will result in just a cheap imitation by the Syrians of the surface things American…They say that…the whole House has changed—and is very much better—really friendly and alive. Formerly these people used just to try to get into the Syrian houses, and then they'd sit down and ask questions. And the Syrians are a shy people. They don't understand that.

One afternoon there, he met Joseph Hitti, brother of the Middle Eastern scholar Philip K. Hitti. Kahlil questioned Joseph about the rationale of the settlement project.

> What did it all amount to? Each one of those women came with a question and I had gone without an answer…Once there I throw my whole heart into it for the hour or two hours or three hours and I enjoy it. Then I go home and it is all over and I say to myself, "Why did I go to that place? What was it worth to anybody?"[20]

But despite his objections and reservations, he loyally continued to visit.

~

Returning from Europe in August 1926, Mary tried to see Kahlil in New York, only to learn that he was in Boston. No word about "C. J." appeared in her diary for the next eight months. Finally, on April 16, 1927, she wrote: "Kahlil—? Ever so many questions. How is your book of Jesus? How has the winter been? What has happened with you? Please write me a letter." In the following pages of her diary, she described her life, recounting a touching scene.

> And the other day an Alabama woman, a stranger, dining here and looking at my portrait, suddenly said, "It reminds me of another painter—I wonder if you know any of his work—named Gibran." I took her upstairs to my room and showed her the twenty-seven pictures on the walls…Wherever your work meets its own, here as elsewhere, its own recognize it and love it.[21]

It is unclear whether or not he replied to this message. The few notes Mary received from him became more remote in tone. Then, in the second week of December 1927, she received the manuscript of *Jesus the Son of Man*.

She began to edit the work. Throughout the winter and into early spring of 1928, he continued to send her revisions and additions, which she often worked on while her household slept. "*March 8, 1928*. Remainder of 'Son of Man' arrived. *March 30*. 'Son of Man' 3:00 A.M. to 7:00 A.M. *April 4*. At night I finished 'Son of Man'—so as to return it before leaving."

Four days after returning the pages to him, Mary was in New York preparing to embark on another trip to Europe. In the midst of shopping, theatergoing, and family reunions, she stopped over at 51 West Tenth Street. "Work with C. J. on S. of Man and saw the beautiful drawings for the book—to be 250 pp." On May 2, they met once more. "Return to Gibran his 'Beautiful Necessity.'"[22]

~

Kahlil's ambitious work had taken its toll. Over the past December, an increasing desire to pull back from the world had begun to pervade a series of his poems.

> Pity it is
>> We drowse too soon;
> Pity it is
>> We fall asleep
> Ere our song
>> Encompass the height,

And ere our hand
    Inherit the deep.
Thanks unto the Lord,
We have no possessions,
Nor have we a possessor.
And we have no mate nor descendant nor kin.
We walk the earth a shadow
Seen only by those in whose eyes the shadow is hidden.
We laugh for the tragedy and the day;
And we weep for the laughter thereof.
And we are a spirit,
And you say "How strange."
But we say, "How strange is your body"…

In his own formerly trim physique there were symptoms of bloat. That summer in Boston, his legs and feet swelled. His appetite, often limited, dwindled. Marianna was replacing empty *arak* bottles at an alarming rate. He remained inside 76 Tyler Street all throughout July and August, and refused Corinne Roosevelt Robinson's annual invitation to Henderson House. When she sent her consolations, he thanked her and added, "I did not mind a bit my not going to Russia to attend the Tolstoy Fete. I only wanted to be once again under your roof…They tell me that 'Jesus,' my little book, will be out on the 12th of October. Of course I shall send the very first copy that reaches my hand to you."[23]

Pain was besetting him, and by 1928 he medicated by drinking to excess. Requesting *arak* in letters to Marianna, he couched his pleas in jest. "New York is a wasteland," he wrote, "There is not a drop of arak to drink before dinner and no song by Maroon after dinner…If you have a little, send my share."[24]

He was entrusting Assaf George—his procurer of alcohol during the height of Prohibition—with more responsibilities than supplying his means of coping. First, he jointly purchased two buildings in Boston with George and put them in Marianna's name. More modest than his earlier venture, he made sure he wasn't involved in its management. The houses at 180-182 Broadway were not far from Tyler Street, and agreement for mutual ownership ensured that Marianna would always have somewhere to go if she was forced to leave their tenement. He also commissioned George to investigate the sale of a monastery near Bsharri. It was not Mar Mema, but a similar site owned by the Carmelites. "I was very happy because you called about Mar Sarkis," he wrote George. "We must obtain that holy piece of land. And I beg you to do all you can about that matter."[25]

Mary did not know until November how sick Kahlil had been. While he was suffering from what he called summer rheumatism, her husband Florance too was ailing and occupying her time. She made no attempt to communicate with Kahlil until after the book's publication, and by then he was back in New York and somewhat cheered by its reception. On November 7, 1928, he wrote to tell her that she had been sent a copy.

> I hope you will like it, when you see it, in spite of the many little mistakes. My publishers seem to be extremely happy over it, and my friends here, as well as others throughout the country, say such kindly things about it...My summer was not a happy summer. I was in pain most of the time. But what of it? I wrote much in Arabic, songs and prose poems...you know, Mary, that I am homesick and that my heart longs for those hills and valleys. But it is better that I should stay here and work. I can do better in this strange, old room than anywhere else.[26]

~

In contrast to the mainly negative reception of *Sand and Foam* ("arid and thin," the *New York Herald Tribune* called it), *Jesus the Son of Man* was praised widely. In November 1928, the *Springfield Republican*, in Massachusetts, featured "Mystic Drawings by the Poet Gibran." The article discussed Kahlil's art in *Jesus the Son of Man*.

> In a time when book illustrations are apt to be the work of a person totally unacquainted with and unrelated to the book and its creator, Gibran has chosen the more difficult way, that of being his own artist...In Gibran...it is indeed the revery of a soul, bemused by the dream as harmonious as the music of the spheres...In his latest work, "Jesus the Son of Man," this can be seen perhaps more pointedly than in his earlier work. The subject lends itself to serenity. But after all, the serenity must first exist in the mind of the artist and the poet. The chief thing about Gibran's drawings for this book is that they are by no means literary. They do not tell a story or rely upon a caption for understanding. They are to be seen as pictures; to be understood as design and drawing. Balance, rhythm...relation of parts, movement suggested and significant, these qualities are self-evident.[27]

The *New York Times*, which had not reviewed *The Prophet*, devoted the front page of its Christmas book review section to two books on the life of Christ: *The Master* by Walter Russell Bowie and *Jesus the Son of Man*. "It is as a fellow-countryman that [Gibran] approaches the Man of Nazareth," wrote P. W. Wilson. "What we have in his case is not history but drama, a series of soliloquies, poetic in structure

Above left: Sketch for *Jesus the Son of Man*. Graphite and watercolor, 1923. (Courtesy © Metropolitan Museum of Art. Gift of Mrs. Mary H. Minis, 1932. Image source: Art Resource.)

Above right:
Mary Magdalen, from *Jesus the Son of Man*, 1928. Graphite. (Courtesy Private Collection.)

Bottom left: John, son of Zebedee, from *Jesus the Son of Man*. Charcoal and graphite, 1928. (Courtesy Private Collection.)

and beauty, which are attributed to the contemporaries of Jesus…Here is a treatment, certainly unusual, possibly unique."

John Haynes Holmes, the former minister of the Community Church in New York, wrote a sincere and moving appreciation.

> Readers of Mr. Gibran's earlier work *The Prophet*, published in many editions in this country and translated into more than twenty languages, will know what to expect in this book. Here is the same poet, with the same austere purity of thought, the same amplitude and beauty of phrase, the same wisdom, serenity and lofty vision…[He] has attempted a unique and daring experiment. He has told the story of Jesus…episode by episode…somewhat after the fashion of Browning in *The Ring and The Book*…It is as though a contemporary sat down, at a belated hour, to write another and different gospel.
>
> Nor is this as imprudent as it sounds, for Gibran is, secondly, a poet. It is difficult to describe the mystery of his verse. It has a simplicity which is disarming and yet a majesty which at times is overwhelming.[28]

That December 1928, Claude Bragdon, architect and critic, published a feature article about Kahlil in the *New York Herald Tribune*. Bragdon attempted to articulate the quality of "Gibranism."

> Just what this word means Gibran's English readers will have no difficulty in divining: mystical vision, metrical beauty, a simple and fresh approach to the so-called "problems" of life…His major interest is in *life*. He aims to discover some workable way of feeling, thinking, living, which shall lead toward *mastery*—how to serve the forces which enslave us until they are by us enslaved…[29]

Acknowledging his admiration, Bragdon offered his own concise portrait of Gibran the person.

> He is compact, strong, swarthy…he loves society as well as solitude, is an enjoyer of small things as well as great, of things physical as well as metaphysical; although he is austere in one sense, there is none of the ascetic about him…I shall have to leave the description stand as it is with the assurance that he isn't, after all, quite like it—he evades…and escapes me…

Following the article, which was elaborately illustrated with six of his drawings, came Kahlil's Christmas piece, a reflection on the Nativity called "The Great Recurrence." The same essay appeared in the editorial section of the December 23, 1928 edition of the Washington, D.C. *Sunday Star*, as part of a holiday issue, featuring articles on global militarism.

The Great Recurrence

By Kahlil Gibran
Famous Poet and Writer of Lebanon.

MADONNA OF THE OLIVE BRANCH.

SISTINE MADONNA.

MADONNA OF THE HARPIES.

MANY centuries ago they said that the humble shepherds of Judea and the wise Kings of Persia came to a manger to worship the infant Jesus. They also said that the shepherds sang of peace and good will, and of love that binds man to man; and that the wise Kings laid gold and frankincense at the feet of the blessed babe.

Now we children of the vast yesterday come to a manger, which is in truth our solitude; each one of us a shepherd who would have peace in the pasture of his thoughts, and the good will of all the other shepherds—and each one of us a king of his own destiny, who would lay gold and frankincense at the feet of his greater self; gold for assurance and frankincense for dreams.

You and I and all our neighbors would kneel before the anointed genius of mankind, which is in us all.

And they say that Jesus was born in a cave even like his forerunners, Orpheus and Methra and Zoroaster. They said this for they knew that only the secret depths can give birth to great heights.

And today, we, too, believe that vast souls, even as vast worlds, move from darkness to light, and from oblivion to recognition, from hidden roots to blooms that laugh in the sun and dance in the wind.

But they said that the King of Judea decreed, in his fear, the slaughter of all the newborn in the land, for he was told even by the Persian seers that the infant Jesus should overrule him and deprive him of scepter and diadem.

Today we in our fear of the unknown tomorrow would slay the innocence in us that it may not be a stumbling block in the path of our governing intelligence.

But, thanks be to the heavens above, there is for some of us an Egypt for an escape and golden sands and palm trees for safety.

We go there in faith, knowing that that which we would save in us is the truth and the beauty which the angel of our white nights so graciously taught us to love and protect.

Yea, it was in that distant yesterday when the genius of our heart's desire was born, and the secret in our depth was revealed to us, and the innocence in us sought escape from the designing which is in us also.

And all this shall come to pass many times before we reach our homecoming. It is the mystic recurrence of the divine mystery before the face of the Son.

Gigantic Sums for Warfare

Nations Spend Lavishly in Spite of Moves for World Peace—Five and One-Half Million Men Under Arms

Kahlil's reflection on the Nativity, December 1928. (Courtesy Private Collection.)

Restating themes expressed in "O Mist, my sister," Kahlil recast the Nativity story and Herod's slaughter of the newborns as a rite of escape of our innocence from our destructive "designing" natures.

THE GREAT RECURRENCE

Many centuries ago they said that the humble shepherds of Judea and the wise Kings of Persia came to a manger to worship the infant Jesus. They also said that the shepherds sang of peace and good will, and love that binds man to man; and that the wise Kings laid gold and frankincense at the feet of the blessed babe.

Now we children of the vast yesterday come to a manger, which is in truth our solitude; each one of us a shepherd who would have peace in the pasture of his thoughts, and the good will of all the other shepherds—and each one of us a king of his own destiny, who would lay gold and frankincense at the feet of his greater self; gold for assurance and frankincense for dreams.

You and I and all our neighbors would kneel before the anointed genius of mankind, which is in us all.

And they say that Jesus was born in a cave even like his forerunners, Orpheus and Methra and Zoroaster. They said this for they knew that only the secret depths can give birth to great heights.

And today, we, too, believe that vast souls, even as vast worlds, move from darkness to light, and from oblivion to recognition, from hidden roots to blooms that laugh in the sun and dance in the wind.

But they said that the King of Judea decreed, in his fear, the slaughter of all the newborn in the land, for he was told even by the Persian seers that the infant Jesus should overrule him and deprive him of scepter and diadem.

Today we in our fear of the unknown tomorrow would slay the innocence in us that it may not be a stumbling block in the path of our governing intelligence.

But thanks be to the heavens above, there is for some of us an Egypt for an escape and golden sands and palm trees for safety.

We go there in faith, knowing that that which we would save in us is the truth and beauty which the angel of our white nights so graciously taught us to love and protect.

Yes, it was in that distant yesterday when the genius of our heart's desire was born, and the secret was revealed to us, and the innocence in us sought escape from the designing which is in us also.

And all this shall come to pass many times before we reach our homecoming. It is the mystic recurrence of the divine mystery before the face of the Son.

~

The first week of 1929 featured celebrations of Kahlil's creativity, publicly and privately. Just before his forty-sixth birthday, Alma Reed organized a lively party at her studio in Greenwich Village. Reed was a respected journalist and archaeologist. The sponsor in New York of the Mexican painter Jose Clemente Orozco, she was also a key figure in the Delphic group, an association of artists and writers who promoted Hellenic philosophy and poetry. The Delphic group especially promoted the work of the poet Angelos Sikelianos.[30]

Her account of the two artists highlighted their shared ties. Champions of the peasant classes in their native countries, both were expatriates living in New York, in Greenwich Village. Labels had been stamped on their respective talents—the "Mexican Goya" and the "Blake of the twentieth century." Both had drawn likenesses of the captivating Alma Reed, with Orozco—not a fan of Gibran's style—sheepishly admitting that Gibran's crayon drawing was the better likeness.[31] Each artist had an American benefactress—Orozco, Alma Reed; Gibran, Mary Haskell.

Recalled Alma Reed,

> From the very beginning of their acquaintance, there had existed a well-controlled but active antagonism between the two artists. While Orozco maintained a discreet and somewhat ominous silence on the subject of Gibran's pictures, Kahlil would indulge in an occasional defensive fling at what he called "the violent art of Mexico."…Widely divergent views of art, however, did not seem to prevent their enjoyment of each other's company at their frequent meetings. Their mutual regard was never more in evidence than at Gibran's birthday party, which launched the… [studio's] international social activities for the New Year.

Among the members of the Delphic group gathering that night were Syud Hossain, the poet Estelle Duclo, the critic José Juan Tablada, and members of the New York Craftsman's Poetry Group, headed by Elizabeth Crittenden Percy, as well as writer Leonard Van Noppen and Kahlil's good friend Claude Bragdon. "Also present," according to Reed, "was Judge Richard Campbell, genial New York host to visiting Irish intellectuals and patron of the Abbey Theater Players."

Years later, Alma Reed recalled a mercurial Kahlil savoring his attentive and loving friendships, yet somehow emotionally wary. Another honored guest, Sarojini Naidu, described the event to her daughter.

> The delight was a party at the house of a lovely woman who translates Greek poetry, Alma Reed…a gathering of international admirers of the Syrian poet Kahlil Gibran, to celebrate his birthday and the jubilee of his literary life…Syrians in New York are holding a special festival tomorrow to…chant his praises in Arabic. He

read some of his English poems but the rest were recited…by an American woman with a gift for…interpretation…[32]

Kahlil also read from his early English works, *The Madman* and *The Forerunner*, along with some parables. Then, Alma Reed recalled,

> …in their appreciation of Kahlil's delightful fantasy, the guests kept pressing him for more parables and aphorisms. He continued to read in a voice that betrayed deep emotion, until at last he appeared no longer able to control his feelings. Abruptly he asked the company to excuse him. He rushed into the dining room where he sat down and wept. Shaken by sorrow, he explained to me between heavy sobs that as he read the parables he suddenly realized there was nothing in the much publicized books of his maturity to equal these spontaneous little works of his youth…
>
> I tried to console him by pointing out that creative periods are never duplicated in any true artist's life. I assured him that we all thought *The Prophet* and…Lazarus… as great as the parables, if in a different way. But he continued to weep and, as he sat there, Orozco joined us…In a few moments; he succeeded in giving Kahlil a more hopeful outlook.
>
> "Hombre," he said, as he held the poet in one of those cordial, familiar *abrazos* that pass between men friends in Spain and Latin America, "don't regret that your latest work is different from your early work. I find it good—in fact, wonderful— that you change. It would indeed be a calamity if you did not. Who knows—your new work may be even better than your old. Give it time. You are not the sole judge of its worth. Meanwhile, be happy that you are still young enough to grow—that you are not an ossified academician. To stagnate even at a good point is living death for the artist!"
>
> They talked for a little while and Kahlil regained his poise. Then together they walked back into the living room, their faces wreathed in smiles.[33]

The next day, on January 5, 1929, Kahlil was the recipient of tributes from the Syrian community. In honor of his twenty-five years as a contributor to Arab letters, the Pen League sponsored a testimonial dinner at the Hotel McAlpin in New York. Among the eighteen speakers was Philip K. Hitti, chair of the Department of Oriental Languages at Princeton University, who summarized the pride that his countrymen took in the artist and his works.

> The influence which Gibran exercises in modern Arabic literature can be measured, in a way, not only by the multitude of people who have been benefited by reading him but also by the big crop of would-be Gibrans, quasi-Gibrans and Gibran-imitators who have in recent years, mushroom-like, sprung up and flourished all over

Pen League banquet for Kahlil, honoring twenty-five years of artistic activity, January 5, 1929. Gibran is seated in front of the portrait, to the right of the flag. (Courtesy Museo Soumaya.)

the Arabic speaking world. So much so that you can hardly nowadays pick up an Arabic paper printed in Beirut, Cairo, Baghdad, Sao Paulo or Buenos Aires without finding somebody consciously trying to write Gibran-like. Of course, the esoteric, figurative, imaginative style…is not a new thing in Arabic literature…But our hero of tonight, through his unmatched mastery of this art, through his pure and rich imagery, through his lofty and noble idealism, through his unexcelled diction and composition—be it in Arabic or in English—has become the father of a new school of thought all of his own. While others use empty words, are affected and artificial, Gibran unfailingly produces gems of thought and is always natural and sublime.

Kahlil's colleague and Pen League member William Catzeflis, as toastmaster, presented him with gifts and tributes from organizations around the country. A specially bound edition of *Al-Sanabil* (*The Spikes of Grain*), a commemorative anthology of his earlier works, was issued for the occasion. "With visible emotion," as one observer described it, "Gibran then spoke of his pride in his race."[34]

~

Unbeknownst to those who may have witnessed his uncharacteristic displays of intense emotion at these events, Kahlil was by now seriously ill. He soon left for his

Boston refuge on Tyler Street. But the disease he had been trying to evade persisted. By the end of January, X-rays revealed enlargement of the liver.

On the day he was scheduled for an examination, his relatives gathered at the Tyler Street studio. For Marianna, her impressions of the hospital were mingled with death and bereavement. Marianna's cousin and her husband, Maroon and Assaf George, were both reluctant to let him leave for what could end in a fearful operation, or worse. So Kahlil decided to avoid further diagnosis and turned away from medical help.[35] The cirrhosis began to ravage him, but he insistently tried to work. In March he wrote Naimy from Boston: "My ailment is seated in something much deeper than muscle and bone. I have often wondered if it was not a state of health instead of illness."[36]

Publicly he chose not to divulge his weakened state, and in April *The Syrian World* announced the fall publication of *The Garden of the Prophet*. But a month later, from Boston, he wrote Mary about his fatigue. Soon afterward, he again abandoned the book. He turned instead to a work previously conceived nearly two decades earlier.

In February 1911, back from Paris, he had told Charlotte about an idea for a poem.

> The earth-God has gone mad, and destroyed all life save one man and one woman. The earth is in the form and likeness of a skull—its hollows dry, riverbeds, gray—its surface cinders…The man and woman are to water it with their tears, make it fruitful again and re-people the earth.[37]

But to make earth fruitful again, its domain and sovereignty have to be recognized. Continuing to expand this theme, in 1925 Kahlil's poem "Earth" was published in Cairo in *Al-Badayi wa Tarray'if* (*Best Things and Masterpieces*), an Arabic compilation of his poetry. Confiding to the earth, he vowed,

> You are my sight and my discernment.
> You are my acknowledgment and my dream.
> You are my hunger and thirst.
> You are my sorrow and joy.

As if asking for forgiveness, he confesses the ways that humans have violated earth's domain and become blind to its lessons.

> How generous you are, Earth, and how strong is your yearning for your children
> lost between that which they have attained and that which they could not obtain.
> We clamor and you smile, we flit but you stay.
> We blaspheme and you consecrate, we defile and you sanctify.

We sleep without dreams; but you dream in your eternal wakefulness.
We pierce your bosom with swords and spears and you dress our wounds with oil and balsam.
We plant your fields with skulls and bones and from them you rear cypress and willow trees.
We empty our wastes in your bosom and you fill our threshing floors with wheat sheaves and our wine presses with grapes.
We extract your elements to make cannons and bombs,
but out of our elements you create lilies and roses.
How patient you are, Earth, and how merciful![38]

Returning over time to his initial idea for *The Earth Gods,* the one earth god evolved into three. He wrote Elizabeth Selig, his editor at Knopf, that they symbolized "the three primal elements in man…the desire for power, the desire to rule a greater world, and Love, a greater desire for Now and this Here." It became a story of three gods watching the drama of two people falling in love and one god's belief in human beings as "divinity"; a praise poem to love through earth's bounty.[39]

Said Kahlil, "I'm going to change every thou in it to you—as in *The Prophet* and my other English books—and I'll cut out some of the phraseology, shorten the way of saying things, and someday finish it."[40] He would continue to work on it for the next year and a half. Published in March of 1931, a review appeared in the *New York Times* later that spring.

Although the…author of "The Earth Gods" was a resident of this country, it is the thought and the mysticism of the land of his birth, Asia Minor, which dictate his utterance. And the literature of the East has shaped the utterance. There is in his lines something of the sensuous surge of the Song of Solomon. His three gods, earth-born and master Titans of life, that appear on the mountains are no mere intellectual concepts. They are corporeal beings, capable of high thought, but also are of their native earth. They are gorgeous gods, as were those of Babylon…This is not verse penned by an Occidental, toying with worn philosophies…

Weary is my spirit of all there is.
I would not move a hand to create a world
Nor to erase one…
Could I but strip my divinity of its purpose
And breathe my immortality into space,
And be no more;
Could I but be consumed and pass from time's memory
Into the emptiness of nowhere!

Drawing, from *The Earth Gods*. Graphite, charcoal, and watercolor. (Courtesy Peter A. Juley / Smithsonian.)

But looking down upon the earth…these gods…had been assailed by the sound of a youth singing; and that singing has awakened the sleeping maiden…to claim her love. The gods perceive…the purpose of one greater than they, one who had himself created them, as he had created maiden and youth…

> We shall pass into the twilight;
> Perchance to wake to the dawn of another world.
> But their love shall stay,
> And his finger-marks shall not be erased.
> …
> The blessed forge burns….

Kahlil Gibran was the author of many books in Arabic before he undertook to write in English…[*The Earth Gods*] is something new, not grandiose but very nearly grand, sweeping and invigorating. In it the voice of older civilizations speaks...with something of sadness, yet with a large tolerance, like elders...to children concerned with small and perishable things.[41]

~

In the fall of 1929, after seeking solitude in Boston for almost ten months, Gibran felt able to return to New York. The Hermitage was becoming cluttered with magazines, books, drawings, and paintings, which he always promised would go to the library he was planning for Bsharri. It was time to put his house in order, and he wrote Mary.

> My responsibilities in the East are over...It was in my heart to help a little because I was helped much, and I am glad of it all. The next time I shall measure, and measure well, the distance between my desire and my ability...I have had the studio repainted. It is now so clean and shiney, and there is in it some kind of order. My Arabic work, my English work, my drawings and my paintings are so separated and arranged so I can put my hand on anything without going through the torture of finding it. And I am going on with the work; rather slowly to be sure, but with a certainty in my heart.[42]

In December, "Snow," a poem he had been saving for *The Garden of The Prophet*, appeared in the *Herald Tribune* magazine section, edited by the respected journalist Marie Mattingly Meloney.[43] It was one of his last published pieces.

He tried to convince his closest friends that his condition was improving, and they in turn screened his dependency on alcohol—the thing that numbed the pain, yet hastened the disease.[44]

In March 1930, Kahlil made the final copy of his will, which provided for Marianna, Mary, and Bsharri. This, along with his few securities, he entrusted to Edgar Speyer. By July he was in Boston with Marianna. Despite her husband's disapproval, Mary continued discreetly to meet with Kahlil to edit both *The Earth Gods* and *The Wanderer*, referring to this only cryptically in her diaries.[45]

While Mary continued editing, Kahlil tried to maintain a normal schedule in Boston. As he had the summer before, he refused invitations. One note from his favorite hostess conveyed her anxiety. "I have thought of you so often," wrote Corinne Roosevelt Robinson, "and asked my son to telephone and find out how you were...All my F. D. R. family are hoping you are coming sometime...I was greatly worried about you, dear Kahlil, and felt so helpless to be of assistance. Yours with real affection and concern."[46]

~

That summer of 1930, Kahlil longed to recreate the days he and Marianna had spent by the sea. With the help of his cousin Zakia Gibran Diab, who located a house on the water, he and his sister stayed for two months at 122 Ocean Street in Squantum. He lingered there far into the fall, and although he wrote Knopf that he was working hard, he rejected his publisher's suggestion that he return. "It is not possible for me to go back to New York just now in order to have new negatives made of the original drawings of *The Prophet* for the Czechoslovakian publishers."[47]

Correspondence from Kahlil to Gertrude Stern, an office worker in New York's garment district and admirer of his work who had first met Kahlil through the Yiddish translator of *The Prophet*, Isaac Horowitz, describe his health that summer.

Portrait of Kahlil in March 1931, shortly before his death, by artist Eleanor Small Fisk. (Courtesy Private Collection. Reprint: Interlink.)

It delights me to hear that you are flaming with health. It is your youth singing before the face of the sun! And how else can it be with doctors who know how to doctor themselves? As for me, I am really getting well. They tell me that I must do no work and that I must be at perfect peace with the world and what there is in it. It is rather hard for a burning bush to be a cabbage—but what would you, if your doctors say so?...And may our God keep you.[48]

Kahlil was trying to elude the disease sapping his creative will and capacity to work.

Leaving Squantum was difficult, but leaving his sister was even more so. He commissioned Zakia to look for an apartment, some place within the city and near public transportation. By 1930, South Enders were leaving the inner city and settling in surrounding greenbelts, and he insisted to a reluctant Marianna that it was time for her to leave the crowded streets. When a comfortable apartment was found across the street from Franklin Park, he stayed in Boston until mid-October to be sure that she was settled in, promising to return for Christmas.

In November, Kahlil signed another contract with Knopf, knowing there was no time for *The Garden of the Prophet*. Already the bloat of the past two years was giving way to a sudden wasting away. He worked on parables left over from *The Madman*.

His last work would be *The Wanderer*—"a man with but a cloak and a staff, and a veil of pain upon his face."[49] Christmas came, and he stayed in New York. By January, he was confined to his studio, but he insisted to old friends that it was only a temporary setback. He did, however, share his condition with May Ziade.

My health at present is worse than it was at the beginning of the summer...This strange heart that used to quiver more than one hundred times a minute is now slowing down and is beginning to go back to normal after having ruined my health and affected my well-being...I am, May, a small volcano whose opening has been closed. If I were able today to write something great and beautiful, I would be completely cured. If I could cry out, I would gain back my health...

Please, for God's sake, don't tell me, "You have sung a lot, and what you have already sung was beautiful." Don't mention to me my past deeds, for the remembrance of them makes me suffer, and their triviality turns my blood into a burning fire, and their dryness generates thirst in my heart, and their weakness keeps me up and down one thousand and one times a day. Why did I write all those articles and stories?...I was born to live and to write a book—only one small book—I was born to live and suffer and to say one living and winged word, and I cannot remain silent until Life utters that word through *my* lips. I was

The Wanderer. Charcoal and watercolor. (Courtesy Peter A. Juley / Smithsonian.)

unable to do this because I was a prattler…However, my word is still in my heart, and it is a living and a winged word which I must utter in order to remove with its harmony the sins which my jabbering has created…[50]

In mid-March, with *The Earth Gods* published, he sent Mary a copy and message.

No, I have not been so very well but getting on nicely now. I am preparing another book, The Wanderer…My publishers wish to bring it out next October…I must turn over the manuscript and the drawings within a month. I wonder if you should care to see the manuscript with your seeing eyes and lay your knowing hands upon it before it is submitted?

By March 31, she had received it. "*Saturday, April 4.* Reading *The Wanderer* since last Tuesday. It goes slowly." Two days later she sent her reply. "Ever so happy with The Wanderer—and will return it as soon as I possibly can."[51]

~

In 1931, Easter fell on the 5th of April. Disregarding published reports of his final days, the following letter from Barbara Young to Margaret Lee Crofts seems to be a spontaneous account of the events.

> For some weeks…he had been keeping [to] his bed most of the time, getting up and down, but seldom dressing as for the street. Easter evening I spent with him, and he was feeling much better, his voice was strong and he got up and walked about but was pitifully thin and with a drawn look in the darling face. I had a habit of calling him every day on the phone. Monday I called and his voice was fine, he said he had Syrian friends coming in the evening. Tuesday he sounded tired, but said he had letters to dictate. Then he would go to sleep early. I told him I would be out of town for the day Wednesday if he was *sure* he would be all right. He laughed and said "I *will* be all right."
>
> Thursday I called and his voice frightened me, so I went at once and found that the janitor's wife [Anna Johansen, who daily brought Kahlil his breakfast] had sent for Mrs. Jacobs that morning—Leonebel Jacobs, who used to live in the building.[52] They had brought a doctor and would take him to St. Vincent's Hospital Friday morning. I sat beside the precious being doing all that there was to do. He talked and was playful, perfectly himself, sleeping a little—and just a short time before the ambulance came in the morning there was a sudden change. Before he went downstairs he said—seeing my terrible anxiety—"Don't be troubled. *All is well*," and these were his last conscious words.[53]

Barbara Young wired Marianna, whose last long trip had been her journey with her family to Boston in 1895. Feeling helpless, it was up to Assaf George and Zakia Gibran Diab to accompany her to New York. When she arrived, a sea of unknown faces greeted her. The only face she was able to recognize was Kahlil's.

Word had spread. The *Herald Tribune Sunday Magazine* editor Marie Mattingly Maloney joined the vigil with painter Adele Watson and Mikhail Naimy. Barbara became intermediary. She told Naimy that when a nun had asked him if he were a Catholic, he had answered, "No." By the time a pastor of Saint Joseph's Maronite Church had arrived at St. Vincent's, he was unconscious.

Kahlil Gibran died on April 10, 1931, at 10:55 p.m. A death certificate would confirm the cause of death to be cirrhosis of the liver. It also noted incipient tuberculosis in one lung—the same disease that had touched Kahlil's family and so many other immigrants to America's urban centers at the turn of the twentieth century.[54]

Welcoming the Gibran cortege as it passed on the road to his native Bsharri. (Courtesy Museo Soumaya.)

21

HOMECOMING

"And verily he will find the roots of the good and the bad,
the fruitful and the fruitless,
all entwined together in the silent heart of the earth."[1]

With his passing, myths surrounding Kahlil Gibran would proliferate, obscuring the person and the story behind his creative vision. Jessie Fremont Beale, elderly and eking out her days at the height of the Depression in a Beacon Hill room, remembered the precocious immigrant youth. Of the many letters, memorials, and tributes to appear that year, hers returned to the place where his early efforts to paint and write began to form. Once again Beale wrote to the sponsor she had first asked to help nurture Kahlil's promising talent.

> Dear Mr. Day:
> Miss Brown [poet Alice Brown] passed on to me the Kalil clipping. That dear little Syrian boy did a lot of thinking! His interest in his fellowman was great. Did you see him when he was in Boston the year before his death, I think? He was visiting his sister on Tyler Street or somewhere in that neighborhood. The Congregational book store on Beacon Street was interested in keeping his books on sale. I hope sometime to read his *Life of Christ*.
> Jessie Fremont Beale[2]

~

Marianna had agreed to a two-day vigil in New York. On Saturday and Sunday, Kahlil's body lay at a funeral home on Lexington Avenue where, *The Syrian World* reported, "hundreds filed by...in a continual stream."[3] The next day Marianna, members of the Pen League, Barbara Young, and a few other American friends accompanied the cortege to Boston.

Friends and relatives gathered at South Station. Front row, left to right: Marianna Gibran, Zakia Gibran Diab, Maroon George, Rose Gibran, Amelia Parent, Back row: Barbara Young, Assaf George, Mike Eblan, N'oula Gibran, Fr. Stephen el-Douaihy. (Courtesy Museo Soumaya.)

Obituaries appeared in metropolitan newspapers. *The Sun*, New York's popular broadsheet, featured an editorial referring to Kahlil as the "chief poet and artist of the Arabic-speaking peoples of the world." Within a week, educational, religious, and other social reform-oriented journals across the country were remembering him. "Kahlil Gibran is dead," was a lead article in the Ohio *Penitentiary News*.[4]

Kahlil's small circle of family feared that the Catholic Church would not allow a consecrated burial, since rumors of his refusal to receive the sacrament of Extreme Unction ("last anointing") had reached Boston. A few hours after he had met the train at South Station, Monsignor Stephen el-Douaihy promised a distraught Marianna that he would conduct the traditional ritual for her brother. His assurance was courageous. Years later, letters from the Chancery's archive documented that his decision caused friction between the Roman Catholic hierarchy and the local Maronite church. The crux of the disagreement was whether Catholic rites were wrongfully administered. William Cardinal O'Connell, archbishop of Boston, was never completely satisfied with the Maronite priest's defense of the poet's character and his writings.[5]

~

Seventeen years earlier, in 1914, Mary Haskell had written,

> I often think of his death—and of myself after that. This Sunday night before I left
> for my train I lay by his side…looked at his profile…and thought again of the day
> when it will not turn to me.

Unaware of his last days, Mary had convened a convention of the Southern States
Arts League. On Sunday morning, April 12, Marianna's telegram finally reached
her. When she earned of his death, she reacted quickly. Two hours later, Mary was
on the northbound train. She arrived on Monday evening and went immediately to
Marianna. "Found her waiting for me. She had on her mother's…black lace scarf. We
went by cab to 44 West Newton Street—Syrian Ladies Club, where Kahlil was laid
out." To Mary, Kahlil appeared "stern, determined, kind, remote, concentrated."

Among the long line of Syrians that night were the relatives about whom
she had heard for years—N'oula and Rose Gibran, Zakia Gibran Diab, Maroon
and Assaf George. She also for the first time met his Arab and New York associates—Nasib Arida, Najib Diab, Mikhail Naimy, Barbara Young, Adele Watson, and
Gertrude Stern.

The next day hundreds of mourners followed the cortege through the streets to
the church of Our Lady of the Cedars of Lebanon.

> As the cortege passed by, many dropped upon their knees…and the scores of traffic
> officers of Boston stood at salute as the flag-draped casket went by. It was impossible
> for the many hundreds of friends to find places inside the little church, and they
> waited in silence on the sidewalk during the service.[6]

At the hillside vault in Mount Benedict Cemetery, several of Kahlil's friends stepped
forward and spoke.

~

Two days later, Marianna and her cousin Zakia traveled to New York, where Mary
began the process of establishing that the document Kahlil had written in March
1930, and given to Marianna in July that year, was his last will and testament.
Provisions for Marianna and Mary differed little from his earlier wills.

> In the event of my death I wish that whatever money or securities Mr. Edgar
> Speyer has been gracious enough to hold for me should go to my sister Mary K.
> Gibran who now lives at 76 Tyler St., Boston, Mass.

There are also 40 (forty) shares of the Fifty-one West Tenth St. Studio Association stock lying in my safe deposit box with the Bank of Manhattan Trust Company, 31 Union Square, New York. These shares are also to go to my sister… Everything found in my studio after my death…pictures, books, objects of art, etcetera go to Mrs. Mary Haskell Minis, now living at 24 Gaston Street West, Savannah, Ga. But I would like to have Mrs. Minis send all or any part of these things to my home town should she see fit to do so.

But two additional paragraphs would turn this simple bequest into a legal nightmare.

There are in addition to the foregoing, two (2) bankbooks of the West Side Savings Bank, 422 Sixth Avenue, New York, which I have with me in my studio. I wish that my sister would take this money to my home town of Becharri, Republic of Lebanon, and spend it upon charities.

The royalties on my copyrights, which copyrights I understand can be extended upon request by my heirs for an additional period of twenty-eight years after my death, are to go to my home town.[7]

Even among relatives and close friends, only Mary had heard his dream of helping his village and understood what he had wanted. On May 29, 1923, he had told her:

If I had 50,000 dollars to spend, I could get three or four hundred acres in Lebanon…and make a model agricultural station of it. And Syria needs that. For in Syria, as all over the world, the people are leaving…and many of the farms are abandoned…Syria needs one man with five or ten millions who will deliberately work for her growth and development and consciousness of herself. I could get any amount of money from the Syrians here—but I don't want to do that and go over there. They would say, "Gibran the poet has turned

Kahlil's death mask. (Courtesy Museo Soumaya.)

farmer"—But I could be back of the project if the money were my own—and really help it…

There is a valley in the Lebanon—at the northern end of the range—like a platter in shape—the mountains rise around the sides of it—and from the far end a bold stream comes that waters it all…The Gibrans owned that valley—and it was let out in farms where people had lived for ages…But now all that is changed. All the Gibrans but one have moved away…The lands are sold…wild again and feeding no one.[8]

On April 17, 1931, Mary, Marianna, and Zakia visited Edgar Speyer's office, where his assistant, Henry Lorch, produced a copy of the 1930 will and confirmed that he and an associate had witnessed it. The women, joined by Barbara Young, spent the rest of the day in the studio, where no later document was found. Another search was conducted on Saturday at the bank. Accompanied by Walter Shea, assistant to Kahlil's lawyer William Saxe, they found only the West Tenth Street Studio shares in his safe deposit box.

For Mary, however, the search in the studio had been successful. Among hundreds of papers unearthed were notebooks and manuscripts she had worked on, plus several packets of her letters. Faced with so much printed material that she was unable to read, Marianna begged to leave. Mary agreed to travel with her and Zakia to Boston, and Marianna promised to accompany her brother to his final resting place in Bsharri.

Back in New York early Monday morning, Mary asked Mikhail Naimy to meet with her at Thompson's Spa, a restaurant near Grand Central Station. She knew that he was planning to write a biography in Arabic, and her concern was that he should understand Kahlil's work from her viewpoint. Naimy, who had been close to Kahlil ever since the founding days of *Al-Funun* and the Pen League, was unfamiliar with Kahlil's Boston years. For four hours she explained to him details of her sponsorship. Their conversation continued from the restaurant to the studio. "Mischa asked many wonderful questions about Kahlil," she wrote that night as she traveled to Savannah, "and I was glad it is he who will write Kahlil's life for the Arabic speaking world. I understood as we talked why Kahlil trusted him to write, above even other men friends."[9]

Then Mary set herself to the task of securing the studio. "My fears were for the safety of his writings, his drawings and paintings," she explained in a letter to Marianna.

First I went out and bought two rather large locked suitcases. Then I had [the caretaker] put latches on the windows and a padlock on the closet door…Until 6

p.m. I worked alone. Then Naimy came back and we worked together till 9:55…
and now in the closet, locked up, are all the portfolios…all the small treasures…
all the manuscripts that we found; and in my 2 suitcases I put my notebooks that
had been found on Saturday and *all* the letters, mine, his, and other peoples, locked
them up and marked them with my name.

Knowing that immediate problems had been faced and resolved, Mary left
feeling secure. But once in Savannah, hundreds of miles from New York, she encountered difficulties in trying to oversee the estate. Not only was she still editing
The Wanderer, but her constant communication with Saxe forced her to act as
intermediary between him and Marianna. Turning to Barbara for help, Mary sent
her keys to the studio and detailed instructions about readying it for dispersal. She
also entrusted Barbara to deal with Knopf in regards to *The Wanderer* and answering condolences.[10]

Barbara and her
daughter in Kahlil's
studio. (Courtesy Peter A.
Juley / Smithsonian.)

The task of arranging a tribute was undertaken by someone who had known
Kahlil since his early days in Boston. Charles Fleischer, former rabbi of Temple
Israel in Boston, gathered everyone together—New York friends, Boston col-
leagues, Arab and American editors and writers. "A Tribute to the Spirit of Kahlil
Gibran" was held on the afternoon of April 29 at the Master Institute of United
Arts and Roerich Museum, then the Riverside Drive home of the Russian artist
Nicholas Roerich. Fleischer, recently an editor of *New York American*, was then
broadcasting his own CBS Radio program. His efforts in sponsoring and organiz-
ing Kahlil's memorial reflected their lifelong friendship. Fleischer sent personal

invitations to key people in Kahlil's life, referring to him as "our common friend" when he wrote Corinne Roosevelt Robinson; and in his invitation to Marianna, described the program to be "sweet, simple, significant in keeping with Kahlil's own rare soul."[11]

Fleischer's welcoming words echoed Kahlil's sentiments. "His passing from our sight and ken is really only a reclamation by the Eternal Spirit...we mourn not; because we can easily take...his own words from *Sand and Foam*: 'Mayhap a funeral among men is a wedding feast among angels.'"[12] Three members of the clergy offered eulogies: Robert Norwood, rector of St. Bartholomew's Church in New York; Abraham Mitrie Rihbany, from Boston's Church of the Disciples; and Reverend W. A. Mansur, a contributor to *The Syrian World*, who once described Kahlil as "the singer of the Syrian American soul."

Speakers included Claude Bragdon, Syud Hossain, Salloum Mokarzel, Percy MacKaye, along with poetry readings by Estelle Dulco, Mikhail Naimy, Leonora Speyer, and Barbara Young. Music also honored Kahlil's life and work, as Bragdon remarked, "This bird of God is free at last." Cellist Prince Mohammed Mohiuddin began with Shubert's "Due bist die Ruh," while baritone Hubert Linscott, accompanied by composer-pianist Anis Fuleihan, sang adaptations of Kahlil's poetry, followed by Prince Mohiuddin's oud performance.

With former rabbi Charles Fleischer presiding, with Syud Hossain praising the poet's "deep insight into the history and psychology of the Islamic peoples," and with Reverend Robert Norwood calling attention to the "intimacy and understanding" with which Kahlil "knew God and Christ," the tribute personified Kahlil's own stated vision.

> You and I are sons of one faith—the Spirit. And those who are set up as heads over its many branches are as fingers on the hand of a divinity that points to the Spirit's perfection.[13]

Death had sparked international attention to Kahlil's work. *The Syrian World* said, "The Arabic press of Egypt, Syria, Lebanon, Iraq, and other Arabic-speaking countries eulogized him as they have no other Syrian emigrant before, and as they have few of the outstanding literary personalities of the homeland in recent times."[14] On May 24, two major memorial meetings were held within the Syrian community. A tribute in Brooklyn included official representation from several Arab countries. At the Municipal Building in Boston's South End, a thousand Syrian and Lebanese gathered to remember their native son.

For over twenty years, Mary had known how ardently Kahlil had wanted to be buried in Lebanon. In June 1911, he had described the grotto chapel of Mar Mema: "It is there I came to myself, I learned, was shown. There I went oftenest and I loved it most…Is it selfish, extravagant, for me to want to be buried in Syria?" He had also spoken about a sanctuary he wished to have in a house there. He envisioned a square room of gray stone, "simple, with one narrow door like the Egyptians, and light from above…" Opposite the door would be an old Buddha from India, with a crucifix hanging above it. An Islamic prayer rug would cover the floor, and on the rug would stand a silver incense bowl. He wished that when he died his friends would bury him "under the stones of the floor." Mary may have had these conversations in mind when she answered Marianna.

> Yes, I think that the town of Becharri…has the right…idea…It seems to me, as I know it seems to you, that it will be the most beautiful thing, for his body to rest in Lebanon…And there should be also a collection there…some pictures, some treasures from the studio, some mementoes of the poet.[15]

By June 1, Marianna again traveled to New York, where she and Saxe were appointed administrators of the estate. The lawyer advanced her two thousand dollars, half for charity in Bsharri and half for expenses, and with this assurance she relented. Assaf George and Zakia Gibran helped Marianna write to Mary: "I am preparing for my trip with the body…it is a hard task for me."[16]

~

Kahlil's final journey home began on the morning of July 23, 1931. A long line of cars accompanied the casket and embarking party—Marianna and the Georges—to Providence, where speeches were read before several hundred mourners from Boston and New York, and Barbara read several of his poems. Music played, while the casket was lowered into the Fabre Line's SS *Sinaia*, by chance a ship with a storied history of transporting World War I refugees to safe havens. At 2:00 p.m., the ship sailed.

Arriving in Beirut Harbor on August 21, 1931, after an arduous four-week voyage from Providence, Marianna was overwhelmed by the multitude of ceremonies organized by political, religious, and literary communities. Before the *Sinaia* docked, an official delegation boarded and draped the flag of the French Mandate State of Greater Lebanon around Kahlil's coffin. Then the bier, accompanied by Marianna with Assaf and Maroon George, was transferred to a launch that steamed to the pier.

Memorial service in Bsharri. Marianna (*center*), between Minister of Interior Mousa Bey Nammour (*left*) and Bishop Boulos Akl (*right*), along with French and Lebanese military figures. From *Al-Barq*, August 26, 1931. (Reprint: George Lynde/Art Imaging.)

Upon landing, the coffin was opened, and Minister of Education Gebran Tueni placed a posthumous Decoration of Fine Arts medallion on Kahlil's remains. Then led by governmental dignitaries, French military officers, consular representatives, and members from Christian, Muslim, and Jewish societies, along with scores of schoolchildren, the entourage processed to the music of a police band down Beirut's broad avenues, past the Grand Serail, the historic government palace of the Ottoman and then the French Administration. There a company of soldiers saluted.

Memorial Service at Beirut's Grand Theater, with (seated, *left to right*) wife of speaker Edmund Wehbe, Maroon George, and Marianna; and (standing) members of the Gibran Committee: (*left to right*) Boutros Al Fakhri, Assaf George, Yusuf Zakhia, Edmund Wehbe, Emil Hanna Dahir, Fouad Mufarej, Sheik Farid Geagea, al-Chartouni, Toufigh Hassan, Tanous Kayrouz, Toufiq Sasen, Sheik Tanous Geagea. From *Al-Maraad*, August 30, 1931. (Reprint: George Lynde/Art Imaging.)

The cortege as it wound through the streets of Beirut. Photo from *Al-Barq*, September 3, 1931.

The procession ended at the Cathedral of Saint George, where Archbishop Ignatius Mobarak, amid chanting and incense, blessed Kahlil's body with holy water and ut-

Service at St. George Cathedral in Beirut. From *Al-Barq*, August 26, 1931. (Courtesy Private Collection.)

tered prayers for the dead in the Syriac language the poet loved so well. Young men who had traveled from Bsharri to stand watch through the night completed the Maronite ritual.[17]

That evening, an even larger crowd assembled at the Grand Theater, where President of the Republic Charles Debbas led the tributes and poems. First to speak was publisher Gebran Tueni, grandfather of revered journalist Gebran Ghassan Tueni, this time fondly remembering meeting Kahlil in Paris. He recalled visiting the Louvre and together gazing at Leonardo da Vinci's *Mona Lisa*. Reflecting on his friend's spirituality and universal appeal, he referred to Kahlil as a "Sufi sage" and "genius for all mankind."[18]

Praising *their* native son were government officials and religious figures, including the president of the Islamic Society, a Druze representative, and a priest from Bsharri. Eulogizing for his family was Kahlil's cousin Assaf George. Perhaps the most fervent expressions were from attending authors. *Al-Barq* (*Lightning*), a magazine of "literature, art and politics," devoted its front and back covers and ten pages to the memorial events. Poet Khalil Mutran, who had most likely traveled to Beirut from his home in Egypt, recited a farewell poem he had composed. Poet Beshara el-Khoury, editor of *Al-Barq*, spoke, drawing on their decade-long correspondence.[19]

Ameen Rihani began by describing Kahlil's love of the ancient pre-Islamic poets, then compared him with other historic figures—David, Solomon, Socrates, Blake, Chopin, and Rodin. Rihani spoke of Kahlil's duality. "Through Arabic, he conquered our minds. And through English he conquered our hearts." Then he addressed the soul of his good friend who had finally returned. "My brother and colleague, Gibran, nothing makes me sadder than your return to Lebanon…I would have given my eyes and heart to see you here, alive once again." Expressing his sorrow, he concluded,

> This generous loving mountain that holds you today and will hold me tomorrow will deliver a message from the soil that we share: from the shade of the pine trees shading my grave, the wind will carry warm greetings night and day to you lying under the shade of the cedars.[20]

The procession to Bsharri. Photo from *Al-Barq*, September 3, 1931.

Marianna's family photo of "Aunt Sardi," from the memorial in Bsharri. (Courtesy Private Collection.)

In a sense, the eulogies by Lebanese writers with whom Kahlil had long conversed were a gathering of lost friends, reunited again. Throughout the ceremony, musical settings of Kahlil's poems, created by local composers, were played.

The next day, the fifty-mile route—from Beirut, along the coast and up the steep mountain to Bsharri—was lined with townspeople. Twenty times, the swelling cortege stopped for local ceremonies. Accompanying the body, men chanted martial songs and improvised poetry, as villagers responded. At a town near Byblos, ancient ceremonies recalling the local goddess Astarte were enacted, as young men in traditional dress brandished swords and women danced, scattering perfume and flowers before the hearse. Impressed by the evergreen arches erected at each town and by the companies of Bedouin horsemen, one American traveler wrote back that the entire event appeared "more like a triumphal entry than a funeral."[21] After two more days of ecclesiastical and lay ceremony, the body remained at Saint John's in Bsharri, while Marianna and the Georges negotiated with the Carmelite Mission to purchase Mar Sarkis.

Mar Sarkis Monastery, Kahlil's burial place.

Accounts of the welcome appeared in the *New York Times* on September 20. His friends appreciated the ritual. In a letter to old friends, Rose O'Neill wrote, "Kahlil died this year...If *he* could lay down his heavy tools, any of us can lay down ours. For no one was so faithful..."[22]

By early January 1932, word finally was received that Marianna had negotiated the purchase of Mar Sarkis Monastery. Again amid eulogy and chanting, on January 10, his body was moved from the Maronite church to its final resting place.

In a letter to Barbara, Mary reflected that now, "Kahlil is in the care of Life."

> All of time still lies before him; he stands in his own power, and does not depend on the service or the upholding of another. Those who are ready will hear him... And one of the things one can learn from Kahlil is a certain firmness in self preservation. He was his own first responsibility...and I know of no instance where he sacrificed that responsibility to anyone else...The whole tenor of his writing is to value one's self and to expect others to value themselves.

By the end of June, Mary had fulfilled most of her responsibilities. Thirty crates holding most of the studio effects, along with 73 paintings, 366 drawings, and hundreds of books from his library, had arrived at Beirut on the *Sinaia*. Marianna was back from Lebanon, where she had been asked incessantly for money. Although Saxe reported that her income from the studio and stock shares was "meager," she could support herself.

Following the memorial events, Maroon George and Assaf George (standing, *center*) beside Marianna Gibran, during their visit to Bsharri, 1931. (*Courtesy Museo Soumaya.*)

Mary sent a letter to the mayor and township of Bsharri. In presenting the mementoes to the town, her words reflected her lifelong generosity: "This complete gift comes to Becharre in the name of Gibran himself, and of his sister Marianna— and I am but a loving instrument."

~

Inevitably over time, friends and relatives who had inhabited and enriched Kahlil's life grew old and departed.

Poet *Josephine Preston Peabody* had passed in 1922 when she was just forty-eight, leaving behind her husband Lionel Marks and two young children. Four months after Kahlil's death, *Micheline* also died. Her marriage to lawyer Lamar Hardy produced one daughter, and she had remained actively involved in the life of New

York City's French community. *James Oppenheim*, editor of *The Seven Arts* little magazine, who would be remembered for his working-class anthem, "Bread and Roses," died one year later, in 1932.

For years, *Fred Holland Day*'s self-imposed exile confined him to his family's mansion, where he died in 1933. With the passage of time, his estate became the site of the Norwood Historical Society, and Day's reputation as one of America's finest publishers and the founder of pictorial photography in the country slowly was acknowledged.

After leaving America and traveling widely, *Ameen Rihani* continued his work as a prolific author, scholar, and reform advocate. He met with heads of state, religious leaders, and international figures, including Ibn Saud, former president Theodore Roosevelt, British Prime Minister Sir Ramsey MacDonald, and Pope Benedict XV. A "messenger of peace and cooperation among the Arab rulers," Rihani represented Arab interests at the Hague Peace Conference and at the Reduction of Armaments Conference in Washington, D.C. An early voice to speak up for the rights of Arabs in Palestine to American and European audiences, he continued to do so throughout his life.[23] His final years were spent writing in his birthplace of Freike, Lebanon, where a bicycling accident took his life in September 1940. With his epic work, *The Book of Khalid,* Project Khalid was launched in 2011 to recognize and honor Rihani's groundbreaking work as a pioneer of Middle Eastern literature and cultural exchange between the region and the West.[24]

Following the deaths of her parents, a close friend, and then Kahlil, *May Ziade* traveled throughout Europe from 1932 to 1934. Returning to Lebanon, she was hospitalized for depression. Friends of May's, including Ameen Rihani, helped to secure her release.[25] By 1938, she had recovered and delivered a widely recognized lecture, "The Message of the Writer to Arab Life," at the American University of Beirut. Returning to Cairo, she died there in 1942.

The Pen League's congenial and respected mentor *Nasib Arida* and his wife Najiba Haddad remained in Brooklyn, where they raised their niece Nora, after her mother's death. With the demise of *Al-Funun,* the magazine that had contributed so much to the Arab literary renaissance, Arida edited his brother-in-law Abd al-Massih Haddad's newspaper *As-Sayeh,* while also contributing to *Al-Hoda* and *Mirat al-Gharb.* A collection of his poetry, *Al-Arwah al-Hairah (The Confused Souls)* was published shortly before his death in the spring of 1946. One spring, more than a half century later, "The Black Stones of Homs," Arida's poem honoring his birthplace, would be sung by Syrians seeking to reclaim their homeland.[26]

Peripatetic *Charlotte Teller* published *The Diary of an Expectant Mother* in 1917. After stays in Germany and Washington, D.C., she settled with her family in Paris. Tragically, her husband Gilbert Hirsch committed suicide, and Charlotte struggled alone to bring up her son.[27] During the 1930s, she wrote *Everybody's Paris* and *Reasons for France.* Surviving the Depression and the German occupation, she moved to Versailles, where she died in 1953.

Unbeknownst to Mary, *Barbara Young* died in 1962 at eighty-two after three decades of writing about Gibran and dealing with his art. Acknowledged as one of the last people to care for Kahlil in his final days, her book, *This Man from Lebanon,* published in 1945, described his life in words of praise.

Kahlil's close friend *Youssef Howayek,* who had studied painting and sculpture with him in Paris, returned to Lebanon and devoted his life to creating monumental

Youssef Howayek's *Martyrs' Monument,* commissioned by Beirut Municipal Council as a tribute to sacrifices made for independence from Ottoman rule. Carved from local limestone, it depicts two women—Muslim and Christian—standing at an urn symbolizing the ashes of martyrs. It was first displayed at Martyrs' Square, then moved to Sursock Museum Gardens, Beirut. (Courtesy Library of Congress.)

sculptures. These included statues of the Lebanese national hero Youssef Bey Boutros Karam, Youssef's uncle Patriarch Elias Howayek, and painter Daoud Corm. His monument sculpture of two women—Christian and Muslim—was first installed in Beirut's Martyrs' Square and later transferred to the Sursock Museum Garden. Howayek died in 1962.[28]

Arranging for the studio contents to be shipped to Bsharri, *Mary Haskell* continued to look after Kahlil's manuscripts, journals, and letters, and corresponded with Marianna. For the next five years, she cared for her husband and his properties. In 1936, Florance Minis died, and after settling his estate she moved to a modest apartment. Free to travel on her own, she did visit Kahlil's family in Boston and gazed at his art in Barbara Young's New York art gallery. Throughout the years, she kept in close touch with her nieces and nephews.[29] Although World War II and age slowed her down, she served on the local ration board and volunteered at a kindergarten. On October 9, 1964, she passed away in a nursing home at the age of eighty-nine, her last five years blurred by senility and debilitating arthritis.

Probably the longest lived of all of Kahlil's friends was his fellow Mahjar writer *Mikhail Naimy*. Returning to his family's ancestral farmland in Baskinta, Lebanon, shortly after Kahlil's death, he continued to write, living in solitude for most of the remainder of his life. There in 1934, he completed his Arabic biography of Kahlil, with a less controversial English-language edition appearing in 1950. Two years earlier in 1948, he published his signature work, the religious classic, *The Book of Mirdad: The strange story of a monastery which was once called the Ark*. Naimy died in February 1988, at the age of ninety-nine.

Marianna Gibran returned to Boston from Bsharri after Kahlil's burial ceremonies and continued to live simply. As always, she was known for her caring generosity, ensuring that relatives and friends were well supplied with the basic provisions of food and clothing. She did her best to manage the Gibran estate from Boston until 1968, when illness confined her to nursing care. She died on March 28, 1972, at the age of eighty-eight. But before her passing, the sister who could not read saw to it that the Gibran Kahlil Gibran Scholarship was established in memory of her brother, providing funds for young people of Middle Eastern background to receive college support in his name.

~

Religion, or *Brotherhood.* Mikhail Naimy described the snake twisted around the ankles of the figures as the "serpent of fanaticism, or religious bigotry, of lowly passions aroused by foolish notions of man's servitude to God, and of criminal trafficking for material gain carried on in the name of religion." Graphite and watercolor, 1918. From *Al-Mawakib* (*The Processions*), Mirat al-Gharb edition, 1919. (Courtesy Houghton Library, Harvard University.)

For how long shall we [be] scattered like dust before this cruel storm and quarrel like hungry whelps around this stinking corpse?...Until when will brother continue to slay brother on his mother's bosom? Until when will neighbor threaten neighbor by the grave of the beloved? Until when will the Cross be separated from the Crescent before the face of God...[30]

By the mid-1970s, travelers had begun to visit Bsharri and the Gibran Museum, even as civil war was beginning to engulf Lebanon, foreshadowing future decades of violence that would overwhelm the Near East, producing new generations of emigrants. One visitor, an American columnist, wondered why his nineteen-year-old daughter was so excited about receiving a Gibran book. "I couldn't understand why this strange, brooding genius, who died more than forty years ago, appealed so strongly..." In writing about a family visit to Bsharri to find out, he was struck by the "stately grandeur of its snowy peaks, eroded crags and great grove of cedar trees"—a place where mysticism had sown fertile fields.[31]

Visitors to Gibran Museum in Bsharri. (Courtesy: National Council of Tourism, Lebanon.)

The same writer remembered growing up in New York on West Tenth Street in Greenwich Village, opposite Kahlil's studio building. "He was just a name to me then, but I used to see him occasionally entering and leaving his building, a wispy, shy… figure." While at the Gibran Museum in Bsharri, admiring views of the majestic gorges outside, he stopped to read a passage from a poem hanging on the wall.[32]

> *Come, my beloved, let us walk among the little hills, for the snows have melted and life is awakened from its sleep and wanders through the hill and valley.*[33]

Kahlil's words continued to offer solace. He had created a body of work suggesting that, through our elemental links to one another and to the Creation, we are "far greater than we know"—and "all is well." His artfully expressed faith would continue to touch new generations. Kahlil had returned to Mount Lebanon and to Bsharri, but his homeland now reached beyond geographic borders, recalling words of the Greek poet Meleager, some two thousand years earlier.

> *If Syrian, what the marvel then?*
> *Stranger, we all have yet*
> *one homeland—the world;*
> *all people*
> *one Chaos did beget.*[34]

The Qadisha Valley and Bsharri. (Courtesy Library of Congress.)

Bronze plaque from the Copley Square memorial in Boston, by Kahlil G. Gibran. The Cedar of Lebanon bough commemorates Kahlil's devotion to his birthplace. (Courtesy George Lynde/Art Imaging)

LEGACIES

I n the heart of Boston is Copley Square, the city's historic plaza. The expansive square is surrounded by public landmarks that are iconic of the city. On the north side sits Trinity Church, "Boston's church" and a hub of interfaith activity. On the south side stands the Boston Public Library, with the welcoming message "Free to All" carved above its granite entrance. In 1896, the recently opened library invited Gibran as a youth to read and draw there. Eighty-one years later, on September 25, 1977, in a small park facing the library, a memorial was dedicated to Gibran's life and art.

The dedication drew guests and speakers including Charles H. Malek, former president of the United Nations General Assembly and a leading author of the Universal Declaration of Human Rights; Fouad Boutros, foreign minister of Lebanon; and Helen Thomas, journalist from the White House Press Corps. Also taking part in the ceremonies were a Melkite Greek Catholic archbishop, a Maronite priest, a Greek Orthodox priest, a rabbi, an imam, and a Presbyterian minister. The dedication program featured declarations from the Boston City Council, the governor, the Office of the Mayor, and an Apostolic Blessing from the Patriarch of Antioch.

The memorial itself is a pink granite stand, upon which is mounted a portrait of Gibran, created by his godson and cousin. Originally crafted in wax and cast in the lost-wax process, the bronze bas-relief pictures a youthful Gibran, seated and gazing directly ahead, one hand to his forehead, and in the other a slim book, entitled *The Prophet*. As if shading him, a carefully modeled Cedar of Lebanon bough conveys Kahlil's devotion to his birthplace. The richly patinated green of the plaque contrasts with the pink granite upon which it is mounted. Carved on the face of the stand is an inscription.

KAHLIL GIBRAN, A NATIVE OF BESHARRI LEBANON, FOUND
LITERARY AND ARTISTIC SUSTENANCE IN THE DENISON
SETTLEMENT HOUSE, THE BOSTON PUBLIC SCHOOLS,
AND THE BOSTON PUBLIC LIBRARY. A GRATEFUL CITY
ACKNOWLEDGES THE GREATER HARMONY AMONG MEN AND
STRENGTHENED UNIVERSALITY OF SPIRIT GIVEN BY
KAHLIL GIBRAN TO THE PEOPLE OF THE WORLD IN RETURN.

On the front side of the stand are carved Gibran's own simple view of his legacy.

IT WAS IN MY HEART TO HELP A LITTLE
BECAUSE I WAS HELPED MUCH.

Copley Square Gibran Memorial, Boston. (George Lynde/Art Imaging.)

The Copley Square Gibran memorial is a fitting tribute to an adopted son. Yet, its serene beauty belies the fraught relations between the West and the Near East, the ongoing hostilities that have benumbed Gibran's homelands and rippled globally, touching Boston Marathon runners near this Copley Square monument itself. Complex forces continue to consign streams of humanity to exile, triggering frustration and despair.

Rediscovering his story in the light of the present brings Gibran as a person more clearly into focus. An artist in exile, a pioneer and peer among his emigrant compatriots, Gibran's "universality" reflects not just his individual talent as an artist but issues of dispossession and loss, belonging and justice, with which so many people contend.

~

A sister monument can be found on a wall in Beirut. Street artist Yazan Halwani through his mural portraits seeks to memorialize the faces of Lebanese and other Arabs who have offered a unifying and harmonizing influence on the country's fractious history, one often erased and overwritten by political banners, logos, and messaging that cover the city's walls. Halwani's portraits include the legendary singers Fairuz and Sabah; martyred historian and journalist Samir Kassir; Ali Abdallah, a local homeless person who died from exposure to the cold; twelve-year-old Fares Al-Khodor, *The Flower Seller*, who sold roses in Beirut to help support his family and was killed in an airstrike when he returned to Syria; and poets Mahmoud Darwish and Kahlil Gibran.[1]

Gibran mural in Beirut, by Yazan Halwani. (Courtesy the artist.)

Recalling Gibran's commitment to portrait art, Halwani searches his subjects' faces for the stories they tell of a wished-for Lebanon, for insights from familiar faces in which the Arab world especially may take pride. Among them, Halwani honors those who modeled another way of responding to the conflicts of Beirut, of Lebanon, and of the region; who resisted divisive patterns, but loyally and with affection. His pictorial rescues of memory welcome viewers from beyond the city, prompting cross-cultural conversations, with Arabic calligraphy used to convey motion and dynamic in ways that can be understood by Arabic and non-Arabic speakers alike.

Halwani's portrait of Gibran adorns an enlarged 100,000 Lebanese Lira note on a building wall. In it, Gibran gazes downward toward the brick walkway at the foot of the wall. It is tempting to read into his gentle, downcast glance, despair at the calamity that has beset his region, and at the fearful repercussions triggered in all directions. But as Gibran's own poem of defeat suggests, his glance can redirect us toward more than fear, fury, or resignation. In his gaze we can also find solace, and his legacy can help us to reclaim memory from the debris of collective failure.

Gibran's art sprang from the joy of persistent hard work and the willingness and imagination to face failure and loss. At the heart of his legacy was a "tear and a smile": the compassion and courage to acknowledge and embrace defeat, to find in it sources of renewal, and turn loss into promise—together to "dig graves for all that die in us" in order to be able to "stand in the sun with a will."

The passage of time and dynamics of the marketplace in various ways stripped Gibran of facets of his identity, features which time now more clearly restores to view. Gibran's life story and art never were divorced from the suffering, struggles, or aspirations of ordinary people, but were rooted in and spoke to them. Gibran Khalil Gibran, a youth from Mount Lebanon, through exile became a faithful citizen artist without borders, who worked to reconcile issues of spiritual unity and justice. These were sources of the suggestive power and reach of his art.

While the catastrophic consequences of destructive and divisive self-interest— our "designing nature"— may rupture bonds between us, work like Gibran's, and that of other citizen artists, like Yazan Halwani, restore living strands of memory that unite us. Gibran's legacy preserves a language of survival: one of gratitude and self-respect, compassion and resilient self-reliance, mutual recognition and belonging. "Until we reach our homecoming," we need such legacies that repair, sustain, and encourage.

NOTES

Introduction

1. Mary Haskell, journal, July 21, 1916, no. 46, Minis Family Papers, University of North Carolina, Chapel Hill, N. C., collection no. 02725.

2. Haskell, journal, September 19, 1915, no. 46; Haskell, journal, November 12, 1916, no. 47.

3. Hani Bawardi's groundbreaking study, *The Making of Arab Americans: From Syrian Nationalism to U.S. Citizenship* (Austin: University of Texas Press, 1914), reclaims a history of Arab American advocacy, offering a fresh context for considering Gibran's activism. Bawardi retraces the community's advocacy to the early years of the twentieth century, when a wave of immigration to the U.S. from Ottoman-ruled "Greater Syria" first incubated Arab American political identity. Adel Beshara's *Origins of Syrian Nationhood: Histories, Pioneers, and Identity* (London: Routledge, 2011) and Tanyss Carol Ludescher's insightful research also informed this book's portrait of Gibran's Syrian nationalism. Lively studies on the Arab immigrant press by Stacy Fahrenthold, Richard Alan Popp, Elizabeth Saylor, and others contributed to a picture of how an Arab American immigrant writers' movement first took root. And projects like the Khayrallah Center for Lebanese Diaspora Studies at North Carolina State University and the Washington Street Historical Society in Lower Manhattan provided invaluable resources on the community from which Gibran's work grew.

Chapter 1: *Born in Bsharri*

1. Kahlil Gibran, "On Time," *The Prophet* (New York: Knopf, 1923).

2. Mary Haskell, journal, June 9, 1915, no. 45, Minis Family Papers, University of North Carolina, collection no. 02725. Marianna Gibran often repeated her brother Kahlil's comments about his birth. His friend Mary Haskell once asked him how a French magazine had been able to publish 1883 as his definite birth year. He responded, "My birth year is known." In 1883, Lebanon (officially Mount Lebanon) was an autonomous

province of Turkey. To Westerners it was commonly referred to as Syria, and Kahlil himself often referred to the Lebanese people as "Syrians."

3. Rose Gibran was the daughter of Christina Towk and Melham Gibran. She and her husband N'oula Gibran (biographer Kahlil George Gibran's father) were second cousins to the poet, often a close relationship within Middle Eastern culture.

4. Henry Harris Jessup, *Syrian Home-Life*, comp. Isaac Riley. (New York: Dodd, Mead, 1874), 97.

5. Antiin Ghattas Karam, *Muhadarat fi Jubran Khalil Jubran* (Cairo, 1964), 10.

6. Kahlil Gibran, *Blue Flame: The Love Letters of Kahlil Gibran to May Ziadah* (London: Longman House, 1983), 30.

7. Tanyss Carol Ludescher, "'The Orient is Ill': Kahlil Gibran and the Politics of Nationalism in the New York Syrian Colony 1908–1920" (Ph.D. dissertation, University of Connecticut, 2010).

8. Gibran, *Blue Flame*, 30.

9. N'oula Gibran, personal interview, n.d.

10. Alexandre Najjar, *Kahlil Gibran* (Paris: Pygmalion/Gerard Watelet, 2002). Subsequently published in English as *Kahlil Gibran: A Biography* (London: Saqi, 2008). For decades, Gibran biographers wrote that Kamila's marriage to Khalil Saad Gibran was preceded by her marriage to Hanna Abd al-Salaam Rahme, ending with his death in Brazil. Then, according to oral history, townspeople claimed that Kamila accompanied her first husband to Brazil. After his death, she returned to Bsharri and married Yusuf Elias Geagea, although the union was subsequently annulled. While documentation does not seem to confirm these details, Gibran Museum administrators in Bsharri agree that this version may be true. Whether or not Kamila did marry Geagea, family oral history does confirm her final marriage to Khalil Saad Gibran. Responding to an email in 2015 from William Nix (of the Gibran National Committee), Joseph Geagea (director of the Gibran Museum) confirmed that Kamila married three times and that her marriage to Yusuf Elias Geagea was short-lived. A copy of the divorce/annulment is not recorded in Bsharri.

11. Haskell, journal, March 22, 1911, no. 41.

12. Gibran, *Blue Flame*, 30.

13. John Carne, *Syria, the Holy Land* (London: Fisher, 1836), 47.

14. Haskell, journal, January 14, 1922, no. 59.

15. Ibid., November 1915, no. 46.

16. Manuscript, 1913, Mary Haskell folder 68.

17. Haskell, journal, August 27, 1915, no. 46; Haskell, journal, August 29, 1913, no. 44; Haskell, journal, June 1, 1924, no. 68; Haskell, journal, July 26, 1916, no. 46.

18. Haskell, journal, June 30, 1915, no. 45.

19. Abdul Latif Tibawi, *American Interests in Syria 1800–1901* (Oxford: Clarendon Press, 1961), 16.

20. Riley and Jessup, *Syrian Home-Life*, 158.

21. Haskell, journal, December 7, 1910, no. 41.

22. Ibid.

23. The date of Marianna Gibran's first entry to the United States was stamped on her passport when she returned to Lebanon in 1931 (see Certificate of Registry, no. 27256, file R–33017).

Chapter 2: A City Wilderness

1. Mary Haskell, journal, April 11, 1915, no. 45, Minis Family Papers, University of North Carolina, collection no. 02725.

2. Ellis Island Records, SS *Spaarndam*; Arrival: June 17, 1895; Port of departure: Rotterdam via Boulogne.

3. Literary Notes. Review of *The Poor in Great Cities,* by Robert A. Woods, *Wellesley Prelude* 3, 30 (May 14, 1892): 391.

4. Alan Kraut, *Public Health Report 2010*, vol. 125, suppl. 3 (Maryland: National Center for Biotechnology Information, 2010): 123–133.

5. Robert A. Woods, *The City Wilderness* (Boston: Houghton Mifflin, 1899), 7, 36, 37.

6. Ibid., 46.

7. *Twentieth Annual Report of the Associated Charities of Boston* (1899), 56–57.

8. Ibid., 58.

9. Ibid., 57.

10. Ibid., 58.

11. Haskell, journal, September 19, 1915, no. 46.

12. Quincy School records now at Abraham Lincoln School, Boston, show that "Kahlil Gibran Jr. alias Assad" entered school on September 30, 1895, and was discharged September 22, 1898. The source of the name Assad is unknown.

13. Woods, *The City Wilderness*, 40.

14. Haskell, journal, July 23, 1916, no. 46.

15. Haskell, journal, March 22, 1911, no. 41; Haskell, journal, April 11, 1915, no. 45.

16. Haskell, diary, April 29, 1911, no. 40.

17. Haskell, journal, September 19, 1915, no. 46.

18. Haskell, journal, September 3, 1920, no. 52.

19. Woods, *The City Wilderness*, 234–235.

20. Ibid., 235.

21. Ibid., 184, 197.

22. Ibid., 111–112.

23. Ralph Waldo Emerson, "Self Reliance," in *Essays* (1841).

24. Woods, *The City Wilderness*, 245, 248.

25. Robert Treat Paine, in *Twentieth Annual Report of the Associated Charities of Boston* (1899), 2.

26. Ibid.

27. *Time and the Hour* 3 (November 7, 1896): 15.

28. *Time and the Hour* 3 (November 28, 1896): 7.

29. Kahlil Gibran's sketchbook, long in the possession of a parishioner, was retrieved by Monsignor Joseph Lahoud of Boston's Maronite Church and acquired by the biographers. It is now at the Museo Soumaya in Mexico City.

30. *Time and the Hour* 5 (June 12, 1897): 1.

31. *Twenty-Sixth Annual Report of the Boston Children's Aid Society* (1890): 13–15.

32. Denison House Records, 1890–1984, Schlesinger Library, Radcliffe College. Descriptive statement: 2.

33. Jesse Beale to Fred Holland Day, November 25, 1896. F. Holland Day Papers, 1793–2010, Library of Congress Manuscript Division, Washington, D.C.

Chapter 3: Bookmaking and Bohemia

1. *Statement of the Boston Children's Aid Society for the Year 1897*, 4.

2. John Howard Brown, *Lamb's Biographical Dictionary of the United States*, vol. 2 (Boston: James H. Lamb Company, 1900), 390.

3. *The Mahogany Tree*, January 2, 1892.

4. *Boston Evening Transcript*, April 2, 1892.

5. *Publishers Weekly* 65 (February 17, 1894): 333.

6. *Boston Evening Transcript*, May 13, 1899, 9.

7. William Dana Orcutt, "Frederick Holland Day," *Publishers Weekly* 125 (January 6, 1934): 54.

8. Ralph Adams Cram, *The decadent: being the gospel of inaction: wherein are set forth in romance form certain reflections touching the curious characteristics of the ultimate years and the divers causes thereof.* (Boston: Privately printed for the author by Copeland and Day, 1893), 15.

9. Florence Peirce to Fred Holland Day, 1896. F. Holland Day Papers, Library of Congress Manuscript Division, Washington, D. C.

10. Peirce to Day, 1896.

11. Peirce to Day, January 9, 1897.

12. Fred Holland Day, "Photography Applied to the Undraped Figure," *American Annual of Photography and Photographic Times Almanac* (1898): 192.

13. *Photograms of the Year 1900* (London: Dawbarn & Ward, Ltd.,1900), 114.

14. Edward Steichen, "The Age of Corporate Patronage: Advertising Accelerates the Demand for Photography," Chapter 2 in *A Life in Photography* (New York: Doubleday, 1963), 25–41.

15. *Boston Evening Transcript*, March 9, 1898, 6.

16. Herbert Whyte Taylor, "F. Holland Day: An Estimate," *Photo Era* 4 (March 1900): 77–78.

17. Sadakichi Hartmann, "A Decorative Photographer," *The Photographic Times* 32 (March 1900): 105.

18. Haskell 46, August 27, 1915 and April 21, 1916.

19. Sadakichi Hartmann, "A Purist," *The Photographic Times* 31 (October 1899): 451.

20. Minna A. Smith to Day, December 24, 1917.

21. Smith to Day, December 11, 1917.

22. Day, "Photography Applied to the Undraped Figure," 194.

23. In the time since the publication of the first edition of this biography in 1974, increased attention has been given to the nature of Fred Holland Day's photographic gaze. For a useful encapsulation, see Shawn Michelle Smith, "F. Holland Day, Imperial Masculinity, and the Intimacy of Photography," *The Photographic Situation* (blog): January 31, 2013, https://thephotographicsituation.wordpress.com/2013/01/31/f-holland-day-imperial-masculinity-and-the-intimacy-of-photography/.

24. Peirce to Day, May 21, 1897.

25. Jesse Beale to Day, June 10, 1897.

26. Beale to Day, July 9, 1897.

27. Beale to Day, September 22, 1897.

28. *Time and the Hour* 5 (July 17, 1897): 9.

29. Josephine Peabody Marks, diary, December 8, 1898, Josephine Preston Peabody Diaries, Houghton Library, Harvard University, MS Am 2162.

30. Ibid.

31. Haskell, journal, September 7, 1912, no. 43.

32. Maurice Maeterlinck, *The Treasure of the Humble*, trans. Alfred Sutro (New York: Dodd, Mead, 1899), 25, 52, 79, 164.

33. *Time and the Hour* 6 (December 4, 1897): 14–15.

34. Examples can be found in the authors' collection.

35. Haskell, journal, April 21, 1916, no. 46.

36. *Annual Report of the Trustees of the Public Library of the City of Boston 1896.* (Boston: J. H. Eastburn, 1896), 22.

37. Lilla Cabot Perry to Day, n.d.

38. *Time and the Hour* 7 (March 19, 1898): 11–12.

39. *Boston Evening Transcript*, March 9, 1898, 6.

40. Haskell, journal, August 27, 1915, no. 46.

41. Ibid.

42. Haskell, April 18, 1922, no. 59.

43. Peabody Marks, diary, December 8, 1898.

44. Perry to Day, March 12, 1899.

45. *The Critic: a weekly review of literature, fine arts, and the drama* 29, 841 (April 2, 1898): 232.

46. Day, "Photography Applied to the Undraped Figure," 188.

47. Marianna Gibran in discussion with Zakia Gibran Rahme.

48. Louise Guiney to Day, August 4, 1898.

49. Peirce to Day, 1898.

50. Guiney to Day, September 4, 1898.

51. Peirce to Day, September 10, 1898.

52. Peabody Marks, diary, November 1903; Peabody Marks, diary, May 30, 1897.

53. Peabody Marks, diary, December 19, 1898. Inscription translated by Professor Toy.

54. Peabody Marks, diary, September 15, 1898.

Chapter 4: *Beirut*

1. Antiin Ghattas Karam, *Muhadarat fi Jubran Khalil Jubran* (Cairo: Ma'had al-Dirasat al-Arabiyah, 1964), 26.

2. Maha Shuayb, ed. *Rethinking Education for Social Cohesion: International Case Studies* (Basingstoke, United Kingdom: Palmgrave MacMillan, 2012).

3. Marun Abbud, *Judud wa Qudama* (Beirut: Dar al Thaqafah, 1954), 118–121.

4. Josephine Peabody Marks to Frederick Sherman, 1898, in *Diary and Letters of Josephine Preston Peabody* (Boston: Houghton Mifflin, 1925), 5.

5. Peabody Marks, diary, May 1894, Josephine Preston Peabody Diaries, Houghton Library, Harvard University, MS Am 2162.

6. Peabody Marks, diary, February 1895; Peabody Marks to Horace E. Scudder, September 7, 1894; Peabody Marks, diary, October 1895. July 1895 (ibid., 56, 48, 73, 59).

7. Peabody Marks to Scudder, January 6, 1895; Peabody Marks, diary, April 1896 (ibid., 55, 77).

8. Peabody Marks, diary, October 1895.

9. Ibid., February 1, 1897.

10. Ibid., October 5, 1898.

11. Ibid., December 8, 1898.

12. Ibid., December 12, 1898.

13. Ibid., December 8, 1898.

14. Peabody Marks to Kahlil Gibran, draft, December 12, 1898.

15. Peabody Marks, diary, March 24, 1899.

16. Peabody Marks to Fred Holland Day, March 25, 1899.

17. Peabody Marks, diary, March 30, 1899.

18. Haskell, journal, July 23, 1916, no. 46, Minis Family Papers, University of North Carolina, collection no. 02725.

19. Khalil S. Hawi, *Kahlil Gibran: His Background, Character and Works* (Beirut: Arab Institute for Research and Publishing, 1972): 87n.

20. Haskell, journal, June 5, 1912, no. 43.

21. Hawi, *Kahlil Gibran*, 87n.

22. Haskell, journal, April 19, 1911, no. 41.

23. Haskell, journal, March 24, 1911, no. 41.

24. N'oula Gibran, personal interview, n.d.

25. In July 1998, shortly before Kahlil departed for Beirut, an article in *Camera Notes* described the photo: "Possibly Mr. Day's most successful effort...is the study entitled 'Hypnos' in which sleep is represented by an Ephebe with closed eyes, breathing the soporific odor of a poppy. In this the idealism is wonderfully aided by the wing of a bird, a pigeon's possibly." That same article pointed out English painter George Frederick Watt's influence on Day: "In fact, in loftiness of aim Mr. Day bears no slight resemblance to that great painter of mysteries." Kahlil's youthful expression may be viewed as conceived in Mount Lebanon, where he may have recalled the idealizations of a Boston pictorial photographer who, in turn, borrowed his aesthetics from an English painter.

26. Fred Holland Day, "Portraiture and the Camera," in *American Annual of Photography and Photographic Times Almanac* (1899).

27. Alvin Langdon Coburn, "American Photographs in London," *Photo Era* 6 (January 1901): 209–215. "The New School of American Photography Supplemented by An Additional Collection of One Hundred Examples of the Work of F. Holland Day of Boston."

28. Royal Photographic Society, *Program* (London: Royal Photographic Society, November 8, 1900); "Portrait of M.G.K.G.," *American Annual of Photography and Photographic Times Almanac* (1901): 36. Catalogue numbers 323, *Kahlile*, 343, *Syrian Boy*, and 363, *Portrait of Master G. K. G.* Also shown was *Portrait of Miss S. G.*—one of Day's efforts to capture Sultana Gibran's solemn beauty.

29. Sadakichi Hartmann, "A Decorative Photographer: F.H. Day," *The Photographic Times* 32 (March 1900): 103; Thomas Bedding, "The English Exhibitions and the American Invasion," *Camera Notes* 4 (January 1901): 163; Hartmann, "Decorative Photographer," 106.

30. Day to Louise Guiney, April 23, 1901, private collection.

31. Haskell, journal, March 10, 1914, no. 44.

32. American Line, *List of Manifest of Alien Immigrants for the Commissioner of Immigration*, list no. Y (May 10, 1902).

33. Haskell, journal, March 10, 1914, no. 44.

34. Ibid.

Chapter 5: "Pegasus Harnessed To An Ash-Wagon"

1. Josephine Peabody Marks, diary, May 1899, Josephine Preston Peabody Diaries, Houghton Library, Harvard University, MS Am 2162; ibid., October 1899.

2. Ibid., March 30, 1899; Peabody Marks to Mary Mason, July 8, 1899.

3. Peabody Marks, diary, September 13, 1900.

4. Daniel Gregory Mason, *Music in My Time and Other Reminiscences* (New York: Macmillan Company, 1938): 118–119.

5. Peabody Marks, diary, January 1, 1901; Peabody Marks, *Diary and Letters of Josephine Preston Peabody* (Boston: Houghton Mifflin, 1925), 159; Peabody Marks to Dreyfus, June 1902, in *Diary and Letters*, 169–170.

6. Peabody Marks to Mason, September 30, 1899, in *Diary and Letters*, 122.

7. Peabody Marks to Mason; Peabody Marks, diary, March 3, 1900.

8. Peabody Marks, diary, November 17, 1902. Dr. Charles Fleischer, who was in 1902 a rabbi at Temple Israel in Boston, would serve as chair of a memorial service for Gibran twenty-nine years later.

9. Peabody Marks, diary, November 21, 1902.

10. Ibid.

11. Peabody Marks, diary, November 25–27, 1902. Peabody Marks later wrote a different poem titled "Return."

12. Peabody Marks, diary, December 6, 1902.

13. Peabody Marks, diary, December 1902; Peabody Marks, diary, December 13, 1902.

14. Peabody Marks, diary, December 13, 1902; Peabody Marks, diary, December 22, 1902.

15. Peabody Marks, diary, December 13, 1902; Peabody Marks, diary, December 23, 1902.

16. Peabody Marks, diary, December 23, 1902.

17. Peabody Marks, diary, January 1, 1903; Peabody Marks, diary, January 12, 1903.

18. The month of Khalil Gibran's birth may have been December (Kanoon I) or January (Kanoon II). In transliteration the two are easily confused. He chose to observe his birthday on Twelfth Night, or the Epiphany.

19. Kahlil Gibran to Margarethe Müller (Josephine Peabody Marks, January 6, 1903).

20. *Twenty-third Annual Report of the Associated Charities of Boston* (1902), 23.

21. Peabody Marks, diary, January 15, 1903; Peabody Marks, diary, January 19, 1903.

22. Ibid.

23. Peabody Marks, January 26, 1903.

24. Peabody Marks to Mary Mason, January 25, 1903.

25. Written in Arabic in a dummy (blank) copy of Copeland and Day's *Lyrics of Earth*, Mexico City: Museo Soumaya, Fundacion Carlos Slim.

26. Peabody Marks, diary, February 21, 1903.

27. Peabody Marks to Mary Mason, March 9, 1903.

28. Mary Haskell, journal, March 10, 1914, no. 44, Minis Family Papers, University of North Carolina, collection no. 02725.

29. Kahlil Gibran to Day, March 12, 1903.

30. Peabody Marks, March 13, 1903.

31. Peabody Marks, diary, March 16, 1903.

32. Peabody Marks, March 24, 1903.

33. Peabody Marks, April 21, 1903.

34. Peabody Marks, May 9, 1903.

35. Written in *Lyrics of Earth*.

36. *The Iris* (Wellesley, Massachusetts: Wellesley College, Tau Zeta Epsilon Society, 1903): 4–5.
37. Peabody Marks, May 30, 1903.
38. Peabody Marks, June 15, 1903 (*Diary*, 177).
39. Peabody Marks, June 9, 21, and 24, 1903.
40. Kahlil Gibran to Fred Holland Day, private collection.
41. Haskell, journal, March 10, 1914, no. 44.

Chapter 6: "A Gallery of Gracious and Novel Heads"

1. Josephine Peabody Marks to Louise Guiney, July 5, 1903, Guiney Family Papers, Archives and Special Collections, Dinand Library, College of the Holy Cross.
2. Peabody Marks, diary, August 9, 1903, Josephine Preston Peabody Diaries, Houghton Library, Harvard University, MS Am 2162.
3. Rosina Hassoun, "Arab-American Health and the Process of Coming to America," in *Arabs in America: Building a New Future*, ed. Michael Suleiman (Philadelphia: Temple University Press, 1999), 159.
4. Fred Holland Day subsequently bought the property from Louise Guiney.
5. Khalil Gibran to Fred Holland Day, August 20, 1903, F. Holland Day Papers, Library of Congress Manuscript Division, Washington, D.C.
6. Peabody Marks, diary, September 24, 1903.
7. Peabody Marks, diary, October 2, 1903; ibid., October 21, 1903.
8. Kahlil Gibran to Peabody Marks, draft, in a dummy copy of Copeland and Day's *Lyrics of Earth*, Mexico City: Museo Soumaya, Fundacion Carlos Slim.
9. Written in *Lyrics of Earth*.
10. Lilian Whiting, *Boston Days* (Boston: Little, Brown, 1902), 352–353, 358.
11. Gertrude Smith to Day, November 3, 1903.
12. Draft of letter to Josephine Peabody Marks, in *Lyrics of Earth*.
13. Peabody Marks, diary, December 25, 1903.
14. Ibid., January 8, 1904.
15. Thomas Langryl Harris painted miniature portraits of fashionable men and women. These impressionist works labeled him "an embryonic genius" in Kansas City where he grew up, and were admired by arbiters like Edward Steichen. The young artist traveled to Canada seeking fame and fortune. By the time he reached Boston in 1898, he was known for his art and his habit of conning merchants, and even friends. Despite warnings, Day photographed Harris and let him stay in his Pinckney Street studio. The photos attracted notice, but some homoerotic frontally nude images were not publicly displayed. Leaving Boston, Harris met Day again in London and Paris during the photographer's New School of American Photography exhibits. Tragically, early in 1901, his body was found in the Seine River, probably as a result of suicide. Day's exhibit of both artists showed not only admiration for his young protégés but also demonstrated grief over Harris's

terrible death. See Patricia Fanning, "F. Holland Day and 'the Beautiful Boy': The Story of Thomas Langryl Harris and Day's Nude Study," *History of Photography* 33, no. 3 (2009): 249–261.

16. Day had met Gertrude Käsebier in 1898 at the First Photographic Salon of Philadelphia. The two admired each other's work and visited each other in their summer places, hers in Newport, Rhode Island, his in Five Islands, Maine. He exhibited her photos in March 1904 just before Gibran's and Harris's exhibit. Known for her handsome portraits of the Lakota Sioux Native Americans who toured with Buffalo Bill's Wild West Show, Käsebier also produced loving images of mothers and children, including her famous "Blessed Art Thou Among Women," a portrait of young Peggy Watts Lee and her mother. Agnes Rand Lee, author of Copeland and Day's popular children's book *The Round Rabbit* was then married to printer photographer Francis Watts Lee. Another talented couple contributing to Day's circle was newspaper illustrators Beatrice Baxter Rüyl and Louis H. Rüyl. Beatrice Rüyl also posed for Käsebier in the well-known portrait "The Hand That Rocks the Cradle," ca. 1905. For more on this creative group of Bostonians who influenced and inspired the maturing Kahlil, see Patricia J. Fanning, *Artful Lives: The Francis Watts Lee Family and Their Times.* Amherst: University of Massachusetts Press, 2016. See Barbara L. Michaels, *Gertrude Käsebier, The Photographer and her Photographs* (New York: H. N. Abrams, 1992). See also "Gertrude Käsebier (1852–1934): Introduction and Biographical Essay," Library of Congress Prints and Photographs Reading Room, last modified May 21, 2014, accessed September 18, 2015, http://www.loc.gov/rr/print/coll/womphoto/kasebieressay.html, accessed 9/18/2015.

17. Peabody Marks diary, March 11, 1904.

18. *Boston Evening Transcript*, May 3, 1904, 10.

19. Haskell, diary, August 16, 1937, no. 71.

20. Haskell, journal, December 7, 1910, no. 41; Peabody Marks diary, May 10, 1904.

21. Haskell, diary, May 10, 1904, no. 35; Haskell, journal, December 7, 1910, no. 41.

22. Haskell, journal, March 12, 1922, no. 60.

Chapter 7: Al-Musiqa

1. Kahlil Gibran, *Al-Musiqa* (New York: Al-Mohajer, 1905).

2. Mary Haskell, journal, December 7, 1910, no. 41, Minis Family Papers, University of North Carolina, collection no. 02725; Alicia M. Keyes (1855-1924) was an "artist and art teacher/lecturer" born to a prominent family in Concord, Mass. Her close ties with the Emerson family, her art studies with May Alcott and extensive European travels led to teaching art at Wellesley College, 1899-1902, and lecturing in art at the Museum of Fine Arts in Boston ca. 1911 to 1924. Haskell journals indicate she also taught at the Haskell School for Girls during the early twentieth century. See the Papers of Alicia M. Keyes, 1877–1941 at the Concord Free Public Library, Concord Massachusetts.

3. Louise Haskell Daly, *Alexander Cheves Haskell* (Norwood, Massachusetts: Plimpton Press, 1934), 173.

4. Haskell, diary, February 9, 1894, no. 32.

5. *The Wellesley Magazine*, April 14, 1894, 372–373; *Wellesley College News*, November 1896, 110.

6. Haskell, diary, January 27, 1894, no. 32.

7. Ibid.; May 17–20, 1904, no. 35.

8. Josephine Peabody Marks, diary, May 23, 1904, Josephine Preston Peabody Diaries, Houghton Library, Harvard University, MS Am 2162.

9. Haskell, diary, June 17, 1904, no. 35.

10. Peabody Marks diary, June 27, 1904; Haskell, diary, June 29, 1904, no. 35.

11. Peabody Marks, diary, July 1, 1904; Peabody Marks diary, July 5, 1904; Peabody Marks, July 8, 1904.

12. Peabody Marks, diary, July 4, 1904; Peabody Marks, diary, July 1, 1904.

13. Thomas Richard Barrabee to Fred Holland Day, July 4, 1904. "My Expaients [*sic*] with Mrs. J. M. Spears." F. Holland Day Papers, Library of Congress Manuscript Division, Washington, D.C.

14. Najib Diab, "The Story of a Young Syrian," *The Independent*, v. 55, no. 2839 (April 30, 1903): 1007–1013.

15. Ameen Ghorayeb, "Jubran Khalil Jubran," *Al-Haris* 8 (1931): 689–704.

16. Gibran, *A Tear and A Smile* (New York: Alfred A. Knopf, 1950), 30–31.

17. Peabody Marks, diary, October 15, 1904.

18. Kahlil Gibran to Fred Holland Day, October 29, 1904, private collection.

19. *Boston Herald*, November 12, 1904, 1, 5; *Boston Herald*, November 13, 1904, 6.

20. "Artists' big loss, work of many years wiped out by flames. Value of Harcourt Building Studio contents put at $200,000," *Boston Sunday Globe*, November 13, 1904, 5.

21. Peabody Marks to Margarethe Müller, November 19, 1904; Peabody Marks, diary, November 26, 1904; Peabody Marks to Day, November 27, 1904; Haskell to Day, November 28, 1904; Kahlil Gibran to Haskell, n.d.

22. Peabody Marks, diary, February 23, 1905; ibid., March 1, 1905.

23. Draft of letter written in the dummy copy of Copeland and Day's *The Arabella and Araminta Stories*, Mexico City: Museo Soumaya, Fundacion Carlos Slim.

24. Gibran, *A Tear and A Smile*, 32–34.

25. Ibid., 5–8.

26. Ibid., 58ff.

27. Illuminated birthday greeting in the private collection of Lionel P. Marks.

28. A copy can be found at Harvard College Library.

29. Peabody Marks, diary, July 1, 1905.

30. Ibid., November 29, 1905.

31. Haskell, diary, August 20, September 17, October 31, 1905, no. 36.

32. Haskell, diary, November 10, 1905, no. 36; ibid., April 23, 1906, no. 37.

33. Gibran to Peabody Marks, December 25, 1905; Peabody Marks, diary, December 28, 1905.

34. Haskell, diary, February 11, 1906, no. 37; Peabody Marks, diary, February 13, 1906.

35. Gibran to Peabody Marks, February 25, 1906.

36. Peabody Marks, diary, February 27, 1906.

37. Peabody Marks, diary, May 2, 1906; Peabody Marks, diary, May 30, 1906.

38. Peabody Marks, diary, 202; "Wedding Book," private collection of Alison P. Marks. The day before the event, Kahlil sent his regards: "May the morrow be a golden link between the beautiful past and the joyous future" signing his note, "Your godchild Kahlil Gibran." Kahlil and she would meet again only occasionally. After her death in 1922, in response to Lionel's offer to return the little silver ring Kahlil gave Josephine during Christmas of 1903, Kahlil again graciously recalled her influence: "If it is your desire that I should have the ring, of course, I would like to have it; not only for early associations but also for the sweet and gentle memory of Mrs. Marks herself." See Kahlil Gibran to Josephine Preston Peabody, June 20, 1906, Josephine Preston Peabody Papers, Houghton Library, Harvard University, MS AM 1990. See also Kahlil Gibran to Lionel P. Marks, March 14, 1924, Josephine Preston Peabody Papers, Houghton Library, Harvard University, MS AM 1990.

Chapter 8: "The Presence of a She-Angel"

1. Khalil Gibran to N'oula Gibran, December 28, 1905, private collection.

2. *New York Times*, February 1, 1906, 1.

3. Khalil al-Ghurayyib, "Dhikrayat Jubran, al-Rihani, Rustum, Mukarzel, al-Ghurayyib," 10, and "Marakat al-Tan al-Samit bayn Jubran wa Asad Rustum," 56–63.

4. Gibran, *A Tear and A Smile* (New York: Alfred A. Knopf, 1950), 38–41.

5. Ibid., 18–20.

6. Ibid., 82–84.

7. Ibid., 14, 24.

8. Ibid., 60.

9. Ibid., 27, 37, 44.

10. Khalil al-Ghurayyib, 57–58.

11. Gibran, *A Tear and A Smile*, 89–91.

12. Josephine Peabody Marks to Fred Holland Day, May 3, 1907.

13. Salim Sarkis to Gertrude Barrie, June 24, 1904. All Gertrude Barrie manuscripts and material are in the authors' collection.

14. Diploma from the New England Conservatory of Music in Boston, Massachusetts, presented to Gertrude Barry. She preferred spelling her name "Barry" until 1910, when she adopted "Barrie" consistent with family usage. Gibran's postmarked envelopes reflect this change.

15. Kahlil Gibran to Gertrude Barrie, October 3, 1906.

16. Annie Wright Seminary, *Seminary Catalogue* (Tacoma, Washington: Amy Wright Seminary: 1902–1903).

17. Newspaper review, unsigned and undated, of Gertrude Barry's piano recital, in Jersey City, New Jersey.

18. Kahlil Gibran to Gertrude Barrie, July 5, 1907.

19. Gibran to Barrie, pre-1909.

20. A few years later, Salim Sarkis would write Gertrude from his Cairo office: "When I wanted to give you a sample of the Syrian I gave you Gibran. And I do not regret it. Do you?" (See Salim Sarkis to Gertrude Barrie, February 20, 1908.) As intense as Barrie's relationship with Gibran was, her ties with Salim Sarkis would last longer. The few existing notes from correspondence between Sarkis and Barrie reveal a perspective on the Middle East's early nineteenth-century Arab literary renaissance that was little known in the West at that time. Sarkis writes:

    "At night I meet a few intelligent friends. Shall I tell you about them? You may ask Gibran. He may have heard about some of them. We meet usually of an evening in a library or in my office. They are Dr. Shemail our philosopher and anarchist, George Zaiden our historian, Rachid Riza the Mohammedan reformer, Sheikh Youssif Al Khazen our wit, Solaiman Bustani the translator of Homer and the Iliad, and others. We are nearly all good editors and writers. We discuss different subjects and tell good stories. You may have heard that Gibran has been writing for the last years some articles to *Al-Mohajer* under the heading of 'Tears and Smiles.' I read every one. I copy some for my magazine." (See Salim Sarkis in *Sarkis Magazine*, May 1, 1908, 1–5).

21. Mary Haskell, diary, September 3, 1894, no. 32, Minis Family Papers, University of North Carolina, collection no. 02725.

22. Haskell to Sarah Armstrong, August 23, 1906.

23. Haskell, diary, January 11, 1907, no. 38.

24. *New York Tribune*, February 11, 1906, sec. 4, p. 4, as quoted in Gerald W. McFarland, *Inside Greenwich Village: A New York City Neighborhood 1898–1918* (Amherst: University of Massachusetts Press, 2001), 121.

25. Laura Skandera Trombley, *Mark Twain's Other Woman: The Hidden Story of His Final Years* (New York: Alfred Knopf, 2010), 103–105.

26. Sometime in October, Clemens's secretary Isabel Lyon accused Teller of being an adventurer with marital designs on the famous writer. Years later, Charlotte described the incident in a self-published pamphlet. According to her, Clemens reacted to Lyon's insinuations and begged his protégé that she "leave 3 Fifth Avenue with my grandmother, and live somewhere else conspicuously so that he could come and see me." (See *S.L.C. to C.T.*, privately printed, 1925). Charlotte cancelled his endorsements, even his introduction to her book, and promised to pay back the money he had loaned her. The Teller/Twain friendship ended, but national papers, including *The San Francisco*

Call, picked up the story. "There is a rumor in literary circles that Mark Twain is going to marry Charlotte Teller the novelist." Charlotte tried hard to escape the embarrassing publicity. See Barbara Schmidt, "Mark Twain's Angel-Fish Roster and other young women of interest," Twain Quotes, accessed June 2, 2015, http://www.twainquotes.com/angelfish/angelfish.html.

27. Review of *The Cage* in *The Independent*, March 7, 1907, 559–560.
28. Haskell, diary, December 7, 1907, no. 38.
29. Ibid., January 27, 1908, no. 39.
30. Kahlil Gibran to Mary Haskell, January 26, 1908.
31. Haskell, diary, January 30, 1908, no. 39; Peabody Marks, diary, January 30, 1908.
32. Charlotte Teller to Mary Haskell, January 29, 1908.
33. Haskell, journal, December 25, 1912, no. 43.
34. Haskell, diary, February 4, 1908, no. 39.
35. Haskell, diary, February 6–11, 1908, no. 39.
36. Gibran to Ghorayeb, February 12, 1908 in *Kahlil Gibran: A Self-Portrait* (1959), 22–24.
37. Gibran to Haskell, February 17–20, 1908.
38. Gibran to Haskell, January 28, 1908; Teller to Haskell, January 22, 1908.
39. Teller to Haskell, March 7, 1908; ibid., January 22, 1908.
40. Haskell, diary, March 26, 1908, no. 39.
41. Copies at University of North Carolina.
42. Gibran to Haskell, March 25, 1908.
43. Haskell, diary, March 27, 1908, no. 39.
44. Ibid., March 28, 1908, no. 39.
45. Ibid., April 26, 1908, no. 39.
46. Gibran to Haskell, January 28, 1908.
47. Haskell, diary, April 1908, no. 39.
48. Mary Haskell misc. folder, visit on May 5, 1908, recorded on May 10.
49. Ibid.
50. Gibran, *A Tear and A Smile*, dedicated to M.E.H., "The Beauty of Death," 168.
51. Gibran to Day, June 1908, private collection.

Chapter 9: Rebellious Spirits in Paris

1. Kahlil Gibran, "On Freedom," in *The Prophet* (New York: Knopf, 1923).
2. Kahlil Gibran to Mary Haskell, July 9, 1908, Minis Family Papers, University of North Carolina, collection no. 02725.
3. Ibid., July 13, 1908.
4. Ibid., July 29, 1908.
5. Kahlil Gibran, *Al-Arwah al-Mutamarridah* (*Spirits Rebellious*) (New York: Al-Mohajer, 1908).
6. Kahlil Gibran, *Spirits Rebellious*, translated by H. M. Nahmad (New York: Alfred A. Knopf, 1948): 16.

7. Ibid., 61.

8. Ibid., 37.

9. Mary Haskell, journal, August 20, 1920, no. 52, Minis Family Papers, University of North Carolina, collection no. 02725.

10. Ameen Ghorayeb, *Al-Arwah al-Mutamarridah*, Introduction, 7.

11. Kahlil Gibran to N'oula Gibran, March 15, 1908, in *Kahlil Gibran: A Self-Portrait* (1959), 27–28.

12. Ibid., 32.

13. Kahlil Gibran, *Spirits Rebellious*, copyright page.

14. Kahlil Gibran to Mary Haskell, July 4, 1909.

15. See Claire Freches-Thory and Antoine Terrasse, *The Nabis: Bonnard, Vuillard, and Their Circle* (New York: Abrams, 1991).

16. Gibran to Haskell, October 2, 1908.

17. Ibid., November 8, 1908.

18. Ibid., October 2, 1908; ibid., November 8, 1908.

19. Ibid., October 2, 1908.

20. Haskell, diary, November 20–27, 1908, no. 39.

21. Gibran to Haskell, December 20, 1908; ibid., January 2, 1909.

22. The painters of the self-named group, the Nabis, from the Arabic word for prophets, valued mystical and poetic expression. Their symbolist leanings influenced aesthetic theory in the late nineteenth and early twentieth centuries. See Freches-Thory and Terrasse, *The Nabis*.

23. Gibran to Haskell, January 2, 1909; ibid., February 7, 1909.

24. Haskell to Gibran, April 3, 1909; Gibran to Haskell, April 17, 1909.

25. Gibran to Gertrude Barrie, April 18, 1909. Authors' collection.

26. Gibran, *A Tear and A Smile*, 137; Gibran to Haskell, January 6, 1909.

27. Gibran to Haskell, March 14, 1909; Haskell to Gibran, April 3, 1909.

28. Gibran to Haskell, February 7, 1909; ibid., April 17, 1909.

29. Ibid., March 14, 1909.

30. "Exhibition of Mr. Kahhl Gilran's Studies," *College News* [Wellesley College], 8, 28 (May 26, 1909): 4.

31. Charlotte Teller to Mary Haskell, June 2, 1909. "His work shows an immense improvement. He has touched reality and he has learned to draw. His color sense is his own and I feel that his whole nature has matured and strengthened in this year. He is doing a portrait of me for you. No—dear, he does not—no one—loves me as you do, nor do I love anyone as I love you. He cannot understand that which is modern and occidental in me—but we get on beautifully and he will be a fine companion to see the art of Paris."

32. Gibran to Haskell, June 23, 1909.

33. Ibid.

34. Ibid., May 10, 1910.
35. Ibid., July 31, 1909.
36. Ibid.
37. Ibid., March 14, 1909; ibid., June 23, 1909.
38. Frances Keyzer, "Eugene Carriere," *The Studio* 8 (August 1896): 135–142.
39. Gibran to Haskell, October 20, 1909.
40. Ibid., November 10, 1909.
41. Ibid., December 19, 1909.
42. Ibid.
43. Henry James, introduction to *Impressions*, by Pierre Loti (Westminster: Constable, 1898): 4.
44. Gibran to Haskell, May 10, 1910.
45. Ibid.
46. Youssef Howayek, *Dhikrayati ma Jubran* (Paris, ca. 1910).
47. Haskell, journal, September 2, 1914, no. 44.
48. Ibid., September 3, 1914, no. 44.
49. Gibran to Haskell, May 10, 1910.
50. Kahlil Gibran, *Les Mille Nouvelle Nouvelles*, "Martha La Banaise," November 1910, 142.
51. Ameen Rihani, "A Syrian Symbolist," *Papyrus* 8 (February 1908): 18–22.
52. Gibran to Haskell, December 19, 1909; ibid., August 30, 1910.
53. Ibid., August 30, 1910.
54. Ibid., June 5, 1910; ibid., December 19, 1909.

Chapter 10: *Frontiers of Friendship*

1. Mary Haskell, journal, April 17, 1911, no. 41, Minis Family Papers, University of North Carolina, collection no. 02725.
2. Kahlil Gibran to Gertrude Barrie, November 10, 1910. Author's collection.
3. Haskell, journal, April 10, 1915, no. 45.
4. Haskell, diary, November 7, 1910, no. 40.
5. Haskell, journal, March 1, 1911, no. 41.
6. Haskell, diary, November 16, 1910, no. 40; Haskell, journal, November 28, 1910, no. 41.
7. Kahlil Gibran to Mary Haskell, January 2, 1909.
8. Tanyss Carol Ludescher, "'The Orient is Ill': Kahlil Gibran and the Politics of Nationalism in the New York Syrian Colony 1908–1920" (Ph.D. dissertation, University of Connecticut, 2010).
9. Ibid.
10. Ibid.
11. Haskell, diary, December 10, 1910, no. 40; Haskell, journal, April 10, 1915, no. 45; Haskell, journal, March 12, 1922, no. 60.
12. Haskell, journal, December 10, 1910, no. 41.

13. For a description of this encounter, see Paul M. Wright, "The President Meets the Prophet: Charles W. Eliot's 1910 Encounter with Kahlil Gibran," *Harvard Library Bulletin* 23, no. 3 (Fall 2010): 79–92.

14. Haskell, diary, December 26, 1910, no. 40; ibid., December 30, 1910, no. 40.

15. Kahlil Gibran, "We and You," in *A Treasury of Kahlil Gibran*, ed. Martin L. Wolf (New York: Citadel, 1951): 86–91.

16. Haskell, diary, January 4, 1911, no. 40; ibid., January 7, 1911, no. 40; ibid., January 24, 1911, no. 40.

17. Haskell, diary, January 28, 1911, no. 40.

18. See Mary Haskell's annotation of John Polos' letter to her. See also Haskell, diary, January 28, 1911, no. 40.

19. Haskell, journal, January 28, 1911, no. 41.

20. Ibid., January 26, 1911, no. 41; ibid., June 20, 1915, no. 45.

21. Ibid., December 21, 1910, no. 41; Haskell, diary, February 3, 1911, no. 40.

22. Haskell, diary, February 17, 1911, no. 40.

23. Haskell, journal, March 17, 1911, no. 41; ibid., March 22, 1911, no. 41.

24. Ibid., February 18, 1911, no. 41.

25. Ibid., February 19, 1911, no. 41.

26. Ibid., March 22, 1911, no. 41; ibid., March 12, 1922, no. 60.

27. Ibid., March 17, 1911, no. 41; ibid., March 22, 1911, no. 41.

28. Charlotte Teller to Mary Haskell, November 1, 1910.

29. Haskell, journal, March 1, 1911, no. 41; ibid., March 9, 1911, no. 41.

30. Haskell, journal, April 14, 1911, no. 41.

31. Ibid.

32. Haskell, journal, April 15, 1911, no. 41.

33. Ibid.

34. Ibid.; Haskell, journal, April 11, 1915, no. 45.

35. Haskell, journal, April 17, 1911, no. 41.

36. Haskell, diary, April 18, 1911, no. 40.

37. Teller to Haskell, April 18, 1911; Haskell, journal, April 20, 1911, no. 41.

38. Gibran to Haskell, April 27, 1911; ibid., May 1, 1911.

39. Ibid., May 1, 1911; ibid., May 2, 1911.

40. Ibid., May 2, 1911; ibid., May 16, 1911.

41. Teller to Haskell, May 15, 1911.

42. Gibran to Haskell, May 16, 1911; ibid., May 22, 1911.

43. Haskell, diary, May 28, 1911, no. 40; ibid., May 24, 1911, no. 40.

44. Haskell, journal, June 1, 1911, no. 41; Teller to Haskell, May 20, 1911; Haskell, journal, June 3, 1911, no. 41.

45. Haskell, diary, June 3, 1911, no. 40.

46. Haskell, journal, April 11, 1915, no. 45.

47. Ibid., June 7–24, 1911, no. 41.

48. Jennifer Ratner-Rosenhagen, *American Nietzsche: A History of an Icon and His Ideas* (Chicago: University of Chicago Press, 2011), 168–172. Ratner-Rosenhagen details Kahlil's interest in Nietzsche. For another mention of Gibran's interest in Nietzsche, see George Nicolas El-Hage, "The God-Man and the Antichrist," ch. 5 in *William Blake and Kahlil Gibran: Poets of Prophetic Vision* (Create Space Independent Publishing Platform, 2013): 141–165.

49. Haskell, journal, June 6, 1911, no. 41.

50. Ibid.

51. Haskell, journal, June 7, 1911, no. 41. "K.G.'s memo of bequest and direction in case of his death."

52. Haskell, journal, June 10, 1911, no. 41; ibid., March 29, 1911, no. 41.

53. Haskell, diary, June 24, 1911, no. 40.

Chapter 11: *From Boston to New York*

1. Dante Gabriel Rossetti, *Poems by Dante Gabrielle Rossetti*, vol. 11, ed. Elizabeth Luther Cary (New York: G. P. Putnam's Sons, 1903), 79. Kahlil's lovers' cry, "Have mercy on me and mend my broken wings" also recalls "have pity on all broken wings," the final words of the ascetic figure in Josephine Preston Peabody's one-act play *The Wings* (New York: Samuel French Publisher, 1917): 28.

2. Kahlil Gibran, *The Broken Wings* (New York: Citadel Press, 1957), 92.

3. Mary Haskell, journal, December 2, 1911, no. 42, Minis Family Papers, University of North Carolina, collection no. 02725.

4. Haskell, journal, September 16, 1911, no. 42.

5. Kahlil Gibran, "Slavery," in *A Treasury of Kahlil Gibran*, ed. M. L. Wolf, trans. A. R. Ferris (New York: Citadel Press), 63–67.

6. M. M. Badawi, *A Critical Introduction to Modern Arabic Poetry* (Cambridge: Cambridge University Press, 1975), 181–182.

7. Mary Haskell to Kahlil Gibran, January 27, 1912.

8. Haskell, journal, September 16, 1911, no. 42.

9. Gibran to Gertrude Barrie, n.d, authors' collection.

10. Haskell, journal, September 26, 1911, no. 42.

11. Ibid., no. 42, September 28, 1911; ibid., no. 42, September 29, 1911.

12. Ibid., October 1, 1911, no. 42.

13. Laura E. Lockwood, "A Christmas Mystery Play at Denison House," *The Survey: A Journal of Constructive Philanthropy* 29, no. 10 (December 7, 1912): 309–310.

14. Haskell, journal, February 26, 1911, no. 41.

15. Kahlil's use of the term "Golden Links" (as opposed to "Golden Circle," which was the preferred translation of Al-Halaqat al-Dhahabiyah) may well have originated with

his knowledge of Fred Holland Day's membership in the Linked Ring, a British-based group, committed to photography as art.

16. Lockwood, "A Christmas Mystery Play," 310.

17. Haskell, journal, February 26, 1911, no. 41.

18. Hani J. Bawardi, *The Making of Arab Americans: From Syrian Nationalism to U.S. Citizenship* (Austin: University of Texas Press, 2014): 57–66. According to Dr. Bawardi (whose translation appears here), a copy of the address is located in the Jafet Memorial Library at the American University of Beirut. It was published in *Mirat al-Gharb* on March 3, 1991, and some weeks later in *Al-Barq*.

19. Haskell, journal, September 29, 1911, no. 42.

20. Ibid., October 2, 1911, no. 42.

21. Haskell, diary, October 6, 1911, no. 40; ibid., October 7, 1911, no. 40.

22. Ibid., October 9, 1911, no. 40.

23. Ibid., October 10, 1911, no. 40; ibid., October 19, 1911, no. 40.

24. Haskell, journal, October 13, 1911, no. 42; ibid., February 14, 1911, no. 41.

25. Haskell to Gibran, October 18, 1911.

26. Ibid., October 28, 1911; Haskell, diary, October 23–24, 1911, no. 40.

27. Haskell, diary, October 25–26, 1911, no. 40; ibid., October 29, 1911, no. 40.

28. Haskell to Gibran, November 3, 1911.

29. Gibran to Haskell, November 10, 1911.

30. Haskell, diary, November 6, 1911, no. 40; ibid., November 17, 1911, no. 40; Haskell, journal, November 30, 1911, no. 42,.

31. Haskell, journal, November 30, 1911, no. 42.

32. Linda K. Jacobs, "If You Are Wearing Pearls, Wear Nothing But Pearls": Marie El-Khoury, Jeweler to New York Society," *Kalimah Press* (blog), August 24, 2015, http://kalimahpress.com/blog/if-you-are-wearing-pearls-wear-nothing-but-pearls-marie-el-khoury-jeweler-to-new-york-society/; Linda K. Jacobs, *Strangers in the West: The Syrian Colony of New York City, 1880–1900* (New York: Kalimah Press, 2015), 298–299.

33. Charlotte Teller to Haskell, December 13, 1911.

34. Ameen Rihani, *The Book of Khalid*, illustrated by Kahlil Gibran, afterword by Todd Fine (Brooklyn: Melville House Publishing, 2012).

35. Haskell, diary, January 17, 1912, no. 40; ibid., January 31, 1912, no. 40; ibid., February 1, 1912, no. 40.

36. Gibran to Haskell, January 26, 1912; ibid., January 31, 1912.

37. Teller to Haskell, January 21, 1912.

38. Haskell to Gibran, March 8, 1912; Gibran to Haskell, March 10, 1912; Gibran to Haskell, March 24, 1912.

39. Haskell, journal, April 5, 1912, no. 42; Haskell, diary, April 14–15, 1912, no. 40; Haskell, diary, March 27, 1912, no. 40.

40. Haskell, diary, March 24–25, 1912, no. 40; ibid., March 27, 1912, no. 40; ibid., March 28, 1912, no. 40.

41. Haskell, diary, March 31–April 2, 1912, no. 40.

42. Haskell, journal, March 12, 1922, no. 60.

43. Gibran to Haskell, April 16, 1912.

44. Ibid., April 19, 1912.

45. Marzieh Gail, "Juliet Remembers Gibran: As told to Marzieh Gail," *World Order* 12, no. 4 (1978): 29–31, http://bahai-library.com/gail_thompson_remembers_gibran.

46. Free Religious Association, *Proceedings at the Annual Meeting* (Boston: Free Religious Association, May 23–24, 1912), 86.

47. Charles Fleischer, *American Aspirations* (New York: B. W. Huebsch, 1914).

48. Haskell to Gibran, August 16, 1912; Mary Haskell events of September 7 entered under August 26–27, 1912.

49. [Charlotte Teller], "America Facing Its Most Tragic Moment," *New York Times*, September 29, 1912, 74.

Chapter 12: *Growing Partnerships*

1. Mary Haskell, journal, January 10, 1914, no. 44, Minis Family Papers, University of North Carolina, collection no. 02725.

2. Haskell, diary, August 6, 1912, no. 40 (retrospective account recording the events of September 7, 1911).

3. Haskell, diary, August 6–9, 1912, no. 40 (recording the events of September 7).

4. Charlotte Teller to Haskell, May 21, 1912.

5. Kahlil Gibran to Haskell, September 29, 1912.

6. Gibran to Haskell, October 22, 1912.

7. Haskell, journal, December 1, 1912, no. 43; Gibran to Haskell, December 7, 1913.

8. Haskell, diary, May 2–3, 1912, no. 40; Haskell to Gibran, September 22, 1912.

9. Haskell, diary, October 3, 1912, no. 40 (recording the events of November 9); Haskell, journal, November 9, 1912, no. 43.

10. Teller to Haskell, April 13, 1912.

11. Gibran to Haskell, February 16, 1913.

12. Haskell, journal, December 21, 1913, no. 44.

13. Ibid., June 20, 1914, no. 44.

14. Gibran to Haskell, February 14, 1913; Haskell, diary, February 6, 1913, no. 40 (originally written at "the end of April 1913").

15. Haskell, journal, April 6, 1913, no. 43; ibid., February 12, 1913, no. 40 (originally written at "the end of April").

16. Kahlil would continue to refer to "the work" or "the collection" in terms of an investment shared by them both.

17. Gibran to Haskell, February 18, 1913; ibid., April 30, 1913.

18. Sarah M. A. Gualtieri, *Between Arab and White: Race and Ethnicity in the Early Syrian American Diaspora* (Berkeley: University of California Press, 2009), 148–150.
19. Haskell to Gibran, May 11, 1913.
20. Ibid.
21. Gibran to Haskell, May 16, 1913.
22. Haskell, journal, June 25, 1913, no. 43.
23. Haskell, diary, March 27, 1912, no. 40; ibid., March 28, 1912, no. 40; ibid., March 24–25, 1912, no. 40.
24. Haskell, journal, June 25, 1913, no. 43.
25. Ibid., August 29, 1913, no. 44.
26. Ibid., August 31, 1913, no. 44.
27. Ibid.
28. Ibid., March 12, 1922, no. 60.
29. Ibid., September 2, 1913, no. 44.
30. Ibid.
31. Ibid., September 3, 1913, no. 44; Bennard B. Perlman, *The Lives, Loves, and Art of Arthur B. Davies* (Albany: State University of New York Press, 1998): 242.
32. Haskell, diary, from letter of September 21, 1913, no. 69.
33. Haskell, journal, n.d. (ca. 1912), no. 43.
34. Ibid., June 11, 1915, no. 45.
35. Haskell to Gibran, February 6, 1912; Haskell, journal, June 12, 1912, no. 43; Haskell, journal, June 15, 1912, no. 43.
36. Haskell, diary, February 8, 1912, no 40.
37. Haskell, journal, June 10, 1912, no. 43; ibid., December 27, 1912, no. 43.
38. Ibid., April 6, 1913, no. 43.
39. Ibid.; Gibran to Haskell, February 8, 1912; Haskell to Gibran, April 19, 1913.
40. Haskell to Gibran, December 7, 1913; Gibran to Haskell November 4, 1913.
41. Haskell, journal, December 21, 1913, no. 44.
42. Haskell, diary, October 27, 1913, no. 40.
43. Richard Alan Popp, "Al-Funun: The Making of An Arab-American Literary Journal" (Ph.D. dissertation, Georgetown University, 2000), 119.
44. Ibid., 242.
45. For the publishing dates of *Al-Funun*, see its Table of Contents: http://www.al-funun. org/al-funun/contents/index.html, accessed October 10, 2015.
46. Gibran to Haskell, January 21, 1914; ibid., February 8, 1914.
47. Haskell to Gibran, May 1914; Gibran to Haskell, March 8, 1914.
48. Haskell, journal, June 20, 1914, no. 44.
49. Haskell, journal, pre-March 10, 1914, no. 44.
50. Gibran to Haskell, January 19, 1914; ibid., January 21, 1914.
51. An inscribed copy can be found at Chapel Hill.

Chapter 13: *Work Made Visible*

1. For more on Harry Leon Wilson—editor of *Puck Magazine* (one of America's earliest humor and political satire magazines) from 1892 to 1902—see the Harry Leon Wilson Papers, Bancroft Library, University of California, Berkeley.

2. Rose O'Neill, *The Story of Rose O'Neill*. Edited by Miriam Formanek-Brunell (Columbia: The University of Missouri, 1997): 119.

3. Ibid.

4. Haskell, journal, August 30, 1914, no. 44, Minis Family Papers, University of North Carolina, collection no. 02725.

5. Ibid.

6. Haskell, journal, September 2, 1914, no. 44; ibid., August 31, 1914, no. 44.

7. Haskell to Gibran, December 8, 1914.

8. Gibran to Haskell, December 13, 1914.

9. See Helen Johnson Keyes, "Ameen Rihani's 'The Book of Khalid,'" review of *The Book of Khalid* by Ameen Rihani, *Bookman*, December 1911, 438–439. See also Marguerite Mooers Marshall, review of *The Book of Khalid* by Ameen Rihani, *The Nation*, March 21, 1912, 291. See also their introductory essay based on both the 1911 and 1912 reviews in Ameen F. Rihani, *The Book of Khalid* (Beirut: Librairie du Liban, 2000): foreword a–d.

10. Marguerite Mooers Marshall, *Buffalo Times*, December 15, 1914, 16.

11. Haskell, journal, December 19, 1914, no. 45; Charlotte Teller to Mary Haskell, December 25, 1914.

12. Haskell, journal, December 27, 1914, no. 45; Haskell, journal, December 20, 1914, no. 45. Kahlil may have been referring to the painter Kenneth Miller.

13. See bibliography: Selected Book Illustrations, Exhibitions, and Catalogues, 1914.

14. Chamberlain to Gibran, December 24, 1914.

15. Jean Hamilton, "Woman's Influence," *New York Evening Sun*, December 28, 1914, 8.

16. Henry McBride, *New York Sun*, December 20, 1914, 2.

17. Henry McBride, *New York Sun*, April 1, 1917, sec. 5, p. 12.

18. Haskell, journal, April 26, 1915, no. 44.

19. Gibran to Haskell, January 11, 1915.

20. Haskell to Gibran, February 2, 1915.

21. Haskell, journal, April 11, 1915, no. 45; Gibran to Haskell, March 14, 1915; Haskell, journal, April 11, 1915, no. 45.

22. Author Corinne Roosevelt Robinson (Mrs. Douglas Robinson) was the sister of Franklin Delano Roosevelt and aunt of Eleanor, who would become Franklin Roosevelt's spouse and the First Lady. Scribner's had recently published *The Call of Brotherhood: And Other Poems*. Her initial negative reaction to Kahlil's work soon was replaced with admiration, and she became his close friend and champion.

23. Haskell, journal, June 3, 1915, no. 45; Haskell to Gibran, April 22, 1915.

24. Ibid., June 3, 1915, no. 45.

25. Ibid., June 11, 1915, no. 45.
26. Haskell to Gibran, July 1915.

Chapter 14: *War and Famine*

1. Kahlil Gibran to Mary Haskell, May 16, 1912.
2. Haskell, journal, June 22, 1913, no. 43, Minis Family Papers, University of North Carolina, collection no. 02725; Gibran to Haskell, June 21, 1918.
3. Haskell, journal, June 20, 1915, no. 45.
4. Gibran to Haskell, May 16, 1912.
5. Gibran to Haskell, October 22, 1912; ibid., June 10, 1913.
6. Haskell, journal, June 22, 1913, no. 43.
7. Gibran to Haskell, July 10, 1913.
8. Kahlil Gibran, "Ila al-Muslimin min Shacir MasHu," *Al-Funun* 1, no. 8 (November 1913): 37–39.
9. "Min Sharit Masihi Il al Muslimin," *Al-Funun* 1 (November 1913): 37–39; "Bad Thawrah" [The beginning of revolution], *As-Sayeh*, March 9, 1914 (clipping found in Mary Haskell folder no. 71); Gibran to Haskell, March 8, 1914.
10. Haskell, journal, August 30, 1914, no. 44; Haskell to Gibran, October 2, 1914; Gibran to Haskell, October 14, 1914.
11. Haskell, journal, November 14, 1914, no. 45.
12. Ibid., December 20, 1914, no. 45.
13. *Syria during March, 1916* (London: Causton, 1916), 22. This book contains a collection of articles originally printed in the journal *Mokattam* of Cairo.
14. "Gibran wa-Muhammad," *As-Sayeh* 4, no. 368 (May 25, 1916): 1.
15. Ibid.
16. Gibran and Haskell, May 26, 1916.
17. Ibid., May 26, 1912; ibid., June 29, 1912.
18. "Washington Asked to Give Syrians Aid," *The Washington Times*, June 21, 1916, 4.
19. Richard Popp, "Al-Funun: The Making of an Arab-American Literary Journal" (Ph.D. diss.) Georgetown University, 2000), 192.
20. Haskell, journal, April 23, 1916, no. 46.
21. Amin Mushriq, "Rabitah Qalimiyya," *As-Sayeh* 5, no. 378 (June 29, 1916): 4–5.
22. The scholar M. M. Badawi emphasized the importance of emigrant writers in the development of the Arab renaissance. "By introducing a new conception of poetry, by adding a spiritual dimension to it…by turning away from rhetoric and declamation, by concentrating on the more subjective experience of man in relation to nature…by introducing biblical themes and images into their poetry, by their preference for short metres and stanzaic forms, the *Mahjar* poets, especially of the United States, exercised a liberating influence upon modern Arabic poetry." See M. M. Badawi, *A Critical Introduction to Modern Arabic Poetry* (New York: Cambridge University Press, 1975), 192.

23. See Michael Malek Najjar, *Arab American Drama, Film and Performance: A Critical Study, 1908 to the Present* (Jefferson, North Carolina: McFarland, 2015): 81–87.

24. Ibid., 81. Variant translations of this title include "The Colored Faces," in contrast to Michael Suleiman's "Chameleon-like Personalities," Nefertiti Takla's "The Chameleons," and in this volume, Abdul Mohsen Al-Husseini's "The Two-Faced Characters." See Kahlil Gibran, "Al-Wujuh 'al-mulawana," *As-Sayeh* 4, no. 358 (April 20, 1916): 3–6.

25. The article criticized by the characters was Jean Hamilton's "Woman's Influence is to Be Found Somewhere Behind All the Creations of Man Throughout the Centuries," which appeared on page 8 of the *New York Evening Sun* on December 28, 1914.

26. Kahlil Gibran, "Al-Wujuh al-mulawana," *As-Sayeh* 4, no. 358 (April 20, 1916): 3–6.

27. Ibid., 4.

28. Ibid., 5.

29. Ibid., 6.

30. Salloum Mokarzel, "Gibran's Tears," *Syrian World* 3, no. 8 (February 19, 1929): 32–33. (From "Tributes to Gibran"—speeches delivered at a January 5, 1929 testimonial dinner).

31. Haskell, journal, July 21, 1916, no. 46.

32. Ibid.; Haskell, journal, October 5, 1916, no. 46.

33. Originally published in 1890. For a more recent edition, see Knut Hamsum, *Hunger*, trans. Robert Bly (New York: Farrar, Straus and Giroux, 2008).

34. Kahlil Gibran, "Dead Are My People," in *Treasury of Kahlil Gibran* (New York: Citadel, 1951), 339–345. This piece was orignially published as "Mata Ahli," *Al-Funun* 2 (October 1916): 385–390.

35. Gibran to Marianna Gibran, Jan 15, 1919.

36. Gibran to Bynner, September 22, 1916; ibid., n.d. (ca. 1916).

37. Haskell, journal, October 5, 1916, no. 46.

38. Frederick J. Hoffman et al., *The Little Magazine* (Princeton: Princeton University Press, 1946): 87; Haskell, journal, July 23, 1916, no. 46.

39. Randolph Bourne, "Trans-national America," *The Atlantic*, July 1916, accessed January 5, 2016, www.theatlantic.com/past/issues/16jul/bourne.htm.

40. Gibran to Oppenheim, July 12, 1916; ibid., n.d. (ca. 1916), New York Public Library.

41. Haskell to Gibran, November 2, 1916.

42. Gibran to Haskell, November 5, 1916.

43. Haskell, journal, November 11, 1916, no. 47.

44. Ibid., February 3, 1917, no. 47.

45. Ibid., September 19, 1915, no. 46; ibid., November 12, 1916, no. 47.

46. Gibran to Haskell, January 3, 1917; ibid., January 12, 1917.

47. Gibran to Haskell, January 31, 1917.

48. Haskell, journal, February 3, 1917, no. 47.

49. Ibid., February 3, 1917, no. 47 (recording the events of February 4, 1917).

50. Ibid.; Alice Raphael, "The Art of Kahlil Gibran," *The Seven Arts* 9 (March 1917): 531–534.

51. Haskell, journal, August 27, 1915, no. 46; ibid., May 9, 1917, no. 47.

52. Henry McBride, *New York Sun*, April 1, 1917, sec. 5, p. 12.

53. Haskell to Gibran, April 18, 1917; ibid., April 22–23, 1917.

54. F. W. Coburn, "Syriac Suggestions," *Boston Sunday Herald*, April 22, 1917, 5; Haskell to Gibran, April 22–23, 1917.

55. Haskell, journal, May 9, 1917, no. 47; Gibran to Haskell, April 20, 1917.

56. Letter sent to Theodore Roosevelt, April 5, 1918, Roosevelt Collection, Harvard College Library, reel 271. The letterhead reads, "Syria-Mount Lebanon League of Liberation."

57. Haskell, journal, July 27, 1917, no. 47; Haskell to Gibran, April 22, 1917; Charlotte Teller to Haskell, June 2, 1918.

58. Amy Lowell to James Oppenheim, July 30, 1917, Harvard College Library.

59. Jeff Riggenbach, "The Brilliance of Randolph Bourne," Mises Institute, May 27, 2011, accessed January 10, 2016, https://mises.org/library/brilliance-randolph-bourne.

60. Haskell, journal, November 10, 1917, no. 47.

61. See "A Rebel Syrian. Gibran Kahlil Gibran," in Adel Beshara's *The Origins of Syrian Nationhood: Histories, Pioneers and Identity* (London: Routledge, 2011), 143–161.

62. Haskell, journal, December 26, 1917, no. 47.

Chapter 15: A People's Poet

1. Kahlil Gibran to Corinne Robinson, January 26, 1918, Corinne Roosevelt Robinson Papers, 1847–1933 (MS AM 1785–1785.7). Theodore Roosevelt Collection, Houghton Library, Harvard University.

2. Gibran to Mary Haskell, February 5, 1918.

3. Haskell to Gibran, February 10, 1918; Gibran to Haskell, February 26, 1918.

4. Gibran to Haskell, February 26, 1918.

5. Witter Bynner Papers, Houghton Library, Harvard University. Their friendship was demonstrated in letters to Bynner from the artist Barry Faulkner, who was then serving in the army. By April 1918, he alluded to Bynner journeying to Syria along with Gibran and Julia Ford. (See Barry Faulkner to Witter Bynner, Syracuse University Library). The intended trip never occurred, but Bynner's memories of Gibran confirm his key presence among a circle of artists in New York that included Poetry Society members.

6. Howard Willard Cook, *Our Poets of Today* (New York: Moffat, Yard, 1919). This was published as part of the Modern American Writers series (1908–1924) which also included *The Men Who Make Our Novels*, *Our Essayists of Today*, *Our Short Story Writers*, *Our Humorists of Today*, and *Our Playwrights of Today*.

7. Haskell, journal, March 22, 1918, no. 47, Minis Family Papers, University of North Carolina, collection no. 02725.

8. Haskell, journal, March 24, 1918, no. 47.

9. Ibid., September 10, 1917, no. 47; ibid., March 24, 1918, no. 47.

10. Haskell, journal, June 12, 1912, no. 43; ibid., September 7, 1912, no. 43.

11. Ibid., April 6, 1913, no. 43; ibid., September 4, 1914, no. 44; ibid., November 14, 1914, no. 45.

12. Haskell, journal, April 11, 1915, no. 45.

13. Ibid., April 21, 1916, no. 46. Kahlil's reference recalls Act I of *The Tempest*, when wise Gonzalo describes his natural state: "I' the commonwealth I would by contraries/ Execute all things, for no kind of traffic/Would I admit, no name of magistrate." He clearly would have been familiar with the term, not only from living more than half his life in the Commonwealth of Massachusetts, but from his Denison House days when young immigrant audiences memorized Shakespearean speeches and performed in frequent productions of his plays.

14. Haskell, journal, July 30, 1917, no. 47.

15. Gibran to Bynner, March 15, 1918, Houghton Library, Harvard University.

16. Marie Tudor Garland, *The Potter's Clay: Poems* (New York: G. P. Putnam's Sons, 1917); Marie Tudor Garland, *Hindu Mind Training* (London: Longmans Green, 1917).

17. See *The Garland Book*—Dick Cowen's unpublished papers tracking Marie Tudor Garland's family history. Housed at the Lillian Goldman Law Library, Yale University and available online at:
http://documents.law.yale.edu/sites/default/files/garland%20unpublished%20bio.pdf.
William Z. Foster, Elizabeth Gurley Flynn, and Norman Thomas served as board members for the American Fund for Public Service. Bay End Farm continues to operate in Buzzards Bay, Massachusetts.

18. Gibran to Haskell, April 10, 1918.

19. Mrs. Hope Garland Ingersoll, personal interview, July 24, 1973.

20. Gibran to Marianna Gibran, n.d., author's collection; Gibran to Haskell, April 14, 1918; Haskell to Gibran, April 17, 1918.

21. Haskell, journal, May 6, 1918, no. 47.

22. Ibid.

23. Ibid. The line from *The Prophet* is from page 18 of the Knopf edition.

24. Haskell, journal, May 11, 1918, no. 47; Haskell to Gibran, May 12, 1918.

25. Gibran to Haskell, June 5, 1918.

26. Haskell, journal, November 13, 1915, no. 46; ibid., December 30, 1915, no. 46.

27. Ibid., May 11, 1918, no. 47.

28. Ibid.

29. Haskell to Gibran, June 20, 1918.

30. Gibran to Haskell, July 11, 1918.

31. Gibran to Haskell, May 29, 1918; Haskell to Gibran, June 4, 1918; Gibran to Haskell, June 21, 1918.

32. Haskell to Gibran, June 20, 1918; ibid., June 4, 1918.

33. Haskell, journal, June 20, 1915, no. 45; ibid., April 3, 1912, no. 42; Haskell to Gibran, June 20, 1918.
34. Haskell to Gibran, July 24, 1918; ibid., August 9, 1918.
35. Gibran to Haskell, August 26, 1918.
36. Ibid., May 21, 1918; Haskell, journal, August 31, 1918, no. 48.
37. A copy can be found at Minis Family Papers, University of North Carolina; Gibran to Haskell, November 7, 1918; ibid., November 17, 1918.

Chapter 16: *Awakenings in the Immigrant Press*

1. Mary Haskell to Kahlil Gibran, October 27, 1918.
2. *Al-Funun* 2, no. 4 (September 1916): vi–vii. This special issue of *Al-Funun* announced a contest for best contributor. Offering a word about the judges—Gibran, Rihani, Naimy, and Catzeflis—beginning with Kahlil, editor Nasib Arida commented, "He has the admiration of the people and I must mention the readers' fondness for the subject. Gibran was born in 1883 in Bsharri, Lebanon (and it is said that he was born in Bombay, India)."
3. Kahlil Gibran to Blanche Knopf, March 11, 1928, Knopf Papers, Harry Ransom Center, University of Texas at Austin.
4. Mary Haskell, journal, June 20, 1914, no. 44, Minis Family Papers, University of North Carolina, collection no. 02725; Haskell, journal, September 7, 1912, no. 43; Haskell, journal, September 4, 1914, no. 44; Haskell, journal, September 19, 1915, no. 46.
5. See books by Kahlil Gibran published in 1918 in the bibliography.
6. Joseph Gollomb, "An Arabian Poet in New York," *New York Evening Post*, March 29, 1919, sec. 1, p. 10.
7. *The Nation* 107 (December 28, 1918): 812.
8. Harriet Monroe, "Journeymen Poets," *Poetry: A Magazine of Verse* 14 (August 1919): 278–279.
9. *The Dial* 65 (November 30, 1918): 510.
10. Kahlil Gibran to Gertrude Barrie, n.d. This letter was sent from 51 West Tenth Street in New York, to Tetlow Street in Boston.
11. Charlotte Teller to Mary Haskell, December 23, 1918.
12. Kahlil Gibran, *The Madman* (New York: Knopf, 1918): 7–8.
13. Haskell, journal, January 11, 1919, no. 48.
14. Marguerite Wilkinson, *New Voices* rev. ed. (New York: Macmillan, 1929), 27, 95.
15. Haskell, journal, April 14, 1919, no. 49; ibid., April 20, 1920, no. 51.
16. James Waldo Fawcett, *Unity* 83 (March 6, 1919): 10.
17. H. P. S. review of Gibran's *The Madman*, *The Liberator* 1, no. 11 (January 1919): 44.
18. See Edward Abrahams's *The Lyrical Left: Randolph Bourne, Alfred Stieglitz and the Origins of Cultural Radicalism in America* (Virginia: University of Virginia Press, 1986).
19. Haskell, journal, April 14, 1919, no. 49.

20. Ibid., April 20, 1920, no. 51.

21. Ibid., June 9, 1919, no. 49; ibid., November 9, 1919, no. 50.

22. Rose O'Neill, *The Story of Rose O'Neill: An Autobiography*, ed. Miriam Formanek-Brunell (University of Missouri Press, 1997), 204, 198; O'Neill to Lie, n.d., in the collection of Jean Cantwell, Branson, Missouri.

23. Haskell, journal, November 8, 1919, no. 50; Gibran to Haskell, May 4, 1919.

24. "Kahlil Gibran," Poetry Foundation, accessed September 12, 2015, www.poetryfoundation.org/bio/kahlil-gibran.

25. Suheil Bushrui and Joe Jenkins, *Kahlil Gibran: Man and Poet* (Oxford: One World, 1998), 181.

26. Emile Zaidan, "Natharat min ras'el. Lam funshar li Jubran Khalil Jubran," *El-Hilal* 42 (March 1934): 513. Zaidan explains that these "fragments" are from Gibran's letters, written to him between 1919 and 1922.

27. Haskell, journal, April 14, 1919, no. 49.

28. Ibid., July 30, 1919, no. 49; Kahlil Gibran, "To Young Americans of Syrian Origin," *The Syrian World* 1, no. 1 (July 1926): 4–5; Haskell, journal, July 30, 1919, no. 49.

29. Haskell, journal, August 4, 1919, no. 49; ibid., November 8, 1919, no. 50.

30. Ibid., December 30, 1919, no. 50; Gibran to Haskell, April 10, 1920.

31. Ibid., April 17, 1920, no. 50; Glen Mullin, "Blake and Gibran." Twenty Drawings. By Kahlil Gibran; *The Nation* 110 (April 10, 1920): 485–486.

32. As described by Howard Willard Cook, "those who know Bojer…will find in this drawing a study of infinite power and penetrating character analysis." From *Johan Bojer: The Man And His Works*, trans. Elizabeth Jelliffe MacIntire, with an introduction by Carl Gad (New York: Moffat, Yard, 1920), 27–29.

33. Haskell, journal, April 17, 1920, no. 50; ibid., April 18, 1920, no. 51; ibid., April 20, 1920, no. 51.

34 Haskell, journal, November 15, 1914, no. 45; Mikhail Naimy, "Fajr al-Ami ba'd Layl al-Ya's," *Al-Funun* 1, no. 4 (July 1913): 50–70.

35. Mikhail Naimy, *Kahlil Gibran: A Biography* (New York: Philosophical Library, 1950), 154–155.

36. William Catzeflis, introduction to *The Life of Gibran Khalil Gibran and His Procession*, by G. Kheirallah (New York: Arab-American Press, 1947).

37. Gibran, *Al-Funun* 3, no. 3 (October 1917): 191–193.

38. Ibid., 3, no. 2 (September 1917): 142–144.

39. Ibid., 2, no 2 (July 1916): 152–154.

40. Ibid., 2, no. 3 (August 1916): 258; Al-Ghazali (1056–1111), Ibn Sina (980–1037), Ibn al-Muqaffa (d. 756) (Kahlil Gibran *Al-Funun*, v. 3, no. 4. November 1917, 297.), al-Khansa (*Al-Funun* v.2, no. 10. March 1917, 297).

41. Ibid., 5.

42. Ibid., 120.

43. Haskell, journal, May 20, 1920, no. 51; ibid., May 22, 1920, no. 51; Gibran to Haskell, July 19, 1920.

44. "Lakum Lubnanukum wa Li Lubnani," *Al-Hilal* 29 (August 31, 1920): 19–23; Haskell, journal, August 31, 1920, no. 52.

45. Haskell, August 20, 1920, no. 52; ibid., August 25, 1920, no. 52.

46. Ibid., September 3, 1920, no. 52; ibid., September 7, 1920, no. 53.

47. Ibid., September 7, 1920, no. 52; ibid., September 14, 1920, no. 52.

48. Ibid., September 14, 1920, no. 53; ibid., September 7, 1920, no. 53.

49. William Stanley Braithwaite, "The Lutanists of November: Three Books of Selections by Makers of Poetry," *Boston Evening Transcript*, November 3, 1920, 2.

50. *Poetry* 18 (April 1921): 40–41.

51. Gibran to Haskell, December 12, 1920.

Chapter 17: "No Longer Apart"

1. Mary Haskell, journal, December 18, 1920, no. 54.

2. Kahlil Gibran, "Lakum Lubnankum wa Lya Lubnani" ("You Have Your Lebanon and I Have Mine"), *Al-Hilal* 29, no. 1 (1920): 19–23.

3. Haskell, journal, December 18, 1920, no. 54.

4. Kahlil Gibran to Zaidan, published in *Al-Hilal* 42 (March 1934): 517.

5. Haskell, journal, December 18, 1920, no. 54.

6. Ibid., December 30, 1920, no. 54.

7. Kahlil Gibran to Mikhail Naimy in Mikhail Naimy, *Kahlil Gibran: A Biography* (New York: Philosophical Library), 252–253.

8. John Daye from chapter "Mikha'il Nu'aymayh" in *The Origins of Syrian Nationhood: Histories, Pioneers, and Identities*, edited by Adel Beshara. (London: Routledge, 2011), 202.

9. Ibid., 203

10. "Syrian Plaque for Wilson," *New York Times* (January 25, 1921): 2.

11. Nathalie Sedgwick Colby, *Remembering*. (Boston: Little Brown and Company, 1938), 238, 253.

12. Haskell, journal, March 29, 1921, no. 55.

13. Kahlil Gibran, "Al-Ahd al-Jadid" ("The New Era"), *Al Hilal* (April 1, 1921): 636–640.

14. Haskell, journal, December 30, 1920, no. 54.

15. Ibid., February 5, 1921, no. 55.

16. Mikhail Naimy, "If Thorns But Realized the Secret of Flowers," translated by Abdul Mohsen al Husseini:

    Oh you wine serving soul, by god, don't fill my cups.

    Fill others' cups. As for me, consider me not seated.

    Move along. Leave me. Don't say that the wine doesn't appeal.

    But I have a wine that nothing like it can quench It is my own wine squeezed from my hardened heart.

Oh you player sending tunes from the oud like magic that arouses the lover
to madness, haven't you seen my constricted face and the eyes beneath my brows?
Don't say I'm lovesick (bewildered). No I'm not lovesick, my friend. For my heart
is hard as ice.
But I am listening to myself. For in myself, there are strings and songs. Go and leave
me among my tunes.

Oh you resident of a glamorous mansion,
have pride and enjoy your beautiful home, my friend.
And may the days give you abundant pleasures and long life. May you reap bliss
year after year.
Don't say your lofty mansion didn't appeal and that I didn't enjoy its breeze.
But I have a castle in my thoughts and dreams and I have a castle where my soul
seeks solace.

Oh you, seated among graves whose inhabitants have become soil and worms.
No doubt the soul you grieve is a lover or a close friend. Or, if you wish, you may
save the best of people.
But tomorrow, you will forget them, whereas in my life, there's a person buried
every day.
For I extract who has become a worm to me, along with the many who represent
great hope.

Oh, you accumulator of money, toiling nights and days for dime after dime,
whose days are yellow and years colorless, except for gold, blinded by money that
goes who knows where.
Know by he who holds thee; know by god who portions out our fate, I don't have
a lump in my throat or anguish in my heart by your wealth. For fortune has granted
me another kind of wealth.
Accumulate and don't pity my poverty.

Oh you carrying the Bible, calling for abandoning evil deeds and warning of
punishment, bring glad tidings and save souls that have gone astray, so that they will
be rewarded on judgment day.
My ears are deaf to your call. So forgive me and let me remain astray, for I have a
heart that contains paradise and god knows what hell fire it contains. Go and leave
my heart in its impurities.

Oh flower among thorns unnoticed but for your fragrance

Do the thorns realize, my flower, that the spreading scent is your fragrance?

Do the thorns realize that the scent that is spread is not theirs but yours?

Do the thorns realize what you know?

Have leaches scented their tails while you absorb their fragrance?

Or do the thorns weave nothing but thorns

while you weave the finest fabric?

The thorns may become chrysantemums if they realize what you know.

17. Haskell, journal, February 5, 1921, no. 55.

18. Ibid., April 1924, no. 56.

19. Naimy, *Kahlil Gibran: A Biography*, 168–169, 171.

20. Naimy to Kahlil Gibran, July 21, 1921, authors' coll.

21. Haskell, journal, July 12, 1921, no. 57.

22. Ibid., July 22, 1921, no. 57.

23. Ibid., August 8, 1921, no. 56.

24. Ibid., August 12, 1921, no. 58.

25. Ibid., August 30 and September 6, 1921, no. 58.

26. Ibid., September 9, 1921, no. 58.

27. Ibid., January 5, 1922, no. 58.

28. Ibid., January 9, 1922, no. 58.

29. Ibid., January 12, 1922, no. 59.

30. Haskell to Kahlil Gibran, October 10, 1920.

31. Haskell, journal, January 14, 1922, no. 59.

32. Haskell to Kahlil Gibran, February 22, 1922.

33. Haskell, journal, March 12, 1922, no. 60.

34. Ibid.

35. Ibid.

36. Ibid.

37. Haskell, journal, April 14, 1922, no. 59.

38. Ibid., April 25, 1922, no. 60.

39. Ibid., May 5, 1922, no. 61.

40. Ibid., April 21, 1922, no. 59; September 17, 1920, no. 53.

41. Ibid., May 5, 1922, no. 61.

42. Ibid., May 9, 1922, no. 61.

43. Ibid., May 19, 1922, no. 61.

44. Ibid., May 30, 1922, no. 62.

45. Ibid., April 25, 1922, no. 60.

46. Ibid., June 16, 1922, no. 62.

47. Ibid., May 12, 1922, no. 61; September 11, 1922, no. 62.

48. Ibid., September 11, 1922, no. 62.

49. Ibid., October 7, 1922, no. 63.

50. Ibid., November 12, 1922, no. 64.

51. Ibid., November 9 and 12, 1922, no. 64.

52. Ibid., December 31, 1922, no. 65.

53. Ibid., January 2, 1923, no. 65.

54. Kahlil Gibran to Mary Haskell, March 19 and April 17, 1923.

55. Haskell, journal, June 16, 1923, no. 66.

56. Ibid., June 23 and 16, 1923, no. 66.

57. Ibid., May 30, 1923, no. 66.

Chapter 18: "O Mist, My Sister"

1. Mary Haskell, journal, December 31, 1922, no. 65, Minis Family Papers, University of North Carolina, collection no. 02725.

2. Margo Badran, *Feminists, Islam, and Nation: Gender and the Making of Modern Egypt* (Princeton: Princeton University Press, 1996), 48–60.

3. Antje Ziegler, "Al-Haraka Baraka! The Late Rediscovery of Mayy Ziyada's Works," *Die Welt Des Islams* 39, no. 1 (March 1999): 103–115, accessed March 12, 2014, jstor.web.

4. Kahlil Gibran to Ziade, draft, July 25, 1919, private collection.

5. Gibran to May Ziade, January, 28 1920 in *Blue Flame: The Love Letters of Kahlil Gibran to May Ziadeh*, edited and translated by Suheil Hadi Bushrui and Salma Haffar Kuzbari (New York: Longman, 1983), 33.

6. Kahlil Gibran, "Bayn al-Laylwa al-Sabah" [Between night and morn], trans. Abdul Mohsen al-Husseini, *As-Sayeh*, January 16, 1919.

7. Gibran to Haskell, February 27, 1919.

8. Haskell, journal, December 31, 1922, no. 65..

9. *Al-Mashriq* 15 (1912): 315–316 (author, title unknown); Louis Cheikho, "Badai Jubran Khalil Jubran wa Taraifuh," 487–493; *Al-Mashriq* 21, no. 12 (1923): 910–919; Fuad al-Bustani and Edward Sab, "Bayn al-Mashriq wa al-Saih," 910–919.

10. Haskell, journal, September 7, 1920, no. 53.

11. Alfred A. Knopf, *Portrait of a Publisher, 1915–1965: Reminiscences and Reflections*, vol. 1 (New York: The Typophiles, 1965), 48.

12. Haskell to Gibran, October 2, 1923.

13. Haskell, journal, November 26, 1923, no. 67.

14. Marjorie Allen Seiffert, "Foreign Food," *Poetry* 23, 4 (January 1924): 216–218; Haskell, journal, June 5, 1924, no. 68.

15. Haskell, journal, August 25, 1915, no. 46.

16. Sarah M.A. Gualtieri, *Between Arab and White Race* (Berkeley: University of California Press, 2009), 216. See note from Congressional Record 71, pt. 1, April 29, 1929.

17. *Daily Boston Globe*, May 1, 1929, 32.

18. Salloum Mokarzel, "Syrians, whether at home or abroad, unhampered by religious intolerance, unfettered by political autocracy, and unhindered by race prejudice will force their way to the forefront in commerce, education, religion, science and politics," *The Syrian World*, V. III, No.13 (September 1928): editorial, 16.

19. Kahlil Gibran, "To Young Americans of Syrian Origin," *The Syrian World* 1, no.1 (July 1926): 4–5.

20. For more on Afifa Karam (1883–1924), see Elizabeth Claire Saylor, "A Bridge Too Soon: The Life and Works of Afifa Karam: The First Arab American Woman Novelist," (Ph.D. diss., Near Eastern Studies, U.C. Berkeley, 2015) and also Gualtieri, 148–149. Mokarzel also introduced in *The Syrian World* the script of Anna Ascends, a Broadway play and silent movie produced in 1922, two years before the Immigration Act. The play's heroine, a young Syrian waitress from Boston, overcomes social and economic obstacles. Portraying the efforts of newly arrived Arabs to win citizenship, author Harry Chapman Ford in the issue of *The Syrian World* featuring the script reflected on how personally getting to know a Syrian family had affected his views on race. "Their family life, their clean way of living impressed me…I figured here is a people who could read and write probably 6,000 years before the northern 'blue eyes'…" See Harry C. Ford, "Why I Wrote a Syrian Play," *The Syrian World* 2, no. 1 (July 1927): 33–40.

21. "Gibran Widely Quoted," About Syria and Syrians, *The Syrian World* 3, no. 28 (July 1928): 55.

22. See advertisement in *The Syrian World* 6, no. 5 (January 1932): 59.

23. Katherine K. Crosby, "How Boston Syrians Make Themselves Real Americans: Glimpses of Home Life in the Colonies, Where 'Aristocrats of the Immigrants' with 6000 Years of High Civilization Behind Them, Became Settled Citizens of the Hub." *The Boston Sunday Herald*, November 2, 1924.

24. Haskell, journal, November 26, 1923, no. 67.

25. After Josephine's death, Mary wrote, "[Mr. Marks] has been looking for some of her letters to him in the old days—because he wants them for a biography of her." A year later, when the *Diary and Letters of Josephine Preston Peabody* was published, Gibran's name was mentioned three times. Her letters to him were not included—and the story of their friendship remained untold.

26. She identified more of his friends—the Hutchinsons (Hesper Hutchinson was the daughter of Richard Le Gallienne) and Mariita Lawson, a model whose face he had been drawing.

27. Haskell, journal, November 26, 1923, no. 67; Haskell, journal, June 18, 1924, no. 68.

28. Kahlil Gibran, *The Garden of the Prophet* (New York: Alfred A. Knopf, 1933), 62.

29. Kahlil Gibran, *The Garden of the Prophet* (New York: Alfred A. Knopf, 1933), 556–557.

30. Costas Constantinou, *States of Political Discourse: Words, Regimes, Seditions* (Oxfordshire: Routledge, 2004), 81–82.

31. Ibid., 82.

32. Gibran to Ziade, November 11, 1920 in *Blue Flame*, 38–39.

33. Gibran, *The Garden of the Prophet*, 40–41.

34. Kahlil Gibran, "Mustaqbal al-Lughah al-Arabiyah" ("The Future of the Arabic Language"). *As-Sayeh* 8, no. 729 (March 1920): 5–6. See excerpt translated by Adnan Haydar in Reza Aslan, *Tablet & Pen: Literary Landscapes from the Modern Middle East* (New York: W. W. Norton, 2011): 6–11.

35. Gibran, *The Garden of the Prophet*, 49.

Chapter 19: After All the Debts Are Paid

1. Kahlil Gibran, "On Buying and Selling," in *The Prophet* (New York: Knopf, 1923).

2. Gibran to Mary Haskell, August 28, September 4, and October 3, 1924.

3. The first mention of "C.J." occurs in a letter from Mary Haskell to Kahlil Gibran, October 19, 1924.

4. Gibran to Haskell, October 16, 1924.

5. Haskell to Gibran, March 19, 1925; Gibran to Haskell, March 30, 1925; Gibran to Marianna Gibran, n.d., private collection.

6. Gibran to Haskell, July 8, 1925.

7. Haskell to Gibran, Easter 1913; and May 5, 1912.

8. Elias F. Shamon's unpublished article from 1931, in the author's collection. For more about Elias Shamon, see "Syrians protest Reed's remarks," *Boston Globe*, May 1, 1929; "Governor's Council Elias Shamon named judge," *Boston Globe*, January 27, 1944, 22.

9. Mikhail Naimy, *Kahlil Gibran: A Biography* (New York: Philosophical Library, 1950), 133–134.

10. Alfred A. Knopf, *Portrait of a Publisher 1915–1965* (New York: The Typophiles, 1965), 96–97.

11. Ibid., 44.

12. Ibid., 72.

13. Mikhail Naimy, *Kahlil Gibran*, 198.

14. Ibid., 162–163.

15. Kahlil Gibran, *Blue Flame: The Love Letters of Kahlil Gibran to May Ziadeh*, edited and translated by Suheil Hadi Bushrui and Salma Haffar Kuzbari (New York: Longman, 1983), 76–79. See esp. Gibran to Ziadeh, January 17, 1924.

16. Ibid., 88–90. See esp. Gibran to Ziade, February 6, 1925.

17. Ibid., 93–94. See esp. Gibran to Ziade, March 28, 1925.

18. Konrad Bercovici, *Around the World in New York* (New York: Century, 1924), 40.

19. The whereabouts of Gibran's drawing of Alfred A. Knopf is unknown. It is reproduced in *The Borzoi 1925: Being a sort of record of ten years of publishing* (New York: Alfred A. Knopf, 1925). See esp. the insert between pages 100–101, signed "Kahlil Gibran 1925, Alfred A. Knopf Drawing by Kahlil Gibran." See also signed letter to authors from A. Knopf in 1972, confirming that the drawing of Blanche Knopf was housed with the

Alfred A. Knopf, Inc. Records, at the Harry Ransom Center. Austin: University of Texas Library. Authors' collection.

20. Gibran to Haskell, September 4, 1924; Haskell, journal, May 23, 1924, no. 67.

Chapter 20: *The Final Years*

1. Kahlil Gibran to Antony Bashir, November 10, 1925, private collection. Sent to the Antiochian Orthodox Christian Archdiocese of North America, 358 Mountain Road, Englewood, NJ, from the Metropolitan Philip Saliba via Father George Corey, St. George Antiochian Orthodox Church, Boston.

2. Francesco Medici, "Un abito arabo per "Il Profeta": Lettere inedited di Kahlil Gibran a Antony Bashir" [An Arabic garment for "The Prophet": the unpublished letters of Kahlil Gibran to Antony Bashir], *Kervan* 7–11 (January 2012): 37–57.

3. Personal correspondence with Metropolitan Antony Bashir's nephew, Dr. Antony Bashir, November 20, 2015. See also Gibran to Bashir, November 10, 1925.

4. Konrad Bercovici, *Around the World in New York* (New York: Century, 1924), 40.

5. *The New Orient* 2, no. 1 (May/June 1924): 96.

6. Ibid. nos. 4–7 (April/May/June 1925).

7. Sarojini Naidu, *Selected Letters 1890s to 1940s*. Edited by Markarand R. Paranjape (New Dalhi: Kali for Women, 1996). Naidu to Jawaharlal Nehru, 29 September 1929, 230.

8. *The New Orient* 3, no. 2 (July 1926): 76.

9. Syud Hossain, *The New Orient* 2, no. 1 (May/June 1924): 96.

10. *The New Orient* 2, no. 2 (October/ November/December 1924): 7.

11. Haskell, journal, July 22, 1921, no. 57, Minis Family Papers, University of North Carolina, collection no. 02725.

12. Haskell, diary, May 10, 1926, no. 69; ibid., May 13, 1926, no. 69.

13. Gibran to Mr. Smith, May 22, 1926.

14. Gibran to Haskell, April 29, 1909; Haskell, journal, December 7, 1910, no. 41; Haskell, journal, April 19, 1911, no. 41; Haskell, journal, January 10, 1914, no. 44; Haskell, journal, April 19, 1911, no. 41. *Shahbi* means "my people"—Kahlil may have said "wood of my people" (meaning "cedar"), and Mary Haskell may have misheard or left out the phrase.

15. Haskell, journal, May 27, 1923, no. 66.

16. Barbara Young, *This Man from Lebanon* (New York: Knopf, 1945), 100, 103.

17. *Palms* was a magazine devoted to poetry, published and edited in Mexico by Idella Purnell (Stone) (1901–1982). *Palm* lasted for approximately ten years, with Witter Bynner often acting as a contributing editor, and featuring well-known writers including Countee Cullen, D. H. Lawrence, and Hildegarde Flanner. Purnell Stone's review of Mikhail Naimy's English edition of *Kahlil Gibran: A Biography* corroborated his revelation of Kahlil's excessive drinking. Sometime in 1930 she and Chilean poet Gabriela Mistral (1889–1957) visited Kahlil in New York and observed him excusing himself, retreating behind a screen, and taking "a swig out of a bottle which in the unfortunately arranged

mirror, didn't look like a medicine bottle." Sadly this scene was reported to friends and family members who resented both Naimy and Purnell for portraying Kahlil in his final years. Idella Purnell, "Gift of Mimicry Harms Poet," *Los Angeles Daily News*, November 4, 1950, 9. See Idella Purnell Stone and *Palms* at the Harry Ransom Humanities Research Center, University of Texas at Austin.

18. Felix Wray, review of *The Prophet* in *Palms: A Magazine of Poetry* (March 1927): 186.

19. Table Gossip, *Boston Daily Globe*, August 28, 1927, A58. Two years later, Kahlil's play *Lazarus and His Beloved* appeared at the Try-Out Theater in Wellesley. See Table Gossip, *Boston Daily Globe*, May 27, 1928, B58.

20. Haskell, journal, May 19, 1922, no. 61; ibid., May 26, 1922, no. 62.

21. Haskell to Gibran, April 14, 1927.

22. Haskell, diary, March 8/April 4, 1928, no. 69; ibid., April 30/May 2, 1928, no. 69.

23. Gibran to Robinson, September 11, 1928, Harvard College Library.

24. Gibran to Marianna Gibran, n.d., private collection.

25. Gibran to Assaf George, n.d., private collection.

26. Gibran to Haskell, November 7, 1928.

27. "Gibran's Latest Drawings Reveal Innate Mysticism," *Springfield Republican*, November 25, 1928, 63.

28. John Haynes Holmes, "A Poet Interprets a Prophet: *Jesus The Son Of Man* by Kahlil Gibran," *New York Herald Tribune*, December 2, 1928, 6.

29. Claude Bragdon, "A Modern Prophet from Lebanon," *New York Herald Tribune*, December 23, 1928, 16–18.

30. Angelos Sikelianos (1884–1951) was a lyric Greek poet and playwright who visited the United States with his wife Eva Palmer in the late 1920s in an effort to revive interest in a Greek-sponsored Delphic festival of games, theater, and arts. Alma Reed, whose Delphic Studios attracted Mexican artists like Orozco, was also a major supporter of Sikelianos's dreams for a revival of the Delphic arts.

31. Antoinette May, *Passionate Pilgrim: The Extraordinary Life of Alma Reed* (New York: Marlowe, 1993), 225.

32. Sarojini Naidu, *Selected Letters 1890s to 1940s*, 220, to Lelamani Naidu (daughter), at The Mayflower, Washington, D.C., 5 January 1929.

33. Alma Reed, *Orozco* (New York: Oxford University Press, 1956).

34. Philip K. Hitti, Tributes to Gibran, "Gibran's Place and Influence in Modern Arabic Literature," *The Syrian World* 3 (February 1929): 31–33; unsigned article probably by Mokarzel in idem., 52.

35. Dr. Samuel A. Robins to Dr. William J. Brown, January 24, 1929, reporting results of roentgen examination; in 1972 conversations with Mary Kawaji, Zakia Gibran Diab, N'oula Gibran.

36. Gibran to Naimy, Mikhail Naimy, *Kahlil Gibran: A Biography* (New York: Philosophical Library), 260.

37. Haskell, journal, February 24, 1911, 41.

38. al-Badayi' wa Taray'if (Best Things and Masterpieces] (Cairo: Maktabi al-'Arb, 1925). 522-526. English translated selections from "Earth" in *A Second Treasury of Kahlil Gibran*, translated by Anthony R. Ferris (New York: Citadel Press, 1962),108–112.

39. Gibran to Elizabeth Selig, received November 25, 1930. Alfred A. Knopf, Inc. Records.

40. Gibran to Haskell, June 16, 1923, no. 66.

41. "The Earth Gods" *New York Times*, Books, May, 17, 1931.

42. Gibran to Haskell, November 8, 1929.

43. At the time, Marie Mattingly Meloney was known professionally as Mrs. William B. Meloney.

44. His drinking was not publicly acknowledged until 1934, when Mikhail Naimy referred to it in his biography.

45. Haskell, diary, June 18, 1930, no. 70; ibid.; July 12/August 2, 1930.

46. Robinson to Gibran, July 28, 1930, private collection.

47. Gibran to Mr. Stimson, September 18, 1930.

48. Gibran to Gertrude Stern, July 10, 1930. Sent to 76 Tyler Street, Boston, postmarked August 25, 1930. Gertrude Stern Collection; authors' copies. In an effort to clarify her friendship with Kahlil, Stern, then, in 1977, Gertrude Stern Grey, gave the authors copies of her correspondence with Mikhail Naimy soon after his return to Lebanon in 1931. Along with Mary's description of Gibran's early years, Naimy also relied on Stern's perception of Kahlil during his final years and explained his reasons to write a biography of his colleague and friend.

49. Kahlil Gibran, *The Wanderer: His Parables and His Sayings* (New York: Knopf, 1932), 3.

50. Gibran to Ziade, 1930 in *Kahlil Gibran: A Self-Portrait* (New York: Citadel, 1959), 91–92.

51. Gibran to Haskell, March 16, 1931; Haskell, diary, April 4, 1931, no. 70; Haskell to Gibran, April 6, 1931.

52. Jacobs (widely known for her portraits) and her husband had long been Kahlil's neighbors. Jacobs included her painting of him in her 1937 book, *Portraits of Thirty Authors*.

53. Barbara Young to Crofts, April 23, 1931, private collection; Jesse Beale to Fred Holland Day, January 11, 1932.

54. City of New York, Department of Health, Bureau of Vital Records, stamped March 15, 1974. Cause of death signed by Maurice C. O'Shea, M.D.

Chapter 21: *The Homecoming*

1. Kahlil Gibran, "On Crime and Punishment," in *The Prophet* (New York: Knopf, 1923).

2. Jesse Beale to Fred Holland Day, January 11, 1932. F. Holland Day Papers, 1793–2010, Library of Congress Manuscript Division, Washington, D.C.

3. Haskell, January 11, 1914, no. 44, Minis Family Papers, University of North Carolina, collection no. 02725; "The Last Days of Gibran," *The Syrian World* 5 (April 1931): 21.

4. "A Seer Departed," *New York Sun*, April 15, 1931, 37; *Ohio Penitentiary News*, April 18, 1931, 1.

5. Monsignor F. A. Burke, Chancellor to El-Douaihy, June 5, 1931, Archives of the Boston Archdiocese.

6. Barbara Young, "Gibran's Funeral in Boston," *The Syrian World* 5 (April 1931): 23–25.

7. Private collection.

8. Haskell, journal, May 29, 1923, no. 66.

9. Haskell to Marianna Gibran, April 21, 1931, private collection.

10. Haskell to Young, May 8, 1931; Young to Haskell, May 19, 1931; Haskell, diary, May 29, 1931, no. 70; Haskell to Marianna Gibran, July 1, 1931, private collection.

11. Charles Fleischer to Corinne Roosevelt Robinson from, April 20, 1931; Fleischer to Marianna Gibran, April 23, 1931.

12. *The Syrian World* 5 (April 1931): 28–29.

13. Kahlil Gibran, "Voice of a Poet," in *A Tear and A Smile* (New York: Knopf, 1950), 193.

14. "The Arabic Speaking World Mourns Gibran," *The Syrian World* 5 (May 1931): 50.

15. Haskell, journal, June 17, 1911, no. 41; ibid., June 4, 1911, no. 41; Haskell to Marianna Gibran, May 2, 1931, author's private collection.

16. Marianna Gibran to Haskell, June 4, 1931; ibid., June 18, 1931.

17. Salloum A. Mokarzel, "Touching Reception of Gibran's Body in Lebanon," *The Syrian World* 6, no. 1 (September 1931): 14–17. Mokarzel's information was also reported in "Gibran is Honored in Native Lebanon," *New York Times*, September 20, 1931, 82.

18. Photos and details of this event as translated by Abdul Mohsen Husseini and Joelle Solé Maguire are from the August 26, 1931 memorial issue of *Al-Barq* (*Lightning*), edited at that time by Bechara El-Khoury (1890–1964). Certain discrepancies exist between those ten pages and *The Syrian World* version. For example, Gebran Tueni is described as the Minister of Culture in *Al-Barq*. Tueni, from the esteemed Tueni family, founded the widely read journal *Al-Nahar* (*The Awakening*) in 1933 and was a key figure in the services.

19. See mention of El-Khoury: "GKG to MN, letter written Boston, 1921," in *A Second Treasury of Kahlil Gibran*, ed. Anthony Ferris (New York: Citadel, 1962), 63.

20. Ameen Rihani's speech was later published in a sixteen-page pamphlet that was distributed throughout the country (currently in the author's private collection). He also adapted several lines from the speech into a poem that was published in *Al-Baraq* on September 17, 1931.

21. A.C. Harte, letter to the editor, *The Christian Century*, September 30, 1931, 1212.

22. O'Neill to Lies, Christmas 1931, in the collection Jean Cantwell.

23. More than a half century after Rihani's death, United Nations Secretary-General Kofi Annan would pay tribute to him: "Ameen Rihani, one of the earliest Arab Americans, devoted his life to bringing the East and the West together. 'We are not of the East or the West,' [Rihani] wrote. 'No boundaries exist in our breast: We are free.'" See Kofi Annan,

Speech to the 17th National Convention of the Arab-American Anti-Discrimination Committee in Arlington, Virginia, June 9, 2000, United Nations Meetings Coverage and Press.

24. "The 100th Anniversary of the First Arab-American Novel," Project Khalid, http://www.projectkhalid.org.

25. "A Google Doodle for May Ziadeh," Arabic Literature, accessed September 20, 2015, arablit.org/2012/02/11/a-google-doodle-for-may-ziadeh/.

26. Richard Alan Popp, "'Al-Funun': The Making of an Arab-American Literary Journal" (Ph.D. diss., Georgetown University, 2000); Nasib Arida, "The Black Stones of Homs," http://www.syrianmemorycollective.net; accessed December 1, 2015; http://beyondcompromise.com/2014/04/28/the-black-stones-of-homs/, accessed December 1, 2015.

27. She privately published and subsequently sold nineteen letters to her from Mark Twain. See "Rare Books, Autographs, and Prints," *Publisher's Weekly* 101, no. 2 (January 7, 1922): 1768.

28. Howayek's 1976 work, *Gibran Kahlil Gibran in Paris*, continues to be the most reliable account of the two years the artists spent together there. Howayek's work is featured on the website of Lebanese Grand Artists.

29. By the early 1950s, she donated her Gibran art to the Telfair Academy of Arts and Sciences in Savannah, transferred a huge archive of Haskell/Minis/Gibran papers to the University of North Carolina at Chapel Hill, and entrusted Marianna with the manuscripts Gibran had given her.

30. Kahlil Gibran, *Spirits Rebellious*, translated by H. M. Nahmad (New York: Alfred A. Knopf, 1948).

31. Homer Metz, "Memories of Gibran," In Perspective, *Providence Journal*, March 14, 1974.

32. Ibid.

33. Kahlil Gibran, "The Life of Love," in *A Tear and A Smile* (New York: Knopf, 1950), 5.

34. Gerald Heard, "Kahlil Gibran: Comforter and Friend," *New York Times Book Review*, February 19, 1950, 98.

35. Meleager, *Fifty Poems of Meleager*, trans. Walter George Headlam (London: Macmillan, 1890), poem 49, p. 99.

BIBLIOGRAPHY

WORKS BY KAHLIL GIBRAN

Written and Self-Illustrated Works

1905 "Nubthah fi Fan Al-Musiqa" [Music]. *Al-Mohajer.*

"Hayat al-Hubb" [The life of love]. *Al-Mohajer*, April 1.

1906 *Ara'is al-Muruj* [Nymphs of the valley]. *Al-Mohajer.*

1908 *Al-Arwah al-Mutamarrida* [Spirits rebellious]. *Al-Mohajer.*

1909 "Yawm Mawlidi" [My birthday]. *Al-Mohajer.*

1910 "Martha La Banaise." *Les Mille Nouvelle Nouvelles* 10 (November): 141–150.

1912 "Al-Ajnihah al-Mutakassira" [Broken wings]. *Mir'at al-Gharb.*

1911 "Nahnu wa Antum" [We and you]. *Mir'at al-Gharb*, January 6.

"Yasu' al-Maslub" [The crucified]. *Mir'at al-Gharb*, April 14.

"Al-'Ubudiyah." *Mir'at al-Gharb*, September 13.

Al-Hilal 19 (February 1): 302–304.

Al-Hilal 20 (November 1): 118–120.

1912 "Abna' al-Alihah wa Ahfad al-Qurud." *Mir'at al-Gharb*, April 5.

1913 *Al-Funun* 1 (April): 1–4.

Al-Funun 1 (June): 17–21.

Al-Funun 1 (August): 1–3.

Al-Funun 1 (September): 57–58.

Al-Funun 1 (November): 1–3, 37–39.

Al-Funun 1 (December): 70.

1914 *Kitab Dam'ah wa Ibtisama* [A Tear and a Smile].

"Bad' Thawrah." *As-Sayeh* (March).

1915 *To Albert Pinkham Ryder.* New York: privately printed by Cosmos & Washburn.

1916 *Al-Funun* 2 (June): 61–63, 70–71.

Al-Funun 2 (July): 97–99, 152–154.

Al-Funun 2 (August): 211–212, 258–259.

Al-Funun 2 (September): 289–291.

Al-Funun 2 (October): 385–390.

Al-Funun 2 (November): 481–486.

Al-Funun 2 (December): 589–590.

Al-Hilal 24 (April 1): 554–556.

"Al-Wujuh 'al-mulawana" [The two-faced characters]. *As-Sayeh* 4, no. 358 (April 20): 3–6.

"Night and the Madman." *The Seven Arts* (November): 32–33.

"The Greater Sea." *The Seven Arts* (December): 133–134.

1917 *Al-Funun* 2 (January): 673.

Al-Funun 2 (February): 781–782.

Al-Funun 2 (March): 885–887, 931–932.

Al-Funun 2 (May): 1201–1203.

Al-Funun 3 (August): 1–6.

Al-Funun 3 (September): 81–95, 143–144.

Al-Funun 3 (October): 163–164, 171–172, 191–193.

Al-Funun 3 (November): 275–276.

"The Astronomer." *The Seven Arts* (January): 23.

"On Giving and Taking." *The Seven Arts* (January): 37.

"The Seven Selves." *The Seven Arts* (February): 345.

"Poems from the Arabic." *The Seven Arts* (May): 64–67.

1918 *The Madman: His Parables and Poems*. New York: Knopf.

Al-Funun 3 (January): 465.

"Defeat, My Defeat." In *Serbia. 'O Grave Where Is Thy Victory?* privately printed.

1919 *Twenty Drawings*. Reprint, New York: Knopf, 1974.

Al-Mawakib [The procession]. New York: Mir'at al-Gharb al'Yawmiyah.

"Bayn al-Laylwa al-Sabah" [Between Night and Morn]. *As-Sayeh* (January 16).

1920 *The Forerunner: His Parables and Poems*. New York: Knopf.

"Al-'Awasif" [The tempests]. *Al-Hilal.*

Al-Hilal 28 (May 1): 745–752.

Al-Hilal 29 (October 1): 19–23.

"Lakum Lubnankum wa Lya Lubnani" [You have your Lebanon and I have mine]. *Al-Hilal* 29, no. 1 (August 31): 19–23.

1921 "Seven Sayings." *The Dial* 70 (January): 69.

1922 *Al-Hilal* 30 (March 1): 520.

1923 *The Prophet*. New York: Knopf.

Al-Bada'i̧' wa al-Tara'if [Best things and masterpieces]. Cairo: Yusuf Bustani.

Al-Hilal 31 (February 1): 463–469.

Al-Hilal 32 (November 1): 20–23.

1924 "Al-Majnun" [The madman]. *Al-Hilal.*

Al-Hilal 33 (October 1): 21–24.

1925 *As-Sabi* [The forerunner]. Translated by Antonius Bashir. Cairo: Yusuf Bustani.

Al-Hilal 34 (October 1): 35–37.

"The Blind Poet." *The New Orient* (July/September 1925).

1926 *Al-Nabi* [The prophet]. Translated by Antonius Bashir. Cairo: Yusuf Bustani.

Sand and Foam: A Book of Aphorisms. New York: Knopf.

"Lullaby." *The New Orient* (July 1926): 68.

"To Young Americans of Syrian Origin." *Syrian World* (July 1926): 4–5.

1927 *Kalimat Jubran* [Spiritual sayings of Kahlil Gibran]. Edited by Antonius Bashir. Cairo: Yusuf Bustani.

Ramal wa Zabat [Sand and foam]. Translated by Antonius Bashir. Cairo: Yusuf Bustani.

"O Mother Mine." *Syrian World* (March 1927): 13.

"I Wandered among the Mountains." *Syrian World* (May 1927): 11–12.

"Three Maiden Lovers." *Syrian World* (August 1927): 13.

1928 *Jesus the Son of Man. His Words and His Deeds as Told and Recorded by Those Who Knew Him.* New York: A. A. Knopf.

"The Great Recurrence." *New York Herald Tribune*, December 23, 1928.

1929 *Der Novi* [The prophet]. Translated into Yiddish by Yitzshak Horowitz. New York: Yatshkovskis Bibliotek.

Al-Sanabil [The spikes of grain]. New York: As-Sa'ih.

"Snow." *New York Herald Tribune*, December 22, 1929.

1931 *The Earth Gods.* New York: Knopf.

Al-Hilal 40 (December 1): 238.

1932 *Alihat al-Arrd* [The earth gods]. Translated by Antonius Bashir. Cairo: Elias's Modern Press.

The Wanderer: His Parables and His Sayings. New York: Knopf.

Yasu' Ibn al-Insan [Jesus The Son of Man]. Translated by Antonius Bashir. Cairo: Elias's Modern Press.

1933 *The Garden of the Prophet.* New York: Knopf.

Al-Hilal 41 (May 1).

1934 *Prose Poems.* Translated by Andrew Ghareeb. New York: Knopf.

Al-Hilal 42 (March 1): 513–517.

1947 "*Al-Mawakib* [The procession]." In Sirat Jibran Khalil Jibran wa-al-Mawakib [The life of Gibran Kahlil Gibran and his procession]. Translated by George Kheirallah. With an introduction by William Catzeflis. New York: Arab-American Press.

1948 *Nymphs of the Valley.* Translated by H. M. Nahmad. New York: Knopf.

Spirits Rebellious. Translated by H. M. Nahmad. New York: Knopf.

1950 *A Tear and a Smile.* Translated by H. M. Nahmad. New York: Knopf.

1951 *A Treasury of Kahlil Gibran.* Edited by Martin L. Wolf. Translated by Anthony R. Ferris. New York: Citadel.

1957 *The Broken Wings.* Translated and with a foreword by Anthony R. Ferris. New York: Citadel.

1958 *The Voice of the Master.* Edited and translated by Anthony R. Ferris. New York: Citadel.

1959 *Al-Majmu'ah al-Kamilah li Mu'allafat Jubran Khalil Jubran.* Edited by Mikhail Naimy. Beirut: Dar Beirut.

Kahlil Gibran: A Self-Portrait. Translated by Anthony R. Ferris. New York: Citadel.

1962 *Spiritual Sayings of Kahlil Gibran.* Translated by Anthony R. Ferris. New York: Citadel.

A Second Treasury of Kahlil Gibran. Translated by Anthony R. Ferris. New York: Citadel.

1965 *Mirrors of the Soul.* Translated by Joseph Sheban. New York: Wisdom Library.

1973 *Lazarus and His Beloved.* Edited by Jean Gibran and Kahlil Gibran. Greenwich, CT: New York Graphic Society.

1974 *The Prophet: A Musical Interpretation.* Read by Richard Harris. Music by Arif Mardin. New York: Atlantic Recording Corporation. Vinyl.

1982 *Dramas of Life: Lazarus and His Beloved* and *The Blind.* Edited by Jean Gibran and Kahlil Gibran. Philadelphia: Westminster Press.

1995 *The Kahlil Gibran Companion.* Read by Stephen Lang. New York: Random House Audio Publishing.

1998 *Blue Flame: The Love Letters of Kahlil Gibran to May Ziadah.* Edited by Suheil Badi Bushrui and Salma Haffar al-Kuzbari. Translated by Suheil Badi Bushrui. New York: Longman, 1983.

2005 "Gibran's Unpublished Letters to Archbishop Antonious Bashir." Translated by George N. El-Hage. *Journal of Arabic Literature* 36, no. 2: 172–182.

2007 *The Collected Works: With Eighty-Four Illustrations by the Author.* New York: Knopf.

2015 *The Processions: Al-Mawakib.* Edited by Nicholas Martin. Translated by Abdullah Halawani and Lama Nassif. Publisher: Nicholas R. Martin.

Selected Book Illustrations, Exhibitions, and Catalogues

1896 Sketchbook. Includes scenes from Gibran's childhood in Lebanon and his drawing of the Bacchante sculpture at Boston Public Library. Museo Soumaya, Mexico City.

1898 Cover design of Nathan Haskell Dole's *Omar Khayyam*. Boston: L.C. Page & Company.

1899 Embossed book binding of Maurice Maeterlinck's *Wisdom and Destiny*. Gibran created bindings for all Maeterlinck works published by Dodd & Mead Company from 1898 to 1918.

1903 Wellesley College. First exhibition of Gibran's artwork, presented by Tau Zeta Epsilon Society. May.

1904 Harcourt Building, Boston. Exhibition: Drawings, *Studies, and Designs by Gibran Kahlil Gibran, with a Small Collection by the Late Langrel Harris*. April 30–May 10.

1909 Wellesley College. Exhibition, presented by Tau Zeta Epsilon Society. May.

1910 Salon du Printemps de la Société Nationale des Beaux-Arts, Paris. April 15–June 30. Catalogue illustration no. 548, *L'automne*.

1914 Montross Gallery, New York. *Exhibition: Pictures by Kahlil Gibran*. December 14–30.

1914 Frontispiece portrait of Percy MacKaye, *Saint Louis: A Civic Masque*. New York, Doubleday Press.

1917 M. Knoedler & Company, New York. *Exhibition: Forty Wash-Drawings*. January 29–February 10.

1919 Frontispiece portrait, *Selected Poems: The Works of Witter Bynner*. Edited by James Kraft. New York: Alfred A. Knopf.

1920 Frontispiece portrait, *Johan Bojer: The Man and His Works*, by Carl Gad. New York: Moffatt, Yard and Company.

1922 Boston Women's City Club. *Exhibition: Wash Drawings*. Jan. 10–31.

1922 Frontispiece portrait for *The New World* by Witter Bynner. New York: Alfred A. Knopf.

1922 *Companions: An Anthology*. Illustrated by Khalil Gebran [sic]. New York: Samuel A. Jacobs.

1925 Five drawings in *Hill Fragments* by Madeline Mason-Manheim. New York: Brentano's.

1925 Portrait of Alfred A. Knopf in *The BORZOI, 1925, Being a sort of record of ten years of publishing*. New York: Alfred A. Knopf.

1928 Dust jacket portrait of Jiddu Krishnamurti in *The Immortal Friend*. New York: Boni & Liveright.

1932 Gibran Gallery, Tenth Street Studio Building, New York. *Exhibition: Pencil and Wash Drawings by Kahlil Gibran*. January 21–March.

BIBLIOGRAPHY

Posthumous

1983 Boston Public Library. *Exhibition: Kahlil Gibran Lithographs and Photographs* from the Gibran Museum, Bcharre, Lebanon.

1989 Barbican Center, London. Exhibition presented by the British Lebanese Association: *Lebanon—The Artist's View: 200 Years of Lebanese Paintings.* April 18–June 2. Catalogue essays: "The Lebanese Vision: A History of Painting," by John Carswell, p. 11; "A Longstanding Artistic Tradition," by Camille Aboussouan, pp. 120–124.

1989 Vrej Baghoomian Gallery, New York. *Exhibition: Kahlil Gibran: Paintings and Drawings, 1905–1930.* May 25-June 25. Catalogue by Aram Saroyan.

1991 Library of Congress, Washington, D.C. Exhibit of twelve original drawings from *The Prophet.* See Jean E. Turner, *LC Information Bulletin,* Summer, May 25–June 25, p. 296.

1994 Telfair Academy of Arts and Sciences, Savannah, Georgia. *Exhibition: To Discover Beauty: The Art of Kahlil Gibran.* Aug. 24–Sept. 11.

1995 Detroit Institute of Art. *Exhibition: Speak To Us of Beauty: The Paintings and Drawings of Kahlil Gibran,* from the Telfair Academy of Arts and Sciences.

1996 UNESCO Palace, Paris. *Exhibition: The World of Kahlil Gibran: A Pictorial Record of his Life and Work.* Edited and assembled with biographical notes by S. B. Bushrui. March 19–22.

1999 Gibran Museum. *Kahlil Gibran: Horizons of the Painter.* Reproductions of over 180 images contained in the Gibran Museum collection. Beirut: Nicolas Sursock Museum.

2001 Telfair Museum of Art, Savannah, Georgia. *Exhibition: Kahlil Gibran: Artist and Visionary.* From the Permanent Collection.

2004 Kahlil Gibran Exhibit at Antiochian Heritage Museum, Bolivar, Pennsylvania.

2006 Arab American Museum, Dearborn, Michigan. *Exhibition: To Discover Beauty: The Art of Kahlil Gibran,* Selections from the Collection of the Telfair Museum of Art.

2009 Fundacion Carlos Slim, in coordination with Museo Soumaya, Mexico City. *Exhibition: Opening of exhibit,* "Gibran El Profeta." Dec. 12. Catalogue introduction by Soumaya Slim De Romero, essay by Hector Palhares Meza. http://www.cultura.gob. mx/noticias/artes-escenicas/2678-celebra-el-museo-soumaya-sus-15-anos-con-la-exposicion-&quot%3Bgibran-el-profeta&quot%3B.html.

2013 Huntington Museum of Art, Huntington, West Virginia. *Exhibition: Visions of The Prophet: The Visual Art of Kahlil Gibran,* works from the Telfair Museum.

2015 Sharjah Art Museum, United Arab Emirates. *Exhibition: Drawings of Gibran: A Humane Perspective.* October 7–December 10.

Art in Permanent Collections

Brooklyn Museum of Art
Brooklyn, New York

"The Burden" 1919, watercolor and graphite
https://www.brooklynmuseum.org/. Accessed May 12, 2016.

Harvard Art Museums
Cambridge, Massachusetts

Three drawings, "The Flame," "And the Lamb prayed in his heart," "The Slave"
http://www.harvardartmuseums.org/art/298638. Accessed February 7, 2016.

Gibran Museum
Bsharri, Lebanon

The Gibran National Committee manages this major collection, featuring 440 of the poet's paintings and drawings, his library, personal effects, and manuscripts.
http://www.gibrankhalilgibran.org/Museum/. Accessed February 7, 2016.

The Metropolitan Museum of Art
New York City

The museum's Modern and Contemporary Art Department includes five drawings and three watercolors by Gibran.
http://www.metmuseum.org/collection/the-collection-online/search?&noqs=true&ft=Kahlil+Gibran&deptids=21&pg=1. Accessed February 7, 2016.

Museo Soumaya
Mexico City

The museum includes "the personal collection of Gibran's personal objects, letters, manuscripts, annotated editions, videos, and photographs." A complete catalogue is accessible at their web site.
http://gibrankgibran.org/eng/catalogo/. Accessed February 7, 2016.

Museum of Fine Arts
Boston

The museum's printing and drawings Collection of the Americas includes 6 art works by Gibran. http://www.mfa.org/search?search_api_views_fulltext=Kahlil+Gibran. Accessed February 7, 2016.

BIBLIOGRAPHY

Newark Museum
Newark, New Jersey

The museum's drawing collection includes two works by Gibran, including "Portrait of Judge Thomas L. Raymond of Newark."
http://www.newarkmuseum.org/. Accessed May 12, 2016.

Princeton University
Princeton, New Jersey

William H. Shehadi Collection of Kahlil Gibran, in the Library Department of Rare Books and Special Collections, consists of manuscripts, photographs, and ephemera.
http://findingaids.princeton.edu/collections/C1178. Accessed Feb. 7, 2016.

Telfair Museums
Savannah, Georgia

Mary Haskell Minis donated nearly 100 works by Gibran to the art center in 1950.
http://www.telfair.org/view/collections/about-the-collections/. Accessed Feb. 7, 2016.

ARCHIVES, LETTERS, AND UNPUBLISHED MATERIAL

Austin, Texas. University of Texas at Austin. Harry Ransom Center. Alfred A. Knopf, Inc. Records, 1873-1996.

Boston, Mass. Authors' collections: copies of correspondence from Kahlil Gibran to Gertrude Barrie; copies of correspondence from Kahlil Gibran and Mikhail Naimy to Gertrude Stern; copies of letters and photos from Barbara Young to Madeleine Vanderpool, Harpursville, New York.

Cambridge, Mass. Houghton Library. Harvard University. Bynner, Witter, 1881-1968. Witter Bynner papers (MS Am 1891-1891.7)

Cambridge, Mass. Houghton Library. Harvard University. Peabody, Josephine Preston, 1874-1922. Josephine Preston Peabody papers, 1896-1924 (MS Am 1990); Josephine Preston Peabody additional papers, 1874-1922 (MS Am 2161)

Cambridge, Mass. Houghton Library. Harvard University. Robinson, Corinne Roosevelt, 1861-1933. Corinne Roosevelt Robinson papers, 1847-1933. (MS Am 1785-1785.7).

Cambridge, Mass. Schlesinger Library, Radcliffe Institute, Harvard University. Records of Denison House, 1890-1984.

Chapel Hill, N. C. University of North Carolina. Minis Family Papers, 1739–1948. The Southern Historical Collection at the Louis Round Wilson Special Collections Library, collection number 02725. This collection contains Mary Haskell's writings. Volume 32–40 and 69–71 refer to the "line-a-day" diary; volume 41—68 refer to the journal about Gibran.

Concord, Massachusetts: Concord Free Public Library. Alicia M. Keyes Papers, 1877–1941.

New Haven, Conn. Yale University. Beinecke Rare Book and Manuscript Library. Alice Raphael Papers, 1917-1977.

New Haven, Conn. Yale University. Lillian Goldman Law Library, Yale University. "The Garland Book" by Dick Cowen. (unpublished); (http://documents.law.yale.edu/sites/default/files/garland%20unpublished%20bio.pdf), accessed July 6, 2015.

BIBLIOGRAPHY

New York, N.Y., New York Public Library. Samuel Langhorne Clemens collection of papers, 1856-1938.

Statue of Liberty-Ellis Island Foundation, Inc. Passenger search. Rhame (Gibran) family arrival Ellis Island on June 17, 1895. http://www.libertyellisfoundation.org. Accessed Jan. 17, 2015.

Washington, D. C.: Manuscript Division, Library of Congress. F. Holland Day papers, 1793-2010.

Worcester, Mass. College of the Holy Cross Archives & Special Collections. Guiney Family Papers.

HERITAGE AND IMMIGRATION

Kahlil Gibran Memorial Garden by sculptor Gordon Kray, Washington, DC.
(Courtesy © Fiona Clem / dcmemorialist.com.)

American–Arab Anti-Discrimination (ADC)
Washington, DC

ADC is a civil rights organization committed to defending the rights of people of Arab descent and promoting their rich cultural heritage. Founded by former U.S. Senator James Abourezk in 1980, it is today the largest Arab American grassroots organization. Supporting the human and civil rights of all people, it sponsors the Kahlil Gibran Appreciation Initiative dedicated to furthering Gibran's legacy. http://www.adc.org/initiatives/kahlil-gibran-appreciation-initiative/. Accessed September 9, 2016.

Arab American Heritage Council
Flint, Michigan

Established in 1980, the Arab American Heritage Council preserves, celebrates, and promotes the Arab heritage and culture of Flint, Michigan, a city described by historian Hani Bawardi as "the birthplace of Arab American identity" (*The Making of Arab Americans*). The Council provides immigration, naturalization, and language services to Arab Americans and to the greater Flint community. http://www.aahcflint.org/. Accessed September 9, 2016.

Arab American Institute (AAI)
Washington, DC

Established in 1985 by James Zogby, AAI was created to nurture and encourage the direct participation of Arab Americans in political and civic life in the United States. Its affiliate, the Arab American Institute Foundation, promotes greater public awareness by serving as a national resource on the demographics, contributions, and concerns of Americans of Arab descent. It annually sponsors the Kahlil Gibran Spirit of Humanity Awards for International Commitment, Institutional Excellence, and Public Service. http://www.aaiusa.org/. Accessed September 9, 2016.

Arab American National Museum (AANM)
Dearborn, Michigan

The Arab American National Museum—along with its Russell J. Ebeid Library & Resource Center—documents, preserves, and presents the history, culture, and contributions of Arab Americans. Celebrating the ways that Americans of Arab descent have enriched the economic, political, and cultural landscape of American life, AANM is the first and only museum in the U.S. devoted to Arab American history and culture. By bringing the voices and faces of Arab Americans to mainstream audiences, the museum dispels misconceptions about Arab Americans and other minorities. Since opening in 2005, the Museum has shed light on the shared experiences of immigrants and ethnic groups, paying tribute to the diversity of our nation. http://www.arabamericanmuseum.org/. Accessed September 9, 2016.

Faris and Yamna Naff Family Arab American Collection
Smithsonian Institution, Washington, DC

In the summer of 1962, Alixa Naff began recording oral histories of the early generations of immigrants to America from the Middle East, collecting photos and family memorabilia as she traveled the country in her blue Volkswagen beetle ("the camel"). Over five decades, Naff's labors would lead to a collection of 450 oral histories, 500 artifacts, and over 2,000 photos, as well as articles, newspapers, and books on the experience of Arabs in America, on topics ranging from conflict, exile, and discrimination; to the role of women, family life, work and achievement; to the Doumars of Norfolk, Virginia, legendary for inventing the ice cream cone. Named for her parents and now permanently housed at the Archives Center, National Museum of American History, this legacy bequeathed by "the mother of Arab American studies" is a treasure trove of the memory, history, and dignity of immigrants to America from the Middle East. http://www.sova.si/edu/record/NMAH.AC.0078. Accessed September 9, 2016.

The George and Lisa Zakhem Kahlil Gibran Chair for Values and Peace
University of Maryland, College Park

The Kahlil Gibran Chair for Values and Peace is an endowed academic program that strengthens understanding between Eastern and Western cultures in general, and the Arab ethos and American values in particular. Lebanese poet and scholar Kahlil Gibran dedicated his life and works to demonstrating the importance of universal values, the interconnectedness of religions, common ground among cultures, the importance of dialogue, and the goodness of humanity as a whole. He believed the more we explore our interconnectedness as humans, the more we understand and respect the universal values that underpin different cultures. Gibran wrote about and advocated for social justice, freedoms, equality, unity and peace.

Director May Rihani joined the Gibran Chair in May 2016. Ms. Rihani works to expand upon the legacy and foundation created by the Chair's inaugural incumbent, Professor Suheil Bushrui. The Gibran Chair's active program addresses major global topics such as: Studying the Pursuit of Peace; Exploring Paths toward Peace; Examining Common Ground; Understanding Cultural Pluralism; Highlighting the Contributions of Women toward Peace; Deepening Cross-Cultural Understanding; Transcending the Barriers of East and West; Revisiting Poetry, Literature and Art as Connectors within the Global Village; and Celebrating Universal Values. This program is implemented through research, lectures, seminars, workshops, symposia, conferences, and academic publications. http://www.gibranchair.umd.edu/#. Accessed September 9, 2016.

Immigration History Research Center (IHRC)
University of Minnesota, Minneapolis

Founded in 1965, IHRC aims to transform the way in which we understand immigration in the past and present. Along with its partner, the IHRC Archives (University Libraries), it is the oldest and largest interdisciplinary research center and archives devoted to preserving and understanding immigrant and refugee life in North America. The Center promotes interdisciplinary research on migration, race, and ethnicity in the United States and the world through monthly seminars and research grants. It connects U.S. immigration history research to contemporary immigrant and refugee communities through our Immigrant Stories project. It advances public dialogue about immigration with timely programs that draw audiences from around the corner and around the world. It supports teaching and learning at all levels, and develop archives documenting immigrant and refugee experiences for future generations. https://www.cla.umn.edu/ihrc. Accessed September 9, 2016.

Lebanese Emigration Research Center
Notre Dame University, Louaize, Lebanon

The Center is dedicated to the study of migration, global identity, ancestral roots, and genealogical heritage. The Center's Lebanon Migration Nucleus Museum provides a window into the historical and contemporary experience of emigrants to very different parts of the globe. Photographs, artwork, documents, and a variety of cultural items enrich the stories of communities and families in the diaspora. Rare items are displayed from the LERC Archives, the Lebanese National Archives, and private collections. https://www.cla.umn.edu/ihrc. Accessed September 9, 2016.

BIBLIOGRAPHY

Lebanese Syrian Ladies' Aid Society
Boston

Records of the Lebanese Syrian Ladies' Aid Society, 1917–2005, Schlesinger Library, Radcliffe Institute, Harvard University. This invaluable collection includes minutes, correspondence, financial records, printed material, photographs, memorabilia, etc., from the Senior and Junior chapters of the Lebanese Syrian Ladies' Aid Society in Boston. https://oasis.lib.harvard.edu/oasis/deliver/~sch01178. Accessed September 9, 2016.

Moise A. Khayrallah Center for Lebanese Diaspora Studies
North Carolina State University, Raleigh, North Carolina

The Khayrallah Center is a research and outreach center for the production and dissemination of knowledge about the Lebanese Diaspora in the United States and throughout the world. The Center fosters new scholarship on the historical and contemporary Lebanese Diaspora. Its activities include: a biennial conference on the Lebanese Diaspora; a post-doctoral fellowship in Lebanese diaspora studies; funding for visits for affiliated scholars from across the world; an online digital research archive for the history of the Lebanese in the United States; and the journal, *Mashriq & Mahjar*, dedicated to Middle East diaspora studies. The Center supports, produces, and disseminates public history projects, including work by public history students; video productions; museum exhibits; K-12 curriculum development; the training of volunteers to collect oral histories; and an annual artistic production. The Center believes that the best way to knowledge and learning about the Lebanese Diaspora is through collaborative projects with individuals, organizations, and other research institutes. http://www.lebanesestudies.ncsu.edu/about/. Accessed September 9, 2016.

Washington Street Historical Society (WSHS)
Lower Manhattan, New York

Washington Street Historical Society fosters education and awareness about the history of immigration to the Washington Street neighborhood of the financial district of Lower Manhattan. Also known historically as the Lower West Side, the area was once the center of Arab life in the United States, and from the 1880s to the 1940s referred to as the "Mother Colony"—or "Little Syria." Founded by Carl Antoun and Todd Fine, and sustained by a board of dedicated local history and neighborhood preservation activists, the Society maintains artifact collections; works to install plaques, memorials, and signs in the neighborhood; supports local historic preservation campaigns; and advances independent historical research. WSHS welcomes contact and collaboration from media, scholars, artists, students, and other interested parties to help tell the story of this vital part of New York City and locus of the cultural memory of immigrants to America from the Middle East. http://www.savewashingtonstreet.org. Accessed September 9, 2016.

GENERAL SOURCES

'Abbud, Marun. *Judud wa Qudama': Dirasat, Naqd wa Munaqashat* [Grandparents and veterans: surveys/studies, criticism, and discussions]. Beirut: Dar al-Thaqafah, 1954.

———. *Mujaddidun wa Mujtarrun* [Renovations and ruminants]. Beirut: Dar al-Thaqafah, 1961.

———. *Ruwwad al-Nahdah al-Hadithah* [The pioneers of the modern Renaissance]. Beirut: Dar al-Thaqafah, 1966.

Abdulrazak, Fawzi. "Adab al-Mahjar: Bibliyugrhrafiyah." *Mundus Arabicus* 1 (1981): 89–230.

Abrahams, Edward. *The Lyrical Left: Randolph Bourne, Alfred Stieglitz and the Origins of Cultural Radicalism in America.* Charlottesville: University of Virginia Press, 1986.

Abroad in America: Visitors to the New Nation 1776–1914. Edited and with an introduction by Marc Pachter, Marc, and co-edited by Frances Wein Boston: Addison Wesley Publishing, 1976.

Acocella, Joan. "Prophet Motive: The Kahlil Gibran Phenomenon." *New Yorker,* January 7, 2008.

Adams, J. Donald. "Speaking of Books." *New York Times,* September 29, 1957.

Adler, Renata. "The Screen: 'Life is a Feather,' the Wise Man Said." Review of *Broken Wings. New Yorker,* March 16, 1968.

Allen, Henry. "President Bush and the People's Kinder, Gentler Poet," *Washington Post,* May 25, 1991, D1, D4.

Allen, Roger, and Hilary Kilpatrick and Ed de Moor, eds. *Love and Sexuality in Modern Arabic Literature.* London: Saqi Books, 1995.

Amirani, Shoku, and Stephanie Hegarty. "Kahlil Gibran's The Prophet: Why is it so loved?" *BBC World Service,* May 12, 2012. Accessed April 7, 2015. http://www.bbc.com/news/magazine-17997163.

Anderson, Scott. "The Arab American Identity was Born in Flint: Scholar Shows Research in Exhibit at Sloan Museum." Accessed March 14, 2016. http://www.mlive.com/entertainment/flint/index.ssf/2014/01/dearborn_scholar_argues_the_ar.html.

Ansara, James Michael. "The Immigration and Settlement of the Syrians." Thesis, Harvard University, 1931.

Antonius, George. *The Arab Awakening.* 1938. Reprint, London: Hamish Hamilton, 1945.

al-'Aqqad, 'Abbas Mahmud. *Al-Fusul* [The seasons]. Beirut: Dar al-Kitab al-'Arabi, 1967.

Aramco World. "A Land, a Poet, a Festival." *Aramco World* 21, no. 4 (July/August 1970).

Arida, Holly, and Richard Allen Popp. "Writing Together: Two Generations Of Arab Americans Serve The Public Purpose." *Al Jadid* 16, no. 63 (2010): 6–9. www.ALJADID.com.

Arnett, Mary Flounders. "Marie Ziyada." *Council for Middle Eastern Affairs* 7 (1957): 288–294.

Aslan, Reza. "Collection Spans Modern Mideast's Literary Landscapes." By Renee Montagne. *National Public Radio* (Fall 2010). Accessed April 3, 2015. http://www.npr.org/templates/story/story.php?storyId=131208970.

Aslan, Reza. *Tablet and Pen: Literary Landscapes from the Modern Middle East*. New York: W. W. Norton, 2011.

Assad, Carlos Martinez. "Gibran: Child of the Cedars." *Academic Review* (2012).

"Awards and other news." Poetry Society of America, May 1931. Roerich Museum tribute, p. 6. and Gibran obituary, p. 12.

Badawi, M. M. *A Critical Introduction to Modern Arabic Poetry*. Cambridge: Cambridge University Press, 1975.

Badi Bushrui, Suheil, and Salma Haffar al-Kuzbari, eds., trans. *Blue Flame: The Love Letters of Kahlil Gibran to May Ziadeh*. New York: Longman, 1983.

Badran, Margo. *Feminists, Islam, and Nation: Gender and the Making of Modern Egypt*. Princeton: Princeton University Press, 1996.

Bawardi, Hani J. *The Making of Arab Americans: From Syrian Nationalism to U.S. Citizenship*. Austin: University of Texas Press, 2014.

BBC World Service. "The Man Behind the Prophet." Aired May 5, 2012. Accessed April 7, 2015. http://www.bbc.co.uk/programmes/p00r49dp.

Bercovici, Konrad. *Around the World in New York*. New York: Century, 1924. First published as "The Syrian Quarter." *Century Magazine* 86 (1924): 354.

Beshara, Adel. *Origins of Syrian Nationhood: Histories, Pioneers, and Identity*. London: Routledge, 2011.

Blau, Evelyne. *Krishnamurti: 100 Years*. New York: Stewart, Tabori & Chang, 1995.

Bliss, Frederick Jones. *The Religions of Modern Syria and Palestine*. New York: Scribner, 1912.

Bloom, Harold, and Jesse Zuba, eds. *American Religious Poems*. New York: Literary Classics of the United States, 2006.

Boston Daily Globe. "Artists' big loss, work of many years wiped out by flames. Value of Harcourt Building Studio contents put at $200,000." November 13, 1904.

Boston Evening Transcript. "Obituaries, Tributes, and Accounts of Burial in Besharri." April 14, 1931.

Boston Globe. "Gibran's Legacy of Love is Twisted by His People into Hatred and War." December 14, 1972.

Bragdon, Claude. *Merely Players*. New York: Knopf. 1929.

———. "A Modern Prophet from Lebanon." *New York Herald Tribune*, December 23, 1928.

———. *More Lives Than One*. New York: Knopf, 1937.

Braithwaite, William Stanley, ed. *Anthology of Magazine Verse for 1919 and Yearbook for American Poetry*. Boston: Small, Maynard, 1919.

[Braithwaite, Willliam Stanley], "The Lutanists of November. Three Books of Selections by Makers of Poetry." *Boston Evening Transcript*, November 3, 1920.

Brangwyn, John [Charlotte Teller]. *Everybody's Paris*. New York: R. M. McBride, 1935.

———. *Reasons for France*. London: Bodley Head, 1939.

Brockelmann, C. *Geschichte der arabischen Litteratur. Supp. vol. 3*. Leiden: E. J. Brill, 1942.

Brown, Milton W. *The Story of the Armory Show*. New York: Joseph H. Hirshhorn Foundation, 1963.

Buck, Christopher. "Kahlil Gibran." In *American Writers: A Collection of Literary Biographies*, edited by Jay Parini, 113-129. Detroit: Charles Scribner's Sons, 2010.

Bush, George H. W. *Public Papers of the Presidents of the United States: George H. W. Bush, 1991, Book I—May 24, 1991, 556–557*. Washington, DC: Government Printing Office, 1991. Accessed April 7, 2015. http://www.gpo.gov/fdsys/pkg/PPP-1991-book1/html/PPP-1991-book1-doc-pg556.htm.

Bushrui, Suheil. *An Introduction to Kahlil Gibran*. Beirut: Gibran International Festival, 1970.

———, *Kahlil Gibran of Lebanon*. Gerrard's Cross, England: Colin Smythe, 1987.

———, and Joe Jenkins. *Kahlil Gibran: Man and Poet*. Oxford: Oneworld, 1998.

———, and Tania June Sammons. *The Art of Kahlil Gibran at Telfair Museums*. Georgia: Telfair Books, 2010.

al-Bustani, Fu'ad. " 'Ala Dhikr Jubran" [Gibran remembered]. *Al-Mashriq* 37 (1939): 241–268.

al-Bustani, Fu'ad, and Edward Sa'b. "Bayn al-Mashriq wa al-Sa'ih" [Between the Orient and as-Sayeh, the traveler]. *Al-Mashriq* 21 (1923): 910–919.

Bynner, Witter. *Selected Letters: The Works of Witter Bynner*. Edited and with an introduction by James Kraft. New York: Farrar, Strauss & Giroux, 1981.

———. "Kahlil the Gibranite." In *The Borzoi: Being a Sort of Record of Ten Years of Publishing*, edited by Alfred A. Knopf, 43–46. New York: Alfred A. Knopf, 1925.

———. *Selected Poems: The Works of Witter Bynner*. With introductions by Richard Wilbur and James Kraft. New York: Farrar, Strauss & Giroux, 1978.

Campbell, Robert. "The Newest Copley Square Is Better But…" *Boston Sunday Globe*, June 11, 1989.

Carne, John. *Syria, the Holy Land*. London: Fisher, 1836.

Chandler, Paul-Gordon. "Behind Egypt's Revolution. Away from news cameras, Christian, Muslim youth rediscover common ground." *Christianity Today*, March 7, 2011. Accessed April 2, 2015. http://www.christianitytoday.com/ct/2011/marchweb-only/behindegyptrevolution.html.

———. "Behind Egypt's Revolution." *Christianity Today*, March 7, 2011. Accessed April 2, 2015. http://www.christianitytoday.com/ct/2011/marchweb-only/behindegyptrevolution.html.

Chapin, Louis. "Another Side of Gibran." *Christian Science Monitor*, February 7, 1973.

Chaudhuri, Indrani Datta. "The 'Blue Flame': An 'Elliptical' Interaction between Kahlil Gibran and Rabindranath Tagore" *Rupkatha Journal on Interdisciplinary Studies in Humanity* 2, no. 2 (June 2010). Accessed April 6, 2015. http://rupkatha.com/V2/n2/KahlilGibranandRabindranathTagore.pdf.

Cheikho, Louis. "Bada'i' Jubran Kahlil Jubran wa Tara'ifuh" [Wonders and anecdotes of Gibran Kahlil Gibran]. *Al-Mashriq* 21 (1923): 487–493.

———. "Difa' al-Sa'ih 'an Jubran Khalil Jubran" [*As-Sayeh*'s defense of Gibran Kahlil Gibran]. *Al-Mashriq* 21 (1923): 876–877.

Clattenburg, Ellen Fritz. *The Photographic Works of F. Holland Day*. Wellesley, MA: Wellesley College Museum, 1975.

Clements, Amy Root. *The Art of Prestige: the Formative Years of Knopf, 1915-1929*. Amherst, MA: University of Massachusetts Press, 2014.

Colby, Nathalie Sedgwick. *Remembering*. Boston: Little, Brown, 1938.

Cole, Juan. "Kahlil Gibran Page." http://www-personal.umich.edu/~jrcole/gibran/gibran1.htm.

Cole, William I. *Immigrant Races in Massachusetts: The Syrians*. Boston: Massachusetts Department of Education, n.d., ca. 1919.

Cook, Howard Willard. *Johan Bojer: His Life and His Works*. Translated by Elizabeth Jelliffe MacIntire, with an introduction by Carl Gad. New York: Moffat, Yard, 1920.

———. "Kahlil Gibran, Poet of the East." *New York Sun Books and Book World*, December 15, 1918.

———. *Our Poets Today*. New York: Moffat, Yard, 1923.

Cooley, John K. "A Man with a Flair in His Soul." *Christian Science Monitor*, June 4, 1970.

Cotter, Holland. "A Photography Pioneer, Semi-Obscure no More." *New York Times*, February 25, 2001.

Cowen, Dick. "The Garland Book." Unpublished manuscript tracking Marie Tudor Garland's family history. Available online at http://documents.law.yale.edu/sites/default/files/garland%20unpublished%20bio.pdf.

Cram, Ralph Adams. *My Life in Architecture*. Boston: Little, Brown, 1936.

Crosby, Katherine K. "How Boston Syrians Make Themselves Real Americans: Glimpses of Home Life in the Colonies Where 'Aristocrats of the Immigrants' with 6000 Years of High Civilization Behind Them, Became Settled Citizens of the Hub." *Boston Herald*, November 2, 1924.

Daghir, Yusuf. *Masadir al-Dirasah al-Adabiyah* [Sources of literary studies]. Beirut: Manshurat Ahl al-Qalam, 1956.

Dalrymple, William. *From the Holy Mountain: A Journey among the Christians of the Middle East*. New York: Henry Holt, 1999.

Daly, Louise Haskell. *Alexander Cheves Haskell: The Portrait of a Man*. Norwood, MA: Plimpton Press, 1934.

Daoudi, M. S. *The Meaning of Kahlil Gibran*. Secaucus, NJ: Citadel Press, 1982.

Davis, William A. "Gibran's 'The Prophet' spells profit in Besharre." *Boston Globe*, August 5, 1973.

Ditelberg, Joshua Lee. "Kahlil Gibran's Early Intellectual Life, 1883–1908." Master's thesis, University of Pennsylvania, 1987.

Doty, Robert M. *Photo-Secession: Photography as a Fine Art*. New York: George Eastman House, 1960.

Eldredge, Charles C. *American Imagination and Symbolist Painting*. New York: Grey Art Gallery at New York University, 1980.

Fadda-Conrey, Carol. *Contemporary Arab-American Literature*. New York: New York University Press, 2014.

Fairbanks Trevor, *Making a Presence: F. Holland Day in Artistic Photography*. Andover: Addison Gallery of American Art, 2012

Fahrenthold, Stacy. "Transnational Modes and Media: The Syrian Press in the Mahjar and Emigrant Activism During World War I." *Mashriq & Mahjar* (2013): 30-54.

Fanning, Patricia J. *Artful Lives: The Francis Watts Lee Family & Their Times*. Amherst: University of Massachusetts Press, 2016.

———. *Through an Uncommon Lens: The Life and Photography of F. Holland Day*. Amherst: University of Massachusetts Press, 2008.

Firanescu, Daniela Rodica, "Renewing thought from exile: Gibran and the New Era." *Synergies Monde Arabe* 8 (2011): 67–80.

Fleischer, Charles. *American Aspirations*. New York: B.W. Huebsch, 1914.

Forgey, Benjamin, "The Memorial: Oasis From the Din," *Washington Post,* May 25, 1991, D1, D4.

Freches-Thory, Claire and Antoine Terrasse. *The Nabis: Bonnard, Vuillard, and Their Circle*. New York: Abrams, 1991.

Free Religious Association of America, Proceedings of the Annual Meeting. Boston: May 1912.

Freeland, Elana. "Kahlil Gibran on Kahlil Gibran." *East West Journal* (February 1975): 36.

Al-Funun. "Kalimah 'an Udaba' al-Funun" [A word on the literary figures of al-Funun] September 1916.

Gad, Carl. *Johan Bojer, The Man and His Works*. With an introduction by Howard Willard Cook. New York: Moffat, Yard, 1920.

———. *Johan Bojer: The Man And His Works*. New York: Moffatt, Yard, 1920.

Gail, Marziah. "Juliet Remembers Gibran." *World Order* 12, no. 4 (1978): 29–31.

Geagea, Agnatiyus [Ja'ja', Agnatiyus]. "Bisharri Madinat al-Muqaddamin" [Bshirri, city of ancients]. *Al-Mashriq* 30 (1932): 464–469, 538–544, 685–691, 779–787.

"Gertrude Käsebier (1852-1934)." The Library of Congress Prints & Photographs Reading Room. http://www.loc.gov/rr/print/coll/womphotoj/kasebieressay.html. Accessed September 18, 2015.

Ghougassian, Joseph P. *Wings of Thought: Kahlil Gibran, the People's Philosopher*. New York: Philosophical Library, 1973.

al-Ghurayyib, Khalil. "Dhikrayat Jubran, al-Rihana, Rustum, Mukarzil, al-Ghurayyib" [Memories of Gibran, Rihani, Rustum, Mokarzel, Gharayyib]. *Awraq Lubnaniyah,* January (1958): 6–10.

————, "Ma'rakat al-Ta'n al-Samit bayn Jubran wa As'ad Rustum" [The silent battles between Gibran and As'ad Rustum]. *Awraq Lubnanlyah,* February (1958): 56–63.

————, "Min Mudhakkarat al-Rassam Khalil al-Ghurayyib 'an Zamilih Jubran Khalil Jubran" [From the diary of painter Khalil al-Ghurayyib about his friend Gibran Kahlil Gibran]. *Al-Baidar,* January 31, (1960): 14–15.

Ghurayyib, Rose. *Jubran fi Atharih al-Kitabiyah* [Gibran in his own words]. Beirut: Dar al-Makshuf, 1969.

Gibb, H. A. R. "Studies in Contemporary Arabic Literature I–IV." *Bulletin of The School of Oriental Studies* 4 (1926): 745–760.

Gibran, Jean, and Kahlil Gibran. *Kahlil Gibran His Life and World.* With a new introduction by the authors and a foreword by Salma Khadra Jayyusi. New York: Interlink Books, 1991. First published 1974 by New York Graphic Society.

————. "The Symbolic Quest of Kahlil Gibran: The Arab as Artist in America." In *Crossing the Waters: Arabic-Speaking Immigrants to the United States before 1940*, edited by Eric James Hoogland. Washington, DC: Smithsonian Institution Press, 1987.

Gollomb, Joseph. "An Arabian Poet in New York." *New York Evening Post*, March 29, 1919.

Goode, James, M. Washington Sculpture: *A Cultural History of Outdoor Sculpture in the Nation's Capital.* Baltimore: Johns Hopkins University Press, 2009.

al Ghurayyib, Amin [Ghorayeb]. "Jubran Khalil Jubran." *Al-Haris* 8 (1931): 689–704.

————. "Mahrajan Jubran fi Lubnan" [Gibran's festival in Lebanon]. *al-Haris* 9 (1931): 139–147.

Grover, Edwin. *Osgood, ed. Annals of an Era. Percy MacKaye and the MacKaye Family 1826–1932.* Washington, DC: Pioneer Press, 1932.

Gualtieri, Sarah M. A. *Between Arab and White: Race and Ethnicity in the Early Syrian American Diaspora.* Oakland: University of California Press, 2009.

Guerrieri, Matthew. "Combined choirs deliver a stellar Son of Man." *Boston Globe*, May 17, 2011.

Guiney, Louise Imogen. *Letters.* Edited by Grace Guiney. 2 vols. New York: Harper, 1926.

Guthrie. William Norman. *Modern Poet Prophets: Essays Critical and Interpretative.* Cincinnati: R. Clarke, 1897.

El Hage, George Nicolas. *Gibran Kahlil Gibran: The Man Versus the Legend.* Printed by Createspace Independent Publishing Platform, 2014.

————. *William Blake & Kahlil Gibran: Poets of Prophetic Vision.* Louaize, Lebanon: Notre Dame University Press, 2002.

Hamilton, Jean. "Woman's Influence is to be Found Somewhere Behind All the Creations of Man Throughout the Centuries." *New York Evening Sun*, December 28, 1914.

Hamsum, Knut. *Hunger.* Translated by Robert Bly. New York: Farrar, Straus & Giroux, 2008. First published 1890.

————. *Hunger.* Translated by Robert Bly. New York: Farrar, Straus & Giroux, 2008.

Hamza, Dyala. *The Making of the Arab Intellectual: Empire, Public Sphere and the Colonial Coordinates of Selfhood.* London: Routledge, 2013.

Hanna, Suhail ibn-Salim. "Gibran and Whitman: Their Literary Dialogue." *Literature East and West* 12 (December 1968): 174–198.

Harte Jerusalem, A. C. "Burial of a Poet." *Christian Century* 48 (1931): 1212.

Hassan, Wail S. "Gibran and Orientalism." In *Arab Voices in Diaspora: Critical Perspectives on Anglophone Arab Literature*, edited by Layla Al Maleh. New York: Rodopi, 2009.

Hassoun, Rosina. "Arab-American Health and the Process of Coming to America." In *Arabs in America: Building a New Future*, edited by Michael Suleiman. Philadelphia: Temple University Press, 1999.

Huwayyik, Yusuf [Howayek, Youssef]. *Dhikrayati ma' Jubran, Baris 1905–1910* [Some of my memories of Gibran, Paris, 1905–1910]. Edited by Edvic Shaybub. Beirut: Dar al-Ahad, n.d.

Hawi, Khalil S. *Kahlil Gibran: His Background, Character and Works*. Beirut: Arab Institute for Research and Publishing, 1972.

Al-Hilal. Review of *The Broken Wings*. *Al-Hilal* 20 (1912): 383.

Hill, Hamlin. *Mark Twain: God's Fool*. New York: Harper Row, 1973.

Hillyer, Robert. "Three Ornamented Parables." Review of *Nymphs of the Valley* by Kahlil Gibran. *New York Times*, April 18, 1948.

———. "Thoughts of a Mystic." *New York Times*, April 3, 1949.

Hilu, Virginia, ed. *Beloved Prophet: The Love Letters of Kahlil Gibran and Mary Haskell and Her Private Journal*. New York: Knopf, 1972.

Hinkle, Beatrice M. *The Recreating of the Individual*. New York: Dodd, Mead, 1923.

Hishmeh, Richard E. "Strategic Genius, Disidentification, and the Burden of The Prophet in Arab-American Poetry." In *Arab Voices in Diaspora: Critical Perspectives on Anglophone Arab Literature*, edited by Layla Al Maleh. New York: Rodopi, 2009.

History Project. *Improper Bostonians*. Foreword by Barney Frank. Boston: Beacon Press, 1998.

Hitti, P. K. "Tributes to Gibran, Gibran's Place and Influence in Modern Arabic Literature." *Syrian World*, 3, no. 8 (February 1929): 30–32.

Hitti, Philip K. *Lebanon in History: From the Earliest Times to the Present*. London: Macmillan, 1957.

Al-Hoda 1898–1968: The Story of Lebanon and Its Emigrants Taken from the Newspaper Al-Hoda. New York: Al-Hoda Press, 1968.

Hoffman, Frederick J., and Charles Allen and Carolyn F. Ulrich. *The Little Magazine: A History and a Bibliography*. Princeton: Princeton University Press, 1946.

Holman, Louis and Ferris Greenslet. *The Life of Fred Holland Day*. TS manuscript. Library of Congress.

Hooglund, Eric J., ed. *Crossing the Waters: Arabic-speaking Immigrants to the United States before 1940*. Washington, DC: Smithsonian Institution Press, ca. 1987. http://gibrankgibran.org/eng/revision-teorica/gibran-el-hijo-de-los-cedros/.

IOL News. "Mandela funeral: rolling updates." Last modified December 15, 2013. Accessed April 2, 2015. http://www.iol.co.za/news/south-africa/eastern-cape/mandela-funeral-rolling-updates-1.1622772#.VR6F_CiSKCc.

'Intabi, Fu'ad. "Jubran wa Atharuh fi al-Adab al-'Arabi" [Gibran and his impact on Arabic literature]. *Al-'Irfan* 17 (1929): 337–341.

Irwin, Robert. "I Am a False Alarm." Reviews of *Kahlil Gibran: Man and Poet* by Suheil Bushrui and Joe Jenkins, and *Prophet: The Life and Times Kahlil Gibran* by Robin Waterfield. *London Review of Books* (September 1998): 17.

Jabir, Jamil. "Gibran's Message: the Essential Unity of Mankind." *Hongkong Standard*, September 13, 1984.

———. *Jubran, Siratuh, Adabuh, Falsafatuh wa Rasmuh* [Gibran: his biography, literature, philosophy, and painting]. Beirut: Dar al-Rihani, 1958.

———. *Mayy wa Jubran* [May Ziade and Gibran]. Beirut: Dar al-Jamal, 1950.

Jacobs, Leonebel. *Portraits of Thirty Authors*. New York: Charles Scribner's Sons, 1937.

Jacobs, Linda K. *Strangers in the West: The Syrian Colony of New York City, 1880–1900*. New York: Kalimah Press, 2015.

Jayyusi, Salma Khadra. *Modern Arabic Poetry: An Anthology*. New York: Columbia University Press, 1987.

———. *Trends and Movements in Modern Arabic Poetry*. Leiden: E. J. Brill, 1977.

Jessup, Henry Harris. *Syrian Home-Life*. Compiled by Isaac Riley. New York: Dodd, Mead, 1874.

John, Divya. "The Cybernetics of Love: A Study of Kahlil Gibran." Thesis, University of Calicut in India, 2007.

Johnny Cash Infocenter. "Favorite Books of the Man in Black." Posted by Jeff Emond. Last modified December 30, 2014. Accessed April 6, 2015. http://www.johnny-cash-infocenter.com/Articles/johnny-cash-s-favorite-books.html.

Jonathan Yardley. "The Eternal Kahlil Gibran." *Washington Post*, October 8, 1984.

Jones, Kenneth. "Sons of the Prophet, Dark Comedy About Pain, Loss and Legacy, Ends Off-Broadway Run; Is Broadway Next?" *Playbill*, January 1, 2012. Accessed April 7, 2015. http://www.playbill.com/news/article/sons-of-the-prophet-dark-comedy-about-pain-loss-and-legacy-ends-off-broadwa-186002.

Journeys in Film. "The Prophet." Accessed July 2015. http://journeysinfilm.org/films/the-prophet/.

Jussim, Estelle. *A Slave to Beauty: The Eccentric Life and Controversial Career of F. Holland Day: Photographer, Publisher, Esthete*. Boston: David R. Godine, 1981.

Kanfer, Stefan. "But Is It Not Strange That Even Elephants Will Yield-and That The Prophet is Still Popular?" *New York Times Magazine*, June 25, 1972.

Karam, Antoine G. "Gibran's Concept of Modernity." In *Tradition and Modernity in Arabic Literature*, edited by Issa J. Boullata and Terri DeYoung. Fayetteville: University of Arkansas Press, 1997.

————. Unpublished review of *Kahlil Gibran: His Life and World* by Jean Gibran. c. 1973. Author's collection.

Karam, Antun Ghattas. *Muhadarat fi Jubran Khalil Jubran* [Lectures about Gibran Kahlil Gibran]: Ma'had al-Dirasat al-'Arabiyah, 1964.

Karam, Nicoletta. "Kahlil Gibran's 'Pen Bond': Modernism and the Manhattan Renaissance of Arab-American Literature." Ph.D dissertation, Brandeis University, 2005.

Karamah, Nabil. *Jubran Khalil Jubran wa Atharuh fi al-Adab al-'Arabi* [Gibran Kahlil Gibran and his impact on Arabic literature]. Beirut: Dar al-Rabitah al-Thaqafiyah, 1964.

Käsebier, Gertrude. *The Photographer and Her Photographs.* New York: H. N. Abrams, 1992.

Kemp, Ted. "Carlos Slim Reads One of His Favorite Poets." By Michelle Caruso-Cabrera. *CNBC Telecom.* Accessed April 8, 2015. http://www.cnbc.com/id/100804725?__source=fincont&par=fincont.

Kennedy, Edward. *Decisions for a Decade.* New York: Doubleday, 1968.

Keyes, Helen Johnson. Review of *The Book of Khalid* by Ameen Rihani. *The Bookman* 34 (1911): 438–439.

Al-Khazraji, Nidaa Hussain Fahmi, and Mardziah Hayati Abdullah and Wong Bee Eng. "Universal Themes and Messages in Gibran's *The Prophet.*" Special issue, *Arab World English Journal* 1 (2013). Accessed June 13, 2015. http://www.awej.org/index.php?option=com_content&view=article&id=374:nidaa-hussain-fahmi-al-khazraji-mardziah-hayati-abdullah-wong-bee-eng&catid=43:special-issue-on-literature&Itemid=138.

Kheirallah, G. *The Life of Gibran Khalil Gibran and His Procession.* With an introduction by William Catzeflis. New York: Arab-American Press, 1947.

Khuri, Alfred. *Al-Kalimah al-'Arabiyah fi al-Mahjar* [The Arabic word in the diaspora]. Beirut: Dar al-Rihani, n.d.

Khuri, Ra'if. "Jubran Khalil Jubran." *Al-Tariq* 3 (1944): 4–5.

Kickme, Vellum. "Offered Az Iz Beloved: Do we have a female literary vamp in our midst?" *The Biblio* 1 (May 1922): 226–227.

King, Alexander. "Profiles: Kewpie Doll." *New Yorker* (1934): 22–26.

Knopf, Alfred A. *Portrait of a Publisher, 1915–1965: Reminiscences and Reflections.* 2 vols. New York: The Typophiles, 1965.

————. *Sixty Photographs. To Celebrate The Sixtieth Anniversary of Alfred A. Knopf, Publisher.* New York: Alfred A. Knopf, 1975.

————. *Some Random Recollections: An Informal Talk Made at The Grolier Club, 21 October 1948.* New York: The Typophiles, 1949.

Krachkovsky, Ignaty. "Die Literatur der arabischen Emigranten in Amerika (1895–1915)." *Le Monde Oriental* 21 (1927): 193–213.

Kraus, Joe Walker. "A History of Copeland & Day (1893–1899); with a Bibliographical Checklist of Their Publications." Master's thesis, University of Illinois, 1941.

————. *Messrs. Copeland & Day, 69 Cornhill, Boston 1893–1899.* Philadelphia: George S. MacManus, 1979.

Krishnamurti, Jiddu. *The Immortal Friend*. New York: Boni & Liveright, 1928.

Kuehl, Linda. "Talk With Mr. Knopf." *New York Times*, February 24, 1974.

Kunitz, Stanley J. *Twentieth Century Authors: A Biographical Dictionary*. New York: H. W. Wilson, 1967.

"The Last Days of Gibran." *Syrian World* 5 (April 1931): 21.

Lecerf, Jean. "Djabran Khalil Djabran et les origines de la prose poétique moderne." *Orient* 3 (July 1957): 7–14.

———. "The Lounger." *The Critic* no. 841 (April 1898): 232.

Literary Digest. "Syrians in the United States." 61 (May 3, 1919): 43.

Lockwood, Laura E. "A Christmas Mystery Play at Denison House." *The Survey: Social, Charitable, Civic: A Journal of Constructive Philanthropy* 10 (1912): 309–310.

Longrigg, Stephen Hemsley. *Syria and Lebanon under French Mandate*. New York: Oxford University Press, 1958.

Ludescher, Tanyss Carol. "'The Orient is Ill': Kahlil Gibran and the Politics of Nationalism in the New York Syrian Colony 1908-1920." Ph.D dissertation, University of Connecticut, 2010.

Luxner, Larry. "A Garden for Gibran." *Aramco World* (March/April 1990): 2–5.

Lystra, Karen. *Dangerous Intimacy: The Untold Story of Mark Twain's Final Years*. Berkeley: University of California Press, 2004.

Madey, Elia D. "Jubran Tahta Mabadi 'al-Nu'ayma'" [Gibran under the principles of "al-Nu'ayma"]. *As-Sameer* 18 (January 15, 1935): 17–23.

Majallat al-Majma'al-'Rmial-'Arab. Review of *The Madman*. 14 (1924): 468–69.

Majdoubeh, Ahmad Y. "Gibran's 'The Procession' in the Transcendentalist Context." *Arabic* 49, no. 4 (October 2002): 477–493. http://www.jstor.org/stable/4057703.

Majmu'at al-Rabitah al-Qalamiyah li Sanat 1921 [The Pen League group, 1921]. Beirut: Dar Sadir, 1964.

Al Maleh, Layla, ed. *Arab Voices in Diaspora: Critical Perspectives on Anglophone Arab Literature*. New York: Rodopi, 2009.

Mann, Arthur. "Charles Fleischer's Religion of Democracy: An Experiment in American Faith." *Commentary* 17 (1954): 561, 564.

Marshall, Marguerite Mooers. "Set Womankind Free and There'll Be No War, Says Oriental Painter, Born on Mt. Lebanon." *Buffalo Times*, December 15, 1914.

Al-Mashriq. Review of *The Broken Wings*. *Al-Mashriq* 15 (1912): 315–336.

———. Review of *The Madman*. *Al-Mashriq* 22 (1924): 555.

———. Review of *The Procession*. *Al-Mashriq* 22 (1924): 75.

———. Review of *The Prophet*. *Al-Mashriq* 24 (1926): 633.

Mas'ud, Habib, ed. *Jubran Hayyan wa Mayyitan* [Gibran alive and dead]. Sao Paulo, 1932.

Mason, Daniel Gregory. *Music in My Time and Other Reminiscences*. New York: Macmillan, 1938.

May, Antoinette. *Passionate Pilgrim The Extraordinary Life of Alma Reed*. New York: Marlow, 1993.

McCanse, Ralph Alan. *Titans and Kewpies: The Life and Art of Rose O'Neill*. New York: Vantage, 1968.

McDowell, Edwin. "Who Says Most Books Are Losers?" *New York Times*, December 30, 1983.

McFarland, Gerald W. *Inside Greenwich Village: A New York City Neighborhood, 1898–1918*. Amherst, MA: University of Massachusetts Press.

McNulty, Francine H. "Mahjar Literature: An Annotated Bibliography of Literary Criticism and Bibliography in Western Languages." *Mundus Arabicus* 1 (1981): 65–88.

Melhem, D. H. "Gibran's 'The Prophet' Outside the Canon of American Literature." *Al Jadid* 8, no. 40 (Summer 2002). Accessed June 2015. http://www.aljadid.com/content/gibran's-'-prophet'-outside-canon-american-literature.

Metz, Homer. "In Perspective: Memories of Gibran." *Providence Journal,* March 14, 1973.

Miller, Lucius Hopkins. *Our Syrian Population: A Study of the Syrian Communities*. Reprint, San Francisco: R & E Research Associates, 1968.

Mokarzel, Mary. "Besharri Youth Violent Over Gibran Committee," *Lebanese American Journal* 20, no. 4 (April 29, 1971): 10.

———. "Poor Gibran!" *Lebanese American Journal* 20, no. 4 (April 29, 1971): 4.

Moreh, Shmuel. *Studies in Modern Arabic Prose and Poetry*. Leiden: E. J. Brill, 1988.

Morton, Andrew. *Diana: Her True Story*. London: Michael O' Mara Books Limited, 1997.

Moses, John G., and Eugene Paul Nassar and Judith Rosenblatt. *Annotated Index to the Syrian World, 1926–1932*. Minneapolis, MN: University of Minnesota Immigration History Research Center, 1994. http://conservancy.umn.edu/handle/11299/175685.

Mukerji, Dhan Gopal. *Caste and Outcast*. Edited by Gordon H. Chang, Purnima Mankekar and Akhil Gupta. Stanford, CA: Stanford University Press, 2002.

Mushriq, Amin. "Rabitah Qalimiyya." *As-Sayeh* 5, no. 378 (June 29, 1916): 4–5.

Naef, Weston. *The Painterly Photograph, 1890–1914*. New York: Metropolitan Museum of Art, 1973.

Nahas, J. *Seventy-eight and still musing: Observations and Reflections: With Personal Reminiscences of Gibran as I Knew Him*. Hicksville, NY: Exposition Press, 1974.

Naidu, Sarojini. *Selected Letters 1890s to 1940s*. Edited by Markarand R. Paranjape. New Delhi: Kali for Women, 1996.

Naimy, Mikhail. "Fajr al-Amal ba'd Lail al-Ya's" [Dawn of hope after night of desperation]. *Al-Funun* I (1913): 50–70.

———. *Al-Ghirbdl* [Expatriation]. Cairo: Al-Matba'ah al-'Asriyah, 1923.

———. *Kahlil Gibran: A Biography*. New York: Philosophical Library, 1950.

———. *Jubran Khalil Jubran: Hayatuh, Mawtuh, Adabuh, Fannuh* [Gibran Kahlil Gibran: his life, death, literature, art]. Beirut: Dar Sadir, 1960.

———. *Al-Majmu'ah al-Kamilah* [The complete collection]. Beirut: Dar Al-'Ilm, 1970.

———. *Sab'un* [Seventy]. Beirut: Dar al-'Ilm, 1970.

———. "A Strange Little Book," *Aramco World* 15, no. 6 (November/December 1964): 10–15.

Naimy, Nadeem N. *The Lebanese Prophets of New York*. Beirut: American University of Beirut, 1985.

———. *Mikhail Naimy: An Introduction*. Beirut: American University of Beirut, 1967.

Najjar, Alexandre. *Kahlil Gibran: A Biography*. Translated by Rae Azkoul. London: Saqi, 2008.

Najjar, Michael Malek. *Arab American Drama, Film and Performance: A Critical Study*. Jefferson, NC: McFarland, 2014.

al-Na'uri, 'Isa. "Bayn Jubran wa Nu'aymah" [Between Gibran and Naimy]. *Al-Adib* 15 (1956): 12–15.

Nash, Geoffrey P. *The Arab Writer in English, Arab Themes in a Metropolitan Language, 1908–1958*. Brighton, UK: Sussex Academic Press, 1998.

———. "Khalil Jibran: From Arab Mahjar to Consumerist Prophet." In *The Arab Writer in English: Arab Themes in a Metropolitan Language 1908–1958*. Brighton, England: Sussex Academic Press, 1998.

Nassar, Eugene Paul. "Cultural Discontinuity in the Works of Kahlil Gibran." *MELUS* 7, no. 2 (Summer 1980): 21–36.

Nassar, Eugene Paul, and Kahlil Gibran. "Between Margin and Mainstream." *MELUS* 7, no. 2 (Summer 1980): 21—36.

National Committee of Gibran v. Shiya U.S. Supreme Court Transcript of Record with Supporting Pleadings, U.S. Supreme Court Records And Briefs, 1932-1978, MOML (The Making of Modern Law) Print Edition, Washington D.C. Thiel Press, 1967.

New York Times. "Syrian factions fight: 1 dead, another dying." February 1, 1906.

———. "Syrian plaque for Wilson. Presented in recognition of his efforts in behalf of small nations." January 25, 1921.

O'Neal, Denise. "Antiochian Heritage Museum Opens With Kahlil Gibran Exhibition." *Washington Report on Middle East Affairs*, September 2004.

O'Neill, Rose Cecil. *The Story of Rose O'Neill: An Autobiography*. Edited and with an introduction by Miriam Formanek-Brunell. Columbia, MO: University of Missouri Press, c.a. 1977.

Orfalea, Gregory. *The Arab Americans: A History*. Northampton, MA: Olive Branch Press, 2006.

———. *Before the Flames: A Quest for the History of Arab Americans*. Austin: University of Texas, 1988.

———, and Sharif Elmusa, eds. *Grape Leaves: A Century of Arab American Poetry*. Salt Lake City: University of Utah Press, 1988.

Otto, Annie Salem. *The Parables of Kahlil Gibran*. New York: Citadel, 1963.

Parks and Recreation Department. *The Dedication of Kahlil Gibran Park at Copley Square, Boston, Sunday 25, 1977*. Boston: City of Boston Printing Section, 1977.

Parrish, Stephen Maxfield. "Currents of the Nineties in Boston and London: Fred Holland Day, Louise Imogen Guiney, and Their Circle." Ph.D dissertation, Harvard University, 1954.

Peabody, Josephine Preston. *The Collected Plays*. Foreword by George P. Baker. Boston: Houghton Mifflin, 1927.

———. *The Collected Poems*. Foreword by Katharine Lee Bates. Boston: Houghton Mifflin, 1927.

———. *Diary and Letters*. Edited by Christina Hopkinson Baker. Boston: Houghton Mifflin, 1924.

———. *The Wings: A Drama in One Act*. New York: Samuel French Publisher, 1919.

Perlman, Bennard B. *American Artists, Authors, and Collectors: The Walter Pach Letters 1906–1958*. Albany, NY: State University of New York Press, 2002.

———. *The Lives, Loves, and Art of Arthur B. Davies*. New York: SUNY Press, 1998.

Pilpel, Harriet, and Theodora Zavin. *Rights and Writers*. New York: Dutton, 1960.

Popp, Richard Alan. "Al-Funun: the Making of an Arab-American Literary Journal." PhD diss., Georgetown University, 2000.

———. "Al-Rabitah al-Qalamiyah 1916." *Journal of Arabic Literature* 32, no. 1 (2001): 30–52.

Prial, Frank J. "Library Offers Prisoners a Key to Need." *New York Times*, February 6, 1978.

Public Broadcasting Company. "Kahlil Gibran's Legacy." Aired July 12, 2012. Accessed April 7, 2015. http://www.pbs.org/video/2365044477/.

Publishers' Weekly. "Fifteen Years of Mounting Sales." April 2, 1938.

Rabbat, Antun. "al-Muhajir al-Suri" [The Syrian Immigrant]. *Al-Mashriq* 13 (1910): 926–929.

Ratner-Rosenhagen, Jennifer. *American Nietzsche: A History of An Icon and His Ideas*. Chicago: University of Chicago Press, 2011.

Reed, Alma. *Orozco*. New York: Oxford University Press, 1956.

Rihani, Ameen F. *The Book of Khalid*. With a foreword by Marguerite Mooers Marshall and Helen Johnson Keyes. With illustrations by Kahlil Gibran. Beirut: Librarie du Liban, 2000.

———. *The Book of Khalid*. A Critical Edition. Edited and with an introduction by Todd Fine. Syracuse NY: Syracuse University Press, 2016.

———. "Selected Ameen F. Rihani International Publications, July 1897–December 1940." http://www.ameenrihani.org/pdf/intlpub.pdf.

Rihbany, Abraham Mitrie. *A Far Journey: An Autobiography*. Boston: Houghton Mifflin, 1914.

Rollins, Hyder Edward, and Stephen Maxfield Parrish. *Keats and the Bostonians*. Cambridge: Harvard University Press, 1951.

Roosevelt, Eleanor. *My Day: A Comprehensive Electronic Edition of Eleanor Roosevelt's Newspaper Columns*. Accessed June 10, 2015. http://www.gwu.edu/~erpapers/myday/displaydoc.cfm?_y=1936&_f=md054517.

Ross, Martha Jean. "The Writings of Kahlil Gibran." Master's thesis, University of Texas, 1948.

Rossetti, Dante Gabriel. *Poems by Dante Gabriel Rossetti, Volume II.* Edited by Elizabeth Luther Cary. New York: G. P. Putnam's Sons, 1903.

Russell, George W. *The Living Torch.* New York: Macmillan, 1938.

Saal, Rollene W. "Speaking of Books: *The Prophet.*" *New York Times,* May 16, 1965.

Sabagh, Elias. *Wahi al-Ku'us* [The inspiration of al-Kuus]. Boston: Al-Matba'ah al-Suriyyah, 1932.

Said, Edward W. *Orientalism.* New York: Penguin, 1978.

Sa'igh, Tufiq. *Adwa Jadidah 'ala Jubran* [A new aggression on Gibran]. Beirut: Al-Dar al-Sharqiyah, 1966.

Sarraj, Nadirah Jamil. *Dirasat fi Shi'r al-Mahjar, Shu'ara' al-Rabitah al-Qalamiyah* [Studies in diaspora poetry, poets of the Pen League]. Cairo: Dar al-Ma'arif, 1964.

Sawalha, Nadim. *Rest Upon the Wind.* Synopsis accessed April 7, 2015. http://gibrantheplay.com/synopsis/.

Saylor, Elizabeth Claire. "A Bridge Too Soon: The Life and Works of 'Afifa Karam, The First Arab American Woman Novelist." PhD diss., University of California, Berkeley, 2015.

Schillinger, Liesl. "Pioneer of the New Age." *New York Times,* December 13, 1998.

Shadid, Irfan. "Gibran and the American Literary Canon: The Problem of *The Prophet.*" In *Tradition, Modernity, and Postmodernity in Arabic Literature: Essays in Honor of Professor Issa J. Boullata.* Fayetteville: University of Arkansas Press, 1997.

——— "Gibran Kahlil Cibran Between Two Millennia." Farhat J. Ziadeh Distinguished Lecture in Arab and Islamic Studies Series from the Department of Near Eastern Languages and Civilization at the University of Washington, Seattle, April 30, 2002.

Shakir, Evelyne. "Arab-American Literature." In *New Immigrant Literatures in the United States: A Sourcebook to Our Multicultural Literary Heritage,* edited by Alpana Sharma Knippling, 3. Westport, CT: Greenwood, 1966.

———. "The First Philip K. Hitti International Symposium on Near Eastern Studies." *Spectrum* (University of Minnesota) 4, no. 3 (1984): 3–6.

———. "Good Works, Good Times: The Syrian Ladies' Aid Society of Boston. 1917–1932." In *Crossing the Waters: Arabic-Speaking Immigrants to the United States before 1940,* edited by Eric James Hooglund. Washington, DC: Smithsonian Institution Press, 1987.

Shea, Tom. "Translating art for love's sake. Kahlil Gibran poems live through a 93-year old [*Andrew Ghareeb*]." *The [Springfield] Sunday Republican,* August 4, 1991, B-1.

Shehadi, William. *Kahlil Gibran: A Prophet in the Making.* Beirut: American University of Beirut, 1991.

Sherfan, Andrew Dib. *Kahlil Gibran: The Nature of Love.* Secaucus, NJ: Citadel, 1972.

Sherry, Jay. *Carl Gustav Jung Avant-Garde Conservative.* New York: Palgrave Macmillan, 2010.

"Sights and Characters of New York's 'Little Syria.'" *New York Times,* March 29, 1903.

"Sixteen Craters on Mercury Have New Names." Press release from Carnegie Institution, July 15, 2009. www.spaceref.com/news/viewpr.html?pid=28744 accessed Aug. 8, 2016.

Stevens, E. S. *Cedars, Saints and Sinners in Syria*. London: Hurst & Blackett, 1927.

Stokes, Rose Pastor. *I Belong to the Working Class: the Unfinished Autobiography of Rose Pastor Stokes*. Edited by Herbert Shapiro and David L. Sterling. Athens: University of Georgia Press, c.1992.

Sukik, 'Adnan Yüsuf. *Al-Naz'ah al-Insaniyah 'inda Jubran* [Gibran's human integrity]. Cairo: Al-Hay'ah al-Misriyah al-'Ammah, 1970.

Suleiman, Michael, ed. *Arabs in America: Building a New Future*. Philadelphia: Temple University Press, 1999.

Suleiman, Michael W. *The Arab-American Experience in the United States and Canada: A Classified, Annotated Bibliography*. Ann Arbor, MI: Pierian Press, 2006.

Sussman, Vic. "The Prophet Motive." *U.S. News & World Report*, June 3, 1991.

al-Talisi, Khalifah Muhammad. *Al-Shabbi wa Jubran* [Al-Shabbi and Gibran]. Tripoli: Maktabat al-Farjani, 1957.

Taylor, Robert. "Bohemia Revisited." *Boston Globe*, January 7, 1975.

Teller, Charlotte. "America Facing Its Most Tragic Moment–Dr. Carl Jung." *New York Times*, September 29, 1912.

———. *The Cage*. New York: D. Appleton, 1907.

———. *The Diary of an Expectant Mother*. London: A. C. McClurg, 1917.

Thomas, Jack. "Centerpiece: Kahlil Gibran: The Poet Who Fit No Mold Had Roots in Boston." *Boston Globe*, January 5, 1983, 2.

Tibawi, Abdul Latif. *American Interests in Syria 1800–1901*. Oxford: Clarendon Press, 1961.

Time Magazine. "Profits from The Prophet." May 15, 1972.

"Tributes to Gibran…at the Hotel McAlpin in New York…on the Occasion of the Twenty-fifth Anniversary of the Publication of His First Literary Work." *Syrian World* 3 (February 19, 1929): 29–33.

Trombley Skandera, Laura. *Mark Twain's Other Woman: The Hidden Story of His Final Years*. New York: Alfred A. Knopf, 2010.

Turner, Sheila. "Tales of a Levantine Guru." *Saturday Review*, March 13, 1971.

Vincent-Barwood, Aileen. "Gibran Remembered." *Saudi Aramco World* (March/April 1983): 4–7.

"The Vision of Gibran." Conference on Arab-American Literature, Library of Congress, September 23, 1983.

Walbridge, John. "Gibran: His Aesthetic and his Moral Universe." *Al-Hikmat* 21 (2001): 47–66. http://www.personal.umich.edu/~jrcole/gibran/papers/gibwal1.htm.

Waterfield, Robin. *Prophet: The Life and Times of Kahlil Gibran*. London: Penguin, 1998.

Weakley, Sonya. "Kahlil Gibran in the U.S.: A Symbol of Unity." *IIP Digital*, December 30, 2011. Accessed April 8, 2015. http://iipdigital.usembassy.gov/st/english/article/2011/06/20110603212155aynos0.2846491.html#axzz3Wjxa4Qvj.

Weir, David. *Decadent Culture in the United States: Art and Literature Against the American Grain 1890–1926*. Albany: State University of New York Press, 2008.

White, Laura. "Talent to Spare." *Saudi Aramco World* (September/October 1996): 36–37.

Wilkinson, Marguerite. *New Voices*. Rev. ed. New York: Macmillan, 1929.

Wilson, P. W. "Jesus Was the Supreme Poet." *New York Times*, December 23, 1928.

Woods, Robert A. *The City Wilderness: A Settlement Study*. Boston: Houghton Mifflin, 1898.

Wright, Neva Marie. "Gibran Kahlil Gibran. Poet, Painter and Philosopher." Thesis, University of New Hampshire, 1938.

Wright, Paul M. "The President Meets the Prophet: Charles W. Eliot's 1910 Encounter with Kahlil Gibran." *Harvard Library Bulletin* 23, no. 3 (Fall 2010): 79–92.

Yakun, Waliy al-Din. "Al-Ajnihah al-Mutakassirah" [The broken wings]. *Al-Muqtataf* 40 (1912): 297–298.

Yamin, Mousin A., and Nazib Khafir. *Yaqthat al-Hajar (The Stone's Awakening)*. Introduction by Ghassan Tueni. Beirut: Dar An-Nahar, 2004.

Yardley, Jonathan. "The Eternal Kahlil Gibran." *Washington Post*, October 8, 1984.

Young, Barbara. "The Great Survival." *The Poetry Review* 23 (1932): 343–347.

———. *No Beauty in Battle: A Book of Poems*. With illustrations by Kahlil Gibran. New York: Paebar Company, 1937.

———. "The Son of Man." *Pictorial Review* 36 (December 1934): 15, 31–32.

———. *A Study of Kahlil Gibran: This Man from Lebanon*. New York: Syrian American Press, 1931.

———. *This Man from Lebanon: A Study of Kahlil Gibran*. New York: Knopf, 1945.

Zakka, Tansi. *Bayn Nu'ayma wa Jubran* [Between Naimy and Gibran]. Beirut: Maktabat al-Ma'arif, 1971.

Zaidan, Emile. "Natharat min ras'el. Lam funshar le Jubran Khalil Jubran" [Unpublished everyday letters by Gibran Kahlil Gibran]. *Al-Hilal* vol. 42 (March 1934): 513.

al-Zayn, Ahmad al-'Arif. "Lailah fi al-Arz, hawla Hflat Jubran" [Night in the cedars, about Gibran's parties]. *Al-'Irfan* 22 (1931): 410–416.

Ziade, May. "Jubran Khalil Jubran li Munasabat Sudur Kitabih Yasu ibn al-Insan" [Gibran Kahlil Gibran on the occasion of publishing his book, "Jesus the son of man"]. *Al-Muqtataf* 74 (1929): 9–13.

———. "Jubran Khalil Jubran Yasif Nafsah Biyadih fi Rasa'ilih" [Gibran Kahlil Gibran as described in his own letters]. *Al-Hadith* 5 (1931): 363–366.

———. "al-Mawakib" [The processions.] *Al-Hilal* 27 (1919): 874–881.

Ziegler, Antje. "Al-haraka Baraka! The Late Rediscovery of Mayy Ziyada's Works." *Die Welt Des Islams* 39, no. 1 (March 1999): 103–15. http://www.jstor.org/stable/1570914.

Zipser, Arthur, and Pearl Zipser. *Fire and Grace: The Life of Rose Pastor Stokes*. Athens, GA: University of Georgia Press, 1989.

EXTENDED IMAGE AND QUOTATION CREDITS

All unattributed quotations and artwork are by Kahlil Gibran.

The poem "Mist, My Sister" on p. 365 is from *The Garden of the Prophet* by Kahlil Gibran, copyright © 1933 by Alfred A. Knopf, copyright renewed 1961 by Mary G. Gibran. Used by permission of Alfred A. Knopf, an imprint of the Knopf Doubleday Group, a division of Penguin Random House LLC. All rights reserved.

All images described as appearing in books by Kahlil Gibran refer to the original Knopf editions, unless otherwise noted, including *The Prophet* by Kahlil Gibran, copyright © 1923 by Kahlil Gibran, copyright renewed 1951 by Administrators C.T.A. of Kahlil Gibran Estate and Mary G. Gibran.

All images credited: (Courtesy Private Collection.) with no further attribution indicates images provided directly by the collector, or reproduced on behalf of the collector by the Interlink Gibran Project.

All images credited: (Courtesy Alfred A. Knopf, Inc.) are
(Used by permission of Alfred A. Knopf, an imprint of the Knopf Doubleday Group, a division of Penguin Random House LLC. All rights reserved.)

All images credited: (Courtesy Gibran Museum) are
(Courtesy Gibran National Committee, Gibran Museum, Bsharri, Lebanon).

All images credited: (Courtesy Museo Soumaya) are
(Courtesy Museo Soumaya, Fundacion Carlos Slim, Mexico City).

All images credited to: (Courtesy Peter A. Juley / Smithsonian) are
(Courtesy © Peter A. Juley and Son Collection, Photograph Archives, Smithsonian American Art Museum).

All images credited: (Courtesy Telfair Museum of Art) are
(Courtesy Telfair Museum of Art, Savannah, Georgia. Gift of Mary Haskell Minis).
except p. 51 (Courtesy Telfair Museum of Art, Savannah, Georgia).

All images credited: (Courtesy Wilson Library, University of North Carolina, Chapel Hill)are
(Courtesy the Minis Family Papers #2725, Southern Historical Collection, Wilson Library, University of North Carolina, Chapel Hill).

Collections and call numbers for all images credited to the Library of Congress:

p. 19 (Courtesy Library of Congress, LC-M32-456, G. Eric and Edith Matson Photograph Collection. Prints and Photographs Division.)

p. 38 (Courtesy Library of Congress, LC-USZC4-3904, Prints and Photographs Division.)

p. 42 (Courtesy F. Holland Day Collection from Norwood Historical Society, now at Library of Congress. PR 13 CN 2013:008, Prints and Photographs Division.)

p. 43 (Courtesy Library of Congress, LC-USZ62-48305, the Louise Imogen Guiney Collection. Prints and Photographs Division.)

ACKNOWLEDGEMENTS

For years, the poet's Boston relatives and friends generously shared memories and materials. This included ongoing conversations with the poet's sister Marianna, and his cousins: N'oula Gibran and Rose Gibran, Assaf George, Maroon George, Zakia Rahme (often referred to as Rose Diab), and Joseph Rahme. Also helpful were several oral history sessions with Mary Kawaji (Mary Kellan), and LaBeeBee Hanna, the young Boston poet who contributed to *Syrian World* and attended Gibran's Boston and New York memorial services, eventually becoming an art teacher in the Boston Public Schools.

We are grateful to the staff of the Southern Historical Collection at the Library of the University of North Carolina, Chapel Hill. J. Isaac Copeland, director of this collection, and Carolyn A. Wallace, curator of manuscripts, greatly facilitated the Minis Family Papers, Haskell–Gibran series. Richard Teller Hirsch has graciously allowed us to publish writings by his mother, Charlotte Teller, which are deposited at the Southern Historical Society.

The Josephine Preston Peabody Papers and Gibran letters to Witter Bynner and Corinne Roosevelt Robinson at Houghton Library at Harvard College, Carolyn E. Jakeman, assistant librarian for reference, added immeasurably to this work.

Along with staff members of the Boston Public Library, we acknowledge the Boston Athenaeum staff, particularly Donald C. Kelley, art department assistant.

Deserving thanks are New York Public Library personnel, especially John L. Mish, chief of the Oriental division, Francis W. Paar, assistant, and John D. Stinson, research librarian at that library's manuscripts and archives division. David A. Randall, librarian at the Lilly Library, Indiana University, encouraged and advised us.

We also acknowledge: David Farmer, assistant to the director, Humanities Research Center, the University of Texas; Donald Gallup, curator, the Beinecke Rare Book and Manuscript Library, Yale University; Reverend Eugene J. Harrington, S.J., curator of manuscripts at Dinand Library, College of the Holy Cross; Paula Lichtenberg, senior reference librarian, the Public Library of Newark; Eva Moseley, curator of manuscripts, at the Arthur and Elizabeth Schlesinger Library on the History of Women in America, Radcliffe College; Mary Faith Pusey, assistant in manuscripts, Alderman Library, University of Virginia; E. Rosenfeld, curator, Abernethy Library, Middlebury College; Joseph W. Slade, editor of *The*

ACKNOWLEDGEMENTS

Markham Review, Horrmann Library of Wagner College, Staten Island; Wilma R. Slaight, archivist, Wellesley College Library; Ronald S. Wilkinson, manuscript historian, the Library of Congress (where Gibran's letters to Margaret Lee Crofts are on deposit); and Walter W. Wright, chief of special collections, Baker Memorial Library, Dartmouth College.

Alan McNabb, director of the Telfair Academy of Arts and Sciences, Savannah, Georgia, and his assistant, Feay Shellman, have shared reproductions from their Haskell collection of Gibran's art. We are also grateful to the following individuals and institutions for granting us permission to reproduce works of art: Gail Buckland of the Royal Photographic Society of Great Britain; Jerald C. Maddox, curator of photography, the Library of Congress; Grace B. Mayer, the Edward Steichen Archive, the Museum of Modern Art; the Museum of Fine Arts, Boston; the Fogg Art Museum; Harvard College Library; Peter A. Juley & Son, New York; the Metropolitan Museum of Art; the Lebanon Tourist and Information Center, New York; and the New York Historical Society.

Our research at Norwood Historical Society was greatly facilitated by Margaret Alden, Miriam and Charles Lennon, George Mahoney, then president of the Norwood Historical Society, and Francis Morrison. For supplying further information on Day, we thank James Baker, Lilla Cabot Leavitt, Nathaniel Hasenfus, Anna E. Tanneyhill, Clarence White, and Ruth Rüyl Woodbury.

Stephen Maxfield Parrish, whose unpublished dissertation, "Currents of the Nineties in Boston and London: Fred Holland Day, Louise Imogen Guiney, and Their Circle," deserves special acknowledgment. Researching Josephine Preston Peabody Marks has been rewarding due to the generous sharing of the Peabody material owned by Alison P. Marks and Lionel P. Marks. We also thank Nancy Lee Lewis, a president of Wellesley College's Tau Zeta Epsilon society, for locating material about Gibran's first public exhibition in 1903.

The following individuals have provided key information about Mary Elizabeth Haskell Minis and Charlotte Teller Hirsch: Elizabeth Belcher, Mrs. William B. Clagett, Adelaide Collier, Jean E. Crossman of the Wellesley College Alumnae Association, Suzanne Davis Durham, Gertrude Elsner, Dr. David McLean Greeley, Hetty Shuman Kuhn, Agnes Mongan, Marion Raoul Stewart, Gladys and William Teller, and Hilda Washburn, guidance counselor at the Cambridge School of Weston (formerly the Cambridge School).

For their recollections about Gibran's Greenwich Village days we are grateful to Margaret Lee Crofts, Alice Raphael Eckstein, Philip K. Hitti, Hope Garland Ingersoll, Mariita Lawson, Matta and Birger Lie, Dorothy Maadi, Madeline Mason, and Mikhail Naimy. Also contributing to our understanding of Gibran's friends have been Henry Bragdon, Mrs. Malcolm S. MacKay, Madeleine Vanderpool, Jean Cantwell, president of the International Rose O'Neill Club, and Marcia Sullivan for information about Barbara Young.

Alfred A. Knopf, Inc. has been a major resource. We are appreciative of William Koshland, president of that publishing house, and its founder, Alfred A. Knopf, for sharing Gibran correspondence with us.

Compiling and synthesizing the materials by or about Gibran would have been impossible without the assistance of Charles H. Flanigan, who also transcribed the Haskell and Peabody papers. Nabila Mango of the Oriental studies department, University of Pennsylvania, retrieved and translated voluminous Arabic material consulted. We are indebted to Susan Holcombe for her research at New York libraries. We also acknowledge Elizabeth Lansing for her research at the rare book section of the University of North Carolina Library, and Martine Loufti for her work at the Bibliothèque Nationale. Photography by Morton Bartlett and Stephen F. Grohe has been invaluable.

We are privileged to thank other friends and institutions. Salma Hayek, award-winning actress, and producer of the animated film Kahlil Gibran's *The Prophet*, has sought to introduce Gibran's story to a new generation, and we are grateful for her preface. We also salute William Nix, that film's executive producer, and chairman of Creative Projects. Faithful to the preservation of this poet's legacy are Stuart Denenberg and his wife Beverly of Denenberg Fine Arts, Los Angeles. Paul Wright, former acquisitions editor at the University of Massachusetts Press, has been a fount of information. His article "The President Meets the Prophet," describing Gibran's interaction with Harvard president Charles Eliot, rekindled interest in the poet's early years. Charles Fineman, translator and retired Harvard librarian has answered key questions and has helped solve challenging research problems. Jean and Kahlil G. Gibran's daughter Nicole Rose Gibran's rigorous research skills have made her an invaluable supporter and honest critic. F. Frank Isik generously shared his photographic skills to secure key materials. Sustaining our purpose have been annual Writers' Workshops at the William Joiner Institute for the Study of War and Social Consequences at the University of Massachusetts, Boston. Inspirational workshop leader, author Lady Borton (*After Sorrow: An American Among the Vietnamese*), deserves a special thanks. Information specialist Judith Charvat Watkins has made work on notes and bibliography immeasurably easier. We are grateful to friends and neighbors, especially Alice Andrus, Ann Hershfang, Herbert Hershfang, Judith Klau, Patricia Wanner Serues, and Norma Zack, who have responded to calls for assistance and shared their talents and expertise.

Bridgewater State College professor and former president of Norwood Historical Society Patricia Fanning, has provided essential updates on that institution's holdings. Adding to earlier contributions of Francesco Carbone, Dennis Ditelberg, Paul Ward English, Monseigneur Joseph Lahoud, Gertrude Stern, and Eleanor Barrie Trowbridge have been, Antony Bashir, Fr. George Kevorkian, Fr. Michael Massouh, Mary Rahme, Paula Hajar, Jay Sherry, and Elizabeth Saylor.

Throughout the decades, Gibran scholars and Arab American leaders have supported and acknowledged our research. For their dedication and devotion to our subject we are grateful to Robert Andrews, William Baroody III, Sheryl Ameen Fiegel, Greg Gormanous, Albert Johary, Eugene Paul Nassar, Gregory Orfalea, Kareem Roustom, Charles Samaha, Evelyn Shakir, Simon Shaheen, Helen Hatab Samhan, James Zogby, along with Suheil Bushrui and the many contributors to The George and Lisa Zakhem Kahlil Gibran Chair for Values and Peace (University of Maryland).

ACKNOWLEDGEMENTS

We have tried hard to portray several stages of Gibran's art, from his early bookmaking, through his mid-career paintings, to his illustrations for the immigrant press and Knopf's Borzoi publications. We are especially grateful to Amy Root Clements, author of *The Art of Prestige: The Formative Years at Knopf, 1915–1929*, and to the distinguished bibliographer, scholar, and collector G. Thomas Tanselle who helped us learn more about the design and production of Gibran's books.

Curators, museum personnel, and art experts who have graciously provided advice and images for our visual tour include Hubbard Toombs, Gallery Manager, Adelson Galleries, New York City; Julia Ritter, curator and librarian at the Antiochian Heritage Museum and Library; the staff of the Arab American National Museum in Dearborn, Michigan; Patricia M. Boulos, digital programs librarian, Boston Athenaeum; Cynthia Van Ness, director of Library and Archives at the Buffalo History Museum; Joseph Geagea, director of the Gibran Museum in Bsharri, Lebanon, along with Sarah Fakhry, Lina Haidar, Nathalie Hobeika, Hoda Zohrob, and Walid Nasser, legal counsel for the Gibran National Committee, Beirut, Lebanon.

At Houghton Library, Harvard College Library, thanks also to Leslie Morris, curator of modern books and manuscripts, Heather Cole, assistant curator of books and manuscripts, along with reference librarians James Capobianco, Mary Haegert, Susan Halpert, Micah Hoggatt, and the entire staff; to Kenneth Turino, manager of community engagement and exhibitions, Historic New England; Akram Khater, director of the Khayrallah Center for Lebanese Diaspora Studies at North Carolina State University; Ann Miniutti, Erica Garber, and Michael Slade, New York Art Resources for the Metropolitan Museum of Art; William Mater of One Fine Art, Beirut, Lebanon; Beth Moore, assistant curator, Telfair Museums; Nicole C. Dittrich, reference assistant of special collections, at the Research Center, Syracuse University Library; Lindsay Sprechman, Temple Adath Israel, Boston; Alfonso Miranda Marquez, director, Daniela Diaz Olivera, assistant director, and Soumaya Slim de Romero, editorial board of Museo Soumaya, Fundación Carlos Slim, Mexico City. Patricia Jacobs Barquet, director of Archivo Immigrantes Notables en Mexico, will always be remembered for her brilliant scholarship, thoughtful generosity, and contributions to the Gibran website created by the Museo Soumaya staff.

Supporting our search for specialized materials have been Mervat Kobeissi, Samar Mikati, and Kaoukab Chebaro of the Archives and Special Collections Department, Jafet Library, American University of Beirut; Sean Casey, Rare Books Department, and Melisa Theroux along with countless reference librarians at the Boston Public Library; and the dedicated staff at the South End Branch; Connie Manoli, assistant archivist, the Concord Free Public Library in Concord, Massachusetts; Joseph Greene, deputy director and curator, Harvard Semitic Museum, Harvard University; Janet M. Careswell, executive director of the C.G. Jung Foundation for Analytical Psychology; Richard Foster, manager, New York Public Library Research Services; Amber Paranick and several reference librarians, the Library of Congress; Rick Watson, head of reference services, Harry Ransom Center, the University of Texas at Austin, along with Hannah Rainey, graduate research associate at that Center; Todd

Fine, president, of the Washington Street Historical Society, devoted to Manhattan's Little Syria; Michael Frost of the Sterling Library and Matthew Rowe, Beinecke Rare Book and Manuscripts Library Yale University; and Catherine Madsen, bibliographer, Yiddish Book Center, Amherst, Massachusetts. We also gratefully remember past New York Graphic Society editor-in-chief, Donald A. Ackland, editor, Robin Bledsoe, and designer Betsy Beach. A final acknowledgment goes to many friends and countless strangers—the readers who have valued Gibran's work. To these and more, we are deeply indebted.

    —Kahlil George Gibran (1922–2008), Jean Gibran,

       and the Interlink Gibran Project

To My Colleagues

For two decades, Interlink publisher Michel Moushabeck encouraged me to sustain Gibran's timely legacy. Joining together with the remarkable staff at Interlink Books, and with far-flung individuals who gave generously of their time and talents, the Interlink Gibran Project made it possible collaboratively to research and rewrite this story in the light of the present. The forming of this ad hoc team came full circle with the addition of a translator, who with her daughter had fled the most recent Syrian conflict. Together, we have worked to conceive and find language for this new biography's themes and form. To John Sobhiea Fiscella, editor and project coordinator; to Dr. Hani Bawardi, University of Michigan–Dearborn, research advisor; Ann Childs, assistant editor; Pam Fontes-May, designer; Julian Ramirez, designer; Jennifer Staltare, document manager and proofreader; Judith Charvat Watkins, bibliographer and research advisor; Abdul Mohsen Al-Husseini translator, Joelle Solé Maguire and Raghad Qattan, assistant translators; Karen Gracie Kowles, indexer; George Lynde, photographer and proofreader; Whitney Sanderson and Meredith Madyda, proofreaders; Leyla Moushabeck, assistant publisher at Interlink; and Mhani Alaoui, manuscript reader; to all my heartfelt thanks.

    —Jean Gibran, Boston, 2016

INDEX

Al-Aam al Jadid al-Nis'i (The New World for Women) (journal), 213
Abd al-Hamid II, 161m
Abd al-Qadir Rahme, Istifan (grandfather), 5–6
the "Absolute", 157, 192, 289, 309, 384
Abu al-Nawwas, 320, 323
Abu Nuwas (classical poet), **322**
Academy Julian, 146, 149, 152
A Club cooperative home, 133–134, 309
Agora Society, 112
Almustafa ("island man"), 287–289, 313–314, 325, 349, 364–367, 384
American Aspirations (Fleischer), 204
American Fund for Public Service, 290
American University of Beirut, 425, 59
Antar (Ghanim), 161
"the Arab Encyclopedia" (Arida), 323
Arabic language and literature
    and *Al-Badayi wa Tarray'if* compilation, 402
    Hitti on KG and, 400–401
    and immigrant press, 102
    initials design in, 85
    during Islamic ascendency, for Maronites, 13–14
    KG's definition of poet in *Future of Arabic Language*, 367
    KG's speech on Islamic influences, 259
    KG's style of, 116
    literary scene, 152, **221**–223

Mahjar writers, 260–261, 320–323
    and *al-Nahda,* 354
    poetry renaissance, KG's influence on, 377
    publishing community in New York's Little Syria, 172
    translations of KG's work, 383–385
    translations of writers in *Al-Funun,* 222
    See also Pen League; Ziade, May
Ara'is al-Muruj (Spirit Brides) (stories), 129, 135
The Archer (watercolor), **346**–347
Arida, Nasib
    as "the Arab Encyclopedia," 323
    Al-Funun editor, **221**–222, 281
    KG's portrait of, **323**
    life and work of, 425–426
    member of Al-Rabitah, **319**
    publisher, *Tears and Laughter,* 225
    publisher, *The Processions,* 296, 297, 311
    tribute gift to KG, 260
Armistice Day, 300, **301**
Armory Show (International Exhibit of Modern Art), 210, 214–215
Armstrong, Sarah, 132–133
Around the World in New York (Bercovici), 385
The Arts (periodical). See *Funun Al-*
Al-Arwah al-Hairah (The Confused Souls) (Arida), 425
Arwah al-Mutamarida, dedication to, 149

Associated Charities of Boston, 30
Association of American Painters and Sculptors, 210, 216
Ata Allah, Ilyas, 260
Aunt Sardi, **422**
Autumn (painting), **163**
Avicenna (Ibn Sina), 320, **321**
Al-Awasif (The Tempests), 324
Ayoub, Raschid, **319**

Bacchante statue, Boston Public Library, 273, **32**–34
Badawi, M. M., 188
Al-Badayi wa Tarray'if (Best Things and Masterpieces), Arabic compilation, 349, 402
Badiyah, Bahithat al-, 353
Baha, Abdul, **203**–204, 231, 255, 387
Bahout, Wadi, **319**
Balkan states, 213, 255–256, 359
Al-Barq (Lightning) (magazine), 421
Barrie, Gertrude, 130–132, **131,** 152, 169, 189
Bartlett, Paul, 159
Bashir, Antony, 383–385, **384**
Bashir II, 15
The Beacon (magazine), 68
Beale, Jessie Fremont, 34–35, 37, 41, 411, 45–46
Beardsley, Aubrey, 181, 55
The Beholder (painting), 189–**190,** 191
Beirut
    French in, 16, 355
    memorial services, 418–422, **419, 420**
    missionaries in, 16
    port (photograph), **19**

Tower Square, renamed
    Martyr's Square, **58**
vegetable market (photograph),
    69
wall portrait of KG, **435**–436
Bercovici, Konrad, 378–379, 385
Bergson, Henri, 210
Bernhardt, Sarah, 159, 208, **213**
Béronneau, Pierre Marcel, 151–152,
    159
Best Things and Masterpieces (*Al-
    Badayi wa Tarray'if*), Arabic
    compilation, 349, 402
"Between Ourselves" (column in
    New Orient), 386
Beyk, Raji, 17, 71, 72
The Black Riders and Other Lines
    (Crane), 218, 41, 55
"The Black Stones of Homs"
    (Arida), 426
Blake, William, 106, 303, 305
The Blind (play), 388
Bodenheim, Maxwell, 304
Bojer, Johan, **315**
book design. *See* Gibran, Kahlil
    (*book design craft*)
Book of Khalid, The (Rihani), 185,
    187, **199**–201, **200**, 425
Book of Mirdad, The (Naimy), 427
The Book of the Dead, Boston
    Brahmin interest in, 103
borzoi colophon, **312**
Boston
    Back Bay culture, 103, 29–30
    charities, 30–35
    Little Syria described (Crosby),
        361–363
    Oliver Place 20-26, 28, 169-
        170, 197-198, 211
    patrons, not interested in KG's
        work, 236
    Public Library, 32–34, 433, 49
    public school system, 25–27
    settlement houses, 31, 45–46
    Syrian enclaves of, 21–23
Boston Evening Transcript
    (newspaper), 106
Boston Herald (newspaper), **117,**
    261–363, **362**
Boston Sunday Herald (newspaper),
    250
Boughton, Henrietta. *See* Young,
    Barbara
Bourne, Randolph, 269, 281
Bowie, Walter Russell, 394
Bradley, Will, 55m

Bragdon, Claude, 385, 386, 396, 399
Braithwaite, William Stanley, on *The
    Forerunner,* 326
Brazilian gift to President Woodrow
    Wilson, 330, 331
"Bread and Roses" (Oppenheim),
    268, 425
"Breath on a Windowpane"
    (drawing), 324
Broken Wings, The (book), 185, 187,
    189, 354, 72
Brooks, Phillips, 30
Brown, Alice, 40, 64
Bsharri
    versus Beirut (studies), 70
    description, 3, 429
    emigration from, 17–19
    environment, KG and, 72
    funeral procession to, **421,**
        422, 423
    Gibran Museum in, **429**–430
    KG on, 415
    KG's book royalties donated
        to, 376
    in KG's will, 405, 414–415
    MH's letter and mementos
        to, 424
    and missionaries, 16
    photographs of, **14, 2**
    and Qadisha Valley, **431**
    villagers welcoming cortege,
        410
    visitors to Gibran Museum,
        429, 430
Buffalo Times illustration, **230**
Burgess, Gelett, 79
Bushrui, Suheil, on *The Processions,*
    311 The Procession for
        mention of publication
Bustani, Suleiman al-, 380
Bustani, Yusuf, 336
Bynner, Witter, 211, 266–267, 273,
    286, 295, 379, 386

Cabot, Richard and Ella Lyman,
    132, 173, 178
Caffin, Charles H., 237
Cage, The (Teller), 135
Cambridge School, MH's move to,
    294–295
Campbell, Judge Richard, 399
"The Capitalist" in *The Madman,*
    308
card (ink and watercolor) (to
    Josephine), **121, 245**
Carman, Bliss, 47, 48

Carmelite Mission, 422
Carpenter, Edward, 48, 93
Carrière, Eugène, 158, 159, 180,
    220, 222, 237
Case, Bertha, 307
Catzeflis, William, 318–**319,** 401
"The Cedars" (Peabody), 102, 85
Cedars of Lebanon, 8–9
centaur (drawing), **275**
Centaur and Child (wash drawing),
    254
Chamberlain, Joseph Edgar, 237
Chapbook (magazine), 39
charities. See Boston charities
Cheikho, Louis, 356–357
Children's Aid Society, 34
Christmas Nativity essay, 396
City Wilderness, The (Woods), 23
Classical Dictionary (Lemprière), 47
Clemens, Samuel, **134**
Coburn, Alvin Langdon, 105
Coburn, F. W., 280
Colby, Bainbridge, 331
Colby, Nathalie Sedgwick, 331
colonialism. *See* European powers
colophon(s)
    for Copeland & Day, **40**
    hand and flame, on Borzoi
        Books, **206**
    hand and flame linoleum block,
        222
    for Knopf, 311–**312**
    Twenty Drawings, 311
color section, 245–252
Colum, Padraic, 310
Commonwealth (early title *for The
    Prophet*), 288
Companions (poetry anthology), 379
Compassion (painting), 78
"Concord Soul," 195–197
*The Confused Souls (A l-Arwah al-
    Hairah*) (Arida), 425
Constantinou, Costas, 366
Cook, Howard Willard, 286, 304,
    315
Copeland, Herbert, 306, 39, 64
Copeland & Day (publishers),
    39–41
Copia, Isis. *See* Ziade, May
Copley Greenes, 178, 180, 191, 195
Copley Square Memorial, **432**–434
cosmopolitanism, 269
"the Counsels," 290, 292, 295, 307,
    312, 345, 347. *See also The
    Prophet*
Craftsman's Poetry Group, 399

Cram, Ralph Adams, 39, 40
Crane, Stephen, 218, 41, 55
The Crescent (Al-Hilal) (journal), 311, 312, 354, 356
The Critic (weekly review), 54
Crofts, Frederick and Margaret Lee, 380, 409
Crosby, Katherine, 361–363

Dahir, Hala, 72
Dahir, Selim, 10–11, 72
Dahir, Tannous Asad Hanna, 72
Al Da'ira al Adabiya (The Literary Circle), 198
Daly, Reginald, 104m
Dam'a wa Ibtisama (Tears and Laughter) (book), 225
Daughter of Heaven, The (Loti), 208
Davenport, Butler, 358, 385
Davies, Arthur, 210, 216, 217
Day, Fred Holland, XIV, 37–57, 39, 377
  and art photography, 105, 42, 44, 45, 52, 73, 74, 77, 90, 91
  Beale on KG, 35, 411
  and Beardsley death, 55
  books lent to library exhibits, 49
  on censorship, 55–56
  critics on, 42
  death of, 425
  on fire devastation, 117
  gift of *Age of Fable,* 59
  and Guiney, 38, **39,** 75
  invitations for Boston Symphony, 116
  on KG's Temple of Art series, 177
  later years at Norwood estate, 306
  letter from KG before Paris, 142–143
  and Maeterlinck, 46–47
  in Paris, 75
  photographing children, 43–45
  romanticization of KG, 377, 89
  sponsorship of KG, 100, 103, 105, 64, 72–73, 92
"Dead Are My People" (poem), 263–264
Dean, Sarah M., and school reform, 132
"Death Beautiful" (poem), 142
"Death Staying the Hand of the Sculptor" (French), 33

Debussy, Claude (charcoal and graphite), **232**
"Decadence-or Renascence" (Hovey), 48
"Defeat, my Defeat" (poem), 298–299
de Lanux, Pierre 286, 295
Delphic Group, 399
Denison House
  art teacher Peirce, 34–35, 41
  Baha's speech at, 204
  and cultural exchange, 192
  growth of, 31–32, 391
  and Marianna, 125, 197, 391
  performance participants, **192**
Detroit Free Press, on *Twenty Drawings,* 349
Diab, Najib, 172, 174, 189, 256, 281, 413
Diab, Zakia Gibran *See* Gibran, Zakia
The Dial (magazine), 282, 315, 324
Diary of an Expectant Mother, The (Teller), 423
Dibs, Yusuf al- (Archbishop), 59, *60*
Dole, Nathan Haskell, 54
Doll and Richards gallery show, 279, 280
Doro, Marie, 159
Douaihy, Stephen el- (Pastor), 391, 412, **424**
Dream Flowers (Fleurs de Rêve) (Ziade), 353
The Dream of Life (painting), 113
Druze sect, 15
Duclo, Estelle, 399
Dugan, Ethel, 290
"Dust of the Ages and the Eternal Fire" (story), 129

"Earth" (poem), 402–403
The Earth Gods (poems), 242, 403–405, **404,** 408
Eckstein, Alice Raphael, 273, 280, 311
Egyptian Feminist Union, 353
Egyptian Ladies Literary Improvement Society, 354
Eliot, Charles, W. (graphite drawing), **173**
Elzevir Press, 39
Emerson, Ralph Waldo, 103, 164, 30, 47, 48
The Emigrant (Al-Mohajer) (newspaper), 115, 120, 127, 129, 152–**153**

European powers, in Middle East, 15–16, 355–356
Evans, Frederick, photograph of Day, **42**
Everybody's Paris (Teller), 426
Everyday Ethics (Cabot), 132

The Face of My Mother, the Face of My Nation (drawing), **328**
Fakhr ad-Din II, 15
Farid, Umar Ibn al-, 320, **321**
Far Journey, A (Rihbany), 204
Farwell, Arthur, 181
Fatat Boston (newspaper), 312–**313**
Feminist Pieces (Nisaiyat) (al-Badiyah, aka Nasif), 353
"Festival of Death" (illustration), **265**
Fiddler's Farewell (Speyer), 380
Fields, Annie S, 64
fire, in Harcourt Studios, 116–119
First Arab Congress, 256–257
Fisk, Eleanor Small, 406
Five Islands, Maine, 100, 125, 56
Fleischer, Charles (Rabbi), 204, 387, 416–417, 80–**81**
Fleurs de Rêve (Dream Flowers) (Ziade), 353
Flight (wash drawing), **277**
Ford, Julia Ellsworth, 211, 223–224
Foreign Language Information Service, 361
Forerunner, The (book), 314, 316, 326–327
Fortune and Men's Eyes (Peabody), 79
Fournier, Pierre Simon, type founder, 349
Free Religious Association of America, 204, 308
French, Daniel Chester, 33
Al-Funun (The Arts) (journal)
  "An Open Letter to Islam" in, 257
  Arida and, 281, 323
  Bercovici on, 385
  ceasing publication, 225
  cover design, **320**
  forming and features of, **221–223**
  influence of, 425
  revival of, 260
  Syrian Crisis issue 263–265

Gandhi, Mahatma, 387

Garden of the Prophet, The (book), 364, 388, 402

Gardner, Isabella Stewart, 178, 195, 196

Garibaldi II, Giuseppe, 213, **214**

Garland, Charles, 290

Garland, Marie Tudor, 289–291, 298

Gates, Lewis, 79m

George, Assaf (cousin), 376, 393, 402, 409 **412** 418, 422, **424**

George, Maroon (cousin), **266,** 376, 402, **412** 419 **424**

Ghanim, Shukri, 161

Ghazali-Al, 320, **321**

Ghorayeb, Ameen
  afterword in KG's *Spirit Brides,* 129
  on Gibran, 115, 148
  KG published by, 119–120
  KG's letters to, 137–138, 148–149
  in KG's will, 184
  Al-Mohajer newspaper established, 115

Gibbs, Frances, 100

Gibran, Kahlil (KG) *(Arab literary movement)*
  and *Al-Funun,* **221**–223
  Al-Rabitah member, 318–320, **319**
  essays (Arabic) in Ghorayeb's newspaper 119-120
  Hitti on KG's influence on, 400–401
  and oral tradition, 384
  on Pen League, 326, **334**
  and Pen League banquet, 400–**401**
  speech on Islamic influences, 259, 324
  as voice for immigrants, 119–120, 353
  See also KG *(Syrian community);* KG *(Middle East interest)*

Gibran, Kahlil (KG) *(art influences)*
  on Beronneau, 159
  on Carrière, 158, 159
  on da Vinci, 378
  on de Chavannes, 158, 378
  on his naive informal training, 136
  and J.M.W. Turner's paintings, 165
  on Mantegna, 378
  on Armory Show painters, 215–216

pluralistic and cosmopolitan embrace, 377
and Rodin, 154, 183, 236, 239, 271, 421
on Ryder, 239–241
on Western works, 103, 219–220

Gibran, Kahlil (KG) *(art work and opinions)*
  and the Absolute, 157, 192, 193, 289, 309, 384
  and Blake comparison, 303
  and *Book of Khalid,* 185, 187, 199–201
  on Boston, 177
  on "Defeat, my Defeat," 300
  on drawing as breathing, 283
  on earth-God poem, 402–403
  on exile and loss, 378
  on exile and return (after Paris), 167
  on his early *versus* later work, 400
  illustrations in *Companions,* 379
  on madness in Syria, 218–219
  on mist metaphor, 364–366
  on need for beauty and truth, 285
  on peace movement, 255–256
  on 'political farewell,' 324
  on *The Processions,* 287, 311
  on Roosevelt family life, 380
    under Corinne Roosevelt Robinson
  self portraits, **124, 149, 84**
  on socialism and progressive movement, 220, 308–309
    Is there a Socialism heading?
  work in 10th Street studio (photograph), **229**
  on writing and painting, 337

Gibran, Kahlil (KG) *(book design craft)*
  Knopf's support for, 327
  on *Al-Mawakib* and printing craft, 311
  on book size, 357
  on *The Prophet* editing and typography, 343–344, 349
  on *The Prophet* printing production, 349–350
  on *Sand and Foam,* 389
  skills gained at Copeland & Day, 53 55
  Twenty Drawing 311, 327

Gibran, Kahlil (KG) *(death and tributes)*
  burial in Lebanon l, 418–419, 421
  continual appeal and solace of, 429–430
  death mask, **414**
  debts and estate planning, 376
  Burial in Lebanon for l, 418–419, 421
  Eulogies for, 417, 421, 422
  Fleischer tribute at Roerich Museum, 416–417
  Graffiti mural in Beirut, **435–436**
  legacy of "universality," 434–436
  obituaries, 412
  vigil in New York, 411
  will of, 183–185, 373, 405, 413–415
  Young's recounting of death, 409

Gibran, Kahlil (KG) *(early youth drawings)*
  Cedars of Lebanon, **9**
  in copy of Smith's Arabella and Araminta, **49**
  Gibran family tree, **8**
  for Josephine, **101**
  self-portrait as shepherd, **84**

Gibran, Kahlil (KG) *(English language)*
  and Arabic, 377
  on Bible as Syriac English, 289
  critical attacks on style and thinking, 357
  initial work on *The Prophet,* 290
  MH's literature tutorial program, 219–221
  on poet's use of second language, 289

Gibran, Kahlil (KG) *(exhibits)*
  Autumn painting at Beaux-Arts, 163–164
  at Day's Harcourt Studios, 106–107
  Doll and Richards show, 279, 280
  invitation card, **106**
  Knoedler, 272, 273, 274, 275
  lecture tour offer, 314–315
  Montross, **226,** 229–231, 236–238

at Wellesley, 112–113, 154–156, 85–86, 87, 94

Gibran, Kahlil (KG) *(health)*
during 1930 summer, 406–407
alcohol as self-medication, 377–378, 393, 405
and cirrhosis, 401–402
described to Day, 106
described to Ziade, 407–408
on doctor visit, 343, 344
"ongoing malaise" of, 333–335, 376
on poor health, 266–267
and real estate failure, 377

Gibran, Kahlil (KG) *(Syrian Concerns))*
after Young Turks, 161
on Balkans, Turkey, Syria, 256–257
critique of Arab culture, 377
on Dr. Tabet, 263
on emerging nations, 330
essays (Arabic) in Ghorayeb's newspaper, 119–120
and Garibaldi, 213
Islamic culture speech, 259
on nationalism, 191–193, 255–256, 283, 286, 356
and Orient Society, 386
against Ottoman rule, 172, 377
on pacifists and peace movement, 255–256, 281–282
"To Muslims from a Christian Poet," 257
"To Young Americans...", 360–361
on traditional *versus* spiritual principles, 148–149
on Ottoman Empire, 192–193, 256, 263
on West *versus* East, 356
during WW1, 255–265, 281–283
"You Have Your Lebanon and I Have Mine" 329
Ziade's encouragment of, 355

Gibran, Kahlil (KG) *(romanticization of)*
after death, 411
background speculation on, 211
as "dangerously Oriental," 307
Day's "young sheik," 377, **43**
"Easternness," 223

as idealist, 374–375
origins submerged by critics, 280–281, 109, 89
throughout his life, 377
within transcendentalist legacy, 47
as visionary, 103
when *The Madman* published, 304
"young Arab writer Joubrane," 164

Gibran, Kahlil (KG) *(Syrian community)*
faction dispute and KG's drawing, 126–127
"Ila Suriyeen," 172
on immigrant's position in America, 192
influence on, 400–401
interview in Boston *Herald*, 362–363
and KG's association with pacifists, 269–270
nationalist *versus* pacifist communities, 255
in New York, 180–181
as Relief Society secretary, 260
royalties donated to, 256
on social workers, 391
"To Young Americans...", 360–361

Gibran, Kamila (mother)
background and marriages, 5–7
death of, 94–95
dressing KG for Day's photo exhibit, 52
and emigration, 17, 19
KG on the mother, 187–188
and peddling, 24
photograph with Sultana and Marianna, **74**
relationship with KG, 28–29, 56
sickness and, 86, 87
Towards the Infinite portrait, **98**

Gibran, Marianna (sister)
apartment arrangements, 169–170, 282, 407
in Cohasset, **266**–267
on Denison House, 197, 391
on family health, 86, 90–91
as housekeeper and wage earner, 125–126
illiteracy, 125–126, 27
income from KG, 369, 371

on Kamila's death, 94–95
KG estate planning for, 376, 393
at KG's death, 409, 411, **412, 419, 424**
on KG's homecoming after Sultana' death, 76–77
and KG's will, 405, 413, 415
and Mar Sarkis purchase, 422, 423
and MH, 140, 179–180, 197
and Miss Teahan, 114, 180, 295–296
and Peter, 27–28, 90–91, 93
photograph by Day, **90**
on Sultana's passing, 75–76

Gibran, Melham 17, 21
Gibran, N'oula (cousin), 71, 72, 73, 126, **266**, 363, **412**
Gibran, Peter. *See* Rahme, Peter
Gibran, Rose (N'oula's wife and also KG's cousin) 412, 413
Gibran, Sultana (sister), 27–28, 74, 75, **77**
Gibran Diab, Zakia (Melham Gibran's daughter), 192, 406 412, 413, 415, 418
Gibran Museum, in Bsharri, **429**–430
Giller, Jacob, 373
Golden Links Society, 191–193
Gollomb, Joseph, 304–305, 361
Good Friday (drawing), **107**
Goodhue, Bertram Grosvenor, 39, 40, 55
Gorky, Maxim, 134
Grant, Percy (Vicar), 241, 309
Greater Syria, xix, 19, 21–22, 161, 191–193, 359, 377
Great Migration (until 1924), 21, 359
"The Great Recurrence" (essay), 396, **397,** 398
Greek-Syrian Relief Society, 204
Greenwich Village 134, 180, 27, 289, 295, 305, 309, 399, 430
The Guidance (Al-Hoda) (newspaper), 213, 359, 425
Guiney, Louise Imogen
and Beardsley death, 55
character and background, 38
and Day, 38, **39,** 75
and Five Islands, 56
KG reminiscing on, 193

on KG's leaving for Lebanon, 56
and Peabody, 100, 64, 99
and "The Yellow Hair Library," 40–41
Guthrie, William Norman (Reverend), 310

Haddad, Abd al-Massih
and Arida at *Al-Funun,* 323, 425
League of Liberation board, 281
photographs, **221, 319**
President meeting, 330
As-Sayeh hosts writers gathering, 318
tribute to KG, 260
Haddad, Father Yusuf, 59–60, 69
Haddad, Nadra, 318, **319,** 323
Hale, Edward Everett, 30–31, 80–81
Halwani, Yazan, 435–436
Hamilton, Jean 237, 460n
Hanna, Labeebee, 361
Hanna Dahir clan, in Lebanon, 17
Harcourt Exhibit, 107–108
Harcourt Studios fire, 116–119
Hardy, Lamar, 224, 424
Hartmann, Sadakichi, 42
Haskell, Louise (MH's sister), 100, 104, 116, 138, 139, 154, 156, 280
Haskell, Mary (MH))
as English translator, 217–219
attitudes on money, 220–221, 372–374
Haskell Gibran collection, 212–213, 373–374
initial work on *The Prophet,* 290–293
on KG's progress, 242–243
and literature discoveries, 219–221
mentorship discussions, 373
on Marianna, 99–100, 115, 150–151, 197–198, 295–296, 413
on Maronite suppression, 162–163
money arrangement argument, 216–217
and Mount Hermon tuitions, 212–213
on need for corrections, 316
plan for Montross show, 225

securing KG's papers and work, xiii, 415–416, 426
Spirit Brides gift, 135
Haskell, Mary (MH) *(education reformer)*
Haskell-Dean school, 132, 209
photograph, **294**
Haskell, Mary (MH) *(family)*
and "Aunt Loulie" Minis, 263, 339
background and character of, 100, 111–113, 132–133
influences on, 132–134
Sierra Club outing, **122**
Hassoun, Rosina, 99–100
Hellenic philosophy and poetry (Delphic group), 399
hermit (sketch), **243**
Hermitage studio apartment, **374–375,** 405
Higginson, Thomas Wentworth, 112
Al-Hilal (The Crescent), 311, 312, 354, 356
Hindu-Muslim friendship, 386
Hinkle, Beatrice Moses, 204, 210–211, 268, 273
Hirsch, Gilbert, 205, 236, 271, 426
Hitti, Joseph, 391
Hitti, Philip, 400–401
Al-Hoda (The Guidance) (newspaper), 213, 359, 425
Hoernlé, Alfred, 307–308
Holmes, John Haynes, 204, 308, 309, 386, 396
home libraries (Children's Aid Society), 34, 37
Horowitz, Isaac, 385, 406
Hossain, Syud, 386, 399, 417
Housman, Laurence, 273
Hovey, Richard, 48
Howayek, Youssef
on Beaux-Arts reception, 163–164
on KG, 68–69
in KG's will, 184
life and work of, 426–427, **68**
in Paris with KG, 157–159, **158,** 377
on Paris years, 161–162
Howe, Julia Ward, 64
Hubbard, Elbert, 42
"Hypnos" (Day), 72

Ibn Khaldun, **322**
"If Thorns But Realized the Secret of Flowers" (Naimy), **334**

"Ila Suriyeen" (To Syrians) (poem), 172
immigration
described in *Book of Khalid,* 200–201
on emigrant newspapers 114, 115
from Greater Syria, xix, 19, 21–22, 359
Immigration Act of 1924, 359, 361, 374
KG on émigré status as artist, 207
through New York, 134, 19, 21
and transnationalism, 269
The Immortal Friend (Krishnamurti) (dust jacket), **388**
Impressions (Perry), 50, **54**
International Exhibit of Modern Art (Armory Show), 210, 214–215
The Interpreter (newsletter), 361
Iram, City of Lofty Pillars (play), 329
Irish Catholics, 32
Isis (painting), 187
Islamic and Christian heritage, 13–14, 259, 320–323
"island man." *See* Almustafa

James, Henry, 160
Jesus, the Son of Man (book), 375, 389–390, 394, **395,** 396
John, son of Zebedee (charcoal and graphite), **395**
Johnson-Reed Quota Act, 359
Julian, Rudolph, 149
Jung, Carl, 204, 205, 210–**211,** 267–268

Karam, 'Afifa, 213–**214,** 361
Käsebier, Gertrude, **38, 73,** 105, **228**
Kawkab Amirka (Star of America) (newspaper), 204
Kelmscott Press, 49
Kent, Charles Foster, 259
Keyes, Alicia, 111, 195–197, 215
The Keys of Heaven (Young, aka Broughton), 386
Khoury, Beshara el-, 421
Khoury, Esau el- and Marie el-, 198
Kimball, Ingalls, 39
The Knight Errant (magazine), 39
Knoedler and Co., 271, **272, 274, 275**
Knopf, Alfred A.
bookcraft support by, 327

contract with, 407m
drawings of, **297,** 379
KG's introduction to, 295
and *The Madman,* 295
on money advances to K, 375
on *The Prophet,* 335, 357
and *Twenty Drawings,* 311
Knopf, Blanche, **297,** 303, 327, 379
Krishnamurti, Jiddu, 387–**388**

Labor and the Angel (cover sketch),
50
Lady Gregory, 191, 194–**195**
Lafayette (Bartlett), 159
Lanux, Pierre de, 286, 295
Larger Aspects of Socialism (Walling),
220
"Lark and the Serpent" (parable),
314
laurel leaf (bronze) for Miss
Haskell's School, **242**
Lazarus and His Beloved (poems),
388
League of Liberation, 281
Lebanon
achieving autonomy, 355
and European colonialism,
15–16
landscape, inspiration of, 8–10
Mount Lebanon described, 3
as Ottoman province, 14–15
sects in, 15–17
Lee, Agnes Rand, 446n
Lee, Francis Watts, 39, 446n
Lemprière, John, 47
letter opener (photograph), **372**
"Letters of Fire" (essay), 119
The Liberator (magazine), 309, 349
Life of Jesus (Renan), 389
"The Life of Love" (essay), 119
Life of St. Genevieve (Puvis de
Chavannes), 158
Lifted Figure (wash drawing), **278**
Lights of Dawn (Phoutrides), 289
Lilien, Ephraim Moses, 222
Linked Ring (Royal Photographic
Society), 73
*The Literary Circle (Al Da'ira al
Adabiya),* 198
"little magazines," 38–40
Little Syria
Arab-American publishing in
(NYC), 115, 172
Bercovici on KG and,
378–379

Herald writer in Boston's,
361–363
See also Boston
Lord Dunsany, 310
"Lost Mind" (drawing), 155–156
Loti, Pierre, 159–161, 208
Lowell, Amy, 227, 267, 270, 282
Ludescher, Tanys Carol, 172, 5

Macbeth, William, 181, 225
MacKaye, Percy, 223, **233**
MacMonnies, Frederick, 32, 33,
273
Madey, Elia D., 281m, **319**
Madman, The
attempt to find publisher for,
289
Charlotte on, 306–307
frontispiece, **284**
MH collaboration on, 225,
227–229, 243
published during armistice,
300
reading at MH's school, 307
reviews and reception of,
303–309, 349
sold to Knopf, 295
source narratives for, 218–219
submitted to Morrow, 286
Wilkinson on, 308
writings, nucleus in *Al-Funun,*
222
Madrasat al-Hikma, École de la
Sagesse, 59, **60**
Madrasat al-Hikma Golden Book
(from Beirut school alumni),
70
Maeterlinck, Maurice
Arabic translation of, 222, 385
Day's reading to KG from,
46–47
desire to draw portrait of, 159
Hovey on, 48
KG influenced by, 103, 139,
219, 47, 64
KG's designs for *Wisdom and
Destiny* cover, 53
Peabody and, 120, 130, 65
Treasure of the Humble, 385,
46–47
al-mahjar, New York as, 19
Mahjar writers, 260–261, 320–323.
See also Arabic language and
literature
The Mahogany Tree (magazine), 39

Maloney, Marie Mattingly, 409
Malouf, Faris, 369–370
Al-Manarah (magazine), 68
Manheim, Madeline Mason, 379
Marcel-Béronneau, Pierre, 151–**152**
Marks, Lionel, 106, 108, 109, 114,
121, 123, 424
Marlowe (Peabody), 79
Maronite Christians
church, and last rites, 412
clergy on KG's work, 148,
162, 383
Crosby's visit to church, 362
École de la Sagesse in Beirut,
56–57
history of and influences on,
13–17, 5
on KG, 393
versus Orthodox Christians,
126–127, 129
and Protestant missionaries, 16
Syriac language of, 116
See also Bashir, Antony; el-
Douaihy, Stephen
Mar Sarkis (Saint Sergius)
Monastery, **14,** 422, **423**
Marshall, Marguerite Mooers, 230
"Martha La Banaise" (story), 128,
164
Martyrs' Monument (Howayek), **426**
Martyrs' Square, Beirut, **58**
Mary and Kahlil (sketch), **168**
Mary Magdalen (graphite), **395**
Masefield, John, 273
Al-Mashriq (journal), 356–357
Mason, Daniel Gregory, on
Peabody, 79
Mason, Mary, 80, 87, 89
Master, The (Bowie), 394
The Master-Mistress (poetry)
(O'Neill), 227
Al-Mawakib (The Processions), 287,
296–297, 311, 354, 357
McBride, Henry, 237–238, 279
Medusa (pastel), **235**
Meleager (Greek poet), 430
Meloney, Marie Mattingly, 405
"mental chemistry," and
transcendentalists, 102–103
"The Message of the Writer to
Arab Life" (Ziade), 425
Metropolitan Museum, 236
Michael, Monahan, and *Papyrus,*
164
Michel, Emilie ("Micheline")

and Hardy, 224, 363, 424
on KG, 140, 224
and KG art sessions, **137,** 138, 140
and KG friendship, 150, 165–166, 173, 181–182, 363
KG introduction at Morten's, 210
in KG's will, 184
later life and death of, 424–425
and Marianna, 182
MH friendship, 139, 140–142, 150, 271, 389
MH sponsorship, 135, 172, 212
in Paris, assisting KG, 145
as teacher at MH's school, 135
Michelangelo, sonnets of, 220
Middle East. *See* Gibran, Kahlil (*Middle East interest*)
Les Mille Nouvelle Nouvelles (A Thousand New Stories) (journal), 164
Minis, Jacob Florance, 339–341, 343, 345–346, 350, 370, 380, 389, 427
Mirat al-Gharb (Mirror of the West) (journal), 172, 174, 188, 281, 311, 425
Miss Haskell's School for Girls, 100, 111, **113, 242**
missionaries, in the Levant, 16
"Miss May." *See* Ziade, May
mist metaphor, 364–367
Mitraj, Raghib, 222
Al-Mohajer (The Emigrant) (newspaper), 115, 120, 127, 129, 152–**153**
Mokarzel, Salloum, 262, 359, 361
money box, from Peter's store (photograph), **376**
Monroe, Harriet, 305, 326
Montross, N. E., 225
Montross exhibition, **226,** 229–231, 236–238
Moody, William Vaughn, 79
Moreau, Gustave, 151, 158
More Songs from Vagabondia (Carman and Hovey), 47
Morris, William, Boston library show, 49
Morrow, WIlliam, 286
Morten, Alexander, 210, 211, 225
Morten, Marjorie, 210, 211, 229, 231, 363
Mother and Child (painting), **234**

Mother and Child (wash drawing), **276**
Moulton, Louise Chandler, 64
Mount Lebanon, 13, *2, 3*
Mukerji, Dhan Gopal, 290
Müller, Margarethe, 113, 138, 154, **156,** 85–86, 87, 94
Musa, Nabawiyyah, 353
Mushriq, Amin, 260–261
Al-Musiqa, (book cover), **110**
Muslim
and Christian relations, 13–16, 257, 353–354, 426–427, 5
Declaration of Faith, 259
and Hindu friendship, 386
Mustafa ("island man"), 287–289, 313–314, 325, 349, 364–367, 384
Mu'tamid ibn Abbad Al-, **322**
Mutran, Kahlil, 354, 421

al-Nahda, the Arab awakening, 261, 354
Naidu, Sarojini, 387, 399
Naimy, Mikhail
and Catskills vacation, 335–**336**
drawing by KG, **317**
and *Al-Funun,* 221–222
on 'hermitage' at West Tenth Street, 375
on KG and literary organization, 316–**319**
KG on "If Thorns But Realized," **334**
on KG's *Religion,* or *Brotherhood,* **428**
and League of Liberation, 281
life and work of, 427
and MH meeting, 415–416
and Pen League, 261
review of The Tempests, 324
on *Scales of Justice,* 368
and White House visit, 330–331
on writers union meeting, 318
Nasif, Malak Hifni, 353
Nasim, Nazmi, 222
National Association for the Advancement of Colored People (NAACP), 134
nationalism. *See* Syrian nationalism
National Women's Trade Union League, 134
Nativity story (essay), 396, **397,** 398
Nehru, Jawaharlal, 387

"The New Era" (poem), aka "The New Frontier," 332–333
The New Orient (magazine), 386–387
"The New School of American Photography" (exhibit), 73
The New World for Women (Al-Aam al Jadid al-Nis'i) (journal), 213
New York Herald Tribune (newspaper), 396
New York Times (newspaper), 394, 403–404, 423
Nicola, Franklin, 298
Nietzsche, Friedrich, 102, 106, 180, 190, 219, 220, 338
Nisaiyat (Feminist Pieces) (al-Badiyah, aka Nasif), 353
Norwood Historical Society, 425
Nubthah fi Fan Al-Musiqa (On Music) (Gibran), 120
Nymphs of the Valley (stories), 129

O'Connor, Thomas Power, 165
oil lamp (photograph), **373**
Old Greek Folk Stories (Peabody), 63
Oliver Place, *see* Boston,
Omar the Tentmaker, KG's cover for, **36**
"O Mist, My sister" (poem), 365, 396
O'Neill, Callista, 290, 310
O'Neill, Rose, 227–**228,** 290, 309–310, 423
One Thousand and One Nights, Abu al-Nawwas in, 323
On Music (Nubthah fi Fan Al-Musiqa) (Gibran), 120
"On Prayer" (drawing), **366**
"An Open Letter to Islam" (article), 257
Oppenheim, James, 268–270, 273, 281–282, 295, 425
Orient Society, 386
Orozco, Jose Clemente, 399, 400
Ottoman Empire, 15, 161, 172, 21, 213, 255, 377
Our Poets of Today (Cook, ed.), 286

Pach, Walter, 215, 216
pacifists, xviii, 281–282
Paine, Robert Treat, 30
Pan, A Choric Idyl (Peabody), 116
Papyrus (magazine), 164
Paris, and Middle Eastern dissidents, 161

"Passage to Men and Women" (poem), 286–287
Peabody, Charles (critic), 107–108, 280, 52
Peabody, Josephine
    after marriage, 130, 136
    background, studies, and KG introduction, 61–67
    death of, 363, 424
    on Harcourt exhibit, 106, 108
    KG's drawing of, **57**
    on KG's drawings, 119, 64, 65, 80, 99
    and KG's exhibit, 106, 108
    letter to KG in Beirut, 65–66
    on women and men relations, 64
    works and lectures of, 116, 120–121, 123, 177
peddling, as Syrian labor, 24–25
Peirce, Florence, 34–35, 41–42, 45, 56–57
Pen Bond *See* al-Rabitah al-Qalamiyah,
pencil doodles (Gibran), **48**
Pen League, *See* al-Rabitah al-Qalamiyah,
Percy, Elizabeth Crittenden, 399
"The Perfect World" (poem), 242
Perry, Lilla Cabot, 256, 50–**51**, 53, **54,** 89, 149, 236
Photo-Secessionists, 105, 108
Phoutrides, Aristides, 289, 363, 373
"The Poem of the Sufi Way," 323
"The Poet and Scholar" (parable), 314
"The Poet from Baalbek" (poem), 354
Poetry (journal), 326–327, 358
Poetry House bookshop, 386
Poetry Society of America, 241, 285, 289
"The Poet's Death is His Life" (story), 128
"The Poets of *al-Mohajer*" (essay), 127
"The Political Farewell" (essay), 329
Pond, James, and lecture tour, 335
Portrait of an Angel (drawing), **108**
portrait of a woman and nudes (inscribed to Speyer), **379**
Portrait of F. H. Day (Käsebier), **38**
Portrait of Kahlil (Perry), **51**
"Portraiture and the Camera" (Day), 73

The Potter's Clay (Garland), 290
Prendergast, Maurice, 215
Prescott, Kate, 67
The Processions (Al-Mawakib) (poem), 287, **296**–297, 311, 354, 357
Project Khalid, 425
Prophet, The (Gibran)
    final typography for, **350**
    illustrations for, 346–47
    KG distracted from, 312–314
    KG on prologue to, 291–292
    notebook, **292**
    "On Marriage," 287
    production and process, 344–45, 349–350
    reception of, 357–359, 375, 385, 390, 394
    Yiddish translation of, 385, 406
"The Prophet" (Peabody), 84
Psychology of the Unconscious (Jung), 267
"psycho-physics," and transcendentalists, 102–103
A Publisher Is Known by the Company He Keeps (16mm stills), **382**
Puvis de Chavannes, Pierre, 33, 158, 387

Qays, **322**
Quincy School, Boston, 25–27, **26**

Al-Rabitah. (al-Rabitah al-Qalamiyah, Pen League, Pen Bond)
    aims of, 318–320
    cover design for collection, **302**
    KG describing to MH, 326
    at KG's death, 411
    and KG tribute dinner, 400–**401**
    members (photograph) and logo design, **319**
    origins of, 260–261
    response to *Al Mashriq* and Cheikho, 357
    tributes to Bustani, 380
Rahme, Peter (brother)
    in Bsharri, 6
    description of, **18**–19, 28
    dry goods store, **27,** 43, 86, 88
    family concern about KG, 56
    illness and death of, 86, 88, 90–92, **91,** 99
    during Sultana's death, 75–77
Rankine, Mrs. A.K., 268, 282

Raymond, Thomas Lynch, 223–**224,** 285
Reasons for France (Teller), 426
Reed, Alma, 386, 399–400
Reed, Ethel, 41, 49, 55
Reed, John, 281
Reedy, William Marion, 273
"Reflections" (column), 119–120
Religion, or *Brotherhood* (graphite and watercolor), **428**
Renan, Ernest, 389
Resnikoff, Vladimir, 308
Richards, Joseph Dudley, 279
Rihani, Ameen
    background similarity with KG's, 165, 204
    The Book of Khalid, 185, 187, **199**–201, **200,** 230, 425
    Charlotte on, 201–202
    drawings of, **127, 165, 182**
    "Hunger" in *Al-Funun* Syrian Crisis Issue, 263
    on KG at memorial, 421
    League of Liberation vice-president, 281
    life and work of, 425
    member of Al-Rabitah, **319**
    and Syrian immigrant community, 127
    and Syrian Relief Committee, 260
Rihbany, Abraham Mitrie, 204
Riis, Jacob, Boston alley photograph, **20**
Robinson, Corinne Roosevelt, 242, 285, 380, 393, 405
Robinson, Edwin Arlington, 119, 79
Rochefort, Henri (charcoal and graphite), **233**
Rodin, Auguste, 154, 159–**160,** 283, 303, 305
Roerich, Nicholas, 416
Rostand, Edmond (charcoal and graphite), 159, **232**
Rubaiyat of Omar Khayyam, The (trans. Dole), 54
Rüyl, Beatrice Baxter, 105, 177, 184
Rüyl, Louis R.
Russell, Charles Edward, 181
Russian writers, published in *Al-Funun,* 222
Ryder, Albert Pinkham, 238, **239**–240, **241,** 279–280

Sahat al-Burj, Beirut, **58**

Salomey, Edna K., 361

Al-Sanabil (The Spikes of Grain) (anthology), 401

Sand and Foam (parables), 385, 389, 394

Sargent, John Singer, **81**

Saxe, William, 415, 416, 418, 423

As-Sayeh (The Traveler) (newspaper)
  and Arida's *(Al-Funun)* relationship, 323, 425
  covers, **301**
  on KG's Islam speech, 259
  and literary group, 318
  revival of and writers in, 260–261
  role in forming Mahjar writers, 320
  on self-rule during WW1, 281
  special edition, 334

Scales of Justice, from *A Tear and a Smile,* **368**

Scott, Duncan Campbell, 50

Sears, Sarah Choate (Mrs. Joshua Montgomery Sears) 105, 106, 107, 108, 52–53

Sedition Act of 1918, 282

Seiffert, Marjorie Allen, 358

Selig, Elizabeth, 403

Selikovitsch, George (Goetzel), 387

Serbia pamphlet, **298**

Serbia poem, to "Defeat," 378

settlement houses. *See* Boston charities

The Seven Arts (magazine), 268–**270,** 273, 281, 282

Shamon, Elias, 374–375

Sharawi, Huda, 353

"The Shepherd Girl" (Peabody), 62

Shidiaq, Assad (Lebanese martyr), 129

"A Ship in the Mist" (story), 336

Sikelianos, Angelos, 399

The Singing Leaves (Peabody), 102, 79, 85

The Singing Man (Peabody), 84

"Slavery" (story), 188

Sleeping angel (pencil), **73**

Small, Maynard & Co., 39

Smith, Gertrude, 103

"Snow" (poem), 405

Société Nationale des Beaux-Arts, 163

Song Offerings (Tagore), 220

Songs from Vagabondia (Carman and Hovey), 47

The Souls of Men Flying before the Face of the Inevitable (chalk and ink), **155**

South End. *See* Boston

South Station cortege (photograph), **412**

Speyer, Edgar, 310, 331, 351, 405, 413, 415

Speyer, Leonora, 331, **379**–380

The Spikes of Grain (Al-Sanabil) (anthology), 401

Spirit Brides (stories), 129, 135

Spirit of the Centaurs (painting), **11**

Spirits Rebellious (book), **144,** 146–148, **149,** 162–163

Squantum house, on the water, 406–407

Star of America (Kawkab Amirka) (newspaper), 204

St. Augustine, 320

St. Denis, Ruth (drawings), **223, 234**

Steichen, Edward, 105, 75

Steiglitz, Alfred, 105

Stern, Gertrude, 406, 413

Sterner, Mrs. Albert, 271

Stieglitz, Alfred, 44

St. Louis Mirror (newspaper), 273

St. Mark's Church-in-the-Bowery, 310, 358, 385

Stokes, Frederick A., 286

Stokes, Graham Phelps, 308–309

Stokes, Rose Pastor, 308, 309,

Stone, Herbert, 39

"Street Arabs" (Riis photograph), **20**

Strunsky, Anna, 134

Sunday Star (newspaper), **397**

"Sweet Monsters" (O'Neill), 227

Syria
  early Christians of, 13, 5
  French in, 355
  and gift to U.S. President, 331
  and home rule, 165, 256, 377
  immigrant poets from, 260–261

Syriac language, 116

"Syriac Suggestions" (Coburn), 280

Syrian American immigrants
  Bashir and, 383
  in Boston, 23–25, 361–363
  common illnesses of, 376, 76, 86
  and Denison House, 32
  Fatat Boston newspaper, 312–**313**

and feuds between sects, 126–127, 172

on Garibaldi, 214

and Golden Links Society, 191–193

and KG memorials, 417

KG's colleagues on Oppenheim, 269

and Lebanese immigrants, during WW1, 259

Little Syria described, 361–363

mourning KG's death, 413

in New York, 172, 180, 378

and peddling, 24–25

and Pen League, 400

response to racism and immigration ACT, 359

and self-rule advocacy, 281

and social clubs, 191–193

"To Syrians" controversy, 172

writers, **221**–223

(*See also* KG *(Middle East interest);* KG *(Syrian community)*)

Syrian American Society, 191

Syrian Christ, The (Rihbany), 204

"The Syrian Crisis Issue" (*Al-Funun* 1916), 263–265

Syrian nationalism
  and dissidents in Paris, 161
  and integration with adopted country, 269
  KG and activists in New York, 180
  KG on Syrian's self-reliance, xvii, 191–193, 283
  and KG's "To Syrians" challenge, 172
  and meeting Irish nationalist O'Connor, 165
  versus pacifism, xvii–xviii

Syrian Relief Committee, 260, 262

The Syrian World (monthly review), 359, 360–361, 402, 411, 417

Tabet, Ayub, and 1st Arab Congress, 259, 281

Tabit, Sultana, **142**

Tablada, José Juan, 399

Tagore, Rabindranath, 220, 304–305, 329

Tchaikovsky, Nikolai, 134

Teachings of Buddha in Biblical Hebrew (Selikovitsch), 387

A Tear and a Smile (book), 258

"Tears and Laughter" (column), 127
Tears and Laughter (Dam'a wa
    Ibtisama) (book), 225
Teller, Charlotte Hirsch
    background and work of,
        133–135
    and Clemens, 134, 135
    A Club resident, 133–134, 309
    and Jung interest, 204, 205
    on KG, 138, 177–178, 208,
        307, 377
    KG's portrait of, **182, 187**
    in KG's will, 184
    on The Madman, 306–307
    marriage and family with
        Hirsch, 205, 224, 271
    in Paris with KG, 156
    photograph of, **133**
    on Rihani and KG, 182–183,
        199–200, 201–202
    rivalry with KG for MH
        approval, 125, 174–175
    on "the East" and Montross
        exhibit, 236, 340
The Tempests (Al-Awasif), 324
Temple of Art series, 213, 223,
    239–**241,** 379. See also Gibran,
    Kahlil (artist meetings)
Tenth Street Studio building, New
    York, **186,** 189
Terry, Ellen, 159m
This Man from Lebanon (Young), 426
Thompson, Juliet, 203, 260
A Thousand Years Ago (MacKaye),
    223
The Three Are One (Madman
    frontispiece), **284**
The Alexander Tisons, 216
"To Syrians" ("Ila Suriyeen")
    (poem), 172
Towards Democracy (Carpenter), 93
Towards the Infinite (Kamila portrait),
    98
Tower Square, Beirut, **58**
"To Young Americans of Syrian
    Origin" (in The Syrian World),
    360–361
Traherne, Thomas, 220
transcendentalism, 102–103, 164,
    47–48
transnationalism, and Seven Arts, 269
Treasure of the Humble, The
    (Maeterlinck), 385, 46–47
Turkish-Italian conflict, 193. See
    also Gibran, Kahlil (Middle East
    interest)

Twenty Drawings, 311, 315, 349
The Two-Faced Characters (Al-Wujuh
    'Al-Mulawana) (play), 261–262
Tyler Street IX, 25, **30**–**31,** 34, 282,
    295, 337, 363, 391, 393, 402,
    411.

Union Internationale des Beaux-
    Arts et des Lettres, **166**
Unity (magazine), 308
untitled, early pastel, **352**
U.S. exclusion of immigrants, 359

Van Noppen, Leonard, 399
"Victory over Savagery" (As-Sayeh
    cover), **301**
"Vision" (essay), 115
"Vision" (story), 128
Vogeler, Heinrich, illustrator 263
The Vision of Adam and Eve
    (drawing), **108**

Walling, William English, 134, 220
Wanderer, The (book), 407, **408**
watercolor box (photograph), **372**
Watson, Adele, 409, 413
The Wayfarers (Peabody), 64, 66
"The Way of The Seven Days"
    (short sayings), 324–326
"We and You" (poem), 174
Wellesley College, 32, 79, 100, 112
West Tenth Street studio, 169,
    186, 189, 198, 209, 212, 363,
    374–**375,** 405
White, Clarence, 105
Whitman, Walt, 48, 93, 102–103,
    164
Wilde, Oscar, 37, 181, 55
Wilkinson, Marguerite, 308
Wilson, Woodrow, 281, 330–331
Wisdom and Destiny (Maeterlinck),
    53
"The Woman of It" columns
    (Marshall), 230
Women's City Club (exhibit), 339,
women's movement illustration
    (Buffalo Times), **230**
Women's Refinement Union, 354
woodcarvings, 344, **345,** 348
Woods, Robert, 23
World War 1. See Gibran, Kahlil
    (Middle East interest)
Al-Wujuh 'Al-Mulawana (The
    Two-Faced Characters) (play),
    261–262

Yeats, William Butler, **191,** 224
Yellow Book (Beardsley), 55
"The Yellow Hair Library" (juvenile
    series), 40–41
Yiddish translation, of The Prophet,
    385, 406
"You Have Your Lebanon, and I
    Have Mine" (poem), 329, 356
Young, Barbara ("Netta")
    account of KG's death, 409
    background, work, and
        pseudonyms of, 385–386,
        424
    and daughter in KG's studio
        (photograph), **416**
    estate organizing, 385, 413, 415
    on hearing The Prophet, 385
    at KG's funeral, 411, **412** 413,
        418, 424
    on KG's monologues about
        Jesus, 390
    published in The Syrian World,
        361
    secretarial assistance, 388
Young Turks, 161
"Yuhanna the Mad" (story),
    128–129

Zaidan, Emile, editor Al-Hilal (The
    Crescent), 311, 312, 330, 336
Zanzos social world, 310
Ziade, May ("Miss May")
    background, work, and
        correspondence, 353–**355,**
        425
    and KG correspondence, 366,
        378, 407–408, 98
Ziegler, Antje, 354